Educating Children with Multiple Disabilities

Educating Children with Multiple Disabilities

A Collaborative Approach

Fourth Edition

edited by

Fred P. Orelove, Ph.D.
Partnership for People with Disabilities
Virginia Commonwealth University
Richmond, Virginia

Dick Sobsey, Ed.D.
JP Das Developmental Disabilities Centre
University of Alberta
Edmonton, Alberta, Canada

Rosanne K. Silberman, Ed.D.
Department of Special Education
Hunter College, The City University of New York
New York, New York

·P·A·U·L·H·
BROOKES
PUBLISHING CO®

Baltimore • London • Sydney

Paul H. Brookes Publishing Co.
Post Office Box 10624
Baltimore, Maryland 21285-0624

www.brookespublishing.com

"Paul H. Brookes Publishing Co." is a registered trademark of
Paul H. Brookes Publishing Co., Inc.

Typeset by Auburn Associates, Inc.,
Baltimore, Maryland.
Manufactured in the United States of America by
Sheridan Press, Fredericksburg, Virginia.

This book is in no way meant to substitute for a physician's advice or expert opinion;
readers should consult a medical practitioner if they are interested in more information.
The alternate assessment methods described in Chapter 4 may not apply under the
mandates of specific states.

Most individuals described in this book, with the exception of Claire Dickey (whose
name and story are used with her consent) in Chapter 6, are composites, pseudonyms,
or fictional and are based on the authors' actual experiences. Individuals' names have
been changed and identifying details have been altered to protect confidentiality.

Purchasers of *Educating Children with Multiple Disabilities: A Collaborative Approach* may
download free of charge from the Brookes Publishing web site various resources related
to the book. The forms are available at the following address:
http://textbooks.brookespublishing.com/orelove. Use of these materials is granted for
educational purposes only; the duplication and distribution of these materials for a fee
is prohibited.

Library of Congress Cataloging-in-Publication Data

Educating children with multiple disabilities : a collaborative approach / edited by
Fred P. Orelove, Dick Sobsey, Rosanne K. Silberman—4th ed.
   p. cm.
  Rev. ed. of: Educating children with multiple disabilities / by Fred P. Orelove and
Dick Sobsey; with invited contributions. 3rd ed. ©1996.
  Includes bibliographical references and index.
  ISBN 1-55766-710-1 (pbk. : alk. paper)
  1. Children with disabilities—Education.   2. Children with disabilities—Care.
  I. Orelove, Fred P., 1951–   II. Sobsey, Richard.   III. Silberman, Rosanne K.
  IV. Orelove, Fred P., 1951–Educating children with multiple disabilities.
LC4015.068 2004
371.9—dc22

                                       2004005333

British Library Cataloguing in Publication data are available from the British Library.

Contents

Contents

About the Editors

Fred P. Orelove, Ph.D., Executive Director, Partnership for People with Disabilities, Virginia Commonwealth University, Post Office Box 843020, Richmond, Virginia 23284-3020

In addition to serving as Executive Director of the Partnership for People with Disabilities at Virginia Commonwealth University (VCU), Dr. Orelove is a professor of education and directs VCU's program in severe disabilities, which is a participant in the Virginia Consortium for Teacher Preparation in Severe Disabilities. Since the 1970s, Dr. Orelove has taught children and has directed numerous training and demonstration projects related to individuals with disabilities. In addition to this book, he has co-authored two books on teamwork and one on inclusive education. Dr. Orelove remains actively involved in public policy involving individuals with disabilities and families.

Dick Sobsey, Ph.D., Director, JP Das Developmental Disabilities Centre, 6-123 Education North, University of Alberta, Edmonton, Alberta T6G 2G5, Canada

Dr. Sobsey is a Professor of Educational Psychology and Director of the JP Das Developmental Disabilities Centre at the University of Alberta in Canada, where he also serves as an adjunct professor at the John Dossetor Health Ethics Centre. He has worked with children and adults with severe disabilities since 1968 as a nurse, a teacher, and a researcher. His current research explores the relationship between disability and violence. Dr. Sobsey is also the father of two children, including a teenager who has severe and multiple disabilities and is fully included in his neighborhood school.

Rosanne K. Silberman, Ed.D., Professor, Department of Special Education, Hunter College, The City University of New York, 695 Park Avenue, New York, New York 10021

Dr. Silberman is Professor in the Department of Special Education at Hunter College, The City University of New York in New York City, where she coordinates the graduate teacher preparation programs in blindness and visual impairment and severe disabilities including deafblindness. Currently, in addition to serving as Project Director of a training grant from the Office of Special Education Programs (OSEP) in Severe Disabilities including Deafblindness, she is Project Director of a long-term training grant from Rehabilitation Services Administration (RSA) in Rehabilitation Teaching/Orientation and Mobility. Dr. Silberman also is project director of training grants from private foundations including The New York Community Trust, the Allene Reuss Memorial Trust, and the Lavelle Fund for the Blind. She has served as a consultant for many school districts and has conducted educational evaluations of preschool, elementary, and secondary-level students with visual impairments and multiple disabilities in general education classrooms. Dr. Silberman is a member of the Board of Trustees of The New York Institute for Special Education, a member of the advisory board of DB-LINK, and a consulting editor for *Deaf-Blind Perspectives*. She is co-editor with Sharon Z. Sacks of *Educating Students Who Have Visual Impairments with Other Disabilities* (Paul H. Brookes Publishing Co., 1998). Dr. Silberman is the recipient of several distinguished awards including the 2000 Harold Ladas Award for Exemplary Teaching in the School of Education at Hunter College and the 2002 George E. Keane Award for Distinguished Service and Contributions to the Field of Blindness and Visual Impairment from the New York State Association for Education and Rehabilitation of the Blind and Visually Impaired.

About the Contributors

Susan M. Bruce, Ph.D., Assistant Professor, Boston College, 120 Campion, 140 Commonwealth Avenue, Chestnut Hill, Massachusetts 02467

Dr. Bruce coordinates the master's degree programs in intensive special needs. Her research interests include communication intervention and effective instructional practices.

Julie Causton-Theoharis, Ph.D., Lecturer, Department of Rehabilitation Psychology and Special Education and Department of Curriculum and Instruction, University of Wisconsin–Madison, 602 West Olin Avenue, Madison, Wisconsin 53715

Dr. Causton-Theoharis has worked with students who have severe and multiple disabilities as a special educator and consultant since the mid-1990s. She consults with school districts on national and local levels to help teachers and paraprofessionals to appropriately educate students with disabilities in inclusive school and community environments. Her research focuses on the education of students with disabilities within inclusive environments and effective support strategies.

Deborah Chen, Ph.D., Professor, Department of Special Education, California State University, Northridge, 18111 Nordhoff Street, Northridge, California 91330

As a professor in the Department of Special Education at California State University, Northridge, Dr. Chen teaches in the Early Childhood Special Education program. She has been an early interventionist, teacher of children with severe and multiple disabilities, and a program administrator. Her research and publications focus on working with families of diverse backgrounds, promoting early communication with young children who have multiple disabilities and sensory impairments, and providing training to early intervention personnel through distance education methods.

Chigee Jan Cloninger, Ph.D., Executive Director, Center on Disability and Community Inclusion, University of Vermont College of Education and Social Services, 208 Colchester Avenue, Burlington, Vermont 05405

During her career teaching children and adults, Dr. Cloninger has emphasized the importance of providing technical assistance and research, sharing leadership, and working as a team to making a difference in the lives of people with disabilities, their families, and service providers.

June E. Downing, Ph.D., Professor, Department of Special Education, California State University, Northridge, 18111 Nordhoff Street, Northridge, California 91330

Dr. Downing prepares teachers to meet the needs of students with moderate to severe and multiple disabilities. In this capacity, she teaches courses, advises students, and guides teachers in their practicum experiences. Dr. Downing has provided in-service training to teachers, administrators, parents, and support staff around the country. Areas of research include investigating related topics such as educating all students together, enhancing the social-communicative skills of students with severe disabilities, adapting for the unique needs of individual students, developing paraprofessional skills, and preparing teachers for inclusive education.

Paula E. Forney, P.T., B.S., M.M.Sc., Technical Assistance Specialist, Babies Can't Wait/Georgia Department of Human Resources, 2 Peachtree Street NW, Suite 11-204, Atlanta, Georgia 30303

Ms. Forney received her bachelor's degree in physical therapy from Simmons College in Boston and her master's of medical science degree in pediatric physical therapy from Emory University in Atlanta. She is also certified in pediatric Neurodevelopmental Treatment (NDT) and in administration/interpretation of the Sensory Integration and Praxis Test (SIPT). Ms. Forney has worked as a pediatric physical therapist for 30 years, developing and working in both school-based programs and programs based on natural environments. She has worked in early intervention for the past 16 years. Ms. Forney has authored or co-authored a number of special education textbooks, curricula, instructional videotapes, and articles and has made numerous presentations on providing family-centered and collaborative services to families of young children with multiple disabilities.

Kathleen Gee, Ph.D., Associate Professor, Department of Special Education, Rehabilitation, and School Psychology, California State University, Sacramento, 6000 J Street, Sacramento, California 95819

Dr. Gee, president of TASH in 2004, has been involved in personnel preparation, research, and demonstration in the field of severe and multiple disabilities for 25 years. Dr. Gee has worked with numerous schools, districts, and state departments of education to facilitate effective, inclusive schools that serve students with severe and multiple disabilities.

Kathryn Wolff Heller, B.S.N, M.Ed. Ph.D., Professor, Department of Educational Psychology and Special Education, Georgia State University, MSC 6A0820, 33 Gilmer Street, Unit 6, Atlanta, Georgia 30303

Dr. Heller is the program coordinator for the Orthopedic Impairments program (physical and health disabilities) and draws from her nursing and special education background to conduct research and service activities and to teach. One of her primary interests is in providing effective educational instruction and health care for students with physical, sensory, and health impairments.

Jacqui Farmer Kearns, Ph.D., Associate Director, Inclusive Large-Scale Standards and Assessment Group, Interdisciplinary Human Development Institute (IHDI), University of Kentucky, 320 Mineral Industries Building 0051, Lexington, Kentucky 40506

Among her many accomplishments at the IHDI, Dr. Kearns has directed two groundbreaking initiatives for students with disabilities: The Kentucky Statewide Alternate Portfolio Project and the Including Students with Deafblindness in Large-Scale Educational Assessments Project. Dr. Kearns previously directed the Kentucky Statewide Systems Change Project for Students with Severe Disabilities and has extensive experience as a classroom teacher for students with moderate and severe disabilities.

Harold L. Kleinert, Ed.D., Interdisciplinary Human Development Institute (IHDI), University of Kentucky, 320 Mineral Industries Building 0051, Lexington, Kentucky 40506

Dr. Kleinert has published widely in the area of alternate assessment for students with severe and multiple disabilities under the Individuals with Disabilities Education Act, including research on the impact of the inclusion of students with disabilities in large-scale assessment and accountability systems. Dr. Kleinert has served as a teacher of students with severe and multiple disabilities for more than a decade.

Dianne Koontz Lowman, Ed.D., Associate Professor and Director of Academic Performance, Department of Occupational Therapy, Virginia Commonwealth University, 1000 East Marshall Street, Post Office Box 980008, Richmond, Virginia 23298

Dr. Lowman's research interests in the area of pediatrics include focusing on working with infants, toddlers, and young children with oral motor feeding difficulties, severe disabilities, and complex health care needs. Using an action research model, she has worked cooperatively with local child care centers and the Head Start program to develop partnerships that incorporate both service learning and research. She teaches content related to child and adolescent development, infants, toddlers, and preschoolers with disabilities, and qualitative research.

Cathy Miles, M.A., Department of Special Education, California State University, Northridge, 18111 Nordhoff Street, Northridge, California 91330

Ms. Miles has extensive experience working with children and families. She is licensed in marriage and family therapy and has a master's degree in early childhood education and a teaching credential in early childhood special education. She is the parent of three children, one of whom has disabilities.

Catherine Nelson, Ph.D., Clinical Assistant Professor, Department of Special Education, University of Utah, 1705 East Campus Center Drive, Room 221, Salt Lake City, Utah 84112

Dr. Nelson teaches in the areas of early childhood special education and deafblindess. In addition, she consults extensively in the United States and Europe with programs serving children and youth with deafblindness. Her current research interests include assessment of children with deafblindness and early social and communication development in young children with deafblindness and young children with autism.

Margery Szczepanski, M.A., O.T.R., Assistant Professor, Division of Occupational Therapy, Long Island University, One University Plaza—HS 514, Brooklyn, New York 11201

Margery Szczepanski currently teaches pediatric occupational therapy to graduate and undergraduate students. She has specialized training in neurodevelopmental treatment (NDT) and more than 25 years of clinical experience with children with varied disabilities. Ms. Szczepanski conducts workshops and continuing education programs both locally and nationally for teachers and allied health professionals.

Madhavan Thuppal, M.B.B.S., M.D., Medical Director, Southwestern Human Services, and Clinical Assistant Professor of Psychiatry, Western Psychiatric Institute and Clinic, 24 Woodland Drive, Pittsburgh, Pennsylvania 15228

Dr. Thuppal, a practicing child psychiatrist, works with children with complex medical needs, developmental disabilities, and pervasive developmental disorder-not otherwise specified (PDD-NOS). He regularly consults in schools on emotion control and behavior problems of children and adolescents in general and special education schools. Previously, Dr. Thuppal served as the medical director of the John Merck Inpatient Unit for persons with severe and multiple disabilities at the Western Psychiatric Institute and clinic of the University of Pittsburgh Medical Center.

Alice Udvari-Solner, Ph.D., Faculty Associate, Department of Curriculum and Instruction and Office of Education Outreach, University of Wisconsin–Madison, 225 North Mills Street, Room 244a, Madison, Wisconsin 53706

Dr. Udvari-Solner is a national consultant in education. The graduate and undergraduate courses she teaches on accommodating diverse learners in general education settings are integral to the elementary, secondary, and special education teacher certification programs. Differentiation, the design of effective curricular adaptations, collaborative teamwork among educators and paraprofessionals, and systems change toward inclusive education are areas that are central to her research and teaching.

Jennifer York-Barr, Ph.D., Associate Professor, Department of Educational Policy and Administration, University of Minnesota, College of Education, 86 Pleasant Street, SE, Minneapolis, Minnesota 55455

Dr. York-Barr's research development interests are collaborative instructional teamwork, teacher leadership, school change, and professional development. She has authored or co-authored numerous publications in the areas of collaborative learning, the inclusion of children and adults with severe and multiple disabilities in schools and communities, and school and family partnerships.

Preface

What a difference 17 years makes! In 1987, when the first edition of *Educating Children with Multiple Disabilities* was published, the field of special education and opportunities for children with severe and multiple disabilities were radically different. The term *inclusive education* did not even exist in the professional literature, let alone serve as an acceptable (if still not universally accepted) educational practice. Strategies for preparing, recruiting, and hiring related services personnel to work in schools did not take into consideration the multifaceted nature of teaching students with severe and multiple disabilities. Most school districts did not view themselves as coordinators of social services for children, and for the most part, alternate assessment was of low priority in practice and in law.

The terminology used in the field of special education has become more person-first since the first edition of this book was published. A term we used in the first line of the Preface for the first edition, *handicaps,* would sound offensive today but was acceptable when this book was first published. For example, PL 94-142, which governed special education practice, was called the Education for All Handicapped Children Act; it was not until a few years later that legislation reflected more appropriate terminology, with the passage of the Individuals with Disabilities Education Act (IDEA) of 1990 (PL 101-476) and the Americans with Disabilities Act (ADA) of 1990 (PL 101-336).

Other aspects of what is considered important in this field have changed, as well. "Part H" of what is now known as "Part C" of the IDEA, the amendments governing and encouraging early intervention, did not exist in 1987, nor did the Assistive Technology Act of 1998 (PL 105-394) and several other key federal laws emphasizing new focuses and services for people with disabilities.

Of course, technology itself has evolved dramatically. In today's world of wireless communication, personal computers, e-mail, and the Internet, it is a marvel that much of the first edition was actually written longhand on legal pads, with research performed using card catalogs. Most learners with severe and multiple disabilities did not have access to the assistive technology available today. When technology was available, it consisted of highly specialized hardware and rarely showed any evidence of the software solutions or universal design essential to much of today's assistive technology.

Finally, the demographics continue to shift. In 1987, our country was less diverse, and we were less aware of or sensitive to the importance of understanding and respecting the differences among individuals. Today, the climate has changed to include individuals of varying skills and abilities, and attempts are made to respect, value, and accommodate individuals' needs in school and in the workplace.

Although many changes in practice, legislation, and terminology have occurred, there still is room for positive change. Some individualized education programs (IEPs) for learners with severe and multiple disabilities continue to be developed in an atmosphere of intimidation rather than of collaboration. Some schools continue to separate individuals with disabilities from their peers without disabilities without giving rationales for specialized placements. Some school officials continue to see family members as obstacles—people to be accommodated rather than respected and involved. When shortages of trained personnel occur, some schools have to resort to hiring teachers and other personnel who lack sufficient professional preparation in their fields.

This fourth edition was written in a climate of welcome change and openness to new possibilities. Overall, we believe the need is greater than ever for professionals from many disciplines to work collaboratively for the benefit of learners with severe and multiple cognitive, physical, and sensory challenges. Therefore, this edition's contributors represent an even broader range of professions. The practices they describe derive not only from the special education literature but also from research and effective practice in physical and occupational therapy, speech-language pathology, and nursing and medicine, among other disciplines. The authors of this new edition have strived to maintain the book's goals of adhering to a strong empirical base and to include up-to-date research and presentation of classroom strategies in a straightforward manner. Finally, we remain firmly convinced that families must be afforded the respect and role they deserve in their children's education.

Although the book has retained its overall purpose and approach, the fourth edition is, in essence, almost entirely new. We welcome Rosanne K. Silberman, Professor in the Department of Special Education at Hunter College, The City University of New York, as a new editor. Her close association with the chapter authors and extensive work in developing and editing the content were invaluable. She brings to the book a wealth of expertise and knowledge, including extensive experience in the field of sensory impairments. She and 15 other experts in the field are new contributors.

The chapters have been reordered and several renamed to reflect new practices and terminology, and a new chapter has been added on alternate assessment. The book reflects an enhanced emphasis on supporting learners in inclusive environments. An added feature in this edition is the inclusion of resources in the form of web sites, organizations, and related products. Many chapters also include vignettes describing the experiences of children with severe and multiple disabilities and those who serve and care about them, in addition to successful classroom practices. These stories reflect diversity in all senses of the word.

Readers will continue to gain a broad sense of the characteristics and needs of learners with severe and multiple disabilities and their families in Chapters 1, 2, 8, and 10. Almost half of the book (Chapters 3, 4, 5, 6, 7, and 9) is devoted to describing approaches for assessing and instructing children with significant physical, sensory, and health impairments. These approaches include ways to appreciate and accommodate learners' overall development, as well as strategies for designing curriculum, developing adaptations, and providing appropriate handling and positioning. Finally, the last three chapters (11, 12, and 13) detail specific strategies in the critical areas of communication, mealtime, and self-care skills.

We hope that the fourth edition of *Educating Children with Multiple Disabilities* will provide information and resources for further personal research and exploration for those professionals who are studying to be or already employed in the most challenging and important jobs in the world. We continue to be inspired by professionals and family members who care deeply about children and who work hard to encourage those children to achieve a higher quality of life. Of course, it is the children themselves who motivate people like us to continue to write books. Since the first edition of this book was published, a new generation of children has been born, and these children need professionals who have the passion and the tools to support and encourage, to teach and to assess, and to work together to build on each other's strengths. May this fourth edition serve as one small resource in this circle of support.

REFERENCES

Americans with Disabilities Act (ADA) of 1990, PL 101-336, 42 U.S.C. §§ 12101 *et seq.*
Assistive Technology Act of 1998, PL 105-394, 29 U.S.c. §§ 3001 *et seq.*
Education for All Handicapped Children Act of 1975, PL 94-142, 20 U.S.C. §§ 1400 *et seq.*
Individuals with Disabilities Education Act (IDEA) of 1990, PL 101-476, 20 U.S.C. §§ 1400 *et seq.*
No Child Left Behind Act of 2001, PL 107-110, 115 Stat/1425, 20 U.S.C. §§ 6301 *et seq.*

CHAPTER 1

Designing Collaborative Educational Services

Chigee Jan Cloninger

Putting the student with severe and/or multiple disabilities at the core of all planning is the key to truly making a difference in that student's life. Effective individualized education programs (IEPs) are created through the dynamic, syner-
gistic collaborations of team members who share a common focus and purpose
and bring together diverse skills and knowledge (Reiter, 1999). This chapter
focuses on these dynamic, collaborative relationships, specifically the 1) rationale for collaborative teams, 2) importance of a variety of disciplines, 3) organizational models of teams, 4) the collaborative approach applied to educational programming, 5) challenges to implementing a collaborative model and approaches
to ensure success, and 6) essential components for successful collaborative services. Although the emphasis is on supporting students with severe and multiple disabilities, all students can benefit from a collaborative approach to educational planning and supports (Idol, Nevin, & Paolucci-Whitcomb, 2000).

WHY COLLABORATIVE TEAMS: A RATIONALE

Students with severe and multiple disabilities are those "with concomitant
impairments (e.g., mental retardation/blindness, mental retardation/orthopedic
impairments), the combination of which causes such severe educational needs
that they cannot be accommodated in the special education programs solely for
one of the impairments" (CRF Chapter III, Section 300.7 [c][7], 1999). These students, because of their combinations of physical, medical, educational, and social/

Thanks to Ruth Dennis, Susan Edelman, Michael Giangreco, and Ginny Iverson for sharing their
invaluable assistance and support.

emotional challenges, require collaborative, concerted effort so that their IEPs result in learning outcomes that make a difference in their daily lives. Thus, they need the profound and foundational interconnectedness of a diverse group, including family members, to see that learning *does* happen (Selby, 2001). The many needs of students with intense, numerous educational challenges call for a collaborative approach in the educational environment to ensure the following:

- *Services are coordinated rather than isolated and fragmented.* Team members who work together, complement, and support the student's goals and each other provide connected and integrated educational programming. Coordination of services takes place through the actions of team members who learn and implement the components of educational collaboration. Through collaboration, team members experience a sense of collegial belonging and satisfaction (Snell & Janney, 2000).

- *All team members share a framework for team functioning.* An operational framework is shared for team functioning, program assessment, implementation, and evaluation. Team members define their roles in relation to direct and indirect supports that they provide to the student's educational plan and to other team members. Within a collaborative framework, the contributions of every team member are educationally relevant and necessary to the student's educational success; gaps in services and overlapping functions are avoided. Involvement in the development of a student's total plan helps ensure commitment and ongoing collaboration.

- *The student's goals belong to the student, and all team members work collaboratively to ensure that those goals are met.* Goals, objectives, and general supports are developed from the context of valued life outcomes for the student, family, and team members. Valued life outcomes are those basic components that reflect quality-of-life issues, such as being safe and healthy, having a home now and in the future, having meaningful relationships and activities, having choice and control that matches one's age and culture, and participating in meaningful activities in various places. Individualized planning, including supports, accommodations, and specialized instructional strategies based on these valued life outcomes and subsequent learning outcomes will be unique for each child and can be seen as benchmarks for determining the success of the student's program (Giangreco, Cloninger, & Iverson, 1998).

- *The student's needs are addressed through a coordinated, comprehensive approach.* Students with severe and multiple disabilities face challenges in a number of areas, including 1) physical and medical conditions, such as movement restrictions; skeletal abnormalities; vision and hearing loss; seizure, breathing, and urinary disorders; susceptibility to infections; and management of medications; 2) social and emotional needs, such as friendships, expression of feelings, affection, giving to others rather than always being passive recipients, and making decisions; and 3) educational challenges, such as appropriate positioning and handling and best use of vision, hearing, and movements for gaining access to materials and people. Appropriate communication methods and modes to match students' cognitive, visual, hearing, and motor functioning are essential to ensure that students can make choices, have some control over their lives, express basic needs, engage with others, and have access to pre-academics and academics. Although students with severe and multiple disabilities may have physical, medical, social, and emotional challenges, any student's IEP should be based on individually identified educational needs, not on presumed disability characteristics.

IMPORTANCE OF A VARIETY OF DISCIPLINES

To develop IEPs for students with severe and multiple disabilities, it is necessary to call on individuals from diverse disciplines such as special education, general education, nursing, social work, occupational therapy, physical therapy, and speech-language therapy, as well as from fields less traditionally associated with education, such as rehabilitation engineering, nutrition, and respiratory therapy. Whitehouse recognized in 1951 that one or two people from different disciplines could not meet all of the needs or deliver all of the services for these students. Many others in the field of special education have stressed the importance of multiple services (Giangreco, Cloninger, Dennis, & Edelman, 2000; Snell & Janney, 2000; Thousand & Villa, 2000). According to the Individuals with Disabilities Education Act (IDEA) Amendments of 1997 (PL 105-17), what is key to determining the involvement of any of these professionals in a particular student's IEP is whether a professional's services and skills are deemed necessary for a student to benefit from his or her IEP. Within a collaborative framework, the contributions of every team member are educationally relevant and necessary to the student's success, and, for the most part, gaps in services and unnecessary and contradictory overlapping functions are eliminated.

Although they are called on to work collaboratively, family members and professionals have distinct training backgrounds, philosophical and theoretical approaches, experiences, and/or specialized skills. The success of an educational team depends in part on the competence of the individual team members and on a mutual understanding and respect for the skills and knowledge of other team members.

Roles and Responsibilities of Team Members

All members of a student's collaborative team share in carrying out their roles so that the team can function successfully and address goals intended to increase the quality of life of the student. Some roles and responsibilities are generic and shared by all members; some are carried out individually or together; and some are specialized to a specific professional, although shared as necessary and appropriate. Team members include those who provide "specialized education services" as well as those who provide "related services." "Related services" defined in IDEA include

> Transportation, and such developmental, corrective, and other supportive services (including speech-language pathology and audiology services, psychological services, physical and occupational therapy, recreation, including therapeutic recreation, social work, counseling services, including rehabilitation counseling, orientation and mobility services, and medical services, except that such medical services shall be for diagnostic and evaluation purposes only) as are required to assist a child with a disability to benefit from special education, and includes the early identification and assessment of disabling conditions in children. (20 U.S.C. § 1401 [Sec. 602] [22])

Team members, other than family members and the student, provide specialized education services and/or related services to enable the student to reach his or her IEP goals and objectives. Special education can be provided without related services, but for the most part, related services cannot be provided without special education services. In a few states speech-language pathology services can be provided as special education services, if the only identified goals and objectives for the student relate to speech-language skills.

Related services providers, as well as other team members, engage in a variety of functions. Research by Giangreco and colleagues (Giangreco, 1990; Giangreco, Prelock, Reid, Dennis, & Edelman, 2000) found that the four most important functions of related service providers for serving students with severe and multiple disabilities were 1) developing adaptations, equipment, or both to allow for active participation or to prevent negative outcomes (e.g., regression, deformity, discomfort, pain); 2) transferring information and skills to others on the team; 3) serving as a resource, support, or both to the family; and 4) applying discipline-specific methods or techniques to promote active participation, to prevent negative outcomes, or both.

Team membership may be configured differently for each student depending on the array of services required to support his or her educational program. Most often, membership will reflect the people whose discipline-specific roles are emphasized in the following sections.

Student

The student is the core of the team; the reason the team exists is to address his or her educational needs. The student should be present at all team functions, either in person or through representation by family members, peers or advocates, and other team members. Team members are responsible for educating the student to participate as a team member and teaching self-advocacy skills and ways to have choice and control over decisions affecting him or her.

Family Member or Legal Guardian

Although not always present in the school on a daily basis, a family member or legal guardian or caregiver is an important member of the educational team. Apart from the fact that parents have the right to participate in assessment and planning, it simply makes good sense to invite them to participate in all team meetings as the individuals with the most knowledge of their children and the greatest stake in their children's future (Giangreco et al., 1998). See Chapter 2 for more on working with families.

Special Educator

The special educator primarily is responsible for the development and implementation of the student's IEP (IDEA, 1997). The special educator sees that the student with severe and multiple disabilities learns, through direct instruction and by sharing expertise and skills with the student's peers and others (e.g., paraprofessional, general education teacher, occupational therapist, nurse, bus driver) who interact with the student. The special educator may also serve in roles shared by other team members, such as liaison between the parents and school personnel, supervisor of paraprofessionals, member and coordinator of the team, and advocate for the student.

General Educator

The general education teacher provides services for and represents students on his or her class roster, as well as those who spend time in a general education class most of the day. The general educator's role on the team is to contribute expertise and experience about the general education curriculum and standards; weekly, monthly, and yearly curricular plans; class schedule; class routines; class rules and expectations; and the general culture of his or her class. He or she also ensures that students with severe and multiple disabilities have opportunities to participate in class lessons and activities and to interact with other students. He or she shares responsibility for designing or delivering general education components of the student's program, such as evaluating student progress. IDEA '97 (PL 105-17) requires that at least one of the student's general education teachers be on the IEP team, especially related to discussions and decisions about the student's access to and participation in the general education curriculum.

Paraeducator

Paraeducators are vital to the daily operation of the classroom. Their core functions include

> Providing academic instruction; teaching functional life and vocational skills; collecting and managing data; supporting students with challenging behaviors; facilitating interactions with peers who do not have disabilities; providing personal care (e.g., feeding, bathroom assistance); and engaging in clerical tasks. (Giangreco, Edelman, Broer, & Doyle, 2001, p. 53)

Physical Therapist

The physical therapist (PT) focuses on physical functions including gross motor skills; handling, positioning, and transfer techniques; range of motion; muscle strength and endurance; flexibility; mobility; relaxation and stimulation; postural drainage; and other physical manipulation and exercise procedures.

Occupational Therapist

The occupational therapist (OT) focuses on the development and maintenance of an individual's functional skills for participation in instruction and daily living activities, which include use of the upper extremities, fine motor skills, sensory perception, range of motion, muscle tone, sensorimotor skills, posture, and oral-motor skills.

Speech-Language Pathologist

The speech-language pathologist (SLP) focuses on all aspects of communication in all environments, including receptive and expressive levels, modes, and intent; articulation and fluency; voice quality and respiration; and the use of augmentative and alternative communication (AAC). He or she also may be trained in assessing and facilitating mealtime skills.

Assistive Technology Specialist

The assistive technology specialist focuses on the use of high- and low-technology devices and adaptations to facilitate participation in instruction and routine living skills, including communication, environmental management, instruction, social relationships, mobility, and recreation.

School Psychologist

The school psychologist focuses on social-emotional issues, including assessment and evaluation, interpretation of testing information, counseling of students and families, behavioral and environmental analysis, and program planning.

Social Worker

The school social worker focuses on helping the student gain access to community and other services and resources; advocating for the child and family; and acting as a liaison among school, home, and community.

Administrator

Administrators may include the school principal, special education supervisor or coordinator, and program coordinator. At IEP meetings, one of these or another designated person acts as the local education agency (LEA) representative. All of these administrators work together to ensure compliance with local, state, and federal regulations in areas such as placement, transition, curriculum development, transportation, related services, equipment, and scheduling. The school and district administrators are very important in promoting a school culture of high quality, success, openness, and inclusion for all students.

Teacher of Students with Visual Impairments and Certified Orientation and Mobility Specialist

The teacher of students with visual impairments (TVI) provides instruction to meet the unique needs of students with vision impairments and other multiple disabilities. The TVI is responsible for providing direct instruction and adaptations and accommodations in content areas such as tactile communication, use of optical devices, and daily living skills; and adapting general education classroom materials and consulting with the general education teachers. The certified orientation and mobility specialist (COMS) provides instruction in helping students with visual impairments learn how to maneuver safely and efficiently in the environment and may provide adapted equipment and strategies for those with significant challenges (see Chapter 10).

Audiologist

The audiologist identifies different types and degrees of hearing loss using traditional and alternative assessment techniques and equipment. The audiologist also provides consultation on equipment (e.g., hearing aids, FM devices) and their use, as well as environmental modifications (see Chapter 10).

School Nurse

The school nurse focuses on health-related issues and needs and his or her responsibilities may include administration of medications and other treatments (e.g., catheterization, suctioning, tube feeding), development of safety and emergency procedures, and consultation with other medical personnel (see Chapter 8).

Nutritionist and Dietitian

The nutritionist and dietitian focus on students' diet and nutrition. Responsibilities include adjusting students' caloric intake, minimizing the side effects and maximizing the effectiveness of medications, designing special diets for individuals with specific food allergies or health care needs, and consulting with medical personnel.

Physician

The physician focuses on the total health and well-being of the student, including screening for and treating common medical problems and those associated with a specific disability, prescribing and monitoring medications and other treatments, and consulting with other medical personnel. Physicians may include specialists such as a pediatrician, ophthalmologist, neurologist, otolaryngologist, orthopedist, and cardiologist. As related services providers, medical personnel provide services "for diagnostic and evaluation purposes only" (20 U.S.C. § 1401 [Sec. 602] [22]). (See Chapter 8.)

Other Specialists

Other specialists may be needed to address specific needs and concerns. They function as occasional team members, usually providing services that are time limited in response to a specific question by the educational team. Occupations in the field of severe and multiple disabilities may include dentist, optometrist, respiratory therapist, pharmacist, and rehabilitation engineer.

ORGANIZATIONAL MODELS OF TEAMS THAT SERVE STUDENTS WITH SEVERE AND MULTIPLE DISABILITIES

How well children are served in educational environments by the variety of people involved in their programs is influenced greatly by how these people work together. Each team member, as noted previously, brings a unique set of professional and personal skills and experiences to the team relationship. The manner in which teams are formed and the way in which they operate influence both the process and outcomes of children's education. The collaborative team model has proven to be an exemplary model for people working together to bring about differences in the lives of students with severe and multiple disabilities.

This section describes a progression of team models representing a hierarchy of increasingly more coordinated and connected approaches (Giangreco, York, & Rainforth, 1989), with the focus on four organizational structures: multidisciplinary, interdisciplinary, transdisciplinary, and collaborative. Although each of these models may be appropriate in a given environment or situation, many of the models first adopted by special education originated in medical environments in which people may not have even thought of themselves as belonging to a team. Team models have progressed to best meet the unique needs of students with severe and multiple disabilities in educational environments by following the development of educational best practices, research, and legal mandates. They also are based on the realization that educational teaming requires an educational model—the "collaborative" approach—not a medical model for student assessment, program planning, and delivery.

Multidisciplinary Model

Organization

In the multidisciplinary model, professionals with expertise in different disciplines work with the child individually, in isolation from other professionals. Evaluation, planning, priority setting, and implementation are not formally coordinated with other professionals, although each discipline acknowledges the other disciplines, and information may be shared through reports or informally. The overlaps and gaps in services are addressed only minimally, if at all. Team members may cooperate in scheduling and sharing information in writing with each other or the family, much as one might see in hospital charts or medical specialists' reports. In the medical profession, where this model originated, various disciplines co-exist to meet the needs of patients whose problems are typically isolated within one particular domain (Heron & Harris, 2001).

Disadvantages

Although the multidisciplinary model may be effective for children with short-term challenges, children with severe and multiple disabilities have more complex needs that require ongoing interaction among family members and professionals. Team members using the multidisciplinary model carry out isolated, separate assessment activities, write separate assessment reports, and generate and apply separate interventions specific to their area of expertise. The probability is very high that assessment information and intervention priorities will be in conflict, inconsistent, and difficult for other team members to implement. Parents, special educators, and case managers are often left with the task of implementing different or incompatible strategies to address various goals.

———————————

Lindsey, a fourth grader with motor (cerebral palsy) and cognitive disabilities, is served by an SLP who has skills in oral-motor eating issues and by an OT who also has skills in feeding issues. They separately evaluated Lindsey on her eating skills and are both working with her on intervention techniques. Although these techniques could be supportive and provide Lindsey more practice with her eating skills, these professionals' intervention techniques are not complementary and have not been taught to other team members who work with her daily.

Interdisciplinary Team Model

Organization

Representing another team model in the continuum of the ways people can work together, the interdisciplinary model provides a structure for interaction and communication among team members that encourages them to share information and skills (Heron & Harris, 2001). Programming decisions are made by group consensus, usually under the guidance of a services coordinator, whereas assessment and implementation remain tied to each discipline. Team members are informed of and agree to the intervention goals of each discipline; however, team members do not participate in selecting a single set of goals that belong to the student, that is, that are reflective of the student's needs and supported by all team members.

Disadvantages

Although the interdisciplinary model supports group sharing of information and decision making, individual members, often in isolation, carry out assessments. Implementation remains the responsibility of each discipline and occurs separately. Both the multidisciplinary and interdisciplinary models are discipline-referenced models, which means that decisions about assessment, program priorities, planning, intervention, evaluation, and team interactions are based on the orientations of each discipline. Such structures "are more likely to promote competitive and individualistic professional interactions resulting in disjointed programmatic outcomes" (Giangreco et al., 1989, p. 57).

An additional problem with the multidisciplinary and interdisciplinary models is their tendency to rely on intervention services that are direct and often isolated from each other (Giangreco, Prelock, et al., 2000). Direct services represent hands-on intervention by therapists, rather than the therapists serving as consultants and/or supports to other team members in a more "indirect" approach.

Why does a direct, isolated therapy approach *not* best serve students with severe and multiple disabilities?

- Assessments generally do not take place in natural environments, thus the outcomes may not be representative of what the student can do in those environments.

- Assessments often test specific, isolated skills instead of clusters of skills used in everyday activities.

- Assessments often result in diagnostic labels and descriptions of students' performances, but do not include suggestions for specific goal attainment or accommodations and supports.

- Team members cannot collaborate on the performance of individual students in natural situations.

- Limitations of time for direct service may result in children receiving less instruction and practice on learning outcomes—such as communication and mobility—that could be addressed throughout the day.

- Limited resources may lead to centralized service delivery systems in which students with severe and multiple disabilities are grouped together in order to receive multiple services, thus preventing or minimizing interactions with peers without disabilities and access to the general education curriculum (Orelove & Sobsey, 1996; Rainforth, York, & Macdonald, 1992).

Transdisciplinary Team Model

Organization

Originally designed for assessment of infants at high risk for disabilities (Hutchison, 1978; United Cerebral Palsy Association National Organized Collaborative Project to Provide Comprehensive Services for Atypical Infants and Their Families, 1976), the transdisciplinary model is the next in the continuum of people working together in a more collaborative way. This model represents a significant departure from the models of service delivery to which medical professionals are accustomed (i.e., multidisciplinary and interdisciplinary models). The purpose of the transdisciplinary model is to minimize the number of people with whom the young child or family has to interact in an assessment situation.

In contrast to the multidisciplinary and interdisciplinary approaches, the transdisciplinary model incorporates an *indirect* model of services whereby one or two people are the primary facilitators of services and other team members act as consultants (Heron & Harris, 2001; Hutchinson, 1978; Snell & Janney, 2000). Through an *indirect* or *integrative* approach, in contrast to the *direct* approach, therapists involve themselves to a greater extent as consultants to the teacher and other team members (Giangreco, 1996; Giangreco, Prelock, et al., 2000). Assumptions of an indirect therapy model include the following:

1. Assessment of skills and abilities can best be conducted in natural environments.

2. Students are best taught through functional activities.

3. Therapy should be provided throughout the day and in all appropriate environments.

4. Learning outcomes must be taught and verified in natural environments.

Followers of the transdisciplinary approach may provide some direct services to students as well. Clearly, both direct and indirect modes of service delivery have a place in educating students with severe and multiple disabilities. The team needs to decide on using a particular model at a particular moment on the basis of appropriate outcomes for the student being served.

The transdisciplinary model is characterized by planned role release, which is the sharing and exchange of certain roles and responsibilities across team members. One team member releases some functions of one's primary discipline to other team members and is open to being taught by other team members (Giangreco, Prelock, et al., 2000; Snell & Janney, 2000). For team members to serve in consulting positions and for services to be delivered integratively (i.e., integrated therapy approach), traditional roles of teachers, therapists, parents, and other team members must become more flexible. For example, the PT may share his or her assessment goal, strategy, and procedures with another professional who has an established relationship with the child and family and with those who provide primary services to the student. A process of role transition leading to role release includes sharing general information about practices and approaches of the various disciplines, sharing detailed information about specific practices or strategies, and teaching specific strategies to other team members (Lyon & Lyon, 1980; Woodruff & McGonigel, 1988).

Disadvantages

Even though disciplines share in providing services, they often have separate goals, with role release occurring in one direction only. For example, the PT who serves a student named Lindsey releases some aspects of her role, such as positioning Lindsey, to the special education teacher and OT, who position Lindsey throughout the day in various seating situations. But the OT has not released her skills regarding Lindsey's feeding goal to the special education teacher or paraeducator; thus, she is the only person who holds the capability to work with Lindsey on this goal. In this way, various providers may address some of a student's goals separately (Gallagher, 1997; Rainforth, 2002; Rainforth, Giangreco, Smith, & York, 1995).

Collaborative Approach Applied to Education

Organization

The collaborative model is the current exemplary practice in service delivery models for the education of students with severe and multiple disabilities, incorporating all of the best qualities of the transdisciplinary model combined with the integrated therapy model and adding qualities to address the limitations (Giangreco, Cloninger, et al., 2000). Often, the terms *transdisciplinary, integrated therapy,* and *collaborative* are used interchangeably, but there are differences, first identified by Rainforth and others in the early 1990s. To emphasize the need for collaboration, Rainforth and colleagues noted, " 'collaborative teamwork' is now used to refer to service provision that combines the essential elements of the transdisciplinary and integrated therapy models" (Rainforth et al., 1995, p. 137). See Table 1.1 for a comparison of models.

A significant difference between the collaborative model and others is that in a collaborative team, individuals bring their own perspectives to the team but these are purposefully shaped and changed by working closely with other team members (Edelman, 1997). The practice of role release used in the transdisciplinary model is essential, yet the collaborative model goes beyond that concept to embrace influences on one's own practice. The collaborative model is multidirectional and dynamic. All team members acquire not only shared understanding and knowledge of each other's expertise but also the ability to incorporate that into collaborative evaluation, planning, and implementation. New ideas are generated through group interaction that would not be generated by working in isolation.

Another significant difference is that the collaborative model addresses the provision of services in meaningful or functional contexts as well as who provides the services and how multiple team members can provide the same service (Rainforth & York-Barr, 1997). The collaborative team model makes provisions for who is on the team, how each team member's expertise will be used, and the functional contexts in which team members will provide their expertise.

A collaborative team is a group of people working in instructionally and contextually integrated ways on the four major areas of educational programming—assessment, development of instructional goals, intervention, and evaluation—based on student and family valued life outcomes. In the other models, collaboration on these four major areas of educational programming is an option rather than the basis of team expectations and operations.

Table 1.1. Comparison of service delivery models for students with severe and multiple disabilities

Characteristic	Interdisciplinary	Multidisciplinary	Transdisciplinary	Collaborative
Assessment and planning are done separately by discipline.	✓	✓		
Goals are established separately by discipline.	✓	✓		
Interventions are done separately by discipline.	✓	✓		
Intervention may not be of educational benefit or relevance.		✓	✓	
Implementation is done in physical isolation.	✓	✓	✓	
Other disciplines are acknowledged.	✓	✓	✓	✓
Assessment results are shared.	✓	✓	✓	
Medical model is the basis of intervention.		✓	✓	
Assessment is referenced to educational program.			✓	✓
Services (indirect) are integrated and related.			✓	✓✓
Role release is practiced.			(Maybe; not guaranteed)	✓✓
Skills are applied to one set of shared goals.		✓	✓	✓✓✓
Model makes use of natural contexts and functional activities.				✓✓✓
Decisions are shaped and influenced by team members.				
Educational model of intervention serves as the basis.				
Model incorporates team members' expertise into own practice.				✓✓
Program results from melded creativity of all.				✓✓

14

Assessment

The main purpose of assessment in the collaborative approach is to determine relevant educational goals. As York, Rainforth, and Giangreco (1990) observed, the emphasis should be on planned quality assessment conducted in priority educational environments on activities identified by the team, with team members (including the family and student). Once assessment is complete, the team establishes content priorities for the learning outcomes to be taught to the student and writes educational goals and objectives that address those learning outcomes identified as goal priorities for the year.

Development of Instructional Goals and Objectives

Goals and objectives should be selected based on criteria such as whether performing the activity will make a real difference in the student's quality of life— that is, whether the activity will support the student's valued life outcomes.

———————————

Taylor is a sixth-grade student with cognitive, motor, and hearing disabilities. This goal is listed on his IEP: "Taylor will reliably answer 'yes' or 'no' symbolically to a variety of questions to indicate wants and needs." The questions the team needs to address are these: Will teaching Taylor to use a communication device to indicate "yes" or "no" increase his quality of life? Will it provide him the capability to make choices or to participate in more meaningful activities?

———————————

The goals and objectives on students' IEPs dictate the supports and accommodations, schedule, instructional materials and strategies, and the required involvement of specific team members. Therefore, the way in which educational goals and objectives are developed for students with severe and multiple disabilities is absolutely critical to the success of operating within a collaborative model. An IEP developed by a collaborative team is not simply goals and objectives written from individual disciplines and compiled into a single document, with the individual team members responsible for implementing and evaluating progress on their individual goals. No option is given for the members to write separate goals as they are allowed to do in other models. A collaborative IEP is based on goals and objectives that belong to the student and originate from priorities that the student and family select, with input from other team members. It is the responsibility of the team to provide future planning strategies such as Choosing Outcomes and Accommodations for Children (COACH) (Giangreco, Cloninger, & Iverson, 1998) and Making Action Plans (MAPs) (Pearpoint, Forest, & O'Brien,

1996) for the student and family to truly be part of the team and involved in making educational decisions. The goals and objectives are based on what is best for the student educationally for a given year from a family-centered perspective.

The student's goals target educationally relevant learning outcomes that are not tied to any one discipline. For example, "Omar will improve postural stability and increase antigravity of head, trunk, and extremities," is an example of a discipline-specific and jargon-filled goal written by a PT (Giangreco et al., 1998). Instead, a goal should be stated so that everyone can understand clearly what is expected, it can be carried out in natural environments, and it provides an answer to the question, "So what difference will this make in the student's life?" Restating a goal for Omar in a discipline-free, jargon-free manner results in "During lunch, Omar will walk in line, get his lunch tray, reach for two food items, and carry his tray to the table."

In another example, "Moira will extend her dominant hand to an augmentative device for expressive communication requesting of salient items." Stated without reference to disciplines or use of jargon, "Moira will point to pictures on her communication board to make requests for preferred people, toys, and food." For more examples of discipline-free, functional goals, see Chapter 3.

Delivery of Instruction and Related Services

The collaborative model incorporates integrated therapy and teaching, in which team members provide at least some services by consulting and teaching other team members, but all team members have the capability for intervention. Skills and expertise of team members are integrated not only in the writing of the student's goals but also in deciding where and how the student's goals and objectives are taught. The team works together to support the student in all school and community environments and activities as indicated on the IEP. Team members share their personal and professional expertise and skills so that the team can determine how best to address the student's goals and objectives without gaps or unnecessary overlaps in services. In the collaborative model, "planning is referenced to a common set of goals and needs whereby each team member applies his or her disciplinary skill to the shared goals, and therapeutic techniques are implemented in concert with other instructional methods in the context of functional activities" (Giangreco et al., 1998, p. 61).

Evaluation of Program Effectiveness

Teams participate in ongoing evaluation processes by which they make necessary changes in response to the student's needs and priorities. Responsive evaluation addresses questions at various levels, including 1) student-focused questions concerning progress, satisfaction, and needs; 2) program-focused questions concerning methods, curriculum, and environments; and 3) team-focused questions concerning efficacy in implementing the educational program and in working together collaboratively. The last level, team-focused evaluation, can be addressed through two questions:

1. What was the effect of our collaboration on student outcomes? In other words, did team members work together in such a manner to enable the student to be successful in his or her educational program?

2. Did we maintain positive relationships throughout the process?

A later section of this chapter, Essential Components of Collaborative Teaming, lists additional ways to address these two questions.

CHALLENGES TO IMPLEMENTING A COLLABORATIVE MODEL

No matter how useful is the collaborative approach in meeting the educational needs of students with severe and multiple disabilities, collaborative teams inevitably encounter a variety of challenges along the way. These may be similar to challenges or limitations in other models such as the transdisciplinary model. Anticipation and team preparation can alleviate difficulties that often result from lack of understanding, lack of personal experience with the model, and logistics. Challenges in implementing the model are discussed from three perspectives: 1) philosophical and professional, 2) personal and interpersonal, and 3) logistical.

Philosophical and Professional Challenges

Philosophical and professional challenges arise from differences in professional training and philosophy (Edelman, 1997). Team members from different disciplines often approach instruction and therapy differently. Many related service providers, such as OTs and PTs, psychologists, nutritionists, and SLPs, receive their professional preparation in a medical model in which one looks for the underlying cause of a behavior and then directs therapy toward "fixing" the presumed cause. Special educators, especially those who work with children with severe and multiple disabilities, receive their professional preparation in an educational model in which one administers functional or authentic assessment with the goal of teaching functional learning outcomes for the student, not to fix the student (Giangreco, Prelock, et al., 2000).

In too many professions, preparation occurs in isolation from other disciplines; thus, teachers and related services providers neither learn about each other's disciplines or jargon nor have opportunities to work together as members of an educational team. When serving as a member of an IEP team, they are unprepared for the change in roles necessary to be part of a collaborative team (Snell & Janney, 2000).

Releasing part of one's professional role may threaten some professionals' perceived status. Collaborative teams that operate smoothly, however, can actually *enhance* the status of team members by fostering greater respect and interdependence, providing opportunities to share expertise with others, and being part of a creative team (Edelman, 1997; Idol et al., 2000).

In an integrated related services and teaching approach, there may be a few highly specialized procedures for evaluation or intervention that only specifically designated, trained individuals should perform based on their professional judgment or as designated by a physician. For example, in some states only nurses can perform catheterization or dispense medication at school. In other instances, only a PT could appropriately deliver range of motion to a student returning to school after surgery. Other team members should learn and perform only those procedures appropriate for them, with the assurance that legally required supervision by licensed or certified professionals is planned for and regularly occurs.

Team members using the collaborative model may have difficulty deciding who should provide what services because this is not as clear as it is in the other models. The paraeducator and special educator may be carrying out feeding techniques daily at snack time after being taught by the SLP, who provides his or her support to the student via indirect consultation and biweekly direct consultation. Parents or other team members may feel that the child is not receiving adequate related services when the process for integrating related services and instruction is not clear. An important step in enhancing team functioning is for all members to understand the model and the ways in which a specific array of instruction and related services can ensure the best educational results for the student. When team members understand their changing roles, they see the numerous opportunities for involvement in planning, implementation, and evaluation, and consequently, the numerous opportunities for their expertise and resources to benefit the student and other team members.

Personal and Interpersonal Challenges

Team members also encounter personal and interpersonal challenges when implementing a collaborative team model. One of the tenets of the collaborative model is the need for team members to share information and skills with others and to accept and learn from other team members. Some may find meeting this need threatening because it places the team members' skills under scrutiny and requires release of expertise and training on how to teach adults. Thus, sharing one's expertise with others is a matter of trust and a challenge for some team members. Team members can use strategies such as modeling, practice, feedback, and coaching to share their expertise (Heron & Harris, 2001). As these skills increase and trust develops, teaching others and being taught becomes easier, more effective, and enjoyable.

Another source of interpersonal problems may be a lack of clear differentiation of responsibilities among team members. Within a collaborative approach, functions are shared and purposefully melded, which makes it even more essential to clarify roles and responsibilities. At team meetings, members identify who does what (e.g., contact parents, take minutes, repair equipment). Over time, as roles and responsibilities change, team members must be involved in and informed about these changes. The collaborative model advocates strategies to promote shared responsibilities; it does not advocate that related services or accommodations be reduced or that one person provide all of the services needed by the student.

Implementing a new service delivery model takes time and concerted effort as well as administrative support and technical assistance. People respond to change in various ways, from total resistance to exuberance. Understanding how people respond to change should be anticipated and addressed through strategies for fostering dialogue, resolving conflicts, solving problems, and proving the benefits to the student.

Logistical Challenges

Some of the most difficult challenges are ones that often seem out of the control of the team. These include such difficulties as finding the time for meetings and "on the fly" communication, running efficient meetings, and ensuring team communication and consistency among team members. Addressing these challenges often requires the involvement of administrators and others in the school and may include strategies such as training and adapting the collaborative approach for everyone in a school or agency, scheduling team planning time for everyone, training and use of problem-solving processes for a variety of school or agency challenges, and providing e-mail access for all team members (Snell & Janney, 2000; Thousand & Villa, 2000).

Stages of Team Development

The process of working together as a collaborative team does not just happen; the practice of skills must be part of the process. Although all team members enter the process at different levels, new learning occurs for all. Being part of a team is a dynamic, ever-changing process, with most teams going through stages of learning and implementation and then recycling through these stages continuously as new people join the team or as conflict or new situations arise.

ESSENTIAL COMPONENTS OF COLLABORATIVE TEAMING

A collaborative team is defined as an approach to educational programming that exhibits all of the following five components:

1. Appropriate team membership

2. A shared framework of assumptions, beliefs, and values

3. Distribution and parity of functions and resources

4. Processes for working together

5. A set of shared student goals agreed to by the team (Giangreco et al., 1998; Snell & Janney, 2000; Thousand & Villa, 2000)

Component 1: Appropriate Team Membership

Teams include "those who will be most directly affected," rather than "everyone who might be affected" (Giangreco et al., 1998, p. 23). With the potential for a large number of people on a student's team, and the recognition that weekly or biweekly team meetings of all of the team members is neither possible nor necessary, a tiered team membership can be used consisting of core, extended, and situational levels. Membership at each level is related to the student's IEP and is influenced by professional qualifications, regulations, personal skills, and experiences of each member. A thoughtful process for making decisions regarding who is to be involved at each level in each situation facilitates the best use of everyone's expertise and avoids unnecessary overlaps and gaps in delivery of services. Related services providers, serving as other team members, are involved at each level depending on their function (i.e., direct, indirect, consultation) and frequency of contact with the student.

- *Core level:* At the core level, team membership consists of those members who have daily contact and interaction with the child, usually the special and general education teachers, the paraeducator, the parents, and perhaps one or more of the related services personnel such as the SLP, nurse, PT, or peers, as appropriate.

- *Extended level:* The next level or circle of membership, the extended level, includes those who have weekly, biweekly, or some other regular contact with the student such as related services personnel and a school administrator.

- *Situational level:* The last level or circle of membership is at the situational level. It consists of those members such as a dietitian recruited for specific situations and questions and other teachers or related services providers (e.g., psychologist, counselor). Information is shared and solicited from all, but attendance at meetings depends on function and relation to educational planning and implementation and is determined by the agenda (Giangreco et al., 1998).

Component 2: Shared Framework of Assumptions, Beliefs, and Values

Teams need to agree on their beliefs about the purpose of the team, best ways to educate students with severe and multiple disabilities, and involvement of families and professionals. Dialogue takes place in order for members to share perspectives and come to consensus on various educational programming concepts such as valued life outcomes, collaborative relationships, integrated related services and instruction, and team communication strategies.

Component 3: Distribution and Parity of Functions and Resources

Team members value each member's input and expertise and alternately take on the roles of both teacher and learner and giver and receiver of expertise. Ways to share expertise, perspectives, experiences, and resources are applied in meetings; in written communications; and in assessment, planning, and evaluation.

Component 4: Processes for Working Together

Team members use processes for working together in four ways: face-to-face interaction, positive interdependence, interpersonal skills, and accountability.

1. *Face-to-face interactions:* Ongoing, regularly planned times for face-to-face interactions provide members with the opportunities to problem solve creatively, get to know each other, share and receive expertise of others—and most important—plan for the implementation of the student's educational program. Core, extended, and situational tiers of team members are used to designate who needs to be at what meetings. When members are not at meetings, a system of sharing what happened and receiving input is set up so that all can be informed.

2. *Positive interdependence:* Positive interdependence is "the perception that one is linked with others in a way so that one cannot succeed unless they do (and vice versa), and that their work benefits you and your work benefits them" (Johnson & Johnson, 1997, p. 399). Team members agree to provide educational services from a shared operational framework and set of values that not only greatly benefits the student but also benefits each member of the team.

Positive interdependence can be fostered in a variety of ways:

- Stating group and individual goals publicly and in writing

- Sharing team functions, roles, and resources equitably by defining team roles and responsibilities (e.g., recording minutes, facilitating meetings, keeping time, communicating with absent members, using jargon-free language, completing paperwork) and taking turns fulfilling these roles

- Identifying norms or ways team members want to work together (e.g., take turns, listen respectfully, "be nice," give compliments, celebrate successes)

- Creating shared accomplishments and rewards by scheduling time at meetings to present positive achievements of the student and team members, attending workshops together, presenting at workshops together, having a team party, and participating in other wellness activities

3. *Interpersonal skills:* Interpersonal skills are essential to effective team functioning. Adults often need to learn, use, and reflect on the small-group interpersonal skills needed for collaboration. These skills include trust-building, communication, leadership for managing and organizing team activities, creative problem solving, decision making, and conflict management. The priority skills in each of these categories that are reflective of how the team desires to behave and work together can be written in mutually agreed-on group norms and incorporated into the meeting agenda. These products also provide a set of behaviors that can be used as benchmarks for monitoring, discussing, and reflecting as team members learn together and practice teaming skills.

4. *Accountability:* Individual and group accountability is necessary for members to inform each other of the need for assistance or encouragement, to identify positive progress toward individual and group goals, and to recognize fulfillment of individual responsibilities. At each meeting the agenda should include a brief time for *processing,* that is, for sharing observations and suggesting changes in team process as needed. The responsibility for processing is best rotated among members, as are other team roles. The content of the agenda also provides opportunities for accountability reporting (e.g., "Report from physical therapist on co-teaching activity with physical education teacher—5 minutes"). One or two times per year, a team may take more time to evaluate team operations, celebrate, and make adjustments for the next semester or year.

Component 5: Shared Student Goals Agreed to by the Team

The IEP goals and objectives are derived from the needs of the student and indicate what the student will be able to do as a result of instruction. By establishing common student goals, teams avoid the problem of each member having his or her own separate, discipline-specific goals. All team members agree to collaboratively supply their expertise and resources so that the student can achieve his or her goals and objectives. All team members pull in the same direction for the student.

Reasons for a collaborative team approach to the education of students with severe and multiple disabilities stem from the educational difference this approach can make for students. Team members work in a collegial culture, within a community of caring and supportive adults, not in isolation. Team members share a diversity of perspectives and experiences integrated in creative ways to address the many and ongoing learning challenges of students with severe and multiple disabilities. Team members provide context-specific, embedded instruction in meaningful activities that promote learning and generalization. Team members are able to address the learning characteristics of students by designing and implementing coordinated, integrated services.

Just as excellent teaching does not just happen, collaborative teaming does not just happen. Team members must learn from and teach one another. Team members must take the time to learn, practice, and evaluate teaming skills. Team members must take the time to work on challenges and celebrate successes. They do this so that they will provide effective, efficient, creative, truly individualized programs for students.

For other helpful resources on collaborative teamwork, refer to works by Thousand and Villa (2000), Snell and Janney (2000), and Idol and colleagues (2000).

———————————

Zach, who is 11, rides to his neighborhood school on the bus with his brother and other children in his neighborhood to attend a fifth-grade class. Zach likes being in places where there is a lot of activity, and he enjoys music, books, and the outdoors. He presently does not have a formalized communication system; he communicates through facial expressions, vocalizing, crying, and laughing and seems to understand more than he is able to communicate. Zach does not have vision or hearing impairments; however, he does have physical disabilities that affect the use of his extremities. He is beginning to learn to use a power wheelchair for mobility and is beginning to use communication assistive technology.

Zach's IEP was developed using COACH (Giangreco et al., 1998), which identified the priority learning outcomes through an interview process with Zach and his parents followed by general supports and objectives identified by the team working collaboratively. Decisions about the specific roles and responsibilities of each team member for implementation of Zach's IEP were made using the Vermont Interdependent Services

Team Approach (VISTA) (Giangreco, 1996, 2000), a process for coordinating educational support services. Zach's IEP is supported by a special educator, classroom paraeducator, physical therapist, occupational therapist, and speech-language pathologist. See Figure 1.1 for Zach's educational program and support plan. Educational relevance and necessity determine how and where these professionals' expertise is used. By knowing the expertise of each team member, overlaps and gaps can be eliminated, and teaching of goals and objectives occurs more frequently throughout the day. Not all team members will be involved in supporting all educational program components. The PT and OT on Zach's team have shared expertise in a number of motor areas, thus both do not need to be involved on all of the goals (e.g., "doing classroom and school jobs with peers"). The SLP and OT both have expertise in feeding, so the decision was made by the team that the OT would be involved with this general support, not the SLP. As each team member is providing direct instruction to the student for a particular goal, he or she is incorporating the "released" skills from other team members into his or her teaching as well as teaching other adults (e.g., paraeducator).

For Zach's goal of "making requests for food, people, places, and activities using a photo communication system and eye gaze," each of the team members contributes his or her expertise in a specific way as determined by the whole team. All of the team members have the responsibility of assisting in instructional design, in teaching Zach, and in data collection, so that he may attain this goal.

- The special educator designs the specialized instructional program that includes the instructional strategies for teaching "making requests," such as antecedent directions Zach receives, prompting procedures, material and physical cues, consequence reinforcement and correction, and data collection procedures. She also co-teaches with the general educator and teaches Zach in small groups and in pre-group sessions.

- The general educator identifies the class lessons and activities so that Zach can learn and practice "making requests," provides opportunities for Zach to make requests in these lessons and activities, teaches Zach's peers natural supporting and interaction strategies when he makes requests, and shares responsibility for designing and delivering instruction to Zach in general education group activities.

- The paraeducator teaches Zach in various school situations such as small groups in the classroom, provides instructional support in large groups and one-to-one teaching in learning centers and computer labs, records data on Zach's learning outcomes, keeps Zach's equipment in working order, and supports Zach in his personal care activities, using these contexts for Zach to practice "making requests."

Goal or general support	Support needed	Mode of service (Indirect/Direct)	Location of service
Making choices using eye gaze	SE GE PE SLP OT	D/I D D I/D I	Fifth-grade classes
Responding to yes/no questions using eye gaze and head movements	SE GE PE SLP OT	D D D I/D I	Fifth-grade classes
Making requests for food, people, places, and activities using a photo communication system and eye gaze	SE GE PE SLP OT	D D D I/D I	Fifth-grade classes, cafeteria
Doing classroom and school jobs with peers	GE PE PT P	D D/I I D	Fifth-grade classes, around school
Engaging in active leisure by activating devices (e.g., toys, CD player, page turner, computer, appliances) using an adaptive switch	SE GE PE P	D/I D D/I D	Fifth-grade classes, library, computer lab
Personal supports: Needs to be given food and drinks, dressed, assisted with personal hygiene	SE PE OT	D/I D I/D	Cafeteria, bathroom
Physical supports: Needs repositioning at regular intervals, environmental barriers modified to wheelchair access, equipment managed, moved from place to place	SE GE PE PT P	D/I D D I D	Fifth-grade classes

(continued)

Figure 1.1. Zach's individualized education program (IEP) and supports plan reflecting a collaborative approach. (Key: SE = special educator; PE = paraeducator; SLP = speech-language pathologist; OT = occupational therapist; PT = physical therapist; GE = general educator; P = peers)

Figure 1.1.   *(continued)*

Goal or general support	Support needed	Mode of service (Indirect/Direct)	Location of service
Teaching others: Staff and students need to learn about Zach's augmentative and alternative communication system, other communicative behaviors, and how to communicate with Zach	SE GE PE SLP	D D D I/D	Around school
Providing access and opportunities: Access to general education classrooms and activities, instructional and material accommodations prepared in advance for multilevel and curriculum overlap instruction in general education activities	SE GE PE SLP	D/I D/I D I/D	Fifth-grade classes, around school

- The speech-language pathologist takes the lead in identifying Zach's communication system, in designing the sequence in his learning to "make requests," and in teaching other team members how the system works and how to troubleshoot.

- The occupational therapist provides information on positioning of objects, the communication device, and Zach's body for optimal use of eye gaze. He or she also provides instruction to other team members and Zach's peers on placement of objects to teach "making requests." The OT's role in providing accommodations and adaptations for Zach's eating and drinking is related to this goal; he or she could provide input on Zach's preferences used in his "making requests" instructional program.

SUMMARY

The success of students' educational programs and the quality of their lives depends on the team of people who provide services being highly connected and coordinated. The myriad educational, health, social, and emotional needs of students with severe and multiple disabilities require organization for systematic planning, implementation, and evaluation of their programs. Although other models for delivering services were explored, in this chapter the emphasis is on collaborative teaming for designing educational services for students with severe and multiple disabilities. The collaborative teaming model developed from other models of service delivery with subtle and not so subtle transformations along the way. The most similar model, the transdisciplinary model, differs in several ways. The collaborative model arose from an educational emphasis, whereas the transdisciplinary model holds its roots in the medical approach, as do other models (i.e., interdisciplinary, multidisciplinary). The philosophy and practice of the collaborative model is that the team members not only will share their expertise and resources but also will be purposefully changed by other members and will use their acquired skills to influence their own discipline. The collaborative approach offers benefits to the student by having not just a collection of people providing services but also a team with a shared vision, a shared framework, and shared strategies that are more likely to ensure that the student will reach his or her IEP goals and objectives.

The inherent dynamism of teaching and learning, the ever-changing goals and needs of students with severe and multiple disabilities, and the variable nature of people mean there always will be questions without defined answers, and new information to learn. The need for collaborative creativity and flexibility, open minds, and the willingness to share dreams and challenges is ongoing. When team members let values and visions larger than their fears and doubts lead their work, when what they do is designed so that every child attains his or her valued life outcomes, when they are committed to being a team together, then educational programs can lead to meaningful, positive changes in the lives of children with severe and multiple disabilities and their families.

REFERENCES

Code of Federal Regulations. (1999). CFR Chapter III, Section 300.7 (c)(7).

Edelman, S.W. (1997). *The experiences of professional shift of school-based physical therapy leaders.* Unpublished doctoral dissertation, University of Vermont.

Gallagher, J. (1997). *The million dollar question: Unmet service needs for young children with disabilities.* Chapel Hill: Early Childhood Research Institute, Service Utilization, Frank Porter Graham Child Development Center, University of North Carolina at Chapel Hill.

Giangreco, M.F. (1990). Making related service decisions for students with severe disabilities: Roles, criteria, and authority. *Journal of The Association for Persons with Severe Handicaps, 15,* 22–31.

Giangreco, M.F. (1996). *Vermont interdependent services team approach (VISTA): A guide to coordinating educational support services.* Baltimore: Paul H. Brookes Publishing Co.

Giangreco, M.F. (2000). *Guidelines for making decisions about IEP services.* Montpelier: Vermont Department of Education.

Giangreco, M.F., Cloninger, C.J., Dennis, R.E., & Edelman, S.W. (2000). Problem-solving methods to facilitate inclusive education. In R.A. Villa & J.S. Thousand (Eds.), *Restructuring for caring and effective education: Piecing the puzzle together* (2nd ed., pp. 293–359). Baltimore: Paul H. Brookes Publishing Co.

Giangreco, M.F., Cloninger, C.J., & Iverson, V.S. (1998). *Choosing outcomes and accommodations for children (COACH): A guide to educational planning for students with disabilities* (2nd ed.). Baltimore: Paul H. Brookes Publishing Co.

Giangreco, M.F., Edelman, S.W., Broer, S.M., & Doyle, M.B. (2001). Paraprofessional support of students with disabilities: Literature from the past decade. *Exceptional Children, 68,* 45–63.

Giangreco, M.F., Prelock, P.A., Reid, R.R., Dennis, R.E., & Edelman, S.W. (2000). Role of related service personnel in inclusive schools. In R.A. Villa & J.S. Thousand (Eds.), *Restructuring for caring and effective education: Piecing the puzzle together* (2nd ed., pp. 360–388). Baltimore: Paul H. Brookes Publishing Co.

Giangreco, M.F., York, J., & Rainforth, B. (1989). Providing related services to learners with severe handicaps in educational environments: Pursuing the least restrictive option. *Pediatric Physical Therapy, 1*(2), 55–63.

Heron, T.E., & Harris, K.C. (2001). *The educational consultant: Helping professionals, parents, and students in inclusive classrooms* (4th ed.). Austin, TX: PRO-ED.

Hutchinson, D.J. (1978). The transdisciplinary approach. In J.B. Curry & K.K. Peppe (Eds.), *Mental retardation: Nursing approaches to care* (pp. 65–74). St. Louis: C.V. Mosby.

Idol, L., Nevin, A., & Paolucci-Whitcomb, P. (2000). *Collaborative consultation* (3rd ed.). Austin, TX: PRO-ED.

Individuals with Disabilities Education Act (IDEA) Amendments of 1997, PL 105-17, 20 U.S.C. §§ 1400 *et seq.*

Johnson, D.W., & Johnson, F.W. (1997). *Joining together: Group theory and skills* (6th ed.). Englewood Cliffs, NJ: Prentice Hall.

Lyon, S., & Lyon, G. (1980). Team functioning and staff development: A role release approach to providing integrated educational services for severely handicapped students. *Journal of The Association for the Severely Handicapped, 5,* 250–263.

Orelove, F.P., & Sobsey, D. (1996). *Educating children with multiple disabilities: A transdisciplinary approach* (3rd ed.). Baltimore: Paul H. Brookes Publishing Co.

Pearpoint, J., Forest, M., & O'Brien, J. (1996). MAPs, Circles of Friends, and PATH: Powerful tools to help build caring communities. In S. Stainback & W. Stainback (Eds.), *Inclusion: A guide for educators* (pp. 67–86). Baltimore: Paul H. Brookes Publishing Co.

Rainforth, B. (2002). The primary therapist model: Addressing challenges to practice in special education. *Physical & Occupational Therapy in Pediatrics, 22,* 29–51.

Rainforth, B., Giangreco, M., Smith, P.E., & York, J. (1995). Collborative teamwork in training and technical assistance: Enhancing community supports for persons with developmental disabilities. In O. Karan & S. Greenspan (Eds.), *Community rehabilitation services for people with disabilities* (pp. 134–168). Newton, MA: Butterworth-Heinemann.

Rainforth, B., & York-Barr, J. (1997). *Collaborative teams for students with severe disabilities: Integrating therapy and educational services* (2nd ed.). Baltimore: Paul H. Brookes Publishing Co.

Rainforth, B., York, J., & Macdonald, C. (1992). *Collaborative teams for students with severe disabilities: Integrating therapy and educational services.* Baltimore: Paul H. Brookes Publishing Co.

Reiter, S. (1999). *Society and disability: An international perspective on social policy.* Haifa, Israel: AHVA Publishers & The Institute on Disabilities, Temple University.

Selby, D. (2001). The signature of the whole: Radical interconnectedness and its implications for global and environmental education. *Encounter, 14,* 5–16.

Snell, M.E.J., & Janney, R. (2000). *Teachers' guides to inclusive practices: Collaborative teaming.* Baltimore: Paul H. Brookes Publishing Co.

Thousand, J.S., & Villa, R.A. (2000). Collaborative teams: A powerful tool in school restructuring. In R.A. Villa & J.S. Thousand (Eds.), *Restructuring for caring and effective education: Piecing the puzzle together* (2nd ed., pp. 254–291). Baltimore: Paul H. Brookes Publishing Co.

United Cerebral Palsy Association National Organized Collaborative Project to Provide Comprehensive Services for Atypical Infants and Their Families. (1976). *Staff development handbook: A resource for the transdisciplinary process.* New York: Author.

Whitehouse, F.A. (1951). Teamwork—A democracy of processions. *Exceptional Children, 18,* 45–52.

Woodruff, G., & McGonigel, M.J. (1988). Early intervention team approaches: The transdisciplinary model. In J.B. Jordan, J.J. Gallagher, P.L. Hutinger, & M.B. Karnes (Eds.), *Early childhood special education: Birth to three* (pp. 164–181). Arlington, VA: Council for Exceptional Children.

York, J., Rainforth, B., & Giangreco, M.F. (1990). Transdisciplinary teamwork and integrated therapy: Clarifying the misconceptions. *Pediatric Physical Therapy, 2*(2), 73–79.

CHAPTER 2

Working with Families

Deborah Chen and Cathy Miles

At 3 P.M., Linda Petrovich, the special education teacher, is making plans for the next day. Mrs. Chang, the mother of one of Linda's second-grade students, stops by and asks if she has a few minutes. Linda thinks, "Oh no, what does she want from me now? Here we go again. She'll want me to do something else for her son. Doesn't she realize that I have 14 other students? I just don't have time for all of her demands. Maybe she has a problem with something I've already done. I wonder if I should get someone in here as a witness? Maybe I'm making too big a deal of this, but I get so uncomfortable when parents drop by. I just don't know what's worse—being put on the spot during an IEP meeting or these casual visits. Sometimes this job is really stressful! I love teaching. The kids are no problem, but their parents—that's another story!"

———————————

The reactions expressed by Linda Petrovich are far too common among teachers in special education, unfortunately. Although the primary responsibility of any teacher is to his or her students, special educators have an additional obligation to collaborate with families of children with disabilities. Teachers not only must have instructional skills for teaching children but also must have the competency to work effectively with families. Professional standards describe the knowledge and skills that special educators need to promote family involvement and family–professional collaboration in the child's educational program (Council for Exceptional Children, 1995; Trivette & Dunst, 2000). In 1997, the amendments to the Individuals with Disabilities Education Act (IDEA; PL 105-17) strengthened the role of parents as active decision makers in partnership with service providers. Only through collaboration between families and teachers can children with severe and multiple disabilities receive the most meaningful educational experiences and have successful outcomes.

The development of a collaborative working relationship with families requires special effort on the part of teachers for several reasons:

- The national shortage of qualified teachers in special education (U.S. Department of Education, 2002) affects the quality of instruction provided to all students with disabilities.

- Teachers may be very skilled in teaching students with severe and multiple disabilities, but less skilled in working with families.

- The traditional structure and procedures of the educational system may not facilitate home–school partnerships.

- Like any other relationship, the family–professional relationship is a dynamic process of interactions colored by each person's perspectives based on life experiences, roles, values, and beliefs.

- The development and maintenance of an effective family–professional relationship requires concerted effort, an investment of time, ongoing communication, and mutual goals.

Given these challenges, teachers should evaluate their professional roles when working with families, refine their skills for building relationships, and identify ways to collaborate with each student's family. This chapter describes a process of building effective family–professional relationships by 1) analyzing how the structure of educational programs affects family involvement, 2) acknowledging that each family is a complex and unique system, 3) understanding the significant impact that a child with severe and multiple disabilities has on the family, and 4) implementing family-friendly strategies that invite family participation and value their contributions. In this chapter, the term *family* refers to parents, other family members, and significant caregivers who are involved in making decisions about the child's education. This chapter draws on existing literature and uses excerpts from several family stories to illustrate key issues in home–school collaboration and to provide an understanding of family perspectives.

SCHOOL PROGRAMS FOR CHILDREN WITH DISABILITIES

When children with disabilities are younger than 3 years of age, early intervention service providers often have a close working relationship with families. Service providers make regular home visits, families may attend a center-based activity, and services are individualized and family-focused (Chen, 1999). Family members and service providers are in frequent contact, and these partnerships are often strong and long lasting. Sometimes, these natural opportunities for collaboration fade away when the child begins school unless the school program emphasizes family involvement. Depending on the preschool model, families may still receive home visits and have opportunities to participate in center-based activities (Cook, Tessier, & Klein, 2000). Compared with early intervention services, special education services for school-age children are more child-centered than family-centered. By the time a child with a disability enters kindergarten, a family's primary involvement with the school may be at the child's annual individualized education program (IEP) meeting, back-to-school nights, and parent conferences.

The Importance of Family–School Meetings

Teachers of school-age children who have disabilities primarily have three types of meetings with families: 1) the child's IEP meeting, 2) parent–teacher conferences, and 3) parent education meetings on a particular topic. These meetings are formal opportunities for teachers to develop a partnership with families.

Without careful planning, the traditional structure of formal school meetings such as the annual IEP meeting may not invite and may even deter family involvement (Harry, 1992; Kalyanpur & Harry, 1999; Rock, 2000). Parents may work outside the home and often have multiple appointments related to their child's health or other concerns. Some parents do not have the flexibility to attend school meetings during the workday. They may not receive notices about meetings and other school activities in sufficient time to plan for child care, transportation, or time off of work. Meetings at schools add an extra burden to an already busy schedule, especially if the meetings do not invite parents' contributions or address parental concerns. Insufficient time may be scheduled for IEP meetings or parent conferences. For example, parents may encounter several service providers and a busy administrator with only 30 minutes scheduled for the meeting. Assessment reports may be read quickly and papers with computer-generated goals may be presented for the parent to review and sign. In this formal and hurried format, little opportunity is provided for the parent to ask questions or share information and relatively no time is devoted to discussion. The formal and impersonal process of a poorly planned and badly conducted IEP meeting confuses some families to the point that they remain uninvolved in their child's school. Others are very active in their child's educational program but find collaboration with school personnel to be challenging (Harry, Kalyanpur, & Day, 1999; Soodak & Erwin, 2002; Turnbull & Turnbull, 2001).

Linda Petrovich has just completed the annual IEP meetings for her 15 students. The degree of parental involvement varied for each family. She has one student whose parents did not turn up for the meeting and she has not been able to contact them by telephone. The school has mailed the IEP to the family and is waiting for a reply. Five families did not attend their child's IEP meeting, but when Linda telephoned them, they discussed the IEP with her and have signed and returned the document. Other parents attended their child's IEP meetings, but some of them did not have any questions or comments. A few parents discussed their child's goals with Linda before the meeting and had some questions about services. Some of these families even questioned the goals and suggested new ones, and Linda was happy to have their collaboration. Linda wonders what she might do to encourage parents to participate more actively in the IEP meetings and other school events.

Teachers can begin to evaluate family participation in school meetings by asking themselves the following questions:

1. What kinds of meetings do I have with families?

2. How do I prepare for them?

3. How and when are the families notified about meetings? Do parents receive sufficient notice so that they can plan to attend?

4. What can I do to make families feel welcome and valued in meetings about their child?

5. How can I encourage each family to actively participate in meetings?

6. What are the barriers to family participation, and what can I do to overcome them?

Family involvement can be supported with careful planning and consideration of family preferences and by providing sufficient information to families in accessible formats (Beckman & Stepanek, 1996; Woods & McCormick, 2002). If parents are informed and involved in their child's education, then the annual IEP conference is more likely to reflect a home–school partnership and result in meaningful goals and services for the child (Rock, 2000). Table 2.1 includes tips for effective planning meetings.

Family–School Differences in Values, Beliefs, and Goals

If family priorities and perspectives conflict with those of the school system, then unfortunately, the collaborative home–school relationship is challenged

Table 2.1.   Tips for effective planning meetings

- Explain to families that their involvement in their child's educational program is invaluable and will result in learning experiences that benefit the child. Teachers need information about the child's strengths, interests, abilities, and needs and the family's preferences, goals, and concerns about the child. Because children spend more time with their families than with teachers, much of a child's learning will occur out of school, so parents need specific strategies and resources to promote the child's learning.

- Assist families in learning about the educational system by providing information about the services and programs in the school district, their rights under IDEA, and requirements of the IEP process.

- Provide information that is easily understood in a format (e.g., individual discussion, print, video, or internet resources) that is preferred by the family.

- Ask families what they would like to learn that is related to their child's education (e.g., assistive technology, augmentative and alternative communication [AAC] devices or methods, positive behavior supports) or other topics of interest. Based on a family's needs and preferences, teachers may offer information on selected topics in a variety of formats (e.g., group meetings; video, print, or Internet resources).

- Ask the family who should be invited to meetings or the IEP conference and find out who makes the decisions in the family regarding the child's education.

- Schedule the meeting at a time and place that is convenient for family members. If the parents do not have transportation or child care, then problem solve with them and school administrators to identify solutions. For example, can the IEP meeting be held in the evening at the family's home? Is there another parent who is coming to the family education meeting or parent–teacher conference who lives close to that family?

- Prepare the family for the IEP meeting by discussing the agenda; explaining procedures; reviewing assessments; and asking about the family's goals, concerns, and questions about the child's education.

- Arrange for interpreters if needed, plan the meeting with the interpreter, and find out about culturally respectful ways of communicating with families and encouraging their participation in meetings.

- Involve children, as appropriate, in inviting their families to a school activity by creating an invitation, telling their families about the activity, or participating in the event.

- Encourage a parent to bring a friend or relative to the meeting or event if he or she would be more comfortable.

- Create a welcoming atmosphere by providing a comfortable setting for the meeting, offering some refreshments, making introductions, having time for "small talk," and having a conversation about the issue.

- Recognize that some families may not be able to attend meetings despite your best efforts. Nevertheless, make sure that these families understand their legal rights and the educational options for their child. Let these parents know that they are missed and that you understand their particular situation. Continue to keep in touch through home–school journals and call once in a while to find out how they are doing.

(Klein & Chen, 2001; Kroth & Edge, 1997; O'Shea, O'Shea, Algozzine, & Hammitte, 2001; Rothenberg, 1995). Many parents are very involved with their child's school and spend an enormous amount of time and effort to secure the best education for their children. Teachers may view children only within the context of the school system and its resources to provide an appropriate education, which sometimes results in a conflict with the parents' efforts.

Challenges to developing a positive home–school relationship are even more apparent when service providers and families do not share a common culture and language (Barnwell & Day, 1996; Harry, 1992; Kalyanpur & Harry, 1999; Parette & Petch-Hogan, 2000; Schwartz, 1995). Obtaining qualified interpreters may be difficult, and misunderstandings may result because of differences in culture and communication styles. Depending on their cultural background, a family's beliefs about the cause of their child's disability and expectations for this child might vary greatly from those of the teachers. Some families may view the child's disability merely as fate or as bringing an additional purpose to the families' life, whereas others may believe that the disability is a punishment for some past misdeed and reject medical or educational services altogether or be less likely to be involved in their child's educational program (Alvarez, 1998; Chan, 2004; Groce & Zola, 1993; Lamorey, 2002; Sileo, Sileo, & Prater, 1996; Willis, 2004).

A family's culture and community may also promote child-rearing practices and interdependence that conflict with a focus on individualism and independence in school programs and mainstream values (Klein & Chen, 2001; Lynch & Hanson, 2004).

Fung is a 14-year-old girl who has a visual impairment, among other disabilities. She is fully included in an eighth-grade class with special education support. Her annual IEP meeting is attended by her parents, Mr. and Mrs. Woo; Fung's special education teacher, Maxine Lee; her orientation and mobility instructor, Tim Sands; her eighth-grade teacher, Wendy Clark; her instructional assistant, Gina Rivera; the school principal, Stan Williams; and the special education program administrator, Olive Black.

Ms. Lee:	"Mr. and Mrs. Woo, I am very pleased with Fung's progress this year. She has done really well on all of her academic and social objectives. I recommend that we add a vocational objective so that she can participate in our supported employment program. This way she will have work skills to get a job after she leaves school."
Olive Black:	"Our school district has an excellent vocational training program. Our students work in a variety of places: McDonald's, the state utilities

company, the Society for the Prevention of Cruelty to Animals, Target, and in some other companies and businesses. Many of them have gotten jobs after their graduation."

Tim Sands: "I would work with Fung to help her learn to take the bus from school to her job placement. This would be a great opportunity to work on her travel training."

Mr. Woo: "Fung has three sisters and two brothers, so she will always have family to take care of her. She doesn't need to get a job. We don't want her to take the bus."

As demonstrated in the vignette about Fung's IEP meeting, special education programs for students with multiple and severe disabilities emphasize the development of independent daily living skills and focus on supported work after graduation from school. Within some families, caring for a child with a disability is viewed as a lifelong and shared responsibility among family members and such advice from teachers may conflict with beliefs. Parents of all nationalities and cultures, including those who are born in the United States and are English speaking, may encounter differences between their expectations for their children and those of the school and teachers (Turnbull & Turnbull, 2001). Each family's upbringing, experiences, and community will guide their values and beliefs about the child's education.

Barrera and Corso (2002) suggested a Skilled Dialogue approach to assist service providers in responding to cultural and linguistic differences in their work. Two components make up Skilled Dialogue: Anchored Understanding of Diversity and 3rd Space. Anchored Understanding of Diversity requires face-to-face interactions and personal experiences with people of diverse backgrounds so that 1) the range and value of diverse perspectives can be acknowledged, 2) interactions to allow a discussion of all perspectives can be established, and 3) an understanding of the positive intent of others' perspectives can be communicated. In the vignette about Fung's IEP meeting, school personnel should have asked the Woos about their goals and expectations for Fung's future. The discussion should gather information about and reflect understanding of the Woos' perspectives while examining and clarifying the perspectives of school personnel. If, after holding a lengthy discussion and listening carefully, school personnel can understand and respect the Woos' position (i.e., Fung will always live with a family member and will not need to get a job), then they will have achieved an Anchored Understanding of Diversity.

The skill of 3rd Space enables one to consider divergent views at the same time and to shift from an either–or dichotomy to an expanded and comple-

mented possibility—a third choice or 3rd Space. For example, if school personnel can see the Woos' family value (i.e., a lifelong commitment to taking care of
Fung) as complementing rather than conflicting with the school program's vocational goal (i.e., Fung's development of work skills) so that additional choices
are generated to resolve this conflict, then they have created 3rd Space options.

Table 2.2 provides some tips for getting to know families whose cultural,
linguistic, or socioeconomic background is different from your own.

Home–School Communication Difficulties

Many barriers to positive communication exist between families and schools.
Difficulties occur between them from infrequent or nonproductive contacts, the
lack of a shared language, differences in perspectives, the absence of follow-up
on specific concerns, and an unclear commitment to working together. Parents
may feel that they primarily hear from teachers when problems are occurring,
and teachers may have a similar complaint about parents. Teachers often report
that parents do not answer their notes or write in home–school communication
journals. They assume that these parents are uninvolved and unresponsive

Table 2.2.   Tips for getting to know families from diverse backgrounds

- Learn as much as you can about the culture, background, values, and practices of the
  family.
- Find out if there are individuals in the community who can serve as cultural media-
  tors to inform you about the family's culture and to assist the family in learning about
  the special education system.
- Recognize that individual differences exist within a group and that each person has a
  unique way of expressing his or her cultural experience.
- Be wary of stereotypes and assumptions based on a family's ethnicity, language, culture, religion, or socioeconomic status.
- Acknowledge your own cultural and ethnic background, values, and practices.
- Ask open-ended questions to gather information about the family's point of view
  (e.g.,"Please tell me about what you see for Fung after she graduates. Could you give
  me an example of what she would do at home?").
- Examine your own perspective through self-reflection (e.g., "What do I believe about
  family members who do not want their child to get a job or move out of the family
  home?").
- Clarify the family's understanding of your perspective (e.g., "What do you think about
  my recommendation that Fung participate in vocational training?").
- Demonstrate understanding of the family's perspective (e.g., "Tell me if I understand
  what you mean: Fung will always live with you or one of her brothers and sisters,
  so she will never need to get a job. You are worried about her safety if she takes a
  bus.").

without finding out whether this is a convenient or preferred method of communication for the family. Parents may be consumed by work, child care, and other family responsibilities. A teacher may write a note as a means of conveying or obtaining information, as a mechanism to invite family participation, or to promote consistency between home and school in the use of specific child-related strategies. These purposes may not be clear to families. In notes and face-to-face meetings, service providers may use professional jargon, acronyms, or terminology that they do not explain, thus creating barriers to family–professional collaboration (Berry & Hardman, 1998). For example, parents who are new to special education may not know what the terms *IEP, related services,* or *transition meeting* mean. In addition, each school district and professional discipline has unique terminology and acronyms, such as *floor time, DHH* (deaf and hard of hearing), *O&M* (orientation and mobility), and *legally blind,* that should be explained to families.

See Table 2.3 for some tips for developing personalized conversations with families and overcoming conflicts.

OPTIONS FOR FAMILY INVOLVEMENT

Educators can enlist families' involvement in school activities and in their children's education in many ways. Teachers should select the most effective means for communicating with their students' individual families. Some families prefer to read written correspondence from their children's school or attend group meetings. Others prefer a more personal telephone call or home visit. Following are examples of a variety of communication methods.

Print

1. Distribute regular teacher or school correspondence (e.g., newsletters, announcements, invitations).

2. Obtain input from families through questionnaires related to child-centered needs or family-centered interests.

3. Obtain data from families through surveys related to program evaluation or family satisfaction.

4. Encourage the school district to set up web pages and a voice mail system that answers parents' most frequently asked questions. These communication methods are even more useful if they offer the primary languages of families as options.

Table 2.3. Tips for developing personalized conversations with families and overcoming conflicts

- Begin with the premise that most issues are negotiable and then problem-solve conflicts between family priorities and professional recommendations. Provide alternatives for suggestions.
- Let the family know if there is a time limit for the discussion and then do not watch the clock.
- Tailor your comments for the family's situation; for example, use the child's name and provide specific examples of the child's behaviors or activities.
- Explain acronyms and technical terms and use words that are easily understood, but do not "talk down" to families.
- Explain to the family that you are asking questions to learn about their child so that you can provide suggestions that are helpful and instruction that is effective.
- Express a genuine interest in learning about the child (e.g., strengths, interests, needs, typical activities, home routine, social interactions) and understanding the family (e.g., composition, roles, responsibilities, activities).
- Describe the typical school day and how the child participates in school activities.
- Describe your understanding of the child's diagnoses and learning needs.
- Invite the family to share their observations and concerns. Ask them about meaningful goals for their child.
- Explain your professional recommendations and provide information based on experience and expertise.
- Communicate your concerns in a straightforward and nonjudgmental way, and ask the family for help.
- Admit that teachers do not have all of the answers. Share what you think, believe, and know, and identify what you do not know.
- Seek areas of agreement and focus on the child's needs and not on the school or the system.
- Evaluate the child's current performance and base recommendations on measurable outcomes.
- Look at the world from the family's perspective and accept the family's point of view.
- With the family, identify and select educational goals and objectives.
- Discuss strategies to achieve objectives.
- Agree on and record who will do what, where, and when, and develop a written action plan.
- Identify a time for another discussion to obtain feedback from the family on what is working, what needs to be changed, and any results of the intervention strategies.

Meetings

1. Provide an open house or back-to-school night with interpreters as needed.

2. Provide parent or family meetings on selected topics in the family's primary language.

3. Recruit parents to serve on school or program advisory meetings.

4. Sponsor family support groups in the family's primary language.

5. Facilitate a systematic process, such as MAPs (Pearpoint, Forest, & O'Brien, 1996), by which the child, family, and service providers can share information, hopes, and goals for the child.

Personal Contact

1. Communicate with individual parents through telephone calls, letters, a home–school communication book, or e-mail.

2. Make home visits to get to know families and provide in-home instruction.

3. Invite parents to visit the class, to go on field trips, or to volunteer for various school activities.

4. Inform families about opportunities for involvement at their child's school (e.g., at their school-based family resource center).

Effective communication is planned, purposeful, and personalized. Because communication is a two-way process, teachers should demonstrate a sincere desire to collaborate with the family, accurately communicate their intended messages, engage the family in conversation, and listen carefully to family members' comments and questions. Teachers should also recognize that they share a common goal with families, which is to promote the child's education and progress. They need to believe that families care about their children and know a great deal about them. They also need to be open to learning from the family. Based on the literature and clinical experience, a number of communication strategies are described here that facilitate the development of a collaborative relationship (Barrera & Corso, 2002; Beckman, Frank, & Newcomb, 1996; Dennis & Giangreco, 1996; Turnbull & Turnbull, 2001).

One way to develop a collaborative relationship is to practice active listening. Tips for listening actively include the following:

*   Pay attention to the speaker's nonverbal expressions and listen carefully to what is said.

*   Monitor your own nonverbal behaviors and facial expressions.

*   Allow the parent sufficient time to express and describe his or her feelings.

*   Acknowledge and validate the parent's feelings and demonstrate that you understand him or her by reflecting the feelings that the parent has shared (e.g., "This must be a rough time for you," "It's no wonder you feel so worn out").

*   Respond to the families' expression of difficult situations and emotional issues in a sensitive and caring way (e.g., "How are you doing?" "That must

feel terrible," "How can I help?" "Have you thought about....?" "Some families in your situation have found it helpful to....").

- Do not ignore a parent's emotional statement about the child's disability by making superficial comments that ignore the parent's feelings and concerns (e.g., "Don't blame yourself," "Don't worry—things will work out").

- Paraphrase what the parent says by restating the message. Paraphrasing helps to clarify the intended message (e.g., "Let me make sure that I understand what you said....").

- Summarize what the parent has said to communicate that you understand and to check your perception (e.g., "Your main concerns seem to be....").

- Weigh what is being said, and do not make quick judgments. Resist the temptation to give advice or to make recommendations too quickly. It can be more helpful to reflect on the discussion, seek resources, and identify alternatives; then reopen the conversation at a later date.

In the following four examples of parent–teacher interactions, the first teacher response (A) ignores the parent's concern and erodes a collaborative relationship. In contrast, the second teacher response (B) demonstrates the use of active listening strategies that are likely to enhance parent–teacher communication.

Example 1

Teacher: "I'm so glad to have this opportunity to discuss Maya's program. I'd like to begin by showing you the object communication system that she's using at school."

Parent: "But she still can't talk, and I think she needs more speech therapy."

A. Teacher: "Maya is nonverbal and needs a means to communicate."

B. Teacher: "It seems that you feel that learning to talk is the most important goal for Maya right now. Would you like to hear how she is doing in speech therapy?"

Example 2

Parent: "Since Peter has been in this class, his behavior has been horrible at home. He won't listen to me and he has temper tantrums. He wasn't like this when he was in the special education kindergarten class."

A. Teacher: "It's just a phase. Don't worry about it! He'll adjust to the change."

B. Teacher: "You seem to feel that Peter's behavior at home is related to his full inclusion in first grade. Are you wondering if this change is best for him?"

Example 3

Teacher: "You said that you wanted to talk about Juanita's program when she goes to high school next year."

Parent: "Yes, she has been so happy in your class, and high school may be too much for her to handle."

A. Teacher: "Don't worry about Juanita. She'll be fine. The teachers at the high school are excellent and have worked with many students with disabilities."

B. Teacher: "It sounds as if you're worried about how Juanita will adjust to the new school and to different teachers. Are you wondering whether she'll get the individualized help that we have provided in middle school?"

Example 4

Parent: "Angela really loves to use her walker, so we are wondering if she still needs to have her wheelchair at school?"

A. Teacher: "Of course she still needs to use her wheelchair at school! What if she falls, or what happens if we have a fire drill?"

B. Teacher: "That's a good question. I've noticed how well she gets around with her walker. Let's discuss this with the physical therapist and see what would work."

Working with Interpreters

When service providers and families do not share a common language, communication barriers are even greater. IDEA '97 requires that families receive information about their child's program in their primary language and that interpreters be provided for meetings with families when personnel cannot communicate in the family's language. The quality of interpretation and accuracy of communication varies greatly according to the skills of the interpreter and practices of the program and service providers, however. To ensure accurate communication, it is essential to work with a qualified interpreter who is also familiar with the family's cultural background. Certain terms that are commonly used in special education (e.g., *disability, mental retardation*) can have very different meanings in various cultures (Harry, 1992). In some languages, words referring to disability may appear demeaning by the person-first language standards in the United States (Chen, Downing, & Peckham-Hardin, 2002). Some cultures may not include certain disability terminology within its lexicon; for example, an ethnic group may not have a specific word for *disability* (Fowler, 1998). In addition, special education terminology may be difficult to translate into some languages because of vocabulary differences. For example, there is not a word for *plan* in the Hmong language (Chen, Chan, & Brekken, 2000), so translation of the words *transition plan* would require lengthy explanation. With the exception of sign language interpreters, no professional standards are in place for interpreters used in educational environments or policies regarding their practice.

Before the Meeting

Together with the interpreter, teachers should plan the meeting in which interpretation is needed. This preparation is essential for working effectively with interpreters and for building a relationship with families who do not speak English (Al-Hassan & Gardner, 2002; Chen et al., 2000; Ohtake, Santos, & Fowler, 2000). The following are some preparatory steps to planning effective meetings:

- Obtain a qualified interpreter based on the family's language and country of origin and the interpreter's background and experience. If at all possible, avoid using family members or family friends as interpreters because their relationship with the family may interfere with an honest or accurate discussion of personal, sensitive, or confidential topics.

- With the interpreter, plan for the conversation or meeting with the family. Discuss the purpose of the meeting, questions that will be asked, and topics or terms that may come up. Review any written materials (e.g., forms, reports, questionnaires) that will be used. This planning will assist the interpreter in providing a more accurate translation of English words into the family's language.

- Provide the interpreter with a brief description of the family members who will be at the meeting. Stress the importance of confidentiality and discuss expectations of the interpreter's role in the meeting.

- If possible, ask the interpreter to call the family to introduce him- or herself and to get some idea of the family's language, culture, and educational background and to determine whether he or she will be an effective interpreter with this family.

- Ask the interpreter about appropriate ways to address family members in their primary language, the proper pronunciation of their names, and what is likely to be considered respectful and impolite within the family's culture.

- If possible, learn key words in the family's language so that you can attend to them during the conversation. With the interpreter's help, compile an essential vocabulary list (e.g., basic special education terminology, greetings) in the family's language to facilitate direct communication.

- If the meeting with the family is to discuss differences or conflicts between their practices and the program or mainstream values, then ask the interpreter how this issue should be broached with the family.

During the Meeting

The following is a list of some guidelines to consider during the meeting with parents.

- Introduce yourself and the interpreter to the family and describe your roles and the interpretation process. State that the information shared in the conversation will be held in confidence. Reassure the family that their privacy will be respected. Ask the family if they have any questions before you begin the discussion.

- Be respectful in your comments and questions. Do not assume that family members do not understand English. They may prefer to communicate in their primary language, especially when discussing new, complicated, or emotional issues.

- Speak directly to the family members and look at the family member who speaks, not at the interpreter. Watch for nonverbal indicators of confusion or anxiety.

- Monitor your body language, gestures, and other behaviors so that you convey respect for and interest in the family. Do not whisper or have a side conversation with others.

- Speak clearly, slowly, and in a normal conversational voice. Say a few sentences at a time, then pause and allow for interpretation.

- Provide information in a logical sequence, repeat important points, and clarify information if needed.

- Use simple words without "speaking down" to family members and avoid jargon, slang, and idioms that are difficult to translate.

- Check the family's understanding and accuracy of the translation by asking them about what has been communicated or to answer a question related to the information that was shared. Do not ask, "Do you understand?" because people rarely say "no."

- Supplement verbal information with visual aids, modeling, or written materials, if appropriate. Do not assume that because a family member understands or uses a language that he or she also reads that language.

- Allocate sufficient time for the interpretation process to be effective.

After the Meeting

- Evaluate the meeting with the interpreter. Was the conversation understandable and easy to interpret? Did the family seem to understand the information? What worked well during the conversation? What was difficult for the family members, teacher, or interpreter?

- Thank the interpreter for his or her services and provide constructive suggestions if needed.

- If you plan to work with this interpreter again, schedule subsequent meetings.

I worked with one teacher—Suzanne—who was so helpful, you wouldn't believe it! She told me everything about the law, the IEP, different services, and how to help Miguel. She knew a little Spanish, and my English was very bad. There was an interpreter at meetings. With other teachers, some interpreters had used some Spanish words that confused me. They were from different Latin American countries. Spanish isn't the same Spanish everywhere. Suzanne was so patient and went over everything. I was here alone—no family—I was very afraid. I didn't know how to help Miguel or what to do. Suzanne took me to visit different schools. Thanks to her I had hope. I won't forget her.

—Manuel Gonzales

UNRESOLVED PROBLEMS AND NEGATIVE PAST EXPERIENCES

Teachers may have had adversarial encounters with some families and may be hesitant to develop collaborative relationships. Similarly, some parents may have had negative experiences with school personnel previously and may be wary of involvement with their child's program or have come to distrust service providers (Beckman, Frank, & Stepanek, 1996). Others are cynical and exhausted by their continued efforts to advocate and monitor their child's educational program. To overcome these negative experiences, teachers should make every effort to have a positive first contact with families. The following are some tips for getting off to a good start:

- Communicate in a language that the family understands.

- Let the family know that you are committed to their child's education.

- Respond promptly to family inquiries, notes, voice mail, or e-mail messages.

- Ask family members how they would like to be addressed.

- Ask the family what they want you to know about their child.

- Ask about the child's strengths, interests, and needs.

- Inform families about their child's educational program (e.g., send home a schedule of the week's activities).

- Let families know what their child is learning (e.g., send home monthly samples of the child's work and photos of the child's activities, invite the family to visit the class).

- Consider videotaping selected activities to keep the family involved and to support other documentation of the child's progress.

- Describe opportunities for parent involvement (e.g., meetings, specific programs, volunteer tasks, communication books) and ask parents how they would like to be involved in their child's program.

- Describe how you usually keep parents informed about their child's school program and ask them how often they would like to hear from the school.

- If you have a concern, ask the family, "What's the best way for us to talk about this?"

- Discuss a problem or concern in a nonjudgmental way and seek the family's assistance in finding a solution. Ask what has worked at home.

I would like teachers who work with Daniel to recognize that we want to be part of the educational team. I don't want them to feel threatened that we have expectations. We respect the challenges they have, the demands of their job, time, and energy to assist the children. That's why we should be a team. We can problem solve together and try different strategies to see what works. Because we ask questions, we don't think the teacher is inadequate, it's just that we have an understanding of our child's uniqueness and want to support each other in the educational process. We are there to be a resource, not a problem.

—Cynthia Hale

FAMILY PERSPECTIVES

IDEA '97 (PL 105-17) reaffirms the legal rights of parents to be decision makers in their child's education. Parents have the right to informed consent related to assessment plans and procedures, educational goals, objectives and services, and to participate in decisions related to eligibility and placement (National Information Center for Children and Youth with Disabilities, 1998).

I remember a particular teacher who really listened to my concerns and took my observations seriously. This teacher really respected and believed in Brenda and was able to encourage her to accomplish more that anyone could have expected. She recognized Brenda's needs, understood the meaning of her behaviors, and adapted activities so that Brenda could participate and play with other children. She just expected that Brenda would acquire certain skills. This teacher also said that although certain behaviors are cute for a preschooler, they would not be acceptable when Brenda was older, so together we worked on ways to support her communication.

—Mary Collins

Learning About the Family

To develop a positive relationship with families and provide effective interventions for children with severe and multiple disabilities, service providers must understand the family system and how that particular family functions. The structure and characteristics of each family will influence family participation with service providers in the child's educational program.

Our family has lived in California for nearly two generations. We are English-speaking southern Californians with German and Irish heritage. My husband and I were raised to be self-reliant while being loyal and willing to help our families when difficult situations occur. My parents stressed the importance of education, and this value has also influenced my expectations for my own education and for my children's education. We are a blended family, which has reconfigured at different times. When Daniel was born, two older half brothers greeted him, one 15 years old and the other 12 years old. This was a very stimulating and busy time for my husband and me: stepchildren, half brothers, the teen years, an infant with drop seizures—and I was completing graduate school. I have primarily shared child care with my husband, with the added support of Daniel's wonderful grandmother and older brothers who would help out when we were in a pinch. Educational decisions regarding Daniel are always a shared process. Typically, I will initially explore an activity, service, or placement and take the information back to my husband, who will offer his ideas and concerns. We make decisions jointly. We both communicate with the school and exchange responsibilities for medical appointments. My husband provides most of the financial support for our family, and I supplement what I can around Daniel's care and schedule. As for our recreational activities, I give my husband the most votes. He is the creative and imaginative adventurer of our family. His creative talents, observations, masculine influence, and encouragement of Daniel's physical development have enriched our son's confidence and life.

As a family, we are fortunate that we all contribute different qualities and interests and that we can recognize and respect that this benefits all of us.

—Cynthia Hale

The Family System

A family's story provides a snapshot of their family system and a means for understanding the complex and unique structure of each family and how it functions. A family system reflects the composition, socioeconomic status, resources, personal attributes, and special challenges of each particular family. These characteristics influence each member's roles and responsibilities, how decisions are made, and communication within and outside the family. Each member has a role in a dynamic family system (Turnbull & Turnbull, 2001). Moreover, families have many different forms. In the United States, families represent great diversity in composition, lifestyle, and culture (Hammer & Turner, 1996; O'Shea & Riley, 2001).

We are a family of strong women. Toni and I have been together for 10 years, and her mother Esther moved in with us last year. She takes care of Michelle while we are at work. My 18-year-old daughter Katrina also helps out. Michelle goes to a special education class for other children with severe and multiple disabilities at our neighborhood school, so we know some of the other children in the school. Actually, we know a lot of people in this town. There were about 50 people at Michelle's 7th birthday last week. Since she was little, she has been in early intervention programs, and she has had great teachers. I guess we've been lucky because I know other parents have not been happy with their children's teachers or programs. At first, some teachers didn't know quite what to make of Toni and me—two lesbian mothers. From the beginning, we made sure that we both could go to meetings and took Michelle along. We asked for home visits when we were both home. Now, Esther is included as well.

—Louise Davis

Typically, all families function to provide affection, affiliation, economic support, daily care, socialization, recreation, and education to their members. As shown in the Hale and Davis families, some families may have clearly defined responsibilities, whereas others have shared roles for family functions. Within an individual family, certain functions may be clearly identified as a particular member's responsibility, whereas others are not clearly assigned. Traditional families from diverse cultural backgrounds are likely to include extended family members who participate in family decisions and functions (Chan, 2004; Harry, 1992; Sharifzadeh, 2004; Zuniga, 2004).

Families have different stages in their life cycle, also, as determined by their children's ages: infancy and early childhood, childhood, adolescence, and young adulthood. Family life cycles may be far more complicated, however, as the Hale family demonstrates. Families may be blended or some children may be adolescents when a new baby arrives. Family priorities and goals for their child will change during these developmental stages and transitions from one stage to another. Service providers should make the effort to learn about, understand, and appreciate the uniqueness of a family system and recognize that changes in the family life cycle, characteristics, or functions will also influence family involvement in their child's education.

The Effects of the Child's Diagnosis

The diagnosis that an infant or child has severe and/or multiple disabilities thrusts a novice family into a strange, complex, and confusing world of medical, therapeutic, and educational services. This lifelong experience will require Herculean endurance and resources. Children with severe and multiple disabilities may face frequent hospitalizations, numerous medical interventions, and life-threatening crises that disrupt family life. Family interactions between parents, other children, and extended family members can be affected by a child's health and complex needs. The parent's devotion to child care functions may compromise other roles and activities (e.g., career, hobbies, social relationships, relationships with spouse and other family members). The family has to cope with health insurance (if they have it) and other financial issues while managing the child's health, making decisions about medical interventions, and wondering about the child's chances for survival.

An unexpected "bolt from the blue" creates such energy that the force inevitably leads to a transformation during the joyful, sweet, and sometimes sorrowful journey of parenting a child with disabilities. I remember being launched into an early intervention program, physical therapy, occupational therapy, equestrian therapy, and numerous medical and developmental evaluations of my child. I knew something monumental was happening, but I did not know how it would transform our lives. I could not articulate the shock, confusion, and worry, or the underlying sorrow that was not yet experienced. I was venturing through a great portal—pushed along by an invisible force—and there was no turning back. This was not what I had dreamed of when I had happily embraced motherhood for the second time. As a friend reminded me, life is what happens when you are making other plans. It's not that I would give up dreaming, but that my dreams have changed. This is a transformation. Pieces of your life are scattered like a puzzle thrown up into the air. As you pick up the pieces, the puzzle of your life will fit together again—just differently. Now the tasks of feeding, bathing, dressing, positioning, comforting, playing, communicating, transporting, and practicing safety procedures—all normal aspects of child rearing—will demand a new type of vigilance. Your energy that was invested in other aspects of life now must shift. You take on new roles: medical case manager, educational advocate, nurse, medicine dispenser, physical therapist, occupational therapist, speech therapist, adaptive engineer, insurance biller, interpreter, family counselor, and of course, we still remain the parents. As these shifts occur, family life changes also. Adaptability, flexibility, and teamwork are paramount for survival. Unfortunately, many relationships fail to make it over those hurdles. As I go to the many therapies that my child requires, I meet other parents. There seem to be a lot of single mothers doing this juggling act. Perhaps our other children would divorce us too if they had some less-demanding place to go. As parents, we sometimes forget that they, too, have the challenge of this transformation.

—Cynthia Hale

When children have multiple medical and educational needs, parents must learn to work with various agencies and numerous service providers. In addition, the perception that "more is better" may lead families to seek every possible service, thus increasing the steps in an already exhausting, time-consuming, and overwhelming process. Sometimes service providers contradict each other, leading to further confusion. Although children receiving early intervention services and older children with disabilities usually have an identified service coordinator or program manager, true coordination of the child's multiple services and team collaboration is still not a common practice. Coordination of the child's services usually relies on the efforts of families.

I have often thought that we were fortunate because the knowledge of Daniel's disability came to us gradually. There were no known birth complications or preexisting conditions. The awareness of Daniel's disabilities became apparent because of delays in his motor development. I think this gradual awakening allowed for a strong family attachment to occur with our infant without the dark shadows of fear and sorrow. Daniel was a responsive, cuddly infant who startled easily and was sensitive to sound.

He didn't sleep for more then 4 consecutive hours until he was 13 months old because he had terrible eczema and spent hours scratching and rubbing. At 6 months he was still unable to turn over and slouched instead of balancing upright when supported in a sitting position. He had difficulty reaching for objects but could orient well to visual or auditory stimulation. Our pediatrician had noted that Daniel appeared to have some low [muscle] tone but hoped that he might improve over the next several months. By [the time Daniel was] 12 months we were referred to a nearby medical center where he was diagnosed with ataxic cerebral palsy and hypotonia. By 18 months the low tone in his legs had decreased and he exhibited some moderate spasticity. At 20 months he started to have multiple types of seizures, the most devastating being intractable epilepsy with drop seizures. And then finally, the impact of his compromised neurological development, his physical limitations, his language delay, and the sedation of numerous of anticonvulsants, culminated in the additional diagnosis of mental retardation by age 4.

—Cynthia Hale

———————————

Cynthia Hale's experience illustrates how arriving at a diagnosis of a child's disabilities and navigating the medical system are often confusing, anxiety-provoking, heart-wrenching, and time-consuming processes. It may be years before parents know the true scope of a child's special needs. Within this context of turmoil and uncertainty, family reactions to the diagnosis are affected by multiple and complicated factors. These include the family's culture, experience with disability, religious beliefs, socioeconomic status, family structure, availability of support systems, reactions of close friends and extended family members, and the severity of the child's disability and prognosis (Turnbull & Turnbull, 2001). Given the potential range and complexity of a family's experiences, reactions, and feelings about a child's disability, service providers should approach each family with openness and compassion. When a trusting relationship is developed, service providers can introduce new ideas and information regarding the child's disability, development, and education.

———————————

Daniel's ongoing struggle with seizures became increasingly desperate because he became resistant to the few medications that were of any benefit. I think at this point, no one knew how to help us. We were so exhausted, saddened, and caught up in his physical safety while dispensing medication 5 times daily that we became somewhat isolated. It is difficult to communicate to others when you are preoccupied with fear and grief. I think we could have processed these powerful feelings, but there was no time to do so. Our greatest sorrow was that the presence of our little son was fading further and further away—caught in a firestorm of neurological activity for which there seemed to be no answer. Both family and friends have told me that they often wanted to help us during this desperate time but they didn't know what to say and were afraid to assist in his care because of the seizures.

—Cynthia Hale

Feeling States

Much has been written about the range of emotions associated with the birth or diagnosis of a child with a disability (Anderegg, Vergason, & Smith, 1992; Moses, 1991), based on the writings of Kübler-Ross (1969), that described emotional states related to death and dying. Similar feelings (e.g., shock, anger, sadness) have been associated with the processes of grieving the "loss" of the perfect child and therapeutic adaptation to the child with a disability. Some authors have questioned the value of viewing families as being in a particular stage of grief (Howard, Williams, Port, & Lepper, 2001; Miller, 1994; Turnbull & Turnbull, 2001). Individual family members may experience many feelings at a time, in various sequences, and at different times (Bruce & Schultz, 2001). Parents report that many events may trigger these feelings, including any change (e.g., diagnosis, new technology, medical needs, transition to another grade) or milestones (e.g., birthdays, graduation, vocational training). Common feelings that reoccur are anger and sadness. Parents may be angry at the medical system, therapists, and schools. They may have received unhelpful advice or have been disappointed by having unrealistic expectations about medical or educational interventions. Their children may have endured many stressful or unsuccessful procedures. Service providers should recognize that parents have a right to be angry and should not take these feelings personally.

The use of active listening skills, described previously, can acknowledge the parent's feelings and provide a means of building a working relationship. A parent's overwhelming feelings of sadness may result in difficulty managing everyday tasks and keeping appointments, complaining about lack of sleep, or appearing unkempt and tired. In these situations, service providers should ask whether the child receives respite services or if there are family members who can help with child care. They can encourage parents to break down tasks into smaller activities, use family and friends to help out, and identify possible ways for parents to take care of themselves. Service providers need to reassure parents that there may be times when they need to take a break and recharge their personal resources. They should listen for opportunities to have this discussion without giving advice. Surprisingly, a parent may be able to share certain feelings or discuss certain concerns with an empathic service provider that he or she would not tell family members. This may occur because the parent feels protective of or fears the reactions of family members. An empathic service provider can invite discussion about referrals for counseling support if the parent seems open to this suggestion.

———————————

Two of the most vexing aspects of this experience can be the lack of control and the isolation. Whether simple errands or social outings, plans are often difficult to keep because most of what you do will be determined by your child's physical condition. Then there is your own stamina to be considered. Sometimes it feels like you are on a nonstop roller coaster. Depending on your child's disability, you may be heading into a crisis or trying to recover from one. At times, a simple diversion such as going out for coffee with a friend feels like a monumental endeavor. Another mother told me that when she gets a chance for some respite, she goes to bed. It's the only opportunity she has to catch up on her sleep. Control over life's basic necessities such as rest and relaxation, employment, and a personal life can be wrought with adversity. Parents can be physically isolated as the care of their child limits opportunities to connect with others. The poignancy involved in sharing the depth of our feelings, fears, grief, sorrows, and hope often seems like it would be overwhelming to others. Sharing our concerns with those outside our sphere of experience feels futile and frustrating—so we can become emotionally isolated.

—Cynthia Hale

———————————

The most common misuse of the "grief model" that is frequently used by service providers is the overgeneralized reference to parents as being "in denial" (Gallagher, Fialka, Rhodes, & Arceneaux, 2002). What is viewed as denial may serve to actually protect the family when they are not yet able to deal with a problem (Miller, 1994) and provides time for them to integrate complicated information and complex feelings. Service providers should recognize that parents need support and time to understand information about the child's diagnosis, assessment results, and learning needs. It may be of benefit to repeat information at a later date to make sure that the family understands it.

———————————

Others may think we are in denial or we think that they are; nevertheless, we can all be humbled by the feelings of helplessness that arise in these circumstances. I believe that the process of denial may be a misconstrued understanding of a natural process of transformation. In my experience, this transformation contains elements of anticipation, shock, confusion, grief, seeking of information, integration, refocus, and hope. Although hope may look like denial to some, for us as parents it is the belief that with effort, a difference in the quality of our child's life might occur. We need hope.

—Cynthia Hale

When parents have hope, they develop expectations and strive to do what is necessary to support their child's development. This attitude of hope can also be communicated to the child through the parents' actions and encouragement. The intensity and range of feelings that parents experience will differ and change depending on the health, developmental progress, life stages, responsibilities, and resources of the family. What may seem like "denial" may actually be part of an unfolding and gradual process of shifting expectations. Denial may outlive its therapeutic purpose if it prevents a family from advocating for their child's educational needs and from developing a partnership with the educational team, however. Rather than viewing the family's reactions and feelings as a continuum of denial to acceptance, service providers should listen carefully to the family's comments and identify opportunities to offer relevant suggestions for appropriate supports.

Adaptation, Adjustment, and Reorganization

Over time, parents adjust to having a child with a disability or disabilities in the family; but the term *acceptance* may not be an accurate description of the family's adaptation. Certain milestones such as the child's birthday may elicit sadness, especially as the child grows older and the developmental differences with same-age peers become more pronounced. Similarly, transitions to another grade may also trigger certain feelings. Service providers can help families plan for changes such as a new school schedule and transitions including a move to a new class or school by providing sufficient information and time to become accustomed to the change. They should determine whether a change is too sudden for this child and family and how they have handled previous transitions. Together with the family, service providers should identify what supports are needed to facilitate a smooth transition to the new class.

Tips for preparing families for changes in their child's program include the following:

- Discuss plans for any major changes in the child's school program with the family and involve them in making decisions.

- Convene a meeting with the child's family, current educational team, and receiving teacher or team (if already identified) to discuss the child's transition to the new class.

- Provide the family and the child (if appropriate) with information on the new class or school and encourage them to visit.

- Ask the family for suggestions to support the child's and family's adjustment to the new schedule or class.

- Invite the receiving teacher to visit the child in his or her current class.

- Use a systematic, person-centered planning process such as MAPs (Pearpoint, Forest, & O'Brien, 1996) to facilitate the sharing of information, hopes, and goals about the child among the sending and receiving educational teams and the family, friends, and the child, if appropriate.

- Provide follow-up support to the receiving teacher once the child is in the new class.

———————————

I would want a new teacher to know about Daniel's diet treatment for epilepsy, about his fluctuating functional states, and that his processing time is a little slower but that if given encouragement, he will reveal to you much more than you would expect. The teacher needs to know that his receptive language and awareness are far beyond his expressive abilities because he has to communicate through a body that has really compromised his abilities. Expect that he can do more, encourage it, be enthusiastic and reinforce his attempts, and remain positive. Finally, know that positive peer exposure helps development. Find creative ways that Daniel can connect with others and don't expect that this will automatically occur; you must build strategies to encourage this to happen.

—Cynthia Hale

———————————

OPTIONS, ALTERNATIVES, AND CONTROVERSIES ASSOCIATED WITH THE COLLABORATIVE TEAM

The use of a collaborative model enables all members of the team to provide coordinated services and agreed on recommendations to families. Without a collaborative approach, service providers may present conflicting opinions about the most appropriate educational or therapeutic options for a particular child, making it more difficult for families to make decisions about their child's education. For example, if a child is deaf and has developmental disabilities, an SLP might recommend focusing on speech, the teacher in the deaf and hard of hearing area might suggest using sign language, and the classroom teacher might suggest using a picture exchange communication system (PECS) (Frost & Bondy, 1994). The choice of a particular communication method has always been a dilemma for parents of children who are deaf. Options include the auditory/oral method (focusing on listening skills and speech), the simultaneous communication method (speech and manually coded English), or a bilingual-bicultural approach (acquiring American Sign Language as the first language and then learning English). The availability of the cochlear implant has added to the controversy surrounding communication options for children with hearing loss (Samson-Fang, Simons-McCandless, & Shelton, 2000). There are concerns about eligibility criteria for implants as children with severe and multiple disabilities and younger and younger infants are receiving them. Furthermore, members of Deaf culture view the cochlear implant as destructive to their culture and American Sign Language. Although not as marked, similar conflicts surround a focus on speech or alternative communication methods for children with other developmental disabilities such as autism and mental retardation.

Similarly, teachers and families may differ in their views about what constitutes the least restrictive environment for a particular child. For example, a teacher may recommend that a child who is deaf and who has additional disabilities attend a state residential school that emphasizes sign language, because the teacher believes this child will benefit from this language environment. In contrast, the family may want the child to attend the neighborhood school with the other children in the family and never allow any of their children to live away from home. Families should be informed about the range of options and the differing professional perspectives and provided with support so that they can select the method, program, or environment that is most appropriate for their child and family situation.

In addition to the controversies surrounding standard educational options or medical procedures, information about new, alternative, and nonstandard treatments for children with disabilities such as autism, Down syndrome, acquired brain injury, and other developmental disabilities has proliferated in the media and on the Internet (Rosenbaum & Stewart, 2002). These therapies can be categorized as focusing on medications, vitamin and mineral supplements and dietary treatments, behavioral therapies, and surgeries (Nickel, 1996; Starrett, 1996). Medical and educational professionals can support families in making decisions about controversial therapies by 1) providing information about the child's diagnosis and treatment; 2) facilitating access to community resources and services for standard therapies; 3) providing information about specific alternative therapies; 4) discussing parent questions and concerns about their child, standard treatments, and alternative therapies; 5) supporting a trial of the alternative therapy in certain situations; and 6) maintaining communication with the family whatever their decision.

A friend told us of a television special that he had seen, produced by a father who told the story of his own family's journey to stop his son's out-of-control seizures. It was the beginning of a discovery that opened up an entirely different approach to the treatment of our son's disorder; one that did not come through the medical establishment initially, but through the willingness of a family who told the public of a hopeful treatment and our astute friend who called us and said, "Contact the television network; I think this could be an answer to help your son." We have had two neurologists involved with our son's treatment. Regrettably, neither of them suggested the use of diet therapy to control seizures as it was not considered the current standard of treatment. Nevertheless, they have continued to listen, educate us, and monitor his development through the control of his seizures by the supervision of his diet.

—Cynthia Hale

FAMILY-FRIENDLY PRACTICES

Family–professional partnerships, collaboration among service providers, and coordination of services are essential for the child and family to receive effective services. Given the challenges previously identified in this chapter, teachers should review their program policies and practices to determine whether they facilitate service coordination and family–professional collaboration.

Phases of the Evolving Relationship

The literature has identified at least four general phases of the evolving family–professional relationship: 1) the initial "getting acquainted" phase, 2) the exploration phase, 3) the collaboration phase, and 4) the closure phase (Beckman, Newcomb, Frank, & Brown, 1996; Walker & Singer, 1993).

Phase 1: Getting Acquainted

In the initial phase or "getting acquainted" stage, families and service providers exchange information to identify the family's concerns and available resources and services to address these needs. These initial contacts lay the foundation for the working relationship, and the service provider's interactions with the family are likely to set the tone for the relationship.

Phase 2: Exploration

In the exploration phase, intervention goals are identified and families often have specific requests (e.g., equipment, help with child care difficulties, additional services). The service provider's commitment and ability to address these concerns will contribute to the development of a trusting relationship.

Phase 3: Collaboration

In the collaboration phase, services are provided to meet the goals and concerns identified previously. During this phase, service providers should check on the family's satisfaction with the current services, acknowledge any other concerns that the family may identify, and follow up on these concerns. During this period, families may demonstrate increased trust in service providers by seeking their opinions about intervention options, in making decisions, or in sharing personal family information.

Phase 4: Closure

The closure phase marks the end of a working relationship between a specific service provider and family (e.g., the child may be graduating from the program or going to another grade, the family may be moving out of the area). In some cases, the relationship may be abruptly terminated under sad circumstances (e.g., the child's health deteriorates, the family is experiencing other crises). Even under the best of circumstances, planning for this separation may be an emotional time for both the service provider and the family. It is helpful to use this time to make transition plans, to reflect on experiences, and to recognize and celebrate accomplishments.

The questions provided in Table 2.4 are intended to assist teachers in gathering information that is relevant for working with individual families. Information may be obtained though observations during home visits, review of records, discussion with family members themselves, and self-reflection by the teacher.

A collaborative relationship is enhanced by the efforts of both teachers and families to develop mutual respect and trust in each other's expertise and to understand the constraints and resources of the system in which the family lives and the service provider works (Singer & Powers, 1993; Soodak & Erwin, 2000). It is also important to remember that teachers have a professional obligation to work with families and that they may need to make the extra effort or compromise. As Perl (1995) pointed out, some parents may be difficult to work with

Table 2.4.   Questions to guide interaction with families

- Who are the members of the family?
- What is considered respectful and disrespectful in the family?
- Who makes decisions in the family?
- To whom does the family turn for support, assistance, and information?
- What are the family's values and customs?
- What are the family's child-rearing practices, forms of discipline, and expectations of children?
- What are the family's concerns and priorities related to their child with a disability?
- How can I learn about the family's perspectives?
- What do I believe about the family based on their perspectives and beliefs?
- How do my assumptions influence my interactions with the family?
- Have I explained and clarified my perspectives to the family?
- What community resources can I use to better serve this family?
- What information do I need to help this child?
- Have I clarified what the family expects of me and other service providers?
- Have I provided information on the family's legal rights regarding their child's educational program?
- Are there any concerns about my interaction with the family that need to be discussed or clarified?

From Chen, D., Downing, J.E., & Peckham-Hardin, K.D. (2002). Working with families of diverse cultural and linguistic backgrounds: Considerations for culturally responsive positive behavior support. In J.M. Lucyshyn, G. Dunlap, & R.W. Albin (Eds.), *Families and positive behavior support: Addressing problem behaviors in family contexts* (p. 154). Baltimore: Paul H. Brookes Publishing Co.; adapted by permission.

and not easy to like. Nevertheless, teachers should strive to demonstrate genuine caring for the child and family by monitoring reactions to and interactions with families and readjusting attitudes and practice as indicated to better serve families. Service providers can demonstrate genuine caring by building rapport, being empathic, using active listening skills, and maintaining a positive attitude. Service providers should help the family identify the engaging characteristics of their child and how he or she has contributed to their lives. Some parents have viewed the emotions associated with their child's diagnosis of disability as an impetus toward empowerment and have identified the positive effects of the child on their family (Leyser & Heinze, 2001; Turnbull & Turnbull, 2001).

———————————

Daniel has a wonderful temperament. He is friendly, fun-loving, enthusiastic, kind, and patient. He has been an inspiration to us through his fortitude, willingness to try, and sense of humor. He has taught us to be more patient, to be more accepting of differences, and to embrace the simpler experiences to be shared with others. I think he has really developed in me an appreciation for the uniqueness in each individual. I have also learned to recognize and to admire the sacrifices and dedication of families and other caregivers.

—Cynthia Hale

Brenda has contributed positively to my life in many ways. She has helped me to become more patient and has developed in me a greater ability to feel compassion. I take less of the everyday experiences for granted, and I don't look on material possessions as that important. I think I understand more about the true meaning of love. I have learned to live more for today. I think that my experiences with my daughter have allowed me to slow down and appreciate many things in a different way.

—Mary Collins

SUMMARY

The learning needs of children with severe and multiple disabilities are complicated and intensive and involve many service providers and agencies that interact with the child and family. Service providers should demonstrate their willingness to meet the learning needs of each individual child and their commitment to high-quality educational services and to working in partnerships with families. They can implement a collaborative team approach to coordinate services and provide meaningful interventions across the child's day. They can develop and maintain family-friendly practices that invite family collaboration and promote ongoing communication. They can learn about and respect each individual family's lifestyle and culture. They can listen carefully to a family's stories, observations, concerns, and goals for their child. They can develop interventions that fit within a family's routine to increase opportunities for practice and the likelihood that the interventions will benefit the child and family. They can continue their own professional development to increase their knowledge and skills in working with families and their children who have severe and multiple disabilities.

I think teachers need skills that will assist them in building rapport with families. They should try to take the pressure off themselves as the "experts" and cultivate instead a collaborative approach to understand the children and share strategies and methods with others. I think teachers need to be creative and thus explore what might work for a particular child. I really think parents are okay with exploration, knowing you are attempting to discover what works best. Each child is unique and is a bit of a mystery. Teachers should observe the child and build on what he or she can already do. They need to be extremely patient and remember that children develop at their own rate.

—Cynthia Hale

REFERENCES

Al-Hassan, S., & Gardner, R. (2002). Involving immigrant parents of students with disabilities in the educational process. *Teaching Exceptional Children, 34*(5), 52–58.

Alvarez, L.I.G. (1998). A short course in sensitivity training: Working with Hispanic families of children with disabilities. *Teaching Exceptional Children, 31,* 73–77.

Anderegg, M.L., Vergason, G.A., & Smith, M.C. (1992). A visual representation of the grief cycle for use by teachers with families of children with disabilities. *Remedial and Special Education, 13,* 17–23.

Barnwell, D.A., & Day, M. (1996). Providing support to diverse families. In P.J. Beckman (Ed.), *Strategies for working with families of young children with disabilities* (pp. 47–68). Baltimore: Paul H. Brookes Publishing Co.

Barrera, I., & Corso, R.M. (2002). Cultural competency as skilled dialogue. *Topics in Early Childhood Special Education, 22,* 103–113.

Beckman, P.J. (Ed.). (1996). *Strategies for working with families of young children with disabilities.* Baltimore: Paul H. Brookes Publishing Co.

Beckman, P.J., Frank, N., & Newcomb, S. (1996). Qualities and skills for communicating with families. In P.J. Beckman (Ed.), *Strategies for working with families of young children with disabilities* (pp. 31–46). Baltimore: Paul H. Brookes Publishing Co.

Beckman, P.J., Frank, N., & Stepanek, J.S. (1996). Resolving conflicts with families. In P.J. Beckman (Ed.), *Strategies for working with families of young children with disabilities* (pp. 109–126). Baltimore: Paul H. Brookes Publishing Co.

Beckman, P.J., Newcomb, S., Frank, N., & Brown, L. (1996). Evolution of working relationships with families. In P.J. Beckman (Ed.), *Strategies for working with families of young children with disabilities* (pp. 17–30). Baltimore: Paul H. Brookes Publishing Co.

Beckman, P.J., & Stepanek, J.S. (1996). Facilitating collaboration in meetings and conferences. In P.J. Beckman (Ed.), *Strategies for working with families of young children with disabilities* (pp. 91–107). Baltimore: Paul H. Brookes Publishing Co.

Berry, J.O., & Hardman, M.L. (1998). *Lifespan perspectives on the family and disability.* Needham Heights, MA: Allyn & Bacon.

Bruce, E.J., & Schultz, C.L. (2001). *Nonfinite loss and grief: A psychoeducational approach.* Baltimore: Paul H. Brookes Publishing Co.

Chan, S. (2004). Families with Asian roots. In E.W. Lynch & M.J. Hanson (Eds.), *Developing cross-cultural competence: A guide for working with young children and their families* (3rd ed.). Baltimore: Paul H. Brookes Publishing Co.

Chen, D. (1999). *Essential elements in early intervention: Visual impairment and multiple disabilities.* New York: AFDB Press.

Chen, D., Chan, S., & Brekken, L. (2000). *Conversations for three: Communicating through interpreters* [video & booklet]. Baltimore: Paul H. Brookes Publishing Co.

Chen, D., Downing, J.E., & Peckham-Hardin, K.D. (2002). Working with families of diverse cultural and linguistic backgrounds: Considerations for culturally responsive positive behavior support. In J.M. Lucyshyn, G. Dunlap, & R.W. Albin (Eds.), *Families and positive behavior support: Addressing problem behaviors in family contexts* (pp. 133–154). Baltimore: Paul H. Brookes Publishing Co.

Cook, R.E., Tessier, A., & Klein, M.D. (2000). *Adapting early childhood curricula for children in inclusive settings* (5th ed.). Upper Saddle River, NJ: Prentice Hall.

Council for Exceptional Children. (1995). *What every special educator must know: The international standards for the preparation and certification of special education teachers.* Reston, VA: Author.

Dennis, R.E., & Giangreco, M.F. (1996). Creating conversations: Reflections on cultural sensitivity in family interviewing. *Exceptional Children, 63,* 103–116.

Fowler, L. (1998). Native American communities. A more inclusive society? *TASH Newsletter, 24,* 21–22.

Frost, L., & Bondy, A. (1994). *PECS: The Picture Exchange Communication Symbol Training Manual.* Cherry Hill, NJ: Pyramid Educational Consultants.

Gallagher, P.A., Fialka, J., Rhodes, C., & Arceneaux, C. (2002). Working with families: Rethinking denial. *Teaching Young Exceptional Children, 5,* 11–17.

Groce, N.E., & Zola, I.K. (1993). Multiculturalism, chronic illness, and disability. *Pediatrics, 91,* 1048–1055.

Hammer, T.J., & Turner, P.H. (1996). *Parenting in contemporary society* (3rd ed.). Needham Heights, MA: Allyn & Bacon.

Harry, B. (1992). *Cultural diversity, families, and the special education system: Communication and empowerment.* New York: Teachers College Press.

Harry, B., Kalyanpur, M., & Day, M. (1999). *Building cultural reciprocity with families: Case studies in special education.* Baltimore: Paul H. Brookes Publishing Co.

Howard, V.F., Williams, B.F., Port, P.D., & Lepper, C. (2001). *Very young children with special needs: A formative approach for the 21st century* (2nd ed.). Upper Saddle River, NJ: Merrill.

Individuals with Disabilities Education Act Amendments of 1997, PL 105-17, 20 U.S.C. §§ 1400 *et seq.*

Kalyanpur, M., & Harry, B. (1999). *Culture in special education: Building reciprocal family-professional relationships.* Baltimore: Paul H. Brookes Publishing Co.

Klein, M.D., & Chen, D. (2001). *Working with children from culturally diverse backgrounds.* Albany, NY: Delmar.

Kroth, R.L., & Edge, D. (1997). *Strategies for communicating with parents and families of exceptional children.* Denver, CO: Love Publishing.

Kübler-Ross, E. (1969). *On death and dying.* New York: Macmillan.

Lamorey, S. (2002). The effects of culture on special education services: Evil eyes, prayer meetings, and IEPs. *Teaching Exceptional Children, 34*(5), 67–71.

Leyser, Y., & Heinze, T. (2001). Perspectives of parents of children who are visually impaired: Implications for the field. *Review, 33*(1), 37–48.

Lynch, E.W., & Hanson, M.J. (2004). *Developing cross-cultural competence: A guide for working with young children and their families* (3rd ed.). Baltimore: Paul H. Brookes Publishing Co.

Miller, N.B. with Burmester, S., Callahan, D.G., Dieterle, J., & Niedermeyer, S. (1994). *Nobody's perfect: Living and growing with children who have special needs.* Baltimore: Paul H. Brookes Publishing Co.

Moses, K. (1991). *Shattered dreams and growth: Loss and the art of grief counseling.* Evanston, IL: Resource Networks.

National Information Center for Children and Youth with Disabilities. (1998, June). The IDEA Amendments of 1997. *News Digest, 26.*

Nickel, R.E. (1996). Controversial therapies for young children with developmental disabilities. *Infants and Young Children, 8*(4), 29–40.

Ohtake, Y., Santos, R.A., & Fowler, S.A. (2000). It's a three-way conversation: Families, service providers and interpreters working together. *Young Exceptional Children, 4*(1), 12–18.

O'Shea, D.J., O'Shea, L.J., Algozzine, R., & Hammitte, D.J. (2001). *Families and teachers of individuals with disabilities: Collaborative orientations and responsive practices.* Needham Heights, MA: Allyn & Bacon.

O'Shea, D.J., & Riley, J.E. (2001). Typical families: Fact or fiction. In D.J. O'Shea, L.J. O'Shea, R. Algozzine, & D.J. Hammitte (Eds.), *Families and teachers of individuals with disabilities: Collaborative orientations and responsive practices* (pp. 25–50). Needham Heights, MA: Allyn & Bacon.

Parette, H.P., & Petch-Hogan, B. (2000). Approaching families: Facilitating culturally/ linguistically diverse family involvement. *Teaching Exceptional Children, 33,* 4–10.

Pearpoint, J., Forest, M., & O'Brien, J. (1996). MAPs, Circles of Friends, and PATH: Powerful tools to help build caring communities. In S. Stainback & W. Stainback (Eds.), *Inclusion: A guide for educators* (pp. 67–86). Baltimore: Paul H. Brookes Publishing Co.

Perl, J. (1995). Improving relationship skills for parent conferences. *Teaching Exceptional Children, 28,* 29–31.

Rock, M.L. (2000). Parents as equal partners: Balancing the scales in IEP development. *Teaching Exceptional Children, 32,* 30–37.

Rosenbaum, P., & Stewart, D. (2002). Alternative and complementary therapies for children and youth with disabilities. *Infants and Young Children, 15*(1), 51–59.

Rothenberg, B.A. (1995). *Understanding and working with parents and children from rural Mexico.* Menlo Park, CA: The CHC Center for Child and Family Development Press.

Samson-Fang, L., Simons-McCandless, M.A., & Shelton, C. (2000). Controversies in the field of hearing impairment: Early identification, educational methods and cochlear implants. *Infants and Young Children, 12*(4), 77–88.

Schwartz, W. (1995). *A guide to communicating with Asian American families: For parents/ about parents.* ERIC Clearinghouse on Urban Education, New York. (ED396014).

Shapiro, J., & Simonsen, D. (1994). Educational/support group for Latino families of children with Down syndrome. *Mental Retardation, 32*(6), 403–415.

Sharifzadeh, V.S. (2004). Families with Middle Eastern roots. In E.W. Lynch & M.J. Hanson (Eds.), *Developing cross-cultural competence: A guide for working with young children and their families* (3rd ed.). Baltimore: Paul H. Brookes Publishing Co.

Sileo, T.W., Sileo, A.P., & Prater, M.A. (1996). Parents and professional partnerships in special education: Multicultural considerations. *Intervention in School and Clinic, 3,* 145–153.

Singer, G.H.S., & Powers, L.H. (1993). *Families, disability, and empowerment: Active coping skills and strategies for family interventions.* Baltimore: Paul H. Brookes Publishing Co.

Sontag, J.C., & Schacht, R. (1994). An ethnic comparison of parent participation and information needs in early intervention. *Exceptional Children, 60,* 422–433.

Soodak, L.C., & Erwin, E.J. (2000). Valued member or tolerated participant: Parents' experiences in inclusive early childhood settings. *The Journal of The Association for Persons with Severe Handicaps, 25,* 29–44.

Starrett, A.L. (1996). Nonstandard therapies in developmental disabilities. In A.J. Capute & P.J. Accardo (Eds.), *Developmental disabilities in infancy and childhood: Vol. I. Neurodevelopmental diagnosis and treatment* (2nd ed., pp. 593–608). Baltimore: Paul H. Brookes Publishing Co.

Trivette, C.M., & Dunst, C.J. (2000). DEC recommended practices. Family-based services. In S. Sandall, M.E. McLean, & B.J. Smith (Eds.), *DEC recommended practices in early intervention/early childhood special education* (pp. 39–46). Denver, CO: Division of Early Childhood Council for Exceptional Children.

Turnbull, A.P., & Turnbull, H.R. (2001). *Families, professionals and exceptionality: Collaborating for empowerment* (3rd ed.). Upper Saddle River, NJ: Prentice Hall.

U.S. Department of Education. (2002). *Twenty-third annual report to congress on the implementation of the Individuals with Disabilities Education Act.* Washington, DC: U.S. Government Printing Office.

Walker, B., & Singer, G.H.S. (1993). Improving collaborative communication between professionals and parents. In G.H.S. Singer & L.E. Powers (Eds.), *Families, disability, and empowerment: Active coping skills and strategies for family interventions* (pp. 285–316). Baltimore: Paul H. Brookes Publishing Co.

Willis, W. (2004). Families with African American roots. In E.W. Lynch & M.J. Hanson (Eds.), *Developing cross-cultural competence: A guide for working with young children and their families* (3rd ed.). Baltimore: Paul H. Brookes Publishing Co.

Woods, J.J., & McCormick, K.M. (2002). Toward an integration of child and family-centered practices in the assessment of preschool children: Welcoming the family. *Young Exceptional Children, 5*(3), 2–11.

Zuniga, M.A. (2004). Families with Latino roots. In E.W. Lynch & M.J. Hanson (Eds.), *Developing cross-cultural competence: A guide for working with young children and their families* (3rd ed.). Baltimore: Paul H. Brookes Publishing Co.

CHAPTER 3

Developing Curriculum and Instruction

Kathleen Gee

Emil is a wonderful kindergartner who goes to his neighborhood elementary school. He likes school—but it took a while for him to get used to it. Emil loves to move, but needs help to do it. He likes to swim, likes to be pushed very fast in his wheelchair, and loves to be carried. Emil loves music. He also likes toys that move and make noise when he hits a microswitch, such as his adapted racecar.

Emil is totally blind and has a bilateral moderate hearing loss primarily in the high frequencies, which responds somewhat to amplification (he wears hearing aids). At school he uses an FM phonic ear system. He also has quadriplegic cerebral palsy and severe cognitive disabilities.

Emil is working on sitting with some position supports during the circle time. He has a specially designed wheelchair but also spends time in a mobile prone stander, an adapted chair, and on the floor with his peers.

Emil lets people know how he feels by crying, whining, or banging his head back on his wheelchair. He hates to stop, and he hates to wait. He doesn't like new places unless someone takes enough time to help him understand what is going on. He doesn't like the process of eating and to ensure that he gets enough nutrition, he has tube feedings as well as eating by mouth.

Emil is working hard on his ability to make his own needs known and to direct others to assist him. He has some gestures, including one that means *want,* which he uses to request his favorite things. He makes happy sounds when he is pleased about something. Emil has been working on the beginnings of a tangible object system paired with activities. He has an object calendar notebook. He also has a small, portable voice output device that has been adapted for him. This device includes tangible symbols as an object communication system. He uses this in conjunction with tactile gestures and signs. Helping Emil communicate is definitely a high priority for his family and teachers. Emil's parents are extremely interested in increasing the ways he can demonstrate what he knows and tell other people things.

Emil is also working on learning to understand where things are in space in relationship to himself and how to scan and find items, push things away, and generally take charge more. He is learning how to interpret what things are. In addition, Emil has numerous curricular goals related to the kindergarten standards. He recognizes people he knows by their touch, and his friends, teachers, and family greet him in individual ways. Emil loves being with the friends he has made.

————————————

Holly is a 9-year-old fourth grader who has spastic hemiplegic cerebral palsy that affects her left side. Holly wears contact lenses paired with glasses for near vision, after having her cataracts surgically removed. Holly has cognitive challenges. She is being served inclusively in her neighborhood school this year. Prior to this, she was in a segregated "special day class" in a different elementary school.

Holly is outgoing and interested in the other children. She wants to help and to be a part of things. Sometimes she touches the other children too much, but she is working on how to physically connect in a positive way. Sometimes she touches to keep her balance, and she is working on walking with the use of a three-pronged cane. She primarily uses her right hand to do things. Inside, she often cruises along furniture to get around. She is interested in learning to use a bike or scooter, and her team is looking for ways to adapt the equipment so that Holly can use it.

Holly is eager to communicate. She expresses herself through a few spoken words, some use of American Sign Language (ASL), pictures, and facial expressions. Her receptive vocabulary is better than her expressive vocabulary, and this frustrates her sometimes. Her individualized education program (IEP) team is thinking of developing a communication book with pictures to augment her gestures and words so that she can talk with friends and teachers more effectively. Holly likes to play on the computer, and she is very interested in other children and what they are doing.

————————————

Jose is a young man in the seventh grade who has serious spasticity, which limits his ability to control his movements. This is his second year in middle school. Jose had difficulty getting used to the school routines last year when it meant changing classes more often, but once he got used to it, he really liked his schedule. Jose plans to be an assistant for a math teacher he got to know last year, along with an eighth grader assigned as an aide.

Jose has learned to allow other people to assist him to engage in things, but he likes to be in charge of how and when that will happen. Jose doesn't like to wait or be left alone (without personal contact with anyone) for very long. Jose is working on driving a motorized wheelchair. His IEP team feels he should have had access to one when he was much younger, so this is a big priority.

Jose likes riding in a wagon hooked up to his dad's bicycle. He likes the feel of the bumpy ride. He likes going in the car but doesn't like to stop. Jose likes being outdoors and enjoys activities that keep him physically engaged.

Jose is working on increasing his use of a voice output system that uses pictures and words to develop messages. He has more receptive than expressive communication capabilities right now and the plan is to increase Jose's use of the system expressively. Jose is also working on beginning literacy, concept, and vocabulary development in social studies and science; following picture sequences to complete tasks; and using the computer.

Carrie, a 17-year-old senior in high school, is blind and has autism. Carrie is quite a character! She is well known in the school; she has many acquaintances and a special relationship with the principal.

Carrie was in integrated programs (spending some time in general education classes with a special education class base) for elementary school, but she was able to attend an inclusive middle school; in the last few years, her high school has been in the process of changing to an inclusive school. Carrie has been fortunate to be in on the change process. Her team has been doing a lot of transition planning with the help of a university project. Some of the classes in which Carrie's team has been able to support her successfully and in which Carrie has been most successful are biology, Ethnic and Identity Studies, computer technology, drama, chemistry, and choir.

Carrie loves to go out to eat. She also likes going to the school basketball games and getting popcorn at the snack stand. She likes to listen to the band and sometimes goes right up and touches the instruments. Carrie is interested in things in the kitchen but hasn't yet had much instruction in functional daily living skills.

Despite her many successes in school, Carrie has experienced some ups and downs in the high school years. Part of this is communication related; she has both functional and nonfunctional echolalia. Carrie also does not like having routines disrupted. When frustrated, she used to react by scratching and biting, which earned her a reputation for challenging behavior. She has worked hard over the past year to learn to replace the scratching and biting with words and communication signals for *want, stop,* and *no*. She is working on using gestures, words, and a tactile communication book. Carrie's positive behavior support plan is multifaceted and includes a number of strategies for prevention, instruction, ecological support, relaxation, and self-management.

––––––––––––––––––––

Emil, Holly, Jose, and Carrie all have severe and multiple disabilities. Their cognitive, sensory, and physical abilities are unique. What is compelling about each of these students is the rich ways in which they connect to the people and places in their homes, schools, and communities. It is important that we—as educators and team members—critically listen and observe, analyze, and process the wonderfully unique ways in which each child with severe and multiple disabilities learns. Interacting and learning are ultimately two of the keys to quality of life.

A common assumption is that desirable school outcomes improve quality of life; therefore, it is important for teams to identify desirable life outcomes for students with severe and multiple disabilities before discussing a process to achieve these outcomes. Envisioning a desirable future for a student helps guide the IEP team as it designs a meaningful educational program.

Rainforth and York-Barr stated that "a desirable future is one in which a person with disabilities is a participating member of a family and an integrated community" (1997, p. 97). Billingsley and colleagues and Staub and colleagues identified three desirable outcomes that students with severe disabilities achieved when they attended quality inclusive schools: *skills, membership,* and *relationships* (Billingsley, Gallucci, Peck, Schwartz, & Staub, 1996; Staub, Schwartz, Gallucci, & Peck, 1994). Snell and Brown (2000) highlighted these same three outcomes as descriptive of what effective educational programs hope to achieve. The skills outcome refers to all of the relevant skills that students need to acquire to increase their participation in activities of daily living, the activities of their peers without disabilities at school and in nonschool environments, and activities in the community and the workplace. The membership outcome refers to belonging (Kunc, 2000). Belonging to peer groups in school and after-school activities, as well as groups in the community, the neighborhood, and in the workplace, provides students with severe and multiple disabilities the opportunity to develop relationships. The relationships outcome refers to the development of interactions, social relationships, and friendships at all levels. All children and youth need meaningful relationships with peers and adults that are based not on academic prowess but rather on the wide variation of typical relationships that are reciprocal: helpers, play partners, companions, or confidantes, to name a few.

Another critical outcome of effective educational programs is *self-determination.* This chapter refers to learning to make choices; having an effective way to communicate with others; and having a means to exercise responsible control of various aspects of life routines, one's own behavior, and one's own relationships (Wehmeyer, Agran, & Hughes, 1998). The student and his or her family and educational team will ultimately be influenced in their educational decision making by the group's views of who the student's classmates will be; who the student will spend leisure time with, live with, and work with; and how the student will get around and gain access to the community.

This chapter discusses effective practices central to the development of high-quality curriculum and instruction for students with severe and multiple disabilities. The discussion begins by establishing a guiding framework for program development, and then moves to development of the individualized program plan, and then to individualized instruction.

A FRAMEWORK FOR DEVELOPING CURRICULUM AND INSTRUCTION

The process for curriculum development that follows is grounded in research and demonstration efforts that have been conducted in the field with students with severe and multiple disabilities. Effective practice may be supported at a systemic level through agreed-on guiding values and practices.

The research-based framework for educational program development in this chapter is guided by the following five principles: 1) person-centered/family-centered planning; 2) ecologically based assessment and design; 3) functional and social relevance; 4) individualized systematic instruction; and 5) active and informed participation. A *person-centered/family-centered* approach seeks input first from the family. The individual and his or her family focus the team on key priorities through their vision of quality of life, important relationships, and access (Albin, Lucyshyn, Horner, & Flannery, 1996; Demchak & Greenfield, 2000; Turnbull & Turnbull, 2001). An *ecologically based curriculum* is based on the environments, the school curriculum, and the activities of same-age peers without disabilities. Through ecological inventories of the community, school, curriculum standards, classrooms, and home, the team is able to determine chronological age–appropriate environments and activities within which to not only assess the student's strengths and needs but also to provide instruction (Snell & Brown, 2000).

The resulting priorities are *functionally and socially relevant* to the current and future contexts in which the child or youth is expected to participate and engage in learning and social activities. Functional relevance means that the curricular goals and methods of instruction are socially valid, representing areas of need that will truly have a significant impact on the student's life. Parents and team members should be able to quickly and easily answer the question, "Why are we teaching this?" Functionally relevant priorities ultimately increase the student's skills, membership and participation, relationships, and self-determination. Functional relevance does not preclude, however, the team's important task of analyzing the cognitive, sensory, and motor skills of the student within the general education curriculum and other priority learning contexts in order to determine goals and define systematic instructional methods. Research conducted since the 1980s has shown that effective outcomes for students with severe and multiple disabilities in inclusive schools and communities are achieved when the instruction provided is systematic, responsive, and functionally relevant (Halvorsen & Sailor, 1990; Hunt, Farron-Davis, Beckstead, Curtis, & Goetz, 1994; McGregor & Vogelsberg, 1998; Sailor, Goetz, Anderson, Hunt, & Gee, 1988; Snell & Brown, 2000).

Individualized, systematic, yet responsive, instruction means that the outcomes desired are behaviorally specific, the teaching strategies are carefully selected to match learners' needs, and instruction is implemented consistently. Errors are analyzed, and reflective modifications are data-based. At the same time, educators need to be flexible, assess within the context of teaching, observe and adjust, and respond to changes in cognitive initiations from their students. Responsive educators both perceive and utilize critical moments for instruction to provide optimal opportunities for growth and success (Gee, Graham, Sailor, & Goetz, 1995; Thousand, Villa, & Nevin, 2003).

Active and informed participation refers to the structuring of curriculum and instructional adaptations and methods to ensure that all students are not only included in school and community activities but also are truly active and informed participants within each setting or activity (Gee, 1995; Gee, Alwell, Graham, & Goetz, 1994). An *informed* participant has a means to get information about what is going on and an understanding of the context and has been given adequate support to be connected to both the social and task demands of the situation. An *active* and informed student has been given a meaningful way to contribute to social and academic activities or tasks. Teachers working within this framework analyze how each student will receive information and how to best connect the student with the natural cues for cognitive responding (Beukelman & Mirenda, 1998). Teachers structure supports and instruction to ensure that a student's actions and initiations result in functionally relevant events that are, again, connected to the activities and environments in which the student is engaged (Gee et al., 1995; Rainforth & York-Barr, 1997).

Systemic Supports

Achieving the valued outcomes described previously through utilization of the five research-based principles is easier when school districts make systemic commitments to inclusive education, positive behavioral supports (PBS), and collaborative teaming. Although not all schools have these three systemic supports in place, the literature cites these practices as being central to effective programs for students with severe and multiple disabilities. When these practices are not in place, it becomes the role of educational team members to work toward these systemic changes while still providing the best possible educational program within the constraints of the school environment.

1.   *Inclusive schools:* Because a great deal of evidence suggests that students with severe and multiple disabilities are most successfully served in inclusive school environments (see Downing, 2002; Halvorsen & Neary, 2000; Halvorsen & Sailor, 1990; Hunt & Goetz, 1997; McGregor & Vogelsberg, 1998; Sailor, 2001), the examples and processes provided in this chapter are set in inclusive classrooms and school environments. An inclusive school provides the support and environment within which true membership and relationships can form. Without this systemic support, teachers who serve students only in special education classes need to work harder at creating opportunities for their students to spend time with peers without disabilities, become members of their grade-level activities, and develop friendships (Thousand et al., 2003). Although it is possible to practice some communication and self-determination skills in self-contained special education classrooms, fewer opportunities exist in these environments for students to use important skills related to communication, socialization, and academics in natural and functional situations (Snell & Brown, 2000). It is beyond the scope of this chapter to discuss all of the relevant research or to provide the strategies for systemic change that are often required to facilitate the transition to the inclusive school organizational structure. This chapter does provide a process for curriculum development that can be used whether students spend only a small part of or the entire day in inclusive environments.

2.   *PBS:* The second critical systemic support for effective educational programs is both a schoolwide and individual commitment to the use of PBS (Horner & Carr, 1997; Todd, Horner, Sugai, & Sprague, 1999). The technology of PBS has been developed since the 1980s through a National Research and Training Center directed by Dr. Robert Horner, with numerous colleagues from other universities. Efforts toward providing effective and positive support of all students, especially those with the most serious problem behaviors, can challenge schools, teachers, and parents. Schoolwide PBS provide strategies for schools to develop a set of principles and practices that guide students to behave positively. These proactive strategies are focused more on teaching students positive ways to behave than what type of conse-

quences will ensue if students misbehave (Lewis & Sugai, 1999). Individual PBS plans are developed for those students who need intensive support to learn positive ways of communicating, interacting, and maintaining a sense of control (Sugai et al., 2000). Because many challenging behaviors are communication based (Carr et al., 1994), students with severe and multiple disabilities are at a greater risk of developing challenging behaviors if their teams do not pay close attention to providing communication systems, predictability, a means to engage actively in their environment, and opportunities to form relationships that are responsive and reciprocal.

3. *Collaborative teams:* Effective curriculum and instruction is also supported by a systemic belief in the power of collaborative teams. *Collaboration* is a word that has been used widely in the literature regarding students with severe and multiple disabilities (Johnson & Pugach, 1996; Rainforth & York-Barr, 1997; Thousand et al., 2003; see also Chapter 1). Because students with severe and multiple disabilities have a range of challenges in their lives, professionals and family members need to combine their expertise and experience in ways that will benefit, not fragment, the child's educational day and home life.

The remainder of this chapter provides a practical, curricular, and instructional planning process that is based on these concepts.

GATHERING INFORMATION AND SETTING PRIORITIES

Where do we get our information? What do we need to know? Collaborative team members usually have these questions when beginning to set curriculum and instructional goals for a student with severe and multiple disabilities. Multiple sources of information are available for the team to consider when determining educational priorities for the student. But before the information is gathered, the first step is to form the student's team, then enlist the support of all team members in sharing information and contributing to the collaborative decision-making process. Students' teams will vary in their makeup but should include the family member or caregiver, special education teacher(s), general education teacher(s), the key related services personnel (e.g., occupational and physical therapists, speech-language pathologists, vision specialists), close friends, and any other individuals that the family considers critical to the team.

Assembling the Team to Develop a Cohesive Vision

It is important for the student's team to have agreed on a vision for the student's future and a clear sense of long-term outcomes. Chapter 2 of this text provides information and methods for developing reliable alliances with families. True partnerships and collaborative problem solving with families are often enhanced through the use of processes designed to help team members envision desirable futures and formulate priorities (Giangreco, Cloninger, & Iverson, 1998; Halvorsen & Neary, 2000; Turnbull & Turnbull, 2001). One process is called "personal futures planning" or "person-centered planning" (Holburn, 2002; Holburn & Viest, 2002; Kincaid & Fox, 2002; Malette, O'Brien, O'Brien, & Mount, 1997). Another commonly used process is Making Action Plans (MAPs) (Pearpoint, Forest, & O'Brien, 1996), formerly known as the McGill Action Planning System (MAPS) (Lusthaus & Forest, 1987; Thousand, Villa, & Nevin, 2003). Other teams use *Choosing Outcomes and Accommodations for Children* (COACH) (Giangreco et al., 1998).

The most important aspect of these processes related to our discussion of setting educational priorities is that the student and his or her parents and other family members are truly central members of the team, with equal participation in all aspects of the meeting. Thus, a person-centered/family-centered meeting should be held prior to the actual IEP meeting to develop a personal profile of the student that emphasizes strengths and abilities, a vision for the individual's future, and plans for getting there. The team will then be able to address issues in the community and the school and to begin determining ways to work together and support each other in the implementation of the student's educational and/or transition plan. The meeting often begins with the parents and/or the special education teacher providing a short summary of previous experiences in school, and any other issues that are important for setting the stage.

Jose's person-centered planning meeting was held with his team, which included his mother and father; his grandmother; his friends David, Alberto, Maria, and Garrett; his general education science teacher from sixth grade, Mr. Kim; his physical therapist; and his special education teacher, who served as the facilitator. Following is a summary of the meeting:

Jose's family wanted the new team members to know what some of the issues had been in previous environments, so they spent a little time discussing some of the challenges and solutions. Mr. Kim shared the positive experiences from the previous year.

Jose's family felt strongly that he should live near the same community in the future. They had a large, extended family and wanted him to continue to have that support. The whole team envisioned the types of jobs that Jose might enjoy and in which he might be most successful with supports. Jose's dad and his friends speculated that because Jose loves motion and being outdoors so much and "isn't afraid," he would like jobs that included outdoor activity. Mr. Kim also indicated that Jose enjoyed using the adaptations made last year in his class that allowed Jose to run certain pieces of equipment. It was important to his friends and other team members that Jose have a future with lots of friends and ways to gain access to recreation and other services in the community. They also felt that Jose should have the opportunity for post–high school educational options because he had so much curiosity.

Several participants shared their concerns about his future. His parents were worried about his physical health and the continuing issues that he and his team faced related to mobility and medical needs. The special education teacher noted these concerns, and she and the physical therapist acknowledged and supported the family as they openly discussed their fears. Mr. Kim and Jose's friends expressed concern that Jose continue to be challenged in school and that people give him the opportunity to learn as much as he possibly can and not limit him based on his disabilities. His friends wanted to be sure that Jose could remain in classes with them—because they know him and want him to be happy.

Jose's parents and his teachers talked about his natural curiosity, his sense of humor, his desire to be "in charge," his genuine friendships, and how much he has shown everyone he can do since coming to the middle school and being included in the general education program. His grandmother said he was "stubborn," but she thought this was an important quality in many ways. She knew how hard he worked to participate in all of their family events. Other team members talked about his receptive language skills and his increasing expressive communication skills using the computerized, verbal output system with pictures.

Jose's friends reiterated their belief that Jose continue on with them in school classes so they could help other people get to know him and show other kids how to use his communication system. They also believed that he was happier when he was with his friends. Jose's mom and dad felt strongly that he needed to improve his communication system and were hopeful about some of the literacy work that had begun last year. They were a little anxious, but very excited, about the power wheelchair that Jose was learning to use. They were hopeful that this would prove to be successful for him, but they were also worried about access—they had no way to transport his wheelchair and had limited accessibility at their home. Jose's grandmother expressed concern about afterschool time, when she often took care of Jose while his mom and dad were at work. She felt he needed more things to do after school; that he got bored; and that he should be doing things other children do after school involving homework, friends, and recreation.

The special education teacher and the physical therapist added that it was important to make sure that Jose was challenged to improve his cognitive and communication skills in every class period of seventh grade and that it would be important to work closely with Mr. Kim and the other general education teachers to make sure that Jose had another really productive year. They also talked about the need for training time with various staff at the school, time for training with his new power wheelchair, and communication needs.

Jose's friend David said that Jose didn't like people to physically help him without asking. He added that Jose wanted to do it himself. Even when he needed help, he wanted to feel that he was doing it himself. The physical therapist said that she had learned "the hard way" that Jose needed to have the opportunity to try something and that he liked it better when she had him physically shadow her hands versus when she took his hands and helped him do something. Mr. Kim said that Jose needed to get to know people first, and that after there was a relationship, he was able to show people what he knew. Mr. Kim also added that when the communication system was adequately programmed and Jose was given assistance with it, he could see how much Jose could communicate. He was frustrated sometimes with the communication system and believed that Jose was, too.

Jose's dad said that when Jose learned to ride in the adaptive equipment hooked up to his bicycle, Jose needed short rides at first with lots of encouragement. In fact, they used to just sit in the cart and talk and have something to eat, then get out and come back and try again the next day. Jose's special education teacher acknowledged this and said that Jose seemed to perform best when new skills were carefully planned so that there was a gradual increase in expectations and Jose could be successful right away.

Jose's team agreed on many issues, including some of the classes in which he might be most successful, and certain priorities, including continuing to use his power wheelchair, developing his communication skills, and working with Mr. Kim—possibly as an instructional assistant—and that they wanted him to be challenged in all of his classes. The team also agreed that it was important for Jose to begin after-school activities this year, and they worked on ways to connect his family with outside supports for adaptations at home and funding for a wheelchair-accessible van.

Participants in a person-centered planning meeting share their visions and their concerns for the individual's near and distant future. The student's strengths and needs, preferences, and learning styles are discussed from a *personal* point of reference. This means that the "language" of the meeting is not the language of a psychological or discipline-specific assessment tool but is, instead, the language of people who know the student, talking together about who the individual student "is," what they want for him or her, and how they can help. Assessment tools and reports are left at the office. In other words, people who spend the most time with an individual (at home, in school, and in the community) share and discuss their concerns and ideas about the individual's education and quality of life. Information regarding the student's previous school and community integration, social networks, and age-specific program issues are a natural part of the discussion.

The facilitator prompts the discussion by asking some key questions, such as, "When we look at the dreams we have listed here on the wall, the visions we have for Jose, what strengths does he bring? What are the qualities and abilities that he already has that will help him achieve his dreams/our dreams for him?" The facilitator also asks about the student's needs. For example, "What are some of the things Jose needs in order to fulfill his vision for his future?" Another important part of a family-centered meeting is discussing learning and support from a holistic point of view. Jose's special education teacher put the question to the team as follows: "What do we know that really works for Jose? When he has been really successful at something, what did it look like?" And, "What do we know that *doesn't* work? Let's make two lists." With some additional prompting, Jose's team began to talk about what they knew.

The final step of the person-centered planning meeting is to summarize what the team has learned and to make recommendations for the IEP and school program. The team makes a list of priorities for the coming year and also looks at long-term planning and support ideas that may involve bringing in other resources. The results of the person-centered/family-centered planning meeting are extremely helpful for the IEP process (Kincaid & Fox, 2002). Because the primary team members have already come together and agreed on what they think are the most important aspects of the student's program for the coming year, finding agreement on the more specific goals and objectives, adaptations, and supports at the IEP meeting is much easier. Using person-centered planning strategies puts everyone on "equal ground." It changes the way the person with disabilities is discussed and encourages common terminology. The group is focused on increasing the quality of life of the individual through choices and empowerment, creating a common bond, which greatly enhances the IEP process. By continuing to meet on a regular basis, this group can positively influence the implementation of actions that will have a direct impact on the individual's future (Holburn & Viest, 2002; Malette et al., 1992). (Other methods for soliciting input from families and partnering with parents in the IEP process are described in Chapter 2.)

Determining Instructional Activities Across Ecological Domains

Another important source of information in the development of the IEP is the student's current performance and participation levels across age-appropriate and ecologically relevant domains. Brown and his colleagues (1979) identified four functional curricular domains that must be considered when planning IEPs for students with severe and multiple disabilities: home, school, community, and work. This ecological model of curriculum development requires teams to take an inventory of the coursework and activities that same-age children and youth who are typically developing are engaged in across all domains (Browder, 2000; Downing, 2002; Rainforth & York-Barr, 1997; Snell & Brown, 2000). The general education, school, and community activities of same-age peers provide the context for goals that are functional and relevant and also provide the instructional context for teaching important basic skills such as communication, social, motor, and sensory skills.

Since the mid-1990s, the wide body of research and experience with including students with severe and multiple disabilities in general education classrooms and schools has greatly expanded the school domain in the ecological model (Downing, 2002; Falvey, 1995; Gee, 1995; Hunt & Goetz, 1997; Snell & Brown, 2000). Now, students have access not only to the general education curriculum but also to membership in general education classrooms. Many teams consider this domain the top priority for instructional environments (Sailor, Gee, & Karasoff, 1993).

Taking an inventory of the academic curriculum, the extracurricular activities, and the other activities that occur at school yields important information for the IEP (Falvey, 1995). With an understanding of the general education curriculum and how it is implemented in the student's general education classroom, the team can plan to assess the student's performance and determine modified goals/outcomes within each subject area (see section on the general education curriculum that follows). Let's look at each student's particular situation:

The kindergarten curriculum at Emil's school was highly focused on language and literacy. Teaching activities emphasized reading and oral language development throughout various social studies themes and science themes. The school had a farm and garden center that afforded students with hands-on experiences in nature activities within an urban setting. In addition to interaction and membership, the general education kindergarten curriculum afforded Emil with multiple opportunities to practice basic communication, motor, and social skills.

Fourth graders at Holly's school focused on California history, reading for meaning, literacy that used historical lessons, and math. The curriculum also included science and the arts.

The curriculum for seventh graders at Jose's school consisted of pre-algebra, social studies, science, English, physical education (PE), and one elective (either a foreign language, art, computers, or drama). An additional "zero period" was available for orchestra or band.

Carrie attended a fully inclusive high school with numerous options in both academic and extracurricular coursework.

A well-done inventory helps the special education team connect to the typical structures, policies, and procedures for all students in the school. For example, an inventory at Emil's school prompted the school inclusion team to re-examine the after-school activities to determine whether all students had access to activities. Holly's elementary school teachers already worked in teams and had time on Wednesday afternoons for planning. These Wednesday-afternoon planning and in-service opportunities were important for the new structures and skills being put into place given that this was the first year for the school to move to an inclusive model. Jose's middle school had a new principal but maintained a strong core group of faculty with whom his special education teacher had collaborated the previous year. At Carrie's high school, an inventory revealed three different types of programs through which high school students could volunteer and do internships both on and off campus.

An inventory of the neighborhood surrounding the school can yield information as to whether community environments are readily available for community-based instruction of various functional skills or whether other arrangements will need to be made. Holly will now be attending the same school the other children in her neighborhood attend. Many of her neighbors walk to school and some are driven. Her family belongs to the YMCA, where Holly takes swimming lessons and attends summer camp. An inventory of Jose's community revealed that while the school is located near the town center, Jose and many of his friends live quite a distance from community services in this rural-suburban area. Jose's family did not yet have adequate transportation for Jose's power wheelchair, making connections difficult. Helping Jose gain access to friends and the community and supporting the family to gain transportation, became team priorities.

Starting with the general education curriculum and courses as a base, each student's team must prioritize how to designate the instructional time during school hours. In Tables 3.1–3.4, the reader can see that each of our focus student's teams considered all of the curricular domains, provided input in note form, then prioritized a daily and/or weekly schedule of context-specific courses and activities that were determined to be the most efficacious for each student. In these tables, notes and schedules vary to show different ways this can be done.

Another important source of information to consider is discipline-specific information and skills that can be taught within and across the general education curriculum and other functional activities in the school, home, and community.

Embedding Priority Skills Throughout the Instructional Day

Conducting an analysis of the student's current strengths and challenges related to academic skills, cognitive processes, sensory abilities and challenges, motor strengths and challenges, and receptive and expressive forms of communication is critical to determining priority goals. Although some of this information is generated through the person-centered plan and/or family interviews, input from all relevant team members should be synthesized for practical and functional use across contexts. Best practice indicates that assessments and analyses done by discipline-specific team members such as physical or occupational therapists should be conducted within and across the home, school, and community contexts in which the student spends his or her time (Dunn, Brown, & McGuigan, 1994; Giangreco, Edelman, Luiselli, & MacFarland, 1996; Rainforth & York-Barr, 1997). (See Chapter 1 for more on collaborative teaming.)

The physical and occupational therapists on Holly's team were working with all team members to ensure that Holly received the right support for the use of her three-pronged cane; mobility routes around the school; and the use of specific adaptive equipment for writing, eating, and other activities. The special education teacher and vision resource teacher recommended instruction on classroom participation skills such as finding materials, using her desk, and using various low-vision aids to enhance instruction in cognitive areas. In the area of language and literacy, the team also prioritized picture communication, a conversation book, computer, and picture sequencing skills as part of beginning literacy. Because it was Holly's first year to be fully included in the general education classroom, her team members indicated on the action plan that they would need to do further assessment within the fourth-grade environment to determine other needs and ways in which Holly could best be supported. After further analysis, additional priorities and supports were added.

Several communication and movement priorities were established for Emil. His team members all agreed that these skills and management strategies needed to be consistently implemented across all of the kindergarten activities. High priorities for Emil included consistently using his FM system (i.e., getting both Emil

Table 3.1. Summary information for Emil

Input from person-centered planning meeting, family interviews, and other sources	Age-referenced activities	Basic skills or areas to address across all contexts
Communication system is highest priority	*Kindergarten curriculum:*	*Communication system:* Work out specific gestural dictionary for all staff and peers; work on tactile symbol/voice output system, systematic instruction, and use throughout the day
Encourage friendships, ways for Emil to play and interact with others	Morning circle: calendar, planning for the day, projects from previous days, integrate the day	
Find ways to ease transitions from place to place	Language and literacy groups	Make sure there is positioning for all of the various kindergarten activities that is most advantageous and functional for Emil
Need staff training	Recess	
Make sure that Emil's physical positioning and movement is done very positively	Math groups	
	Stories and large group language activities	Movement: Work on increasing range and use of arms and hands
Make sure that Emil gets enough to eat and that there is adequate training for his tube feeding	Lunch/recess	FM system: Make sure everyone knows how to use it
	Quiet reading time: books on tape, partner read, independent reading	
Find ways to work on his skills within the kindergarten activities—making sure that his mom and dad know how this is going	Rotating schedule: M/W farm and garden, Tu/F music, and Th community library	
Communicate regularly with teachers		
Child care provider wants more training/support	*Home:* Personal care activities: Making choices for clothes, toys, food, and so forth; assisting in toothbrushing and washing up; socializing; play activities	
Find ways to make family outings easier (e.g., eating out, going to events)	*Community:* Eating out, going shopping—participate with parents	

Emil's schedule as determined by the team	The priority goals that will be taught in the schedule
Arrival, time on playground with friends	*Communication system:* Gestural and tactile
Transition	—Use FM system to add to receptive skills
Morning circle: calendar, planning for the day, projects from previous days, integrate the day	—Direct others
Language and literacy groups	Direct transitions, anticipating changes
Recess	Use arms and hands to participate in the various activities in math and literacy groups, microswitch
Math groups	Morning circle/calendar planning: Use tactile schedule book
Stories and large-group language activities	*Literacy groups:* Access stories on tape with FM system, use computer to access voice output stories, distinguish books on tape versus books being read, choose from two favorite stories based on the tactile symbol on the cover, activate the books on tape using a microswitch and holding the book with the tactile symbol for the story
Lunch/recess	*Motor skills:* Use stander and adapted chairs to participate in different activities; use arms to bring things to himself and push things away
Quiet reading time: books on tape, partner reading, independent reading (tube feeding done during this time)	Initiate invitations to play at recess and other free times; respond to invitations to play
Rotating schedule: MW farm and garden, Tu/F music, and Th community library	Invite peers to play after school and on weekends
	Eat soft foods from spoon, drink liquids

Table 3.2. Summary information for Holly

Input from person-centered planning meeting, family interviews, and other sources	Age-referenced activities	Basic skills or areas to address across all contexts
Communication system is highest priority	Fourth-grade subjects: language arts, math, social studies (California history), science, physical education, art; three fourth-grade teachers—students work in teams for science and art; several field trips planned for the year; school has arts and drama magnet grant; fourth graders do one culminating drama performance per semester—need to determine outcomes	Work on class/school participation skills such as using a desk, organizing materials, finding places in the school; knowing routes to and from class, bathroom, other parts of the school
Friendships with other kids in the class		
Communication: Ways to talk to other kids and socialize		Communication skills: Use conversation book with pictures and words, assess whether a portable voice output system would be more motivating to Holly
New ways to start interactions		
Keep improving her physical capabilities and ways to compensate	After-school tutoring programs, sports clubs, and Wednesday afternoon classes in a variety of things such as chess and Spanish	Improve self-care skills
Ride a bike or a scooter like other neighborhood kids		Walk with the three-pronged cane
Improve her ability to use visual aids and other adaptations		Use adapted utensils and writing tools
Fourth-grade curriculum activities: Modified outcomes	Holly will now be in the same school as her neighbors—priority to develop friendships; most students are driven to school, but there are some school buses; some students walk to school	Use low-vision aids
Money—what it is and how to buy something at the store or pay for something		Literacy: Work on picture sequencing to put sentences together
Self-care activities—brushing teeth, dressing (need adaptations)	Holly's family belongs to the YMCA, and Holly takes swim lessons there and attends day camps in the summer with support from an older cousin—priority to increase participation.	Improve computer access
Use the computer		Practice skills in lunchroom, recess, assemblies
Take part in some of the Wednesday classes and other after-school activities		Improve purchasing skills

Decisions that were made for Holly:
What the student's school day/week will look like

Fourth-grade schedule (often varies, however):

8:15   Language arts: reading, writing
9:45   Recess
10:05 Math and math workshop
11:00 Science or art/drama
12:00 Lunch/recess
12:45 Sustained silent reading
1:15   Social studies/language arts
2:45   School ends

Need to allow time for self-care activities in restroom
Need to allow for longer transitions during certain periods to get mobility practice with cane
Need to determine practical times for purchasing and other access skills

After-school class on Wednesday with peer support

The priority goals that will be taught in the schedule

Communication skills: Conversation book and other methods
Friendships/social relationships
Literacy: Picture sequencing to put sentences together
Math kindergarten standards modified:
—Standard 1.1 modified: Holly will learn to count out objects from 1 to 5 when asked
—Standard 1.4, modified: Holly will group similar objects into same and different groups
—Standard 1.5, modified: Holly will recognize and sort coins and one dollar bills
Social studies: Holly will identify and match pictures of people and events in California history
Science: Holly will demonstrate the ability to work in a small group to carry out science project activities
Class/school participation skills: using organizer adaptations; following routines; raise hand/use communication system
Learning to ride a bike or scooter
Computer skills: Using computer to access information in social studies and science; use picture sequencing software
Improving self-care skills: dressing, using restroom, brushing teeth
Walking with the three-pronged cane
Using adapted utensils and writing tools
Using vision aids
Improving skills in lunchroom, recess, assemblies
Improving purchasing skills

Table 3.3. Summary information for Jose

Input from person-centered planning meeting, family interviews, and other sources	Age-referenced activities	Basic skills or areas to address across all contexts
Desired future: Jose will have a job and live supported in the community, have friends, have access to recreation and ways to get around	*School:* Seventh- and eighth-graders change classes every period but have a core of four teachers that work with their sections in the four main subject areas: English, social studies, math, and science	Motorized wheelchair use—mobility routes
For this year: Continue to improve use of picture based voice output communication system	Seventh graders have one elective and can select from foreign language, art, or drama or can be an instructional assistant to one of the sixth-grade teachers; band and orchestra are additional zero period classes.	Increase use of voice-output communication system initiation
Work very hard on emerging literacy skills		*Friendships:* Develop after-school relationships and options with family
Instructional assistant: Make sure this works	*Extracurricular:* sports, yearbook, newspaper	*Literacy:* Beginning word recognition; functional word/picture match
Seventh-grade schedule: probably all classes except math and foreign language; try band even though it is zero period (early morning optional class)	*Community:* Town center is new; rural-suburban community	Understand and identify from pictures concepts related to academic curricular activities (e.g., mountains, rivers, oceans, valleys, deserts, volcanoes, floods)
Community access skills: Driving motorized chair!!!! Yeah!!	Middle school is located close to various shops and services: video store, grocery, library, dry cleaner, post office, bicycle store, other	Put picture sequences together to illustrate the order and results of concepts discussed in classes
Friendships: Develop more after-school and weekend relationships—HIGH priority	Students are bused to school	Jose will use his voice-output communication system to respond to yes/no and short-phrase answers to concept questions in social studies science, and English
Challenge Jose cognitively!!	Jose's family does not have a wheelchair van, making community access more difficult	Work on motor extensions, maintain range and use of physical adaptations for eating and drinking
Extracurricular: Possibly help manage a team that one of his friends plays on		Work on anticipating schedule using schedule book and making smooth transitions and following picture sequence for various tasks
Could Jose take computer class again?		
Need to explore wheelchair van funding		
Make sure he is enrolled with some of his friends for key classes like English and science		

Decisions that were made for Jose:

What the student's school day/week will look like	The priority goals which will be taught in the schedule
Period 0: Band	*Motorized wheelchair use:* Learn mobility routes, practice motor extensions, maintain range and use of physical adaptations
Period 1: Computer class (make sure seventh-grade instructional assistant is peer who knows Jose)	Increase communication skills, initiate use of voice output system
Period 2: English	*Friendships:* Develop after-school relationships
Period 3: PE	*Literacy:* Improve beginning word recognition, functional word/picture match
Lunch	
Period 4: Science	*Science:* Understand and identify from pictures the concepts, including mountains, rivers, oceans, valleys, deserts, volcanoes, and floods; put picture sequences together to illustrate the order and results of catastrophic events; use voice output communication system to respond to yes/no and short phrase answers to the concept questions
Period 5: Instructional assistant with Mr. Kim	
Period 6: Community based instruction and extra mobility instruction	*Social studies and English:* Understand and identify from pictures and some beginning word concepts related to stories and novels being read aloud and related to ancient religions and cultures; match symbols on maps and match clothing and other pictures to particular civilizations
After school: In fall, assist in managing soccer team	
Find ways to provide Jose with the physical motion he enjoys and needs during PE/other	Anticipate schedule using schedule book and make smooth transitions—know how to end one activity and move on to another
Find a way for Jose to get a snack sometime in the a.m. because the morning will be long	Eat and drink using adapted equipment
	Various clerical jobs—instructional assistant related jobs
	Computer use—both academic and recreational

Table 3.4. Summary information for Carrie

Input from person-centered planning meeting, family interviews, and other sources	Age-referenced activities	Basic skills or areas to address across all contexts
Future plans: Stay living in same city as parents, supported living with a couple of friends, part-time job, community college classes, friends, recreation, clubs	*Large comprehensive high school program—what is available:* Typical 11th-grade schedule: math analysis; English, anatomy, or chemistry; government/economics; foreign language; electives	Team needs to meet early with teachers for academic course periods to plan for embedded instruction of priority skills and ways to interact with the class activities
Priorities for this year:	Carrie needs courses that provide opportunities for interaction and skill building	Positive behavioral support (PBS) plan is high priority
Improve communication system—HIGH priority	Numerous clubs and extra-curricular activities and sports	*Communication system:* Put serious focus on it—across academic subjects and other activities
Positive behavioral support (PBS) plan needs fine tuning, training for everyone, monitored regularly—this is another HIGH priority	*Community:*	*Orientation and mobility:* Work on in school and community
Continue orientation and mobility work	School is located near public transit stops, shops, restaurants, services, middle school, veterans hospital, art museum, and zoo	*Jobs in community:* Try dentist office, zoo, and veterans hospital this year
Friendships/social relationships:	Takes about 30 minutes to get downtown by bus	Use fast-food and sit-down restaurants
Join a club with some acquaintances	Optometrist and dentist office complex nearby	Shop in the community
Try different types of jobs in the community, see what Carrie likes best		*Exercise skills:* Try stationary bike, adapted bike with partner, bicycle built for two, treadmill, swimming
Classes for this year might include anatomy (with the teacher who taught the biology class), choir, government, aerobics/biking		*Self-care skills:* Work on adaptations for dressing and finalizing skills in certain areas

Decisions that were made for Carrie:

What the student's school day/week will look like	The priority goals that will be taught in the schedule
	PBS plan, replacement skills, new communication strategies
Period 1: Anatomy (with the teacher who taught the biology class)	*Communication system:* Work on verbal input with tactile object system; work on expressive verbal skills—making echolalia meaningful and moving echolalia to direct speech; use voice output device and computer as part of strategy
Period 2: Choir	
Period 3: Dance—fall; aerobics—spring	
Lunch	
Period 4: Government—fall; Economics—spring	Orientation and mobility—school and community
Periods 5 & 6: Off-campus job and other community instruction, mobility, and so forth	Take care of school supplies and belongings
	Develop goals in government, anatomy, and choir in conjunction with general education teachers after 2–3 weeks of experience in the class
Period 7: Yearbook staff	Follow schedule at job
Club: Determine a club that some of her friends are in and arrange for peer support along with after-school or lunch-time paraprofessional availability	Eat in fast-food and sit-down restaurants
	Shop in the community
	Practice exercise skills
	Self-care skills: Work on adaptations for dressing and finalizing skills in certain areas
	Enjoy friendships/social relationships

and the teachers used to using it), pairing a tactile/object system and tactile gesture system with verbal input for receptive communication, using a tactile-object voice output system in addition to gestures for expressive communication, and using hand and arm movements more regularly. Emil also needed a positioning and handling protocol across all periods of the day and a specialized health care plan to ensure adequate nutrition and hydration.

Many of the skills and priorities the special education teacher and discipline-specific team members identified for Holly and Emil were not bound to any particular instructional context. Instead, these skills and priorities were "non–context-bound," meaning that they were basic and underlying to almost all of the activities in which the students were involved. Instruction of these skills can, thus, be embedded into the student's activities in the general education curriculum, the school, at home, and in the community.

Prioritizing Goals and Planning the School Day and Week

Educators at nearly every school lament that there is never enough time in a school day or week. Making the most efficacious use of school time while providing an educational context that is flexible, fosters relationships, and allows teachers to be responsive is a challenge that each team, and especially the primary support teacher, must meet. An important step is the formulation of a plan that delineates each student's schedule of class periods, educational activities, and contexts in which instruction will take place over the school week and the prioritized educational goals that will be incorporated within and across the schedule. Some goals will require specific environments or contexts in order for instruction to take place. Other goals will be taught across multiple environments and situations. For elementary and middle school students, the contexts and activities generally consist of the general education class schedule; other school environments such as the gym, the cafeteria, and the playground; and any other alternative but integrated environments that the team determines are necessary to meet the goals (Rainforth & York-Barr, 1997).

Secondary students' teams often have more flexibility in the selection of courses and how the student's day is structured (Thousand et al., 2003). Teachers of secondary and postsecondary students sometimes struggle with how much time to spend in general education classes and how much time to spend in other school and community environments. Preparation for the world of work and adult supported living requires a balance between time spent with peers without disabilities and the acquisition of important academic, social, and communication skills versus time spent in learning community access, developing job interests, and determining other recreational and social interests. Unfortunately, many programs give up a substantial amount of integration when they organize community or work activities that are conducted in isolation from peers or co-workers without disabilities. It is important to remember to reference the student's day to other young people of the same age. High school students who are typically developing are in school all day but may have part-time jobs or other internships related to future career planning. The school experience provides a rich set of opportunities within which to grow cognitively and socially alongside peers of the same age. If the team develops some goals that can best be met in community or work environments, these environments should be inclusive and provide rich opportunities for interaction and the development of other important skills (Wehmeyer, 2002).

IEPs allow for variation in the amount of time spent in different educational activities. Quality inclusive schools promote fluid instructional options for all students. As stated previously, Tables 3.1–3.4 depict the decisions made by the collaborative teams for the four students described in this chapter. In each case, the team considered the information from the person-centered/family-centered plan, the general education curriculum, the school, the community, the home, and the discipline-specific input. The next step is to analyze, more specifically, each chosen educational context and how skills will be instructed.

INDIVIDUALIZING OUTCOMES, SUPPORTS, AND SERVICES WITHIN GENERAL EDUCATION CLASSES

The general education curriculum and the instructional activities that are designed to support it are primary contexts within which students with severe and multiple disabilities receive instruction. Students with disabilities may have curricular outcomes that are the same as their peers without disabilities, or their outcomes may be quite different. Aligning learning outcomes with the general education curriculum and modifying the expectations for individual students within the curriculum requires the ability to scaffold skill development and determine underlying skills within a large subset of skills. The design of modified outcomes for students with disabilities has been discussed in numerous sources in the literature (Snell & Janney, 2000; Wehmeyer, 2002) as well as in Chapters 4 and 5 of this text.

For definitional purposes, *modified outcomes* refers to changes the team makes in expected academic or cognitive outcomes for individual students. The student may be working on the same or similar goals but at a different grade level. For example, Jose was working on early literacy skills that can be found in the kindergarten standards while his peers were working on seventh-grade English content standards. Specifically, one of his goals was to identify the characters, settings, and important events in a story that was read to him while he listened. In his science class, Jose was working on understanding the concept of mountains, rivers, valleys, deserts, volcanoes, and floods while one goal for the other seventh graders was to demonstrate an understanding of catastrophic events and how these events affect life on earth.

Some students may have outcomes within the general education curriculum that are similar to, but not reflected in, grade-level content standards. Table 3.5 depicts some contextually aligned goals related to core curriculum content standards from the California frameworks (http://www.cde.ca.gov/cfir/curfrwk.html) for Emil, Holly, Jose, and Carrie. This type of information is used to develop specific planning for objectives and instruction for each class period. Initial goals may need to be revised based on the problem-solving process described later. In Table 3.5, for example, while Emil's same-age kindergarten peers are working on Language Arts Standard #3: *Students listen and respond to stories based on well-known characters, themes, plots, and settings,* he is working on how to activate the books on tape using a microswitch and how to recognize the tactile symbol for "story." Within the fourth-grade math curriculum at Holly's school, her peers were learning the place value of whole numbers and the concept of negative numbers, among other outcomes, while Holly's outcomes included counting and using coins.

Other outcomes that may get identified within the general education activities are those not necessarily reflective of the curricular area but are basic or underlying to the educational activity. Many general education activities provide excellent, motivating instructional opportunities for basic communication, sensory, motor, cognitive, and social skills. Research has shown not only that students with severe and multiple disabilities can learn these basic skills within the same activities of the general education peers but also that these instructional situations are motivating and highly effective (Gee et al., 1995; Hunt, Farron-Davis et al., 1994; McGregor & Vogelsberg, 1998; Snell & Janney, 2000).

Emil is working on sitting with supports in the kindergarten morning circle; he is also working on his tactile communication symbols within the math activities of his peers. In addition to the beginning literacy skills outcomes in English class, Jose has expectations for learning particular social skill goals, organizational skills, and communication skills. Holly is working on using her three-pronged cane while moving from one activity to the next in her fourth-grade class. She is also working on her computer skills and using her conversation book during the fourth-grade math activities. During anatomy class, Carrie is working on identifying body parts, following sequences of steps for lab activities, and learning various vocabulary words; but she also works on several skills related to her PBS plan including following a schedule book, how to indicate "no" using her words, and how to use her conversation book. She also works on carrying her backpack, finding her materials in it, and organizing lab materials.

Table 3.5. Sample of contextually aligned goals and objectives modified from state curriculum framework

Sample goals from California Curriculum frameworks	Modified goals/outcomes for each student
Kindergarten: Language Arts Standard #3: *Students listen and respond to stories based on well-known characters, themes, plots, and settings.* 3.1. Distinguish fantasy from realistic text 3.2. Identify types of everyday print materials 3.3. Identify characters, settings, and important events	**For Emil:** Emil will learn to distinguish books on tape versus books being read to him. Emil will choose from two favorite stories based on the tactile symbol on the cover. Emil will learn to activate the books on tape using a microswitch and hold the book with the tactile symbol for "story."
Fourth grade: Math Standard #1: Number Sense *Students understand the place value of whole numbers and decimals to two decimal places and how whole numbers and decimals relate to simple fractions. Students use the concepts of negative numbers.*	**For Holly:** Holly will learn to count out objects from 1 to 5 when asked. Holly will group objects into same and different groups. Holly will recognize and sort coins and $1 bills.
Seventh grade: Life Science Standard #4: Earth and Life History *Students know that earth processes today are similar to those that occurred in the past and that slow geological processes have large cumulative effects over long periods of time.* *Students know the history of life on earth has been disrupted by major catastrophic events, such as major volcanic eruptions or the impacts of asteroids.*	**For Jose:** Jose will understand and identify from pictures the concepts of mountains, rivers, oceans, valleys, deserts, volcanoes, and floods. Jose will put picture sequences together to illustrate the order and results of catastrophic events. Jose will use his voice output communication system to respond to yes/no and short phrase answers to the concept questions.
12th grade: Government Standard 12.2.: *Students evaluate and take and defend positions on the scope and limits of rights and obligations as democratic citizens, the relationships among them, and how they are secured.*	**For Carrie:** Carrie will understand the rules of her PBS plan and respect others' safety rights. Carrie will follow a tactile schedule paired with verbal input for class activities. Carrie will work in a group to develop case arguments that she will tape-record and play back for students practicing their presentation. Carrie will learn to say the Pledge of Allegiance and sing the "Star Spangled Banner" by listening to tapes.

During some courses or class activities, alternative or substitute curricular outcomes may need to be designed. When alternative activities are created because the team feels it is more beneficial to the student, these activities should be integrated with small groups of peers or peer partners without disabilities as much as possible (Halvorsen & Neary, 2000). When Jose leaves school in seventh period to work on community mobility in his power wheelchair, peer tutors taking the class as their elective accompany him to various stores to provide modeling and social interactions.

Adaptations and accommodations refer to the types of changes the team makes in the ways in which information is both provided and required (Snell & Janney, 2000). In other words, a student's outcomes may be the same as all the other students, with adaptations in either *input* (the ways in which the student receives information) or *output* (the ways in which the student produces information or lets people know what she knows). A student may require both modified outcomes and adaptations to benefit most from the curricular activities. Some adaptations are standard practices that teams always agree to do for a child. Some examples include specific seating arrangements or physical equipment, a longer time for a child to produce a product, or an agreement that answers will be spoken rather than typed, and so forth. Other adaptations are specific to certain subjects or particular teaching activities. For example Emil, Holly, Jose, and Carrie all require adaptations in the ways in which information is provided throughout all activities. Their receptive communication systems require more than just verbal input. Carrie and Emil both use tactile object systems in addition to verbal input, and Emil also uses tactile gestures. Holly and Jose both use picture communication systems for following sequences and learning other concepts.

Within each general education activity, Emil, Holly, Jose, and Carrie require adapted ways of demonstrating what they know (their output systems). Emil uses his tactile symbol voice output device and specific gestures to let people know what he needs, what he chooses, and who he wants to be his partner. Holly expresses herself through a few spoken words, some use of American Sign Language, pictures, and facial expressions. Jose uses physical adaptations to indicate picture choices and make selections. Carrie uses her words and her tactile symbol book to let people know what she wants and to respond to questions from the teacher.

Each student's IEP should include goals that describe the expected outcomes within each general class period/course/subject in which the student is enrolled or participating. This is crucial for several reasons. It gives general education teachers a specific frame of reference for the expectations for the student within the class or subject area, it organizes the IEP around the educational contexts selected by the team; and it provides a clear guide for what the student is working on and when. IEPs should reflect the student's educational program and educational day (Rainforth & York-Barr, 1997). Teams will find it especially helpful if each period of the day has goals that indicate the purpose and outcomes related to the general curriculum.

Designing Support Plans

One of the most important phases of instructional planning is the development of support plans for each curricular period of the student's day. Whether this is done prior to entry in the class or shortly after the school year begins, the process can have a significant influence on the success of the student in the general education classroom. The planning process recommended here has been documented in other sources and has been used with numerous educational teams across the country (Gee, 1995; Gee, Alwell, et al., 1994). Basically, the planning process begins with setting a tone for collaborative ownership of the curriculum, responsibility for the students in the class, and the special needs of the child with severe and multiple disabilities.

The focus begins with the general education curricular unit. Depending on whether the special education and general education teachers have collaborated previously for other students and how well they know each other, various levels of this process can be utilized. The suggested planning process assumes that team members are new to working with each other and learning about the specific focus student and/or the curricular units.

The planning process with the general education teacher/team may start with a unit of material—or the way in which the general education teacher organizes his or her teaching. Some English teachers, for example, may organize their course around units for each novel with various ongoing assignments related to the novel. A history teacher may organize units of material based on particular periods of history or major historical events. A science unit may revolve around a creek study or a garden project. Language arts units may be organized based on particular reading curriculum units, whereas direct reading and math instruction may be ongoing and individually monitored. The time spent on a given unit may vary as well as subject matter; for example, elementary school units may take place over a shorter period of time than secondary school units.

The special education teacher may be a part of a grade-level team, which fosters collaboration. Some schools are more readily organized for team meetings than others. It is important to stress to the general education teachers and the principal that getting some substantive time to focus just on curriculum and the instructional outcomes and supports will save a lot of on-the-spot crisis planning later on. Rather than expecting teachers to meet often, a carefully planned brainstorming and planning session can yield positive, sustained results if the meeting is focused. The following focus questions have been found to be useful to numerous teams. Some special and general education teachers plan units jointly under a team or co-teaching structure (Brown et al., 1979). These questions must still be answered, however, in order to specifically determine what the outcomes for the special education student will be and when and where instruction will occur. Using the planning process carefully can be a valuable means for in-service training, as well.

1. *What are the primary outcomes/expectations for the students during this curricular unit?* What is the range of expectations within the class? What are the social expectations? These questions prompt the general education teacher to talk generally about the class, the focus for the unit, the social expectations, and so forth. For example, Jose's English teacher said that the class was going to be doing a unit on a fantasy novel called *A Wizard of Earthsea,* by Ursula K. LeGuin (1984) (see Figure 3.1). The teacher's overall goals were related to the language and literacy goals from the frameworks, but she also wanted the students to love to read and to share her interest in this particular novel. She indicated that she had a wide range of reading levels in the class. Some students were very advanced and would probably read ahead; others were behind grade level and would no doubt struggle with this particular text. She already differentiated her instruction for these students. The classroom had a set of class rules and expectations that were posted on the wall. The students helped develop these at the beginning of the school year.

2. *What are the main teaching activities and routines you will be using to engage students in the learning process during this unit?* In the second column, the person recording the information writes down the key teaching activities to be used in the unit. This is not a place to write detailed lesson plans; instead, it is a place to get a projection of all of the different types of teaching activities that will be happening over the next few days or weeks and the ways in which these activities will be organized. This gives the special education teacher and team a clear picture of what the student will be participating in during class time. For example, Jose's English teacher was quick to say that they would not be doing the same thing every day, but when prompted, she was able to list some of the key activities that would regularly occur, such as journal writing and reading aloud; various projects, such as developing a "mandala" or a "sociogram"; and the types of assignments students would be given (see Figure 3.1).

3. *In order to get more information, the special education teacher might ask: How does each of the activities look? Tell me more about how they are organized.* It is important to understand the formats for instruction, the instructional groupings,

Team Planning Tool
(Active and informed participation)

Student: Jose

Unit: A Wizard of Earthsea by Ursula K. LeGuin

Typical class activities and routines within the unit	Typical teaching strategies	Expectations for all students/content standards	Expectations (outcomes) for the focus student	How will the student receive information?	How will the student provide information?	What additional types of supports are needed?
Reading aloud	Large group, vary readers, discuss in between passages	Follow reading, reading aloud, participate in discussion	Follow class schedule/transitions, work on emergent literacy skills	Picture schedule system, verbal input and peer supports to re-emphasize directions and sequences, research fact sheets	Computer output and voice output system will be programmed for his participation in discussion, in provision of group information and so forth.	Circle of friends Set aside 5 minutes on a regular basis to train the peers in Jose's support him during particular activities and tasks
Journal and homework written assignments in Thoughtful Ed. model with four styles	Independent work or with partner	Complete assignments after every two chapters. Grammar, spelling, reading for comprehension and understanding, critical thinking	Journal time: Use computer—work on literacy program		Vocabulary lists on Jose's computer—all students must access it from him • Other information for class in Jose's computer	Make sure peers know how to use Jose's communication system and how to prompt him to use it

(continued)

Figure 3.1. Team planning tool for Jose.

97

Figure 3.1. *(continued)*

Debate	Room divides in half on a position; students who change their mind physically move	State arguments clearly, determine agree or disagree, share thoughts, articulate positions	Use communication system		Provide the peers with feedback
Mandalas	Students design mandalas based on the themes from the book	Critical thinking, creative approaches to themes, understanding story themes	Picture sequences to tell stories		At support circle meetings, discuss upcoming projects and look at possibilities for Jose
Sociograms	Students work on sociograms of the characters over the course of the book in groups	Understanding the relationships between the characters in the book	Practice word recognition and matching	Computer	• Generate picture sequences to tell stories and provide input	Arrange for how Jose will do homework, class discussions, and projects
				Peer input for group projects		
Play: Fantasy	Four groups of students: Students design a one-act play that is a fantasy and perform it for the class	Writing, articulating story plots and themes, understanding fantasy as a literary form, work skills	Using communication system, transitioning, social skills			Support literacy goals with special education teacher or trained paraprofessional in class

and types of peer-mediated learning activities that typically occur. Questions 2 and 3 allow the opportunity for collaborations and for team members to receive suggestions from other professionals and the chance to get to know each other's strengths. For example, Jose's teacher indicated that students typically engage in journal writing and start on their homework assignments but that some people work as partners. Participating in the sociogram projects and writing the play are done in groups. The students will have time in class several times a week and can come into the teacher's room during lunchtime if they want more time. Jose's teacher also describes the debate included in the lesson. During the debate, the students divide the room in half and each side takes one side of the argument. As the debate ensues, students physically switch sides when they agree or disagree with a particular point. This makes the debate very active. The teacher then gives the special education teacher a sample of the chapter homework and journaling activities so he can see how these activities are constructed. Using his voice output system, Jose is expected to state his arguments clearly, assert whether he agrees or disagrees, and convey his thoughts and positions.

4. *What are the primary products or assignments for students within these activities, and how will students be evaluated?* In the third column of the planning tool (see Figure 3.1), the special education teacher writes down key expectations/outcomes/products that will be generated and how the evaluation will take place. For example, during debates, the expectation for the seventh graders in Jose's class is that they state arguments clearly and use complete sentences to articulate their positions and that they respect other points of view. Grading on written assignments is done with a rubric that has been developed by the English department.

Determining Expectations for a Student with Disabilities

At this point, the special education teacher takes a short time to review key information about the student with disabilities who will be in the class and participating in the unit. More than one student with disabilities may be in the class, and/or the general education teacher may have several different students in different sections of the same class completing the same unit. Although the unit is the same, the modifications and adaptations will be different for each student. The special education teacher should provide a short student summary, what the student's strengths and needs are, and the IEP goals that have been aligned to the subject area. If the general education teacher has been involved in the person-centered planning process, then this will be review. A brief "IEP at a glance" should be left with the teacher, including a summary of "best practices" for this individual (e.g., best ways of communicating).

Now the team is ready to brainstorm.

5. *Will the outcomes/expectations need to be modified or alternative outcomes provided within the primary teaching activities?* The team members, with the knowledge of the student's academic, cognitive, sensory, and communicative abilities, brainstorm the modified outcomes that will meet IEP goals for the focus student, and put the ideas in the fourth column of the planning tool. These are the objectives that will require specific instructional plans. For example, one outcome for Jose is to increase his ability to gain access to information on the computer. He works on this in connection with the research fact sheets, the vocabulary lists, and the journal writing time (see the fourth column of Figure 3.1). Two of Emil's expected outcomes during reading and language are to use his tactile symbol system to replay stories and to determine with whom he wants to sit (see the fourth column of Figure 3.2).

In the beginning it may be hard for general education teachers or other team members to generate ideas under columns four, five, and six of the Team Planning Tool (regarding how the student will receive and provide information and what supports are needed) because they are usually less experienced or do not know the student as well. This usually changes over the year.

6. *Are there any adaptations that need to be made in the way information is provided to the student (input)?* How will the team ensure that the student is an informed participant? In the fourth column of Figure 3.2, the reader can see that Emil receives input through his FM system and through tactile symbols and physical gestures. Peers and/or adults take responsibility for letting him know what is happening and giving new information to him. In Figure 3.1, column four shows that Jose's picture/word communication system is utilized for input in addition to verbal instructions.

7. *Are there any changes/adaptations that need to be made in the ways in which the student will provide information to the teachers and his or her peers?* How will the student be a contributing member of the class both socially and academically? The recorder puts the ideas in the fifth column of the planning chart. Emil uses his tactile gestures and his tactile symbol/voice output system to make choices and indicate responses during the kindergarten calendar time. He also uses a prerecorded loop tape to respond to specific questions from the teacher that is recorded daily and as needed. Jose contributes to the class by producing the vocabulary lists on his computer for his peers, accessing the research information, and generating picture sequences to tell stories and provide input. Designing specific ways in which the student will contribute and/or produce products and other assignments is highly important for both academic and social inclusion.

Team Planning Tool
(Active and informed participation)

Student: Emil

Unit: _Kindergarten Morning Circle_

Typical class activities and routines within the unit	Typical teaching strategies	Expectations for all students/content standards	Expectations (outcomes) for the focus student	How will the student receive information?	How will the student provide information?	What additional types of supports are needed?
Class meeting	Teacher talks about schedule for the day, collects any materials, reads roll	Listen, turn in notes	Use FM system, listen, sit in special seating, tolerate proximity of peers	Tangible symbols for each activity, FM system	Loop tapes/tape recorder Voice output system	Daily partner who rotates
Lunch count	Students indicate yes/no to school lunch	Respond when asked	Respond using voice output system Pass notes and items	Peers: Model/voice/ tangible and tactile input Proximity of general education peers	Gestures Microswitch	
Calendar	Students read day/date and yester-day, today, and tomorrow	Think about concepts presented, participate in verbal group recitation, keep hands and feet to self	Follow tactile object calendar; use tactile schedule system, listen to group recitation	Tape player and voice output system		Paraprofessional support or special education teacher support during this period
Read story	Look for patterns	Listen to story, respond to questions	Range of motion and stretching while listening to story	Choices presented tactilely and verbally		
Give directions for language arts activity		Participate	Use communication system	Tactile signs/gestures		

Figure 3.2.   Team planning tool for Emil.

101

8. *What types of instructional supports will be needed, and what types of social supports will be needed for success?* In the seventh column of the planning tool, the team determines when extra direct instructional support, either individually or in small groups, is needed, and plans for peer and other support structures. Jose's team decided that peer buddies could provide a certain amount of support during the class activities. They also determined that extra adult support was needed during the work on literacy goals and some communication goals and that peer tutors could accompany and support him in certain classes. Explicit instructional programs were also needed to provide consistent methods for implementing Jose's objectives within the unit.

Finally, the special education teacher makes sure that everyone is clear on responsibilities and lets the general education teacher know that a support plan will be generated from the planning meeting. This support plan will outline the information just generated. Then she asks the following question: How should we plan to spend some time together with [student's name] so that you can get to know [him or her] better? Depending on the teaching structures at the school, obtaining collaborative teaching time may be easier in some schools than in others. The presence of the special education teacher—working closely with the general education teacher and/or paraprofessionals—has been highly correlated with positive results in inclusive classrooms. A significant amount of the special education teacher's time should be spent in providing direct small- and large-group instruction in the general education classrooms versus simply managing people.

After the special and general education teachers have been working with each other within this framework and planning method for a while, the ideas come easier and the roles begin to merge. It may not be necessary to utilize the planning chart, and teams may move directly to the support plans. The key questions become natural to the problem-solving process after the team has more specifically addressed each question over a couple of curricular units.

In follow-up to the brainstorming session, the special education teacher develops support plans that are one page long, easy to read and follow, and distributed to everyone. One key component in the support plan is to indicate which objectives are the focus and who will have training on implementing the specific instructional programs designed to teach each objective. Sample support plans for Carrie in government and Holly in math are provided in Figures 3.3 and 3.4.

INDIVIDUALIZING INSTRUCTION, SUPPORTS, AND
SERVICES WITHIN OTHER SCHOOL AND COMMUNITY CONTEXTS

The process for developing supports and services within other educational contexts is similar to what was described previously, except that the special education

Student: _Carrie_

Unit: _Government: The Constitution_

Participation and Support Plan

Primary teaching activities and purpose/expectations for class	Any modifications and/or adaptations necessary	Instructional support strategies
Reading chapters in book—homework Get more information Read, answer questions at end of chapter	Carrie will follow a tactile schedule paired with verbal input for class activities. Carrie will understand the rules of her positive behavioral support plan and respect others' safety rights. Carrie will assist teacher with holding example sources, passing papers, using the overhead and other equipment—goal from IEP on following task sequences.	Update schedule book daily Follow PBS plan Use paraprofessional or special education teacher support at start of period to get oriented and determine tasks for Carrie and review them with her; provide general education teacher with ideas and support Peer buddies follow through with plan
Test preparation and prep for class discussion	Carrie will learn five concept words related to the Constitution, demonstrated by her ability to complete the sentence for the definitions.	
Class lectures and discussion Listen, follow outline Take notes on key concepts Understand key concepts Test preparation	During lecture, Carrie will listen for the key words and identify to peer partner or adult when they occur. _Homework_ Carrie will learn to recite the pledge of allegiance and sing the "Star Spangled Banner" by listening to tapes and working with her peer tutors after school.	Arrange time with peers at lunch time and after school

(continued)

Figure 3.3. Participation and support plan for Carrie.

103

Figure 3.3. *(continued)*

Primary teaching activities and purpose/expectations for class	Any modifications and/or adaptations necessary	Instructional support strategies
Class notebook Include notes, answers to questions, in-class assignments, and so forth, and turn in for grade at end of unit	Carrie will use her elf-monitoring check-list for PBS	Notebook in backpack—list gets checked at end of period with staff and peer buddies
Class projects Purpose is to further understanding through applications. Usually groups, also includes group process objectives	Carrie will work in a group to develop case arguments—PBS plan; tape record and play back for students practicing their presentation. Carrie will work on the five concepts/vocabulary words within the group.	Paraprofessional or special education teacher support during project time
In-class assignments such as reading articles and responding—usually asks for independent responses and discussion Use real sources; discuss; further understanding	Carrie will assist teacher with tasks, use tape recorder to play out audio information.	
Pop quizzes Purpose is to make sure students are reading the chapters	Carrie will use time to evaluate PBS self-monitoring checklist or listen to tapes of pledge/song.	Special education teacher support or paraprofessional
Unit tests Evaluate what students know	Carrie will be tested on pledge and song.	Homework practice with family

General support strategies

Everyone knows positive behavioral support (PBS) plan
Use schedule book and communication system
Paraprofessional or special education teacher support in room at all times for now
Make use of peer buddies

Reminders

Make sure all necessary materials are with Carrie in backpack, especially tape recorder and alternative items to hold and use for relaxation—see PBS plan
If substitute is coming, alert special education teacher/para-professional ahead of time; do the same for big changes in class activities

Participation and Support Plan

Student: Holly
Subject: Math

Activities: See activities below for unit on fractions

Student considerations

- The list of partners and Holly's support circle is in the folder.
- Make sure Holly's peers receive short instruction at start of period.
- Make sure Holly's picture schedule is in place and her communication system is out and ready and her conversation book is handy.

Goals/objectives

- Primary objectives for Holly are beginning sorting of objects, understanding same and different, counting out objects from 1 to 5, and recognizing coins and dollars.

Support Needed

What the class does	Provide information and support in the following ways	How Holly participates
Large group Review daily problems	Use communication book and conversation book	Holly follows directions, uses communication device
One concept each day—compare and contrast whole numbers with fractions	Provide teacher with daily concepts to give Holly related to her goals, and daily problem that is different from class	Completes problem with support from peer buddy
Provide a visual or verbal rationale for each concept/individual		Shares answer with class by physically showing and peer buddy describes

(continued)

Figure 3.4. Participation and support plan for Holly.

105

Figure 3.4. *(continued)*

What the class does	Provide information and support in the following ways	How Holly participates
Small groups Daily cooperative group work on fractions—collect a journal of examples of using fractions in daily life Design a handbook of fractions or construct a model	Paraprofessional or special education teacher provides instruction to group at start of activity Adaptations for participation planned ahead Holly's book will be similar in design and look, but will contain example (photos) of her work with objects and coins.	Holly will work on her problems using the same materials and objects as the group but at her level. Holly's book will be similar in design and look, but will contain example (photos) of her work with objects and coins.
Independent work Daily fraction problems; word problems: Generates visual chart and each child has sample book of each type of fraction concept Design a problem of your own representing the concept for the day	Provide individual support and direct instruction for the number concept goal and same/different sorting	Provide individual support and direct instruction for the number concept goal and same/different sorting
Unexpected events	Use communication system	Can be spontaneous

106

and related services staff have more responsibility for the design of the activities and the contexts. The special education teacher analyzes the context in which the activities will occur (e.g., the locker room, the cafeteria) and determines what the primary teaching activities will be during the period of time the student spends there. A similar instructional analysis is completed in which the teacher outlines the key activities based on what typical peers do in that context and determines the modified outcomes for the student with severe and multiple disabilities. In some instances, alternative outcomes will be the focus. The teacher and other team members determine adaptations in the ways in which both input and output will be provided. In other words, how will the student be connected to the activity context and to peers/people without disabilities who are present? How will the student get information about what is going on and what the expected behaviors are? How will this student's participation be modified for success? How and by whom will systematic instruction be provided? Let's look again at the focus students and how their educational team members helped them to translate skills in other contexts.

Emil's teacher analyzed the lunchroom environment to determine what skills would be priorities and what adaptations would be required. Emil is working on eating and drinking a small amount within the lunchroom context (he also has tube feedings). He also works on using his tactile object/voice-output device to communicate with friends and how to handle the transition from one place to the next.

At recess, Holly is learning mobility skills with her three-pronged cane and working on riding an adapted bicycle. She is also working on her communication skills with friends and on participating in some of the games her friends play on the playground. The focus is on developing her friendships.

In the community, Jose is working on using adaptations to purchase small numbers of items at stores, using his power wheelchair, and socializing with his peer buddies through his conversation book and other nonsymbolic communication methods.

Carrie receives instruction on a variety of objectives while at her part-time job at the veterans hospital. The job specifications have been modified for her, and she is learning to do a variety of office tasks; but she is also working on her communication skills, orientation and mobility skills, and self-care skills. She is working on community mobility skills on her way to and from work, and she is learning to use her money in a vending machine when she takes her breaks.

———————————————

Summarizing Where and When Instruction Will Occur

A matrix such as the one for Holly depicted in Figure 3.5 can be a great tool to help people on the team realize how all of the priority goals and objectives are embedded into meaningful activities across the general education classes and the other various environments in which the student spends time.

In the row across the top, the teacher puts the student's schedule as agreed on in the action plan. In the far-left column, the student's IEP priorities and goals are listed. It is helpful to group priorities that are context-specific (i.e., require a specific place to be instructed, such as dressing in the locker room), and then the priorities that can be embedded within a variety of activities and environments. In each corresponding cell in the matrix, the teacher checks whether the educational priority is going to be instructed or facilitated during that class/activity. The team then looks back over the matrix and asks the following questions:

- Are there any underlying skills or content skills that we still think are important that aren't getting enough opportunities for practice with this plan? Can we do something about this? If not, when would be an appropriate time to create some alternative activities to accommodate the student's priority needs?

- Are there any priorities we would now drop? These are things the team may have thought were highly important, but after the contextual assessments, decide otherwise, because the need for the skills proved to be minimal or less important.

In this way, the matrix provides a place for accountability of instruction by giving an overview that can indicate where and when instruction is taking place. When Holly's matrix was first developed, the team determined that there were not enough opportunities for Holly to have time to work on some key self-care goals that were important to her family. Holly is now able to get enough practice on those goals, but she misses the time period for sustained silent reading in her class. Because there are other opportunities for Holly to be read to, the team felt this alternative would be useful.

The matrix shown in Figure 3.5 falls short in terms of specific information, such as how to facilitate an activity, so it should not be used alone or in place of specific instructional or support plans. A matrix can be very detailed or very sim-

Matrix for Prioritizing and Initial Action Planning

Student: Holly Date: 9/30 Team members participating: Various Page: 1

(In the far left column, list the context-specific priorities first, then the embedded content priorities, and then the underlying skill priorities).

Daily schedule	8:15	9:45	10:05	11:00	11:00	12:00	12:45	1:15	2:45
Priority goals	Arrival and language arts/reading	Recess	Math and math workshop	Science M/W	Art/drama Tu/Th/F	Lunch and recess	Self-care activities	Social studies and language arts	Going home
Dressing and using restroom	X	X					X		
Lunchroom skills						X			
Riding a bike		X				X			
Using money						X			
Communication skills–using picture system	X	X	X	X	X	X	X	X	X
Social skills	X	X	X	X	X	X		X	X
Computer skills	X		X	X				X	
Literacy: Pictures	X		X	X	X			X	
Using cane	X	X	X	X	X	X		X	X
Math skills: same and different, counting 1–5, using coins			X	X		X	X X		
Classroom participation skills	X		X	X	X			X	

Figure 3.5. Holly's matrix for prioritizing and initial action planning. Team members indicate in which activities priority goals are met.

ple, depending on the team's preference. When the matrix is complete, it offers a nice summary to parents and other team members, outlining where and when instruction is occurring. Utilizing the matrix early in the planning, and later as a summary, assists the team in making the instructional day and week most productive for the student with severe and multiple disabilities.

IMPLEMENTING INSTRUCTION

Systematic, data-based instruction has proven to be the most effective means for teaching students with severe and multiple disabilities in inclusive schools (Lehr & Brown, 1996; McGregor & Vogelsberg, 1998; Sailor et al., 1988; 1990; Snell & Brown, 2000). A systematic instructional plan has a clearly written objective with measurable outcomes, a clear delineation of the natural cues and situations in which the student will need to use the skill, a plan for providing opportunities to practice the skill (both specifically organized and incidental in nature), a clearly stated method for teaching the skill, a plan for when errors occur, a method for evaluating progress, and a plan for teaching team members how to consistently provide the needed instruction.

Providing systematic instruction within the contexts described previously, however, requires team members to provide a strong connection between the natural cues for behaviors and functional responses that are available within the activities. Instruction is still systematic and data-based, but moves beyond traditional models (Snell & Brown, 2000; Wehmeyer, 2002). The team must determine whether direct or indirect instruction is necessary for the student to accomplish the objective. Instructional methods may include having peers provide prompts or other assistance and may include other types of peer-mediated instruction (Thousand et al., 2003). Instructional methods may include some direct and planned instruction and some incidental instruction.

A systematic plan for how each of the students' priority objectives will be taught is the responsibility of the special education teacher, who trains other team members and ensures consistent and accountable delivery of instruction, data collection, and ongoing reflection of the data. Instructional methodology is beyond the purview of this chapter. The reader is also referred to Halvorsen and Neary (2000) and Snell and Brown (2000) for more information on systematic instructional methods within inclusive classrooms.

SUMMARY

Curricular design for individuals with severe and multiple disabilities involves consideration of input from several sources: the student's person-centered planning team, ecological inventories, discipline-specific information, and functional skill needs. Collaborative planning within the general education curriculum makes it clear what goals and objectives will be the expected outcomes of the educational activities of same-age peers who are typically developing. Alternative environments are used to teach context-specific skills and skills that the team determines cannot be taught within the general education classroom. Modified outcomes are designed and adaptations are provided to ensure that students are both active and informed participants. Relationships are fostered through an emphasis on facilitation of interactions and friendships in both social and academic activities. The resulting program plan should specifically outline where and when instruction on all priorities occurs, and how the instruction will be delivered.

REFERENCES

Albin, R.W., Lucyshyn, J.M., Horner, R.H., & Flannery, K.B. (1996). Contextual fit for behavioral support plans: A model for goodness of fit. In L.K. Koegel, R.L. Koegel, & G. Dunlap (Eds.), *Positive behavioral support: Including people with difficult behavior in the community* (pp. 81–98). Baltimore: Paul H. Brookes Publishing Co.

Beukelman, D., & Mirenda, P. (1998). *Augmentative and alternative communication* (2nd ed.). Baltimore: Paul H. Brookes Publishing Co.

Billingsley, F., Gallucci, C., Peck, C., Schwartz, I., & Staub, D. (1996). "But those kids can't even do math": An alternative conceptualization of outcomes for inclusive education. *Special Education Leadership Review*, 43–55.

Browder, D. (2000). *Curriculum and assessment for students with severe disabilities*. New York: Guilford Press.

Brown, F. (2000). Development and implementation of educational programs. In M. Snell & F. Brown (Ed.), *Instruction of students with severe disabilities* (5th ed.). New York: Merrill.

Brown, L., Branston, M.B., Hamre-Nietupski, S., Pumpian, J., Certo, N., & Gruenewald, L. (1979). A strategy for developing chronological age appropriate and functional curricular content for severely handicapped adolescents and young adults. *Journal of Special Education, 13*, 81–90.

Carr, E.G., Levin, L, McConnachie, G., Carlson, J.I., Kemp, D.C., & Smith, C.E. (1994). *Communication-based intervention for problem behavior: A user's guide for producing positive change*. Baltimore: Paul H. Brookes Publishing Co.

Demchak M.A., & Greenfield R. (2000). A transition portfolio for Jeff, a student with multiple disabilities. *Focus on Exceptional Children, 32*(6), 44–49.

Downing, J.E. (2002). *Including students with severe and multiple disabilities in typical classrooms: Practical strategies for teachers* (2nd ed.). Baltimore: Paul H. Brookes Publishing Co.

Dunn, W., Brown, C., & McGuigan, A. (1994). The ecology of human performance: A framework for considering the effect of context. *The American Journal of Occupational Therapy, 48*(7), 595–607.

Ferguson, D., & Baumgart, D. (1991). Partial participation revisited. *Journal of The Association for Persons with Severe Handicaps, 16,* 218–227.

Gee, K. (1995). Facilitating active and informed learning and participation in inclusive school settings. In N.G. Haring & L.T. Romer (Eds.), *Welcoming students who are deaf-blind into typical classrooms: Facilitating school participation, learning, and friendships* (pp. 369–404). Baltimore: Paul H. Brookes Publishing Co.

Gee, K., Alwell, M., Graham, N., & Goetz, L. (1994). *Inclusive instructional design: Facilitating informed and active learning for individuals with deaf-blindness.* Manual produced on the Active Interactions Project, OSERS Validated Practices: Children and Youth with Deaf-Blindness, #HO 86G00003, 1990–93. Department of Special Education, San Francisco State University.

Gee, K., Graham, N., Sailor, W., & Goetz, L. (1995). Use of integrated, general education and community environments as primary contexts for skill instruction of students with severe, multiple disabilities. *Behavior Modification, 19*(1), 33–58.

Giangreco, M.F., Cloninger, C., & Iverson, V.S. (1998). *Choosing outcomes and accommodations for children (COACH): A guide to educational planning for students with disabilities* (2nd ed.). Baltimore: Paul H. Brookes Publishing Co.

Giangreco, M., Edelman, S., Luiselli, T., & MacFarland, S. (1996). Support service decision making for students with multiple service needs: Evaluative data. *The Journal of The Association for Persons with Severe Handicaps, 21*(3), 135–144.

Halvorsen, A., & Neary, T. (2000). *Building inclusive schools.* Needham Heights, MA: Allyn & Bacon.

Halvorsen, A., & Sailor, W. (1990). Integration of students with severe and profound disabilities. In R. Gaylord-Ross (Ed.), *Issues and research in special education* (Vol. 1). New York: Teachers College Press.

Holburn, S. (2002). How science can evaluate and enhance person-centered planning. *Research and Practice for Persons with Severe Disabilities, 27*(4), 250–260.

Holburn, S., & Vietze, P.M. (Eds.). (2002). *Person-centered planning: Research, practice, and future directions.* Baltimore: Paul H. Brookes Publishing Co.

Horner, R.H., Albin, R.W., Sprague, J.R., & Todd, A. (2000). Positive behavior support. In M.E. Snell & F. Brown (Eds.), *Instruction of students with severe disabilities* (pp. 207–243). Upper Saddle River, NJ: Merrill.

Horner, R.H., & Carr, E.G. (1997). Behavioral support for students with severe disabilities: Functional assessment and comprehensive intervention. *Special Education, 31*(1), 64–104.

Hunt, P., Farron-Davis, F., Beckstead, S., Curtis, D., & Goetz, L. (1994). Evaluating the effects of placement of students with severe disabilities in general education versus special classes. *Journal of The Association for Persons with Severe Handicaps, 19,* 200–214.

Hunt, P., & Goetz, L. (1997). Research on inclusive educational programs, practices, and outcomes for students with severe disabilities. *Journal of Special Education, 31,* 3–29.

Hunt, P., Staub, D., Alwell, M., & Goetz, L. (1994). Achievement by all students within the context of cooperative learning groups. *Journal of The Association for Persons with Severe Handicaps, 19,* 290–301.

Johnson, L.J., & Pugach, M.C. (1996). Role of collaborative dialogue in teachers' conceptions of appropriate practice for students at risk. *Journal of Educational and Psychological Consultation, 7*(1), 9–24.

Kincaid, T., & Fox, L. (2002). Person-centered planning and positive behavior support. In S. Holburn & P.M. Vietze (Eds.), *Person-centered planning: Research, practice, and future directions* (pp. 29–49). Baltimore: Paul H. Brookes Publishing Co.

Koegel, L.K., Harrower, J.K., & Koegel, R.L. (1999). Support for children with developmental disabilities in full inclusion classrooms through self-management. *Journal of Positive Behavior Interventions, 1*(1), 26–34.

Kunc, N. (2000). Rediscovering the right to belong. In R.A. Villa, J.S. Thousand, W. Stainback, & S. Stainback (Eds.), *Restructuring for caring and effective education: Piecing the puzzle together* (2nd ed., pp. 77–92). Baltimore: Paul H. Brookes Publishing Co.

LeGuin, U.K. (1984). *A wizard of Earthsea.* New York: Bantam.

Lehr, D.H., & Brown, F. (1996). *People with disabilities who challenge the system.* Baltimore: Paul H. Brookes Publishing Co.

Lewis, T.J., & Sugai, G. (1999). Effective behavior support: A systems approach to proactive schoolwide management. *Focus on Exceptional Children, 31*(6), 1–24.

Lusthaus, E., & Forest, M. (1987). The Kaleidoscope: A challenge to the cascade. In M. Forest (Ed.), *More education integration* (pp. 1–17). Downsview, Ontario, Canada: G. Allan Roeher Institute.

Malette, P., Mirenda, P., Kandborg, T., Jones, P., Bunz, T., & Rogow, S. (1992). Application of a lifestyle development process for persons with severe intellectual disabilities: A case study report. *Journal of The Association for Persons with Severe Handicaps, 17*(3), 179–191.

McGregor, G., & Vogelsberg, R.T. (1998). *Inclusive schooling practices: Pedagogical and research foundation: A synthesis of the literature that informs best practices about inclusive schooling.* Philadelphia: Allegheny University of the Health Sciences, Consortium on Inclusive Schooling Practices. (Available from Paul H. Brookes Publishing Co, 1-800-638-3775; http://www.brookespublishing.com)

Pearpoint, J., Forest, M., & O'Brien, J. (1996). MAPs, Circles of Friends, and PATH: Powerful tools to help build caring communities. In S. Stainback & W. Stainback (Eds.), *Inclusion: A guide for educators* (pp. 67–86). Baltimore: Paul H. Brookes Publishing Co.

Rainforth, B., & York-Barr, J. (1997). *Collaborative teams for students with severe disabilities: Integrating therapy and educational services* (2nd ed.). Baltimore: Paul H. Brookes Publishing Co.

Sailor, W., Gee, K., & Karasoff, P. (1993). Full inclusion and school restructuring. In M.E. Snell (Ed.), *Instruction of students with severe disabilities* (4th ed., pp. 1–30). Upper Saddle River, NJ: Merrill Prentice-Hall.

Sailor, W., Goetz, L, Anderson, J., Hunt, P., & Gee, K. (1988). Research on community intensive instruction as a model for building functional generalized skills. In R. Horner, G. Dunlap, & R. Koegel (Eds.), *Generalization and maintenance in applied settings* (pp. 67–98). Baltimore: Paul H. Brookes Publishing Co.

Snell, M.E., & Brown, F. (Eds.). (2000). *Instruction of students with severe disabilities* (5th ed.). Upper Saddle River, NJ: Merrill Prentice-Hall.

Snell, M., & Janney, R. (2000). *Teachers' guides to inclusive practices: Modifying school work.* Baltimore: Paul H. Brookes Publishing Co.

Staub, D., Schwartz, I.S., Gallucci, C., & Peck, C.A. (1994). Four portraits of friendship at an inclusive school. *Journal of The Association for Persons with Severe Handicaps, 19,* 314–325.

Sugai, G., Horner, R.H., Dunlap, G., Heineman, M., Lewis, J.J. Nelson, C.M. et al. (2000). Applying positive behavioral supports and functional behavioral assessments in schools. *Journal of Positive Behavior Intervention, 2*(3), 3–27.

Todd, A.W., Horner, R.H., Sugai, G., and Sprague, J.R. (1999). Effective behavior support: Strengthening school-wide systems through a team-based approach. *Effective School Practices, 17*(4), 23–37.

Turnbull, H.R., & Turnbull, A. (2001). *Families, professionals, and exceptionality: A special partnership* (3rd ed.). Columbus, OH: Charles E. Merrill.

Thousand, J.S., Villa, R.A., & Nevin, A.I. (Eds.). (2003). *Creativity & collaborative learning: The practical guide to empowering students, teachers and families* (2nd ed.). Baltimore: Paul H. Brookes Publishing Co.

Wehmeyer, M.L., Agran, M., & Hughes, C. (1998). *Teaching self-determination to students with disabilities: Basic skills for successful transition.* Baltimore: Paul H. Brookes Publishing Co.

Wehmeyer, M.L. (with Sands, D.J., Knowlton, E., & Kozleski, E.B). (2002). *Providing access to the general curriculum: Teaching students with mental retardation.* Baltimore: Paul H. Brookes Publishing Co.

For More Information

The reader is encouraged to get more information on positive behavioral supports through the following organizations and publications:

Journal of Positive Behavior Interventions
http://www.education.ucsb.edu/autism/jpbi.html

OSEP Technical Assistance Center
on Positive Behavioral Intervention and Supports
http://www.pbis.org

Positive Behavioral Interventions and Support Technical Assistance Center
5262 University of Oregon
Eugene, OR 97403-5262
541-346-2505

TASH (formerly known as The
Association for Persons with Severe Handicaps)
29 Susquehanna Avenue, Suite 210
Towson, MD 21204
410-828-8274
410-828-6706 fax
http://www.tash.org

CHAPTER 4

Alternate Assessments

Harold L. Kleinert and Jaqui Farmer Kearns

Teaching students with severe and multiple disabilities presents exacting challenges and enduring rewards. Among those rewards is the sense that one has enabled a student to accomplish a valued life skill, to become more independent in daily routines, to have a greater sense of self-efficacy and control over his or her environment, and to have a deeper sense of membership with his or her age-peers. These accomplishments are important for any child; yet, until July 2000, such achievements for students with severe and multiple disabilities were never reflected in state and district large-scale educational assessments, or in measures of school or district effectiveness (e.g., school district "report cards"). Rather, students with severe and multiple disabilities were excluded from all such measures; thus, their achievements were overlooked in our nation's rush to improve educational results (McGrew, Thurlow, & Spiegel, 1993).

Students with severe and multiple disabilities have been included in state and district educational assessments only since the provision of the Individuals with Disabilities Education Act (IDEA) Amendments of 1997 (PL-105-17). Specifically, at the state level, IDEA '97 requires that "children with disabilities be

The work on which this chapter is based was supported, in part, by the U.S. Department of Education, Office of Special Education and Rehabilitation Services (Grant No. H324D990044). However, the opinions expressed do not necessarily reflect the position or policy of the U.S. Department of Education and no official endorsement should be inferred.

The authors thank Jean Clayton, Teacher, Kenton County, Kentucky Schools, for her assistance in developing the IntelliKeys overlays for the first example in this chapter, and Dr. Barney Fleming, Ms. Kathy Sheppard-Jones, and Mr. Mike Burdge, Interdisciplinary Human Development Institute, University of Kentucky, for their assistance in the second student example of this chapter.

included in general state and district-wide assessment programs, with appropriate accommodations, where necessary" (§612[a][17][A]) and "as appropriate, the State or local educational agency: (i) develops guidelines for the participation of children with disabilities in alternate assessments for those children who cannot participate in State and district-wide assessment programs; and (ii) develops and, beginning not later than July 1, 2000, conducts those alternate assessments" (§612[a][17][A][i–ii]).

As of July 1, 2000, states are now required to report both the numbers and the performance of children participating in the alternate assessment (§612[a][17][B][ii–iii]). Alternate assessment scores must be aggregated into overall school, district, and state composite scores; and when it will not result in the disclosure of personally identifiable student information, alternate assessment scores are to be disaggregated from the overall totals as well (e.g., a separate report on the performance of students who participated only in the alternate assessment). States must take into account the performance of all students with disabilities, including those students participating in the alternate assessment, in the State Improvement Plan performance goals and indicators now required under IDEA (§612[a] [16][D]).

At the student level, the individualized education program (IEP) must include a statement of any individual modifications or accommodations needed for the student to participate in the state and/or district assessments. If the IEP team determines that the student is unable to participate in any part of the state- or district-level assessment, then the IEP must include a statement as to why the assessment is *not* appropriate for the student and how the student will be assessed through an alternate assessment (§614[d][1][A][v]).

In short, the question is not *whether* students with disabilities will be included in state and district large-scale assessments, but precisely *how* they will be included (Heumann & Warlick, 2000). Exclusion is no longer an option. With this fundamental change in how we consider the educational results for all students comes a set of important challenges and new opportunities for teachers of students with severe and multiple disabilities.

Benefits to Students

Educational assessment (i.e., measuring what students have learned) and accountability (i.e., ensuring that these results are used to improve instruction) are at the heart of contemporary educational reform efforts (Kleinert & Thurlow, 2001). Yet, a number of teachers have questioned whether students with severe and multiple disabilities can derive any benefit from participation in large-scale assessments—even alternate assessments (Kleinert, Kennedy, & Kearns, 1999).

Teachers have also noted their concerns with the time required for completing alternate assessments with their students and that this added requirement can result in reduced learning time for students (Kleinert et al., 1999).

Despite these concerns, research has indicated important benefits for the inclusion of students with severe and multiple disabilities in educational assessments. For example, we found that 5 years after the implementation of Kentucky's alternate assessment in 1992, teachers reported a substantial increase in the percentage of students with severe disabilities having a formal communication system (Kleinert et al., 1999). Furthermore, alternate assessment scores for students with significant disabilities were directly related to the degree of implementation of best practices in these students' educational programming (Kleinert, Kearns, & Kennedy, 1997; Turner, Baldwin, Kleinert, & Kearns, 2000). In other words, higher alternate assessment scores were indicative of increased educational opportunities and effective levels of individualized student supports. Bennett and Davis (2001) found that, as a result of participating in Indiana's statewide electronic portfolio, students demonstrated increased motivation through listening and viewing their own performances, and parents expressed that they were able to see for the first time what their children *could* do, as opposed to hearing once again what that their children *could not* do. Finally, practitioners and researchers have found that students with severe and multiple disabilities can score at the very highest levels of the alternate assessment (see Denham, Bennett, Edyburn, Lahm, & Kleinert, 2001; Denham & Lahm, 2001). As a result, schools are receiving recognition for exemplary programs for these students just as they are rewarded for exemplary programs for students without disabilities.

Despite such benefits, teacher concerns with the time and increased paperwork required to complete alternate assessments are very real. The concerns expressed by the teachers in the statewide survey conducted by Kleinert et al. (1999) are highly consistent with the increasing paperwork and time requirements expressed by the field of special education in general (Heward, 2000; "Special Educators," 1999). Teachers of students with severe and multiple disabilities may perceive these requirements as even more burdensome given the difficulty in accurately assessing these students in general and the range of people and related disciplines who may be involved in these students' educational teams. Yet, Kampfer, Horvath, Kleinert, and Kearns (2001) found that student scores in one state's alternate assessment were not appreciably related to time outside of instruction that teachers spent on the alternate assessments of their students. Rather, student scores were dependent on the extent to which teachers *embedded* the alternate assessment into their ongoing instructional activities and the extent to which students were *active* participants in the construction and completion of their own alternate assessments. These findings have significant implications for teachers and other team members of students with severe and multiple disabilities. First, embedding assessment into ongoing instruction across a variety of educational environments and people is highly consistent with transdisciplinary and collaborative models of services; in fact, this is one of the hallmarks of the collaborative model, which has evolved from the transdisciplinary approach. Second, the extent to which students can assume ownership for their own learning through the process of planning, monitoring, and evaluating their own performance—and including that self-evaluation as a part of their assessment—is an important element in the broader life outcome of self-determination. Self-determination is an essential educational outcome for all students but is even more so for students with the most significant disabilities, who have often been denied the opportunity for age-appropriate control and decision-making in their lives (Giangreco, Cloninger, & Iverson, 1998). Thus, Kleinert, Denham, and colleagues (2001) and Kleinert, Green, Hurte, Clayton, and Oetinger (2002) have argued that alternate assessment can be an effective teaching vehicle for imparting important component skills of self-determination.

Within this chapter, we provide examples of how alternate assessments can be embedded throughout ongoing instruction and daily routines within the context of a collaborative model. We also show how teachers can use their state's alternate assessment to provide valuable opportunities to teach the component skills of self-determination to their students with severe and multiple disabilities within the context of the general education curriculum.

State Approaches to Alternate Assessment

Ysseldyke and Olsen (1999) have suggested a range of formats that alternate assessments can take, including observations of student performance, structured interviews and checklists, performance records (instructional data, graphs, anecdotal records), and performance tests on specified tasks. In this chapter, we present examples of structured observations of student performance (often called performance event tests), and examples of daily instructional data and graphs. Other forms of alternate assessment include structured interviews, which are designed to elicit reports of student performance from teachers and parents across a range of academic and life-skill domains, and skill checklists, usually completed by teachers, which reflect whether a student can perform a series of targeted skills in one or more academic or life domains. More informal records of student performance include peer, teacher, and parent notes reflecting how the student has used an important skill in specific situations. Portfolios, a type of authentic assessment, are another commonly used assessment of students with severe and multiple disabilities.

As of 2001, approximately half of all states were using student *portfolios* or bodies of evidence as their primary approach to alternate assessments (National Center on Educational Outcomes, 2001). Paulson, Paulson, and Meyer have described a portfolio as "a purposeful collection of student work that exhibits the student's efforts, progress, and achievements in one or more areas. The collection must include student participation in selecting content, the criteria for selection, the criteria for judging merit, and evidence of student self-reflection" (1991, p. 60). Thus, portfolios are structured collections of student work documented over time. Portfolios typically include a broad range of evidence such as student performance or instructional data; student, peer, and parent reflections on the student's performance; student products; and video- or audiotapes of the student's performance. Depending on their purpose, portfolios may allow for considerable latitude in the teacher's and student's selection of the content; they may also specify required entries that all students in that assessment must complete. At least one state, Indiana, has designed a statewide electronic portfolio for alternate assessments (Bennett & Davis, 2001).

The use of portfolios as an assessment strategy is increasing practiced at all levels of education (Denham et al., 2001). Portfolios emphasize *authentic* learning (i.e., directly related to real-life contexts) and may be especially applicable for students who come from culturally and linguistically diverse populations (Pike & Salend, 1995). Finally, a portfolio "provides a broader perspective on the outcomes of learning than can be easily measured through a test" (Denham et al., 2001, p. 149). These characteristics of portfolio assessment make it particularly attractive in documenting performance for students with significant disabilities. (See "For More Information" at the end of this chapter to learn about web sites devoted to portfolio assessment. In this list, we have also included web sites devoted specifically to the use of portfolios for alternate assessments.)

Given the heterogeneous needs of students with severe and multiple disabilities, as well as the complexity and intensity of those needs, portfolios provide valuable opportunities for students to document what they *can* do; allow for the input from a variety of team members, including parents and other students (Anthony, Johnson, Mickelson, & Preece, 1991; Kearns, Burdge, & Kleinert, in press); and promote a sense of self-ownership for students who have often not had significant control in their educational decisions (Ezell & Klein, 2003; Ezell, Klein, & Ezell-Powell, 1999; Kearns et al., in press). Furthermore, portfolios illustrate the relationship between assessment and instruction. Because portfolios are formative in nature, the documentation of student learning can result in changes in instructional practices (Denham et al., 2001; Kearns et al., in press). While teachers of students with severe and multiple disabilities must, of course, use the alternate assessment formats required by their own states or local districts, the use of portfolio assessments as an alternate assessment strategy holds considerable promise for students with significant disabilities. Even in those states not currently using portfolio assessment as their primary vehicle for alternate assessments, portfolio assessment may still prove to be a powerful tool at the classroom and student level (Wesson & King, 1996). Several examples of portfolio assessment entries are provided throughout this chapter.

Some states also are developing performance event tests, which are structured observations of student performance in predetermined tasks. These tasks may reflect either the performance of a functional life activity or be tied more specifically to the content of the general curriculum (e.g., a task designed to address the state learning standards in social studies or science). Performance event tasks provide a greater uniformity in the structure of alternate assessments than the more open-ended formats of portfolios. Yet, without adequate assistive technology and personal and instructional supports, students with severe and multiple disabilities can be at a considerable disadvantage in one-time tests of student performance. This chapter also provides an example of a performance event test for students with severe and multiple disabilities and how adequate instructional supports can be included.

In addition to the form that alternate assessments might take, an even more fundamental question is what *kinds* of learning should be measured—should the alternate assessment focus on student achievement on individualized (IEP) objectives, or should it be more broadly based on the student's achievement within the general curriculum—or should it be based on both? As noted, a few states have based their alternate assessments directly on each student's IEP; thus, students who achieve high percentages of their individual short-term objectives or benchmarks score higher on their state's alternate assessment than students making little progress on their respective objectives. Kleinert and Thurlow noted,

> This approach certainly makes the alternate assessment directly relevant to the student's educational program (and to the goals that are supposedly most important for that student), but in no way does it ensure that the student's learning will address the content standards underlying the general curriculum for all students. (2001, p. 11)

In 2001, the majority of states (68%) were basing the alternate assessment directly on the learner standards for all students or a subset or modified set of those standards that links the standards to functional skills (National Center on Educational Outcomes, 2001). Still other states have based their alternate assessments on a combination of general education standards and a set of life skill standards deemed most appropriate for students with significant disabilities. A memorandum from the U.S. Department of Education Office of Special Education and Rehabilitation Services (Heumann & Warlick, 2000) makes clear the U.S. Department of Education's position: "Alternate assessments need to be aligned with the general curriculum standards set for all students" (p. 9). In our own work (Kleinert & Kearns, 1999), we have found that educational experts on severe and multiple disabilities strongly support the alignment of the alternate assessment with general education outcomes. We have taken the approach that alternate assessments for students with severe and multiple disabilities should clearly reflect the learner standards for all students while providing opportunities for students to show progress on critical skills (target or IEP skills). Browder and Spooner (in press) have noted that as of 2001, "nearly all states have focused their alternate assessments on either functional examples of how to apply state standards or by showing direct links from functional to academic standards."

Alternate Assessments: A Collaborative Approach

Alternate assessments for students with severe and multiple disabilities need to reflect the essential elements of a collaborative approach. First, alternate assessments should reflect these basic assumptions that lie at the heart of a transdisciplinary approach (Orelove & Malatchi, 1996). Let's look at each in the context of students with severe and multiple disabilities:

1. *All children can learn.* This principle is at the heart of the inclusive assessment requirements of IDEA '97. IDEA '97 requires that we must find a way to measure and report the learning of every student, either through participation in the regular assessment with appropriate accommodations or modifications or through the use of an alternate assessment. The point of alternate assessments is that we measure, in ways that connect to the general curriculum, the important achievements of students with severe and multiple disabilities.

2. *A collaborative team is necessary.* The basic assumption of this text is that the collaborative team (including special and general educators, the parents and student, related services providers, and administrators) is essential in the design and implementation of the student's educational program. As a matter of law, this same team is also required to determine how the student will participate in large-scale educational assessments under IDEA '97, as well as how the student will participate in the general education curriculum. How the student will be assessed in state or district assessments and how the student will participate in the general curriculum are challenges that can only be effectively addressed by the whole team, working in a collaborative and

integrated fashion. Successful participation in the general curriculum and documentation of educational results are only possible in the context of shared educational goals and role release across disciplines, so that students have the needed supports throughout the school day and across all critical environments.

3. *Families are vital.* Families know their son or daughter better than anyone else; they are the most vested of anyone in their child's future (Giangreco et al., 1998). Their participation in their child's alternate assessment is also vital. First, they can play an essential role in shaping the content of their child's alternate assessment by working in partnership with the team to identify the most important things for their child to learn and how their child will participate in the general curriculum. Second, they can confirm the contents of their child's alternate assessment. Families can note whether the alternate assessment represents, in their view, a valid picture of their son or daughter's educational achievement. (This parent validation is actually a required component of the alternate assessment in several states.) Third, families can provide evidence of how their child's learning in school has generalized or carried over to other important life domains, including home and community environments.

DESIGNING ALTERNATE ASSESMENTS FOR STUDENTS WITH SEVERE AND MULTIPLE DISABILITIES

The primary focus of alternate assessments should be the extent to which student learning is linked to the standards for all students. This concept challenges the IEP team to consider the general curriculum as an integral part of the program planning process, and to continuously monitor student progress and adjust student programs as necessary. This enables the student not only to achieve the objectives on the IEP but also to demonstrate learning related to the core content for all students.

Browder (1987) noted that the first consideration of assessment for program planning should be the extent to which the selected skills enhance the student's integration with peers without disabilities. Giangreco and colleagues (1998) suggested that the IEP should represent a prioritized subset of skills that enable the student to gain access to a variety of typical school and community activities and environments. Access to the general curriculum provides a framework for designing learning opportunities that allow the student to practice skills from his or her IEP, to engage in activities with typical peers, and to develop academic skills similar to those of his or her peers. The linkage between program planning and assessment of outcomes is thus established by their shared focus on the general curriculum. That linkage should be a continuous process, with outcome assessment providing the basis for subsequent phases of student program planning.

As indicated in Figure 4.1, program planning, instruction, and outcome assessment form a continuous quality improvement loop. Within this larger loop is contained a second, smaller feedback loop between instruction and assessment. Assessment informs instruction not just at the point of program or IEP development but throughout the school year. With effective, data-based instruction, this continuous improvement cycle can occur even on a daily basis.

In this section, we outline a process for merging planning, instruction, and assessment into a single cycle. This process begins with a consideration of the curriculum or content standards for all students and the specific performance standards delineated in the state or district alternate assessment. These two elements provide a road map for collaborative teams in developing appropriate goals and objectives and in achieving desired outcomes. Second, we consider the assessment strategies that can be used to measure and monitor student progress. Third, we outline concrete strategies for merging planning, instruction, and assessment so that a student's progress can be continually monitored and outcomes documented. Finally, we consider how outcome results from the alternate assessment can be used in subsequent IEP planning and ongoing instructional design.

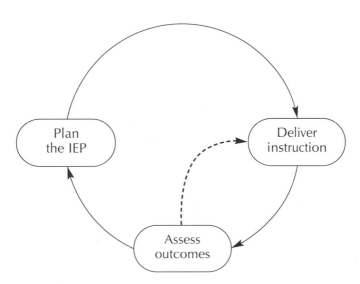

Figure 4.1. The process of program planning, instruction, and outcomes assessment should be continuous.

As an illustration of how this process might work, consider the following example.

———————————————

Ms. Bowling assigned her fourth-grade students a project to investigate consumer choices and to predict which consumer choices were more likely to be made by members of their class. The other fourth-grade class in the school was participating also, and combined, the group had a total "sample" of 50 students for their investigation. At the end of the activity, the students were to present a report to both classes on their findings. Working in groups, students chose from a variety of consumer choices (e.g., ice cream flavors, favorite toys, favorite music, favorite snacks) and planned strategies to investigate their classmates' preferences. Jody, a student with multiple disabilities, was working with the group investigating music preferences. Jody has a moderate cognitive disability, a visual impairment, and a motor impairment limiting his mobility, range of motion, and fine motor responses.

———————————————

Ms. Bowling consulted with members of Jody's team to consider the supports that Jody would need to learn specific math skills taken from the general curriculum, as well as skills from his IEP, during this project. With the help of the student members of Jody's group, the team decided that the interview question "What is your favorite music?" and samples of rock, country, rap, and classical music would need to be recorded. Jody would need a way to ask that question, play the music samples, and record the students' answers. He would also need a way to count the students' responses. With these supports in place, Jody could then ask and answer the project-related question about the students' most likely consumer choices in music.

To enable Jody to participate in this project and to create his own report, his teacher constructed an IntelliKeys (IntelliTools, 2002a) overlay (Figure 4.2) with the use of Overlay Maker (IntelliTools, 2002c). The overlay has pictures representing the four music types of rock, country, classical, and rap. In addition, it has an icon for asking the question, "What music do you like to listen to?" As each student was interviewed, Jody touched that icon and a recorded peer's voice asked the question. Then Jody recorded each student's response by touching the picture icon that represented that student's response. The name of the student's musical choice was spoken aloud as the response was recorded by using IntelliTalk II (IntelliTools, 2002c).

The computer recorded each selection, in turn, for each student; each student's response was represented as a visual musical icon on the computer printout (see Figure 4.3). Jody tallied the responses for each type of music by count-

Figure 4.2. Jody's IntelliKeys overlay for selecting his classmates' musical preferences (produced with Overlay Maker; images used courtesy of IntelliTools, Inc.)

ing the picture icons representing that music category. He sampled 10 students per day, with the data collection phase of the project lasting a total of 5 days.

With the tallied results, Jody and a peer created a bar graph illustrating the students' choices; they then used this graph as a part of their presentation. In order to create the bar graph, Jody and his peer partner decided to simply cut out each of the music icons from the daily computer printouts, sort them by music type, and glue the icons directly onto a bar chart illustrating the number of students who selected each music category. For the presentation to the class, Jody used his IntelliKeys overlay along with PowerPoint (Microsoft Corporation, 2000) to play samples of the music and to illustrate the raw data that the group collected (via the computer printouts); he conducted his part of the presentation from a prone stander as his group described the results. For the conclusion of the presentation, he used his IntelliKeys to select the PowerPoint slide illustrating the students' overall consumer choice in music. Documented outcomes for this activity included instructional data for Jody's independent IntelliKeys use (an IEP objective) and data on counting student responses (an activity involving the general curriculum math skill of counting with correspondence and basic addition of student responses across each of the 5 days). In addition to his IntelliKeys use and math skills, a videotape of the group's presentation illustrated Jody's independent use of his IntelliKeys overlay and his social interaction skills.

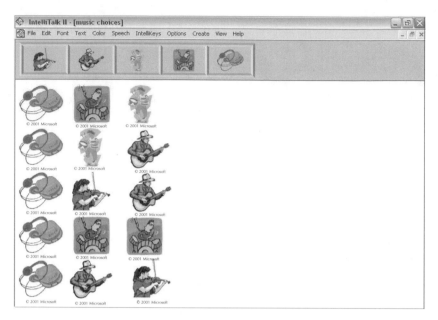

Figure 4.3.   Music choices for 10 classmates (Monday—first day; produced with IntelliTalk II; images used courtesy of IntelliTools, Inc.). The icons in the first column represent the question, "What music do you like to listen to?" The icons in the second and third columns each represent one classmate's choices of his or her favorite music (*N* = 10 classmates).

Each team member contributed to the outcomes in this activity. To extend the skills from this activity to other environments, materials, and people, Jody's special education teacher designed review worksheets and homework for count-ing and basic addition using the music theme. Jody's mother assisted the group by recording a variety of music selections from which to choose the samples. The speech-language pathologist assisted Jody by enlisting his peers in recording the questions and music samples on the IntelliKeys overlay and by ensuring that the questions and voice inflections were age-appropriate. The PT and OT assisted with the correct positioning and placement of the icons on the IntelliKeys over-lay so that Jody could efficiently provide an accurate response. The vision expert ensured that the icons from the IntelliKeys were of high contrast and readily dis-tinguishable from each other. Throughout this process, the collaborative team was essential in designing and providing the supports that enabled Jody to learn in the context of the general curriculum, and in documenting that learning.

Next, we present four key considerations in enabling all of this to happen.

Consideration 1: Start with Standards

The IEP team must consider two types of standards for the student. *Content* stan-dards establish *what* should be learned in language arts, mathematics, science, and social studies. Generally, content standards are defined for particular grade levels and describe what *most* students should know. Content standards are used to design curriculum activities that motivate and engage a wide range of students. For example, for one state's science standard, "Students identify, compare, and contrast patterns and use patterns to understand and interpret past and present events and predict future events," an elementary-age student with a severe or multiple disability may demonstrate that standard through independently following his or her own daily schedule. For each subsequent activity on that student's schedule, he or she could select what comes next and prepare for that activity. Similarly, a middle school student with multiple disabilities could evidence the social studies standard, "Students recognize the geographic interactions between people and their surroundings" by describing three ways in which people who live in extremely cold climates have to adjust to that environment in their daily lives.

In the previous example, Ms. Bowling designed the investigation activity to address mathematics standards related to the concept of using data for predicting certain and uncertain events. Language arts standards are usually divided into reading, speaking, and writing; whereas mathematics standards are generally divided into six areas: number concepts, mathematical procedures, space and dimensionality concepts, measurement concepts, patterns and functions of change, and data concepts. Ms. Bowling integrated the mathematics standards and the language arts standards by requiring the students to give an oral presentation about their data collection. In addition, Ms. Bowling requested that Jody's collaborative team identify strategies for him to learn counting and number skills in the activity. Even though the other students in Jody's learning group already have mastered these skills, the data-gathering activity provided an excellent opportunity for Jody to develop and practice these skills. In addition, the activity provided numerous opportunities for Jody to practice communication skills from his IEP and to create his own report.

Whereas content standards outline what students should know, *performance* standards define the *degree* to which a student should perform at particular levels (i.e., "what the student should be able to do"). Because Jody is participating in the alternate assessment, the performance expectations in a content area may be modified but still should be linked to the content standards. A performance rubric is generally used to describe the extent to which a student can perform at a particular level. A rubric generally has four or more performance levels and may be single or multidimensional. Performance levels typically denote the student's level of competence in that task or activity; several states have aligned their performance levels for their rubrics for their alternate assessments with the performance levels of their regular assessments for all students. For example,

Kentucky's performance levels of "Novice," "Apprentice," "Proficient," and "Distinguished" correspond exactly to the performance levels used to score all students' work in that state's regular assessment.

Figure 4.4 illustrates a single-dimension rubric concerned primarily with the level of support or prompting a student requires to perform certain skills in the activity. This rubric is designed to reflect systematic prompting procedures such as the system of least prompts (Wolery, Ault, & Doyle, 1992) and can be used across activities. Within the system of least prompts, the teacher first provides the student an opportunity to perform each step in a task independently. If the student does not perform that step within a specified time interval (e.g., 5 seconds), referred to as the inter-prompt interval, or if the student starts to make an error, the teacher then provides the next-level prompt (e.g., a verbal prompt). If the student again fails to respond correctly within the specified prompt interval, the teacher provides the next-most-intrusive prompt (e.g., a model prompt or demonstration of the step, paired with the verbal prompt). Finally, if the student does not respond to the model prompt within the specified interval, the teacher provides the final prompt level (e.g., physical guidance, paired with the verbal prompt) so that the student is able to complete the step. The teacher then repeats this procedure with each step in the task analysis, always ensuring that the student first has the opportunity to perform each step in the task independently. According to Browder and colleagues (in press), 60% of the states responding in their national survey included a measure of the level of independence in student performance as a part of their respective scoring rubrics for alternate assessment.

No response 1	Physical prompts 2	Model prompts 3	Verbal prompts 4	Independent 5
Student does not respond, even with extensive physical prompting.	Student performs the skill(s) when the correct response is physically prompted.	Student performs the skill(s) when the correct response is modeled.	Student performs the skill with verbal prompts.	Student performs the skill without assistance.

Figure 4.4. Single dimension rubric to measure the degree of student independence. (From Kearns, J., Burdge, M., & Kleinert, H. [in press]. *Practical strategies for conducting alternate assessments: Research to practice series*. Washington, DC: American Association on Mental Retardation; adapted by permission.)

Figure 4.5 is an example of a multidimensional rubric that addresses not only the level of student independence in skill performance but also 1) the extent to which those skills are linked to the state standards for all students and 2) the generalization of skills across environments, activities, materials, and individuals. Linkage to state standards is a critical element in assuring that the alternate assessment is tied to the general curriculum for all students. Including that dimension as part of the evaluation criteria for students' work ensures that teachers are making that important connection to the general curriculum. Generalization of skills is an area in which students with severe and multiple disabilities often experience

	(1)	(2)	(3)	(4)
Performance	Student demonstrates skills and concepts only with physical assistance	Student demonstrates skills and concepts with a model of the correct performance	Student demonstrates skills and concepts with verbal prompts	Student demonstrates skills and concepts accurately and inde- pendently
Link to standards	Student performance data and products are not linked to the content standards	Student performance data and products link to standards in one content area	Student performance data and products link to standards in two to three content areas	Student performance data and products link to standards in at least four areas
Generalization	Student demonstrates skills and concepts only under familiar conditions	Student demonstrates skills and concepts in at least one novel condition, including settings, people, activities, and materials	Student demonstrates skills and concepts in three novel conditions including settings, people, activities, materials	Student demonstrates skills and concepts in at least five novel conditions, illustrating a range of environments, people, activities, and materials

Figure 4.5.   Scoring rubric across multiple dimensions. [From Kearns, J., Burdge, M., & Kleinert, H. (in press). *Practical strategies for conducting alternate assessments: Research to practice series.* Washington, DC: American Association on Mental Retardation; adapted by permission.]

considerable difficulty (Heward, 2000), and nearly half of the states (43%) responding to the Browder and colleagues (in press) survey indicated that they included a measure of student skill generalization in their alternate assessments. This third rubric dimension thus calls attention to the need for specific generalization planning and for documenting that the student has generalized target skills.

The rubric in Figure 4.5 guides the IEP team to consider these three questions in planning the IEP, providing instruction, and measuring results:

1. What type of instructional strategies or prompting procedures will allow the student the best opportunities to respond as independently as possible?

2. What consideration has been given to including skills from the content standards into a student's IEP and into instruction?

3. How will generalization of skills across environments, individuals, activities, and materials occur?

This rubric also guides the team in determining the measurement strategies that can best capture the student's progress (i.e., the use of instructional data including levels of prompts recorded across environments, materials, and people).

A performance dimension rubric delineating the relationship of content and performance standards and specifying increasingly more proficient levels of student achievement is, thus, a road map for the IEP team. This road map guides the IEP team to always consider these important elements related to student performance throughout planning and instruction.

In the story about Jody, the collaborative team considered each dimension of the performance rubric in Figure 4.5. First, the team carefully documented the level of Jody's independent IntelliKeys use and counting responses. Second, the team ensured that Jody's learning addressed both his IEP objectives *and* the language arts and math content standards for all students. For generalization, Jody's team provided extended activities through additional classroom practice (perhaps with additional peers outside his assigned group) and through counting and basic addition homework centered on the theme of music. We should note that Jody's mother was also a very important part of this team throughout this process, including documenting generalized performance. The importance of well-constructed performance rubrics can be summed up by the title of a paper by Burgess and Kennedy (1998): "What Gets Tested, Gets Taught." How we measure that performance shapes both what we do as teachers and what we expect of our students.

Consideration 2: Determine Alternate Assessment Formats

The IEP team should consider the format of its state alternate assessment in considering measurement strategies to document student learning. The alternate assessment formats described earlier in this chapter—student portfolios and performance events—are both highly consistent with a collaborative team model of planning and instruction. Both portfolio assessment and performance tasks/events lend themselves to measuring student progress in ways that are useful and practical. A portfolio can encompass a variety of measurement strategies and, in fact, can even include performance tasks or events as a part of the total "package" of documentation. In both formats, multiple assessment strategies can enhance the validity of the assessment by providing a more complete picture of the student's overall performance (Kearns, Burdge, & Kleinert, in press).

In a performance event task, the teacher reviews a predetermined, activity-based protocol that incorporates a number of skills from a particular content area. Prior to the assessment, the teacher, along with the team, will need to determine what supports, adaptations, and modifications the student will need in order to perform as many skills listed on the protocol as possible. The collaborative team suggests adaptations, including assistive technology, and helps to determine the types of prompts and task modifications that might be necessary for the student to respond. During the assessment, the teacher provides the task directions to the student and then follows the procedures for assessing each skill. The student's responses are then recorded according to the level of instructional support the student required for each skill in the activity protocol. Figure 4.6 illustrates a sample activity protocol similar to the task that Ms. Bowling developed for her math class. The figure includes the activity, the mathematics skill set (Jody's targeted skills), a coding system for recording data (e.g., system of least prompts), and observer notes. Jody's performance and prompting levels on this mathematics task is directly noted in this figure.

From these data, it is easy to see that Jody independently chose a preference area for interviewing his classmates and that he made predictions about the students' most likely choices and summarized their overall preferences with only verbal prompts. Moreover, with model prompts he interviewed the students, counted their responses, and displayed his results on his IntelliKeys. Because entering his daily counts into tabular form required a more refined motor response and Jody was not able to identify all of the numerals from 1 to 10, he needed physical prompts at first to perform that skill.

Although this performance task can stand alone as an assessment of Jody's skills, it gives only a snapshot of Jody's performance in mathematics on a particular day. If a portfolio assessment format is used, however, then the documentation of Jody's skills can occur over time, usually over a school year, and can give a more complete picture of his increasing competence in mathematics. The daily or ongoing collection of observational data characteristic of portfolios also provides the team with individualized instructional feedback on a more frequent

Activity	Targeted skills for Jody	Student response	Observer notes
Collect and summarize data for 10 students in a particular preference area (e.g., music, ice cream preferences)	Select preference area for interview.	5	Chose a preference area independently
	Make prediction about student preferences	4	Chose between options with verbal prompt
	Interview 10 students.	3	Used IntelliKeys; required model
	Tally student responses (i.e., count with correspondence).	3	Used icons; required model prompt for counting
	Record daily tally for each music category into data preference table.	4	Required physical prompt; need to learn numerals
	Display own data/results.	3	Used IntelliKeys and PowerPoint for presentation with model
	Summarize overall results.	2	Responded with verbal prompt

Figure 4.6. Jody's instructional data for a performance event task. (Key: 5 = performed independently, 4 = performed after verbal prompt, 3 = performed after model prompt, 2 = performed after physical prompt, 1 = not performed, even with physical prompt.)

basis. It can also suggest specific instruction to enhance generalization. The example in Figure 4.7 illustrates math and language arts skill data in Jody's portfolio.

The data sheet in Figure 4.7 and a visual chart of Jody's performance (Figure 4.8) were both included in the portfolio. The performance chart in Figure 4.8 indicates Jody's increasing independence in his counting responses, expressed as an average daily prompt level. Samples of Jody's homework, along with a note from his mother, documented his ability to generalize this skill. A videotape showing Jody's use of his IntelliKeys to interview students was also included in his portfolio.

Activity	Skills	Student responses					Summary
		Dates					
		1/28	1/29	1/30	1/31	2/1	
Interview participants.	Ask each participant his or her music choice.	3	3	3	4	4	
	Record each student's response.	3	4	4	4	5	
Average daily prompt level for interviewing students		3.0	3.5	3.5	4.0	4.5	
	Observer initials	jk	mb	jk	mb	jk	
Count participant responses from computer printout.	Count icons for country music.	2	2	3	3	3	
	Count icons for classical music.	2	3	2	3	4	
	Count icons for rock music.	2	3	3	3	3	
	Count icons for rap music.	3	3	3	4	4	
Average daily prompt level for counting.		2.25	2.75	2.75	3.25	3.50	
	Observer initials	jk	mb	jk	mb	jk	
Display data and summarize results (class presentation).	Use IntelliKeys to provide data display to class.					4	
	Indicate class's overall musical preference.					5	
	Observer initials					jk	

Figure 4.7. Jody's performance data for a portfolio entry. (Key: 5 = independent, 4 = verbal prompt, 3 = model prompt, 2 = physical prompt, 1 = no response after physical prompt.) (From Kearns, J., Burdge, M., & Kleinert, H. [in press]. *Practical strategies for conducting alternate assessments: Research to practice series*. Washington, DC: American Association on Mental Retardation; adapted by permission.)

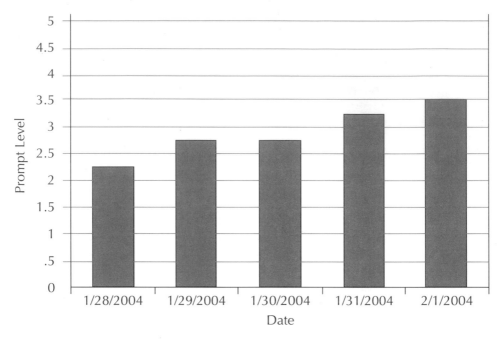

Figure 4.8. Jody's average daily prompt level for counting.

Jody used the Learning Evaluation Form (often referred to as a Planning, Monitoring, and Evaluation Form or PME) depicted in Figure 4.9 to evaluate his own performance and his contribution to the group's learning. PME sheets typically have the following components, each of which is determined or evaluated by the student: 1) the skill or skills on which the student will focus that day or week; 2) how the student will practice or learn that skill (e.g., group work, practice on the computer); 3) the actual performance data, with a place for the student to indicate if his or her performance improved each time; and 4) what skill the student most needs to focus on *next time* in order to continue to improve (Kleinert, Denham, et al., 2001). For example, Jody used his Learning Evaluation Form (Figure 4.9) to set goals for his own performance (i.e., counting, finding the correct numeral, using his IntelliKeys). Student goal setting has resulted in increased acquisition rates of skills for students with mild to profound disabilities (Copeland & Hughes, 2002). In addition, Jody was able to answer the question on his Learning Evaluation Form regarding how he did on his counting that day by reviewing with his teacher or a classmate the brightly colored and contrasted visual chart (shown in black and white in Figure 4.8), which presented his performance data. For other students, performance data can be graphed directly onto the PME sheet, with the student often charting the data him- or herself. Figure 4.10 presents a second example of a student PME

Learning Evaluation Form

Name: _____   Group name: _____

My personal goal: _____

Counting	Find number	Use IntelliKeys
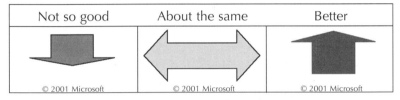 © 2001 Microsoft	© 2001 Microsoft	© 2001 Microsoft

What was the favorite music choice of the class?			
classical music © 2001 Microsoft	country music © 2001 Microsoft	rap music © 2001 Microsoft	rock music © 2001 Microsoft

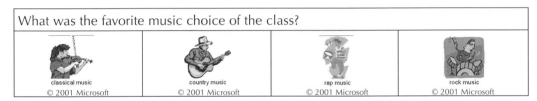

How did I do in my counting?

Not so good	About the same	Better
© 2001 Microsoft	© 2001 Microsoft	© 2001 Microsoft

How did I contribute to the group today?

Offered ideas	Gave help	Praised others	Kept time
© 2001 Microsoft	© 2001 Microsoft	© 2001 Microsoft	© 2001 Microsoft

What skill will I focus on next time?

Counting	Find number	Use IntelliKeys
© 2001 Microsoft	© 2001 Microsoft	© 2001 Microsoft

Figure 4.9. Jody's learning evaluation form.

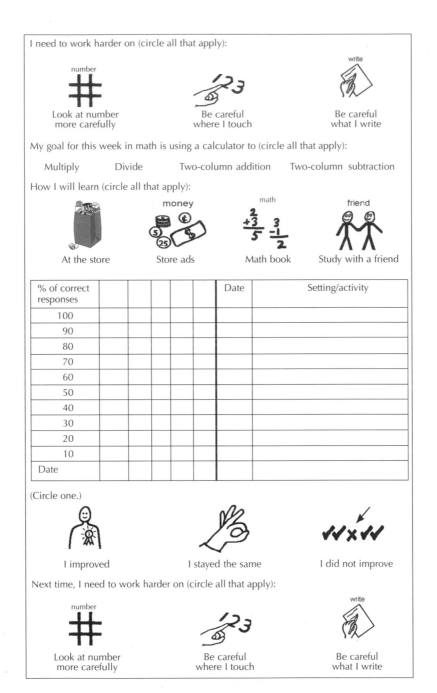

I need to work harder on (circle all that apply):

number

Look at number more carefully

Be careful where I touch

write

Be careful what I write

My goal for this week in math is using a calculator to (circle all that apply):

Multiply   Divide   Two-column addition   Two-column subtraction

How I will learn (circle all that apply):

At the store

money

Store ads

math

Math book

friend

Study with a friend

% of correct responses						Date	Setting/activity
100							
90							
80							
70							
60							
50							
40							
30							
20							
10							
Date							

(Circle one.)

I improved

I stayed the same

I did not improve

Next time, I need to work harder on (circle all that apply):

number

Look at number more carefully

Be careful where I touch

write

Be careful what I write

Figure 4.10. Student planning, monitoring, and evaluation form for math. (From Kleinert, H.L., & Kearns, J. [2001]. *Alternate assessment: Measuring outcomes and supports for students with disabilities* [p. 103]. Baltimore: Paul H. Brookes Publishing Co.; adapted by permission. Picture Communication Symbols © 1981–2004 by Mayer-Johnson, Inc. All Rights Reserved worldwide. Used with permission.)

136

```
┌─────────────────────────────────────────────────────────────┐
│                     Peer Reflection Form                     │
│                                                              │
│  Jody did a super job on our music survey! He counted the    │
│  students in our class who liked each kind of music, and     │
│  we all used his keyboard to do our report. Everybody        │
│  really liked his part, especially when he played the        │
│  class's favorite music! He is a fun partner to work with    │
│  and I learned a lot from him. He taught me how to use his   │
│  computer. His keyboard is bigger and has pictures, too!     │
│                                                              │
└─────────────────────────────────────────────────────────────┘
```

Figure 4.11. Peer reflection form on Jody's performance.

form designed for a general education math class; the PME sheet in Figure 4.10 includes a performance data bar graph that can be completed by the student with peer or teacher support as appropriate.

Finally, peers can provide additional data about how the student's skill acquisition has resulted in increased competence for that student. For example, one of Jody's classmates wrote a peer note describing Jody's performance in this instructional activity (see Figure 4.11). This note was included in Jody's portfolio entry as further evidence of his learning and of his ability to use those skills in integrated class activities.

As educators design data systems to capture student performance, remember that effective observation includes the following assessment practices:

- Skills are observable and measurable.

- Procedures for recording the student's performance are clearly defined.

- Multiple observers verify student performance.

- Adaptations and modifications are provided before the assessment.

- Generalization opportunities are clearly established.

- Data are presented in a chart or graph.

Consideration 3: Merge Instruction with Assessment

Certainly, the previous example of Jody's music project provides ample illustration of how his teacher was able to merge ongoing instruction with assessment. Jody's instructional data sheets, his daily Learning Evaluation Forms, and video-clips illustrating his interviewing skills with his IntelliKeys overlay and his class presentation were all included in his alternate assessment portfolio. All of these samples of his work illustrate the integral relationship of assessment with instruction.

In this section, we provide a step-by-step process for making alternate assessment an ongoing part of students' instructional routines. We also illustrate these six steps with another example, this time for a high school student. In connecting standards-based instruction with assessment, we have found that the most effective teachers follow these steps (Kearns et al., in press):

1. Define the outcome of instruction by answering the question: "What should all students know and be able to do as a result of this work?"

2. Link to the appropriate standard.

3. Identify the instructional activities and how the student with a disability will participate in each step (include supports and adaptations as necessary).

4. Target specific objectives from the IEP that best align with the instructional activity.

5. Select documentation of learning and instruction.

6. Organize the documentation of learning and instruction.

The first four steps of this process focus on activity-based instruction typical of inclusive environments. The final two steps, the documentation of learning and instruction and the organization of documentation, deal primarily with assessment and measuring progress. For students with severe and multiple disabilities, the documentation of student learning presents unique challenges in that assessment strategies are often limited. Direct observation of student performance in either structured or unstructured situations continues to be the primary source of assessment data in both portfolios and performance events. With advances in assistive technology, however, students with severe and multiple disabilities can often demonstrate unexpected levels of achievement in the general curriculum and are producing work samples more consistent with those of their peers without disabilities (see Denham et al., 2001; Denham & Lahm, 2001). These products (e.g., class reports, PowerPoint presentations) can themselves become a part of a student's alternate assessment.

The following science example highlights the important steps for effectively merging instruction and assessment.

———————————

Emilio, a high school student, has multiple disabilities. Although Emilio has some residual vision (he can discriminate sharp contrasts and bright colors), he is not able to read ink print, even with magnification. He is taking a high school science class in which the teacher requires each student to conduct an inquiry or science experiment. In addition to his science class, Emilio enjoys a horticulture class and works part-time at a local greenhouse. His IEP team decided to combine all of these interests for Emilio's science experiment.

Step 1: Define the outcome of instruction. Mr. Howard, Emilio's science teacher, defined the outcome of the science experiment activity as follows: Students will design and conduct a science inquiry into the topic of their choice and share the results of their investigation through appropriate technology media.

Step 2: Link to the appropriate standards. Mr. Howard related this instructional activity to the science content standards of "addressing scientific inquiry" and "application of science concepts to real-world problems" and the language arts standard of "using of technology in making formal presentations." In addition, this activity requires students to collect and chart data, skills that tap math standards of "analyzing quantifiable information" and "predicting patterns." Content-rich instruction often includes standards from multiple areas in a single project. This science activity thus embraced standards from at least three content or discipline areas: science, math, and language arts.

Step 3: Identify instructional activities and how the student will participate. Mr. Howard outlined the following instructional activities:

- *Formulate the research question.* The team decided that Emilio would need assistance in identifying the research question that most interested him. Three sample research questions were recorded on large touch switches, and Emilio chose the question related to his experiences with plants: "How much fertilizer is needed for optimum plant growth?" In his job at the greenhouse, Emilio uses a specially designed liquid fertilizer watering wand to water the plants. This science question was thus important to his job as well!

- *Conduct library/Internet search on the topic.* Emilio and his science partner went to the library and conducted an Internet search on the key words *liquid fertilizer* and *optimum plant growth,* as well as specific plant characteristics. Copies of these documents were used in the results display of the experiment. In addition, Emilio's peer partner extended the experiment by examining the different nutrient mixes in a variety of liquid fertilizers, to see if fertilizer type, as well as fertilizer amount, was a key variable in plant growth. Although Emilio and his partner were both engaged in the same experiment, the level of complexity in their research questions was thus differentiated. Differentiated outcomes, within the context of the same activity, is an important modification for the participation of students with severe and multiple disabilities in general curriculum activities (Giangreco et al., 1998).

- *Design the experiment.* Emilio and his science partner planted three flats of plants and labeled them 1) "water only," 2) "recommended fertilizer," and 3) "double fertilizer." Each day, Emilio used a special measuring device to measure the appropriate amount of fertilizer into the watering wand and he watered the plants. In order to accommodate his motor disabilities, Emilio's occupational therapist designed accommodations that Emilio used for both his science experiment (conducted at the school greenhouse) and for his work site at the community greenhouse. Four-inch containers were used for planting in each flat, as typical flats were too small. Large-handled potting tools were used to facilitate and develop Emilio's grip. The potting bench at each greenhouse was adjusted to wheelchair height, and the watering wand at both sites was mounted from the ceiling to eliminate the need to drag the hose and water wand. The teacher of students with visual impairments (TVI) recommended selecting plants such as marigolds because of their distinctly different flowers and leaves. In addition, marigolds have a unique odor that would add to the multisensory effect.

- *Collect data.* Emilio measured the growth of plants in each flat with a braille measuring tape and recorded their growth on a large bar chart. He also used a digital camera, with an adapted switch, to photograph the growth of the plants in each flat.

- *Report findings.* Plant growth was recorded into spreadsheets to make charts. The photographs were used to illustrate the final results in an IntelliKeys overlay with IntelliTalk II (IntelliTools, 2002c) output.

Mr. Roberts, Emilio's special education teacher, led the collaborative team in the identification of the supports that Emilio required to complete each of the experiment steps. These included modified measuring tools, switch-modified digital camera, environmental modifications (e.g., horticultural tools, watering wand), and development of the IntelliKeys overlays.

Step 4: Target IEP objectives most aligned with the activity. Emilio's IEP objectives that were most aligned with his science project included "asking relevant questions," "using measuring tools," and "staying on the conversation or class topic." Secondary objectives included "working cooperatively with a partner" and "observing time limits in task completion."

Step 5: Select documentation of learning and instruction. The following documentation resulted from Emilio's science experiment:

- Observational data collected on Emilio's targeted IEP objectives

- Observational data collected on his ability to follow the steps of his science experiment (illustrating his achievement of the content standards in science)

- Daily reflection or learning evaluation sheets

- Performance checklists completed by both Emilio's employer at the greenhouse where he worked and Mr. Alexander, the horticulture instructor at the greenhouse at school

- Three 90-second video clips of Emilio completing each step of the experiment at the school greenhouse, using his accommodations, and completing other work-related tasks at the greenhouse where he worked

- Emilio's science experiment class presentation that he made with his IntelliKeys overlay

- Emilio's self-reflection on his learning, dictated to his science partner, at the end of his science experiment. Figure 4.12 presents this self-reflection.

Self-Reflection Form

This is my favorite entry in my portfolio. I think it is my best work. I learned that plants need fertilizer, but too much can hurt. In my job, I have to water each plant with the right amount. I liked telling the class about our results, and working with Larry [Emilio's science partner] and going to the library with him. I had fun taking pictures of the plants with the new [digital] camera and putting the pictures in my portfolio. The marigolds were my favorite plant—I help grow them at work, too! When I graduate, I hope to work at a greenhouse of my own.

—Emilio

Figure 4.12. Emilio's self-reflection on his science entry (dictated to a peer).

Step 6: Organize the documentation of learning and instruction. Mr. Roberts, Mr. Howard, and Emilio's mother worked with him to select and organize the items from the list in Step 5. It is important that students be involved as much as possible in the construction and selection of the content of their own portfolios; in fact, Kampfer, Horvath, Kleinert, and Kearns (2001) found that one of the best predictors of student scores in the alternate assessment was the extent to which students were active participants in this process. Emilio chose to include in his portfolio the photographs, IntelliKeys print-outs from the presentation, the performance checklist completed by his employer at the greenhouse, and his final self-reflection (see Figure 4.12). Mr. Roberts suggested that the performance data demonstrating that Emilio had completed the steps of his science experience and his performance data on his IEP goals and objectives be included as well. Emilio's mother recommended one of the video clips for inclusion in the science entry and another video clip as a part of the videotaped résumé developed to highlight Emilio's vocational skills.

Consideration 4: Using Outcome Results in IEP Planning and Ongoing Instruction

Previously in this chapter, we discussed the integral relationships among instruction, assessment, and program planning. Next, we examine the use of alternate assessment data in making ongoing instructional decisions and in subsequent IEP and program planning.

Teachers who collect student data from observational and/or systematic instructional strategies use these data in determining student outcomes and to adjust instruction to meet the unique needs of individual students on a daily or weekly basis. As we have noted in our examples of Jody and Emilio, direct, systematic observational data may be collected across a variety of instructional activities. Data collection during instruction should occur frequently (i.e., daily or two or three times weekly), with observational data verified by more than one observer. Instruction can be delivered in either a *distributed* trial format (i.e., spaced throughout the day or throughout an activity) or presented in a *massed* trial format (i.e., repeated trials at very close intervals). Activities can include opportunities for *both* massed and distributed trials. For example, Figure 4.7 illustrates how the teacher records Jody's performance on the massed trials of counting each music preference at the end of the activity and also his performance on the distributed trials of asking each student their music preference as the students are interviewed throughout the activity.

Both types of trial formats are necessary for students to acquire, maintain, and generalize skills. For example, if we further consider Jody's targeted skill of counting, his daily counting trials on his classmates' musical preferences and his additional homework practice in counting provided him with the massed practice necessary to acquire and become fluent in that skill.

In order to maintain and generalize a skill, distributed practice is necessary. To identify opportunities for Jody to practice this skill through a distributed trial format, the general and special education teachers developed an activity matrix (Kearns et al., in press) to assist the team in determining other opportunities for Jody to practice counting skills throughout the day. The team also ensured that Jody would have distributed trials in learning to use his IntelliKeys overlays independently in such instructional activities as interviewing students; making his class presentation; completing his homework; and completing other, similar instructional activities. Again, distributed trial practice was essential in order for Jody to maintain and generalize his independent use of IntelliKeys to request information, communicate with peers, and complete reports for his classes. As noted previously in this chapter, generalization of targeted skills is an integral part of the scoring rubric for a number of states' alternate assessments (Browder et al., in press).

Videotape documentation of a student's performance is another data source that has been used successfully by IEP teams in determining appropriate adaptations and ongoing instructional strategies. Videotape documentation has also proven to be a powerful tool for students in modifying their own performance (Dowrick, 2000). Although not always practical for daily or weekly use as an instructional tool, IEP teams can use videotapes successfully to make future planning decisions. Families, in particular, benefit from seeing their son or daughter engage in skills that might be used only at school (Bennett & Davis, 2001). Use of an electronic portfolio storage system makes videotape easy to maintain on a regular basis (Bennett & Davis, 2001; Denham et al., 2001).

Data from both performance events and portfolio assessment can provide useful baseline data to assist IEP teams in determining what skills the student has learned and those that should be targeted for future learning. In both Jody's and Emilio's alternate assessment examples, the collaborative teams gained important information on how these students' learning can be further tied to the content standards for all students and on the supports and modifications that those students need to participate in the general curriculum. Moreover, in Emilio's example, his alternate assessment data, including employer and coworker evaluations of his work, can be used to pinpoint his future vocational interests and goals.

Use of alternate assessment data can thus be part of a continuous feedback loop informing both program planning and ongoing instruction. The breadth of assessment data in alternate assessments, including systematic instructional data, student products, videotape clips, student self-reflections, and peer and parent reflections may assist IEP teams in developing more relevant instructional plans and in creating more consistent instructional opportunities within the general curriculum. The use of a portfolio as an "organizing strategy" for compiling student data (Kleinert, Hurte et al., 2001) can provide yet another opportunity for students to practice important skills in self-evaluation and goal setting. Portfolios used on an ongoing basis can provide invaluable information to IEP teams as students make the transition from teacher to teacher and school to school (Kleinert, Hurte et al., 2001). Portfolios can also highlight important student skills for postschool service providers. For example, Emilio's videotaped resume will be an invaluable tool for his job coach in the development of future employment opportunities.

Finally, portfolio assessment can itself result in the development of new skills for students. For example, several states require that alternate assessment portfolios include a daily, individualized student schedule and instructional data indicating how well the student is learning to independently follow his or her schedule. Managing one's own schedule is an important self-management strategy for all students and has been shown to result in both increased independence and generalization of targeted skills (Heward, 2000). Figure 4.13 includes a sample student pictorial schedule for an elementary-age student. To use this type of schedule, the student indicates what activity comes next, draws the correct starting time on the clock face that corresponds to the printed digital time, and indicates when the activity is completed. This schedule would be included in the student's portfolio along with the instructional data (e.g., average daily prompt level on identifying what activity comes next, accuracy in identifying the correct time) indicating how independently the student was able to identify and prepare for each activity or class throughout the day.

SUMMARY

This chapter has provided an overview of the essential elements of alternate assessment. Alternate assessment for students with severe and multiple disabilities should always embody the basic assumptions of a collaborative model (see Chapter 1). Furthermore, alternate assessment, or assessment for outcomes, is one part of a continuous quality improvement cycle; the other parts of that cycle are program planning and instruction. Four important considerations have been presented for designing alternate assessments, including 1) starting with the standards, 2) determining the format of the alternate assessment, 3) merging assessment with instruction, and 4) using outcome results in IEP planning and in ongoing instruction. As states are using a variety of alternate assessment for-

Dates: _____ to _____

		Monday	Tuesday	Wednesday	Thursday	Friday
Art Music P.E.	8:00	Yes	Yes	(clock)	Yes	Yes
	4th grade 8:15	Yes	Yes	(clock)	Yes	Yes
	9:00	Yes	Yes	(clock)	Yes	Yes
	4th grade 10:30	Yes	Yes	(clock)	Yes	Yes
	11:45	Yes	Yes	(clock)	Yes	Yes
	4th grade 12:15	Yes	Yes	(clock)	Yes	Yes
	4th grade (Monday only) 12:45	Yes	No		No	No
	12:50	Yes	No	(clock)	Yes	Yes
	1:30	Yes	Yes	(clock)	Yes	Yes
	2:30	Yes	Yes	(clock)	Yes	Yes
	2:45	Yes	Yes	(clock)	Yes	Yes
Speech	(Tuesday & Friday) 1:15	No	Yes	(clock)	No	Yes

Figure 4.13. Individualized student pictorial schedule. (From Kentucky Statewide Alternate Portfolio Project. [1999]. *Kentucky alternate portfolio teacher's handbook.* Lexington: Kentucky Department of Education; adapted by permission. Picture Communication Symbols © 1981–2004 by Mayer-Johnson, Inc. All Rights Reserved worldwide. Used with permission.)

mats (including portfolios and performance events), we have used examples of data collection illustrating both of these formats. Because individualized supports, modifications, and adaptations—including assistive technology—are crucial if students with severe and multiple disabilities are to demonstrate all that they have learned, we have provided examples of alternate assessment entries at the elementary and secondary levels that illustrate the use of supports determined by the entire collaborative team. Finally, we have attempted to show how alternate assessment, through its required focus on the content standards for all students, can itself result in enhanced participation and progress in the general curriculum while enabling students with severe and multiple disabilities to achieve important life outcomes of value to themselves and their families.

REFERENCES

Anthony, R.J., Johnson, T.D., Mickelson, N., & Preece, A. (1991). *Evaluating literacy: A perspective for change.* Portsmouth, NH: Heinemann.

Bennett, D.E., & Davis, M.A. (2001). The development of an alternate assessment system for students with significant disabilities. *Diagnostique. Assessment for Effective Intervention, 26,* 15–34.

Browder, D. (1987). *Assessment of individuals with severe handicaps.* Baltimore: Paul H. Brookes Publishing Co.

Browder, D., Ahlgrim-Delzell, L., Flowers, C., Karvonen, M., Spooner, F., & Algozzine, R. (in press). How states define alternate assessments for students with disabilities and recommendations for national policy. *Journal of Disability Policy Studies.*

Browder, D., & Spooner, F. (in press). Understanding the purpose and process of alternate assessment. In D. Ryndak & S. Alper (Eds.), *Curriculum and instruction for students with significant disabilities in inclusive environments.* Needham Heights, MA: Allyn & Bacon.

Burgess, P., & Kennedy, S. (1998). *What gets tested, gets taught. Who gets tested, gets taught.* Retrieved June 24, 2002, from the University of Kentucky, Interdisciplinary Human Development Institute, MidSouth Regional Resource Center web site: http://www.ihdi.uky.edu/MSRRC/publicat.htm.

Copeland, S., & Hughes, C. (2002). Effects of goal setting on task performance of persons with mental retardation. *Education and Training in Mental Retardation and Developmental Disabilities, 37*(1), 40–54.

Denham, A., Bennett, D.E., Edyburn, D.L., Lahm, E.A., & Kleinert, H.L. (2001). Implementing technology to demonstrate higher levels of learning. In H.L. Kleinert & J. Kearns, *Alternate assessment: Measuring outcomes and supports for students with disabilities* (pp. 135–166). Baltimore: Paul H. Brookes Publishing Co.

Denham, A., & Lahm, E.A. (2001). Using technology to construct alternate portfolios of students with moderate and severe disabilities. *TEACHING Exceptional Children, 33*(5), 10–17.

Dowrick, P. (2000). A review of self-modeling and related interventions. *Applied & Preventive Psychology, 8,* 23–39.

Ezell, D., & Klein, C. (2003). Impact of portfolio assessment on locus of control for students with and without disabilities. *Education and Training in Developmental Disabilities, 38*(2), 220–228.

Ezell, D., Klein, C., & Ezell-Powell, S. (1999). Empowering students with mental retardation through portfolio assessment: A tool for fostering self-determination skills. *Education and Training in Mental Retardation and Developmental Disabilities, 34*(4), 453–463.

Giangreco, M.F., Cloninger, C., & Iverson, V.S. (1998). *Choosing outcomes and accommodations for children (COACH): A guide to educational planning for students with disabilities* (2nd ed.). Baltimore: Paul H. Brookes Publishing Co.

Heumann, J., & Warlick, K. (2000, August 24). OSEP memorandum to state directors of special education (OSEP 00-24). Washington, DC: U.S. Department of Education.

Heward, W. (2000). *Exceptional children: An introduction to special education* (6th ed.). Columbus, OH: Merrill Prentice-Hall.

Individuals with Disabilities Education Act Amendments of 1997, PL 105-17, 20 U.S.C. §§ 1400 *et. seq.*

IntelliTools. (2002a). *IntelliKeys.* [Online]. Retrieved from http://www.intellitools.com/index.html

IntelliTools. (2002b). *IntelliTalk II.* [Computer software]. Novato, CA: Author.

IntelliTools. (2002c). *Overlay Maker* [Online]. Retrieved from http://www.intellitools.com/index.html

Kampfer, S., Horvath, L., Kleinert, H., & Kearns, J. (2001). Teachers' perceptions of one state's alternate assessment portfolio program: Implications for practice and preparation. *Exceptional Children, 67*(3), 361–374.

Kearns, J., Burdge, M., & Kleinert, H. (in press). *Practical strategies for conducting alternate assessments. INNOVATIONS: Research to practice series.* Washington, DC: American Association on Mental Retardation.

Kentucky Statewide Aternate Portfolio Project. (1999). *Kentucky alternate portfolio teacher's guide.* Lexington: Kentucky Department of Education.

Kleinert, H., Green, P., Hurte, M., Clayton, J., & Oetinger, C. (2002). Creating and using meaningful alternate assessments. *TEACHING Exceptional Children, 34*(4), 40–47.

Kleinert, H.L., Denham, A., Groneck, V.B., Clayton, J., Burdge, M., Kearns, J.F., & Hall, M. (2001). Systematically teaching the components of self-determination. In H.L. Kleinert & J. Kearns, *Alternate assessment: Measuring outcomes and supports for students with disabilities* (pp. 93–134). Baltimore: Paul H. Brookes Publishing Co.

Kleinert, H.L., Hurte, M.D., Groneck, V.B., Fay, J.M., Roszmann-Millican, M., Hall, M., Clayton, J., & Lester, J.M. (2001). Demonstrating performance across multiple environments. In H.L. Kleinert & J. Kearns, *Alternate assessment: Measuring outcomes and supports for students with disabilities* (pp. 185–211). Baltimore: Paul H. Brookes Publishing Co.

Kleinert, H., & Kearns, J. (1999). A validation study of the performance indicators and learner outcomes of Kentucky's alternate assessment for students with significant disabilities. *The Journal of The Association for Persons with Severe Handicaps, 24*(2), 100–110.

Kleinert, H., Kearns, J., & Kennedy, S. (1997). Accountability for all students: Kentucky's Alternate Portfolio assessment for students with moderate and severe cognitive disabilities. *The Journal of The Association for Persons with Severe Handicaps, 22*(2), 88–101.

Kleinert, H., Kennedy, S., & Kearns, J. (1999). Impact of alternate assessments: A statewide teacher survey. *Journal of Special Education, 33*(2), 93–102.

Kleinert, H.L., & Thurlow, M.L. (2001). An introduction to alternate assessment. In H.L. Kleinert & J. Kearns, *Alternate assessment: Measuring outcomes and supports for students with disabilities* (pp. 1–15). Baltimore: Paul H. Brookes Publishing Co.

McGrew, K.S., Thurlow, M.L., & Spiegel, A.N. (1993). An investigation of the exclusion of students with disabilities in national data collection programs. *Educational Evaluation and Policy Analysis, 15*(3), 339–352.

Microsoft Corporation. (2000). Microsoft PowerPoint 2000 [Computer software]. Redmond, WA: Author.

National Center on Educational Outcomes (2001). *2001 state special education outcomes: A report on state activities at the beginning of a new decade.* Minneapolis: University of Minnesota.

Orelove, F.P., & Malatchi, A. (1996). Curriculum and instruction. In F. Orelove & D. Sobsey, *Educating children with multiple disabilities: A transdisciplinary approach* (3rd ed., pp. 377–409). Baltimore: Paul H. Brookes Publishing Co.

Paulson, F., Paulson, P., & Meyer, C. (1991). What makes a portfolio a portfolio? *Educational Leadership, 48*(5), 60–63.

Pike, K., Compain, R., & Mumper, J. (1994). *New connections: An integrated approach to literacy.* New York: HarperCollins.

Pike, K., & Salend, S.J. (1995). Authentic assessment strategies: Alternatives to norm-referenced testing. *Teaching Exceptional Children, 28*(1), 15–20.

Special educators share their thoughts on special education teaching conditions. (1999). *CEC Today, 5*(9), 1, 5, 15.

Turner, M., Baldwin, L., Kleinert, H., & Kearns, J. (2000). An examination of the concurrent validity of Kentucky's alternate assessment system. *Journal of Special Education, 3*(2), 69–76.

Wesson, C.L., & King, R.P. (1996). Portfolio assessment and special education students. *Teaching Exceptional Children, 28*(2), 44–48.

Wolery, M., Ault, M., & Doyle, P. (1992). *Teaching students with moderate to severe disabilities.* White Plains, NY: Longman Publishing Group.

Ysseldyke, J., & Olsen, K. (1999). Putting alternate assessments into practice: What to measure and possible sources of data. *Exceptional Children, 65*(2), 175–186.

For More Information

ALTERNATE ASSESSMENT WEB SITES

Alternate Assessment Related Links (Mountain Plains Regional Resource Center)
http://www.usu.edu/mprrc/workgroups/aa/links/cfm

American Federation of Teachers Alternate Assessment
http://www.aft.org/edissues/specialed/alternateassess.htm

Charlotte Alternate Assessment Model Project
http://www.uncc.edu/aap/aaphome.asp

Kentucky Alternate Portfolio
http://www.ihdi.uky.edu/kap/

National Center on Educational Outcomes Alternate Assessment
http://education.umn.edu/nceo/

GENERAL, K–12, AND UNIVERSITY WEB SITES ON PORTFOLIO ASSESSMENT

Computers and Writing Course
http://www.cwrl.utexas.edu/~tonya/309m/port/port.html

Discovery Middle School
http://longwood.cs.ucf.edu/~MidLink/portfolios.dms.html

The Kalamazoo Portfolio
http://www.kzoo.edu/pfolio/index.html

CHAPTER 5

Developing Adaptations to Promote Participation in Inclusive Environments

Alice Udvari-Solner, Julie Causton-Theoharis,
and Jennifer York-Barr

All of the students in Mr. Theo's eighth-grade homeroom are assembled to sign each other's yearbooks on the last day of school. The excitement in the room is palpable as students race from person to person, autographing and writing messages to one another. Groups of adolescents are clamoring to say farewell to their friends for the summer. A student named Claire, barely visible in the center of the crowd, can be heard to say, "Will you sign my yearbook?" and "Have a nice summer." She is now signing other students' yearbooks as they sign hers, but instead of using a pen to sign, she is using a programmable voice output device and a name stamp.

————————————————

Claire, like so many other students with severe and multiple disabilities across the country, uses a variety of instructional adaptations to support her academic involvement and membership in her school community. For the purposes of this chapter, an adaptation is considered to be any adjustments to instruction, the environment, or materials that help someone accomplish a task more effectively.

Portions of this chapter appearing in the third edition of this book were rewritten and updated by Alice Udvari-Solner and Julie Causton-Theoharis. Earlier versions contained critical elements that remain pertinent and were therefore preserved. We thank the original authors, Jennifer York-Barr, Beverly Rainforth, and Peggy Locke, for their significant contributions. In addition we acknowledge Claire Dickey and her parents Jacqueline Philpott and Larry Dickey for allowing us to feature Claire in this chapter. Penny Reed and Dave Medaris provided invaluable background to us on current assistive technology. This chapter is dedicated to Sam Theoharis, who was born during the writing of this chapter.

151

Claire, for example, does not have the motor skills required to write her name. Consequently, her name stamp helps her to participate in the signing of yearbooks.

As Claire and other students with severe and multiple disabilities are included in general education environments more frequently, the need for adaptations is significantly intensified. Educators and other professionals must be able to identify the need for, develop, and use instructional adaptations or devices to increase the participation of students with complex learning needs in educational contexts. To educators and others without much experience in this area, this can initially be a formidable task.

This chapter presents a process to assist educators and other service providers in developing and utilizing adaptations to increase the participation of people with disabilities in school, community, and work environments. The strategy is illustrated in the experiences of a middle school student named Claire and applied in various aspects of her educational programming. Claire's story illustrates how creative use of simple adaptive technology can promote meaningful participation, friendships, and contributions in integrated community and general education environments (see also Figure 5.1). This chapter concludes with a discussion of considerations, precautions, and resources related to the effective use of adaptations as a complement to instruction.

IDENTIFYING AND DEVELOPING INDIVIDUALIZED ADAPTATIONS

The use of adaptations is determined by an analysis of individual student abilities and needs. That is, the process starts by identifying learner characteristics, individually relevant goals, and the school and community contexts in which these goals can be achieved. Meaningful, individualized instructional objectives and effective teaching or adaptive strategies are then determined to promote participation or independence in these environments. Figure 5.2 presents guiding questions for identifying and developing adaptations. This process is grounded in an ecological approach and draws from foundational concepts predicated by researchers in the field (Baumgart et al., 1982; Brown, Branston-McLean, Baumgart, Vincent, Falvey, & Schroeder, 1979; Brown et al., 1980; Brown, Shiraga, York, Zanella, & Rogan, 1984a, 1984b; Falvey, 1995; Ferguson & Baumgart, 1991; Piuma & Udvari-Solner, 1993a, 1993b; Udvari-Solner, 1995, 1996). The hierarchy of questions is designed to facilitate dialogue, problem solving, and decision making among team members, resulting in viable interventions that promote active participation and skill development for students with disabilities.

The first step in the process is to clearly understand the capacities, needs, and overarching educational priorities of the student. Second, the actual school, home, community, and vocational environments in which a given student operates are

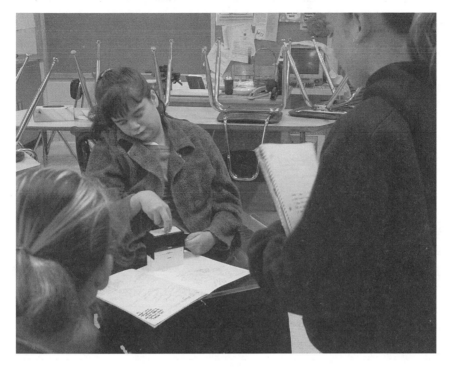

Figure 5.1. Claire, stamping yearbooks with friends at school.

identified. Third, the activities and skills necessary to participate in the selected environments are delineated. Fourth, the ability of the student with disabilities to engage in the required activities and skills is assessed in the actual environments. Fifth, difficulty areas, referred to as *performance discrepancies,* are identified and analyzed. Hypothesizing why these discrepancies exist is part of the analysis. Understanding the potential intellectual, motor, sensory, and behavioral characteristics attributed to performance discrepancies is an essential basis for designing effective interventions (Piuma & Udvari-Solner, 1993b). Sixth, priority skills are targeted for instruction; and seventh, intervention strategies are developed.

Essentially, educators can choose from among three intervention options. One is to teach the student to perform the skill in the same way that a person who does not have a disability would perform it. For example, if a student were not able to carry his or her science lab materials to the lab table, the student would be taught to do so in a way identical to the way his or her classmates without disabilities perform the skill. The second option is to employ instructional adaptations that modify the requirements of the task. For example, the student might be taught to carry each lab item individually. The third option involves using adaptive materials or devices. For example, a student carrying lab items in a bag

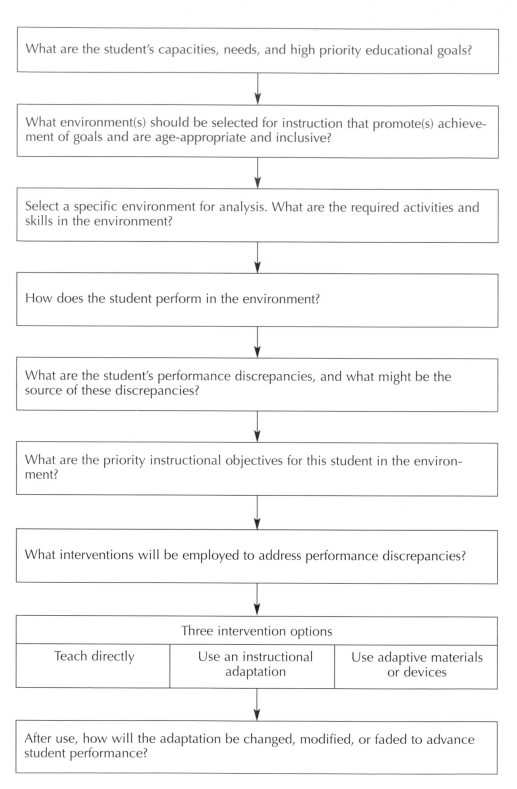

Figure 5.2. A process for developing individualized adaptations. (*Source:* Baumgart et al., 1982).

attached to his or her walker would be using an adaptation to accomplish the task. If a student is unlikely to learn essential intellectual, motor, or sensory requirements for performing a skill in a typical manner, then an adaptation is one way to accommodate the difficulties. The final part of the process is to implement and evaluate the intervention strategy, including providing systematic instruction and engaging in ongoing evaluation of performance (Piuma & Udvari-Solner, 1993b).

Beginning the Process: Asking Guiding Questions

The process to identify and develop adaptations is described next. Actions to take in response to each of the guiding questions are explained and application of the process is illustrated through an example of Claire ordering lunch at a fast-food restaurant with a group of peers who do not have disabilities. Claire is a 14-year-old with physical and intellectual disabilities who requires extensive supports.

What Are the Student's Capacities, Needs, and High-Priority Educational Goals?

To develop effective instructional strategies and useful adaptations, educators begin by extensively learning about their students. Gathering information that results in a positive profile of the student's social and academic abilities, strengths, and learning concerns is an essential first step. These facts help establish a shared vision of the student's active involvement for the team and can reveal pertinent strategies for effective teaching (Udvari-Solner, Villa, & Thousand, 2002).

Knowledge of the student's preferences and learning style, past instructional methods, and reliable physical and motor movements (especially for a student with severe and multiple disabilities) will affect the selection of adaptations. Information gathering and sharing must include the learner, the family, current and previous teachers, peers, and others close to the student. Considering how the student performs in varied environments such as home, school, and community and under different conditions (e.g., with peers versus with a parent) facilitates a global view of the student's capabilities, needs, and educational priorities.

Claire's challenges or disabilities can be described as follows. Claire has severe and multiple disabilities that necessitate the use of a variety of supports and assistance. Claire has muscular dystrophy, which considerably limits her gross and fine motor abilities. She also has a metabolic disorder that causes her to have varying energy levels. She needs frequent breaks and snacks to give her the energy needed to function throughout each school day. She has a significant cognitive disability that affects her ability to respond to questions or engage in academic tasks. She is nonverbal but uses eye pointing or hand selecting to communicate choice. She also communicates through facial expressions and body movements. Her motor skills are affected by her disability, and she requires a wheelchair for mobility. She uses a nonelectric wheelchair because she is unable to drive it independently. Claire is able to move her arms and hands and grasp objects volitionally but has difficulty reaching for items. These abilities vary considerably day to day based on her physical status. Figure 5.3 provides a positive student profile of Claire. This profile accurately describes her skills and abilities for the purposes of designing appropriate adaptations.

Claire's parents and educational team identified the following educational priorities:

1. Increasing self-initiated communication with peers, general educators, and the public, which would include expressing her preferences and needs, making requests, and responding to questions

2. Increasing comprehension of vocabulary associated with instructional units/topics in eighth grade

3. Increasing her access to and use of a computer

4. Reaching and grasping, assisting in movements guided by others, and moving her legs purposefully

Such background information and a student's priority educational goals should guide the next step in selecting relevant environments for instruction.

What Environment(s) Should Be Selected for Instruction that Promote(s) Achievement of Goals and Are Age-Appropriate and Inclusive?

The second phase of the process is to select the "real world" environments in which the student's educational goals can be accomplished. As a priority for a school-age student, these environments should promote access to and participation in general education curriculum and instruction. In addition, home, community, and work environments in which the student is functioning or will be expected to function in the future should be identified. Environments are determined individually for each student with age-appropriate criteria in mind.

Critical environments for Claire are the core eighth-grade classes (e.g., social studies, language arts, science), exploratories (e.g., art, computer lab, industrial technology), and extracurricular clubs. The mall, local restaurants, the neighborhood pool, and the teen community center are other environments of importance to Claire. As she reaches her later high school years, however, businesses in her community will be targeted for vocational instruction. Right now, however, Claire can still learn skills within local businesses such as Big Mike's Subs®. Some of the reasons for selecting this restaurant as an environment for Claire include the following: 1) She can practice her communication and physi-

Student Profile

Name: _Claire Dickey_   Grade: _8_   School: _Lakota Middle_

Age: _14_   Gender: _Female_

General information	Learning style
Claire lives at home with her parents; her brother Max is away at college. She has attended school with her eighth-grade classmates since kindergarten.	Claire learns best with clear and consistent directions. She works best with familiar people and environments. She comprehends both verbal and pictorial information.
Strengths and interests	**Academic information**
Claire has a great sense of humor and a beautiful smile. She is social and enthusiastic. Relationships are important to her, and she is a responsive friend. She enjoys hanging out with her classmates.	Claire does not read and has not demonstrated counting or one-to-one correspondence. She does, however, respond to yes/no questions consistently.
	She recognizes photos and line drawings of familiar or taught vocabulary.
Communication style	**Behavioral concerns**
Claire responds best when she is face to face with her communication partner. She can eye point or hand select to make choices. She also communicates through body language and facial expressions. She is able to hit a switch to activate a voice output device. She enjoys communicating with peers more than with adults.	We are not concerned about Claire's behavior. She is agreeable and cooperative and extremely patient.
	When Claire is experiencing frustration or fatigue, she brings her fist to her mouth in a repetitive pattern.
Social style	**Other information**
Claire works best with partners and in small groups. Her Circle of Friends meets weekly to eat lunch and plan weekend activities. Claire and her friends enjoy socializing and shopping together.	The members of Claire's Circle of Friends are Wendy, Rebecca, Nicole, Laurie, Eliza, and Stephanie.
	Claire and her parents hope that after high school she lives in a supported apartment with a roommate and has a paid job that she enjoys.

Figure 5.3. A positive student profile of Claire Dickey.

cal motor goals; 2) the restaurant is situated near her school where students her age gather to socialize; 3) Claire enjoys going out to eat, and this restaurant expands her local options; 4) Claire's family eats at the restaurant; 5) the restaurant is located near other community environments in which Claire might learn to function (e.g., a grocery store, a community art studio); and 6) Claire will use the skills to order food across her life span.

What Are the Required Activities and Skills in the Environment?

After a specific environment has been selected, the activities and skills required there are identified by delineating a task that a person without disabilities would engage in and what steps would be taken to perform this task. This task is then broken down into steps to serve as a guide for assessing the performance of the student with disabilities. This outline of sequential skills and the assessment that follows has been referred to as a discrepancy analysis (Brown et al., 1984a; Falvey, 1995). It is important to note that there are multiple ways to do any activity; there is not necessarily a right way, a wrong way, or a universal standard. As this outline of skills is generated, the team should try to select what seems like the most logical and efficient method to carry out the task. An activity sequence completed by a person without disabilities who frequents the restaurant is detailed in the first column of Figure 5.4.

How Does the Student Perform in the Environment?

Next, the team assesses the performance of the student with disabilities by comparing his or her skills with those of a person without disabilities (Brown et al., 1984b; Falvey, 1995). Assessment requires taking the student to the specific environment and using the inventory as the tool for recording performance. The student's response to naturally occurring conditions is recorded. A (+) is noted when the student *does* perform a skill as would a person without a disability. A (-) is recorded when the student *does not* perform the skill as would a person without a disability. Any assistance provided to the student to help him or her participate in the activity also should be noted. An example of the assessment information for Claire's performance at the restaurant is provided in the second column of Figure 5.4. Claire is able to push the automatic door button, wait in line appropriately, establish eye contact with the counter person, hear the cue to order, and participate in carrying food wrappers to the trash. During the assessment, acceptable performance of all other skills required teacher assistance.

In practice, some teachers, paraprofessionals, and other specialists stop problem solving once they recognize that the student with disabilities is able to perform such a limited number of skills. Often, educators decide that the majority of the activity will be done for the student, resulting in the student passively

Activity: *Ordering lunch* Person with a disability: *Claire* Location: Fast food restaurant: *Big Mike's Subs©*

Activity sequence of a person without disabilities	Performance of a person with disabilities	Potential reason for discrepancy	Intervention options
(What does a person without disabilities do in this environment?)	(What does a person with disabilities do in this environment?)	(Why can't the student perform the task the same way a person without a disability would?)	(What should the teacher do to remedy the discrepancy?)
		Student learning factors Instructional factors Environmental factors Physical sensory or motor factors Motivation factors	Teach directly Use instructional adaptation Use material or device adaptation
1. Enters restaurant (through correct door)	(+) Claire is able to push the automatic door switch to open the door. (-) Her teacher pushes Claire's wheelchair through the door of the restaurant.	Physical motor factors	*Instructional adaptation:* Provide personal assistance from a peer.
2. Takes off jacket and gets out wallet	(-) Claire keeps her jacket on. She has difficulty managing many belongings at one time.	Student learning factors Physical motor factors	*Instructional adaptation:* Change the instructional sequence. Claire needs to first remove her jacket and set down her belongings so her hands are free to place order and pay.

(continued)

Figure 5.4. A discrepancy analysis of ordering lunch in a fast-food restaurant. (Key: [-] = does not perform skill as would a person without a disability, [+] = performs skill as would a person without a disability.)

159

Figure 5.4. *(continued)*

Activity sequence of a person without disabilities	Performance of a person with disabilities	Potential reason for discrepancy	Intervention options
3. Walks to counter	(−) Claire uses a nonmotorized wheelchair and is unable to maneuver it independently.	Physical motor factors	*Instructional adaptation:* Provide personal assistance from a peer.
4. Stands/waits in the line	(+) Claire sits in her wheelchair while she waits in line.	No significant discrepancy	No intervention necessary
5. Decides what to order while in line	(−) The teacher determines what Claire will eat.	Student learning factors Instructional factors	*Material or device adaptation:* Use a preselected picture menu with a main dish, side order, and beverage. *Instructional adaptation:* Teach Claire to eye point to her choices.
6. Moves forward in line and steps up to the counter	(−) Claire uses a nonmotorized wheelchair and is unable to maneuver it independently. Her teacher pushed her wheelchair.	Physical motor factors	*Instructional adaptation:* Provide personal assistance from peer.
7. Establishes eye contact with counter person	(+) Claire establishes eye contact.	No discrepancy	No intervention necessary
8. On hearing the natural cue of "May I take your order," person states food choices	(+) Claire hears and appears to understand the cue. (−) but cannot verbally order.	Student learning factors	*Instructional adaptation and material or device adaptation:* Claire's friend will program her voice output device so she will press it to order her food.

160

		Student learning factors	
9. After hearing the cost of the meal, person counts money and pays	(-) Claire is unable to count money.	Student learning factors	*Instructional adaptation:* Claire needs to learn to pay with a predetermined amount of money.
10. Receives change and food places change in pocket	(-) Claire is unable to manage the change and the food at the same time.	Physical motor factors	*Material or device adaptation:* When Claire pays with her paper money, clip a note to it that reads, "To go." *Teach directly:* Then teach Claire to grab the bag and place it on her tray.
11. Gets napkin, straw, and so forth	(-) Claire cannot reach the straws and napkins.	Environmental factors Physical motor factors	*Material or device adaptation:* Teach Claire to push a pre-programmed switch that speaks "Can you place a straw and napkin on my tray?" or *Instructional adaptation:* Ask the manager to put napkins and straws on lower counter.
12. Returns to table with food	(-) Claire uses a nonmotorized wheelchair and is unable to maneuver it independently. Her teacher pushes her wheelchair.	Physical motor factors	*Instructional adaptation:* Personal assistance from peer.

(continued)

161

Figure 5.4. (continued)

Activity sequence of a person without disabilities	Performance of a person with disabilities	Potential reason for discrepancy	Intervention option
13. Eats and converses with tablemates	(-) Claire needs her food prepared and positioned in front of her. (-) She is not verbal so conversation is difficult. She seems uninterested in conversing with the teacher.	Physical motor factors Student learning factors	*Instructional adaptation:* Her friend prepares her food and places it within reach. Students are taught to ask Claire yes-or-no questions about specific topics. *Material or device adaptation:* Teach Claire to use her multiple option output device to initiate and sustain conversation. A set of photos of weekend activities can serve as a conversation point.
14. Cleans up trash, table area	(+) Claire can carry rubbish to garbage area, (-) but needs assistance to put it in the receptacle.	Physical motor factors	*Teach directly:* Teach Claire to sweep trash into the garbage.
15. Uses or checks self in bathroom to clean up	(-) Claire cannot maneuver in the bathroom or correct her appearance if necessary.	Physical motor factors Student learning factors	*Instructional adaptation:* Provide personal assistance from peer.
16. Leaves with friends or says goodbye to friends	(-) Claire does not bid farewell to her friends.	Student learning factors	*Material or device adaptation:* Teach Claire to press a switch that activates a programmed goodbye message.

observing others or being physically manipulated through an experience. The next steps of the adaptation process stimulate more complex problem solving. If a student cannot carry out a portion of the activity, team members must ask why, then move forward to develop systems that will teach, compensate for, or circumvent unsuccessful aspects of performance.

What Are the Student's Performance Discrepancies and What Might Be the Source of These Discrepancies?

After the assessment is conducted in the actual environment, student perform-ance discrepancies or problem areas are identified in relation to how a person without disabilities would function in the environment. That is, using a form such as that found in Figure 5.4, information from Column 2 would be com-pared with the sequence in Column 1. In this way, specific activities and skills in which the student requires instruction or intervention could be identified. The skills for which Claire required assistance are noted with a (-) in Column 2 of Figure 5.4. Claire's key areas of difficulty include mobility within the restau-rant, manipulating her money and lunch items, selecting and ordering food items, and having a means to converse with friends.

Educators must question why these performance discrepancies exist. Piuma and Udvari-Solner found that professionals who were skilled at developing adaptations "engaged in a complex discourse of discriminating questions, in a sense theorizing, making educated guesses about the source of the discrepancy" (1993b, p. 16). These educators used their hunches to engage in a process of elimination and ultimately acted on these to determine the origin or cause of the discrepancy. Five causal categories were identified that could lead to the sys-tematic selection of adaptations:

1. *Student learning factors* pertain to the unique learning characteristics, rate of skill acquisition, preferences, and established patterns of behavior of the student.

2. *Instructional factors* refer to the selection, pacing, and delivery of prompts, cues, and teaching strategies used during the activity.

3. *Physical sensory or motor factors* include aspects that relate to the student's physical status, fine and gross motor abilities, vision, hearing, information processing, and mobility.

4. *Motivation factors* concern the affective elements of the student's behavior, what is reinforcing, or whether the student is expressing lack of interest, frustration, boredom, or fear.

5. *Environmental factors* are the general physical conditions, atmosphere, and organization or use of materials.

Table 5.1 provides a sample list of questions, suggested by Piuma and Udvari-Solner (1993b), that educators should consider to reveal the source of the discrepancy. After considering these questions, a "best guess" as to the reason for the discrepancy can be proposed. In all likelihood, one or more causes will surface and lend direction to the nature of the intervention. The third column in Figure 5.4 shows the potential causes for Claire's discrepancies. In her case, answers to these guiding questions pointed to learning factors and physical/motor issues as key reasons.

What Are the Priority Instructional Objectives for this Student in the Environment?

Drawing from the analysis of the identified discrepancies, instructional priorities can be selected and corresponding objectives written. Information gathered during the assessment allows further refinement of broad educational goals to more context-specific objectives. Considerations in selecting priorities typically include such variables as enhancing participation in current and future integrated environments, increasing social inclusion and interactions with peers, having frequent and multiple applications across environments and activities, maintaining health and vitality, and honoring the student's or family's preference (Rainforth & York-Barr 1997). Claire's assessment indicated several instructional priorities, including that she 1) have a means to communicate her lunch choice, 2) participate in paying for her lunch, 3) manipulate and control her money and materials, and 4) converse with friends during lunch. The broad communication and physical/motor goals previously identified are now more specific to the restaurant environment.

INTERVENTIONS TO ADDRESS PERFORMANCE DISCREPANCIES

Next, team members must decide how the discrepancies and the priority skills will be addressed. Teams must use their knowledge of the student, their inferences as to the cause of the discrepancy, and their collective expertise to select from three intervention options. The decision is then made whether to teach the skill directly (i.e., the way that a person without disabilities would perform the skill), employ an instructional adaptation, or generate material or device adaptations that will enable greater and more independent participation.

Teach Directly

The decision to teach directly is only made when it is feasible for the student to learn and perform the skill as would a person without disabilities. Given Claire's

Table 5.1. Sample questions to determine reasons for performance discrepancies related to various factors

Student Learning Factors

- Has the student been observed performing the same or similar action/sequence in other contexts (i.e., at home, in the community, in the classroom)?
- Does past experience with learning rate, style, and abilities indicate that it is feasible for the student to learn the task as expected?
- Do the student's unique learning characteristics preclude him or her from engaging in specific steps (e.g., the student has a very brief short-term memory and is unable to remember more than one direction at a time)?

Instructional Factors

- Has the instructional sequence been communicated to the student in ways that match his or her primary modalities (e.g., picture sequence, written or verbal directions)?
- Does the student need more time to perform the task than is provided?
- Will the student benefit from more intensive instruction?
- Does the instructional sequence need to be modified? (e.g., Are there too many steps or too few? Do the steps need to be rearranged?)
- Is the pacing of instruction correct for the student? (e.g., Does the student need more latency time between steps to perform correctly?)
- Is the level and type of teacher assistance correct?

Physical, Sensory, or Motor Factors

- If the activity requires the use of specific physical movements, does the student have the necessary fine or gross motor movements in his or her repertoire to complete the task?
- If the student has the necessary basic motor movements and responses, but they are weak, without intention, or disorganized, does the student have the potential to build and strengthen these responses through instruction, practice, and/or therapy services?
- What are the student's preferred movements? Have you selected a way to do the activity that builds on these movements?
- What is the student's endurance level? Can the student's endurance be increased through practice, positioning, or better physical arrangements (e.g., standing versus sitting)?
- Does the student experience any sensory difficulties? Do the nature of these impairments preclude the student from performing any parts of the task? Specifically, does the task have inherent tactile, visual, or auditory cues that must be followed?

Motivation Factors

- Is the environment and activity motivating? If not, is there another location that would be more motivating?
- Would the student be more motivated by working with a different peer or co-worker than with the selected instructor?
- Does the student fall asleep during the task? Is the sleepiness caused by the environment, avoidance, or physical/health reasons?
- Is the work activity scheduled at the optimal time for the student's endurance and interest level?
- Are inappropriate behaviors interfering with performance of required skills (e.g., falling asleep, self-stimulation)?

(continued)

Table 5.1. *(continued)*

- Have proactive behavior strategies been employed within the context of the environment and task?
- Does the student have opportunities to express preferences and choices throughout the work day and are communication attempts (both verbal and nonverbal) acknowledged by the instructor, peers, or co-workers?

Environmental Factors

- Does the student have easy access to the environment and necessary materials?
- Is the immediate work area too confining or cluttered for the student to perform?
- If the student uses a wheelchair and needs to be taken out of the chair during instruction, is there a location where this can be done without bringing undue attention, or can alternative seating be arranged for continued participation in the activity?
- Is the lighting sufficient?
- Is the noise level of the environment tolerated or agreeable to the student?

Source: Piuma, C., & Udvari-Solner, A. (1993b).

performance discrepancies at the restaurant, the team decided to teach her the following skills directly: to reach for, grasp, and place her order on her tray and to sweep her trash into a garbage can when done eating. For Claire, the remaining discrepant skills could be better addressed through the use of both instructional adaptations and adaptive material/devices. In the following sections these adaptations are described, and examples specific to Claire are provided. The fourth column in Figure 5.4 summarizes the interventions determined for Claire.

Employ Instructional Adaptations

Four types of instructional adaptations are considered when teaching skills to students with severe and multiple disabilities: 1) modify skills or activities; 2) modify the physical environment; 3) modify rules, policies, or procedures; and 4) provide personal assistance. These forms of adaptation open up options for educators to alter some aspect of instruction, conditions in the environment, or the way in which people exchange support.

Modify Skills or Activities

This type of adaptation involves changing typical skill sequences or the way the task is done. Certain expectations for performance may be revised or even omitted. In Claire's case, she clearly cannot read the menu and make her choice verbally. Rather than ordering from a written menu, she selects from two picture choices by eye pointing. Here, the need for Claire to verbally state her choice is eliminated and replaced with another pertinent communication skill. Along a similar vein, Claire will go to the restaurant with a predetermined amount of money that will cover her purchases. Because of her cognitive learning characteristics, Claire is not able to count out the correct money denominations in response to the stated cost of a purchase because of her cognitive learning characteristics. By bringing slightly more than the amount of money required for a typical lunch purchase, the need to calculate costs is eliminated from the sequence.

Another instructional adaptation that modifies the skills required is employed during Claire's lunch conversation. In a spontaneous social conversation, partners typically ask and answer a jumble of open-ended questions. Claire's communication difficulties do not allow her to express complex responses on the spot. Consequently, the skills required are modified by teaching her peers to ask a range of yes/no questions about familiar topics to which Claire can affirm or negate with facial expressions.

Furthermore, elements of the activity can be reorganized or combined in ways that facilitate participation. Claire had difficulty managing her belongings in the restaurant while waiting in line to order. The instructional sequence was changed to the following: deposit belongings at a table, organize money and order information, then proceed to the counter to order and obtain a meal.

Modify the Physical Environment

The second type of instructional adaptation reflects adjustments that have been made in the physical surroundings or conditions. The most common examples are accommodations that facilitate accessibility such as curb cuts, ramping entryways to buildings, rearranging furniture to create space for maneuvering a wheelchair, and modifying public transportation vehicles with lifts.

Environmental modifications also relate to conditions such as lighting, noise level, visual and auditory input, and location of materials. For students who experience sensory impairments, physical disabilities, information processing, or communication difficulties, elements of the environment may need to be consciously engineered. Accommodations in this category required by the Americans with Disabilities Act of 1990 (PL 101-336) can be found at http://www.ada.gov.

Claire faced only minimal environmental barriers. The entryway was accessible, and there was sufficient room in the restaurant for maneuvering her wheelchair. A potential environmental adaptation identified in the assessment was to change the location of the straws, napkins, and utensils to a lower counter so that Claire could reach them. A more significant environmental adaptation used in the school environment for Claire was to move a futon couch into the student commons area—a place used by all students to gather and socialize during free periods. The futon offered a location for Claire to get out of her wheelchair and sit or recline in a relaxed position. This age-appropriate environment offered Claire an alternative to an isolated physical therapy room when she needed breaks from her wheelchair.

Modify Rules, Policies, or Procedures

The third type of instructional adaptation requires changes in the usual patterns, practices, or customs of a particular environment. The informal or formal guidelines for typical conduct are relaxed or somehow altered. For example, an implicit rule in most high school classrooms is that students sit at their desks while listening to a lecture. For one student with autism, sitting for any length of time was impossible. In response, the typical rules of conduct were loosened and the student was allowed to move to several different seats at will or even stand next to the teacher during the lecture. Learning continued for all students, but under different classroom policies.

"No food or drink" is a general rule in Claire's eighth-grade classes; however, Claire's metabolic condition necessitates that she have snack and juice breaks periodically to boost her blood sugar. Rather than leaving the class and fragmenting her understanding of the curriculum, Claire is allowed to eat and drink while still engaging in instruction. In the restaurant, a simple but important rule was manipulated. A rule adaptation was employed by having Claire order her food "to go" even though she and her friends intended to eat in the restaurant. By doing so, Claire's order was placed in a bag with silverware and napkin, and a cup cover was placed on her drink. This change allowed Claire to reach for and transfer the bag to her tray rather than manipulate single items and an open drink. In all environments it is important to consider the explicit and implicit social rules that have been constructed and determine if any elements require change to promote a better student/environmental match.

Provide Personal Assistance

A fourth instructional adaptation is to provide assistance to the student. A central tenet in inclusive education is to promote positive interdependence among classmates. Reciprocal (i.e., mutually beneficial) social and academic interactions must be fostered between students with and without disabilities. As a student with disabilities enters the adult world, school relationships translate to connections with employers and co-workers who typically do not have disabilities. These individuals are the natural support systems in school and community environments and can provide unobtrusive personal assistance to students and adults with disabilities.

Providing personal assistance as another type of instructional adaptation may be needed on a temporary or ongoing basis in order for some students to learn skills that they are very unlikely to learn using direct instruction or other adaptations. For example, a student who has not been successful learning to move between high school classes independently may require the assistance of a peer on a long-term basis. In the restaurant example, personal assistance from peers was a logical solution to Claire's mobility issues in the restaurant. In addition, peers were easily taught how to present picture menu choices to Claire, interpret her responses, and program her voice output device. When considering the use of personal assistance, it is necessary that students with and without disabilities be apprised of their roles so that excessive or inappropriate help does not dominate the relationship.

Use Adaptive Materials or Devices

During the problem-solving process to address a student's performance discrepancies, teaching directly or using instructional adaptations may be insufficient. The third intervention option, using adaptive materials or devices, may be called for. This category includes portable objects, equipment, tangible devices, or instructional materials individually designed for the student. These types of adaptations, either commercial or teacher-made, can be employed to compensate for intellectual or physical challenges.

A number of adaptive devices and materials were used in response to Claire's instructional needs in the restaurant. First, the teacher constructed a picture menu representing the actual food items available at Big Mike's Subs®. The promotional pictures used by the restaurant for marketing in the local newspaper were made into individual picture symbol cards. These materials allowed Claire to select a main dish, side order, and beverage when given a choice of two preferred items from each category.

Second, the switch-activated Step-by-Step Communicator, commercially available from AbleNet, was selected for use as a voice output device. Programmed by a peer whom Claire selected, multiple messages totaling 75 seconds in length were recorded in a young woman's voice. Sequentially, Claire could push the switch to communicate her order, request a straw or napkin, make comments or ask questions of her peers during their lunch conversation, and say goodbye.

Third, when Claire paid for her lunch, a typed note was clipped to her money stating, "My order is to go; please place my change in the bag. Thanks!" The counter person read the note and carried out the request, thereby reducing the number of items Claire had to manipulate.

Fourth, Claire brought to the restaurant a small photo album that she and her family update weekly with pictures Claire has taken of events or people. This individualized material serves as a conversation starter with her friends during lunch. These simple, low-tech devices or materials sustain Claire's participation throughout the sequence to use in the restaurant.

Implement and Evaluate the Effectiveness of Instruction

Whether teaching skills directly or using instructional or device adaptations, it is important to remember that direct instruction is necessary. Use of an adaptive device serves only to simplify the task in some way—it does not *teach* the student. In fact, the use of adaptations has been criticized for the not-uncommon practice of substituting adaptive devices for skill development and sometimes causing passive involvement (Ferguson & Baumgart, 1991). Instructional programs that delineate systematic cuing and fading strategies should be designed, implemented, and evaluated. Evaluation criteria for determining the effectiveness of adaptive devices should determine whether the adaptation 1) performs its intended functions, 2) is integrated into the instructional sequence, 3) is accompanied by sufficient instruction to learn the adaptation, 4) facilitates independence or interdependence with same-age peers, 5) results in the least-intrusive assistance, 6) is attractive and safe, 7) "fits" in the specific context, 8) results in acceptable rate and quality of performance, and 9) does not interfere with interactions.

Adaptations to Help Claire Participate in Eighth Grade

Claire spends her entire day with her peers without disabilities in general education environments. She is supported by multiple forms of adaptations during each eighth-grade class period. Several examples are illustrated to demonstrate how these adaptations promote independence and interdependence and allow Claire to participate in meaningful ways with her classmates.

Social Studies

A 15-minute student-led activity opens Claire's eighth-grade social studies class daily. Individuals or pairs of students are assigned to present a current news event from written or electronic media sources. The student(s) presenting the current event must read the article and provide a three-point summary of the primary content. This synopsis then launches an open discussion among class members. Claire uses some of the same instructional adaptations and low-tech devices in this school environment as those identified for the restaurant. Claire and a partner prepare for their presentation of a current event in the following ways. Claire's partner reads the article aloud while periodically jotting down main points. The peer then poses yes/no questions to Claire to select the key points to be included in their summary. Three to four statements are recorded on the Step-by-Step Communicator so that Claire can lead the presentation of the summary. Her partner has also selected several points to communicate. Class members are then free to react to the topic, and an informal discussion takes place facilitated by the social studies teacher. When Claire is expected to present alone, the same preparation sequence occurs the night before class at home with her parents. Figure 5.5 features Claire during a current events session, and the Step-By-Step Communicator is depicted in Figure 5.6a.

Language Arts

In language arts class, Claire is able to fulfill various roles within the classroom context, such as in the creative writing and poetry units. For example, every Friday and during the month of May, the language arts teacher focuses on creative guided writing. The students are asked to write with certain story elements as guidelines. Claire uses a device called an All-Turn-It Spinner with blank overlays (see Figure 5.6b). Students brainstorm lists of characters, environments, exclamations, and nouns and verbs that are simultaneously recorded on Claire's overlays by a peer. Claire then pushes her switch to activate the spinner and

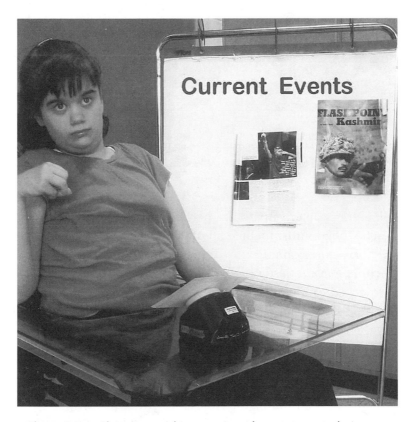

Figure 5.5. Claire engaged in a session of current events during eighth-grade social studies.

a   b

c   d

Figure 5.6. Examples of adapted devices used by Claire in eighth-grade general education classes: a) Step-by-Step Communicator, b) All-Turn-It Spinner, c) Powerlink Environmental Control Unit, and d) Big Red Switch. (Reproduced by permission of AbleNet.)

each story element is determined. The peer then records Claire's selections on the board. Each student must include all of the story elements when writing his or her own story. For example, on one particular day, each student's story needed to include *Captain Cucumber, cruise ship, toilet plunger,* and *sky diving.* The students were asked to include these elements in their story in creative ways while maintaining the proper components of a story: introduction, rising action, climax, falling action, and closing. Claire's participation is clear and has enhanced the experience for everyone. She is a key class member, and students view her as essential in helping them to determine their story.

During a poetry unit, the class was writing haiku poems. With Claire in mind, the instructional grouping was altered to allow students to work in pairs or individually. Claire initiated working with a self-selected partner by eye pointing to a picture of a classmate. She then activated her voice output device, which asked, "Do you want to be my partner?" The student agreed. Claire's partner, who knows her well, wrote three poem topic choices. Claire eye-pointed to the topic of her choice—flowers. Claire's partner continued to write the poem by giving her two choices for each line of the poem. Claire eye-pointed to her selections. When the poem was finished, the two students created a PowerPoint presentation of their haiku. The students took five digital pictures of flowers from the school garden and inserted them into the PowerPoint presentation. A digital camera adapted for single switch use was utilized (see the Adapt JamCam available through ORCCA Technology). Claire used a switch interfaced to the computer to progress through the digital slide presentation that was presented to the class at the end of the poetry unit.

Choir

Claire is in the eighth-grade choir with her peers without disabilities. This choir performs quarterly for the entire school and one evening for parents. They also sing for various community organizations around the city. Much time is spent in class preparing for such performances. One of Claire's many roles in the choir class involves helping the choir to review and assess their performance in preparation for various presentations. Claire's microswitch is hooked up to an environmental control unit called the Powerlink and to a tape recorder. Claire is situated with a peer in the front of the class. The students watch her to determine when to begin singing. She then records the entire musical piece and operates her switch again to rewind and play the song back for the choir to hear. Students listen to their performance and fill out a card for the purposes of assessing their sound. The students determine the musical aspects of the song that need improvement (i.e., diction, pitch, rhythmic accuracy, blend, and dynamics). Students work to perfect their sound, and this activity is repeated for each musical piece. Claire is not a passive member during this activity; instead, she is a central participant responsible for facilitating the rehearsal. The Powerlink is pictured in Figure 5.6c.

Art

During a unit on the study of 20th-century abstract painters, students are assigned to small groups to create a mural in the tradition of a famous artist such as Klee, Miro, or Kandinsky. The painter Jackson Pollock served as the inspiration for Claire's group. Equipped with quarts of paint, paint balls, and paint guns, the group was ready to create! Claire was fitted with a light pointer that could be attached to a hat on her head, her wrist, or her foot. As one of the group's designers, Claire directed the location of the paint splashes and paint bombs with the light streaks or pinpoints created by her volitional movements.

Physical Education

Automatic ball pitchers are available at most discount stores for a reasonable cost. Battery powered and switch operated, these devices discharge balls for slow-pitch games. During physical education Claire consistently acted as the pitcher during games and batting practice. The built-in switch of the pitching device was replaced with a larger micro switch called the Big Red, available through AbleNet. The switch was mounted in various locations so that she could activate it with her head, hands or feet to encourage Claire to use more active physical movements. Figure 5.6d shows the Big Red Switch.

Computer Class

A combination of computer access technology provided a means for Claire to carry out individualized goals in the context of her computer class. All students in the class were expected to advance their keyboarding skills and navigation of the Internet for academic and social purposes.

Claire's computer was equipped with IntelliKeys, an adaptive keyboard. When fitted with overlays and interfaced with the word processing program IntelliTalk, she could select and type preprogrammed phrases into an e-mail or document. During computer lab Claire used this time to e-mail her brother who was away at college and to compose invitations to the weekly Circle of Friends (Falvey, Forest, Pearpoint, & Rosenberg, 1997) meeting with her classmates.

Claire's experiences in eighth grade illustrate key elements of the individualized adaptation process. Careful consideration of Claire, the specific context in which she functions, knowledge of adaptations, and creativity resulted in Claire's enhanced participation and valued membership in an inclusive school community. A useful checklist developed by Reed and Walser (2001) is featured in Figure 5.7. This list outlines areas in which assistive technology or adaptations may be needed and provides an initial menu of options to guide teams in the selection process. A checklist of this type can be attached to the student's IEP so that everyone knows what adaptations were selected.

Vocational Adaptations

The need for vocational adaptations will become central as Claire attends high school and begins job training. Described next are three low-tech vocational adaptations developed for students with intensive support needs similar to Claire's. These devices allowed students to perform real paid jobs in the community. Developed by teaching staff while students were in high school, these adaptations followed them into their postschool job placements.

Assistive Technology Checklist

Writing

Mechanics of Writing

- ☐ Regular pencil/pen
- ☐ Pencil/pen with adaptive grip
- ☐ Adapted paper (e.g., raised line, highlighted lines)
- ☐ Slant board
- ☐ Use of prewritten words phrases
- ☐ Templates
- ☐ Portable word processor to keyboard instead of write
- ☐ Computer with word processing software
- ☐ Portable scanner with word processing software
- ☐ Voice recognition software to word process
- ☐ Other:

Computer Access

- ☐ Keyboard w/accessibility option
- ☐ Word prediction, abbreviation/expansion to reduce keystrokes
- ☐ Keyguard
- ☐ Arm support (e.g., Ergo Rest)
- ☐ Track ball/track pad/joystick w/on-screen keyboard
- ☐ Alternate keyboard (e.g., IntelliKeys, Discover Board, Tash)
- ☐ Mouth stick/Head Master/Tracker w/on-screen keyboard
- ☐ Switch with Morse code
- ☐ Switch with scanning
- ☐ Voice recognition software
- ☐ Other:

Communication

- ☐ Communication board/book with pictures/objects/letters words
- ☐ Eye gaze board/frame
- ☐ Simple voice output device (e.g., BIGmack, Cheap Talk, Voice in a Box, MicroVoice Talk, PictureFrame)
- ☐ Voice output device w/levels (e.g., 6 Level Voice in a box, Macaw, Digivox)
- ☐ Voice output device w/ icon sequencing (e.g., AlphaTalker II, Vanguard, Chatbox)
- ☐ Voice output device w/ dynamic display (e.g., DynaVox, Speaking Dynamically w/laptop computer/Freestyle)
- ☐ Device w/ speech synthesis for typing (e.g., Cannon Communicator, Link Write: Out Loud w/laptop)
- ☐ Software for manipulation of objects
- ☐ Voice recognition software
- ☐ Other:

Recreation & Leisure

- ☐ Toys adapted with Velcro, magnets, handles, and so forth
- ☐ Toys adapted for single switch operation
- ☐ Adaptive sporting equipment (e.g., lighted or beeping ball)
- ☐ Universal cuff/strap to hold crayons, markers, and so forth
- ☐ Modified utensils (e.g., rubber stamps, brushes)
- ☐ Ergo Rest or other arm support for drawing/painting
- ☐ Electronic aids to control TV, VCR, CD player, and so forth
- ☐ Software to complete art activities
- ☐ Games on the computer

(continued)

Figure 5.7. Assistive technology checklist the collaborative team can use to consider and select accommodations for students with severe and multiple disabilities. This checklist can be included in a student's IEP. (From Reed, P., & Walser, P. [2001]. *Wisconsin Assistive Technology Initiative: Assistive Technology Checklist.* Retrieved from http://webschoolsolutions.com/wati/wati-check.htm; adapted by permission.)

Figure 5.7. *(continued)*

Assistive Technology Checklist

Activities of Daily Living (ADLs)

☐ Nonslip materials to hold things in place

☐ Universal cuff/strap to hold items in hand

☐ Color coded items for easier locating and identifying

☐ Adaptive eating utensils (e.g., foam handles, deep sides)

☐ Adaptive drinking devices (e.g., cup with cutout rim)

☐ Adaptive dressing equipment (e.g., button hook, elastic shoe laces, Velcro instead of buttons)

☐ Adaptive devices for hygiene (e.g., adapted toothbrushes, raised toilet seat)

☐ Adaptive bathing devices

☐ Adaptive equipment for cooking

☐ Other:

Mobility

☐ Walker

☐ Grab bars and rails

☐ Manual wheelchair including sports chair

☐ Powered mobility toy (e.g., Cooper Car, GoBot)

☐ Powered scooter or cart

☐ Powered wheelchair w/joystick or other control

☐ Adapted vehicle for driving

☐ Other:

Positioning & Seating

☐ Nonslip surface on chair to prevent slipping (e.g., Dycem)

☐ Bolster, rolled towel, blocks for feet

☐ Adapted/alternate chair, sidelyer, stander

☐ Custom fitted wheelchair or insert

☐ Other:

Reading, Studying, and Math

Reading

☐ Standard text

☐ Predictable books

☐ Changes in text size, spacing, background color

☐ Book adapted for page turning (e.g., page fluffers, 3-ring binder)

☐ Use of pictures/symbols with text (e.g., Picture It, Writing with Symbols 2000)

☐ Talking electronic device/software to pronounce challenging words (e.g., Franklin Speaking Homework Wiz, American Heritage Dictionary)

☐ Single word scanners (e.g., Seiko Reading Pen)

☐ Scanner w/OCR and talking word processor

☐ Electronic books

☐ Other:

Learning/Studying

☐ Print or picture schedule

☐ Low tech aids to find materials (e.g., index tabs, color coded folders)

☐ Highlight text (e.g., markers, highlight tape, ruler)

☐ Recorded material (e.g., books on tape, taped lectures with number coded index, etc.)

☐ Voice output reminders for assignments, steps of task, etc.

☐ Electronic organizers

☐ Pagers/electronic reminders

☐ Single-word scanners

☐ Hand-held scanners

☐ Software for concept development/manipulation of objects (e.g., Blocks in Motion, Toy Store)—may use alternate input device (e.g., switch, touch window)

☐ Software for organization of ideas and studying (e.g., Inspiration, ClarisWorks Outline, PowerPoint)

- ☐ Palm computer
- ☐ Others:

Math

- ☐ Abacus/Math Line
- ☐ Enlarged math worksheets
- ☐ Low tech alternatives for answering
- ☐ Math "Smart Chart"
- ☐ Money calculator and Coinulator
- ☐ Tactile/voice output measuring devices
- ☐ Talking watches/clocks
- ☐ Calculator/calculator with printout
- ☐ Calculator with large keys and/or large display
- ☐ Talking calculator
- ☐ Calculator with special features (e.g., fraction translation)
- ☐ Off-screen/scanning calculator
- ☐ Alternative keyboard (e.g., IntelliKeys)
- ☐ Software with cuing for math computation (may use adapted input methods)
- ☐ Other:

Vision

- ☐ Eye glasses
- ☐ Magnifier
- ☐ Large print books
- ☐ CCTV (closed circuit television)
- ☐ Screen magnifier (mounted over screen)
- ☐ Screen magnification software
- ☐ Screen color contrast
- ☐ Screen reader, text reader
- ☐ Braille translation software
- ☐ Braille printer
- ☐ Enlarged or Braille/tactile labels for keyboard
- ☐ Alternative keyboard with enlarged keys

- ☐ Braille keyboard and note taker
- ☐ Other:

Hearing

- ☐ Pen and paper
- ☐ Computer/portable word processor
- ☐ TDD for phone access with or without relay
- ☐ Signaling device (e.g., flashing light or vibrating pager)
- ☐ Closed Captioning
- ☐ Real Time captioning
- ☐ Computer-aided note taking
- ☐ Screen flash for alert signals on computer
- ☐ Phone amplifier
- ☐ Personal amplification system/ hearing aid
- ☐ FM or loop system
- ☐ Infrared system
- ☐ Others:

Control of the Environment

- ☐ Light switch extension
- ☐ Use of interface and switch to activate battery operated devices
- ☐ Use of interface and switch to turn on electrical appliances (e.g., radio, fan, blender)
- ☐ Radio/ultra sound to remotely control appliances
- ☐ Use of electronic aid to daily living to control environment in connection with an augmentative communication device
- ☐ Other:

Comments:

Stapling Adaptation

Figure 5.8 presents a stapling adaptation created for a high school student to use at a community worksite. It was made of a moveable Plexiglas tray mounted on a stationary base. An electric stapler was placed at the far end of the tray. Letter-sized papers to be stapled were placed in the tray, which kept the pages collated and aligned appropriately. When pushed, the tray moved forward, causing the top, left-hand corners of the papers to be inserted into and stapled by the electric stapler. A spring was mounted under the tray so that the tray returned to its resting position after being pushed and released. The student demonstrated no purposeful arm movement but did occasionally move her arms randomly. A co-worker placed papers to be stapled in the tray, and the student learned to push the tray with firm, controlled movement. As the staple discharged, the adaptation provided immediate feedback to the student regarding the movement.

Stamping Adaptation

The stamping adaptation illustrated in Figure 5.9 was developed for a student to stamp return addresses on various size envelopes at a government office. Prior to development of this adaptation, the student learned to reach and hold a handle extended from a self-inking stamp but was unable to apply sufficient pressure to stamp. The stamping adaptation shown here was made from Plexiglas. The top piece, to which the actual stamp was secured, was attached by two hinges to the base. The resting position for the adaptation was with the stamp raised. Very little pressure was required to depress the stamp onto the brochure. The two pieces of Plexiglas located on the base of the adaptation could be moved to form a guide for varying sizes of envelopes. The stamp position also was adjustable.

Collating Adaptation

The collating adaptation illustrated in Figure 5.10 employed the use of two microswitches. It was made from Plexiglas, two lever microswitches, a metal track, and a control unit for the windshield wiper of a car. The top section of the adaptation consisted of one tray divided into two compartments. The left com-

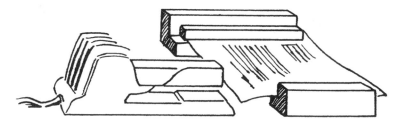

Figure 5.8.   Stapling adaptation. (Developed by Alice Udvari-Solner.)

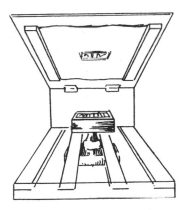

Figure 5.9. Stamping adaptation. (Developed by Kathy Zanella Albright.)

partment held the first page to be collated, and the right compartment contained the second page. The top tray was mounted onto the base in two horizontal tracks. The tray could slide laterally in these tracks. One lever micro switch was placed under each compartment of the top tray, and each was wired to the control unit located behind the device. When each compartment was depressed and the switch was tripped, the tray moved back and forth automatically.

This adaptation was designed by a vocational teacher for a 21-year-old student with severe intellectual and physical disabilities who was in transition from school to a community job. The student had to remain lying on his back in a reclined wheelchair for health reasons. His one reliable movement (besides that of opening and closing his mouth) was extension and flexion of his right elbow. The student wore a forearm and hand splint to keep his wrist near neutral and to prevent his fingers from curling into his palm.

In order to pick up the pages to be collated, Plasti-Tac (a sticky, putty type material) was placed on the tip of his hand splint. To collate a two-page newslet-

Figure 5.10. Collating adaptation. (Developed by Alice Udvari-Solner.)

ter, the student extended his elbow so that the Plasti-Tac landed on the paper in the left compartment. Then he flexed his elbow, thereby pulling the top page off the pile. The weight of his hand touching the first compartment triggered the switch to move the second compartment into reach. As the second compartment moved into place, he waited for the paper to fall off the splint into a box on his right side. He then simply repeated these motor movements, taking papers from compartment two, then compartment one, and so forth, as the device moved back and forth at a speed he controlled with the action of arm flexion.

The ability of this student to collate afforded him the opportunity to work in the community for several mornings a week upon graduation from school. Otherwise, he would have remained at home.

CONSIDERATIONS FOR USING ADAPTATIONS

Team members should consider numerous factors carefully before determining which adaptations individual students should use (Baumgart et al., 1982; Merbler, Hadadian, & Ulman, 1999; Nisbet et al., 1983; York, Nietupski, & Hamre-Nietupski, 1985). These considerations include teaching the skill, soliciting student preference, increasing participation, ensuring longitudinal use, understanding physical movements, and designing and constructing adaptations.

Teaching the Skill

The first consideration when determining the use of an adaptation is whether an adaptation is necessary at all. Sometimes, team members resort to the use of an adaptation before carefully considering or systematically implementing unadapted participation options. If, within a reasonable period of time, a student could learn to engage in an activity without using an adaptation, then the student should be taught to engage in the activity directly and no adaptation should be used. Failure in directly teaching the skill in a reasonable amount of time, however, would indicate the need to consider use of adaptations.

Soliciting Student Preference

A second consideration when contemplating use of an adaptation is preference. Would using an adaptation allow a student to engage in an activity that he or she enjoys or finds interesting? Would use of an adaptation increase participation in activities that are preferred, enjoyed, or highly valued by family members and peers? Research suggests that students have distinct opinions regarding use of classroom and instructional adaptations (Vaughn, Schumm, Niarhos, &

Daugherty, 1993). Student willingness or preference for accommodations is an essential consideration and will likely increase successful implementation (Sax, 2001). Every effort should be made to facilitate participation in preferred, age-appropriate, and family activities. Students who have opportunities to indicate and engage in preferred activities enter into the learning process with greater enthusiasm. For example, one student was taught to choose preferred CDs and to activate the music with a microswitch. He then shared this preferred music with his friends after school at his home.

Increasing Participation

Third, the use of an adaptation should increase active participation in an activity. This is important for many reasons. Active participation can increase responsibility, foster development of age-appropriate attitudes, and increase self-esteem. Increased active participation also can change the perceptions of students with disabilities that are held by people without disabilities. For example, when students with disabilities participate actively in general education classroom routines and activities, this fosters the perception that the students are contributing class members. Using an adaptation to achieve active participation without assistance from an adult can increase a student's opportunity to interact with classmates. Adults assigned to support the students in general education classrooms sometimes unintentionally inhibit interactions between the student and classmates or even between the student and the classroom teacher (Giangreco, Broer, & Edeman, 1999; Giangreco & Doyle, 2002; York, Vandercook, Heise-Neff, & Caughey, 1990).

Postschool functioning in inclusive community environments may occur more frequently when students learn to support each other with the help of adaptations. If the goal of community inclusion for all people is to be achieved, the responsibility cannot rest solely on paid human services support personnel. Instead, support for people with disabilities needs to include assistance from co-workers, employers, and community members. Therefore, during the school years, educational teams must systematically plan for more interdependent participation of students with disabilities with their peers without disabilities. Use of adaptations can be a tool for promoting such interdependence.

Ensuring Longitudinal Use

A fourth consideration is the anticipated longitudinal use of an adaptation. Will it be used in future as well as current environments? Will the adaptation remain age appropriate? For example, the type of picture menu Claire used to select items at a restaurant will most likely remain appropriate throughout Claire's life because she will probably enjoy going to restaurants at any age. An adaptation designed to assist a 2-year-old child in stacking blocks would not remain age appropriate, however, and consequently, it should be used only with young children.

Physical Movement Demands

A fifth consideration is the physical movement demands required from an individual in using an adaptation. Some physical movements (e.g., excessive, rigid extension of the arm), if used to activate adaptations, ultimately can result in more restricted movement and loss of function. If an adaptation promotes more efficient movement patterns, however, the likelihood of developing contractures and deformities is reduced, and long-term functional maintenance is increased. Use of an adaptation sometimes can reduce the physical demands of an activity and enable the individual to move with greater ease and efficiency.

Given the characteristics and abilities of each individual student and the range of instructional priorities, the influence of each of the previously discussed considerations in the adaptation decision-making process will vary. Discussions regarding appropriate use of adaptations require active participation from general educators, special educators, parents, teachers, therapists, classmates, and others to ensure careful consideration of many factors. Appropriate decisions result from the expertise of all educational team members.

Design and Construction Demands

Finally, after considering the myriad pre-existing adaptations on the market, the team may need to build or fashion an adaptation. Design and construction characteristics are another consideration. Some adaptation ideas require more technical expertise than the team has. Is the design of an adaptation so complex or are the construction requirements so time consuming that months will pass before the adaptation is developed? Will frequent repairs be likely? Complex adaptations have a greater likelihood of breakdown. Broken equipment can delay teaching students the skills that will enhance participation in home, school, and community environments.

Determining who is responsible for developing adaptations is a critical decision. As students with more complex needs are educated in general education environments with increasing frequency, anyone on the educational team may take responsibility for developing adaptations. The adaptation is likely to be most successful when all team members are involved in creating, using, and evaluating the adaptation, however.

PRECAUTIONS FOR USING ADAPTATIONS

As with any instructional methodology or educational tool, educators must be thoughtful and use care when employing adaptations. Educators and service providers have in the past made several common and unintentional mistakes when creating or using adaptations. To avoid these potential pitfalls, the following precautions are suggested.

First, remember that each student is an individual and the adaptations that are appropriate and successful with one student may not work with another student. Too often, an adaptation becomes overgeneralized and used with others for whom its use is inappropriate. For example, one student in middle school needed an adaptation for a combination lock, so he was given a key lock. It worked so well for that particular student that the teacher decided to get key locks for all of her students whether they needed them or not. A student in the school was then overheard saying that you could identify all of the students in the school who were in special education by looking at their lockers. As teachers do when designing other individualized instruction, consider the student and his or her particular skills, strengths, and preferences when designing or selecting an adaptation.

A second precaution concerns the critical need for systematic instruction when using adaptations. As mentioned previously, implementation of adaptive devices for some students has resulted in no direct instruction and only passive participation (Ferguson & Baumgart, 1991). Individualized adaptations do not replace the need for instruction. Neither placing a student in a sidelyer nor providing a student with an adaptive device would be considered instruction. For example, when Claire was learning to order from a restaurant, she was not merely handed a picture menu and left to order her food. Intensive instruction was necessary to teach her to accurately eye point to select items. Adaptations are only one means by which performance is enhanced and dependence is decreased. Most students will require direct instruction to learn appropriate use of an adaptation, however.

A third precaution concerns the ongoing evaluation of student performance. Evaluating the student with and without an adaptation will help ensure that appropriate decisions regarding long-term use are made. Adaptations may be required for only short periods of time until student abilities improve. For example, if a student's arm and hand movement improves so that direct activation (i.e., without the use of a microswitch) of an audiotape player is possible, the microswitch should be removed. Similarly, if a student learns to complete a job sequence without a picture sequence, the adaptation should be removed. Adaptations must be modified, replaced, or eliminated based on changes in student abilities and/or task requirements.

A final precaution aimed at reducing frustration for team members and students is to expect that adaptations will require several modifications before an efficient match between student abilities and task demands is attained. Very rarely does the initial adaptation prove most functional. An example is the collating device mentioned in the vocational examples, which underwent more than 10 modifications before optimal efficiency was attained.

SUMMARY

As it is becoming more common for students with severe and multiple physical disabilities to take their rightful place in school, domestic, community, vocational, and recreational environments with their peers without disabilities, educational teams must come together for the purposes of increasing the independence and ease with which students actively participate in such environments. Instructional adaptations can be the key to minimize students' disabilities and maximize opportunities for interaction, participation, and contribution. Selecting and using the right adaptations can be a complex and delicate endeavor. No formula exists when making such decisions. A process does exist for developing individual adaptations with an emphasis on student strengths, knowledge of student goals, and selection of student interventions.

This process should be utilized when selecting and using individualized adaptations. After considering the multitude of preexisting adaptations, teams of professionals may have to design or fashion the adaptive device. Care should be used to avoid potential negative and unintentional problems, however. Useful adaptations are a result of a thoughtful and dedicated team with a willingness to be creative. This combined creativity is necessary to design and use adaptations that allow students to learn, discover, contribute to society, and lead more fulfilling lives. It is critical to remember when working with learners who have complex challenges that student potential is limited only by the bounds of the collective creativity of members of the educational team.

REFERENCES

Americans with Disabilities Act (ADA) of 1990, PL 101-336, 42 U.S.C., §§ 1201 *et seq.*
Baumgart, D., Brown, L., Pumpian, I., Nisbet, J., Ford, A., Sweet, M., Messina, R., & Schroeder, J. (1982). Principle of partial participation and individualized adaptations in educational programs for severely handicapped students. *Journal of The Association for the Severely Handicapped, 7*(2), 17–27.
Brown, L., Branston-McLean, M., Baumgart, D., Vincent, L., Falvey, M., & Schroeder, J. (1979). Utilizing the characteristics of current and subsequent least restrictive envi-

ronments as factors in the development of curricular content for severely handicapped students. *AAESPH Review, 4*(4), 407–424.

Brown, L., Falvey, M., Vincent, L., Kaye, N., Johnson, F., Ferrara-Parrish, P., & Gruenewald, L. (1980). Strategies for generating comprehensive, longitudinal, and chronological age appropriate individualized education programs for adolescent and young adult severely handicapped students. *Journal of Special Education, 14*(2), 199–215.

Brown, L., Shiraga, B., York, J., Zanella, K., & Rogan, P. (1984a). The discrepancy analysis technique in programs for students with severe handicaps. In L. Brown, M. Sweet, B. Shiraga, J. York, K. Zanella, P. Rogan, & R. Loomis (Eds.), *Educational programs for students with severe handicaps* (Vol. XIV, pp. 43–47). Madison, WI: Madison Metropolitan School District.

Brown, L., Shiraga, B., York, J., Zanella, K., & Rogan, P. (1984b). Ecological inventory strategies for students with severe handicaps. In L. Brown, M. Sweet, B. Shiraga, J. York, K. Zanella, P. Rogan, & R. Loomis (Eds.), *Educational programs for students with severe handicaps* (Vol. XIV, pp. 33–41). Madison, WI: Madison Metropolitan School District.

Falvey, M.A. (Ed.). (1995). *Inclusive and heterogeneous schooling: Assessment, curriculum, and instruction.* Baltimore: Paul H. Brookes Publishing Co.

Falvey, M., Forest, M., Pearpoint, J., & Rosenberg, R. (1997). *All my life's a circle.* Ontario, Canada: Inclusion Press.

Ferguson, D.L., & Baumgart, D. (1991). Partial participation revisited. *Journal of The Association for Persons with Severe Handicaps, 16*(4), 218–227.

Giangreco, M.F., Broer, S.M., & Edelman, S.W. (1999). The tip of the iceberg: Determining whether paraprofessional support is needed for students with disabilities in general education environments. *Journal of The Association for Persons with Severe Handicaps, 24*(4), 281–291.

Giangreco, M.F., & Doyle, M.B. (2002). Students with disabilities and paraprofessional supports: Benefits, balance, and band-aids. *Focus on Exceptional Children, 34*(7), 1–12.

Merbler, J., Hadadian, A., & Ulman, J. (1999). Using assistive technology in the inclusive classroom. *Preventing School Failure, 43*(3), 113–117.

Nisbet, J., Sweet, M., Ford, A., Shiraga, B., Udvari, A., York, J., Messina, R., & Schroeder, J. (1983). Utilizing adaptive devices with severely handicapped students. In L. Brown, A. Ford, J. Nisbet, M. Sweet, B. Shiraga, J. York, R. Loomis, & P. VanDeventer (Eds.), *Educational programs for severely handicapped students* (Vol. XIII, pp. 101–146). Madison, WI: Madison Metropolitan School District.

Piuma, C., & Udvari-Solner, A. (1993a). *A catalog of vocational assistive devices for individuals with severe intellectual disabilities.* Madison Metropolitan School District and University of Wisconsin–Madison.

Piuma, C., & Udvari-Solner, A. (1993b). *Materials and processes for developing low cost vocational adaptations for individuals with severe disabilities.* Unpublished manuscript, Madison Metropolitan School District and University of Wisconsin–Madison.

Rainforth, B., & York-Barr, J. (1997). *Collaborative teams for students with severe disabilities: Integrating therapy and educational services* (2nd ed.). Baltimore: Paul H. Brookes Publishing Co.

Reed, P., & Walser, P. (2001). *Wisconsin Assistive Technology Initiative: Assistive Technology Checklist.* http://webschoolsolutions.com/wati/wati-check.htm

Sax, C. (2001). Using technology to support belonging and achievement. In C. Kennedy & D. Fisher (Eds.), *Inclusive middle schools* (pp. 89–103). Baltimore: Paul H. Brookes Publishing Co.

Udvari-Solner, A. (1995). A process for adapting curriculum in inclusive classrooms. In R. Villa & J. Thousand (Eds.), *Creating an inclusive school* (pp. 110–124). Alexandria, VA: Association for Supervision and Curriculum Development.

Udvari-Solner, A. (1996). Examining teacher thinking: Constructing a process to design curricular adaptations. *Remedial and Special Education, 17*(4), 245–254.

Udvari-Solner, A., Villa, R.A., & Thousand, J.S. (2002). Access to the general education curriculum for all: The universal design process. In J.S. Thousand, R.A. Villa, & A.I. Nevin (Eds.), *Creativity and collaborative learning: The practical guide to empowering students, teachers, and families.* (2nd ed., pp. 85–103). Baltimore: Paul H. Brookes Publishing Co.

Vaughn, S., Schumm, J.S., Niarhos, F.J., & Daugherty, T. (1993). What do students think when teachers make adaptations? *Teaching and Teacher Education, 9*(l), 107–118.

York, J., Nietupski, J., & Hamre-Nietupski, S. (1985). A decision making process for using micro switches. *Journal of The Association for Persons with Severe Handicaps, 10*(4), 214–223.

York, J., Vandercook, T., Heise-Neff, C., & Caughey, E. (June, 1990). Does an "integration facilitator" facilitate integration? *TASH Newsletter,* 4.

For More Information

You will notice that our use of written resources is limited in this chapter. The premise of the process to develop adaptations is based on cornerstone concepts in the field of assessing and teaching students with severe and multiple disabilities, which have been noted in this chapter. We believe that Internet sites would prove most useful as resources, however, because they are constantly changed and updated. Here is a sampling of sites organized by topic that were current as of 2004. Readers are also encouraged to access their state assistive technology programs funded by the National Institute on Disability and Rehabilitation Research.

GENERAL

ABLEDATA
8455 Colesville Road
Suite 935
Silver Spring, MD 20918
800-227-0216
http://www.abledata.com

Assistive Technologies: A Guide to Resources, Organizations, and Research
http://www.nal.usda.gov/ttic/assist/atint.htm

Alliance for Technology Access
2175 East Francisco Boulevard
Suite L
San Rafael, CA 94901
800-455-7970
http://www.ataccess.org

Closing the Gap
http://www.closingthegap.com

National Center to Improve Practice
http://www.edc.org/FSC/NCIP

Trace Research and Development Center
http://www.trace.wisc.edu

AUGMENTATIVE AND ALTERNATIVE COMMUNICATION (AAC)

AbleNet
1081 Tenth Avenue Southeast
Minneapolis, MN 55414-1312
800-322-0956
http://www.ablenetinc.com

Adaptivations, Inc.
2225 W. 50th Street
Suite 100
Sioux Falls, SD 57105
800-723-2783
http://www.adaptivation.com

Assistive Technology Inc.
7 Wells Avenue
Newton, MA 02459
800-793-9227
http://www.assistivetech.com

Creative Communicating
Post Office Box 3358
Park City, UT 84060
435-645-7737
http://www.creative-comm.com

DynaVox Systems
2100 Wharton Street
Suite 400
Pittsburgh, PA 15203
800-344-1778
http://www.dynavoxsys.com

Enabling Devices
Toys for Special Children
385 Warburton Avenue
Hastings-on-Hudson, NY 10706
800-832-8697
http://www.enablingdevices.com

Frame Technologies
W681 Pearl
Oneida, WI 54155
920-869-2979
http://www.frame-tech.com

Mayer-Johnson Co.
Post Office Box 1579
Solana Beach, CA 92075-7579
619-550-0084
http://www.mayer-johnson.com

Prentke Romich Company
1022 Heyl Road
Wooster, OH 44691
800-262-1984 x302
http://www.prentrom.com

Saltillo Communication Products
2143 Township Road 112
Millersburg, OH 44654
800-382-8622
http://www.saltillo.com

Tash Inc.
3512 Maryland Court
Richmond, VA 23233
800-463-5685
http://www.tashinc.com

ZYGO Industries, Inc.
Post Office Box 1008
Portland, OR 97207-1008
800-234-6006
http://www.zygo-usa.com

COMPUTER ACCESS, READING, AND WRITING

Academic Software, Inc.
331 West 2nd Street
Lexington, KY 40507
606-233-2332/800-VIA-ADLS
http://www.acsw.com

AlphaSmart
20400 Stevens Creek Boulevard
Suite 300
Cupertino, CA 95014
408-252-9400
http://www.alphasmart.com

Don Johnston, Inc.
26799 West Commerce Drive
Volo, IL 60073
800-999-4660
http://www.donjohnston.com

Franklin Electronic Publishers
One Franklin Plaza
Burlington, NJ 08016-4907
http://www.franklin.com

Freedom Scientific, Inc.
Post Office Box 215
Moffett Field, CA 94035-0215
800-444-4443
http://www.arkenstone.org

IntelliTools
55 Leveroni Court, Suite 9
Novato, CA 94949
800-899-6687
http://www.intellitools.com

Schwab Learning
http://www.schwablearning.com

21st Century Eloquence
http://www.voicerecognition.com/

DAILY LIVING SITES

Adaptability
75 Mill Street
Post Office Box 515
Colchester, CT 06415-0515
800-288-9941
http://www.adaptability.com

Access with Ease
1755 Johnson
Post Office Box 1150
Chino Valley, AZ 86323
http://store.yahoo.com/capability/index.html

Ali Med
297 High Street
Post Office Box 9135
Dedham, MA 02026
800-225-2610/617-329-2900
http://www.alimed.com/

Homecare Products
15824 SE 269th Street
Kent, WA 98042
800-333-4000
http://www.homecareproducts.com

Independent Living Aids
27 East Mall
Plainview, NY 11803
800-537-2118; 516-752-8080
http://www.independentliving.com

Maxi Aids
Post Office Box 3209
42 Executive Boulevard
Farmingdale, NY 11735
800-522-6294; 634-752-0521
http://www.maxiaids.com

Rubbermaid Health Care Products
1147 Akron Road
Wooster, OH 44691-6000
http://www.rubbermaid.com

Sammons Preston Rolyan
An Ability One Company
4 Sammons Court
Bolingbrook, IL 60440
800-323-5547
http://www.sammonspreston.com

RECREATION AND LEISURE

Linda J. Burkhart
6201 Candle Court
Eldersburg, MD 21784
http://www.lburkhart.com

ORCCA Technology, Inc.
317-B South Ashland Avenue
Lexington, KY 40502
606-268-1635
http://www.orcca.com

RJ Cooper and Associates
24843 Del Prado
Suite 283
Dana Point, CA 92629
800-752-6673
http://www.rjcooper.com

POSITIONING AND EQUIPMENT

ADAS, LLC
2728 South Cole Road
Boise, ID 83709
800-208-2020; 208-362-8001
http://www.ad-as.com

Rifton
Post Office Box 901
Rifton, NY 12471-0901
800-777-4244
http://www.rifton.com

SOFTWARE

Attainment Company
Post Office Box 930160
Verona, WI 53593-0160
800-327-4269
http://www.attainmentcompany.com

Edmark Corporation
Post Office Box 97021
Redmond, WA 98073-9721
800-362-2890
http://www.edmark.com

Slater Software
351 Badger Lane
Guffey, CO 80820
877-306-6968
http://www.slatersoftware.com

SoftTouch, Inc.
4300 Stine Road
Suite 401
Bakersfield, CA 93313
877-763-8868
http://www.funsoftware.com

VISION

Ai Squared
Post Office Box 669
Manchester Center, VT 05255
802-362-3612
http://www.aisquared.com

LS & S Group, Inc.
Post Office Box 673
Northbrook, IL 60065
800-468-4789
http://www.lssgroup.com

CHAPTER 6

Sensorimotor Development

Implications for the Educational Team

Paula E. Forney and Kathryn Wolff Heller

Understanding the interaction of the sensory and motor systems in the development of functional movement is critical for families, educators, and therapists. Children interact with their environment through sensory and motor exploration and, thereby, learn about their world, which results in perceptual, language, social, and cognitive development as well as advancement in sensorimotor skills (Campbell, Vander Linden, & Palisano, 2000; Forney, 2001; Larin, 2000). For example, children learn about water through a variety of different contexts and activities: playing in the bathtub, washing hands at the sink, getting a drink, splashing in a puddle, or swimming in a pool. In addition to learning what water is, children performing these activities are simultaneously learning self-help skills such as pouring or drinking from a cup, cognitive skills involving space and mass, language skills including labeling objects and actions, social skills such as imitation and turn-taking, and a wealth of fine and gross motor skills. When infants and young children are unable to experience typical sensory and motor experiences at critical periods in their development, whether through environmental deprivation, developmental delay, or physical disability, many areas of development can be affected. In addition, children and adults with atypical sensorimotor abilities may be unable to accomplish many tasks without appropriate adaptations or interventions.

The sensorimotor system refers to the combination of the sensory and motor systems that work closely together within the nervous system. The nervous system is made up of the brain and the spinal cord (comprising the central nervous system or CNS) and the many nerves that branch out from the spinal cord throughout the body (the peripheral nervous system) to form a communication system regulating incoming sensory and outgoing motor information. Sensory information from many different sources (e.g. vision, touch) provides input to the nervous system, which, in turn, regulates the development and the coordination of functional or adaptive movements in response to the various incoming sensory stimuli. For example, tactile receptors on the skin provide information about touch, pressure, pain, and temperature, whereas receptors in the muscles, joints, and surrounding tissues give information on body position as movement occurs. In the inner ear, the vestibular system responds to movement of the body through space. Taste receptors on the tongue contribute important information related to the development of eating skills. Smell, hearing, and vision are all distance senses contributing important sensory information that helps to arouse, orient, and direct movement. As all of these various forms of sensory information reach the brain, the information is processed and organized, and this typically results in a functional movement response that addresses the environmental demand.

Consider this example. If a person is handed an ice cream cone, receptors in the eyes indicate the location of the ice cream cone in space. Enjoyable past experiences with ice cream, made through taste receptors and memory connections, then motivate the person to reach for the cone. The sensory receptors in the joints and muscles of the arm and hand, with additional visual input, give information about reaching accurately to make contact with the ice cream cone. The tactile receptors in the hand and fingers then provide information about the texture and weight of the ice cream cone and work together with the joint and muscle receptors in the hand and fingers to adjust the grip on the cone so as not to crush it but still maintain a hold on it. Vision, joint, and muscle receptors and the tactile system then continue to work together to guide the cone to the mouth where the taste and touch receptors in and around the mouth (in conjunction with sense of smell) sense the taste, temperature, and texture of the ice cream and the cone. Finally, the receptors in the joints and muscles around the mouth help adjust the type and force of movement of the oral muscles in order to lick the ice cream, bite and chew the cone, and swallow.

Refinement of children's movement skills occurs over time because of a continual interplay between multiple sensory inputs and their resultant motor outputs and the ongoing adjustments made by the nervous system connections in order to achieve optimal motor control and motor performance (Bradley, 2000; Keating, Spence, & Lynch, 2002; Summers, 1992). In the example of the ice cream cone, a young child will require multiple experiences eating an ice cream cone before he or she perfects all of the sensorimotor skills required to be efficient at this skill. The child may drop or crush the cone or may experience a very messy eating experience before he or she refines the skills necessary to handle all sensorimotor aspects of the task optimally. Some children and adults with severe and multiple disabilities may not be able to perform complicated sensorimotor tasks, such as eating an ice cream cone, without using adaptive strategies.

It is important that the educational team, including families as well as professionals, understands sensorimotor development and uses this knowledge when assessing children's skills, selecting desired functional outcomes, and planning strategies to achieve those outcomes. This chapter first describes sensorimotor systems and sensorimotor development and follows with a discussion of atypical sensorimotor development in students with severe and multiple disabilities. Therapy models and methods are discussed next, followed by educational assessment and strategies to address sensorimotor issues across functional tasks and natural learning environments.

DEVELOPMENT AND FUNCTION OF THE SENSORIMOTOR SYSTEMS

The 1970s heralded an extraordinary burst of new scientific information on the development and organization of sensory systems in mammals. Researchers recognized that sensory receptors and their associated pathways within the nervous system provided the interface between the physical world of sensory stimuli and the motor responses of the organism. Study of sensory system development during the 1990s and beyond is now providing answers to how and why sensory processing is acquired (Coleman, 1990b; Keating, Spence, & Lynch, 2002; Shumway-Cook & Woollacott, 2001; Summers, 1992).

Sensory stimulation from the environment, whether it is a noise, something we see, a touch, and so forth, acts on the receptors of that particular sensory system to create an impulse in the central nervous system. The stimulus has to be strong enough for the individual to register it and this threshold for stimulus recognition is particular to the individual, based on both genetic makeup and on previous sensory experiences. For example, some individuals register pain at a much lower threshold than others simply due to inborn factors. Based on previous sensory experiences, individuals who work in relatively noisy environments may learn to ignore sound stimuli of certain frequency or loudness that would typically be distracting (e.g., voices heard in normal conversation around the work station).

Sensory stimulation usually leads either to arousal (when the individual alerts to or notices the presence of the stimulus) or to discrimination of the stimulus (which is usually organizing or calming to the individual). These responses are, in part, based on the individual's previous sensory experiences. Response to sensory stimulation is usually either protective in nature to avoid danger or injury (e.g., quickly moving one's hand off of a hot object) or is part of a functional, adaptive response to the stimulation (e.g., an infant turning his head toward his mother as he hears her voice). Table 6.1 provides information on the types of sensory stimulation related to each of the sensory systems that bring about arousal/alerting versus discriminating/organizing responses (Dunn, 1996). When planning programs for students with severe and multiple disabilities, as discussed later in this chapter, team members can use this information to select sensory inputs and activities that aid in achieving student outcomes. Table 6.2 outlines how each sensory system affects the individual's skill development in various movement, perceptual, and cognitive areas (Blanche, Botticelli, & Hallway, 1995). The potential long-term effects of sensory processing impairments on children's movement, self-esteem, and learning are covered in Table 6.3 (Blanche et al., 1995).

Each of the sensory systems will be explored briefly on an individual basis first and then followed by a discussion of motor development and how the sensory and motor systems work together to coordinate movement responses.

THE SENSORY SYSTEMS

The tactile (somatosensory), proprioceptive, vestibular, taste (gustatory), smell (olfactory), visual, and auditory systems all work together to provide individuals with information about themselves and their world. Most of the developmental maturation associated with the sensory systems occurs early in life, prior to the preschool years. In the first few years of life, the brain combines input received from all of the sensory systems to provide important information about the body and its relationship to other people and objects in the environment. These multiple sensory experiences provide the groundwork for the future development of motor, perceptual, self-help, social, cognitive, and language skills (Campbell, 2000; Colson & Dworkin, 1997; Dunn, 1996; Inamura, 1998).

The Tactile System

The tactile system, sometimes referred to as the *somatosensory* system, is the sense of touch. Tactile information is available to the fetus early in embryonic development as he or she moves within the uterine environment. The tactile system responds to various types of touch input through receptors in the skin. These receptors differ in type, number, and distribution, depending on the area of the body considered. For example, some receptors respond to light touch whereas others respond to firm touch—pressure, pain, or temperature. A greater number

Table 6.1. Arousal/alerting and discriminating/organizing descriptors of the sensory system

Sensory system	Arousal/alerting descriptors[a]	Discriminating/organizing descriptors[b]
For all systems	*Unpredictability:* The task is unfamiliar; the child cannot anticipate the sensory experiences that will occur in the task	*Predictability:* Sensory pattern in the task is routine for the child, such as with diaper changing—the child knows what is occurring and what will come next
Somatosensory	*Light touch:* Gentle tapping on skin; tickling (e.g., loose clothing making contact with skin) *Pain:* Brisk pinching; contact with sharp objects; skin pressed in small surface (e.g., when skin is caught between chair arm and seat)	*Touch pressure:* Firm contact on skin (e.g., hugging, patting, grasping); occurs both when individual touches objects or people or when they touch individual
	Temperature: Hot or cold stimuli (e.g., iced drinks, hot foods, cold hands, cold metal chairs)	*Temperature:* Neutral temperature (e.g., of environment, foods)
	Variability: Changing characteristics during the task (e.g., putting clothing on requires a combination of tactile experiences)	*Repetition:* Characteristics of tasks stay generally the same (e.g., repetition of a game such as rolling a ball back and forth)
	Short duration stimuli: Tapping, touching briefly (e.g., splashing water)	*Long duration stimuli:* Holding, grasping (e.g., carrying a child in your arms)
	Small body surface contact: Using only fingertips to touch something	*Large body surface contact:* Includes holding, hugging; also holding an object with entire palmar surface of hand
Vestibular	*Rotary head movement:* Head moving in an arc (e.g., spinning in a circle, turning head side to side)	*Linear head movement:* Head moving in a straight line (e.g., bouncing up and down, going down the hall in a wheelchair)
	Head position change: The child's head orientation is altered (e.g., pulling the child up from lying on the back to sitting)	*Repetitive head movement:* Movements that repeat in a simple sequence (e.g., rocking in a rocker, slow head/body movements)
	Speed change: Movements change velocity (e.g., the teacher stops to talk to another teacher when pushing the child to the bathroom in a wheelchair)	
	Direction change: Movements change planes (e.g., bending down to pick up something from the floor while carrying the child down the hall)	

(continued)

Table 6.1.　*(continued)*

Sensory system	Arousal/alerting descriptors[a]	Discriminating/organizing descriptors[b]
Proprioceptive	*Quick stretch:* Movements that pull on the muscles (e.g., briskly tapping on a belly muscle)	*Sustained tension:* Steady, constant action on the muscles, pressing on or holding the muscle (e.g., using heavy objects during play)
Visual	*High intensity:* Visual stimulus is bright (e.g., looking out the window on a bright day)	*Low intensity:* Visual stimulus is subdued (e.g., cool colors, lowered illumination)
	High contrast: Great difference between the visual stimulus and its surrounding environment (e.g., cranberry juice in a white cup)	*High similarity:* Small difference between the visual stimulus and its surrounding environment (e.g., classroom desk located in area without visual distraction on walls)
	Variability: Changing characteristics during the task (e.g., a television program is variable visual stimulus)	
Auditory	*Variability:* Changing characteristics during the task (e.g., a person's voice with intonation)	*Rhythmicity:* Sounds repeat in a simple sequence/beat (e.g., humming, singing nursery songs)
		Constancy: The stimulus is always present (e.g., a fan noise)
		Noncompetitiveness: The environment is quiet (e.g., the bedroom when all is ready for bedtime)
	High intensity: The auditory stimulus is loud (e.g., siren, high volume radio)	*Low intensity:* The auditory stimulus is subdued (e.g., whispering)
Gustatory/ Olfactory	*Strong intensity:* The taste/smell has distinct qualities (e.g., spicy food, odor of cinnamon)	*Mild intensity:* The taste/smell has nondistinct or familiar qualities (e.g., cream of wheat, odor of mom's perfume)

From Dunn, W. (1996). The sensorimotor system: A framework for assessment and intervention. In F.P. Orelove & D. Sobsey, *Educating children with multiple disabilities: A transdisciplinary approach* (3rd ed., pp. 40–41). Baltimore: Paul H. Brookes Publishing Co; adapted by permission.

[a]Tend to generate "noticing" behaviors; the individual's attention is momentarily drawn toward the stimulus. Can become part of a functional behavior sequence. May also increase general body muscle tone. Biobehavioral state = arousal.

[b]Create temporal and spatial qualities of body and environments that can be used to create goal-directed movement. May also decrease general body muscle tone. Biobehavioral state = becoming calm, organized.

of tactile receptors are also distributed in a more dense fashion in certain areas of the body where fine tactile discrimination is required (e.g., face, hands, feet). Information from these tactile receptors is transmitted from the body surface to the brain, where it is combined with other sensory information. The brain then sends messages back to muscles to react to the touch stimulus, typically with movement (Stein, Grillner, Selverston, & Stuart, 1997).

Table 6.2. How the sensory systems affect the development and integration of input for skill development.

Sensory system	Modulation/ regulation	Discrimination	End product
Gustatory/ olfactory system	Emotional comfort Rhythms	Feeding	Self-esteem
Tactile system	Emotional comfort Mother–infant bond Oral comfort	Feeding Stereognosis (knowing where touch occurs) Body perception/scheme Oral-motor skills	Self-esteem Praxis (ability to organize and conceptualize a new motor activity) Ability to concentrate
Proprioceptive system	Emotional comfort Gravitational security Comfort with changes in position Comfort in weight-bearing patterns (proximal joint stability)	Calibrating spatial and temporal frames of reference Body percept/maps Grading the force of contraction Timing of movement Perception of movement Movement feedback (internalization of movement patterns) Muscle tone Righting reactions Postural control	Coordinated movement Praxis Perception of space Perception of time Organization of behavior into meaningful activities
Vestibular system	Emotional comfort Gravitational security Enjoyment when moved in space	Equilibrium reactions Postural control Muscle tone Oculomotor control Bilateral motor coordination Timing/sequencing	Organization of movement with other sensory information Praxis Visual skills during movement
Visual system	Orientation to the environment	Oculomotor control Visual perception (space, depth, etc.)	Visual skills during movement
Auditory system	Orientation to the environment	Auditory perception (sound localization, discrimination, etc.)	Language

From Blanche, E.I., Boticelli, T.M., & Hallway, M.K. (1995). *Combining neuro-developmental treatment and sensory integration principles: An approach to pediatric therapy.* San Antonio, TX: Therapy Skill Builders; adapted by permission.

Table 6.3. The long-term effects of sensory processing impairments on children's movement, self-esteem, and learning

Original problems/ sensory processing impairments	Compensations/ coping strategies	Consequences/ long-term impairments
Tactile modulation impairments	Avoidance of social situations that require tactile contact	Social isolation
Poor modulation of tactile and/or proprioceptive input	Seeking large amounts of proprioceptive input such as that received when pushing, pinching, hitting, throwing, and so forth	Labeled as aggressive Behavior problems Acting out
Vestibular processing impairments—inadequate postural control	Leaning on hands Sluggish posture	Rounded upper back
Gravitational insecurity	Staying close to the ground Dragging feet Staying close to supports Avoidance of challenging situations	Apprehension Insecurity Avoidance of challenging situations
Poor constructional skills	Avoidance of manipulative play Avoidance of constructional toys	Low frustration tolerance when presented with activities that require two- and three-dimensional copying
Poor motor planning skills	Avoidance of activities that require motor coordination, such as sports	Inadequate physical fitness Overweight Feelings of inadequacy

From Blonche, E.I., Boticelli, T.M., & Hallway, M.K. (1995). *Combining neuro-developmental treatment and sensory integration principles: An approach to pediatric therapy* (p. 7). San Antonio: TX: Therapy Skill Builders; adapted by permission.

In early development, tactile stimulation plays an important role in facilitating early movements and enabling early interactions with the environment. Tactile input is the stimulus for many of the early motor reflexes that allow infants to react to and interact with the environment. The palmar grasp reflex is one example of these reflexes. When the infant's palm is touched in the first few months of life, the tactile stimulus elicits a motor response in which the infant's fingers flex around the object in his or her palm (see Figure 6.1). This response is not intentional on the infant's part at this stage, but it is an important precursor for the later development of a more mature, intentional grasp.

Figure 6.1. Palmar grasp reflex. (From Alexander, R., Boehme, R., & Cupps, B. [1993]. *Normal development of functional motor skills: The first year of life* [pp. 46–199; illustrations by J. Boehme]. Tucson, AZ: Therapy Skill Builders; reprinted by permission.)

Another important example of these early tactile-based reflexes is the rooting reflex. In this case, a touch stimulus to the infant's lower face near the mouth results in the head turning toward the stimulus in order to locate the nipple and get nourishment. Both of these tactile-based reflex movement patterns, and others, provide the infant with tactile input that leads to early movement responses, which, in turn, result in ongoing sensory feedback and resultant adaptive movements. These tactile–movement loops provide the young child with information about the environment and his or her own movements that are critical for developing sensorimotor control (Bradley, 2000; Dunn, 1996).

Tactile stimulation not only provides one of the primary inputs for developing control over body movements but also has been found to contribute to behavioral state change and psychosocial development. Firm touch (as is used in some massage techniques) can be calming to the central nervous system, whereas light touch tends to be alerting or arousing. When deprived of tactile stimulation, organisms tend not to initiate interactions with other organisms or their environments and may fail to thrive or develop in a typical way. The tactile system plays a critical part in the development of the young child and in maintaining homeostasis throughout life (Heller, Alberto, Forney, & Schwartzman, 1996; Inamura, 1998).

Many children with severe and multiple disabilities have tactile problems, either a decrease in tactile sensitivity, as is sometimes seen in cerebral palsy, or an increase in tactile sensitivity, as seen in tactile defensiveness. In addition, children with severe and multiple disabilities frequently cannot generate the variety of gross and fine motor tactile experiences on their own that their peers who are typically developing can. Children with visual impairments or deafblindness need rich experiences with tactile exploration in order to take in information about their world that they are not able to receive through the visual or auditory systems (see Chapter 10). The tactile system may be one of the primary learning channels for the educational team to consider when planning strategies to achieve functional outcomes for children with severe and multiple disabilities.

The Proprioceptive System

The proprioceptive system is responsible for providing the individual with awareness of body position in space. The muscles, joints, and tissues surrounding the joints (i.e., the joint capsules) house the receptors of the proprioceptive system. These receptors respond to the ongoing repositioning of the body in space during movement and assist with supporting the movement through regulation of muscle tension and by providing the individual with awareness of body position. Stretch and compression activate these receptors, so weight-bearing tasks such as propping on elbows in a prone position or standing and walking activate proprioceptors in the arms and legs, respectively. In addition, tasks such as bouncing, pushing, pulling, and so forth also activate the receptors through stretching or compressing joint structures. Many of the young child's typical exploratory activities naturally stimulate the proprioceptive system and bring about awareness and control of body movements in space (Dunn, 1996; Shumway-Cook & Woollacott, 2001).

Depending on what proprioceptive receptors are stretched or compressed and the force applied, information is supplied to the nervous system to bring about awareness of where the various parts of the body are in space and how fast they are moving. This information also helps the body to adjust the tension in specific muscles in order to ensure efficient movement or to protect the body from extreme ranges of movement and potential resultant injury (Bloedel, Ebner, & Wise, 1996; Green, Mulcahy, & Pountney, 1995).

Children with severe and multiple disabilities, particularly those with disorders of muscle tone, often receive misinformation from their muscles and tendons concerning proprioception. Children with high muscle tone may receive too much proprioceptive information and children with low muscle tone may receive too little, making it difficult for them to modulate movements to support functional actions (Younger, 1999). Physical and occupational therapists can provide information on appropriate strategies to assist children's gross and fine functional movements, how to position children for optimal function, and how to adapt materials or environments to encourage functional movements. Speech-language pathologists can provide similar information on strategies, positioning, and adaptations to encourage functional movements related to communication and feeding. Information from the entire educational team, including therapists, educators, and families, will need to be shared in order to plan for and provide consistent instructional and environmental supports to children with severe and multiple disabilities to promote functional movement and appropriate proprioceptive feedback.

The Vestibular System

The vestibular system provides information about movements of the head in space and helps the individual to maintain an upright position. This sensory system is housed in the inner ear, along with the organ of hearing, the cochlea. Encased in bone, the vestibular receptors include the utricle and saccule and the three semicircular canals, in pairs, one for each side of the body (see Figure 6.2). The utricle lies in the horizontal plane, whereas the saccule lies in the vertical plane. Their combined role is to detect the position of the head with respect to gravity (whether the head is upside down, tilted, and so forth), but the receptors also respond to quick tilting movements of the head and to rapid linear acceleration and deceleration. Motion sickness is caused primarily by prolonged, fluctuating stimulation of the utricle and saccule (Anniko, 1990; Baloh & Halmogyi, 1996).

The semicircular canals are half-circles that lie at right angles to each other. Because the semicircular canals are oriented in each of the major planes of the body, these receptors are in a position to sense specific directions of head movement and rotation.

In the utricle, saccule, and semicircular canals are specialized hair cells that protrude into the fluid that surrounds them. Stated simply, as the head moves, the fluid also moves, causing the hair cells to bend. Depending on the direction that the head is moving and, to some extent, the speed of that movement, specific hair cells move in particular patterns, providing specific information to

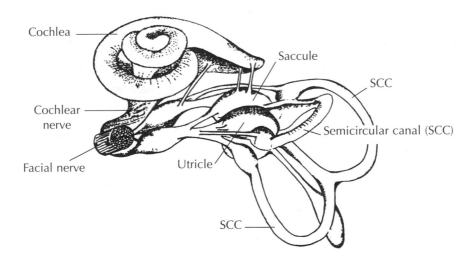

Figure 6.2. The vestibular system. (From Coleman, J.R. [Ed.]. Copyright © 1990. This material is used by permission of Wiley-Liss, Inc., a subsidiary of John Wiley & Sons, Inc. *Development of sensory systems in mammals.* New York: John Wiley & Sons, p. 343.)

the nervous system, which helps the individual to recognize his or her orientation in space (Baloh & Honrubia, 2001; Lysakowski, McCrea, & Tomlinson, 1998).

The vestibular system communicates information to a number of different areas within the nervous system that work together to produce organized, sequenced, and well-timed postural adjustments and body movements. Connections occur between the vestibular system and the following areas: 1) the extensor muscles of the body (those muscles that keep the body and limbs straight in order to facilitate maintenance of upright posture); 2) the muscles of the neck to influence changes in head position in response to movement; 3) the eye muscles to coordinate eye gaze with head movements and to orient one visually to the environment during movement; 4) the part of the brain called the *cerebellum,* which assists with timing and force of adaptive movements; and 5) the vestibular receptors on the opposite side of the body to coordinate sensory input and motor response from both sides of the body (Baloh & Honrubia, 2001; Lysakowski et al., 1998; Parham & Mailloux, 1996).

In addition to playing a major role in coordinating balance, posture, and movement control, the vestibular system also sends input to other areas in the brain that are known to control biobehavioral state. Biobehavioral state refers to the individual's level of arousal, the ability to notice and respond to information in the environment. Certain forms of vestibular stimulation (e.g., fast rotation such as spinning in a swing; irregularly timed, directed movement such as bouncing or swinging a child in your arms at varying speeds or in different directions) can bring about arousal and awareness of environmental stimuli in the nervous system, whereas other types of vestibular stimulation (e.g., slow, rhythmical, repetitive movements such as rocking) are calming and organizing to the nervous system (Fisher, Murray, & Bundy, 1991; Inamura, 1998).

Body movements in many different planes and at many different speeds activate the vestibular system, which then generates appropriate muscle actions that keep the individual upright against gravity, even when balance/equilibrium is threatened. Many children with severe and multiple disabilities have a paucity of independent movements that stimulate the vestibular system. Therefore, the educational team must provide movement experiences that tap this important and multidimensional sensory system, both for learning experiences and to help with regulation of biobehavioral state and arousal. For example, for a child who tends to be lethargic, careful use of controlled bouncing, swinging, or spinning activities prior to a lesson in the classroom could help increase the child's arousal and attention to task, whereas the parents of a different child who is often in an active, aroused state may find slow rocking in a rocking chair assists with calming the child before bedtime.

One caution concerning vestibular system stimulation should be noted. Because of the previously mentioned multiple connections that the vestibular system has within the central nervous system, both biobehavioral state and muscle tone can be affected by vestibular stimulation. Vestibular stimulation that brings about arousal and awareness of environmental stimuli in the nervous system can also result in an increase in overall body muscle tone, whereas vestibular stimulation that is calming and organizing to the nervous system can result in an overall decrease in body muscle tone. It is, therefore, critical that the educational team recognizes the dual nature of vestibular system effects on both muscle tone and biobehavioral state and observes the individual's responses to stimuli to ensure that desired results are being obtained (Fisher et al., 1991; Inamura, 1998). For example, it is possible that some individuals with low muscle tone may be easily overaroused (e.g., a young child with Down syndrome who is easily overstimulated by multiple sensory inputs such as movement, touch, sound, and visual stimulation occurring at the same time). Correspondingly, some individuals with high muscle tone may exhibit low arousal (e.g., an older child with cerebral palsy who is taking medication that makes him sleepy). In these two examples, vestibular stimulation would have to be used carefully in order to balance effects on the motor versus the biobehavioral systems. Using fast rotation as a form of vestibular stimulation might achieve the goal of increasing general muscle tone in the young child with Down syndrome, but overarousal might also occur, making concentration on a task difficult. Conversely, slow rocking could relax too-high muscle tone in the child with cerebral palsy but might also decrease general environmental awareness or even induce sleep.

Obviously, a key factor in providing appropriate vestibular experiences to children with severe and multiple disabilities is that families, educators, and therapists work together to develop safe and appropriate movement activities that tap vestibular input and lead to desired movement and/or biobehavioral outcomes.

The System of Taste

Taste, as ordinarily perceived, is a complex sensation that can be equated with flavor and often includes aspects of smell, texture, temperature, and even pain, as well as "true taste." For example, when a cold interferes with an individual's sense of taste, this phenomenon is the result of a temporary loss of smell, indicating that these systems work together to provide sensory information about taste. The taste system (sometimes referred to as the *gustatory system*) uses chemical receptors located in the mouth, primarily on the tongue, to obtain information about the taste of material in the mouth. These taste receptors are found in the taste buds, which are small cellular areas located on the tongue and in the mouth. Food substances dissolved in the saliva are able to chemically stimulate these cells, and this stimulation is, in turn, passed onto the nervous system for interpretation. Single receptors may be sensitive to one or more of a number of substances characterized as sweet, salty, bitter, or sour, and perhaps others as well. Taste receptors in different parts of the mouth tend to respond maximally to certain chemicals. For example, taste buds on the front of the tongue tend to respond to salts, whereas taste buds in the back of the mouth tend to respond to sugars (Mistretta, 1990; Stein et al., 1997).

Taste buds are among the first sensory receptors to appear in utero, occurring in the human fetus at about 55 days of gestation. During the intrauterine period, the taste system has ample opportunity for chemical stimulation. The developing fetus lives in an environment of amniotic fluid that provides a complex taste environment. Because the fetus swallows large volumes of amniotic fluid during a given day, taste buds frequently are stimulated. Consequently, a newborn infant has a well-developed functional sense of taste. Studies have also shown that, although numerous taste buds are present prenatally, the number of taste buds continues to increase after birth (Mistretta, 1990; Stein et al., 1997). Therefore, the sense of taste continues to change and develop throughout life, and this could explain why patterns of food preferences and aversions, cravings and rejections, are so changeable throughout the lifespan.

In the developing child, taste experiences interact with neural development to establish behavior responses to certain tastes. Taste sensations perceived by the individual can scarcely be separated from behavior responses; for instance, the individual accepts or rejects certain foods based on his or her perception of the taste of the food. Taste preference is strongly tied to the motivation to eat. This link has important implications for the development of feeding programs for children with severe and multiple disabilities. It points to the need to respect children's individual food preferences or dislikes whenever possible, but it also indicates the importance of providing as wide a variety of tastes, textures, and temperatures of food as are accepted. Eating is an important skill that requires specific oral-motor responses such as sucking, biting, chewing, and swallowing, all of which are not only important for the intake of nutrition but also critical to the development of the lip and tongue movements required for speech development. When children with severe and multiple disabilities have not experienced a range of foods that vary in taste, texture, and temperature, aversion to most food can occur. This may result in the child having a limited diet, with serious health consequences.

Depending on the location of the receptors in various oral regions, stimulation of the taste buds can also elicit very different reflexes including swallowing, salivation, insulin release, coughing, gagging, vomiting, and apnea (Hodapp, 1998; Mistretta, 1990; Stein et al., 1997). Because of this link between stimulating taste receptors and eliciting these reflex responses, closely observing a child's overall responses and making necessary adaptations during feeding programs is important for the child's health, comfort, and well being.

The System of Smell

The sense of smell, also known as the *olfactory system*, is a distance sense that uses chemical receptors (similar to the sense of taste) that respond to airborne chemicals or odors. Smell is called a distance sense because an individual can detect a stimulus or the odor that corresponds with it from a distance. The organ of the sense of smell is composed of a sheet of sensory cells—about the size of a postage stamp—that lines a portion of the nasal cavity. Each of these small areas, however, contains as many as 600,000 receptor cells. Even with our relatively insensitive olfactory equipment (as compared with other mammals), humans are still able to discriminate some 10,000 different odors (Axel, 1995).

As odors (molecules that can be smelled) are inhaled, they dissolve in the mucus layer of the sensory cells and a chemical message is sent to the nervous system for interpretation as a particular smell. How can one kind of cell enable us to discriminate among thousands of different odors? Approximately 1,000 separate odor receptors are present in mammals; however, only about 40% of these are functional in humans, which may help to explain why some animals (e.g., dogs) that have use of a greater percentage of these odor receptors are better than humans at detecting odors. Each receptor is probably capable of binding to several different odors. Also, each odor is probably capable of binding to several different receptors. Because of the many diverse combinations that can occur, the brain has a mechanism capable of discriminating among millions of different odors (Axel, 1995).

Researchers have shown that the sense of smell develops very early in the human embryo (in the first to second month of life). This early development, along with other indicators, points to an apparent simplicity and "primitiveness" of the olfactory system, even though the behavioral effects of the system on the life of the organism are profound. Experiments with animals have found that the sense of smell may be functional in utero and may help to determine early postnatal behaviors related to feeding and movement (e.g., locating the nipple to nurse) and maternal bonding issues (Graziadei, 1990). Researchers have also linked the sense of smell to the sense of taste and feeding behaviors; arousal and biobehavioral state issues; and memory of familiar people, places, and things (Axel, 1995).

For children with severe and multiple disabilities, then, the educational team could consider using these individuals' sense of smell in planning strategies to achieve functional outcomes in the areas of alerting to and moving toward environmental olfactory cues, especially when other sensory systems may not be available. For example, allowing a child with severe motor disabilities and deafblindness to smell a food item with a noticeable and pleasant smell while in the classroom could be used as a communication cue that moving to the lunch room is the next event of the day.

The Visual System

One of the most critical distant receptor systems for supplying information about objects and movement in the environment is the visual system. Although quite developed on a cellular level and in its interconnections within the nervous system at birth, the visual system is not active in prenatal development (the womb being a dark environment) and is one of the last sensory systems to mature postnatally (Chalupa & White, 1990; Stein et al., 1997).

The visual receptors, known as the rods and cones, are located in the eye itself. The rods are sensitive to low-intensity, dim light and can detect gross form and movement. Rods are primarily responsible for peripheral vision and night vision. The cones are sensitive to high-intensity illumination and can detect fine detail and color. Other structures of the eye help to focus the image picked up by the visual receptors onto a structure called the retina. The retina then converts the light rays to electrochemical impulses that travel to the brain for interpretation of the visual information.

Visual proprioception is also dependent on vision input combined with movement. If we think of the retina as being "bombarded" with rays of light from objects in the visual field, then the location of where these rays land on the retina is unique for each position that an eye can achieve in space. Moving the head changes the angles of entry of these rays into the eye and therefore their relative locations on the retina. The pattern of light rays is called an *optical array*. The changes in the optical array when the eye is moved from one place to another are called the optical flow. Generally, optical flow gives you information about your movements with respect to objects in the environment and about the environment itself. The visual receptors identify form by transmitting information about multiple contrasting light ray images, thereby creating a kind of "map" of the environment. This environmental map is updated constantly by the nervous system as the individual moves about in space and, thereby, alters the map components. As previously mentioned, the vestibular system also assists in this process (Kiorpes & Movshon, 1990; Movshon & Kiorpes, 1990; Shumway-Cook & Woollacott, 2001; Thelen & Smith, 1994).

Vision, then, is not merely an exteroceptive (relating the information outside the individual) sense, passively providing information about the environment. It is also a proprioceptive (relating to the individual's own movement) sense that tells the individual about his or her own movements. In this way, vision and movement are closely and reciprocally linked. Reseachers have shown the critical part that vision plays in the young child's development of reaching, object use, and locomotion (Shumway-Cook & Woollacott, 2001; Thelen & Smith, 1994). Children with visual impairments are often not motivated to move out into and learn about their world because they are unable to see interesting objects and people in the environment. Delays can occur in fine motor, gross motor, self-help, social, cognitive, and language skills unless intervention occurs (Campbell, 2000; Heller et al., 1996).

Visual impairments (e.g., poor visual acuity, visual field deficits, oculomotor problems, cortical processing problems) are often present in children with severe and multiple disabilities (Campbell, 2000; Heller et al., 1996; Younger, 1999). When working with children with severe and multiple disabilities, particularly children who have vision loss, the educational team must consider the critical link between vision and motor development when planning needed environmental adaptations and implementation of educational strategies. More information about vision and visual impairments can be found in Chapter 10.

The Auditory System

Another of the sensory systems that is traditionally classified as a distance sense is the auditory system. The auditory receptor, the cochlea, is housed in the inner ear and is responsible for hearing. Also in the inner ear is the vestibular apparatus, discussed previously.

Sound energy in wave form is moved from the external ear into the external ear canal and then transferred to the eardrum, which is set in motion by the sound waves. This mechanical energy is then transferred to the bones of the middle ear and into the cochlea.

The cochlea is actually a coiled tube that is snail-like in appearance. The cochlea contains chambers that are filled with fluid. The receptor elements for hearing are hair cells (approximately 20,000 in number) that are surrounded by this fluid. As sound moves through the auditory system, the fluid in the cochlea is set in motion, stimulating these hair cells to move as well. The layout of the hair cells from the base of the cochlea near the eardrum to its apex deep inside the coiled cochlea provides a system for the coding of sound frequency. Hair cells near the base of the cochlea react to high frequency stimulation, and hair cells near the apex of the cochlea react to low frequency stimulation. The loudness of the sound is communicated by an increase in the amplitude of the vibration, which results in increased numbers of hair cells being stimulated and a faster rate of stimulation. Information from the cochlea travels to the brain for interpretation as sound (Heller et al., 1996; Stein, 1997).

Like vision, the sense of hearing gives us information not only about the nature of movements in our environment but also about our own movements. Hearing can, therefore, be considered both exteroceptive and proprioceptive. As a child moves to locate the source of a sound, sensory feedback in the form of sounds made by his or her own movements and correction of movements that are not successful in locating the sound source occur over time to give the child information about the environment and his or her own movements. In this way, hearing and movement, like vision and movement, are closely and reciprocally linked. Hearing is also an early system to develop in utero, so it is a sensory system that has both prenatal and postnatal implications in the role of sensorimotor development (Coleman, 1990a; Herer, Knightly, & Steinberg, 2002). Hearing clearly also plays a critical role in supporting the development of communication.

Hearing impairments may be present in children with severe and multiple disabilities. Individuals may experience different types and levels of hearing loss, depending on the location and degree of impairment. Chapter 10 offers additional information and suggestions for working with children with hearing loss. All members of the educational team must support use of environmental adaptations, special equipment/devices, and communication programs that are selected for each individual student, if optimal functional outcomes are to be met for that student. When vision and hearing loss are combined, even on less-severe levels, the resultant deafblind condition calls for very specific, individualized program plans addressing adaptations across all developmental domains if such outcomes are to be achieved both at home, at school, and in the community.

THE MOTOR SYSTEM

Sensory information from the many sources described in the previous section comes together in the nervous system, and the brain then controls a resultant coordinated movement response. (For definitions of commonly used motor terminologies, see Table 6.4.) The nervous system uses the information from thousands of individual receptors in many sensory modalities (e.g., what is seen by the eye, heard by the ear, felt by the skin, smelled by the nose) to extract the most significant features from events that are occurring in the environment. The

Table 6.4. Definitions of commonly used motor terminology

Abduction	The lateral movement of a body part away from the midline of the body
Adduction	The lateral movement of a body part toward the midline of the body
Asymmetrical	One side of the body assumes a different posture than the other (e.g., one arm bends while the other straightens)
Bilateral	Pertaining to or affecting both sides of the body
Distal	Point farthest away from the central part of the body, the trunk (e.g., the hand is distal to the shoulder)
Extension	Straightening a body part
External rotation	Turning a limb outward, away from the midline of the body
Exteroceptive	Relating to information outside the individual's body
Flexion	Bending a body part
Internal rotation	Turning a limb in toward the midline of the body
Lateral	Pertaining to or relating to the side
Medial	Pertaining to or relating to the middle
Obligatory	Having to occur (as seen in atypical motor development when primitive reflexes cannot be overcome)
Prone	Lying on the stomach
Proprioceptive	Relating to the individual's own movements
Proximal	Point closest to the center of the body (e.g., the shoulder is proximal to the hand)
Reaction (or postural reaction)	Subconscious movement that uses visual, vestibular, tactile, and proprioceptive information to establish the normal relationship of the body in space
Reflex	Movement performed involuntarily in response to a stimulus
Supine	Lying on the back
Symmetrical	Correspondence in shape, size, and position of body parts on both sides of the body
Trunk rotation	Process of turning or twisting the body; movement takes place between the shoulders and hips

From Heller, K.W., et al. (1996). *Understanding physical, sensory, and health impairments: Characteristics and educational implications* (p.16). Pacific Grove, CA: Brooks/Cole; adapted by permission.

nervous system then specifies appropriate responses to numerous muscles in the body, adjusting input to these muscles during the course of the resultant movement based on continual monitoring of the sensory feedback input received. By this means, the vast barrage of incoming sensory information is translated into a form that is useful for action. The nervous system can then choose which outputs will be used during the task and what movement each muscle will make to accomplish an adaptive response. The resultant movements are also continuously monitored by the available sensors, the information is sent to the nervous system during the course of the movement, and necessary changes are made during the movement itself to achieve correction of the adaptive movement, thereby ensuring optimal functional performance (Bloedel et al., 1996; Goldfield, 1997; Greenough, Black, & Wallace, 1987; Grossberg & Kuperstein, 1989).

For example, an individual may be barraged by multiple sensory inputs—sounds, sights, smells, and tastes—and multiple vestibular inputs—tactile, proprioceptive, and vestibular—as he or she is moving about the kitchen listening to music and preparing a meal. If the person's hand suddenly comes into contact with a hot surface on the stove, however, the brain will quickly extract this key information from all of the other sensory information being received at the same time and will send specific input to appropriate muscles so that the hand is immediately withdrawn from the heat source.

Reflex Development

The motor system enables the individual to interact with the environment. Early movements of the typically developing young infant that are reflexive and automatic occur in response to sensory stimuli in the first few months of life and evolve into functional, voluntary movements as the child matures. (Table 6.5 summarizes these early reflexes and the mature postural responses that develop later in life.) Typically developing children develop control and organization over these reflex responses as they mature, and eventually the reflexes fade to be replaced by higher level postural reactions that assist the individual to maintain an upright posture and balance throughout life.

For example, when a young infant moves his or her head to one side or the other in response to visual or auditory stimulation, the resultant stimulation to the vestibular system causes changes in body muscle tone. Extensor tone (i.e., straight body position) increases on the side of the body toward which the face is turned, and flexor tone (i.e., bent body position) increases on the side of the body toward the back of the head. This reflex is referred to as the asymmetrical tonic neck reflex, or ATNR (see Figure 6.3), and is usually present in the first 6 months or so of life. The reflex facilitates the infant's development of visually directed reaching and rolling back to side because of the infant's resultant body position, with his or her eyes being in a position to regard the hand and the asymmetrical body muscle tone enabling rolling to the side to occur (Heller et al., 1996). After approximately 6 months of age, however, this reflex response begins to fade and the older infant begins to develop postural reactions that allow more mature body movements such as pushing up into a sitting position or onto hands and knees. Reflex development of children with severe and multiple disabilities is described later in this chapter.

Table 6.5. Primitive reflexes and postural responses that develop later in life

Reflex	Stimulus	Response	Suppression	Clinical significance
Primitive reflexes: Present at birth, suppressed with maturation				
Asymmetrical tonic neck	Head turning or tilting to the side	Extension of the extremities on the face side, flexion on the occiput side	Suppressed by 6–7 months	Obligatory, abnormal at any age Persistent, suspicious of CNS pathology
Symmetric tonic neck	Neck flexion Neck extension	Arm flexion, leg extension Arm extension, leg flexion	Suppressed by 6–7 months	Obligatory, abnormal at any age Persistent, suspicious of CNS pathology
Moro	Sudden neck extension	Arm extension-abduction followed by flexion-adduction	Suppressed by 4–6 months	Abnormal if persists
Tonic labyrinthine	Head position in space, strongest at 45° angle to horizontal Supine Prone	 Predominant extensor tone Predominant flexor tone	Suppressed by 4–6 months	Abnormal at any age if hyperactive or if persistent
Positive supporting	Tactile contact and weight-bearing on the soles of the feet	Leg extension for supporting partial body weight	Suppressed by 3–7 months and replaced by volitional standing	Abnormal at any age if obligatory or hyperactive; suggests spasticity of the legs
Rooting	Stroking the corner of mouth, upper or lower lip	Moving the tongue, mouth, and head toward the site of the stimulus	Suppressed by 4 months	Searching for nipple Diminished in CNS depression; obligatory persistence may be immature CNS development

(continued)

213

Table 6.5. *(continued)*

Reflex	Stimulus	Response	Suppression	Clinical significance
Palmar grasp	Pressure or touch on the palm, stretch of finger flexors	Flexion of fingers	Suppressed by 5–6 months	Diminished in CNS depression; absent in lower motor neuron paralysis; persistence suggests spasticity (i.e., cerebral palsy)
Plantar grasp	Pressure on sole just distal to metatarsal heads	Flexion of toes	Suppressed by 12–18 months	Absent in lower motor neuron paralysis; persists and hyperactive in spasticity (i.e., cerebral palsy)
Automatic neonatal walking	Contact of sole in vertical position tilting the body forward and from side to side	Automatic alternating steps	Suppressed by 3–4 months	Variable activity in typical infants; absent in lower motor neuron paralysis of the legs
Placing	Tactile contact on dorsum of foot or hand	Flexion to place the leg or arm over the obstacle	Suppressed before end of first year	Absent in lower motor neuron paralysis or extensor spasticity of the legs
Postural reactions: Emerge with maturation, present throughout life, modulated by volition				
Head righting	Visual and vestibular	Align face vertical, mouth horizontal Prone Supine	Emerge at 2 months 3–4 months	Delayed or absent in CNS immaturity or damage or motor neuron disease
Body, head righting	Tactile, proprioceptive, and vestibular	Align body parts	Emerge from 4–6 months	Delayed or absent in CNS immaturity or damage or motor neuron disease

(continued)

Table 6.5. *(continued)*

Reflex	Stimulus	Response	Suppression	Clinical significance
Protective extension or propping	Displacement of center of gravity outside of supporting surface	Extension and abduction of the extremity toward the side of displacement to prevent falling	Emerge between 5 and 12 months	Delayed or absent in CNS immaturity or damage or motor neuron disease
Equilibrium or tilting	Displacement of center of gravity	Adjustment of tone and trunk posture to maintain balance	Emerge between 6 and 14 months	Delayed or absent in CNS immaturity or damage or motor neuron disease

From Heller, K., Alberto, P.A., Forney, P.E., & Schwartzman, M.N. (1996). Understanding physical, sensory, and health impairments (p. 17). Pacific Grove, CA: Brooks/Cole; reprinted by permission. Based on *Pediatric Rehabilitation* by G.E. Molnar. Copyright © 1992 Williams & Wilkins.

Figure 6.3. Asymmetrical tonic neck reflex. (From Alexander, R., Boehme, R., & Cupps, B. [1993]. *Normal development of functional motor skills: The first year of life* [pp. 46–199; illustrations by J. Boehme]. Tucson, AZ: Therapy Skill Builders; reprinted by permission.)

Motor Control Theories

Theories of motor control have undergone significant changes since the early 1990s. Although principles that were previously thought to explain motor development still generally describe the sequence and timing of typical development of motor skills accurately, the motor system is now viewed as being much more complex, with motor development being affected by a much more dynamic interaction of the individual's sensory, motor, and environmental experiences. For example, researchers (Bradley, 2000; Colson & Dworkin, 1997; Hadders-Algra & Prechtl, 1992) have used various developmental principles to explain typical motor development as tending to proceed in certain ways:

- *In a head-to-tail direction (cephalo-caudal):* Children first learn to control head movement, then to control movement of the trunk, arms, and hands and finally to control leg and foot movements.

- *From proximal to distal—in a direction starting from the center of the body and moving away to the periphery of the body:* Children gain control over the muscles of the trunk first, which provides them the stability they need to then gain control over moving their arms and legs.

- *From reflex to volitional:* In the first 6–9 months of life, many early movements are reflex-based. That is, certain incoming sensory stimuli result in predictable patterns of movement responses (see Table 6.5). Gradually, the infant develops more voluntary control over body movements.

- *From gross to fine movements:* Early movements are more random and non-specific, and then become more skilled (e.g., early swiping at a toy within reach versus later use of an accurate, visually guided reach to contact the toy).

- *From movements toward the body (i.e., flexion movements) to movements away from the body (i.e., extension movements):* A balance between these two types of movement is necessary for children to gain postural stability and the control over their bodies to be able to move into upright positions against gravity and to move out into space.

- *From stability to mobility to skill:* Children can first assume and hold various developmental positions (e.g., on hands and knees) before they learn to move while in the positions (e.g., rocking on hands and knees) and before they can perform a skilled action in the position (e.g., creeping).

These principles of motor development generally describe the sequence and timing of typical development of motor skills in young children. Typically developing children can frequently vary from this general skill-acquisition framework, however. For example, many children experiment with a number of motor skills at the same time (e.g., crawling on stomach and pushing up into sitting) and some children skip certain developmental skills entirely (e.g., creeping on hands and knees). Moreover, children with severe and multiple disabilities frequently do not follow a typical sequence of motor skill development, nor do they have typical sensorimotor experiences when they do move independently.

For children with severe and multiple disabilities, a typical developmental approach to sensorimotor skill acquisition is therefore not applicable. Families and professionals may find it more appropriate to describe motor performance and to plan outcomes in relation to functional movement. A functional approach to movement for children with severe and multiple disabilities allows for the development of skills necessary for independence and can be built into many activities naturally occurring throughout the day, providing many opportunities for practice (Campbell, 1997; Dunn, 1996; Haley, Baryza, & Blanchard, 1993).

Sensorimotor control theory of the early 21st century expands on the developmental principles described previously and explains them as a more active and interactive process. This theory underscores both the child's opportunities for practice and repetition of movement in developing useful and functional patterns of movement and the interconnections between sensorimotor experiences and other developmental domains (e.g., cognition, language). Thus, it supports a more functional approach to planning outcomes and activities for children with severe and multiple disabilities.

SENSORIMOTOR CONTROL—DYNAMIC SYSTEMS THEORY

Throughout the years, successive revisions of sensorimotor development theories have been made. Underlying the changes in these developmental theories are varying concepts about the roles of the changing structure and function within the developing individual and the influence of the environment on the course of development. Thelen and Smith (1994) and others (Campbell, 2000; Shumway-Cook & Woollacott, 2001) have proposed the dynamic systems theory, which is a dynamic and functional perspective on sensorimotor development that directs most current research. Basic to this theory of sensorimotor control is that in response to sensory stimulation, movement emerges primarily from the interaction of three basic factors: the individual, the task, and the environment. The individual generates movement based on incoming sensory stimuli to meet the demands of the task at hand, a task being performed within a specific environment. An individual's functional capability is measured by his or her ability to successfully meet the combined demands placed on him or her by both the task and the environment (Shumway-Cook & Woollacott, 2001). For example, a child first learning to walk can successfully respond to his mother who is across the living room encouraging him to walk to her only if he 1) has the prerequisite motor skills to accomplish this, 2) can register the sensory elements related to the task (e.g., seeing and hearing Mom), 3) understands the nature of the task from past walking experiences, and 4) does not encounter environmental obstacles such as toys on the floor or a table in the way.

Dynamic systems theory also emphasizes process rather than product or nervous system hierarchy. The theory also places all structures and processes that interact to promote sensorimotor development on an equal plane. Cooperating systems within the individual include the sensory systems that have been previously discussed, musculoskeletal components, sensorimotor integrative mechanisms in the nervous system, and arousal and motivation factors (Campbell, 2000; Shumway-Cook & Woollacott, 2001; Thelen, 1995; Thelen & Smith, 1994). In the dynamic systems approach, these internal components of the individual and the external context of the task are equivalent because behavior is considered task-specific. Therefore, when considering the developing child in the context of dynamic systems theory, the environment is as important as the child. In the example used of the child first learning to walk, the factor of the environment being unobstructed and conducive to the task of walking across the room was as important to successful completion of the task as was the child's walking skill.

Constraints or limitations on the performance of any specific sensorimotor behavior are also viewed in the context of the cooperating systems. In the case of the developing infant, system components that do not develop at the same time, such as those involving muscle strength or postural control, are seen as limiting to the performance of motor behaviors at certain periods. Environmental factors such as an inability to practice a particular movement skill are also limiting to the development of motor behaviors. An example is a child who is learning to walk inside the house but is not allowed to practice walking on uneven surfaces such as on the grass outside. He or she will be limited in fully developing walking as a skilled movement pattern due to environmental factors (Campbell, 2000; Heriza, 1991)

Thelen and Smith (1994) also described transitional periods, when movement patterns appear more variable, as sensitive periods in development in which intervention might be particularly effective. Studies conducted in the mid-1990s of the development of locomotion and spatial abilities in human infants who were born with movement or vision impairments seem to support this dynamic systems theory. Telzrow, Campos, Kermoian, and Bertenthal (1996) studied seven infants who were born with meningomyelocele. This condition caused the infants to have delayed walking skills, but they performed typically for their ages on tests of cognitive functioning. These infants were tested monthly with two tasks, finding a hidden object and following the experimenter's point and gaze. The infants began to crawl at different ages, ranging from 8.5 months to 13.5 months. Despite this variability, on the object search task, the performance of five of the seven infants dramatically improved after the onset of locomotion and an equally convincing increase occurred in the same group in following the experimenter's point and gaze associated with this motor milestone. This is especially strong evidence against a strictly maturational hypothesis for hidden search behavior because the infants' performances shifted on both tasks, not as a function of age, but of locomotor skill.

Additional intriguing evidence to support the dynamic system theory's tenet that perception and action form an inseparable loop comes from Bigelow's (1992) study of three infants born with visual impairments. Bigelow tracked these infants from before they began to crawl until they walked alone. In all cases, the motor milestones of crawling and walking were significantly delayed despite the infants' having no motor disabilities. Bigelow tested the infants monthly with tasks designed to elicit their understanding of object permanence. He tested whether they could locate (by reaching) toys that made a sound as the toys were moved in increasingly complex locations away from the infants' bodies. Bigelow found that the emergence of locomotor skills was related to the infants' performance on the object permanence task, despite considerable differences in age when the tasks were mastered. For example, the infants showed the highest level of performance—that is, tracking a sound toy and accurately locating it after it had been displaced—just before or at the time of independent walking, which varied from 17 to 36 months.

In summary, then, the current dynamic systems model for sensorimotor development describes the following seven tenets (Campbell, 2000; Shumway-Cook & Woollacott, 2001; Thelen, 1995; Thelen & Smith, 1994):

1. All structures and processes that interact within the individual to promote development are equally important, including the sensory systems, musculoskeletal components, the central nervous system, cognition, perception, and arousal and motivation factors.

2. Each of these internal variables develops at its own rate.

3. These internal variables are equally important as external environmental variables.

4. Constraints or limitations on development occur both within the individual (e.g., adequate strength development to perform certain movements) and within external variables (e.g., opportunities to practice motor skills).

5. Sensorimotor development requires spontaneous, active, self-directed movement exploration.

6. Sensorimotor development requires the opportunity for practice and self-selection of the most appropriate movements for accomplishing goal-directed, functional, meaningful activities.

7. Transitional periods in development, when movement patterns appear more variable, are sensitive periods when intervention might be most effective.

The following section relates this information gained from dynamic systems theory so that families, teachers, and therapists can together plan integrated services and strategies in order to achieve functional outcomes for children with severe and multiple disabilities.

ATYPICAL SENSORIMOTOR SKILL DEVELOPMENT

How do we define functional movement when attempting to plan functional sensorimotor outcomes for children with severe and multiple disabilities? *Function*, according to Fisher (1992), is simply what people do. This definition implies that functional movements are self-chosen, self-directed, result in action on the environment, and are, therefore, meaningful in the life of the individual at his or her particular stage of life (Campbell, 2000). As has already been discussed, typically developing children acquire and develop sensorimotor and cognitive skills through ongoing experimentation with sensory input, resultant attempts at functional goal-directed movement, and the consequences of that movement. This ongoing process of sensorimotor skill development enables young children to learn to play; conceptualize ideas; socialize; communicate; and feed, dress, and bathe themselves. The sensorimotor system supports these functional life skills by providing the mechanism through which children experience and act on the environment in specific ways (Dunn, 1996; Hanft & Place, 1996).

Children with severe and multiple disabilities vary widely in their sensory, motor, and cognitive abilities. Functional skill acquisition is still vital for these children even though their sensorimotor systems operate differently from typically developing children. Although each child with severe and multiple disabilities has individual strengths and limitations, several characteristics of atypical sensorimotor skill development or use are described next: 1) atypical muscle tone; 2), persistence of reflexes; 3) atypical postural control and movement; 4) feeding, gastrointestinal, and respiratory problems; 5) secondary orthopedic changes; 6) difficulty with development of functional skills; 7) specific motor problems associated with hearing loss; and 8) specific motor problems associated with vision loss. These characteristics may or may not be present in children diagnosed with severe and multiple disabilities.

Atypical Muscle Tone

Muscle tone is the state of tension that the central nervous system continuously exerts on all muscles of the body. This normal tension in the muscles enables the body to move against the force of gravity and provides the background for movement, with the muscles ready for movement at any time. When a disturbance of the underlying tension in muscles occurs with damage to the nervous system (related to the brain, spinal cord, nerves, or muscles), muscle tone and body movement will be atypical and motor development and functional movement may be affected. A nonprogressive disorder of muscle tone due to damage to the developing brain in utero or in the first year of life is referred to as cerebral palsy. Cerebral palsy is a common diagnosis for children with severe and multiple disabilities, but children with this diagnosis may present with a variety of movement problems based on the location and severity of damage in the brain. Other disabilities may accompany the diagnosis of cerebral palsy including visual problems, hearing loss, speech difficulties, seizures, learning disabilities, cognitive impairments, and social-emotional problems. Other conditions involving atypical muscle tone (e.g., myelomeningocele, which involves muscle weakness or paralysis and sensory problems due to spinal cord damage; mitochondrial disease, which involves muscle weakness and fatigue due to problems at the cellular level) may also be present in children with severe and multiple disabilities. Descriptors of the different kinds of muscle tone problems follow.

Muscle tone may be lower than expected, resulting in decreased power to move body parts against gravity and an interference with postural alignment. Joints may also be overly flexible. Low muscle tone is sometimes referred to as *hypotonia.* Muscle tone may also be higher than expected, resulting in labored movements that often occur in abnormal patterns and within a limited range of motion. Interference with postural alignment and inflexible joints may be present. High muscle tone is sometimes referred to as *hypertonia* or *spasticity.* Extremely high muscle tone is sometimes called *rigidity.* Muscle tone may also fluctuate in some children; for example, a child's muscle tone may be high at one time and low at another. This fluctuation may make movements imprecise and uncontrolled and sometimes writhing in nature, especially during active movement. This type of movement disorder is referred to as *athetosis.* Ataxia describes movements that are uncoordinated, especially during activities requiring balance and equilibrium such as walking. In some cases, muscle tone problems may be mixed (e.g., the trunk muscles may exhibit low tone, whereas the arm and leg muscles exhibit high tone) (Batshaw, 2002; Heller, Forney, Alberto, Schwartzman, & Goeckel, 2000; Younger, 1999).

Atypical muscle tone may affect the individual's whole body (e.g., quadriplegia), only one side of the body (e.g., hemiplegia), one part of the body (e.g., monoplegia—one limb, paraplegia—legs only), or one part of the body more than the other (e.g., diplegia—legs more affected than arms). The type and location of the atypical muscle tone will depend on the location of the damage in the central nervous system.

Disorders of muscle tone may also occur on a continuum from mild in volvement that only minimally affects a child's movement and functional abilities to severe involvement that makes independent movement and function very difficult without adaptations and supports. The level of involvement will depend on the extent of the damage within the central nervous system. Heller and colleagues (1996) also cited a classification system that defines severity based on limitation of the individual's activity. Table 6.6 defines the various terms used in describing disorders of muscle tone.

Persistence of Reflexes

As has been mentioned in previous discussions, at birth, the typically developing infant's movements are dominated by reflexes or involuntary movements that are stimulated by various kinds of external sensory input (e.g., touch, pressure, vision, movement of the fluid in the vestibular system, stretch on the muscle tendons). These reflexes are automatic but depend on interaction with the environment. Some of these reflex movement patterns are protective and some form the basis of early motor skills. As the young child's central nervous system matures, and due to movement experiences acquired in the first few months of life, these reflex patterns of movement gradually fade by about 6–9 months of age and are replaced by higher level, self-regulated movements.

Table 6.6. Terms used in describing disorders of muscle tone

Term	Definition
Types of muscle tone	
Ataxia	Uncoordinated movements of the muscles, especially during activities requiring balance and equilibrium
Athetosis	Fluctuating muscle tone; may be high at one time and low at another; movements may appear writhing in nature
Hypertonia	High muscle tone or constant tension in the muscles; sometimes called *spasticity*
Hypotonia	Low muscle tone; difficulty moving body parts against gravity
Mixed	Presence of more than one type of muscle tone
Rigidity	Extremely high muscle tone
Area of involvement	
Monoplegia	Involvement of only one limb
Paraplegia	Involvement of the legs only
Triplegia	Involvement of three limbs, usually both legs and one arm
Diplegia	More serious involvement of the legs than the arms
Hemiplegia	Involvement of one side of the body
Quadriplegia	Involvement of all four extremities and usually of the entire body
Level of involvement	
Mild	Minimal impairment with very little limitation of activity or uncoordination
Moderate	Impairments in gross and fine motor movements; affects ambulation and speech; independent functioning is limited without use of assistive devices
Severe	Impairments almost completely incapacitating; inability to perform the usual activities of daily living without extensive adaptations
or	
Class I:	No limitation of activity
Class II:	Slight-to-moderate limitation of activity
Class III:	Moderate-to-great limitation of activity
Class IV:	Individuals are unable to carry out any functional physical activity without assistive technology

Children with severe and multiple disabilities who have damage to their central nervous systems, especially those with cerebral palsy, may exhibit persistence of these reflexive patterns of movement far beyond when they would normally occur. Rather than promoting development at this stage, persistent reflexes interrupt the child's ability to gain control over body movements. As has been described earlier, the typically developing young infant responds to certain stimuli with a reflex motor response, but this response is never obligatory. The infant can move out of the resulting reflex motor response at will. With damage to the central nervous system, however, the reflex response can become obligatory in nature. Every time the stimulus presents, the motor response occurs and can be very difficult for the child with severe and multiple disabilities to move out of. Attempts at functional movement may be interrupted by an obligatory motor response from a reflex pattern. For example, an older child with an obligatory palmar grasp reflex would have difficulty releasing or orienting an object such as a pencil or a spoon held in his or her hand. In addition, higher level postural responses, such as righting, protective, and equilibrium reactions, which help an individual develop upright control against gravity, cannot develop normally when certain persistent, primitive reflex patterns of movement (such as seen with an ATNR) are present (Heller et al., 2000; Younger, 1999).

Atypical Postural Control and Movement

Children with atypical muscle tone or persistent reflexes are unable to make graded movement adaptations to environmental stimuli. They may become fixed in certain positions, held there by the force of gravity or by their own muscle tone. The quality of their movement is also limited by these tone and reflex factors. The result is a decreased effectiveness of movement for functional activities. Because postural control and movement both support children's ability to interact with people and objects, learning and cognitive development may also be affected by an inability to explore and interact with the environment (Stamer, 2000).

Feeding, Gastrointestinal, and Respiratory Problems

A child with atypical muscle tone and primitive reflex patterns may also display these tone and reflex problems in the oral-motor area. The child may find sucking, chewing, and swallowing difficult. Experiencing low or high muscle tone in the face and tongue, a persistent bite reflex (i.e., a touch on the gums or teeth causes a strong clenching of the teeth), a hyperactive or hypoactive gag reflex (i.e., stimulation of the palate or tongue causes gagging or choking), and a strong tongue thrust (i.e., food on the tongue causes a forceful protrusion of the tongue out of the oral cavity) can all cause feeding difficulties. Oral hyper- or hyposensitivity issues may also affect feeding (Heller et al., 1996; Stamer, 2000).

The child with severe and multiple disabilities may have trouble eating enough food to maintain health and growth. Food in the stomach may also be ejected into the esophagus, a condition known as gastroesophageal reflux. This occurs when the esophageal sphincter muscle does not close properly, allowing stomach contents to escape, which irritates the esophagus and causes pain or results in frequent vomiting. Surgery to tighten the sphincter or to implant a gastrostomy tube may be needed to correct this problem (Eicher, 2002).

Feeding problems can also make mealtime extremely frustrating, time-consuming, and frightening for the parent, teacher, support staff, and child and can create behavior and socialization problems. Because feeding is such a critical area to the child's health and well-being, a collaborative team effort is imperative to develop mealtime strategies. Chapter 12 covers feeding issues in more detail.

Constipation is also a frequent problem for children with severe and multiple disabilities. Low or high muscle tone, lack of activity, lack of upright positioning, poor sensation, and lack of necessary abdominal strength can all produce problems with elimination. Atypical muscle control and decreased sensation can also lead to problems with bladder control and resultant urinary tract infections in children with severe and multiple disabilities (Batshaw, 2002).

Children with severe and multiple disabilities who have muscle tone problems may also aspirate (inhale) saliva and food into their lungs. Poor muscle control may make it difficult for these children to cough and thereby clear aspirated material. When this occurs, chronic congestion can result, which can lead to pneumonia if the lungs become inflamed.

Atypical muscle tone may also make it difficult for children with severe and multiple disabilities to breathe deeply enough to take in adequate oxygen. Not only can this lead to fatigue and health problems but also rib cage formation may be affected over time. The lack of coordination between breathing, sucking, and swallowing may further complicate feeding, and the breath support and control required for speech production may also be inadequate (Heller et al., 2000; Stamer, 2000).

Secondary Orthopedic Changes

Atypical muscle tone, persistent primitive reflexes, and limitations in position and independent movement can also lead to secondary changes in joints, muscles, and bones. If the child with severe and multiple disabilities is not moving his or her joints through their normal full range of movement, muscles can shorten and connective tissue can tighten around joints, which then physically limits the child's ability to move or be moved. If intervention to prevent or correct these limitations does not occur, permanent changes in bone muscle, or tendon formation or bone growth may require orthopedic surgery (Younger, 1999).

Difficulty with Development of Functional Skills

When children with severe and multiple disabilities have atypical postural control and movement patterns, they often cannot make the postural adaptations needed to independently perform the functional tasks of playing, eating, dressing, washing, and toileting at an age-appropriate level. In addition, once children reach school age, functional tasks necessary for classroom performance, such as writing, may be impaired. Increasing functional skills in these areas through use of adaptive strategies or adaptive equipment/materials can not only improve the child's motor performance but also can be important to developing cognitive, social, and communication skills.

Specific Motor Problems Associated with Hearing Loss

The child who acquires a sensorineural hearing loss as a result of a disease such as meningitis may also lose motor control and the sense of balance. The disease process may destroy sensory hair cell receptors in both the cochlea, the hearing mechanism, and in the vestibular mechanism of the inner ear. As has been discussed previously, the vestibular mechanism interacts, through the central nervous system, with the visual system, the muscles of the body, and the skin and joint receptors to produce a coordinated muscle response that keeps the body upright against gravity. The child with a hearing loss and balance/motor problems due to vestibular damage has a good prognosis for eventually developing typically in the sensorimotor area. If no brain damage resulted from the disease process, then the visual, tactile, and proprioceptive systems gradually accommodate to the loss of vestibular information and work together to restore balance and equilibrium. Balance and equilibrium, however, may continue to be impaired when vision is removed—when the individual is in the dark or has his or her eyes closed, for example (Heller et al., 1996).

Specific Motor Problems Associated with Vision Loss

Vision plays a central role in enabling children to monitor what is in the environment, make comparisons, anticipate events, understand cause and effect, and gain stimulation and motivation from the environment that is necessary for developmental progress.

Children with visual impairments often exhibit developmental delays in many areas such as language, socialization, and self-help skills, as well as gross and fine motor skills. Young children with vision loss cannot easily monitor their own movements, nor can they easily copy other people as models of movement. Awareness of their own bodies and their position in space, as well as the relation of other objects in space, is delayed. Without adequate vision, children may experience orientation problems caused by difficulties with creating a mental map of the surrounding environment. Loss of vision may also remove an important source of motivation for the young child to move into and interact with the environment. The stability milestones (e.g., sitting and standing) are less delayed than the mobility milestones (e.g., creeping and walking). Fine motor manipulation skills and self-help skills may also be delayed. In the perceptual-motor area, children with visual impairments may also be slower to develop concepts related to time and space, object permanence, and problem-solving strategies. Positional preferences (e.g., supine on back preferred over prone on stomach), food preferences (e.g., bland foods with less texture), tactile defensiveness, fear of movement, and stereotypic behaviors (e.g., hand flapping, eye poking) may also develop as either protective mechanisms or as ways to provide self-stimulation in children with visual impairments (Ferrell, 2000; Heller et al., 1996; Hodapp, 1998).

SENSORIMOTOR SYSTEMS: APPLICATION TO THE NEEDS OF CHILDREN WITH SEVERE AND MULTIPLE DISABILITIES

According to the dynamic systems theory of sensorimotor control described previously, the individual, the task, and the environment are all equally important elements of sensorimotor development. In order to identify the sensorimotor abilities and needs of children with severe and multiple disabilities and to plan integrated services and strategies to achieve functional outcomes for these children, formal and informal assessment of all three of these areas is necessary.

Indicators of Sensorimotor Problems

Educators, therapists, families, and other team members can often gain information on the sensory processing abilities of a child with severe and/or multiple disabilities by observing and recording the specific child's tolerance to and preference for particular sensory input and his or her motor responses during functional daily routines in natural environments. For example, when picking up and moving a toddler with severe and multiple disabilities across the room to begin a new activity, the child's teacher has the opportunity to observe the child's response to being touched and to being moved through space (i.e., vestibular stimulation). The child may indicate pleasure by smiling or assisting with the movement (e.g., reaching toward the teacher) or may show distress by crying or pulling away. Table 6.7 provides examples of observable behaviors that may indicate difficulty with sensory processing during functional daily activities (Dunn, 1996).

In this example, however, a single observation would not be sufficient to indicate the meaning of the child's responses. A child who is smiling may be responding to being moved, to being touched, to the social interaction with the teacher, or to the change from a boring or difficult task. A child expressing irritability may also be responding to being moved or touched, may be reacting to

Table 6.7. Examples of observable behaviors that indicate difficulty with sensory processing during daily life tasks

Sensory system	Personal hygiene	Dressing	Eating	Homemaking	School/work	Play
Somatosensory	Withdraws from splashing water Pushes washcloth/towel away Cries when hair is washed and dried Makes face when toothpaste gets on lips, tongue Tenses when bottom is wiped after toileting	Tolerates a narrow range of clothing items Prefers tight clothing More irritable in loose textured clothing Cries during dressing Pulls hats, head gear, accessories	Tolerates food at only one temperature Gags with textured food or utensils in mouth Winces when face is wiped Extends hand and avoids objects and surfaces (finger food, utensils)	Avoids participation in tasks that are wet, dirty Seeks to remove batter that falls on arm	Cries when tape or glue gets on skin Overreacts to pats, hugs; avoids these actions Tolerates only one pencil, one type of paper, only wooden objects Hands extend when attempting to type	Selects narrow range of toys, similar textures Cannot hold on to toys/objects Rubs toys on face, arms Mouths objects
Proprioceptive	Cannot lift objects that seem heavy (a new bar of soap) Cannot change head position to use sink and mirror in same task	Cannot support heavy items (belt with buckle, shoes) Fatigues prior to task completion Misses when placing arm or leg in clothing	Uses external support to eat (propping) Tires before completing meal Cannot provide force to cut meat Tires before completely eating foods that need to be chewed	Drops equipment (broom) Uses external support (leaning on counter to stir batter) Difficulty pouring a glass of milk	Drops books Becomes uncomfortable in a particular position Hooks limbs on furniture to obtain support Moves arm, hand in repetitive patterns (self-stimulatory)	Unable to sustain movements during play Tires before game is complete Drops heavy parts of a toy/game

Vestibular	Becomes disoriented when bending over the sink Falls when trying to participate in washing lower extremities	Gets overly excited/distracted after bending down to assist in putting on socks Cries when moved around a lot during dressing	Holds head stiffly in one position during mealtime Gets distracted from meal after several head position changes	Avoids leaning to obtain cooking utensils Becomes overly excited after moving around the room to dust	Avoids turning head to look at people; to find source of a sound After being transported in a wheelchair, more difficult to get on task Moves head in repetitive pattern (self-stimulatory)	Avoids play that includes movement Becomes overly excited or anxious when moving during play Rocks excessively Craves movement activities
Visual	Cannot find utensils on the sink Difficulty spotting desired item in drawer Misses when applying paste to toothbrush	Cannot find buttons on patterned or solid clothing Overlooks desired shirt in closet or drawer Misses armhole when donning shirt	Misses utensils on the table Has trouble getting foods onto spoon when they are a similar color to the plate	Cannot locate correct canned item in the pantry Has difficulty finding cooking utensils in the drawer	Cannot keep place on the page Cannot locate desired item on communication board Attends excessively to bright or flashing objects	Has trouble with matching, sorting activities Has trouble locating desired toy on cluttered shelf

(continued)

229

Table 6.7. *(continued)*

Sensory system	Personal hygiene	Dressing	Eating	Homemaking	School/work	Play
Auditory	Cries when hair dryer is turned on Becomes upset by running water Jerks when toilet flushes	Distracted by clothing that makes noise (crisp cloth, accessories)	Distracted by noise of utensils against each other (spoon in bowl, knife on plate) Cannot keep eating when someone talks	Distracted by vacuum cleaner sound Distracted by television or radio during tasks	Distracted by squeaky wheelchair Intolerant of noise others make in the room Overreacts to door closing Notices toilet flushing down the hall	Play is disrupted by sounds Makes sounds constantly
Olfactory/ gustatory	Gags at taste of toothpaste Jerks away at smell of soap	Overreacts to clothing when it has been washed in a new detergent	Tolerates a narrow range of foods Becomes upset when certain foods are cooking	Becomes upset when house is being cleaned (because of odors of cleaners)	Overreacts to new person (new smells) Intolerant of scratch-n-sniff stickers Smells everything	Tastes or smells all objects before playing

From Dunn, W. (1996). The sensorimotor systems: A framework for assessment and intervention. In F.P. Orelove & D. Sobsey, *Educating children with multiple disabilities: A transdisciplinary approach* (3rd ed., pp. 64–66), Baltimore: Paul H. Brookes Publishing Co.; adapted by permission.

his or her inability to anticipate what is about to happen, or may feel displeasure with being taken away from a task of interest. Team members would need to accumulate information on the child's responses, the nature of the task eliciting the response, and the environment in which the task is occurring, observed across many activities and in many different situations, to confirm the meaning of the child's responses and, thereby, to make inferences about the child's sensory processing abilities.

Although recording of multiple observations of sensorimotor behavior across time and tasks can provide the team with important information, specific sensorimotor assessments of the child are also necessary to pinpoint the exact nature of the sensorimotor problems.

Sensorimotor Assessment Considerations

The vast majority of long-familiar assessment tools currently available for examination of sensorimotor control are based on brain maturation or learning theories, but more recently developed assessment tools appear to be reflecting changing views of development, such as those suggested by dynamic systems theory. Many maturational-based or learning-based tools emphasize reflex testing or achievement of motor milestones as their measure of sensorimotor control. Tools incorporating a dynamic systems-based view of development attempt to examine spontaneous, self-produced movements under natural conditions, recognizing that multiple variables contribute to movements. All sensorimotor assessment tools provide some indication of ability or extent of control, but tests have yet to be developed that tell us exactly how or why sensorimotor control is limited (Campbell, 2000; Haley, Baryza, & Blanchard, 1993; Palisano, 1993; Shumway-Cook & Woollacott, 2001).

Although a number of tests are available that will provide valuable information on the sensorimotor system, no single test allows one to collect all of the necessary information about the individual's abilities, the task, and the environment. Therefore, the collaborative team conducting the assessment needs to use multiple assessment measures to get a true picture of an individual's sensorimotor skills. Input from families or caregivers concerning the child's functional abilities should also be an important part of assessing the child with severe and multiple disabilities. Sensorimotor assessment of children with severe and multiple disabilities needs to be performed with input from the entire educational team, including the family, educators, therapists, and support personnel. To gain an accurate portrayal of the student's abilities, it is important that assessments be performed in natural environments, and at natural times of the day, and they should include assessment of the activities necessary to perform successfully in these environments.

When a task-oriented assessment approach is used, the student's performance of the task will need to be examined in conjunction with the sensory and
motor components of the task. This approach, as discussed by Shumway-Cook
and Woollacott (2001), examines sensorimotor behavior at several levels,
including functional abilities based usually on performance-based test measures;
a description of the strategies used to accomplish functional skills; and quantifi-
cation of the underlying sensory, motor, perceptual, and cognitive impairments
that constrain functional movement. Various members of the collaborative team
could administer the assessment, matching their education and experience to
the particular needs of the child, but the whole team should discuss assessment
results in order to draw on the knowledge and expertise of all team members.

A task-oriented approach to assessment of sensorimotor skills is directed at
answering the following questions (Shumway-Cook & Woollacott, 2001):

1. To what degree can the individual perform functional tasks?

2. What strategies does the individual use to perform the tasks, and can he or
    she adapt strategies to changing tasks and environmental conditions?

3. What is the combination of impairments that constrains how the individual
    performs the task, and can these impairments be changed through inter-
    vention/adaptations?

4. Is the individual performing optimally, given the current impairments, or
    can intervention/adaptations improve either the strategies being used to
    accomplish functional tasks or the underlying impairments?

Discrepancy Analysis for Sensorimotor Problems

One type of task-oriented assessment that can be used to identify sensorimotor
problems is a discrepancy analysis. A discrepancy analysis refers to a process in
which the student's current capability to perform specific tasks is examined so
that the areas requiring adaptations or specific interventions are identified. A
discrepancy analysis is a direct measure of the student's performance capability
on a targeted task.

A discrepancy analysis is usually composed of five steps: 1) task analysis,
2) student performance (score), 3) student error, 4) performance discrepancy, and
5) adaptations. As seen in Figure 6.4, the first column contains a task analysis for
Mary, a student eating a sandwich in the cafeteria with her peers. The second column is used to determine the student's score (or determining the prompt level) on
each step of the task analysis. The third column is used to record the precise error
for steps the student is unable to perform independently. The next part of the discrepancy analysis is determining the reason for the error, which is referred to as the

Student: _Mary Robinson_   Teacher: _Ms. White_   Date: _3/5/04_

Domain: _School_   Environment: _Cafeteria_   Subenvironment: _Seating area_

Environmental assessment: Possible problems: Visual distractions, noisy environment, poor lighting, and table height too high

Task analysis for activity: Eating a sandwich	Score I = Independence V = Verbal Prompt P = Prompt	Student error	Performance discrepancy M = Motor S = Sensory H = Health L = Learning C = Communication Mt = Motivation	Adaptations, strategies, or interventions
1. Locate sandwich half	P	Unable to locate sandwich	S	Change to high contrast plate
2. Move hand to sandwich	P	Overshoots sandwich	M	Wrist weights
3. Grasp sandwich	P	Squeezes too hard	S/M	Sandwich holder
4. Bring sandwich to mouth	P	Unable to reach mouth	M	Sandwich holder
5. Open mouth	I			
6. Place part of sandwich in mouth	I			
7. Bite sandwich	I	Tonic bite reflex	M	Special feeding technique
8. Chew and swallow	I			
9. Repeat with rest of sandwich				

Figure 6.4. Discrepancy analysis form for Mary. This analysis shows factors influencing her ability to eat a sandwich in the school cafeteria, her performance score, and interventions that can be put in place.

performance discrepancy. There are six major categories of performance discrepancies: 1) motor, 2) sensory, 3) health (endurance), 4) learning, 5) communication, and 6) motivation (Heller et al., 2000). The last column contains the necessary adaptation, strategy, or intervention to address the performance discrepancy.

The type of performance discrepancy will determine the type of adaptation, instructional strategy, or intervention needed to address the student's error. Careful consideration is needed by the teacher and team members to select the appropriate performance discrepancy category because the adaptations or strategies will typically be very different between categories. For example, very different interventions for each possible performance discrepancy category could be applicable for a student incorrectly bringing a sandwich to his or her mouth:

- A motor problem may result in the recommendation for a sandwich holder.
- A sensory problem (tactile type in which the student drops the sandwich due to the feel of the bun) may result in the use of a different type of bread.
- An endurance problem may point to the need for resting between bites.
- A learning problem may result in the implementation of a specific instructional strategy.
- A communication problem may result in the use of a symbol for *eat*.
- A motivation problem may indicate the need to use a preferred sandwich.

In some instances, it may be difficult to determine which performance discrepancy category is responsible for the student missing the step of the task analysis. In this situation, motor, sensory, and health components are considered first, prior to learning, communication, or motivational ones. This is because learning, communication, and motivational strategies are usually programmed into instruction, but unless a motor, sensory, or health problem is addressed, the student will not typically be able to successfully perform the step. Trying out different adaptations and strategies may be necessary to rule out motor, sensory, or health problems and determine the appropriate intervention.

When a student incorrectly performs part of a task due to a sensorimotor problem, the team will need to carefully examine the student's precise errors and determine the specific motor or sensory area that is resulting in the problem. By pinpointing the exact sensorimotor problem, the appropriate intervention can be selected. The next two sections provide information on assessing motor and sensory task components and describe a sampling of interventions.

Assessing Motor Performance and Interventions

When the discrepancy analysis shows a student error on one of the steps of the task analysis, it is important to determine if a motor problem caused the error. By pinpointing the exact motor problem, accurate interventions can take place.

List of motor categories	Sample problems	Sample interventions
Body position	Student slouching in wheelchair	Be sure student is positioned with buttocks in back of chair with seatbelt over hips
Gross motor movement: abnormal control of movement	Arms have slow, jerking movements toward items	Give student enough time to complete task
Gross motor movement: restricted range of motion	Unable to reach material	Arrange placement of materials within reach of student
Gross motor movement: High, low, fluctuating, or deteriorating muscle tone	Student has deteriorating condition with low muscle tone	Adapt material to accommodate low muscle tone Have desk at appropriate height so student can rest elbows while working Assess gross motor movements frequently and make appropriate changes to match motor ability
Fine motor control	Unable to hold pencil	Use a pencil with a larger grip
Motor strength	Unable to maintain hold on cup and difficult to lift when full	Use an adapted cup with a handle Give student adapted cup half full and refill as needed
Reflexes	The primitive reflex of Asymmetrical tonic neck reflex (ATNR) persists and interferes with tasks	Present items at midline to minimize ATNR from occurring

Figure 6.5.   Sample motor categories, problems, and interventions.

Several subcategories in the motor system may be considered: body position, gross motor movement, fine motor control, motor strength, and reflexes. Each one of these should be considered in order to determine the appropriate intervention (see Figure 6.5).

The teacher or other team members should consider each of the various motor subcategories, looking first at the student's body position. If the student with a physical disability is not positioned properly, the student's ability to use his or her arms and hands optimally can be negatively affected. The physical therapist can assist with appropriate positioning. Adapted equipment may also assist with proper positioning. Handling, positioning, and adaptive equipment is discussed in detail in the next chapter.

The next subcategory is control of gross motor movements (i.e., large body movements, typically made by arms or legs). This category refers to body movements that are not typical, fluid, or purposeful. For example, students with cerebral palsy often exhibit atypical arm movements that make it difficult to move their arms to the correct location needed to perform a task. Problems such as restricted range of motion, abnormal movement control, and high or low muscle tone can all interfere with movement. Various adaptations and strategies may be used to help compensate.

Fine motor control, the next subcategory, most commonly refers to hand use. Just as some students have difficulty with gross motor movements, similar problems may be present with fine motor control. For example, the student may have difficulty grasping items, turning pages in a book, holding a pencil, or manipulating a wide range of school-related material. Various adaptations may be used to address fine motor control problems.

The next subcategory encompasses motor strength. On the one hand, many students lack sufficient motor strength to perform common tasks. When this is the case, the student may be unable to lift relatively lightweight items or maintain a grasp on certain items. Use of lightweight material or adapted material may be needed. On the other hand, some students may be unable to gauge their strength, or lack control of their grasp, and may grasp too tightly. In this case, some consideration may be needed in regard to the type of material being used in the task.

Reflexes are the last subcategory and refer to reflex patterns of movement that may be present and possibly interfere with performance of certain tasks. As discussed previously in the chapter, some students with severe and multiple disabilities will continue to exhibit reflex movement patterns in response to sensory stimuli long after they would have disappeared during typical development. For example, a student with ATNR may find it impossible to engage both hands together in a task if he or she looks to the right or left, due to the resultant asymmetrical involuntary arm movement. In this case, the teacher will need to bring items to the student's midline (directly in front), rather than to the student's side to decrease the likelihood of bringing about this reflex.

In our example describing a student, Mary, eating a sandwich (see Figure 6.4), the performance discrepancy indicated several motor problems. Close examination of what Mary did incorrectly on each step (or part) of the task analysis is needed to determine the type of motor problem so that appropriate adaptations and strategies can be put in place. In Step 2 of the discrepancy analysis, the student overshoots picking up the sandwich. This was determined to be a gross motor movement problem due to her mixed cerebral palsy (spastic and athetoid types). To help correct Mary's gross motor movement, the occupational therapist and teacher decided to try wrist weights. On Step 4 of the task analysis, bringing the sandwich to the mouth, Mary had some contractures (shortening of the muscle) that reduced her range of motion and prevented the sandwich from reaching her mouth. This was attributed to restricted range of motion of the arms, and a sandwich holder was selected to extend her reach. In Step 7 of the task analysis, Mary presented a tonic bite reflex while eating the sandwich. To address this type of motor error, the teacher was instructed in special feeding strategies to try to prevent a tonic bite from occurring and what to do if it occurs. (See Chapter 12 on feeding for more information on feeding problems and interventions.)

Assessing Sensory Performance and Interventions

Just as it is important to determine the type of motor performance discrepancy found in the discrepancy analysis, it is important to examine the sensory components. Careful consideration of all of the sensory categories is important to pinpoint the exact subcategory and problems interfering with correct execution of the step of the task analysis. The subcategories of a sensory performance discrepancy are tactile, proprioceptive, vestibular, visual, auditory, smell (olfactory), and taste (gustatory). Figure 6.6 provides a listing of the sensory systems with sample problems and interventions.

Taking our example of eating a sandwich: Mary missed the first step of locating the sandwich. Because the teacher knew Mary's history of low vision and closely observed her performing this step, this made the teacher suspect the error was specifically because of a vision problem. The specific sensory task required in this activity was to scan and locate one of the sandwich halves on the lunch plate. A possible adaptation is to use a high-contrast plate (instead of a white one) to visually assist Mary in locating the sandwich. Another example of a possible sensory problem is Mary's action of grasping the sandwich so hard that it falls apart. The team decided that the problem was a possible combination of a sensory problem (i.e., being unable to detect the amount of pressure to exert on the sandwich) with a motor problem of executing the correct pressure. The team determined that using the sandwich holder would be an appropriate adaptation that would prevent the sandwich from being crushed, especially because it was required for an earlier step.

Assessing the Environment for Sensory and Motor Elements

In addition to performing a discrepancy analysis, examining the environment for competing sensory and motor stimuli that may interfere with the student

Sensory categories	Sample problems	Sample interventions
Tactile: Touch	Unable to locate/identify items by touch Hypersensitivity to sensory input	Use vision to assist and teach targeted items. Use a desensitization program.
Tactile: Pressure	Unable to exert appropriate pressure on item Unable to detect pressure/pain due to paralysis	Provide adaptations to items that can be crushed or damaged. Schedule position changes, teach student to do skin checks.
Tactile: Pain	Has a condition (e.g., juvenile rheumatoid arthritis) in which student experiences a lot of pain	Provide modifications (e.g., allow time to move, do not have student sit for long periods of time without moving around).
Tactile: Temperature	Cannot detect temperature in paralyzed lower half of body	Have student check items (e.g., water) for temperature before exposing legs to it.
Proprioceptive	Unable to locate paralyzed legs	Use a clear wheelchair tray for student to check on leg positioning.
Vestibular	Becomes dizzy upon leaning over to pick up items	Have student kneel down to get items rather than moving head downward.
Visual	Unable to see items on low-contrast backgrounds (e.g., white paper on white table)	Use contrasting colored paper as background for items.
Auditory	Unable to hear with background noises present	Use auditory trainer.
Olfactory	Smelling strong odors results in self-injurious behavior	Minimize strong odors. Try to determine which specific strong odors result in self-injurious behavior.
Taste	Appears to have no preference for foods. Foods have been pureed together	Separate foods and introduce different items. Observe student response.

Figure 6.6.   Sensory categories and problems and interventions.

performing the task is also necessary. This examination typically includes the way an individual can gain motoric access to the environment as it is set up, the visual or auditory background of the environment, and tactile qualities of the materials in the environment. Our discrepancy analysis of Mary's experience of eating in the cafeteria noted that the environment was noisy with a lot of visual activity, the lighting was poor, and the table height was too tall for her height (see Figure 6.7). All of these factors could interfere with task performance. In our example, Mary became very distracted with the movement of all of the people in the room. To help address this issue, Mary was helped to move to the other side of the table, which that faced toward the side of the cafeteria rather than facing toward all of the other tables. (This had the added advantage of allowing her to direct her attention to the peers sitting across from her to promote socialization,

Category	Sample problems	Sample interventions
Visual	Items not appropriate size in environment	Enlarge the item
	Lighting inappropriate	Add additional lighting/color contrast
	Distracting visual activities	Turn away from distracting activities
	Visual clutter	Decrease visual clutter
	Items out of reach in environment	Lower items whenever possible
Auditory	Noisy environment	Consider alternate environment
	Startling loud noises (bells)	Determine if noise can be changed
Tactile	Items slide on table when being touched by student	Add nonslip material under material
	Student unable to feel different textures	Add verbal description and visual enhancement of item
Motor	Items and their placement not appropriate for student to access	Enlarge items, place within student's range
	Environment not arranged for wheelchair access	Rearrange environment to allow access by wheelchair users
	Height of table is poor	Lower table

Figure 6.7. Environmental assessment of motor and sensory factors affecting Mary's ability to eat a sandwich in the cafeteria.

rather than being overwhelmed by a large number of students.) Although the poor cafeteria lighting was thought to interfere with Mary's ability to locate food on the plate, since the plate color was changed for better contrast, it was felt that the lighting would be adequate at this time. Lighting would be further evaluated at a later date to determine if additional illumination would be necessary. Finally, it was determined that the table height was not optimum. To help accommodate Mary, the table height was lowered, which did not appear to inconvenience the other children at the table.

Planning Functional Sensorimotor Outcomes and Interventions

Based on the results of the collaborative sensorimotor assessment, the educational team can translate the information gained through the assessment into a list of target areas that reflect functional limitations and their underlying impairments, as well as individual strengths. From this list, the team can then work together to identify the most critical issues, which will become the focus for establishing short- and long-term goals on the individualized family service plan (IFSP), in the case of children from birth to 3 years old and their families, or on the individualized education program (IEP) in the case of school-age children. Established goals can then direct initial strategies geared toward achieving functional outcomes for the individual child with severe and multiple disabilities.

How can strategies best be devised to achieve functional goals? According to dynamic systems theory, the educational team needs to ask what constraints in the variety of cooperating subsystems (sensory, musculoskeletal, perceptual, cognitive, arousal, and motivation) and in the environment might be limiting the child's performance. Furthermore, the team has to determine whether the child's selected movement strategy is a stable pattern or is in transition (the latter being more amenable to intervention). Based on task analysis and an interpretation of the child's selected movements, with thought given to functional ability and prevention of further secondary problems, the team would then decide whether to intervene or to leave the child and the environment alone.

If the decision is to intervene, the team must determine whether to adapt the physical environment, verbally or physically prompt the child's movements, and/or instruct the child in a possible new movement solution. After implementing these strategies, re-evaluation would be necessary to determine the effectiveness of the strategies on the desired functional outcomes or goals (Campbell, 2000).

A task-oriented approach to establishing a comprehensive educational plan, such as that suggested by Shumway-Cook and Woollacott (2001), includes intervention strategies designed to achieve the following goals derived from the previously discussed three-level sensorimotor assessment: 1) resolve, reduce, or prevent sensorimotor impairments; 2) develop effective task-specific strategies to promote movement; and 3) adapt functional goal-oriented strategies to changing task and environmental conditions to promote generalization of motor learning. The identified sensorimotor goals are approached not sequentially, but rather, concurrently with each other and also with goals across other developmental domains. For a child with cerebral palsy and deafblindess, a goal to promote independence in feeding, for example, might incorporate strategies whereby caregivers, both at home and at school, do the following: 1) properly position the child in special seating and use preparatory relaxation techniques prior to the meal; 2) use the same adaptive feeding equipment (e.g., nonslip matting and a special plate, spoon, and cup during the meal); 3) provide the same visual adaptations, considering room illumination and color and contrast of materials used, and 4) use the same communication system to guide and provide feedback during the course of the meal.

The Team Process in Planning and Achieving Functional Outcomes

Historically, occupational and physical therapists and speech-language pathologists employed a direct service model of providing intervention to both young and school-age children. In this model, a therapist evaluated the child within discipline-specific parameters and created an individualized intervention plan that focused on carrying out programming with the child on a one-to-one basis. With the passage of the Individuals with Disabilities Education Act (IDEA) Amendments of 1997 (PL 105-17), services have been refocused on including families in assessment and planning and on sharing the process of assessment and intervention among all professionals working with the child, either in the home, school, or community environment. It is important that therapists practicing in early intervention and in school environments function as part of collaborative teams of individuals (refer to Chapter 1) that include families, educators, and other medical and non-medical specialists whose collective expertise is needed to address the complex needs of children with severe and multiple disabilities.

As part of a collaborative team, all professional roles, including therapists' roles, change as the needs of the child and the learning situation dictate. In this model, rather than exclusively providing direct, discipline-specific services to the child with severe and multiple disabilities, professionals' roles are integrated with each other. Planning is set up around a common set of student strengths, goals, and needs, and each team member applies his or her professional skills to meet these shared goals. Therapeutic techniques are implemented in conjunction with other instructional methods in the context of meaningful, functional activities. Professionals teach and learn from each other so that information and instructional strategies are integrated across all developmental domains for meeting children's needs.

Integrated Intervention Strategies

Therapists still may choose to apply discipline-specific intervention strategies to prepare a student to move or to support the student's movement attempts, but these strategies should be explained to the rest of the team; used in the more general context of meeting shared team goals for the child; performed in natural environments; and, if appropriate, taught to other team members. For certain techniques, possible cultural considerations involving touch on the body may need to be explored with and approved by families before they are used. Some therapeutic interventions such as joint mobilization (in which the therapist applies movement to the joints and their surrounding tissues to improve joint mobility), myofascial release (in which the therapist applies gentle stretch to underlying soft tissue structures to improve mobility in an specific body area), and craniosacral techniques (in which the therapist uses specific light touch in the head or pelvic area to change the dynamics of the body's internal hydraulic system and thereby improve mobility) require special knowledge and training to perform.

If deemed appropriate for the child, however, therapists can and should explain and demonstrate some principles surrounding neurodevelopmental treatment (NDT), sensory integrative (SI) treatment, or other types of intervention to other members of the team, including family members, so that these principles can be used with the child to promote adaptive movement responses throughout daily functional activities.

The focus of NDT is to implement handling and positioning strategies that will decrease the effects of atypical muscle tone and reflexes and will increase functional movements by facilitating balanced muscle activity and postural control during movement (Blanche et al., 1995; Bly, 1999; Stamer, 2000). Using NDT as an example for integrated services, therapists can teach other team members ways of positioning a child in order to decrease the occurrence of reflex patterns of movement (e.g., use of side-lying to decrease a strong asymmetrical posture) and ways of handling a child to facilitate active, functional, adaptive movement patterns (e.g., use of slow rocking to decrease muscle tone before assisting a child to push up into sitting from side-lying while on the floor).

The focus of SI intervention is to set up situations and environments that will provide appropriate sensory stimulation to the child in order to elicit adaptive and integrated movement responses (Blanche et al., 1995; Fisher et al.,

1991; Inamura, 1998; Parham & Mailloux, 1996). Integrated services in the SI model might include the therapist showing the teacher and other team members how to do vestibular-based movement activities with a child prior to requiring in-seat performance in order to calm or arouse the child's attention system. In this way all team members who are interacting with the child can be providing consistent, therapeutic input to the child in the way that he or she is positioned and moved by others and in the way that the child's own movements are supported. Treatment techniques and therapeutic interventions will be explained and discussed further in Chapter 7 on handling and positioning children with severe and multiple disabilities.

The team may also need to adapt the presentation of materials and the expectation of the child's response parameters, based on the child's sensorimotor abilities. These adaptations should take into account the child's motor strengths and impairments, as determined on team evaluation. It may be necessary to allow for responses that do not require movement or those that allow for the use of alternative movement that the child is able to accomplish, such as that used to operate switch devices, communication devices, and special adaptive equipment. Whatever adaptations are chosen, they should be available and used across all environments (home, school, and community), and all people working with the child, including the family, should be fully instructed in their use.

The child with atypical motor development will require ongoing assistance from the educational team if his or her sensory and physical needs are to be met and sensorimotor development is to reach its maximum potential. Different professionals may need to act as the primary provider of services at different times in the child's development, based on the priority functional outcomes or goals desired at that time that are determined by the full team and dictated by the needs of the child. Ongoing team assessment will need to occur to ensure that changes in programming are made 1) when children meet their goals and achieve functional outcomes, 2) when children are unable to meet the goals as stated (e.g., in the case of medical conditions in which regression in physical skills occurs), and 3) following surgical interventions or other medical treatments that might change performance parameters.

SUMMARY

The sensorimotor systems are a vital connection between the individual and the environment. The developing child's awareness of the world and response to environmental demands occur through the sensorimotor systems. Sensory systems make up an interdependent network that enables the child to acquire increasingly complex skills across all developmental domains and use these skills in functional ways. Children with severe and multiple disabilities may have impairments in some of the sensorimotor systems. These problems interfere with the acquisition and use of sensorimotor skills to achieve functional outcomes, which can have resultant effects across other developmental domains such as cognition, communication, socialization, and self-help. Effective assessment and intervention include what is currently known about the way children learn sensorimotor skills. The child's ability to produce spontaneous, self-directed movements that lead to functional performance in response to environmental demands is examined in natural environments and contexts. The underlying internal constraints to that performance, including sensory, musculoskeletal, perceptual, cognitive, arousal, and motivation factors are evaluated. Environmental constraints are also examined. Finally, input from all members of the educational team, including families, educators, and medical and non-medical support professionals, is considered together to assist in planning functional goals and effective intervention strategies that serve to minimize the effects of the child's multiple disabilities while maximizing functional potential at home, at school, and in the community.

REFERENCES

Alexander, R., Boehme, R., & Cupps, B. (1993). *Normal development of functional motor skills.* Tucson, AZ: Therapy Skill Builders.

Anniko, M. (1990). Development of the vestibular system. In J.R. Coleman (Ed.), *Development of sensory systems in mammals* (pp. 341–400). New York: John Wiley & Sons.

Axel, R. (1995). The molecular logic of smell. *Scientific American, 273*(4), 154–160.

Baloh, R.W., & Halmogyi, G.M. (1996). *Disorders of the vestibular system.* Oxford, United Kingdom: Oxford University Press.

Baloh, R.W., & Honrubia, V. (2001). *Clinical neurophysiology of the vestibular system.* Oxford, United Kingdom: Oxford University Press.

Batshaw, M.L. (2002). *Children with disabilities* (5th ed.). Baltimore: Paul H. Brookes Publishing Co.

Bigelow, A.E. (1992). Locomotion and search behavior in blind infants. *Infant Behavior and Development, 15,* 179–189.

Blanche, E.I., Botticelli, T.M., & Hallway, M.K. (1995). *Combining neuro-developmental treatment and sensory integration principles: An approach to pediatric therapy.* San Antonio, TX: Therapy Skill Builders.

Bloedel, J.R., Ebner, T.J., & Wise S.P. (Eds.). (1996). *The acquisition of motor behavior in vertebrates.* Cambridge: The MIT Press.

Bly, L. (1999). *Baby treatment based on NDT principles.* San Antonio, TX: Therapy Skill Builders.

Bradley, N.S. (2000). Motor control: Developmental aspects of motor control in skill acquisition. In S.K. Campbell, D.W. Vander Linden, & R.J. Palisano (Eds.), *Physical therapy for children* (2nd ed., pp. 45–87). Philadelphia: W.B. Saunders.

Campbell, S.K. (1996). Quantifying the effects of interventions for movement disorders resulting from cerebral palsy. *Journal of Child Neurology, 11* (Suppl. 1), S61–S70.

Campbell, S.K. (1997). Therapy programs for children that last a lifetime. *Physical and Occupational Therapy in Pediatrics, 17*(1), 1–15.

Campbell, S.K. (2000). The child's development of functional movement. In S.K. Campbell, D.W. Vander Linden, & R.J. Palisano (Eds.), *Physical therapy for children* (2nd ed., pp. 3–44). Philadelphia: W.B. Saunders.

Campbell, S.K., Vander Linden, D.W., & Palisano, R.J. (Eds.). (2000). *Physical therapy for children* (2nd ed.). Philadelphia: W.B. Saunders.

Chalupa, L.M., & White, C.A. (1990). Prenatal development of visual system structures. In J.R. Coleman (Ed.), *Development of sensory systems in mammals* (pp. 3–60). New York: John Wiley & Sons.

Coleman, J.R. (1990a). Development of auditory system structures. In J.R. Coleman (Ed.), *Development of sensory systems in mammals* (pp. 205–247). New York: John Wiley & Sons.

Coleman, J.R. (Ed.). (1990b). *Development of sensory systems in mammals.* New York: John Wiley & Sons.

Colson, E.R., & Dworkin, P.H. (1997). Toddler development. *Pediatrics in Review, 18,* 255–259.

Dunn, W. (1996). The sensorimotor systems: A framework for assessment and intervention. In F.P. Orelove & D. Sobsey, *Educating children with multiple disabilities: A transdisciplinary approach* (3rd ed., pp. 35–78). Baltimore: Paul H. Brookes Publishing Co.

Eicher, P.S. (2002). Feeding. In M.L. Batshaw (Ed.), *Children with disabilities* (5th ed., pp. 549–566). Baltimore: Paul H. Brookes Publishing Co.

Ferrell, K.A. (2000). Growth and development of young children. In A.J. Koenig & M.C. Holbrook (Eds.), *Foundation of education: History and theory of teaching children and youths with visual impairments* (Vol. 1, pp. 111–134). New York: AFB Press.

Fisher, A.G. (1992). Functional measures: Part 1. What is function, what should we measure, and how should we measure it? *American Journal of Occupational Therapy, 46,* 183–185.

Fisher, A.G., Murray, E.A, & Bundy A.C. (1991). *Sensory integration: Theory and practice.* Philadelphia: F.A. Davis Company.

Forney, P.E. (2001). Providing early intervention services in natural environments: Concerns and tips. *American Association for Home-Based Early Interventionists (AAHBEI) News Exchange, 6*(4), 1–4.

Goldfield, E.C. (1997). Toward a developmental ecological psychology. *Monographs of the Society for Research in Child Development, 62*(3), 152–158.

Graziadei, P.P. (1990). Olfactory development. In J.R. Coleman (Ed.). *Development of sensory systems in mammals* (pp. 519–566). New York: John Wiley & Sons.

Green, E.M., Mulcahy, C.M., & Pountney, T.E. (1995). An investigation into early postural control. *Developmental Medicine and Child Neurology, 37,* 437–448.

Greenough, W.T., Black, J.E., & Wallace, C.S. (1987). Experience and brain development. *Child Development, 58,* 539–559.

Grossberg, S., & Kuperstein, M. (1989). *Neural dynamics of adaptive sensory-motor control.* Elmsford, NY: Pergamon Press.

Hadders-Algra, M., & Prechtl, H.F.R. (1992). Developmental course of general movements in early infancy: I. Descriptive analysis of change in form. *Early Human Development, 28,* 201–213.

Haggard, P. (1992). Multi-sensory control of coordinated movement. In J.J. Summers (Ed.), *Approaches to the study of motor control and learning* (pp. 195–231). New York: Elsevier Science Publishing Co.

Haley, S.M., Baryza, M.J., & Blanchard, Y. (1993). Functional and naturalistic frameworks in assessing physical and motor disablement. In I.J. Wilhelm (Ed.), *Physical therapy assessment in early infancy* (pp. 225–256). New York: Churchill Livingstone.

Hanft, B.E., & Place, P.A. (1996). *The consulting therapist: A guide for OTs and PTs in schools.* San Antonio, TX: Therapy Skill Builders.

Heller, K.W., Alberto, P.A., Forney, P.E., & Schwartzman, M.N. (1996). *Understanding physical, sensory, and health impairments: Characteristics and educational implications.* Pacific Grove, CA: Brooks/Cole Publishing Co.

Heller, K.W., Forney, P.E., Alberto, P.A., Schwartzman, M.N., & Goeckel, T.M. (2000). *Meeting physical and health needs of children with disabilities: Teaching student participation and management.* Belmont, CA: Wadsworth/Thomson Learning.

Herer, G.R., Knightly, C.A., & Steinberg, A.G. (2002). Hearing: Sounds and silences. In M.L. Batshaw (Ed.), *Children with disabilities* (5th ed., pp. 193–228). Baltimore: Paul H. Brookes Publishing Co.

Heriza, C. (1991). Motor development: Traditional and contemporary theories. In M.J. Lister, (Ed.), *Contemporary management of motor control problems: Proceedings of the II Step Conference* (pp. 99–126). Alexandria, VA: Foundations for Physical Therapy.

Hodapp, R.M. (1998). *Development and disabilities: Intellectual, sensory, and motor impairments.* Cambridge, United Kingdom: Cambridge University Press.

Inamura, K.N. (Ed.). (1998). *SI for early intervention: A team approach.* San Antonio, TX: Therapy Skill Builders.

Individuals with Disabilities Education Act (IDEA) Amendments of 1997, PL 105-17, 20 U.S.C., §§ 1400 *et seq.*

Keating, R.F., Spence, C.A., & Lynch, D. (2002). The brain and central nervous system: Normal and abnormal development. In M.L. Batshaw (Ed.), *Children with disabilities* (5th ed., pp. 243–262). Baltimore: Paul II. Brookes Publishing Co.

Kiorpes, L., & Movshon, A. (1990). Behavioral analysis of visual development. In J.R. Coleman (Ed.), *Development of sensory systems in mammals* (pp. 125–154). New York: John Wiley & Sons.

Larin, H.M. (2000). Motor learning: Theories and strategies for the practitioner. In S.K. Campbell, D.W. Vander Linden, & R.J. Palisano (Eds.), *Physical therapy for children* (2nd ed., pp. 170–197). Philadelphia: W.B. Saunders.

Lysakowski, A., McCrea, R.A., & Tomlinson, R.D. (1998). Anatomy of the vestibular end organs and neural pathways. In C.W. Cummings (Ed.), *Otolaryngology: Head and neck surgery* (3rd ed., Vol. 4, pp. 2561–2583). St. Louis: Mosby.

Mistretta, C.M. (1990). Taste development. In J.R. Coleman (Ed.), *Development of sensory systems in mammals* (pp. 567–613). New York: John Wiley & Sons.

Movshon, J.A., & Kiorpes, L. (1990). The role of experience in visual development. In J.R. Coleman (Ed.), *Development of sensory systems in mammals* (pp. 155–202). New York: John Wiley & Sons.

Palisano, R.J. (1993). Neuromotor and developmental assessment. In I.J. Wilhelm (Ed.), *Physical therapy assessment in early infancy* (pp. 173–224). New York: Churchill Livingstone.

Parham, L.D., & Mailloux, Z. (1996). Sensory integration. In A.S. Allen & P.N. Pratt (Eds.), *Occupational therapy for children* (3rd. ed., pp. 307–352). St. Louis: Mosby.

Shumway-Cook, A., & Woollacott, M.H. (2001). Motor control: Theory and practical applications. Philadelphia: Lippincott Williams & Wilkins.

Sporns, O., & Edelman, G.M. (1994). Solving Bernstein's problem: A proposal for the development of coordinated movement by selection. *Child Development, 64,* 960–981.

Stamer, M. (2000). *Posture and movement of the child with cerebral palsy.* San Antonio, TX: Therapy Skill Builders.

Stein, P.S.G., Grillner, S., Selverston, A.I., & Stuart, D.G. (Eds.). (1997). *Neurons, networks, and motor behavior.* Cambridge: The MIT Press.

Summers, J.J. (Ed.). (1992). *Approaches to the study of motor control and learning.* New York: Elsevier Science Publishing Company, Inc.

Telzrow, R.W., Campos, J.J., Kermoian, R., & Bertenthal, B.I. (1996). *Evidence for effects of motoric development on psychological processes. Studies of infants with myelodysplasia.* Unpublished manuscript.

Thelen, E. (1995). Motor development: A new synthesis. *American Psychologist, 50,* 79–95.

Thelen, E., & Smith, L.B. (1994). *A dynamic systems approach to the development of cognition and action.* Cambridge: The MIT Press.

Younger, D.S. (Ed.) (1999). *Motor disorders.* Philadelphia: Lippincott Williams & Wilkins.

CHAPTER 7

Physical Management in the Classroom

Handling and Positioning

Margery Szczepanski

Most learning activities in the classroom require posture and movement skills for children to participate. How a child manages learning situations and the school environment is dependent on the child's motor abilities and the demands of the learning experience. For a child with severe and multiple disabilities who has limited motor skills, classroom participation and learning will depend on how the environment supports performance through a daily physical management program that addresses the child's unique motor needs. Although the impact of cerebral palsy and other motor impairments varies with each child, most children with severe and multiple disabilities require teacher assistance and proper positioning to engage in daily activities.

This chapter focuses on physical management of children with cerebral palsy and other neuromotor involvement who have moderate to severe postural deficits and limitations in voluntary movement. It provides teachers and classroom staff with practical information that can be readily applied in the classroom to assist these children in participating optimally in the learning environment with their peers. Readers are advised to refer to Chapter 6 for an overview of the impact of neuromotor impairments on function and sensorimotor development, the role of the sensory systems, and motor control theory.

MOVEMENT IN THE CONTEXT OF FUNCTIONAL ACTIVITY

For most individuals, movement in daily life is automatic and requires so little thought that it is often taken for granted. Yet, even the simplest automatic movements of the whole body, arms, or hands, in isolation or combination, are based on a complex interaction of sensory, motor, and cognitive components that allow purposeful movement to occur. A carefully planned and consistent program of physical management can positively influence components that a child needs for functional movement.

Essential components needed for motor function include postural control and alignment, sufficient muscle tone and strength to allow movement to occur, and control of voluntary movement. Sensory components, discussed in detail in Chapter 6, also have an essential role in eliciting, monitoring, and adapting movement in progress to the demands of the activity and in influencing alertness and arousal level. Cognitive skills that influence attention, interest, motivation, and purposeful intent are important for generating movement that is meaningful and goal directed for function.

Although learning can occur in any position, sitting is the preferred position in the classroom. While seated upright in a chair to look at the teacher, to listen, or to use an augmentative and alternative communication (AAC) device, the child must maintain postural control—that is, position and balance him- or herself on the chair so as not to fall forward or to the side. The nature of the learning activity dictates the voluntary movement, particularly movements of the arms and hands, that will be required to participate in the task. If the activity is looking at a book, movement to turn pages may be required. If the activity involves the computer, movement will be necessary to interact with the computer program. These activities require varied voluntary movements of the head, trunk, and extremities, and components of postural control. The following sections provide information useful to understanding how various components of movement are needed for function.

Muscle Tone

Muscle tone is the readiness of the muscles in the body to act. Every movement requires some degree of muscle tone. Muscle tone needs to be high enough for the muscles to move a body part against gravity, support the position of the body during movement, and maintain stabile postures, yet low enough so that muscles can move the joints freely (Colangelo, 1999). To sit in a chair, one's muscle tone in the trunk must be high enough to align the trunk and spine in an upright position against gravity but low enough to adjust one's posture in order to reach and to use one's arms and hands. When a child's muscle tone is in the typical range, the child can move freely and with control to follow through with the movement required to complete an activity.

As noted in Chapter 6, children with neuromotor impairment have muscle tone that is too high (*hypertonia*), which results in a stiffness that interferes with movement, or muscle tone that is too low (*hypotonia*), which makes it difficult to stabilize joints or maintain a position against gravity. Muscle tone can also fluctuate through a range from being too high to too low, which occurs in children with athetoid cerebral palsy. Children who have abnormal muscle tone, whether it be spasticity, hypotonia, or fluctuating muscle tone in the extremities, tend to have lower muscle tone in the trunk musculature, or what is referred to as *low postural tone* (Schoen & Anderson, 1999). Even when there is spasticity in all four extremities, postural muscle tone in the trunk may be low. In chair sitting, this results in difficulty maintaining an upright posture, and considerable effort will be required on the child's part to maintain the position. Atypical patterns that compensate for spasticity or hypotonia may be present. An atypical pattern is a posture or movement that is not usually observed in a child who is typically developing. An example is when the child extends his or her neck excessively (hyperextension or arching) to keep his or her head up while sitting in a rounded back posture.

Abnormal muscle tone not only affects a child's ability to maintain and move within a position but also interferes with active movement and use of the extremities. The type and distribution of muscle tone and its degree of severity influence both the quantity and quality of movement. For example, a child with severe spasticity in all four extremities (spastic quadriplegia) may not be able to sit independently or use arms and hands without total assistance, whereas a child with a minimal to moderate degree of spasticity might be able to sit in a classroom chair with a supported back and pelvic seat belt and use his or her arms and hands independently if the activity is adapted so that the child can accomplish it.

Muscle Co-activation

Movement and posture require a balance of muscle activation around a joint, which is referred to as *co-activation* (Janeschild, 1996). Co-activation of musculature is necessary for a child to maintain stabile postures and positions (stability) and to move (mobility). During typical movement, stability and mobility occur simultaneously, with some parts of the body maintaining stability while others are mobile. Independent sitting, for example, requires a balance of muscle activation in the front, back, and sides of the trunk that results in the trunk stability needed to maintain a static sitting position. As a child moves when sitting, such as when reaching to obtain an object from a teacher or peer, the trunk continues to maintain stability while it moves to some degree to allow the child to reach.

When abnormal muscle tone is present, muscle activation in the trunk and the extremities is not balanced. The child's movement is then either restricted or is present but poorly controlled. The child will require caregiver assistance to sit or adapted equipment to provide trunk stability while positioned in sitting.

Joint Alignment

In order for muscles to perform their typical action around a joint, the joint must be in proper alignment or have the ability to be moved into an aligned position by the action of the muscles. In order for the child to sit with his or her trunk in an upright, erect position, the vertebrae of the spine must be properly aligned and the whole spine must be aligned over the pelvis. When joint alignment is poor, sitting is difficult, as are typical movements of the extremities. Due to atypical muscle tone and poor postural alignment, the child with neuromotor impairment may sit with a rounded spine (see Figure 7.1), arch the trunk (extend) excessively, or appear to sit toward one side. In these positions, the trunk muscles cannot act in a typical manner to overcome the influence of gravity to erect the spine and maintain the trunk in an upright position, as exhibited by the student shown in Figure 7.2.

Postural Control

Postural control is the ability to assume and maintain posture against gravity during static (e.g., sitting) and dynamic (e.g., crawling, walking) activities (Cupps, 1997; Schoen & Anderson, 1999). It includes the abilities of making small adjustments in posture, shifting body weight over the base of support, and

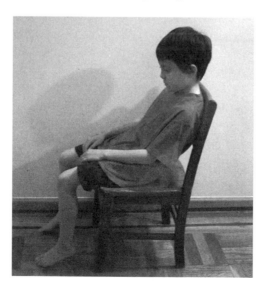

Figure 7.1. Child sitting with a rounded back and poor spinal alignment resulting from insufficient postural control.

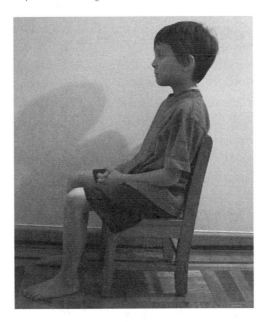

Figure 7.2.   Optimal sitting position with erect spine.

regaining the center of gravity when balance is disturbed. A child sitting slouched in a chair demonstrates postural control when he or she sits up straight after the teacher asks him or her to sit up. To sit in the classroom, the child uses postural control of the head and trunk to maintain the position. To maintain comfort in sitting, the typical child makes periodic small adjustments in posture. These adjustments might be barely perceptible trunk movements or more obvious shifts in body weight. When the child reaches for a coin presented by the teacher during a group counting exercise, the child will shift weight, adjusting posture so that the arm can reach forward to obtain the coin.

Postural control involves what are frequently described as postural reactions: the righting and equilibrium reactions and protective responses of the extremities (Ratliffe, 1998). Righting reactions align the head and trunk toward an upright position in space, whereas equilibrium or balance reactions enable an individual to maintain or regain an upright position when balance is displaced or disturbed. For example, if a typical child reaches too far in sitting so that balance is threatened, then an automatic balance response allows the child to regain balance and maintain the seated position. If a child loses his or her balance in floor sitting, then protective responses in which the arms straighten protect the child from hitting the floor. Postural reactions are an integral component of dynamic movement in space, such as reaching, changing positions, crawling, walking, or riding a bicycle.

Primitive Reflexes

A primitive reflex is an involuntary response of the body to a specific sensory stimulus that appears in early development (birth to 6 months) but disappears with maturation of the central nervous system (VanSant, 1993). In some children with severe and multiple disabilities, abnormal muscle tone and the presence of involuntary primitive reflexes interfere with the development of postural control. When postural control is lacking, adult assistance or adapted equipment will be needed for the child to maintain a sitting position in the classroom. The child will need to be repositioned frequently because small postural adjustments needed for comfort and the prevention of pressure build-up on the buttocks may not be within the child's capability. Primitive reflexes that commonly persist in children with spasticity and suggestions for reducing their influence on a child's motor function are listed in Table 7.1.

Weight Shift

Weight shift is a movement that involves displacement or change of the center of gravity of the body and occurs during postural adjustments and most functional activities (Bly, 1994; Schoen & Anderson, 1999). In any functional position (prone on elbows, sitting, quadruped [on all fours], kneeling, standing), weight shifts can occur forward and backward, to either side, or on a diagonal plane. For example, reaching in front of the body beyond the length of the arm involves a forward weight shift of the trunk (as in reaching for a container of juice on the table during snack time), reaching overhead or to the side beyond the length of the arm involves a lateral weight shift (as in reaching up with one arm to erase the chalkboard), whereas reaching across the body midline involves a diagonal weight shift in which the upper body rotates over the lower body (as in passing paper with the right hand to a child sitting on one's left side).

Weight shift is critical for function because it initiates movement from one position to another. This can be experienced easily by sitting in a chair and then standing up. In order to stand, one must first shift weight by leaning the trunk forward and moving one's center of gravity over the feet. Without this weight shift, it would be impossible to stand up.

A child with abnormal muscle tone and poor postural control has difficulty with weight shift. Functionally, this results in difficulties using the arms freely in sitting, initiating movement from one position to another, and achieving independent mobility. The child may compensate for these difficulties by using spasticity to stabilize him- or herself upright against gravity and by using atypical movement patterns to achieve his or her goals. A child with spasticity may, for example, hold him- or herself in a sitting posture by using spastic muscles at

Table 7.1. Primitive reflexes frequently observed in children with severe and multiple disabilities

Typical age range of appearance and disappearance	Description	Impact on function	Classroom management strategies
Startle reflex: Birth to 2 months	Sudden loud noise results in abduction of the arms with elbow flexion	Interferes with balance in sitting and arm use in all positions	Avoid sudden, loud noises such as doors slamming or unexpected loud music. Develop a collaborative team plan for habituating the child to commonly occurring environmental sounds.
Moro reflex: Birth to 6 months	Sudden change in child's head position when semi-reclined; results in abduction of the arms followed by arms coming together in front of the body toward the midline	Interferes with balance in sitting and arm use	Avoid sudden changes in head position during daily care and movement of the child. Support child's head during transfers
Grasp reflex: Birth to 4 months	Pressure in the palm of the hand toward the ulnar side (little finger) results in grasping of the stimulus	Interferes with voluntary grasp and release of objects and weight bearing on an open hand. Hands may remain fisted	Weight bearing experiences on an open hand may diminish the strength of the reflex. Use pressure on the fleshy area over the thumb (i.e., the thenar eminence) to assist hand opening when the grasp reflex is elicited during functional activities. See handling techniques to open the fisted hand (Figure 7.14).
Flexor withdrawal response: Birth to 2 months	Touch pressure on the sole of the foot in supine position results in flexion of the leg	Interferes with weight bearing on the feet in sitting and standing. Flexor spasticity may increase in legs during dressing	Apply firm, deep pressure to the soles of the feet prior to positioning and weight bearing. Keep the child's orthotics and shoes on during the school day.

(continued)

255

Table 7.1. *(continued)*

Typical age range of appearance and disappearance	Description	Impact on function	Classroom management strategies
Positive support reaction: Birth to 6 months	Pressure/weight on the ball of foot when the child is held upright in standing results in stiffening of the legs in extension	Interferes with standing and walking on a flat foot. Interferes with sitting when feet are not positioned properly, as legs may stiffen	Avoid standing child on ball of foot or toes. Stand child with orthotics on so that feet are properly positioned. Position hips, knees, and ankles at 90 degrees in sitting with weight on flat feet. Use ankle straps positioned at a 45-degree angle in adapted seating.
Tonic labrynthine response (TLR)—supine: Birth to 6 months	Positioning in supine results in increased extension of head, trunk, and extremities. May result in total body extension	Interferes with head control in supine, hands to midline, midline play, and rolling. Increases extensor spasticity	Avoid placing the child with extensor spasticity in supine. Position child sidelying for dressing and rest periods.
Tonic labrynthine response—prone: Birth to 6 months	Positioning in prone results in increased flexor muscle tone in the extremities	Interferes with head lifting in prone, prone skills, and rolling. Increases flexor spasticity	Avoid unnecessary static prone positioning. Position child prone on a wedge while keeping hips extended. Consider use of a prone stander as an alternative to prone positioning.

Reflex	Characteristics	Effect on function	Intervention strategies
Asymmetrical tonic neck reflex (ATNR): Birth to 6 months	Head turning to the side results in extension of arm and leg on the face side and flexion on the opposite side. Also referred to as the fencing position Head flexion in quadruped (all fours) position results in flexion (bending) of the arms and extension of the legs	Interferes with voluntary control of arms. Functions such as arm and hand use in the midline, using two hands together, coordinating eyes and hands (as in visually directed reach), and mobility skills such as rolling and crawling, will be difficult. Contributes to spinal curvature (scoliosis)	Position child with head in midline. Use lateral supports to maintain the head in midline in adapted seating. Position in sidelying (rather than supine) for rest periods with head in midline. Present classroom materials directly in front of the child at the midline.
Symmetric tonic neck reflex (STNR): 6–8 months	Head extension in quadruped (all fours) results in extension (straightening) of the arms and flexion of the hips and knees Influence may also be observed in sitting	Interferes with development of prone activities, such as prone propping, assuming a quadruped position, and reciprocal crawling. Coordinating eye and hand movements in sitting may be difficult.	Avoid excessive head and neck flexion and extension in prone and sitting. Encourage upright head posit on in sitting. Raise wheelchair lap tray to avoid excessive neck flexion in looking down at materials. Present classroom work at child's eye level. Use a slant board or book holder to position books and visual materials at eye level.

Sources: Fiorentino, 1981; Ratliffe, 1998; Trefler, 1984.

the hip (hip flexors and hamstring muscles) to stabilize the pelvis in one position. Another child may rely on using muscles excessively on one side of the trunk to hold an upright posture. In either of these cases, typical weight shift is not possible.

Sensory Input

Adequate processing of visual, auditory, tactile, proprioceptive (from muscles and joints), and vestibular (awareness of movement) information is necessary for postural control and voluntary movement. Movement is dependent on both sensory input from the external environment (visual, auditory, tactile, proprioceptive, and vestibular) and internal sensory feedback from movement in progress. A child uses visual and auditory information from the teacher (e.g., when the teacher shows a picture or calls a child's name), sensory information from the hard seat of the chair, and sensory information from existing posture and movements, in order to sit and participate in learning activities in the classroom.

The child with severe and/or multiple disabilities is likely to have impairments in one or more sensory systems that are important for generating controlled movement. In addition, neuromotor impairments and the presence of atypical muscle tone affect the quality of internal sensory feedback generated from movement. When the child sits in an atypical posture (e.g., with a rounded back) or moves in atypical patterns (e.g., arching the back in order to move the arm), the internal feedback that the child receives will be based on these atypical movements. Repetition of this type of sensory feedback may interfere with the child's ability to learn more functional postural responses and movement patterns.

Volitional Control

Volitional control is the ability to initiate and carry out active and purposeful movement. It is dependent on a child's muscle tone and the ability of the muscles to create motion at a child's joints through a full range of motion in a coordinated manner determined by the demands of the activity. Sitting in a chair, using a manual sign to communicate a desire, taking a cookie from a platter, or reaching toward a communication board are all activities requiring volitional motor control (voluntary movement). Children with severe and multiple disabilities may have difficulty with voluntary movement for a variety of reasons including the presence of abnormal muscle tone, involuntary reflexes, and central nervous system damage to regions of the brain responsible for motor coordination. Basic volitional movements of the body with functional examples that might occur in school are described in Table 7.2.

Table 7.2. Basic volitional movements of body parts, illustrated by functional school-related examples

Proximal body parts	Movement	Functional example
Head	*Capital flexion:* Downward movement of the skull on the first cervical vertebrae. The chin tucks toward the chest with the neck straight.	Gazing down to look at a book while seated or positioned prone on elbows
	Capital extension: Tilting the head backward while the neck is straight. The chin juts slightly forward.	Tilting the head slightly backward to look up at a video monitor or television mounted on the classroom wall
	Flexion: Forward bending of the cervical spine	Tilting the head forward and downward to see pants while fastening a snap
Neck	*Extension:* Straightening the neck as in holding the head upright. Backward bending of the cervical spine	Tilting the head backward to have the front of the neck wiped after lunch or snack
	Lateral flexion: Side bending of the cervical spine. The ear moves down toward the shoulder and the head tilts to the side.	Lifting the head sideways to initiate movement from sidelying to sitting
	Rotation: Twisting of the cervical spine	Turning the head toward the side to look at or talk to a person sitting on the side
Trunk	*Flexion:* Forward bending; rounding of the spine	Leaning forward while sitting in a chair to pick up a paper from the floor
	Extension: Straightening the trunk; arching the back	Keeping the back straight to sit upright at the computer or to walk
	Lateral flexion: Side bending. Lateral flexion occurs in the trunk during most lateral weight shifting of the trunk.	Reaching down to the floor with the right hand while sitting in a chair, to pick up a backpack on the floor on the right side (the trunk bends to the right)
		Reaching overhead to get a box from a high shelf
	Rotation: Twisting movement of the spine. The upper trunk twists on the lower body (pelvis) or vice versa; or the upper trunk twists in one direction while the pelvis twists toward the other.	Reaching with the right arm in front and across the body midline to pick up a book on the left side of a desk
		Crawling and walking require counter-rotation in which the upper body and pelvic rotate in opposite directions
Shoulder girdle (Scapula)	*Elevation:* Upward movement	Shrugging the shoulders in a Simon Says game
	Depression: Downward movement	Pushing up on straight arms to perform a sitting pushup in a wheelchair (the shoulder girdle moves downward)
	Abduction: Movement away from the midline (spine)	Catching a ball with arms in front of the body (the shoulder girdle abducts to allow the arms to reach in front of the body)

(continued)

259

Table 7.2. *(continued)*

Proximal body parts	Movement	Functional example
Shoulder girdle (Scapula) *(continued)*	*Adduction:* Movement toward the midline (spine)	Reaching behind the body during toileting to reach the toilet paper holder on the wall
	Upward rotation: Movement upward on a diagonal to position the arm for reach above shoulder height	Reaching to get a hat from the top shelf of a cubby or locker
	Downward rotation: Movement downward on a diagonal so that the scapula-humeral joint tilts downward	Reaching backward and behind the body to protect self from falling when balance is lost in sitting
Pelvis	*Anterior tilt:* Forward movement. Tilting the pelvic anteriorly creates a slight arch or lordosis in the lower spine that results in good postural alignment in sitting or standing.	Leaning forward while sitting in a chair to have one's coat put on (weight shifting the trunk forward in sitting requires an anterior tilt of the pelvis)
	Posterior tilt: Backward movement. Tilting the pelvis posteriorly creates rounding in the lower back.	Leaning backward in sitting to relax in a soft bean bag chair with the trunk rounded (weight shifting the trunk backward in sitting requires a posterior tilt of the pelvis)
	Lateral tilt: Side tilting upward or downward. A lateral tilt of the pelvic accompanies lateral weight shift of the trunk.	Lifting one leg up in standing in order to kick a ball
	Rotation: Twisting; movement on a diagonal	Moving from prone to sitting, crawling, or walking

Distal body parts—
hip and shoulder

Flexion: The angle of the joint becomes smaller as the joint is bent

Extension: The straightening of a joint

Abduction: Movement of the limb away from the center line of the body

Adduction: Movement of the limb toward the center line of the body

Internal rotation: Turning in or rotating toward the front of the body

External rotation: Turning out or rotating toward the back of the body

PHYSICAL MANAGEMENT IN THE CLASSROOM

For a child who has severe and/or multiple disabilities, addressing his or her physical and motor needs through physical management is essential to maximize daily function in the classroom and quality of life. In general, the goals of physical management are to

- Encourage functional movement in purposeful and meaningful activities in the classroom

- Encourage maximum participation in the environments in which the child functions, including home, school, and community. Postural control and stability, arm and hand use, transfers and mobility, and motor participation are prime areas that need to be addressed in each of these environments (Rainforth, 2003).

- Minimize the negative impact of physical impairments on movement and function and reduce the risk of development of secondary problems (e.g., contractures, deformities)

- Promote the development of posture and movement skills to the extent possible given the child's capabilities

Within the classroom, physical management includes

- Proper positioning so that the child can engage in classroom activities. This frequently involves use of specialized and adapted seating and positioning equipment, splints, and orthotics.

- Preparing a child to participate in tasks and providing physical assistance as needed during activities requiring a motor response

- Carrying out activities with a child that facilitate achievement of functional motor goals designated in the child's individualized education program (IEP). This is accomplished through teaching or practicing new motor skills (e.g., reaching for objects, using a switch to operate an augmentative communication system, holding a spoon for feeding oneself). These activities may include those designed by the physical and occupational therapist to use in the classroom with the child.

- Planning and carrying out a daily schedule that provides a child with experience in a variety of positions based on the child's unique physical needs and IEP

Physical management requires a team approach that involves the child, the family, educators, and health professionals in both planning and implementation. Shared goals, consistency in approach, and daily implementation with repetition are needed (Campbell, 2000; Campbell, McInerney, & Cooper, 1984). Although teachers may encounter numerous approaches to specific motor problems, the information in this chapter is based on the most prevalently applied therapeutic perspectives: the Neurodevelopmental Treatment (NDT) approach, motor learning, and a compensatory approach. A brief overview of these approaches follows.

The Neurodevelopmental Treatment Approach

Karl and Berta Bobath developed the NDT approach in the 1950s for treatment of children with cerebral palsy (Bobath, 1980; Howle, 2002). Since that time, many changes have occurred in how physical and occupational therapists utilize the approach to develop and improve motor skills in children with neuromotor deficits (Bly, 1991). One of these changes has been the recognition that improving motor skill is enhanced when handling is provided within the context of functional activities in the natural environment. Thus, therapists providing intervention in a school environment collaborate with the team to identify the motor skills that are educationally relevant and needed by the child to function optimally in the classroom. NDT techniques that are frequently applied during functional activities include controlling sitting posture during group instructional activities, moving from sitting to standing for transfers, getting from one place to another in the school building, and using the arms and hands during personal care routines such as eating lunch, toileting, and dressing.

The term *handling,* most frequently associated with NDT, refers to "graded sensory input provided by the therapist's hands at key points of control on the child's body" (Shoen & Anderson, 1999, p. 108). Graded sensory input refers to the sensation a child experiences while being assisted to move. This sensory input includes the touch and pressure from the adult's hands on the child and the proprioceptive and vestibular sensation from the actual movement experience. A simple way to think about handling as graded sensory input is to consider the amount of assistance provided to a child. Maximal assistance is needed when a child does not initiate active movement, whereas minimal assistance is needed when a child can actively move but requires guidance for direction and control of movement.

The purpose of handling is to influence muscle tone and to facilitate postural control and the development of movement patterns that contribute to function in daily life (Bly, 1991; Bobath, 1980; Howle, 2002; Ratliffe, 1998; Shoen & Anderson, 1999; Whiteside, 1997). Handling provides sensory input and movement experiences that influence muscle tone during functional movement, thus allowing the child to move more freely and with greater control. Although handling does not repair damage to the central nervous system or permanently alter atypical muscle tone, handling techniques minimize the impact of atypical muscle tone on function and enhance the child's motor development.

Key points of control in handling are parts of the child's body that are used to guide and facilitate movement, and can be proximal (on or near the trunk) or distal (on the extremities or away from the trunk). The most common key points of control are the trunk, shoulders, pelvis, upper arms, forearms, and hands. The use of these key points of control in handling and movement activities is discussed later in this chapter.

Within the classroom environment, handling techniques are used to prepare the child for positioning and motor activities, to assist the child with postural control and the motor components of a task during the activity, and to encourage the child to learn new movement patterns. For example, handling is frequently used to prepare a child to be positioned properly in an adapted seat or to inhibit a child's spasticity when preparing him or her to use an adapted switch to access a computer or a communication device (see sections on facilitation of arm and hand use). Handling techniques can be utilized to assist a child with the arm movements needed to reach and obtain materials during a learning activity or to indicate choices on a communication board. Finally, handling can be used to teach motor tasks, such as rolling, moving from one position to another, reaching in different planes of movement, and utilizing two hands together at the midline of the body.

In the NDT approach, *facilitation* and *inhibition* are used to influence a child's muscle tone, postural control, and quality of movement (Bly, 1991). *Facilitation* refers to handling activities that are intended to encourage more normal postural alignment, postural control, and active movement. Facilitation techniques are also used to influence muscle activity during handling activities when a child's muscle tone is hypotonic. *Inhibition* refers to decreasing a child's spasticity, abnormal reflex activity and postures, and atypical movement patterns. Although frequently discussed as separate entities, in reality, facilitation and inhibition occur simultaneously during handling. For example, if handling is used to facilitate a child's ability to reach in front of the body, then spasticity that interferes with active movement at the shoulder and elbow is inhibited. If handling is used to inhibit the influence of the asymmetrical tonic neck reflex (ATNR), then active head and trunk control in the child is facilitated to diminish the influence of the reflex activity. To clarify, the terms *facilitation* and *inhibition* can refer to activating a child's muscles or diminishing the child's muscle activity, respectively. Facilitation and inhibition are also used to refer to the encouragement of typical movement patterns (facilitating movement) and the discouragement of atypical patterns (inhibiting movement).

Motor Learning Theory and Handling

Since the 1980s, there has been a significant trend toward combining NDT with systematic instruction that incorporates principles from motor learning theory related to how functional movements and motor skills are learned. "Motor learning is the study of what movement processes associated with practice or experience lead to a permanent change in a person's capability for skilled action" (Schmidt, as cited in Kaplan & Bedell, 1999, p. 402). It takes into account the individual, the task, and the environment as critical factors in the learning of functional movement. Based on motor learning theory, Goodgold-Edwards (1993, p. 32) suggested five general principles to apply when guiding the acquisition of motor skills:

1. Motor learning is enhanced when participation is active.

2. Motor learning is enhanced when actions are goal directed.

3. Motor learning is enhanced when sessions include both repetition and problem solving.

4. Motor learning is enhanced by practice in meaningful contexts.

5. Performance is enhanced when the performer assumes an optimal state of readiness for action.

Principles from learning theory indicate that strategies such as providing children with systematic instruction and feedback and opportunities to experiment with movement are also important (Kaplan & Bedell, 1999). Handling techniques that result in a change in muscle action, quality of movement, and improved motor function in daily activity are likely to be more effective when motor learning principles are applied simultaneously and consistently with NDT. Research has demonstrated that the practice of movement occurring in a functional context is more effective than the practice of the movement in isolation (Beauregard, Thomas, & Nelson, 1998; Lin, Wu, Tickle-Degnen, & Coster, 1997; van der Weel, van der Meer, & Lee, 1991). The remainder of this section provides introductory guidance in applying motor learning principles in the classroom.

Active Participation and Goal Direction

In the classroom, active movement should always be encouraged during activities requiring a motor response and while handling a child. Handling is not intended to provide passive movement but, rather, the assistance a child needs to participate actively. Active movement can be elicited by providing activities that have interest and meaning to a child and thus consider the child's preferences. A child is more likely to participate in movement that is being encouraged when the movement has purpose and is used to achieve a goal that is meaningful to the child. For example, a child who is being encouraged to reach for and explore different textures is more likely to participate actively, with the teacher's assistance, if presented with textures that he or she enjoys touching. If the child enjoys touching and exploring rough textures, he or she is more likely to try to reach actively if presented with hard and rough—rather than soft and fluffy—textures. Active participation and goal direction are more likely to be assured when a child chooses the activity. In this case, the teacher follows the child's lead, providing the handling necessary for the child to participate more fully in the chosen activity.

Goal-directed activity provides critically important information about movement. As a child attempts to achieve a goal, successes and failures influence sensory information about the movement that is needed to perform the task successfully. Handling that facilitates and assists a child's achievement of success contributes to the child's ability to learn the initial movement required for the task. Once a child is familiar with a movement, it is important to provide the opportunity for the child to practice it unassisted so that he or she can learn from errors. With sufficient practice, the child is then more likely to initiate the movement independently. Verbal feedback regarding successes and errors is also useful for the child who is cognizant of his or her efforts when learning a movement. For example, the child with athetoid cerebral palsy who is aware of spasticity increasing during an activity involving reaching can be verbally encouraged to relax before and during the task.

At times it might be difficult to identify activities that are interesting and meaningful to a child. In such situations, classroom time should be devoted to carefully observing the child and exploring the child's interests with a wide variety of activities. Care should be taken to repeat exploratory activities because a child may not demonstrate active responses to new and unfamiliar stimuli or experiences the first time. In addition, it may take several presentations of an activity to recognize that a child has responded to it. Changes in mood, alertness, looking, listening, resting muscle tone in the whole body or the extremities (decrease or increase stiffness), or in the sounds a child is producing may indicate interest in activity in the absence of active movement.

Repetition and Problem Solving

Repetition and practice are always required for a child to learn new movements. Handling techniques and proper positioning need to be provided on a daily basis for change to occur in the child's motor function. Many children with severe and multiple disabilities also need repetition and practice to maintain their current level of functioning. Thus, handling and positioning will have the greatest benefit to the child when used consistently by the entire collaborative team, including the child's caregivers, teaching staff, and therapists, both in school and at home. For example, if a child is being positioned in an adapted seat with his or her head in midline to decrease the influence of the ATNR, the reflex is more likely to decrease in strength if the same positioning technique is used by all of the members on the child's team.

When introducing a new movement or activity, it is important in the beginning and until the child is familiar with the task to provide consistency in the task demand, the assistance provided, and the context in which the task is practiced. For example, if the goal is active grasp of a hairbrush, the child should be positioned similarly each time the task is practiced, the same type of hairbrush should be utilized, and the same type or degree of assistance should be provided. Gradually, as the child learns to actively grasp the hairbrush, the assistance provided can be decreased in relationship to the child's gains in motor control.

Once the child has achieved a simple task or goal, opportunity for generalization should be provided. It should be kept in mind, however, that generalization will not occur automatically for many children with severe and multiple disabilities and that certain movements and motor tasks will need to be practiced and repeated in each situation requiring the movement. When it is anticipated that the child is capable of generalizing learned movements to a variety of situations, however, opportunity should be provided on an ongoing basis to use the emerging movement in various contexts. For example, when the objective is to combine reach and grasp of objects, a child should be provided with opportunities to reach and grasp objects during mealtime (cup and utensils), grooming (washcloth, towel, soap, toothbrush), and classroom activity (writing tools, paper, books, counting cubes, containers).

Practice in Meaningful Contexts

Movements are most likely to be attempted and repeated when the context is meaningful to a child. If independent rolling is a goal for a child in a self-contained classroom, then rolling should be practiced as a means of mobility to get from one place to another to obtain a toy during free choice or play/leisure time. If the goal is grasping a spoon, then the child should practice grasping a spoon at each mealtime, preferably while he or she is helped to feed him- or herself an enjoyable food. If the child is learning to move from sit to stand in order to transfer, then this movement should be practiced throughout the school day when the child is actually being transferred.

Optimal State of Readiness for Action

Optimal levels of alertness and arousal are needed for motor learning. Chapter 6 highlights sensory activities that can be used in the classroom to influence alertness and arousal level. In addition, the child with abnormal muscle tone must be prepared for action and readied for participation through handling activities that inhibit spasticity or that increase tone in a child with hypotonia.

The Role of Compensatory Approaches

Although NDT integrated with motor learning theory serves as the foundation for therapeutic intervention to develop and enhance motor control needed for daily function, change in motor control is typically slow in children with severe and multiple disabilities. For many children, it is appropriate to apply a more compensatory approach—one that focuses on adapting activities so that children can participate given their current physical limitations. It may also be appropriate to teach methods of accomplishing a task using children's current level of motor control.

An example of a compensatory strategy is to provide a child with utensils such as spoons, paintbrushes, or toothbrushes with built-up handles that are easily grasped so that the child can feed, paint with peers, and brush teeth him- or herself. The adapted utensils are used so that the child can function in the immediate situation. At the same time, the OT might work with the child to develop more refined control over grasp of utensils without an adapted handle. A suggested guideline is to provide whatever adaptations and assistance are necessary so that the child can function optimally today.

Collaborative team decisions are essential in selecting appropriate and effective compensatory strategies for the child with severe and/or multiple disabilities. The team should consider whether it is realistic to expect the child to learn a task without the assistance of a device or technological aid, whether it will take just as long for the child to learn a task with an assistive device as without it, and whether the child's use of an atypical movement pattern or position to accomplish an activity is appropriate for the child.

Developing a Physical Management Plan

The following questions provide a useful guide to help teachers, therapists, other specialists, and parents on the child's team to develop a physical management program.

1. What are the functional motor goals for the child that will maximize participation in the education environment? Motor goals for the child should focus on the postural control and movement needed to function in the following areas (Rainforth, 2003, p. 21):

    *   Sitting for classroom activities

    *   Changing positions, moving from one position to another, transfers

- Mobility
- Use of arms and hands
- Communication
- Personal care skills

2. What specific motor skills need to be developed for the child to achieve these functional goals?

3. Do abnormal muscle tone, the presence of primitive reflexes, or atypical postures and movements interfere with movement and active participation in activities? Are there health issues and/or orthopedic concerns that need to be considered in the child's educational program? If so, how will these issues be addressed?

4. Will the child need a positioning plan and schedule?

5. What roles will each team member have in implementing the goals outlined in the child's IEP?

6. How will the goals be achieved in an inclusive environment? How can the goals be addressed in naturally occurring daily routines?

GENERAL CONSIDERATIONS FOR HANDLING IN THE CLASSROOM

In general, children with spasticity benefit from an environment that is calm, predictable, and relatively quiet. Excessive noise and bright, flashing lights should be avoided because these tend to create conditions that increase muscle tone. Quick, jerky movements tend to increase a child's spasticity, whereas rhythmic rocking and slow movement tend to decrease it. During position changes, children should always be informed about who will help them move and how and where they will be moved. Usually, moving a child with spasticity unexpectedly has a temporary effect of increasing muscle tone. Firm touch that the child can anticipate is more acceptable than quick, light, unexpected touch. Consider also that the social environment can affect a child's muscle tone. Loud and brisk talking, unfamiliar adults in the room, or excitement over a holiday party or special activity may increase a child's spasticity.

In contrast, children with hypotonia will benefit from an environment and sensory stimuli that tend to generate excitement or an increase in muscle tone. The environment should provide stimuli that are more alerting and arousing to the child with low muscle tone. Quick, arythmical movement tends to be tone generating for these children. The influence of sensory input on muscle tone and arousal is discussed more specifically in Chapter 6.

Each child's responses to sensory stimuli in the environment vary tremendously. Each environmental stimulus must be assessed for its effects on a child. For example, a child with severe spasticity may demonstrate the ability to eat in a quiet corner of the cafeteria with one peer but may have difficulty in a bustling cafeteria at a table with several peers. A child with hypotonia may sometimes withdraw when experiencing a stimulating environment, even though in some situations a stimulating environment may alert the child.

Movement and Task Analysis

Task analysis provides an important interim step between establishing functional motor goals for the child and implementing a handling, positioning, and instructional program that will lead to goal achievement. It can be used to identify what movements the child might need assistance with (or facilitation of) to accomplish a task and what functional tasks might be selected to encourage a particular movement while the child is engaged in activity (Bigge & Best, 2001). If the classroom group is painting in art class, the occupational therapist might work with the child that day to facilitate more controlled reach with greater range of motion and wrist and hand function in controlling strokes of the brush. Or, the therapist might suggest this activity to the art teacher because the activity provides the child with an opportunity to practice reach, grasp, and more controlled arm movement. Figure 7.3 provides an example of a task analysis for a student painting at an easel.

General Guidelines for Handling

The following questions can be used to assess the child's need for handling:

1. What movement does the child need to participate in the activity?

    - Consider the position in which the activity is typically performed and whether an alternate position is possible, as well as the postural control needed during the activity (e.g., maintaining a stabile posture or weight shifting).

    - Consider the arm and hand movements needed to perform the activity.

2. Does the child need to be prepared to participate in the activity? If the child has atypical muscle tone, involuntary reflexes, or atypical postures and movement patterns that interfere with voluntary movement, then some handling to prepare the child to participate in the activity is needed.

3. What types of assistance and handling does the child need during the activity? How should the child be handled?

Activity: <u>Painting at an easel with the preferred hand</u>   Materials required: <u>Stand-up easel with height adjustments</u>   Typical position: <u>Standing</u>

Alternative positions: <u>Sitting in a chair, sitting on the floor with easel lowered, sitting in a wheelchair, standing with the assistance of a walker, standing in a prone or supine stander</u>

	Movements required	Activity adaptations
Trunk	Erect; extended Postural adjustments with weight shift during reach of the arm	Use equipment to provide head and trunk support. Adjust the height of the easel to limit the demands on postural adjustments. Use the nonpreferred hand to assist in postural support by holding onto easel. Adjust the size of the paper to increase or decrease the degree of weight shift necessary during reach. Position the easel within arm's length to decrease demands on anterior weight shift.
Shoulder girdle	Stability while it moves in conjunction with arm Abduction with forward reach Upward rotation as arm reaches above shoulder height	Facilitate shoulder girdle movement with the key point of control at the shoulder. Lower the height of the easel or paper when there is insufficient shoulder girdle mobility and stability to allow reach above shoulder height.
Shoulder joint	Flexion and extension, horizontal adduction and abduction to reach the easel and direct movements to paint Shoulder may be stabile while child moves more distally to direct the brush	Change the height of the easel or size of paper to accommodate limited active range of shoulder motion. Facilitate shoulder movements with the key point of control from the shoulder or upper arm (humerus).
Elbow	Flexion and extension	Move the easel closer to the child when the child's elbow cannot be fully extended. Facilitate elbow movements from the key point of control of the forearm.
Forearm	Forearm pronation (palm facing down) with some movement toward supination (palm facing up) during brush strokes	Facilitate a more neutral position of the forearm from the forearm itself or from the sides of the wrist joint.
Wrist	Extension to position the hand for grasp and proper orientation to the easel	Facilitate a neutral position or wrist extension from the sides of the wrist joint.
Hand	Radial digital grasp with brush held with thumb, index, and middle fingers	Use a large-handle paintbrush when the child has difficulty grasping a tool. Adapt the brush by inserting it into a ball that will fit into the child's hand and facilitate grasping. Provide hand-over-hand assistance for grasp of the paintbrush.

Figure 7.3.   Example of a task analysis for movement required by a student painting at an easel.

Using Key Points of Control

Key points of control facilitating movement vary based on the functional movement being facilitated, the child's muscle tone and postural control, the activity, and the skill of the individual who will be handling the child. The PT or OT working with a child, for example, may use different types of handling techniques to encourage sitting because a variety of key points may be effective. In the next section, which describes specific handling techniques, the suggested key points are those that tend to be the easiest and most effective in encouraging the desired movement. Teachers are encouraged to work with PTs and OTs on each child's team to identify the key points and handling techniques that work best with the child. Prior to handling the child, it is advised that the teacher observe the therapists on the team while they handle the child and then practice techniques under the therapists' guidance.

Teachers are very familiar with the hand-over-hand assistance that is provided in teaching situations. For example, in teaching a child to grasp and move a computer mouse, the teacher gently holds the child's hand around the mouse and guides it, providing firmer pressure on the child's hand if needed to prevent him or her from releasing the mouse. Less pressure is used over the child's hand if the child is familiar with holding and moving the mouse. Handling is similar. The teacher can use a gentle grasp using the hold hand (with fingers together as in a position to scoop) to contact the child's body part. At times, only a light contact will be needed to guide the child's movement, at other times, a firm contact. Firm contact is usually needed when supporting the child's body weight or when moving the child's trunk.

Key points can also be considered response prompts "used to help the student initiate a motor response, provide guided practice of a motor response, and inhibit the student from practicing errors" (Heller, Forney, Alberto, Schwartzman, & Goeckel, 2000, p. 41). Physical prompts include full prompts in which total assistance is provided for performance or partial prompts that are provided to assist initiation and direction of movement. With either type of prompt, the amount of continuous and graduated guidance is modified (increased or decreased) so that the child can be as successful as possible in participating in the activity.

Movement in Handling

Key points during handling and positioning influence abnormal muscle tone when they are paired with movement that either activate muscles (when a child has hypotonia) or diminishes muscle tone (when a child has spasticity). Rhythmic, predictable movements with rotation in the trunk tend to inhibit spasticity in the child, whereas quicker, less-predictable movements tend to generate more muscle activation. When muscle tone fluctuates from very high to low (when a child has athetosis), the type of movement provided varies depending on the child's muscle tone at the time and the child's response to movement. Remember that moving a child always influences the child's muscle tone in some way.

In many instances, spasticity increases as children attempt to move. Although self-generated movement is always positive, a child should be encouraged to move in ways that minimize spasticity so that spasticity will not ultimately limit movement. As the child attempts to move, guiding a child's movement and decreasing the effort involved for the child provides inhibition and facilitation. Some children with spasticity are able to reduce their own muscle tone using techniques they have learned in therapy. An example of this is teaching a child to hold his or her head in midline to inhibit the influence of the ATNR.

Sitting

Most children with severe and multiple disabilities will require some adapted seating equipment to support their posture in good alignment while sitting. To position a child optimally in sitting, the child's weight is distributed equally on both sides of the buttocks and the pelvis is slightly tilted forward. The head and trunk are upright or extended. Hips, knees, and ankles are bent at 90 degrees with feet flat on the floor (as shown in Figure 7.2) (Best, Bigge, & Reed, 2001; Colangelo, 1999; Trefler, Hobson, Taylor, Monahan, & Shaw, 1993; Ward, 1994).

For a child who sits independently without equipment, consideration needs to be given to the chair and work surface so that an optimum and comfortable position is obtained. The chair should have a firm seat that is the proper height so the child's hips, knees, and ankles are at 90 degrees and his or her feet are flat on the floor. The child's thighs should rest on the chair seat, with the seat depth allowing for 1 inch between the back of the knee and the seat edge. As noted previously, the child's pelvis should be anteriorly tilted and touching the back of the chair. The seat back should be firm and straight or slightly angled back (to approximately 100 degrees). A seat that is too deep results in a posteriorly tilted pelvic position with slouching, whereas a seat that is too shallow tends to result in insufficient support whereby the child may feel pushed out of the chair.

When a child will be moving from one classroom to another during the school day, the child should be provided with an appropriately sized chair in each classroom. Plastic bucket-type chairs should be avoided because they encourage slouching and interfere with good postural alignment, even in children who are typically developing.

The height of the work surface (desk or table) is equally important for good posture in sitting and for using the arms and hands efficiently. Table height should allow the forearms to rest on the table surface with the arms in front of the body and create a 30-degree angle between the upper arm and the trunk.

Adapted Seating

The importance of and need for proper positioning of children with cerebral palsy and multiple disabilities and seating options and adaptations available for these children have been documented extensively in the literature (Bergen & Colangelo, 1985; Bergen, Presperin, & Tallman, 1990; Colangelo, 1999; Trefler, 1984; Trefler et al., 1993; Ward, 1994). Adapted seating provides the child with needed support to maintain an upright position in good alignment and is essential for facilitating classroom participation. The checklist for seated positioning provided in Figure 7.4 is a useful guide for assessing proper seating of the child with a physical disability.

Collaborative team decision making involving the contributions of the parents, child, the PT, OT, and SLP; the teacher; and the adapted equipment specialist is essential in selecting an adapted seating system for the child. Although many team decisions are involved in selecting a system, the most important are identifying what adaptations are necessary to provide the assistance the child needs to sit and what modifications will promote function while the child is seated. The teacher's contribution to the team is critical to identifying the child's classroom needs (e.g., identifying which instructional periods require the child to sit upright and for which periods the child can be semi-reclined) and in determining whether classroom staff can realistically manage the equipment. An effort should always be made to minimize the extent to which equipment sets the child apart from peers.

Positioning the Pelvis and Hips

Maintaining the child's pelvis in a stabile, anterior (slightly tipped forward) position is an essential component of seating because pelvic position influences alignment of the head, neck, and trunk. The pelvis, hips, and thighs provide the base of support for the rest of the body (Colangelo, 1999). To maintain the pelvic and hip angle of 90 degrees, a seat belt is usually necessary. As shown in Figure 7.5a, the seat belt should cross the hips at a 45-degree angle and be fastened securely enough to stabilize the pelvis, yet loose enough so as not to cause discomfort or dig into the skin. The seat belt should never be secured from the back of the chair or across the abdomen where it can restrict breathing and create pressure on the child's internal organs (see Figure 7.5b). The seat belt is a necessary component of adapted seating systems and is not a restraint when used for pelvic and hip positioning. Concern about restraining the child can be

PELVIS AND HIPS
_____ Hips flexed to 90°
_____ Pelvis tilted slightly forward
_____ Pelvis centered on the back edge of seat
_____ Pelvis not rotated forward on one side

THIGHS AND LEGS
_____ Thighs equal in length
_____ Thighs slightly abducted (apart)
_____ Knees flexed to 90°

FEET AND ANKLES
_____ Aligned directly below or slightly posterior to knees
_____ Ankles flexed to 90°
_____ Feet supported on footrest
_____ Heel and ball of feet bearing weight
_____ Feet and toes facing forward

TRUNK
_____ Symmetrical, not curved to the side
_____ Slight curve at low back
_____ Erect upper back, slight extension

SHOULDERS, ARMS, AND HANDS
_____ Shoulders in flexed, neutral position (not hunched up or hanging low)
_____ Upper arm flexed slightly forward
_____ Elbows flexed in midrange (about 90°)
_____ Forearms resting on tray to support arms and shoulders if necessary to maintain alignment
_____ Forearms neutral or rotated downward slightly
_____ Wrists neutral or slightly extended
_____ Hand relaxed, fingers and thumb opened

HEAD AND NECK
_____ Midline orientation
_____ Slight chin tuck (back of neck elongated)

Figure 7.4. Checklist for seating positioning. (From York, J., & Weimann, G. [1991]. Accommodating severe physical disabilities. In J. Reichle, J. York, & J. Sigafoos [Eds.], *Implementing augmentative and alternative communication: Strategies for learners with severe disabilities* [p. 247]. Baltimore: Paul H. Brookes Publishing Co; adapted by permission.)

alleviated by providing an auto-type release buckle or Velcro closure that can be released by the child.

When severe extensor spasticity in the low back and lower extremities interferes with sitting and needs to be reduced, a wedge is sometimes used to decrease the child's angle of hip flexion to less than 90 degrees (Colangelo, 1999). The wedge, with the deeper portion placed under the knees, reduces the seat-to-back angle of the chair and decreases the individual's spasticity in sitting (Colangelo,

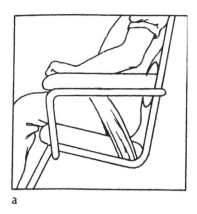 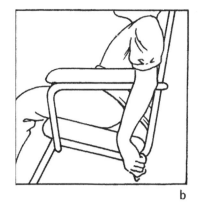

a   b

Figure 7.5. Sitting in a chair a) with a seat belt keeping hips flexed and firm lumbar pad supporting the low back, and b) with the seat belt improperly positioned across the abdomen. (From Rainforth, B., & York-Barr, J. [1996]. Handling and positioning. In F.P. Orelove & D. Sobsey, *Educating children with multiple disabilities: A transdisciplinary approach* [3rd ed., p. 99]. Baltimore: Paul H. Brookes Publishing Co.; reprinted by permission.)

1999). When the lumbar spine tends to be rounded and the pelvis posteriorly tilted, a firm lumbar pad is sometimes effective in providing the additional sensory input needed to the lower back to facilitate more of an anteriorly tilted position of the pelvis.

Positioning the Trunk

A firm seat back is always necessary to support the trunk in adapted seating. To maintain the trunk in a symmetrical position, lateral supports that attach to the back of the chair or the side of the cutout portion of the lap tray are used. The child with little to no trunk control may need to be positioned in a slightly reclined or semi-reclined position. In such cases, the 90-degree relationship between the seat back and the bottom is maintained through use of a tilt-in space seating system in which the whole seat is tilted back as a unit. Harness systems are sometimes used to encourage and maintain alignment of the upper trunk when the child has a tendency to lean forward (Colangelo, 1999). Although these systems can be effective in providing stability to the upper trunk and decreasing the tendency of the child to round his or her shoulders when used appropriately, caution is advised. If the child is not positioned properly or the system is not secured correctly, he or she may be at risk for injury. Finally, a child with no trunk control or severe scoliosis may be fitted with a molded seat back or a complete seat insert to maintain optimal alignment.

Positioning the Head

A child who lacks sufficient control to maintain the head in an upright position in the midline is usually provided with a seat back that extends to the top of the head. Lateral supports may be used to support the child's head in the midline. A small wedge/pad behind the head is effective in decreasing neck hyperextension or pushing the head back forcefully against the chair. For some children, however, a pad behind the head may actually increase the likelihood of the child pushing against the back of the chair. When a child's head tends to fall forward, the whole seating system may need to be tilted backward to provide additional support to both the head and trunk. Molded head and neck supports are used when a child has little to no head control.

Positioning the Lower Extremities

A firm seat bottom that provides proper support for the pelvis, hips, and thighs facilitates an upright position. In general, the sling-type seat of a wheelchair should be avoided for children who sit with their weight distributed unequally on the buttocks or who have trunk asymmetries (lean to one side of the chair or bend on one side of the trunk while seated).

The child's thighs should be positioned symmetrically, slightly separated so that the knees are in line with the shoulders. When there is adductor spasticity (knees pull together), the thighs can be separated by a firm padded wedge positioned between the knees and the distal third of the thigh. These abductor pieces should never be placed between the mid- or the upper thigh because there is a risk for pressure on the genitalia.

In a wheelchair or adapted seat with a footboard, the child's feet are positioned flat, directly under or slightly behind the knees. The back of the feet should rest against the back of the footboard or against the back of the heel loop on the wheelchair footplate. If straps are used, then they are typically positioned to maintain weight on the heel to decrease the influence of the positive support response and extensor spasticity.

Positioning the Arms

When a lap tray is used, the forearms should rest comfortably on the tray in the position described in the previous section on sitting. Otherwise, the armrest of the chair or wheelchair should allow the child's arms to rest comfortably with shoulder abduction (slightly away from the trunk) and elbows and forearms resting in front of the body on the armrest. Armrests are too high when they result in the child raising or elevating his or her shoulders.

Handling Techniques in Sitting

In order to be positioned properly, many children will require some handling and movement to inhibit spasticity prior to being transferred to adapted seating. The handling activities described in the following section are useful for this purpose.

The following handling techniques can be used to align the child's pelvis and trunk and to help him or her obtain a more symmetrical posture prior to sitting in a regular classroom chair or positioning the child in adapted seating equipment. These techniques provide movements needed for function and should be incorporated into daily activities that require weight shift and postural adjustments so that the child has the opportunity to practice them in naturally occurring situations.

Properly handling a child throughout the day necessitates that team members work together to implement the child's physical management program. Teachers are strongly advised to consult with the child's physical or occupational therapist prior to carrying out NDT handling activities. This ensures that selected handling techniques are appropriate to the child's needs and that they are safely and appropriately applied. Handling techniques should always be demonstrated by the child's therapist and practiced by the teacher under the therapist's supervision prior to using them in the classroom with the child.

Forward Weight Shift

Stand in front of the child who is seated in a chair, on a bench, or in a wheelchair or adapted seat. First, gently grasp the upper part of the forearm (as shown in Figure 7.6) while gently bringing the child's arms forward in front of his or her body, externally rotating the child's shoulders. When the shoulders are externally rotated and the arms are extended (elbows straight), the child's palms should face each other. Using the child's upper arm or forearm as the key point of control, gently guide the child's arms overhead while moving his or her trunk

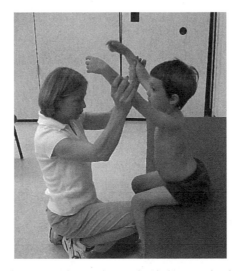

Figure 7.6. Facilitation of anterior (forward) weight shift using the forearm as the key point of control.

and pelvis forward, so that the pelvis tilts more anteriorly and the trunk extends (straightens). The pelvis moves forward over the hips, decreasing the hip angle. The child's weight is now forward and increased over the feet. Alternating this forward weight shift with a backward weight shift (description to follow) can be useful in reducing stiffness around the hips and pelvis so that the pelvis can be anteriorly tilted for sitting.

Some children have considerable instability of the shoulder girdle on the trunk. In such cases, the shoulder girdle can be hypermobile (unstable) on the trunk. When this occurs, the teacher should consult with the child's PT or OT to obtain guidance on an alternate means for weight shifting the child so that hypermobility in the shoulder girdle is not encouraged.

Daily activities for the child in which a forward weight shift should be encouraged include

- Leaning forward while being assisted to remove and replace a jacket
- Leaning forward to prepare for a transfer
- Reaching forward to wash hands at a sink
- Leaning forward on the toilet to be assisted with wiping
- Reaching forward to clean up one's work surface
- Leaning forward to assist with pushing a door open
- Reaching forward to use a reacher to pick up an object that has fallen to the floor

Note that all activities in which the arm reaches forward in front of the body beyond arm's length require a forward weight shift in the trunk.

Backward Weight Shift

Whenever forward weight shift is practiced during activities, the child will need to shift weight backward to erect the trunk and re-align posture. From the child's position of forward weight shift, guide the child's arms down to the level of the shoulders. The upper arms, forearms, or wrists can be used as the key points of control. Gently and simultaneously push the child's arms backward (away from you), as shown in Figure 7.7. The trunk becomes more rounded and the pelvis tilts posteriorly as the child's body weight is shifted backward. Alternate weight shifting the child's weight forward and backward until the pelvis and trunk move more freely and a slight anterior tilt of the pelvis is achieved for proper sitting.

Lateral Weight Shift

During a lateral weight shift, the muscles in the trunk lengthen or get longer on the weight-bearing side as they actively contract to hold weight on the side

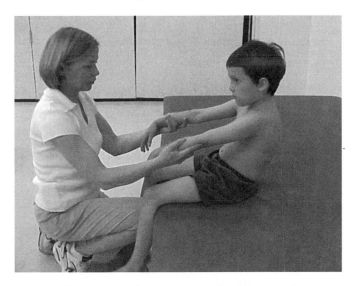

Figure 7.7. Facilitation of a posterior (backward) weight shift using the wrists as the key point of control.

toward which the trunk is shifted. The muscles on the non–weight-bearing side, or the side from which the muscles are moving away, actively shorten. This results in a movement of lateral flexion (bending) in the trunk toward the non–weight-bearing side, the side with less weight. This type of weight shift is needed to achieve full overhead reach of the arm on the weight-bearing side.

Lateral weight shifts are used to decrease spasticity and to obtain mobility in the trunk when the trunk is stiff and in poor alignment. Although lateral weight shifts can be facilitated while the adult stands in front of the child and uses the child's upper arms as the key point of control, it is usually easier to facilitate lateral weight shifts from behind the child, particularly while the child is participating in an activity.

Standing behind the child, gently grasp the upper arms and externally rotate the child's shoulders. Raise the child's arms to the height of the shoulders so that the palms face each other. To shift the child's weight to the left side (weight predominantly on the left buttocks with lengthening on the left side of the trunk), raise the child's left arm overhead (straight up in the air) as in Figure 7.8. If resistance to overhead movement of the arm is felt, raise the arm to the point of resistance, hold it at this point, and gently attempt to raise it further as the muscles relax.

To shift weight to the right side, gently lower the left arm to shoulder height while simultaneously elevating the right arm overhead. Repeat several times, alternating weight shift from right to left sides of the trunk.

When moderate to severe spasticity is present, it may be difficult to raise the child's arm overhead in the full range of shoulder motion. If this is the case, raise

Figure 7.8. Facilitation of a lateral weight shift using the upper arms as the key point of control.

the arm in increments as previously noted, or only move the arm within its cur-rent—but limited—range of motion. Never force a spastic or immobile joint to move by pulling or pushing the joint because injury may occur.

Lateral weight shifting as described previously can be incorporated into the following functional tasks:

- Removing and replacing a hat

- Participating in sleeve removal and replacement by extending arms

- Shifting weight side to side to relieve pressure on the buttocks during extended periods of sitting (more than 30 minutes)

- Reaching overhead to remove and replace objects from high shelves

- Reaching for class materials positioned on the side and/or in front of the body

- Reaching for a paper towel from a towel dispenser after hand washing

- Reaching sideways while in a wheelchair to push a wall switch to activate electric door opener

An alternate form of lateral weight shift occurs when the child reaches down to the side (rather than up) in chair sitting or standing. When reaching down to the right side, for example, the child's body weight shifts to the right side and the trunk bends on the right so that the arm can reach toward the floor on the right. To encourage this movement, use one hand on the child's upper arm to guide reaching down. The opposite side of the pelvis is stabilized gently while it moves in order to assist with trunk control so that the child does not fall to the right side. Although this is a functional movement pattern for a child to learn, the child with poor trunk control may become overly reliant on this pattern in an effort to shift body weight. Care needs to be taken so that the child does not substitute this pattern for lateral weight shifts (previously described) that contribute to improved control of posture and ultimately, more functional movement patterns.

Trunk Movements with Rotation

Trunk movements with rotation can be facilitated from the front, using the upper arm as the key point of control, so that the palms of the child's hands face each other and the child's arms are at shoulder height. While the child's pelvis is stabile, gently move one of the child's arms slightly forward and toward the midline so that the upper part of the trunk on that side rotates forward. Gently move the opposite shoulder slightly backward to allow rotation of the upper trunk to occur.

To facilitate rotation from behind the child, place your right hand on the right side of the child's pelvis to provide pelvic stability. With your left arm, reach around in front of the child from the left side and place your arms under the child's arms so that they rest on your forearm. Raise the child's arms to shoulder height and gently rotate (twist) the upper trunk toward the left, as shown in Figure 7.9. Then gently return the upper trunk to the starting position. Change hands and rotate to the right. While assisting the child to participate in a reaching activity, trunk rotation is best facilitated from behind the

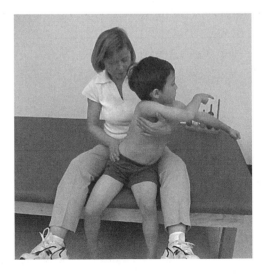

Figure 7.9. Facilitation of a weight shift with rotation using the upper arms and side of the pelvis as the key point of control.

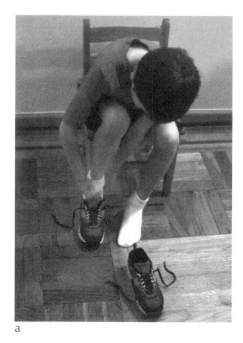
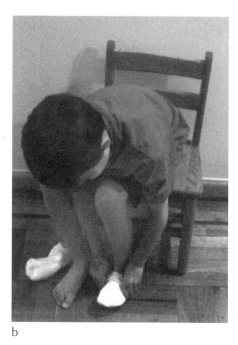

a   b

Figure 7.10.   Reaching down to the floor with upper body rotation to remove a) a shoe, and b) a sock.

child. Use one hand to stabilize the side of the pelvis while the other hand guides reaching toward or across the body midline with upper trunk rotation.

Functional activities incorporating trunk rotation include

- Reaching toward or across the midline to turn on the water faucet at a sink or to reach the soap dispenser

- Reaching for class materials with the preferred hand across the body midline (reaching with the right hand to the left side)

- Reaching down to the feet to remove and replace shoes and socks (see Figure 7.10a and 7.10b)

Handling to Facilitate Arm Use

The child with poor trunk control in sitting and spasticity in the arms will have difficulty reaching for objects and using his or her arms in classroom activities. Atypical posturing of the arms is common and interferes with initiation of controlled movement. The child may posture the arms in a "high guard" position in which the shoulders are abducted and extended, elbows flexed, and hands fisted. The shoulder girdles may tend to pull back or adduct toward the spine in what is commonly referred to as a *retracted* position. This pattern is sometimes seen in children who are typically developing, to stabilize the upper body and balance when learning new motor skills such as sitting or walking. In the child with spasticity, this pattern may be exaggerated when the child is supine or poorly positioned or when the child becomes excited and muscle tone increases.

A second common pattern is for the arms to be internally rotated and adducted at the shoulder and elbows extended and held stiffly in front of the body, sometimes in a scissoring type posture. This pattern tends to be seen more frequently in the child with athetosis in which the tendency is to "lock the joints" in the joints' end range of motion. A third pattern seen in children with spasticity and/or athetosis is the ATNR posture (see Table 7.1).

The child with hypotonia may have difficulty lifting his or her arms and holding them up against gravity sufficiently to participate in activities. The child may be able to reach and grasp, but does so with poor control, lacking the strength to sustain grasp of an object.

When spasticity is present in the arms, the child will need to be handled in ways that inhibit spasticity throughout the school day. This is necessary for the child to move more freely and use any voluntary movement that is present. Active arm movements during activities should be encouraged. Consistently moving and positioning the child so that the arms are in front of the body is perhaps the simplest means of inhibiting an atypical high guard posture secondary to spasticity. This can be accomplished by positioning the child's arms on a table or wheelchair lap tray and keeping the arms in front of the body during lifting, carrying, or transferring the child from one position to another.

The following handling activities are useful in decreasing spasticity in the arms in preparation for arm and hand use and for reducing spasticity during an activity in which effort results in increased tone.

- Movement with weight shift (noted in the previous section) not only influences the child's postural alignment and trunk control but also may be used to reduce muscle tone in the arms.

- Rhythmic rocking of the upper body with rotary movements. Stand in front of the child. Using the upper arm as the key point, externally rotate the child's shoulders gently so that the palms face each other. Gently move the arms so that one moves forward and one moves backward, alternating the forward and backward movement of the upper body in a rhythmic pattern. This provides gentle rotation to the upper body, which inhibits spasticity. Similar results can be obtained by weight shifting the child in a rotary pattern as previously described.

- Approaching the child from the front, gently grasp the side of one of the child's hands with the palm facing downward. Gently shake the child's arm up and down in a small range. Simultaneously move the child's arms toward the front of the body, extending the child's elbow as you feel the child's arm relax. This activity can be done while the child is supine or sidelying, or while seated in adapted equipment.

- On a mat, roll the child with the arms in an overhead or near overhead position (see the section on rolling supine to prone). Roll the child several times in each direction to reduce tone in his or her arms. If the child is very stiff and his or her arms cannot be moved overhead, try gentle shaking of each arm as discussed previously to obtain greater movement at the shoulder and elbow. Never attempt rolling over an arm in the high guard posture because this may result in injury to the child's shoulder.

For the child with hypotonia, weight-bearing activities described in the next section can be used prior to activity to generate increased muscle action. As with activities described in the previous sections, the teacher should collaborate with a child's PT and OT to identify which activities are appropriate for a particular child. The therapist should then demonstrate these activities, and the teacher should practice them. In addition to weight-bearing activities, specific techniques such as tapping on the muscles and joint approximation and traction may be used by therapists to increase muscle activity.

For the child with limited active reach, movement of the arms should first be encouraged in front of the body, then to the side, and finally across the body midline and behind the body. Forward reaching is easiest below shoulder height and may be easier for the child while positioned with the trunk well supported in an adapted seat. As the child acquires active movement in front of the body, reach movements above shoulder height should gradually be encouraged. Similarly, the child should be encouraged, when reaching to the side, to reach below shoulder height, with reach above the shoulder encouraged over time. Initially, the child with limited movement may be more successful attempting reach with one arm at a time, though reaching with two hands should also be encouraged when possible.

To facilitate reaching toward objects,

- Stand behind the child. Using the key point of the upper arm, externally rotate the child's shoulder and guide the arm in the direction of the desired reach, as shown in Figure 7.11a. Reach can be encouraged in this manner for one arm or both arms together. Alternate key points that can be used are the forearm and the sides of the wrist or hand. Remember that the shoulder joint always needs to be externally rotated for reach away from the body (see Figure 7.11b). Do not attempt to facilitate reach when the child's shoulders are internally rotated because this may injure the child's shoulders.

- To encourage reach above shoulder height or overhead, incorporate previously described lateral weight shift activities in the trunk.

As previously discussed, reach in daily function is usually accompanied by postural adjustments in the trunk, that is, weight shifts. Therefore, when it is possible, weight shift through the trunk should be encouraged simultaneously with reaching patterns. When the child is positioned in adapted seating and a seat belt is used to position the pelvis, however, weight shifting the child will not be possible. In this case, reach is facilitated toward objects and activities that are positioned within arms length either in front or to the side of the child, on a table surface, or in space.

Weight Bearing

The child with severe and/or multiple disabilities is likely to have difficulty bearing weight on the extremities (e.g., prone on elbows, weight on extended arms in an all fours position). Controlled movement of the body over the extremities in weight-bearing positions and transitional movement contributes to the development of controlled movement of the extremities in space. PTs and OTs utilize weight-bearing activities to facilitate and inhibit muscle activity necessary for the development of stability and mobility capabilities in the extremities (Boehme, 1988; Chakerian & Larson, 1993; Gudjonsdottir & Mercer, 1997; Schoen & Anderson, 1999).

Functionally, weight-bearing skills in the arms are important to the child for support in sitting (as in forward propping), belly crawling and quadruped crawling

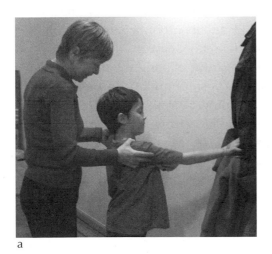

a   b

Figure 7.11.   Facilitation of reach using a) the shoulder as the key point of control, and b) the upper arm as the key point of control.

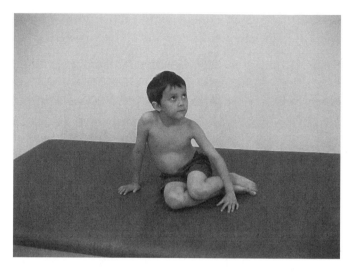

Figure 7.12.　Side sitting with weight bearing on extended arm.

to get from one place to another, supporting him- or herself while moving through position changes, and using a walker or Lofstrand (forearm) crutches. Leaning/ supporting oneself on a table top with one arm while the other is working, pushing on extended arms to adjust one's posture or perform a sitting pushup, or extending one's arms to protect one's self during a fall are functional tasks requiring weight-bearing skill. Weight bearing is also required in all activities requiring a pushing action with the arm, such as when holding on and pushing down on the arm of a chair during a transfer or supporting oneself on a grab bar during toileting. When one of these activities is a functional goal for the child, weight-bearing activities should be documented in the child's IEP and incorporated into the child's handling and positioning program throughout the school day.

The child can be provided with weight-bearing experience on extended arms and elbows through prone positioning and positioning in a prone stander, as described in the section on alternative positioning. During floor activities, the child can be assisted to support him- or herself in side sitting, as shown in Figure 7.12. Side sitting can also be practiced with weight bearing on both arms; however, this position does not allow a child to use his or her arms to participate in an activity. Transitional movements, such as moving from sidelying to sitting, also provide opportunities for weight bearing on the elbow and an extended arm. In addition, the child can be encouraged to practice functional weight bearing on the arms by

- Sitting at a table, positioned with arms in front of the body, bent at the elbow, in an "on elbows" position. The child leans forward so that his or her weight is shifted onto the forearms in sitting. The child is encouraged to use or reach with one arm while weight bearing on the other.

- Sitting in a wheelchair, supporting him- or herself in standing by grasping arms of the wheelchair and performing sitting pushups to alleviate pressure on the buttocks (arms at sides and elbows straight)

- Side sitting propped on one arm on the floor for a group activity

- Pushing with arms while on a prone scooter board during physical education class

- Stabilizing a lunch tray on top of the wheelchair lap tray with two hands, while being pushed from the lunch line to a cafeteria table

- Holding onto a grab bar and supporting self in standing during toileting while being assisted to pull pants up and down

- Standing in a prone stander, supporting upper body with weight on the elbows.

Handling to Facilitate Hand Function

Children with severe and multiple disabilities frequently exhibit tightness in the fingers or closed-fisted hands due to spasticity, the influence of the grasp reflex, and lack of controlled voluntary movement. It is important that hand opening and active hand movements be encouraged to promote and maintain function, maintain range of motion, and prevent joint contractures and hand deformities. Active grasp, release, and manipulative skills (e.g., manipulating fasteners on clothing, pulling a zipper open and closed on a backpack, opening containers, tearing wrappers off packaged foods, self-feeding) should be encouraged whenever opportunity arises.

When a child's IEP includes specific goals related to hand use, the child's team should collaborate on how these goals can be achieved within the natural course of the day. To promote improved hand function and hand use, a child may need weight-bearing experiences, specific exercises and handling techniques for the hands and fingers, and specific sensory experiences if hypersensitivities or hyposensitivities to tactile stimuli are present. Teachers interested in learning more about promoting hand function in the classroom are encouraged to consult Exner (1995), Freeman (1995), Henderson and Pehoski (1995), and Levine (1991).

Facilitating Hand Opening

To facilitate opening a child's spastic fisted hand, first position the child in adapted seating with his or her head and trunk properly aligned. The child's whole extremity should be relaxed through gentle repetitive and rhythmic movements in which the child is assisted in reaching forward in front of his or her body. It is important to note that it may take a teacher several sessions to become proficient at relaxing spasticity in the child's arm sufficiently to allow the child's hand to open.

The anatomy of the hand makes it possible to open a fisted hand by flexing the wrist joint, which automatically extends the fingers. This is done by bending the child's wrist downward toward flexion, as shown by the hand position of the child in Figure 7.13a. If the hand remains fisted, then the teacher can firmly sweep his or her hand from the base of the child's wrist (on the top of the hand) toward the fingers (as shown in Figure 7.13b) several times. These sweeps are similar to a motion one would use to sweep crumbs from a child's sleeve after a snack. The teacher then waits several seconds for the fingers to open. The sweeping can be repeated if only slight or partial opening of the fingers occurs.

When the techniques just described do not seem to be working, never pry the child's hand open from the tips of the fingers. Doing so may cause pain and injury to the child and may even result in increased tightness. An alternative approach is to place pressure on the fleshy part of the child's thumb inside the palm (the *thenar eminence*) for a minute or two and wait for the hand to relax, as shown in Figures 7.14a and 7.14b. A therapist on the team can easily demonstrate this technique.

Use of Hand Splints

Splints may be recommended for a child to inhibit spasticity, maintain range of motion, prevent contractures, and provide proper alignment for function (Hill,

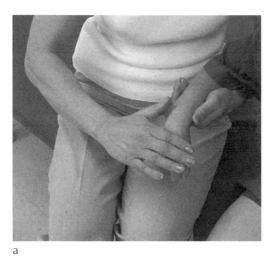
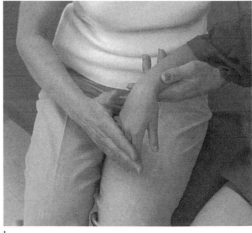

a   b

Figure 7.13. Encouraging the child's hand to open by a) bending (flexing) the wrist downward, and b) sweeping on the top of the hand in a downward motion to facilitate hand opening.

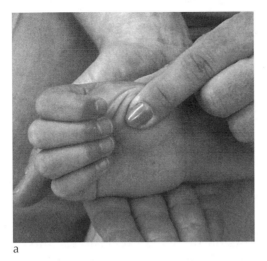
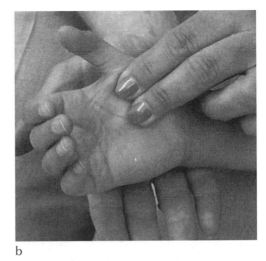

a   b

Figure 7.14. a) Partially fisted hand with thumb in a cortical position, b) Pressure of the base of the thumb (the thenar eminence) to facilitate hand opening.

1998). A hand splint may be worn intermittently throughout the day to inhibit spasticity so that increased function can be obtained once the splint is removed. When a splint is used to stretch tight muscles, prevent progression of contractures, or reduce severe spasticity, the splint is usually worn for an extended period of time (weeks or months) throughout the day. In addition, splints may be used to promote a child's independence and hand use in a specific activity, such as holding utensils, or to allow the child to press the keys on a keyboard or use a writing implement.

Although benefits of splinting have been demonstrated in some children (Exner & Bonder, 1983; Johnson, Lind, & Yates, 1993; Smelt, 1989), splint use is controversial in some cases. One concern is that a child who wears a splint has less opportunity for sensory input to the hand in daily experiences. Restricting sensory input into the hand can be limiting for the child who has decreased hand awareness or the child who is dependent on tactile and proprioceptive input to use the hands. The optimum approach to splinting requires close team collaboration and careful monitoring to evaluate whether the splint is having the desired effect and is, in fact, maintaining or improving the child's hand use. When splints are used, the teacher and the OT will need to communicate frequently about the length of time the splint should be worn each day, the impact of the splint on function, and the need for splint modifications.

Since the 1990s, soft neoprene splints have been used increasingly to position the thumb in a position that inhibits spasticity in the hand or positions the thumb in a position for opposition with the other fingers during grasp (Casey & Kratz, 1988; Hill, 1988; O'Connell, 1998). They can also be used to stabilize the wrist to achieve greater control of the hand. One advantage of neoprene splints is that they are relatively inexpensive, allowing for use on a trial basis without undue financial burden. They are also comfortable and washable and can be applied and removed with relative ease. A disadvantage is that they make the wearer perspire, which can be problematic in hot weather. Removing the splint periodically during the day is usually necessary for the prevention of skin break-down secondary to excessive sweat.

Encouraging Functional Mobility

Rolling Supine to Prone

Because several different key points of control can be used to facilitate rolling, the teacher should consult with the therapists on the child's team to identify which key points of control should be used for a particular child. The method presented here is clinically effective for children with varying needs for partial participation in rolling.

- To roll the child to the right side, begin by positioning the child's right arm to the side and left arm across the body, as shown in Figure 7.15a. The child's right leg is straightened and the left leg is bent at the hip and knee.

- Place your left hand on the front of the child's right thigh and the right hand is placed under the child's left thigh, as shown. The child's left leg is rotated over the right leg to the sidelying position (see Figure 7.15b). Then wait for the child's upper body to follow.

- The left leg is brought down toward the floor while it is straightened (see Figure 7.15c). As the left leg is extended, the child's upper body should automatically rotate down toward the floor.

- Assist the child as needed to adjust the position of his or her arms at the sides of the body or to assume an on-elbows position.

Rolling Prone to Supine

- To roll the child from stomach to back, begin by placing the child's arms in an overhead position with the child's palms facing each other (see Figure 7.16a).

- To roll the child toward the right side, place the right hand on the child's right upper arm and the left hand on the left side of the child's pelvis. Place your hand around the child's arm with the thumb on top so that your arm can rotate externally with ease as the child is rolled over. Begin by rotating the left side of the child's pelvis up and back, simultaneously rotating the

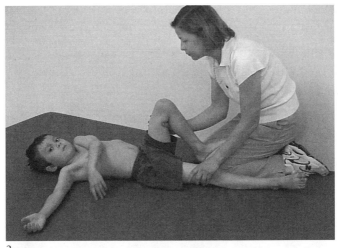

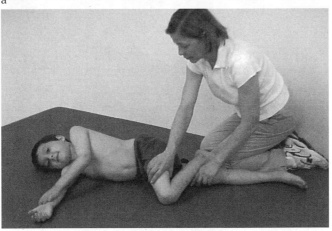

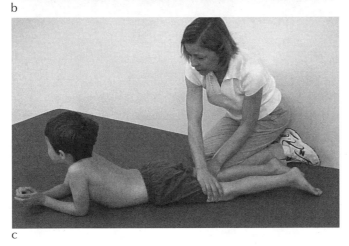

Figure 7.15. Facilitation of rolling supine to prone.

child's right arm externally until the child is in a sidelying position, as shown in Figure 7.16a–7.16b.

- From sidelying, gently guide the left side of the child's pelvis down to the floor. Use your right forearm to support the child's head and to guide it gently down to the floor (see Figure 7.16c).

For many children, controlling the movement of the head down to the floor will be the most difficult part of the roll to control because it requires active head and

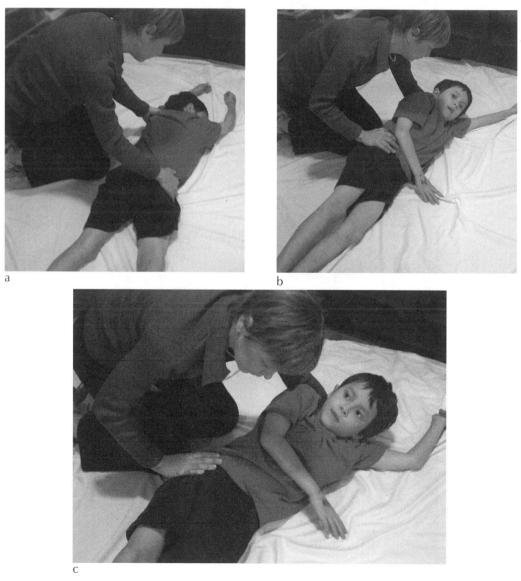

a

b

c

Figure 7.16.   Facilitation of rolling prone to supine.

neck flexion against gravity. The child with extensor spasticity may arch or throw the head backward. The child with hypotonia may not have sufficient head control or may experience loss of partial head control achieved in other positions. These situations can be prevented by supporting the child's head on the teacher's forearm.

Rolling is not only an important means of mobility but also a necessary skill for partially participating in one's daily care from others. If a child can shift body weight in the prone and supine positions, the child can assist caregivers with the weight shifts required during dressing and changing and with bed positioning at home. For a child with spasticity, movements with rotation through the trunk in rolling have the effect of decreasing spasticity and inhibiting atypical postures while facilitating a functional movement pattern.

Facilitating Movement from Prone to Sitting

Begin with the child positioned prone on elbows.

- To facilitate the child to a side sitting position on the left hip, use the child's left shoulder and right side of the pelvis as key points, as shown in Figure 7.17a.

- Shift the child's weight toward the left side (so that there is little to no weight on the right elbow) while rotating the right side of the pelvis toward a sidelying position.

- As the pelvis rotates back, guide the left shoulder up so that the child's left arm extends and supports the child's upper body (see Figure 7.17b).

- As the child's pelvis is rotated to the floor, guide the child's upper body to rotate it until it is in line with the pelvis and the child is sitting upright (see Figure 7.17c and 7.17d)

Functional Mobility in the School Environment

The importance of functional mobility is well recognized. To the extent possible, learning mobility skills should be an essential component of each child's program despite the challenges created by limited time in the child's daily schedule, the physical limitations of the child, and the frequently slow rate of the child's skill acquisition.

The Mobility Opportunities via Education (MOVE) Curriculum (Bidabe, Barnes, & Whinnery, 2001) is an activity-based program designed for children and adolescents with severe and multiple disabilities to teach them functional mobility skills in the context of naturally occurring daily situations in the school environment. The program focuses on basic movement skills such as chair sitting, moving to standing, standing, walking, and functional use of the

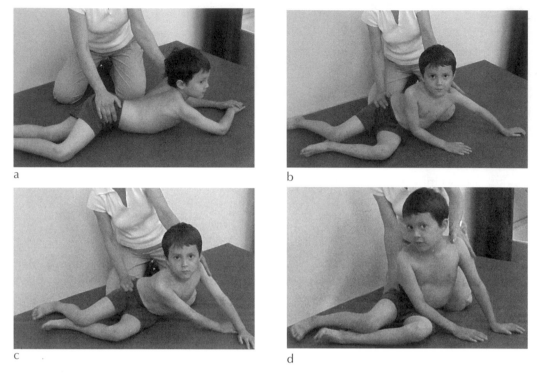

a   b   c   d

Figure 7.17.   Facilitation of movement prone to side sitting

arms. Each functional skill is broken down into small sequential steps accompanied by physical prompts and assistance in instruction of each skill. The program is designed for use by an interdisciplinary team of therapists, teachers, and caregivers who can incorporate opportunities for the child to practice skills throughout the day.

ALTERNATIVE POSITIONING IN THE CLASSROOM

Floor Sitting

Although floor activities are frequently included as part of the school day for preschoolers and older students participating in self-contained classrooms, floor sitting is generally not appropriate in an inclusive environment. When a child with severe and/or multiple disabilities participates in an inclusive classroom and needs experience on the floor to either develop sitting or mobility skills, these experiences can be incorporated into adaptive physical education periods, free periods, or recess. It is suggested that the child's need for floor time experience to achieve functional sitting and mobility goals be documented in the IEP. The remainder of this section addresses the general needs of children in floor sitting.

Many positions provide experience in the upright sitting position. These include ring and crossed-leg sitting, modified ring sitting, side sitting, and heel sitting. Table 7.3 includes descriptions of these and other floor-sitting positions, as well as advantage and disadvantages of each. For the older child, floor sitting provides an alternative to sitting in a wheelchair or adapted seating and an opportunity to develop postural control and sitting balance. Floor sitting also lends itself to the development of transitional movements from one position to another (e.g., moving from sitting to prone and prone to sitting). From floor sitting, some children can more easily initiate moving about the classroom (e.g., rolling, belly crawling, crawling on all fours). To select a floor-sitting position, the child's physical capabilities in sitting and the demands of the activity in which he or she is participating are considered.

Independent floor sitting requires sufficient mobility and stability in the head and trunk, with the accompanying postural control needed to maintain the position. The child also needs to have sufficient joint mobility—particularly at the pelvis, hips, and knees—to be placed in or to assume a sitting position. Children with severe spasticity or with significant hypotonia may be difficult to position on the floor without adapted equipment because the influence of gravity is more pronounced when a child sits on the floor. Spasticity may become more pronounced as the child exerts effort to maintain the position. The child with hypotonia may have a difficult time using available muscle power to counteract the effects of gravity and the quality of sitting posture may, in fact, deteriorate in comparison to that observed in chair sitting.

A child with either spasticity and hypotonia may have a tendency to sit with his or her back more rounded and the pelvis more posteriorly tilted while on the floor in a ring or crossed leg-sit position in comparison to sitting in a chair. Use of a low bench or table in front of the child so that his or her arms can be supported is a simple and effective way to improve the child's trunk posture and alignment. The height of the table or bench should be adjusted upward to facilitate more trunk extension in the child as needed.

Additional suggestions for reducing a rounded back in sitting include the following:

- Position the child in the corner of the room between two perpendicular walls so that the child can take advantage of the wall surfaces for trunk support.

- When the child's balance is inconsistent and the child is fearful of falling, a table surface can be used in front of the child to encourage trunk extension.

- If the child does not yet have sufficient balance to maintain the position, tends to fall to the side, or sits asymmetrically, try a commercially available corner seat or adapted floor sitter.

Table 7.3.   Floor-sitting positions

Position	Advantages	Disadvantages
Ring sit: Legs symmetrical with hips and knees bent	Easiest sitting position for most children Provides wide base of sitting support, which assists the child with poor trunk control Arms can be used easily	Contributes to rounding of the back in child with hypotonia Excessive hip flexion limits lateral weight shift and movement out of sitting
Modified ring sit: One leg straight and one leg bent	Provides opportunity for asymmetrical positioning; a good alternative for the child who habitually ring sits Arms can be used easily Allows lateral shift and movement in/out of sitting	Child may need assistance to develop skill in weight shifting toward side of extended leg
Crossed leg: Tailor-sitting position	Lower extremity position provides stable base for sitting Arms can be used easily	Limits forward/backward, lateral weight shift and mobility Contributes to rounding of back in children with spasticity or hypotonia May be difficult to assume when there is lower extremity spasticity and limited pelvic mobility
Long leg sit: Legs symmetrical, straight out in front of the body	Provides opportunity to practice sit with narrow base of support in comparison to ring or modified ring Provides opportunity to stretch muscles on the back of the leg (hamstrings) Allows lateral movement in and out of sitting	May not be possible for child with tight hamstrings and lower extremity spasticity May increase rounding of back when hamstrings are tight
Heel sit: Hips and knees bent with legs tucked under buttocks, weight of the body on the heels	Allows weight shift forward and backward and movement in and out of sitting	Child easily falls into W sit position Not possible to assume while wearing orthotics Promotes symmetrical movement patterns; limits lateral weight shift and rotary movement

Position	Advantages	Disadvantages
W sit: Weight equally distributed on the buttocks with legs splayed to the side forming a W	Provides a wide base of support Allows weight shift forward and backward to move in and out of the position May be the only position that can be assumed independently	Creates stress on hip and knee joints Promotes symmetrical movement patterns; limits lateral weight shift and rotary movement Tends to limit development of more mature movement patterns in children who are habitual W sitters
Side sit: Weight primarily on one side of the buttocks with trunk lengthened on that side; hips and knees bent toward opposite side Usually assumed leaning on one extended arm for support	Easily assumed from prone, sidelying, or quadruped position Promotes lateral movement of trunk An important component of transitional movement Promotes weight bearing on supporting arm	Requires one or both hands for support to maintain the position Difficult to assume with spasticity in the lower extremities or tightness in the pelvis Reinforces abnormal asymmetries in trunk and legs Arm and hand activities are difficult to perform. Position not recommended for functional activities in the classroom

Source: Rainforth, B., & York-Barr, J. (1996).

When the trunk rounds in floor sitting, rounding is usually accompanied by a posterior tilt of the pelvis. This may be a result of tightness in the hamstring muscles in the child with spasticity and can also be seen—but usually to a lesser extent—in the child with hypotonia. The hamstring muscles, which attach to the pelvis, exaggerate the pull of the pelvis posteriorly when they are tight (as may be the case in a child with hypotonia or spasticity). The impact of this problem can be reduced and a more erect posture obtained, in some cases, by sitting the child on the low edge of a prone wedge. This suggestion will be effective only when the child already has the trunk control and capacity to sit more erect. Combining handling techniques with use of a wedge may also be more effective than use of the wedge alone.

Alternative Positions

Although sitting is the position of choice for classroom activities, children with physical involvement and limited postural control and mobility will require positioning alternatives periodically throughout the school day. In general a child's position should be adjusted or changed approximately every 30–45 minutes. Children with sufficient upper extremity function to adjust their own postures or those who can do "sitting push-ups" should be reminded to do so every half-hour to prevent pressure on bony prominences and skin breakdown resulting from sitting too long in any one position. Children with limited motor ability will need to be adjusted in their chairs or wheelchairs by the teacher, or have their positions changed altogether.

In addition to skin breakdown, prolonged stationary positioning in sitting can result in joint contractures. Children with spasticity are at greatest risk for hip and knee flexion contractures resulting from prolonged sitting on a daily basis. For these children, periods of sitting will need to be alternated with positions in which the hips and knees can be extended (straight), such as in sidelying or prone positions. When there is risk for a progressive scoliosis (curvature of the spine) due to muscle imbalance in the trunk, prolonged sitting is contraindicated. The child will need to be positioned so that his or her trunk can be more relaxed and symmetrical for periods of time to counteract the effects of sitting upright against gravity. For the child with a scoliosis, a daily schedule that limits sitting to 30- to 45-minute periods during the school day is essential.

Finally, it should be kept in mind that upright positioning in sitting may be very fatiguing for children with limited head and trunk control. Alternative positions provide a vehicle for physical rest and relaxation amid a physically challenging school day.

Positioning Schedules

Positioning and meeting the physical needs of a classroom of children with severe and multiple disabilities can be a challenge even for the experienced teacher. Developing a positioning schedule for each student that matches the needs of the child with classroom routines and the daily instructional schedule in the early part of the school year will result in a program that is realistic for adults to carry out. Figures 7.18 and 7.19 are examples of daily positioning schedule alternatives for students in inclusive classrooms. Note that a child may require a different schedule for each week day depending on the schedule of related services and special classes, such as adapted physical education, music, or prevocational training. Table 7.4 describes the most commonly utilized positioning alternatives in the classroom—supine, sidelying, prone, and standing—for children with severe and multiple disabilities. For each alternative, the optimum position is described along with its benefits, risks, and precautions. Common modifications that can be made to the position to meet individual needs are also provided. This information is intended as an introduction to positioning and not as a specific position-

8:30 A.M.	Arrive. Floor play until all children arrive (such as floor sitting, prone on elbows, or independent mobility)
9:00	Sitting for group circle time/group instruction in adapted seat
9:30	Occupational therapy session in the classroom
10:00	Toileting. Sitting for snack in adapted seat
10:30	Free play/work time—floor sitting, prone, or sidelying
11:30	Individual instruction/small group—standing in prone stander
12:00 P.M.	Sitting for lunch in adapted seat
12:45	Toileting
1:00	Rest/nap—sidelying or supine on wedge
2:00	Sitting for afternoon snack and group activity in adapted seat
2:45	Floor play, toileting, preparation for departure
3:15	Transport home in adapted seating system/wheelchair
4:00	Home. Free play on the floor/rest

Figure 7.18. Sample positioning schedule for a preschool-age child who requires adapted seating.

ing prescription for individual children. The team should collaboratively develop the child's daily positioning schedule and the alternative positions that will be used. Teachers should always seek guidance and instruction from the therapists on the team on how to properly position the child and how to utilize any adapted equipment that is needed (e.g., a sidelyer, a stander).

The following questions are useful in guiding the selection of alternative positions for the child:

- Which postures should be avoided (i.e., which reinforce atypical movement patterns and abnormal muscle tone) and which postures should be reinforced?

- Which position(s) provides the inhibition or facilitation the child needs?

- When and during what activity will the position be used?

- What movements will the child need to participate in the planned classroom activity?

- Does the position and use of equipment allow the child the opportunity to participate in the activity with his or her peers?
- Is the position appropriate in the social context of the classroom? Will the child be in a position similar to that of his or her peers?
- Is the position chronologically and developmentally age appropriate?
- Is the positioning alternative realistic given time, space, and equipment availability?
- Is a trained staff member available to position the child? If equipment will be used, is the staff member familiar with how to use it? Is staff training necessary before a positioning program can be implemented?

8:30 A.M.	Arrive. Homeroom. Free time in wheelchair/toileting
9:00	Adapted seating for group instruction (math class)
9:45	Break for changing position in wheelchair
10:00	Adapted seating for group instruction (English class)
10:45	Adapted physical education (mobility activities on the floor)
11:30	Standing (in prone stander) for group instruction (social studies)
12:15 P.M.	Adapted seating for lunch. Toileting
1:00	Recess in sidelying—mat activities
1:45	Adapted seating for group instruction (science) followed by break for adjusting wheelchair
2:30	Adapted seating for group instruction (Spanish)
3:15	Preparation for dismissal. Positioning in wheelchair for transport
3:30	Transport to home
4:00	Home. Rest in sidelying or supine positions

Figure 7.19.   Sample positioning schedule for an adolescent student who requires adapted seating.

Table 7.4. Alternative positions for children with severe and multiple disabilities

Position	Optimum position	Advantages/disadvantages	Appropriateness	Classroom interventions
Supine position	**Head:** midline, neck straight, and chin tucked slightly downward **Trunk:** symmetrical (not bent to either side) and straight (not arched off the floor) **Pelvis:** neutral or posterior tilted with the low back flattened and resting on the surface (not hyperextended or anterior tilted) **Hips and knees:** bent so that feet rest flat on the floor **Shoulder girdles:** down and arms in front of body or resting on the chest (not in a "high guard" position)	**Advantages** Provides opportunity to encourage head control in midline, use of two hands in midline, and symmetrical trunk Provides an alternative position for resting Support surface provides stability the child may need to allow more controlled visual skills **Disadvantages** May reinforce excessive extensor tone and atypical movement patterns such as a "high guard" position of the arms in some children Activities are limited to looking, listening, social interactions, midline play/activities	Appropriate for children of any age for resting or napping; not appropriate in other activities an inclusive setting/classroom	Place child on a wedge so that head and trunk are inclined. To inhibit extensor posturing, the hips and knees should still be bent at 90 degrees by using a roll. Use a thin cushion under the child's head to keep it slightly forward with the chin tucked downward. Use handling techniques to encourage active reach and object exploration. Use with or without the child's ankle/foot orthotics.

(continued)

Table 7.4. *(continued)*

Position	Optimum position	Advantages/disadvantages	Appropriateness	Classroom interventions
Prone position	**Head:** Midline, straight neck (but not hyperextended), chin tucked slightly downward so that eyes can gaze forward or downward **Trunk:** Symmetrical (not bent to either side) and extended **Pelvis:** Neutral position **Arms:** Shoulders forward with the upper arm (humerus) in line with and under the shoulder; elbows bent 90 degrees, forearms resting on surface, wrists extended, and hands open	**Advantages** Lengthens tight hip flexor muscles; good position for preventing hip flexion contractures Provides experience with weight bearing on both elbows and opportunity for weight shifting sideways onto one elbow if the child is encouraged to reach forward with the other arm **Disadvantages/precautions** Requires considerable effort and is fatiguing for most children. Use only for short periods of time. Boys may find positioning in prone uncomfortable due to pressure on the genitalia.	Used for young children for whom floor play and floor positioning are developmentally appropriate. May be appropriate in a preschool setting when peers are engaged in floor play or when the position is commonly being used for several children in the classroom throughout the school day. The developmental appropriateness of prone positioning for older children and adolescents is questionable in the classroom.	Remove orthotics to allow full range of hip extension. Handling in the prone position includes facilitating weight shift from the shoulders, facilitating reach from the shoulder or upper arm, hand opening, and weight shifting over an open hand. Use a wedge under the chest to provide weight-bearing experiences with decreased physical demands.

302

Sidelying position

Head: Midline, neck straight or slightly bent forward; chin tucked slightly downward. This position is achieved by using a cushion of the proper height under the head so that the head rests in the midline.

Trunk: Symmetrical and straight (extended)

Pelvis: Neutral

Hips: Bottom leg is straight at hip and knee joints with neutral rotation at the hip; upper leg is bent 90 degrees at the hip and knee and positioned on a cushion so that it is in line with the shoulder, or slightly abducted (away from the midline of the body).

Advantages

Inhibits abnormal muscle tone and the asymmetric tonic neck reflex

Promotes midline orientation of head and the arms; encourages chin tuck of the head needed for head control and downward gaze

Provides a symmetrical position of the trunk

Restful and relaxing position

Useful position for dressing the child with no or limited head and trunk control

Disadvantages/precautions

If not properly positioned, child may experience increased pressure from the weight of the head and the body on the arm he or she is leaning on

The child will view activities from a horizontal position

Appropriate as a position for rest or nap for most children regardless of age, depending on the classroom situation and whether other children are also being positioned. Not appropriate in an inclusive setting where positioning in sidelying will set the child apart from his or her peers.

Provide opportunity for the child to lie on both sides.

Handling to reduce muscle tone may be needed prior to positioning.

Handling may include facilitation from the shoulder for swiping; reaching, and grasping; tactual exploration of the surface, other textures, and objects presented.

The child with severe spasticity might be positioned more easily while wearing orthotics; however, for an extended rest period, the orthotics should be removed.

(continued)

303

Table 7.4. *(continued)*

Position	Optimum position	Advantages/disadvantages	Appropriateness	Classroom interventions
	Shoulder girdles: Depressed. The arm on the downside is positioned in front of the body at shoulder height. The other arm should be positioned in front of the body and toward the midline.			
Supported standing (stander) position	**Head:** Midline and upright **Trunk:** Erect and symmetrical **Pelvis:** Neutral **Legs:** Hips extended and in neutral alignment under the pelvis; knees extended (but not hyperextended or in a locked position); ankles bent at 90 degrees, feet flat **Arms:** Shoulder girdles depressed and arms in front of the body	**Advantages** Provides weight bearing experience in preparation for ambulation Promotes bone growth, circulation, and respiratory function Promotes alertness and may increase arousal level; provides psychological benefits from the upright experience Provides opportunity for stretching flexor muscles of the hip **Disadvantages** Reinforces atypical postures if the child is not properly positioned;	**Developmental appropriateness** Standing is appropriate for all children after approximately 12 months of age provided that sufficient support can be provided to stand and weight bear on the legs and pelvis and trunk are in good alignment.	Most activities that can be accomplished in sitting can also be done in supported standing if the standing device has a tray.

Supported standing (stander) position (*continued*)	*Note:* If the child wears orthotics, they should always be worn for standing activities.	knees may hyper-extend Obtain instruction from the child's physical therapist prior to placing the child in a stander. Skin should always be checked for reddened areas after removal from the stander. The knees are particularly vulnerable to pressure.

Use of Lower Extremity Orthotics in the Classroom

Most children with severe and multiple disabilities will have lower extremity orthotics that they wear throughout the school day. These devices are prescribed by a physician and constructed by an orthotist, and their wear and use is typically monitored by the PT on the child's team. The purpose of orthotics may vary somewhat from child to child, but in general, their purpose is to maintain proper alignment of the lower extremity joints in order to prevent joint contractures and deformities, to inhibit spasticity, and to provide the child with an optimum base of support in standing (Ratliffe, 1998; Rodstein & Kim, 1999). In addition, orthotics provide the child who is sitting with a point of stability at the feet. This contributes to improved positioning in sitting both with and without adapted seating equipment.

A wearing schedule for the child's orthotics should be provided by the physical therapist. In some cases, the therapist may recommend removing the orthotics for specific activities. For example, a child may have difficulty sitting on the floor, moving from one position to another, or crawling on the floor while wearing orthotics, and the therapist may recommend removing the orthotics to allow the child more freedom of movement.

SUMMARY

An individualized physical management plan for each child with severe and/or multiple disabilities is critical for promoting the child's maximum participation in the school environment and in classroom learning activities with peers. To be most effective in promoting a child's participation, the handling and positioning suggestions presented in this chapter should be incorporated routinely within the context of classroom activity. Not only will the child have the opportunity to develop needed classroom skills but also the child will do so in a manner that addresses his or her unique physical and motor needs.

The implementation of the plan necessitates ongoing team collaboration in problem solving, planning, decision making, and knowledge and skills sharing among team members. Teachers are encouraged to seek guidance from and work closely with the physical and occupational therapist on the child's team in order to develop the skills needed for proper physical management of the child with severe and/or multiple disabilities.

REFERENCES

Beauregard, R., Thomas, J.J., & Nelson, D. (1998). Quality of reach during a game and during a rote movement in children with cerebral palsy. *Physical & Occupational Therapy in Pediatrics, 18*(3/4), 67–84.

Bergen, A.F., & Colangelo, C. (1985). *Positioning the client with central nervous system deficits: The wheelchair and other adapted equipment* (2nd ed.). Valhalla, NY: Valhalla Rehabilitation Publications, Ltd.

Bergen, A., Presperin, J., & Tallman, T. (1990). *Positioning for function: Wheelchairs and other assistive technologies.* Valhalla, NY: Valhalla Rehabilitation Publications, Ltd.

Best, S., Bigge, J., & Reed, P. (2001). Supporting physical and sensory capabilities through assistive technology. In J.L. Bigge, S.J. Best, & K.W. Heller (Eds.), *Teaching individuals with physical, health, or multiple disabilities* (4th ed., pp. 195–228). Upper Saddle River, NJ: Prentice-Hall.

Bidabe, D.L., Barnes, S.B., & Whinnery, K.W. (2001). M.O.V.E.: Raising expectations for individuals with severe disabilities. *Physical Disabilities: Education & Related Services, 19*(2), 31–48.

Bigge, J., & Best, S. (2001). Task and situation analysis. In J.L. Bigge, S.J. Best, & K.W. Heller (Eds.), *Teaching individuals with physical, health, or multiple disabilities* (4th ed., pp. 121–148). Upper Saddle River, NJ: Prentice-Hall.

Bly, L. (1991). A historical and current view of the basis of NDT. *Pediatric Physical Therapy, 3,* 131–135.

Bly, L. (1994). *Motor skills acquisition in the first year.* San Antonio, TX: Therapy Skill Builders.

Bobath, K. (1980). *The neurophysiological basis for the treatment of cerebral palsy* (2nd ed.). Philadelphia: J.B. Lippincott.

Boehme, R. (1988). *Improving upper body control.* Tucson, AZ: Therapy Skill Builders.

Campbell, P.H. (2000). Promoting participation in natural environments by accommodating motor disabilities. In M.E. Snell & F. Brown (Eds.), *Instruction of students with severe disabilities* (5th ed., pp. 291–329). Upper Saddle River, NJ: Prentice-Hall.

Campbell, P., McInerney, W., & Cooper, M. (1984). Therapeutic programming for students with severe handicaps. *American Journal of Occupational Therapy, 38*(9), 594–602.

Casey, C., & Kratz, E. (1988). Soft splinting with neoprene: The thumb abduction supinator splint. *American Journal of Occupational Therapy, 42*(6), 395–398.

Chakerian, D.L., & Larson, M.A. (1993). Effects of upper extremity weight-bearing on hand opening and prehension patterns in children with cerebral palsy. *Developmental Medicine and Child Neurology, 35*(3), 216–229.

Colangelo, C.A. (1999). Biomechanical frame of reference. In P. Kramer & J. Hinojosa (Eds.), *Frames of reference for pediatric occupational therapy* (2nd ed., pp. 257–322). New York: Lippincott Williams & Wilkins.

Cupps, B. (1997, Jan/Feb). Postural control: A current view. *NDTA Network,* 3–7.

Exner, C., & Bonder, B. (1983). Comparative effects of three hand splints on bilateral use, grasp, and arm–hand posture in hemiplegic children: A pilot study. *Occupational Therapy Journal of Research, 3*(2), 75–92.

Exner, C.E. (1995). Remediation of hand skills problems in children. In A. Henderson & C. Pehoski (Eds.), *Hand function in the child. Foundations for remediation* (pp. 197–222). New York: Mosby.

Fiorentino, M. (1981). *Reflex testing methods for evaluating CNS development.* Springfield, IL: Charles C Thomas.

Freeman, J.E. (1995). Treatment of hand dysfunction in the child with cerebral palsy. In A. Henderson & C. Pehoski (Eds.), *Hand function in the child: Foundations for remediation* (pp. 282–296). New York: Mosby.

Goodgold-Edwards, S.A. (1993). Principles for guiding action during motor learning: A critical evaluation of neurodevelopmental treatment. *Physical Therapy Practice, 2*(4), 30–39.

Gudjonsdottir, B., & Mercer, V.S. (1997). Hip and spine in children with cerebral palsy: Musculoskeletal development and clinical implications. *Pediatric Physical Therapy, 9,* 179–185.

Heller, K.W., Forney, P.E., Alberto, P.A., Schwartzman, M.N., & Goeckel, T.M. (2000). *Meeting physical and health needs of children with disabilities: Teaching participation and management.* Belmont, CA: Wadsworth.

Henderson, A., & Pehoski, C. (1995). *Hand function in the child: Foundations for remediation.* New York: Mosby.

Hill, S.G. (1988). Current trends in upper extremity splinting. In R. Boehme (Ed.), *Improving upper body control: An approach to assessment and treatment of tonal dysfunction* (pp. 131–164). Tucson, AZ: Therapy Skill Builders.

Howle, J.M., & the NDTA Theory Committee. (2002). *Neuro-Developmental Treatment Approach: Theoretical foundations and principles for clinical practice.* Laguna Beach, CA: Neuro-Developmental Treatment Association.

Janeschild, M.E. (1996). Integrating the dynamic systems theory with the neurodevelopmental approach. *Developmental Disabilities Special Interest Section Newsletter, 19*(1), 1–4.

Johnson, L.M., Lind, W.R., & Yates, L. (1993, May). Upper extremity orthoses for a child with hemiplegia. *NDTA Network,* 1–9.

Kaplan, M., & Bedell, G. (1999). Motor skill acquisition frame of reference. In P. Kramer & J. Hinojosa (Eds.), *Frames of reference for pediatric occupational therapy* (2nd ed., pp. 401–430). New York: Lippincott Williams & Wilkins.

Levine, K.J. (1991). *Fine motor dysfunction. Therapeutic strategies for the classroom.* Tucson, AZ: Therapy Skill Builders.

Lin, K., Wu, C., Tickle-Degnen, L., & Coster, W. (1997). Enhancing occupational performance through occupationally embedded exercise: A meta-analytic review. *The Occupational Therapy Journal of Research, 17*(1), 25–47.

O'Connell, B. (1998, Jan./Feb.). Tru-Grasp: A new form of splinting. *NDTA Network,* 3–8.

Rainforth, B. (2003). Facilitating motor skills development within general education activities. In D.L. Ryndak & S. Alper (Eds.), *Curriculum and instruction for students with significant disabilities in inclusive settings* (pp. 217–238). Boston: Allyn & Bacon.

Rainforth, B., & York-Barr, J. (1996). Handling and positioning. In F.P. Orelove & D. Sobsey, *Educating children with multiple disabilities: A transdisciplinary approach* (3rd ed., pp. 79–188). Baltimore: Paul H. Brookes Publishing Co.

Ratliffe, K.T. (1998). *Clinical pediatric physical therapy.* New York: Mosby.

Rodstein, B., & Kim, D.D.J. (1999). Orthoses and adaptive equipment in neuromuscular disorders. In D.S. Younger (Ed.), *Motor disorders* (pp. 453–467). Philadelphia: Lippincott Williams & Wilkins.

Schoen, S.A., & Anderson, J. (1999). NeuroDevelopmental treatment frame of reference. In P. Kramer & J. Hinojosa (Eds.), *Frames of reference for pediatric occupational therapy* (2nd ed., pp. 83–118). New York: Lippincott Williams & Wilkins.

Smelt, H.R. (1989). Effect of an inhibitive weight bearing mitt on tone reduction and functional performance in a child with cerebral palsy. *Physical and Occupational Therapy in Pediatrics, 9*(2), 53–80.

Trefler, E. (1984). *Seating for children with cerebral palsy: A resource manual.* Memphis: University of Tennessee Center for Health Sciences.

Trefler, E., Hobson, D.A., Taylor, S.J., Monahan, L.C., & Shaw, C.G. (1993). *Seating and mobility for persons with physical disabilities.* San Antonio, TX: Therapy Skill Builders.

van der Weel, F.R., van der Meer, A.L.H., & Lee, D.N. (1991). Effect of task on movement control in cerebral palsy: Implications for assessment and therapy. *Developmental Medicine and Child Neurology, 33,* 419–425.

VanSant, A. (1993). Concepts of neural organization and movement. In B. Connolly & P. Montgomery (Eds.), *Therapeutic exercise in developmental disabilities.* Hixson, TN: Chattanooga Group.

Ward, D.E. (1994). *Prescriptive seating for wheeled mobility (Vol. 1.). Theory, application and terminology.* Kansas City, MO: Healthwealth International.

Whiteside, A. (1997, Sept/Oct). Clinical goals and application of NDT facilitation. *NDTA Network,* 3–14.

York, J., & Weimann, G. (1991). Accommodating severe physical disabilities. In J. Reichle, J. York, & J. Sigafoos (Eds.), *Implementing augmentative and alternative communication: Strategies for learners with severe disabilities* (p. 239–255). Baltimore: Paul H. Brookes Publishing Co.

CHAPTER 8

Children with Special Health Care Needs

Madhavan Thuppal and Dick Sobsey

All children experience illnesses and injuries from time to time. Even when the effects of these health problems are mild and temporary, they can interfere with learning and place additional demands on children, their families, and others who spend time with them. Children with severe and multiple disabilities experience the same health problems as other children, but for these children, such health problems are often more frequent and severe.

This chapter describes special health care needs common among children with severe and multiple disabilities. It also suggests strategies to prevent special health care needs and to intervene when they occur. It includes practical suggestions for responding to emergencies, with two important cautions. First, this chapter is not intended to provide first aid training. All teachers, especially those working with students with severe and multiple disabilities, should take practical courses in first aid and emergency procedures including cardiopulmonary resuscitation (CPR) and the Heimlich maneuver. Schools should keep appropriate emergency supplies and equipment on hand in places where they can be quickly located and used by school staff in case of an emergency.

Second, individualization is a fundamental principle of quality in health care and education. The general rules discussed here will not always apply to every individual or every situation. When the health care team has made individual plans based on a particular student's needs, those plans, rather than more general rules, should be carried out for that individual. For most children, for example, having more than one seizure in any single day is considered to be a sign of a potentially serious problem and requires immediate notification of the child's family or physician. For some children, however, two or more seizures in a day may be common and not associated with any serious problem, or a child may already be under a physician's care for these seizures. Although a greater frequency of seizures may not indicate the need for special concern about these individuals, a change in the frequency, duration, or pattern of the seizures may be a serious cause for concern. Warning criteria need to be identified and individualized depending on each child's needs and circumstances.

The American College of Emergency Physicians and American Academy of Pediatrics (1999) have established standard forms for briefly summarizing the emergency preparedness information for children with special health care needs. This form or equivalent information should be updated regularly and copies kept both at home and in school. If an emergency occurs, such information can prove valuable and, in some cases, may help those who provide medical assistance to save lives. Blank copies and samples can be found on the American Academy of Pediatrics web site (http://www.aap.org).

Children with severe and multiple disabilities often have unique health care needs as a result of specific neuromuscular damage or conditions affecting other bodily systems. Some of the medical problems commonly encountered in children with disabilities are seizures, gastrointestinal disorders, inadequate ventilation of lungs, kidney and heart problems, sensory impairments, and increased susceptibility to infections (Nehring, 2000). These problems often emerge in infancy or childhood, and many of the same problems remain as major health concerns for people with severe and multiple disabilities throughout their lives. For example, Thuppal (1994) found that seizures; gastrointestinal problems; chronic constipation; and respiratory problems including asthma, aspiration, and choking were among the most frequent problems reported in adults with severe and multiple disabilities. Some health problems may be difficult to prevent because they are direct outcomes of the primary disability. Other health problems, commonly referred to as secondary conditions, are preventable (Marge, 1988). Proper management of health concerns in childhood can help prevent or lessen the effects of secondary problems experienced by many adults with severe and multiple disabilities, such as weight gain, dental disease, deterioration of mobility, sleep problems, and joint and muscle pain (Traci, Seekins, Szalda-Petree, & Ravesloot, 2002).

School personnel play an important role on the health care team. The most common health care needs of children with severe and multiple disabilities and their caregivers include managing infectious diseases, controlling seizures, administering medications appropriately, managing chronic constipation, maintaining nutrition, and optimizing mobility and range of motion (Jackson & Vessey, 2000). In addition to taking part in prevention and intervention, teachers and other school staff play a vital role in observing and reporting health-related information to other members of the health care team. Because they spend much more time with their students than any other collaborative team members other than the parents, their observations are critical to appropriate decision making by physicians and other health care professionals. For example, many children with severe and multiple disabilities are fed through gastric tubes that can increase risk for aspiration of food into lungs. Documentation of signs of aspiration and its timing relative to feedings can help the physician determine if surgery to relocate the feeding tube is needed.

Because many children with severe and multiple disabilities have limited formal communication, common problems such as pain sometimes go untreated. Careful interpretation of behavioral patterns can play a critical role in identifying health concerns (Stallard, Williams, Lenton, & Velleman, 2001). Identifying and providing proper treatment for such problems can greatly facilitate learning and improve the student's quality of life. In addition, recognizing and responding to symptoms such as pain at an early stage may prevent more serious problems from developing. For example, for a child who has abdominal discomfort, identifying and helping the child receive treatment for constipation, if that is the cause, may prevent the development of a life-threatening bowel obstruction. In children with limited communication skills, careful attention should be given to rule out the medical problems before inferring the cause of behavior as solely environmental or as stemming from the child. For example, some students may become aggressive or disruptive to avoid taking part in instructional activities, but this resistance and inappropriate behavior may disappear after a previously undiagnosed sinus infection or dental problem is appropriately treated.

INFECTIOUS DISEASES

An infectious disease results when a disease-producing organism invades a host. This organism may be in the form of a virus, bacteria, fungus, or parasite. A communicable disease is an infectious disease that may be transmitted from one person to another either directly or indirectly. Examples of infections that are communicable are hepatitis B, influenza, and measles. Although a few infectious diseases are not normally communicable (e.g., anthrax, botulism, salmonella), most infectious diseases are communicable (Kennamer, 2002). Exposure to communicable disease may occur by direct person-to-person contact or through contaminated objects such as contaminated needle sticks.

Susceptibility and Effects

Communicable diseases are a particular concern for many children with severe and multiple disabilities for two reasons. First, although some children with severe and multiple disabilities have normal resistance to infection, many contract communicable diseases more frequently than children without severe and multiple disabilities. Second, if infected, these children often experience more severe symptoms and are ill longer than children who do not have disabilities.

This increased vulnerability to communicable disease appears to result from a combination of interacting factors. Some children with severe and multiple disabilities have genetic and metabolic conditions that reduce their resistance to infection. Nutritional problems and reduced levels of physical activity also contribute to these children's vulnerability. In addition, many of the medications that are commonly used by children with disabilities can produce side effects that inhibit the body's natural defenses against infection. Some of these children have not learned the self-care skills that help protect us all from communicable disease. Some behaviors that add to children's risk include handling potentially contaminated objects, drinking from cups left by others, and frequently putting their hands and a variety of other objects in their mouths.

Children with severe and multiple disabilities also are more likely than children without disabilities to experience severe illness because diagnosis is often delayed until the illness becomes more serious. Caregivers may not recognize early signs of illness such as changes in behavior, lethargy, or irritability. Even when caregivers recognize that a child is not feeling well, a precise diagnosis may be difficult to make in the absence of more specific signs because of the child's inability to communicate the nature of the distress.

Some children with severe and multiple disabilities acquired their disabilities as a result of an ongoing illness that began before or just after birth. Many such conditions start in the *perinatal* period (generally considered from about the 28th week of gestation to about a week after birth). For example, 20%–30% of children born to mothers who carry the human immunodeficiency virus (HIV) are likely to be infected before, during, or shortly after birth (Kuhn & Stein, 1995). Central nervous system dysfunction often occurs in children with HIV infections, which leads to developmental disabilities. Aggressive antiviral treatment has been shown to minimize these effects for children who are HIV positive (Englund et al., 1997). When children with HIV have developmental delays or disabilities, early intervention and special education programs should be the same as for children with other conditions requiring these services. Team members should be educated about HIV disease and the potential long-term needs of the infected student. Confidentiality should be maintained and school nurses trained on the use of HIV medications and their side effects (American Academy of Pediatrics, 2000).

Controlling Communicable Diseases

The control of communicable diseases has been an ongoing challenge throughout history. Although the challenge continues, a lot of progress has been made. Most of this progress is the result of improvements in personal hygiene, public sanitation, new and better immunization agents, more effective treatments, epidemic control measures (e.g., case-finding and quarantine measures), and generally improved living conditions.

Educators and other team members working with children with severe and multiple disabilities have a responsibility to do their part both in protecting the children they serve and protecting themselves from the spread of communicable diseases. Because some children with severe and multiple disabilities experience increased risk, additional precautions are sometimes appropriate. All schools should have information available on protecting children from communicable disease. Rapid access to appropriate health care professionals who are knowledgeable about public health measures is essential in some situations. Current information (e.g., Kennamer, 2002; McCulloch, 2000) and Internet resources can serve as valuable supplements. There is one caveat: Although much excellent information is available through Internet resources, anyone using the Internet must exercise caution and careful judgment to select reliable sources and avoid sources that provide outdated, useless, and sometimes even dangerous ideas. See For More Information at the end of this chapter for examples of web-based resources that can provide valuable information for school personnel serving children with severe and multiple disabilities.

Sanitation and Hygiene

Arguably, advances made in sanitizing, sanitary sewers, and modern cooking and hygiene practices have done more to extend the lives of people in contemporary society than all other developments in science and medicine. All children need to be taught personal hygiene and sanitation skills to protect them and those around them. These skills should be reflected in the goals of all students and should be among the highest priorities for training. Normalizing personal hygiene and sanitation behavior is often easier in inclusive environments in which other students provide typical examples, and informal feedback from peers can be a useful supplement to formal training.

The aggressive, disruptive, and self-injurious behaviors sometimes seen among students with severe and multiple disabilities can add to sanitation concerns. For example, students who scratch their skin severely may leave themselves more vulnerable to infection. Effective treatment of such behavior can reduce risk for communicable disease as well as producing other obvious benefits. Until effective treatment changes this behavior, careful attention to sanitary procedures is important to reduce risk to students and staff. Protecting staff members from infection is essential to the welfare of staff and students, because staff members who are infected or contaminated create substantial risk for everyone.

Immunizations

Vaccines can provide complete immunity against some infections and partial immunity against others. Many schools require proof of vaccination against some diseases (e.g., measles, mumps, chickenpox) for all students as a method of preventing the spread of disease, but other vaccinations are strictly voluntary (e.g., influenza). Some students cannot be immunized against some diseases because of conditions that compromise their immune responses or because vaccines may cause allergic or other adverse reactions. Immunizations have come under scrutiny also because some have suggested that autism can result from a reaction to routine immunizations (e.g., Wakefield et al., 1998); however, this claim has been unsupported by further research (e.g., Dales, Hammer, & Smith, 2001; Taylor et al., 1999). Although vaccinations involve some risk and discomfort, for the vast majority of students, the benefits of being inoculated outweigh the risks. Individual families and their physicians are the most qualified to make decisions regarding specific immunizations. Although school personnel cannot mandate certain immunizations for students if families refuse, they should let families know how their decisions might affect classmates. Schools should have current immunization records for each student and work with public health agencies to provide parents with accurate information about the benefits and risks of immunization. Parents should be told to inform teachers when a child is vaccinated because adverse reactions to a vaccination may develop at any time for several days after a vaccination. In some cases, reactions such as fever, pain, swelling, and rashes develop rapidly, and immediate detection and treatment can be important. Classroom staff should work closely with parents, physicians, the school health team, and public health staff members to determine which immunizations are appropriate for each child (while still conforming to school rules surrounding immunizations). These decisions should consider the needs and welfare of both the individual and the group because each child who is not immunized increases the risk for others.

Diagnosis and Treatment of Infectious Diseases

The primary responsibility for the diagnosis and treatment of communicable diseases rests with the family and their physician. Nevertheless, teachers and other program staff can and should play an important role in the detection and treatment of communicable diseases.

The symptoms of a communicable disease may be noticed first in the classroom for at least two reasons. First, many infectious diseases are cyclical. This means that the symptoms may be more apparent at certain times of day, and in some cases, they may be more obvious during school hours. Second, the collaborative team has the opportunity to observe many students over the course of days or weeks. This can provide additional information unavailable to parents. For example, a particular child may be predisposed to allergic rashes, but if several children in close contact with this child begin developing similar rashes, more careful evaluation is required. When communicable diseases are discovered among students, efforts to treat those infected and to protect other students and teachers from exposure should be coordinated among the school, the family, and health professionals. In most cases, treating the individuals who have the illness as soon as possible is essential not only for their own recovery but also for protecting other children from being infected.

Information regarding how and when illness may be spread is essential in determining other appropriate precautions (McCulloch, 2000). For example, chickenpox is infectious for no more than 5 days after the appearance of the first outbreak of a rash. Thus, children returning to school after this time who still have visible signs of a rash cannot transmit chickenpox to other children. Therefore, requiring these children to stay home from school for more than 5 days will provide little or no extra protection for classmates. Children who have never had chickenpox and who have not been vaccinated but have been exposed should be considered potentially infectious from 10 to 21 days after exposure. Careful handling of items that are soiled with nasal or respiratory secretions from children who are potentially infectious can also provide some protection. Children with leukemia or other conditions that compromise their abilities to fight disease may experience prolonged and sometimes fatal effects from exposure to infections such as chickenpox, so they need special protection. In 1996, a vaccine became available for chickenpox, and this has become part of routine immunization for children.

Although individual factors must be considered in each case, students and staff fall into three basic categories of risk, requiring three different approaches to immunization:

1. Those who have already had a particular infectious illness: These individuals are typically immune to reinfection and therefore are at little or no risk and probably need no prevention plans for inoculation against that illness.

2. Those who have not yet had the disease: These children are at greater risk and require moderate precautions.

3. Children with leukemia, AIDS, or other conditions that increase the risk of contracting the disease: These individuals need the highest level of protection from infections.

Occasionally, classrooms may experience epidemics of parasites or other infectious diseases. The term *epidemic* simply refers to the occurrence of more than the usual or expected number of cases among a particular group of individuals. Often, the control of epidemics in the school requires careful coordination of home- and school-based efforts to eliminate the problem. Concurrent disinfection is typically a key element in controlling these outbreaks. Concurrent disinfection requires simultaneous treatment of all members of the group and simultaneous eradication of other sources of infection from the environment. Head lice (*Pediculus capitis*), for example, are a fairly common problem among school children and are transmitted directly from child to child through direct, typically prolonged contact. Although medicated shampoo is generally effective in treating the problem, failure to eliminate sources of reinfection often leads to recurrence. If several children in a classroom have head lice, it may be important to coordinate the treatment of all of them in order to prevent a recurrence.

Often, even if every child in the classroom is successfully treated, non-symptomatic adults (who may be classroom staff or family members) or siblings or other children in close contact outside of school may act as reinfecting agents. Because head lice can occasionally be spread through clothing, contact with clothing that has not been treated may lead to reinfection. To successfully eradicate head lice, it is essential to launder clothing in hot water or dry clean clothing and linens that may be contaminated at the same time that all infected individuals are being treated. Successful treatment may be possible only with careful coordination of home and school efforts.

Children with Increased Vulnerability

All children are vulnerable to communicable diseases, but some children may be more likely to become infected and develop more severe symptoms. Many factors can contribute to increased vulnerability, and the degree of risk varies.

Genetically transmitted immunodeficiency syndromes, leukemia and some other forms of cancer, AIDS, Down syndrome, certain medications (e.g., immunosuppressants used by transplant recipients), nutritional imbalances, and various other factors can greatly increase the risk associated with communicable diseases for some children. These children will require enhanced protection from exposure and special treatment if they become infected.

Children with HIV/AIDS experience a much greater risk of being fatally infected by their schoolmates with a common childhood disease. Hence, they need more attention even for seemingly harmless infections such as the common cold. Treatment teams should take into consideration the increased vulnerability of children infected with HIV and provide appropriate preventative care. Weight loss of more than 10% of baseline weight, fever, and frequent or recurring diarrhea should alert the health care team. HIV and any associated infections should be treated vigorously. Because blood and other body fluids from an infected child could infect others, attention to preventing exposure to these fluids is essential (Caldwell, Todaro, & Gates, 1991; Kennamer, 2002). The educational and social advantages of inclusion, however, must be balanced against potential health advantages of isolation. Because it is almost impossible to fully protect the susceptible child from every source of infection, isolation may be justified only when an unusual risk is present. Children with AIDS or HIV who exhibit severe aggressive (biting) and/or self-injurious behaviors (which expose their body fluids) may need to be isolated until their behaviors are well under control in order to prevent spread of infection.

SEIZURE DISORDERS

Seizures are sudden changes in behavior, sensation, or motor function caused by rapid and disorderly electrochemical discharges in the brain (Freeman, Vining, & Pillas, 2003). Seizures can be caused by a wide variety of factors that interfere with normal brain activity, such as inadequate oxygen, very low levels of blood glucose, toxic substances, or very high fevers. The abnormal electrochemical discharges during seizures may cause strange sensations, emotions, behavior, convulsions, muscle spasms, and loss of consciousness.

Epilepsy is a condition in which seizures occur usually spontaneously (Batshaw, 2002; Freeman, Vining, & Pillas, 2003). It is diagnosed when an individual has repeated seizures that are not the result of another current medical condition (Appleton & Gibbs, 1998). Statistics on incidence and prevalence vary greatly depending on the diagnostic criteria used, but estimates of the prevalence of epilepsy in the American population usually range from 0.5% to 2.0% (Annegers, 2001; Freeman et al., 2003). More than 2 million people in the United

States, approximately 1 in 100, have experienced an unprovoked seizure (National Institute of Neurological Disorders and Stroke, 2001). Approximately 20% of people with epilepsy continue to experience seizures even with the best available treatment.

Epilepsy occurs much more frequently among children with severe and multiple disabilities than among children without such disabilities. As many as 30% of people with mental retardation and up to 50% of children and adults with multiple disabilities also have epilepsy (Ettinger & Steinberg, 2001; Sunder, 1997; Vining & Freeman, 1996). Mental retardation is often accompanied by epilepsy, and the more severe a child's cognitive disability, the greater the chance of epilepsy. Conversely, children with epilepsy have increased risk of mental retardation. In a population study of children between the ages of 6 and 13 who had active epilepsy, Steffenburg, Hagberg, and Kyllerman (1996) found that 38% had mental retardation. The occurrence of epilepsy varies with the syndromes associated with cognitive disabilities. For example, epilepsy is relatively rare for young children with Down syndrome, but as these children mature into adulthood (in their thirties and forties), its frequency increases along with changes in the brain (O'Donohoe, 1994). In tuberous sclerosis, however, epilepsy is very common at younger ages and often increases in severity over the years. Cerebral palsy is also commonly associated with epilepsy. Because mental retardation, epilepsy, and cerebral palsy all result from structural and functional damage to an individual's nervous system and may result from a common cause, the presence of any one is associated with increased likelihood for the others. The severity of motor deficits in cerebral palsy is associated with an increased risk of chronic seizures (Sunder, 1997). Although epilepsy can first manifest itself at any time during a person's lifetime, 75% of cases first occur before an individual reaches age 20. For children with cerebral palsy who have epilepsy, the onset of seizures is typically even earlier, with most having their first seizures before their first birthday (Gururaj, Sztriha, Bener, Dawodu, & Eapen, 2003).

When epilepsy begins early in a child's life, it often becomes more difficult to control later in life (Aicardi, 1994). Structural brain lesions or additional neurological symptoms also can be negative predictors for seizure management. Children with severe and multiple disabilities and epilepsy often have early onset of seizures, frequent seizures, multiple types of seizures, poor response to treatment, and low remission rates (D'Amelio, Shinnar, & Hauser, 2002).

Etiology

Many of the known causes of epilepsy also are causes of cerebral palsy and mental retardation, and many children have more than one of these disabilities.

Typically, these causes are divided into three major categories: 1) prenatal (occurring before the child's birth), 2) perinatal (occurring during or very close to birth), and 3) postnatal (occurring later in life).

Prenatal Causes

A number of events before a child's birth can result in epilepsy. Exposure to radiation, toxic substances (e.g., alcohol, cocaine), or infectious diseases (e.g., toxoplasmosis, herpes simplex, German measles) during pregnancy can damage the developing nervous system of the fetus. Fetal anoxia (i.e., lack of sufficient oxygen) can occur for a variety of reasons (e.g., improperly attached placenta, compression of the umbilical cord) and can damage the child's brain. Despite the excellent natural protection provided in utero, trauma can occur as a result of an accident or violence before birth. Siblings and children of individuals with epilepsy appear to be approximately twice as likely to be affected as other people. It is estimated that the risk of epilepsy is 5%–10% for children who have a parent or sibling with epilepsy. This risk increases to 15%–20% if both a parent and a sibling have seizures (Appleton & Gibbs, 1998). In approximately 70%–75% of instances, no cause may be found for epilepsy. In approximately 33% of children with epilepsy, the cause is likely to be genetic.

Epilepsy is an important feature in numerous single-gene disorders, which are mostly recessive in nature. These disorders are also associated with mental retardation. Some individuals have a genetic predisposition to epilepsy. Chromosomal localizations have been discovered for a large number of epilepsies and other disorders in which epilepsy is a common prominent feature (Appleton & Gibbs, 1998).

Perinatal Causes

Epilepsy may occur as a result of trauma or oxygen deficit during the birth process. Conditions such as a fetal head too large for the maternal pelvis (*cephalopelvic disproportion*), premature separation of the placenta, abnormal uterine contractions, interrupted labor, or excessive loss of blood can produce damage to the infant's brain that results in epilepsy. Incompatible blood types (caused by incompatible Rh factor) between mother and fetus were once a frequent cause of epilepsy; however, medications given to at-risk mothers to reduce the formation of antibodies and the trend toward smaller families (because first children are rarely affected) have greatly decreased the effects of blood type incompatibilities. Nevertheless, when they do occur, they can cause a clumping of blood cells that blocks the flow of oxygen to parts of the brain. As a result, brain damage and epilepsy can occur. A group of infections referred to as TORCH (toxoplasmosis, other infections, rubella, cytomegalovirus, herpes simplex) can harm the developing child if contracted by the mother during pregnancy. These can also result in damage to the central nervous system during gestation or immediately after birth, and epilepsy may result.

Postnatal Causes

Brain injuries and childhood infections that cause encephalitis or meningitis (e.g., measles, tuberculosis, viral infections) also can cause epilepsy. Both accidents and violence are major causes of brain injury in children. About 20% of pediatric brain injuries for children $6\frac{1}{2}$ years old and younger are unquestionably the result of abuse (Reece & Sege, 2000). Of the remaining 80% attributed to accidental injuries, most researchers believe that a significant subgroup are actually the result of abuse, but no one is certain of an exact percentage because so many occurrences go unreported or are difficult to prove. Because violence-inflicted brain injuries are typically much more severe and about nine times as likely to result in long-term disability (Ewing-Cobbs et al., 1998), the 20% of pediatric brain injuries known to result from violence result in as much or more long-term disability as the remaining 80% attributed to accidental causes (Sobsey, 2002). Emotional, sexual, and physical abuse can result in extreme stress that can damage the developing brains of children and, in some cases, produce learning; behavioral; and health problems, including seizures, even when no direct brain trauma is present (e.g., Glaser, 2000; Raskin, 1997). For example, the frequent clinical presentation of seizures among incest survivors, even when no physical trauma was present, was often discounted as "hysterical" or "psychosomatic" until the 1970s, when physiological studies began to show atypical brain wave patterns. Since that time, more sophisticated neuroimaging techniques have provided repeated evidence of anatomical differences in the brain as a result of the extreme stress produced by child abuse (Sobsey, 2002). Note that the occurrence of seizures may not immediately follow a causal event; therefore, certainty regarding the cause for any individual's seizures generally is not possible. Regardless of the cause, however, the physiological process that produces seizures remains the same.

Seizure Mechanisms

The brain is a complex network of approximately 10 billion individual neurons. Nerve impulses are transmitted when the electrical potential across a nerve cell membrane increases. This electrical charge is brought about by exchange of ions (e.g., sodium, potassium, calcium, chloride) across the cell membrane. A charge is transmitted to the neighboring neurons across junctions called *synapses* by chemicals called *neurotransmitters.* Some neurotransmitters excite the neurons they reach, whereas others inhibit the firing of neighboring neurons. During seizures, neurons may discharge impulses as often as 500 times per second, much faster than the typical rate of about 80 times per second (NINDS, 2001). Usually, a balance occurs between the neurotransmitters that excite and the neurotransmitters that inhibit the firing of neurons. This balance can be easily disturbed, particularly in children, which results in abnormal electrical activity. A variety of factors such as scars in the brain, fever, or slight changes in blood chemistry, can result in the initiation of abnormal electrical activity in a group of neurons. If the balance is not restored, abnormal electrical activity spreads to the surrounding neurons and seizures occur (Holmes, 2002).

In people with severe and multiple disabilities, seizures can add further insult to the damaged brain. Although it remains controversial whether seizure activity in itself can do further damage to the nervous system, there is no doubt that anoxia and frequent falls associated with poorly controlled seizures can result in more damage.

International Classification System

Seizures can be classified on the basis of their cause or etiology, on the location of the responsible lesion, or on presumed mechanisms (Aicardi, 1994). Classification is important because medication typically must be prescribed according to the type of seizure to be effective. The International League Against Epilepsy (ILAE) introduced a classification based on clinical seizure type and electroencephalogram (EEG) findings in 1969. Although it has been revised over the years and there are some disputes about its validity, virtually all contemporary clinicians use a version of it. According to this ILAE classification, seizures are grouped into partial, generalized, and unclassified categories. Table 8.1 summarizes this seizure classification system. For additional details, readers may refer to Aicardi (1994), Appleton and Gibbs (1998), and Luders and Wyllie (2001).

An accurate diagnosis of some of the epileptic syndromes requires the individual's participation. Individuals with sensory and psychiatric manifestations of epilepsy need to describe the phenomena as vividly as possible so that the clinician can make a proper diagnosis. Level of consciousness is taken as an important indicator to diagnose seizures. Children with mental retardation requiring extensive supports and children with severe and multiple disabilities are known to show fluctuations in their level of consciousness, as confirmed in studies of biobehavioral states (Guess et al., 1993). Many children with severe and multiple disabilities are also unable to fully describe the sensations and experiences associated with seizures, and doing so may be impossible in young children or individuals with severe communication impairments. As a result, it is sometimes difficult to make precise diagnoses of seizures for these groups of people. For an

Table 8.1.   Classification of seizures

Partial-onset seizures	Generalized-onset seizures
Simple partial seizure	*Absence seizures*
Individual remains conscious	Impairment of consciousness
Individual may engage in repeated or stereo-typed behavior	Typically lasts 2–20 seconds
Typically lasts a few seconds to a few minutes	Previously called petit mal seizure
May include blinking	*Tonic seizure*
	Sudden onset
Complex partial seizure	Impairment of consciousness
Consciousness is impaired	Rigid extension or flexion of the head, trunk, and/or extremities
Aura or prodrome is common	Typically lasts several seconds, occasionally longer
Often includes staring, automatisms (e.g., chewing, lip smacking, mumbling, fumbling with the hands), and posturing (turning to one side or unusual position of one arm)	*Clonic seizure*
	Impairment of consciousness
Typically lasts about 60–90 seconds and is followed by brief period of confusion	Rhythmic, motor, jerking movements of arms, legs, and body
Sometimes previously called temporal lobe epilepsy	Typically lasts more than a few seconds
	Myoclonic seizure
Secondary generalized seizure	Impairment of consciousness may be hard to identify due to brevity
Begins as simple partial or complex partial seizure	Jerking, motor movements that last less than a second
May sometimes generalize to tonic-clonic or other type of generalized seizure	*Primary generalized tonic-clonic seizure*
	Impairment of consciousness
	Generalized tonic extension of the extremities lasting a few seconds
	Clonic rhythmic movements may last from 10 seconds to several minutes
	Previously called grand mal seizures
	Atonic seizure
	Impairment of consciousness
	Brief loss of postural tone, often results in falls and sometimes in injuries

Unclassified seizures
(do not fall in the existing categories)

update on seizures in developmental disabilities, refer to Devinsky and West-brook (2002).

Teacher's Role When a Seizure Occurs

Teachers can provide valuable information for the diagnosis of seizures. When seizures occur in the class, teachers should record observations of the child's behavior as precisely and quickly as possible in order to provide the most useful information to the medical team. They should avoid trying to interpret the behaviors, however. When school personnel witness a seizure, they often feel a great deal of stress and that can make it very difficult to observe and record events objectively. The best way for school personnel to avoid misleading the health care team by mislabeling this or other types of seizures is simply to carefully observe and describe the student's behavior without putting any label on it.

Sometimes, while a child is on medication, a seizure may not manifest itself in a full-blown manner and may be very brief. Such seizures are often misidentified as *petit mal*, an older name for absence seizures (described in more detail later in the chapter). These are more correctly identified as *abortive* seizures because the medication present in the blood stops the seizure before it develops more fully and are often an indication that a dosage adjustment should be considered.

Diagnostic Procedures

Some other medical, neurological, and psychiatric conditions may mimic seizures. A thorough clinical examination, detailed laboratory investigations, and an inpatient observation may be necessary to confirm the diagnosis and start appropriate treatment. In some cases, response to trial treatment may be considered in arriving at a diagnosis. For example, a physician may suspect that the frequent, sudden changes in a child's behavior result from epileptic seizures, but inadequate data may be available to confirm this diagnosis. If episodes of atypical behavior clearly decrease during a trial period of antiepileptic medication, a diagnosis of epilepsy is more likely to be correct. The conditions most often confused with seizures are fainting spells, hypoglycemic attacks (low glucose level in blood), "sleep attacks" such as narcolepsy, breath-holding spells, acute psychiatric manifestations, panic attacks, and hysterical convulsions (Freeman et al., 2003). Because a host of conditions mimic epilepsy, it tends to be overdiagnosed, especially in children. Approximately 20%–30% of individuals referred to specialized epilepsy clinics with a possible diagnosis of epilepsy are found to have nonepileptic conditions (Aicardi, 1994). Several tools are now available to investigate epilepsy, one being the routine EEG.

Electroencephalogram

A routine EEG is the most common diagnostic test for seizure disorder. In 1929, Hans Berger demonstrated that the electrical impulses within the human brain can be measured and recorded by electrodes attached to the outside of the skull (Freeman et al., 2003). The shape, voltage, and frequency of waves from specific sites help determine whether a child has epilepsy and, if so, which type of epilepsy. Many children with epilepsy have abnormal brainwave patterns between seizures, but these will be evident on less than half of EEGs taken on a single occasion and are still not definitive after three EEGs (a number that has been shown to identify abnormal brain waves approximately 90% of the time) (Matoth, Taustein, Kay, & Shapira, 2002). Recording for prolonged periods, during wakefulness and sleep, after sleep deprivation, while lights are flashing, and after 3–5 minutes of deep breathing all can help in the detection of abnormal EEG patterns (Devinsky, 1994). A persistently normal EEG recording usually rules out the possibility of epilepsy (Chabolla & Cascino, 2001); nevertheless, an EEG cannot always conclusively diagnose or rule out epilepsy.

Neuroimaging of the Brain

Computed tomography (CT) scans and magnetic resonance imaging (MRI) of the head are used frequently to get pictures of the brain. The former uses X-rays and the latter uses strong electromagnetic fields. Both procedures produce images of the brain. CT was introduced in the 1970s, whereas MRI revolutionized brain imaging in the 1980s. CT can give good images of the skull and the cavities within the brain called ventricles. MRI scans produce images of the brain with much higher resolution. With an MRI, the gray and white matter of the brain can be differentiated in greater detail. New generations of MRI with greater magnetic strength are now available to produce clearer pictures. A new technique called *diffusion tensor imaging* permits identification of abnormal white matter organization. Positron emission tomography (PET) scans can be used to study the actual functioning of different regions of the brain by determining the amount of glucose being used. The injection of a low dose of radioactive material is necessary for PET scans. Functional magnetic resonance imaging (fMRI) is being used as a noninvasive technique to visualize brain functions with high spatial and temporal resolution without requiring injection of radioactive material. An fMRI is based on the alterations in magnetic fields as a result of the varying oxygen content due to blood flow changes during various functional tasks (Perrine, 1994). Functional MRI gives a measure of the amount of blood flow to different regions of the brain. MRI is not always used routinely in clinical practice. It is an important research tool and clinically valuable in cases highly resistant to treatment. All of these investigations are used to detect structural changes in the brain that can lead to seizures.

Other Investigative Procedures

Brain electrical activity mapping (BEAM), ultrasonography (use of sound waves), magnetic resonance spectroscopy (MRS), and single photon emission computer tomography (SPECT) are some other investigative techniques that are used in the diagnosis of seizure disorders. Procedures other than EEG, MRI, and CT are not routinely used in clinical practice. In cases of vague findings on these investigations, video EEG is used to determine whether a person's behaviors are due to seizures.

Types of Seizures

Seizures are typically described by their symptoms. The specific manifestations seen in any child depend on the area of the brain from which the seizure originates (i.e., focus) and how the abnormal activity spreads through the brain.

Partial Seizures

Partial seizures involve a group of neurons in some part of one cerebral hemisphere.

Simple Partial Seizures   When the epileptic activity remains localized and does not spread to the reticular activating system (i.e., an area of the brain that regulates arousal level), consciousness is not impaired. These are called simple partial seizures. The clinical manifestations depend on the area of abnormal electrical activity. If the epileptic activity is localized to the motor area of the cerebral cortex, the muscles on the opposite side of the body contract in a rhythmic fashion. For example, if there is an epileptic focus in the area of the left brain that controls the hand and the focus slowly spreads toward the area of the brain supplying nerves to the forearm, upper arm, and shoulder, then there will be initial rhythmic contractions of the right hand that spread to the right forearm, upper arm, and shoulder. This kind of progression of epileptic symptoms is sometimes called Jacksonian march. Simple partial seizures can also produce sensory symptoms (e.g., pain, tingling, numbness), special sensory symptoms (e.g., strange visual or auditory perceptions, atypical taste, strange smell), autonomic symptoms (e.g., palpitation, sweating, flushing of face, discomfort in abdomen), or psychic symptoms (e.g., loss of speech, dreamy states, distortion of time sense, illusions, hallucinations). Because simple partial seizures are typically brief and sometimes have few observable symptoms, they often go unnoticed and undiagnosed in children with severe and multiple disabilities.

Complex Partial Seizures   Complex partial seizures (CPS) are associated with additional symptoms. They usually produce loss of consciousness and automatisms (i.e., complex, involuntary movements that occur during loss or impairment of awareness). These can take the form of sucking movements, lip smacking, looking around, searching, grimacing, fumbling with clothes or sheets, or scratching movements. Some children may hum or vocalize (verbal automatisms). Automatisms can also include apparent goal-directed motor behavior (Aicardi, 1994).

Secondary Generalized Seizures   In some cases, seizures that begin as simple or complex partial seizures can become generalized seizures. Although the generalized phases of these seizures are identical to other generalized (typically tonic-clonic) seizures, the best medication to control these seizures may be different. Therefore, it is important to identify if there is a partial seizure phase that precedes the generalized phase.

Generalized Seizures

In generalized seizures, disturbances initially occur in subcortical structures. These may be convulsive or nonconvulsive. Convulsive seizures may be tonic (i.e., muscles become rigid), clonic (i.e., rhythmic jerky movements of the limbs), tonic-clonic (i.e., rigidity followed by jerky movements), or myoclonic (i.e., repeated twitching movements). Generalized tonic-clonic seizures (formerly called *grand mal seizures*) are the most common (approximately 60% of cases) epileptic convulsions. Whereas tonic, clonic, and tonic-clonic seizures are closely related and commonly overlapping categories, myoclonic seizures form a separate group. They are characterized by sudden, jerky movements of the muscles. The movements may be symmetrical, asymmetrical, unilateral, bilateral, confined to a group of muscles, and so forth. Based on the clinical type and age of onset, different syndromes (e.g., infantile spasms, Lennox-Gastaut syndrome, juvenile myoclonic epilepsy) are diagnosed. In all of these syndromes, sudden jerky movements of muscles cause the individual to collapse and he or she may sustain injury. Mental retardation plus a variety of possible seizure types including myoclonic epilepsy occur together in Lennox-Gastaut syndrome (Aicardi, 1994; Weinstein, 2002). Myoclonic seizures also are encountered frequently in children with Down syndrome, tuberous sclerosis, Tay-Sachs disease, and phenylketonuria. Occasionally, generalized seizures occur repeatedly without the individual regaining consciousness between seizures and result in almost continuous seizures. Such a condition is called status epilepticus (continuous seizures) and requires immediate medical attention.

Some individuals experience symptoms for varying periods of time before a seizure begins. These are called a *prodrome,* and if they occur primarily as feeling or sensations, they are commonly called an *aura.* Although many children with severe and multiple disabilities cannot describe an aura if they experience one, other prodromal symptoms can be observed by teachers or caregivers. When these occur with some regularity before seizures, they may provide valuable warnings before impending seizures. These may include changes in behavior, such as unusual hyperactivity, hyperventilation, irritability, or a variety of other behaviors unique to the individual.

Generalized seizures may be primary or secondary. If they are primary, referred to as generalized onset seizures, the epileptic discharge starts suddenly throughout the cerebral cortex. Then, the child immediately loses consciousness, becomes rigid, and often falls over. During this tonic (rigid) phase, breathing does not occur and the person may begin to experience cyanosis (i.e., turn blue). The following clonic (shaking) phase is characterized by alternating, involuntary contraction and relaxation of muscles, which produces undirected movement throughout the body. This movement is usually most noticeable in the arms and legs. The child remains unconscious during this phase and breathing is very inefficient, which may lead to additional cyanosis. Frequently, individuals urinate or defecate involuntarily while unconscious. They sometimes injure themselves while falling or unconsciously flailing their arms and legs. Sometimes they bite their tongue. An entire seizure rarely lasts more than 5 minutes. During the post-ictal (i.e., after-seizure) phase, the individual has no recollection of the seizure and may be confused or irritable. People are typically drowsy at this stage and usually require rest. Sometimes, the individual may remain unconscious after the seizure and require positioning to maintain an open airway.

As mentioned previously, in some partial simple or complex partial seizures, activity spreads to the reticular activating system and triggers generalized seizures. While the seizure activity spreads from the epileptic focus to the subcortical structures, the person may experience a peculiar sensation or group of sensations mentioned previously called an aura. An aura can be an auditory or visual hallucination (e.g., hearing bells, seeing floating patches of color), a feeling of vertigo, a feeling of unfamiliarity or discomfort, or a wide variety of other unusual sensations. Individuals who have seizures generally remember this aura, which typically is experienced similarly during all episodes of seizure. The nature of the aura can help to localize the probable source of epileptic discharge.

Absence Seizures Absence seizures (previously known as *petit mal seizures*) are generalized seizures without convulsions. They occur most frequently in childhood between the ages of 4 and 10. They occur as a series of isolated absence spells. When they occur, the child suddenly loses consciousness for a brief period (usually 5–30 seconds), typically staring into space without moving. The child looks dazed momentarily; stops speaking; becomes immobile; appears pale; and assumes a fixed, glazed appearance with dilated pupils. Posture and balance are maintained and the child may have minor, brief muscular contractions around the eyes. The child is unaware of having had an absence attack but sometimes perceives a change in the environment. Some absence seizures produce clonic movements of the eyelids, head, or (in rare cases) arms. Others may produce repeated chewing, swallowing, or lip-smacking movements. When the seizure is over, the child typically resumes previous activities and is unaware of any interruption (Appleton, Baker, Chadwick, & Smith, 2001). These seizures may be frequent and, if so, disruptive to learning and other activities. When occurring infrequently, absence seizures generally cause few problems and may go unnoticed much of the time. Absence seizures occurring in rapid succession form a condition called *absence status* (petit mal status). Diagnosis of absence seizures is by a characteristic EEG pattern (3 per second spike and waves). Sometimes, rapid breathing (hyperventilation) with eyes closed precipitates a child's absence seizure. When the attack occurs, the eyes open automatically (Aicardi, 1994). The frequency of absence attacks diminishes with increase in age.

Special Forms of Seizures

In addition to partial and generalized seizures, other varieties of seizures include febrile convulsions, neonatal convulsions, and reflex epilepsies (stimulus-sensitive epilepsies). *Febrile convulsions* are a feature of childhood and typically occur between 3 months and 5 years of age. They occur in the presence of fever but without evidence of intracranial infection or other definable cause. Children with febrile convulsions form a heterogeneous group. In the majority there is a genetic susceptibility to convulse in response to increased body temperature. This could be the result of an unrecognized brain injury associated with fever. In some children, febrile convulsions signal the onset of chronic epilepsy (Aicardi, 1994).

Seizures in the neonatal period are considered separately because the brain is not fully developed in the neonatal period. Hence, features of *neonatal* seizures are different from those experienced by adults. Differentiation has to be made from normal movements in the newborn. Most seizures in the neonatal period are subtle. They are either myoclonic, clonic, tonic, or subtle (Appleton & Gibbs, 1998). Eye jerking, sustained eye opening, eye deviation, chewing, low heart rate, and high blood pressure could be subtle manifestations of seizures in the newborn. Seizures in the neonatal period often indicate serious neurological disorders, with 15%–30% mortality. Approximately one third of survivors will have serious aftereffects (Aicardi, 1994). Seizures in the newborn period are extremely complex. EEG recordings do not always aid in the diagnosis.

Environmental stimuli have been known to trigger seizures in some individuals. These individuals are said to have *reflex* or *stimulus-sensitive epilepsy*. For example, photic-induced seizures (triggered by flickering lights such as strobe lights, headlights, helicopter blades, or other visual stimulation) have been reported in some individuals. Similarly, auditory-evoked, movement-evoked, startle-evoked, and even language-evoked epilepsy have been found, but these cases are very rare. Some children have even been found to be selectively sensitive to card games or other highly specific stimuli such as music or running water. Although this phenomenon has been given considerable attention, it is important to note that only a small proportion (5%–6%) of people with epilepsy report that sensory stimulation triggers or exacerbates seizure activity. Therefore, people with epilepsy do not need to be generally restricted from any stimulus (e.g., fluorescent lights, television, cold water) unless their personal histories indicate that a specific stimulus affects them. Restrictions on exposure to stimulation should occur only if justified by demonstrable benefits to the specific child. When sensory-evoked seizures do occur, they may be tonic-clonic, complex partial, or any other type of seizure. In some instances, characteristic behavior may be a manifestation of epilepsy.

Pseudoseizures

Sometimes, apparent seizure behavior is learned behavior and may even be intentional. Some children who are conscious during their seizures learn to imitate the behavior. Others may see other children have seizures and imitate their behavior. Although pseudoseizures may look very much like a real seizure, they are typically longer in duration, breathing rarely stops, and a tonic phase rarely precedes the convulsive stage (Jetdrzejczak, Owczarek, & Majkowski, 1999). In addition, pseudoseizures in children

- Cause fewer injuries
- Do not occur during sleep
- Rarely cause wetting or soiling of clothes
- Generally occur when people are around
- Are less likely to provide secondary gain (e.g., attention, release from a demand)

EEG studies, neuroimaging studies, and analysis of the context in which the seizure episode occurs can be useful in some cases; however, even experts with the benefit of the best diagnostic tools are often unable to clearly differentiate pseudoseizures from epilepsy in many cases (Jetdrzejczak et al., 1999). Children who have atypical seizures—for example, those who are conscious and respond to others while having significant seizure activity—may have real seizure activity ignored by caregivers who are convinced they are "faking" it. Usually the best approach is to treat all seizures routinely without excessive attention but with appropriate attention to health and safety concerns. This reduces the chance that the behavior will be reinforced or imitated while ensuring that health and safety needs are given proper attention. In rare cases, when seizures can be clearly identified as pseudoseizures, nonaversive behavior management or counseling may be employed. For example, one boy with a developmental disability and a confirmed history of epilepsy exhibited pseudoseizures during periods of intense family conflict. These probably functioned to shift family members' attention from their conflict to his health concerns. When caregivers' responses to his pseudoseizures were minimized and the underlying family conflicts were addressed, the frequency of pseudoseizures decreased markedly.

Seizure Management

Seizure management refers to prevention, protection, and first aid measures applied by the collaborative team. Because every child is an individual, seizure management must be tailored to the specific needs of the child, and none of the management provisions discussed here will be appropriate for every child. Rather, these provisions should be thought of as general recommendations to be considered for each individual.

Prevention

Although complete control over seizures is not possible with every child who has epilepsy, reduction in the frequency and severity of seizures can be accomplished for most through a program of prevention. In most cases, the primary prevention method is the careful maintenance of medical treatment. Unless presented with evidence to the contrary, most physicians will assume total medication compliance. Many factors can influence the amount of medication that reaches the bloodstream. Failure to take prescribed medication can be a major cause of difficulty in controlling epilepsy. Some children with severe and multiple disabilities may refuse medication because they do not like the taste or may not swallow the capsules. Some may conceal the medications in their mouths for later disposal. Others may spit them out. These practices may result in an inadequate dosage. The resulting low blood levels of medication may influence the physician to increase the dosage prescribed; subsequently, if the child begins to accept the medication consistently, an overdose may result. When administering medications, it is essential to be certain that the child accepts them.

The manner in which drugs are given also affects blood levels. Currently, a number of anticonvulsants are available in different forms such as sprinkles, syrup, chewable tablets, and long-acting forms. For example, some anticonvulsants are given in suspension form. Unless the suspension is thoroughly mixed before each administration, dosage will be unreliable. Some doses may be too strong, others, too weak. Mixing medications in food can also affect dosage, especially if not all of the food is eaten. Some drugs will be absorbed differently if tablets are crushed or chewed or capsules are opened before swallowing. When these or other factors influence dose maintenance, careful consultation among pharmacist, physician, and individuals administering the medication can help these professionals to develop suitable strategies for ensuring accurate and consistent dosage. The benefits of taking any particular type and amount of medication must be carefully balanced with the negative effects and risks of taking the medication.

Avoiding factors that may precipitate seizures is an important component of seizure prevention for some children with epilepsy. Specific environmental stimuli that trigger seizures may be identified for some children through careful observation. When they occur, they may be eliminated or controlled in the child's environment. Other factors can lower the threshold for seizure. These factors could be stress, fatigue, missed meals leading to low blood sugar, and electrolyte imbalances (e.g., inappropriate fluid or salt intake). Carefully recording events that precede seizures can help identify contributing factors for a specific child. Once identified, these factors can often be eliminated or controlled. Intervention during the prodrome can also help prevent seizures. For example, careful observation may reveal that a child frequently stares out the window and hums prior to having a seizure. Interrupting this behavior can prevent the child from having a seizure in some cases.

Biofeedback has achieved some success in controlling epilepsy that has responded poorly to medication or when the dosage to control seizures has had undesirable side effects (Holzapfel, Strehl, Kotchoubey, & Birbaumer, 1998). The application of biofeedback to control seizures in children with severe and multiple disabilities needs further exploration but could prove valuable. Such interventions are generally done in specialized biofeedback laboratories.

Protection

When seizures do occur, protection against injury is important. Protective measures, like other interventions, need to be individualized to meet the needs of the specific child. For example, absence seizures typically do not require special risk-reduction procedures, but some activities (e.g., riding a bicycle, using scissors, working on machinery) can be hazardous if periods of unconsciousness are long or frequent. In determining the suitability of any potential measure for a specific child, it is important to employ measures that do not overprotect the child. The team must carefully consider the nature and extent of the risk, the extent of risk reduction, and the intrusiveness of the risk-reduction measure before working with the family on seizure management.

Many methods are available for reducing risks. One method is environmental modification. Architectural decisions made during building design stages may greatly influence environmental hazards. For example, long, steep, straight staircases present much greater hazards than stairs interrupted by large landings. Many simple modifications can be made in existing buildings. Padded carpeting will greatly reduce the risk of brain injury for some children with epilepsy. Furniture with rounded corners also reduces the risk of injury during a fall. These and other modifications can be achieved, when needed, within the standards of typical classroom or school environments.

Another common risk-reduction measure, most often used with children with myoclonic epilepsy who have frequent falls, is the use of helmets. The potential benefit to the wearer, however, must be weighed against the intrusiveness of the intervention. Wearing a helmet may contribute to the perception of the wearer as unusual, may restrict the child's movements, and/or may be uncomfortable (especially in warm weather) and thus poorly tolerated by the child. If protective headgear is required, it should be lightweight, well fitting, and as appropriate in the social environment as possible. For example, a bicycle helmet is much lighter than a football helmet and is not necessarily unusual apparel for a school-age child at play. A knit hat or other common type of thick hat will provide considerable protection and is more common in many environments than a helmet. The thick hair typically found on the human scalp provides significant natural protection as well, so it may be helpful for a child to wear his or her hairstyle over areas of the scalp that may otherwise be injured frequently.

Another strategy for risk reduction involves the restriction of hazardous activities. Again, weighing the potential for risk reduction against the restriction of the activity requires careful judgment on the part of the team, and the child's input should be included in the decision-making process regardless of the child's communication and cognitive skill level. Restricting a child from a favorite or highly prized activity should occur only if great risk is present and restriction substantially reduces the risk. Swimming is a common example of an activity that many children with severe and multiple disabilities (including epilepsy) enjoy. It can be dangerous if the individual has a seizure while in the water, however. Children with poorly controlled seizures should not swim, but a child with well-controlled seizures may swim with direct assistance (a child who has seizures should *never* be left in the water alone). The nature of the seizures, size of the child, and other factors may also need to be considered. For example, normally, while an individual is in a tonic phase, water cannot enter the lungs. This provides a brief period for a rescuer to remove a child from the water. A heavy child may be more difficult to bring out of the water, and, once the clonic phase begins, removing the individual from the water without allowing water to get into the lungs is extremely difficult. Particular care needs to be taken around chlorinated and salt water because these are particularly dangerous if aspirated into the lungs, even in small amounts.

First Aid Measures

When seizures occur, simple first aid measures may be required. These are summarized in Table 8.2. In most cases, little intervention is required, and misguided efforts are potentially harmful. First aid measures are aimed at preventing injury caused by the seizure and generally involve simply using common sense.

Table 8.2.   First aid measures for seizures

Type of seizure	Do	Do *not*
Generalized tonic-clonic (grand mal)	*During* Ease to floor Remove hazards Cushion vulnerable body parts *After* Position for clear airway, if required Check for injuries Allow for rest	*During* Put anything in the person's mouth Move the person, unless absolutely necessary Restrain the person's movements *After* Give food or fluids until fully conscious
Generalized absence (petit mal)	Protect from environmental hazards	Give food or fluids until fully conscious
Partial complex with automatisms (psychomotor)	Remove hazards from area or pathway Supervise until fully conscious	Restrain movements Approach, if agitated, unless necessary Give food or fluids until fully conscious

Generalized tonic-clonic and other major motor convulsions often cause injury as a result of the child falling or experiencing powerful involuntary movements. Often, the onset is too sudden for the child to be eased to the floor, but sometimes (usually when the child is sitting in a chair) he or she does not fall immediately. Easing the child to the ground can prevent serious injury. Furniture with hard or sharp edges and other hazardous objects should be removed from the area, if possible. The child should be moved away only if a hazard cannot be moved (e.g., stairwell, swimming pool). Placing a soft object (e.g., cushion, sweater) under the head or other vulnerable body parts can also prevent injury.

Never attempt to put anything in a person's mouth during a seizure. Although people can bite their tongues, which may be injurious during seizures, such injuries are not as frequent or severe as those caused by items placed in the mouth. Items placed in the mouth may force jaws out of joint due to unequal pressure, break teeth, obstruct the airway, or injure oral structures if the child flips over on his or her face. Because the child is unconscious, anything given by mouth may enter the airway, so it is essential to refrain from giving food or fluid. During the seizure, it is usually not useful to attempt to open or clear the airway, but this may be necessary after the seizure is over. If the child remains unconscious, it is desirable to position him or her on the right or left side, with the neck in slight extension and the head slightly lower than the midline of the body to encourage saliva or any other secretions to run out of the mouth and not back into the throat. The child should then be examined for signs of injury. Observation should continue until the child is fully conscious, but it is not generally necessary to call for medical help unless one or more of the following occurs:

- Breathing does not resume (in which case mouth-to-mouth resuscitation should be started)

- One seizure follows another

- The child sustains a significant injury

- The seizure lasts more than 5 minutes

- The child has no history of epilepsy

- The seizure appears substantially different from previously known seizures

Other types of seizures typically require no first aid procedures. Only general precautions, such as removing dangerous objects, are necessary to protect the child from hazards with which he or she might come into contact. For example, a child experiencing a complex partial seizure might walk off a step or ledge, or a child having an absence seizure might not be conscious of an approaching car. Prolonged or repeated seizures, as previously mentioned, require immediate medical attention. Some individuals routinely have two or more generalized tonic-clonic seizures in a day or have seizures that last as long as 7 or 8 minutes, but unless the observer is certain that this represents typical behavior for the child, immediate medical assistance should be requested. In cases of uncertainty, it is better to request assistance when it is not required than to fail to request it when it is needed. Whether a seizure is reported immediately, it should be carefully observed and recorded for the planning of care and treatment.

Observing and Recording

Because most physicians rarely have the opportunity to observe their patients over extended periods of time and seizures generally are unpredictable, physicians must treat most of their patients with epilepsy without ever observing their seizures. Therefore, they depend on parents, teachers, and others who directly observe seizures for accurate descriptions to guide their diagnoses and treatment.

Reports of seizures should be descriptive, not diagnostic (DePaepe, Garrison-Kane, & Doelling, 2002). Using diagnostic labels may mislead the physician and fail to provide important details required for appropriate treatment. For example, reporting that Jenna had a "generalized" or "grand mal seizure" may obscure early events that indicate a partial seizure with secondary generalization. A chronological report of the events of the seizure would describe each phase without attempting to interpret it. The following is an example of a chronological report:

> Jenna stopped moving and made repetitive lip-smacking sounds for about 10 seconds, then her left arm began to shake. After that, her whole body stiffened for a few seconds and she began to convulse. Her whole body shook violently for about 90 seconds. Then she stopped but remained unconscious for about 10 minutes and seemed groggy for several hours.

This description makes it clear that although the seizure became generalized, it began as a partial seizure. This type of information would be much more useful to health care professionals treating the child's epilepsy. A report form can be very useful for organizing this information. Figure 8.1 provides an example of a seizure observation report form. This form organizes events chronologically and provides a checklist for some of the more common components of seizures. Copies of seizure reports should be sent home to parents and kept on file for team consideration, and they should be made available to the physician whenever the child's seizure history is reviewed.

Treatment of Epilepsy

The primary treatment for epilepsy is the administration of anticonvulsant drugs. Research continues to produce many new anticonvulsant medications (see Chapter 8 for a list of anticonvulsant medications). For detailed information on antiepileptic drugs, please refer to Fischer (2000) for a summary of antiepileptic agents.

In addition to medication, surgery, behavioral intervention, and dietary control have been tried as possible treatments. The surgical procedures mainly consist of removing a lesion that acts as an epileptic focus (if one can be identified) or preventing spread of epileptic discharges by cutting some pathways in the brain. Sometimes pressure on the brain can be relieved either by taking out bone fragments or removing excess cerebrospinal fluid. A procedure called *multiple subpial transection* (a series of small cuts in the cerebral cortex) is done in instances in which seizures begin in areas of the brain that are vital to functions such as language, movement, or sensation (Devinsky, 1994). Some of the procedures used are lobectomies (i.e., resecting a portion of a lobe of the brain) and hemispherectomies (i.e., removal of one half of the brain). Surgery is resorted to only in a small percentage of people with intractable seizures. Developmental disabilities are still generally considered to contraindicate surgical treatment of

Seizure Record

Student's name: _____   Date: _____

Time (of occurrence): _____   Location: _____

How did the seizure begin?

_____

_____

What was the student doing before the seizure?

_____

_____

What was happening in the area when the seizure occurred?

_____

_____

Warning signs: ☐ No   ☐ Yes

If Yes, describe:

_____

_____

What was the first indication of seizure activity?

_____

_____

What happened during the seizure?

Duration (if approximate, state it): _____

Did student's body stiffen? ☐ No ☐ Yes

   Parts of body involved: _____

Did student's body shake? ☐ No ☐ Yes   Arms: ☐ Left   ☐ Right

Did the student fall?   ☐ No ☐ Yes   Legs: ☐ Left   ☐ Right

Figure 8.1.   A blank seizure observation report form. (*Source:* Sobsey, 1982.)

338

Figure 8.1. *(continued)*

Any apparent injury? ☐ No ☐ Yes Other: _____

Describe:

_____

_____

Did the student appear to become unaware of the environment? ☐ No ☐ Yes

Was there a change in color of the student's lips, nail beds, etc.? ☐ No ☐ Yes

Describe:

_____

_____

Did student wet or soil? Urine: ☐ No ☐ Yes Feces: ☐ No ☐ Yes

Did student have difficulty breathing?

Before: ☐ No ☐ Yes During: ☐ No ☐ Yes After: ☐ No ☐ Yes

Other/Describe:

_____

_____

How did the seizure end?

Describe first aid given:

_____

_____

Describe student's activity after seizure:

_____

_____

Notifications: ☐ None required ☐ Parents ☐ Physician

Other (Specify):

_____

_____

Reported by: _____ Filed: _____
                                              (Date/Time)

epilepsy by many physicians, but decisions about the appropriateness of such treatment should be made on the basis of risks and benefits to children, not on the basis of diagnostic labels. Because some procedures require patients to remain conscious and to describe their sensations during surgery, patients who cannot participate in this manner may be difficult or impossible to accommodate.

Vagal nerve stimulation (VNS) is a treatment that is being used increasingly to treat people with intractable seizures. The vagus nerve is the tenth cranial nerve that emerges at the base of the brain and passes through the neck to the abdomen. A programmable signal generator powered by a lithium battery is implanted in the patient's brain. Stimulating electrodes connected to the vagus nerve transport the electrical signals from the generator to the vagus nerve. A programming wand and accompanying software are necessary based on the individual needs of the patient (Schachter & Clifford, 1998). Amar, Levy, McComb, and Apuzzo (2001) reported that VNS is a safe procedure for children with intractable seizures and has minimal side effects. Furthermore, VNS does not have the side effects of multiple medications, is reversible, and permits involuntary treatment compliance. Teachers should be aware if a child with seizures has a VNS implant and should avoid providing him or her with toys with powerful magnets. External magnets may interfere with the programmed stimulation from the implant.

Behavioral intervention has also proven useful in treating some children with epilepsy. If a trigger for seizure is identified, systematic desensitization (gradual exposure) to triggering stimuli may help to control seizures. In the case of self-induced seizures, the motivating factors for seizure should be studied, and the child should be rewarded for not inducing seizure. Seizures can be reduced when prodromal behavior chains are interrupted. Each of these approaches has enormous potential for some children. They provide alternatives or supplements to medications, which often have deleterious side effects. Children with epilepsy should be considered good candidates for behavioral intervention if they have one or more of the following: 1) self-induced seizure activity, 2) identifiable preseizure behavior patterns, or 3) identifiable environmental seizure triggers. Careful evaluation and planning by the entire collaborative team is required to determine the appropriateness of behavioral intervention and to evaluate its success.

Dietary intervention is also used to treat epilepsy in some individuals. The *ketogenic* diet, which accumulates byproducts of fat metabolism in the blood, was developed in 1921 to control seizures, primarily in children (Ekvall & Iannaccone, 1993). As awareness of problems related to high fat intake increased and better drug therapy became available, ketogenic diets were used less frequently. In the 1970s, however, the medium-chain triglyceride (MCT) ketogenic diet came into use, which reduced some concern over high intake of saturated fats.

Dietary intervention should be considered when drugs are ineffective or have serious side effects and when decreased seizure activity can be demonstrated during a trial period. A dietitian or nutritionist should be part of the collaborative team considering and monitoring dietary intervention.

Educational Implications

Many of the topics already discussed greatly affect the provision of education for children with epilepsy (e.g., observing and reporting seizures in the classroom, behavioral intervention), but a few specific educational concerns are addressed here as well: 1) the effects of epilepsy on learning and behavior, 2) social implications of epilepsy, and 3) some specific roles of the collaborative team.

Learning and Behavior

Although epilepsy is only weakly correlated with intelligence, it may influence learning in a number of ways. Drugs, intense and frequent seizures, brain damage, related behavior problems, and attention deficits are impediments to learning for some children with epilepsy. Symptoms of confusion, mental impairment, headache, or fatigue following a seizure may interfere with learning. It is important to remember, however, that not all children who experience seizures are affected equally by these factors, and some are not affected by any of these factors. Team decisions must be reached through careful consideration of the effects on specific children. For example, impulsive behaviors, irritability, and attention deficit may be reported and found to be the result of subclinical seizure activity. Although these deficits may be controlled by medication, the medications may occasionally result in sluggishness, lethargy, depression, irritability, or behavior problems that also interfere with learning. Careful evaluation of both liabilities and benefits of treatment must be undertaken by the team based on clear and complete records of the child's social, learning, and seizure behavior.

The role of epilepsy in lack of impulse control, aggression, and violence remains controversial. Interpreting the results of studies of this role are difficult to interpret because there are numerous intervening variables. The majority of children with epilepsy exhibit no special behavior problems. Therefore, behavior problems should not be anticipated simply because a child has epilepsy. When behavior problems do occur in children with epilepsy, they should be treated exactly like behavior problems in any other child. In the rare instances in which behavior problems appear to be the direct results of seizure activity, medical treatment with anticonvulsants may be considered. Teachers should take note of any children who become aggressive during the immediate period following seizures and should provide appropriate supervision to ensure safety.

Social Implications

Epilepsy has a long history of social stigma. Lack of social acceptance and negative public opinion were problems in the past. Over a period of time, the public opinion and attitude toward epilepsy improved (Caveness & Gallup, 1980; Gordon & Sillanpaa, 1997). Attitude changes occur with improved public education. On the one hand, some argue that the stigma associated with severe and multiple disabilities is more prevalent and intense than the stigma associated with epilepsy, and therefore, improved attitudes toward children with epilepsy have little benefit for the child with severe and/or multiple disabilities. On the other hand, if such severe stigma does exist toward people with severe and multiple disabilities, the improved attitudes toward epilepsy provide a hopeful note on how such attitudes may change.

In addition to public opinion, attitudes about epilepsy within the child's family are a special concern. For parents of children with severe and multiple disabilities including epilepsy, seizures are only one aspect of a much larger adjustment and accommodation issue. Nevertheless, the unpredictable nature of seizure activity and the ongoing risk of facing a sudden and sometimes life-threatening health crisis pose special challenges for some families (Farley & McEwan, 2000). It is important to teach families about epilepsy and to encourage acceptance of their children's conditions. Most parents of children with severe and multiple disabilities adjust well, and many eventually see the challenges they face as opportunities for valuable personal growth (Scorgie & Sobsey, 2000). It is important for parents to learn 1) appropriate seizure first aid and when to get medical help, 2) how to administer anticonvulsants properly and reliably, and 3) how to observe and record seizure activity. All of these things usually help restore parents' feelings of purpose and generally help develop self-esteem in addition to enhancing the child's health and quality of life. It is often best to focus on these practical matters first, then to let parents guide the learning process in determining what else they would like to know and when they want to learn it. Although seizures can prove fatal in some cases and the unpredictable nature of epilepsy may add to parental fears, it may be important to help put that risk in perspective. For adults with epilepsy, it is estimated that approximately 2 deaths per 1,000 patients per year occur among individuals with severe epilepsy (Lhatoo & Sander, 2002). For children, the risk appears to be even lower. Camfield and Camfield (2003) pointed out that death is so rare in childhood epilepsy that there is no appreciable difference in life expectancy for children with and without epilepsy. For children with severe and multiple disabilities, seizures may be one of a multitude of factors that has some influence on life expectancy, but their influence should not be exaggerated.

Specific Collaborative Team Roles

Because control of seizures and learning are closely interrelated, decisions affecting either must consider both. The physician should be part of the decision-making team, along with parents, teachers, and other staff. Unfortunately, direct communication between the teacher and the physician regarding a child with epilepsy is rare. It is essential that strategies for communication be put in place. One method of encouraging communication that educators may use is to send seizure records with a brief summary of educational performance to the physician along with a form so that the physician can send a brief report back. Education and training of all team members and other school staff are essential to ensure that they are prepared to handle seizures. Workshops are effective in imparting information about epilepsy, improving teacher attitudes toward epilepsy, and building teachers' confidence in their ability to cope with seizures. Nurses may play a central role in providing training for other team members as well as administering medications and maintaining health records. As of 2003, approximately 50% schools had a full-time school nurse, and many smaller schools had part-time nurses. The National Association of School Nurses recommends 1 nurse per 225 students in inclusive schools and 1 nurse per 125 students in schools that have special education classrooms that serve students with chronic health conditions (Wolfe & Selekman, 2002).

Educating families is one of the important responsibilities of team members in the management of seizures. As mentioned previously, parents should be trained on the nature of seizures, the diagnostic procedures, what to do when the child has a seizure, the effects and side effects of medications, and ways to control seizure triggers and enhance self-esteem. Decisions regarding behavioral intervention for seizure control should include the entire team. Even when treatment is solely medical, team members must participate in the evaluation of treatment by carefully recording the effects of treatment. Similarly, decisions regarding restrictions of activity or protective equipment must include the entire team. Daily activity schedules may require modification to take advantage of a child's peak learning times, especially when medication side effects reduce responsiveness during specific parts of the day. Careful planning and scheduling by the team can work around some of these side effects, and, by allowing some flexibility in scheduling, it becomes possible to compensate at least partially for unpredictable changes.

DUAL DIAGNOSIS

The term *dual diagnosis* refers to the diagnosis of two conditions in the same person. In the area of mental retardation and developmental disabilities, dual diagnosis typically refers to emotional or behavioral disorders and mental retardation. Anyone can have emotional or behavioral disorders, yet research suggests that they are found in children and adults with mental retardation several times more frequently than in the general population (Borthwick-Duffy, 1994; Jacobson, 1990; Reiss, 1990). Disruptive behaviors are three to four times more common in children with intellectual disabilities as compared with other children (Campbell & Malone, 1991). Children with severe and multiple disabilities can manifest the full range of psychopathological conditions and behavior problems seen in other children.

Children with mental retardation are a high-risk group for emotional and behavioral difficulties for several reasons, including 1) the greater likelihood of experiencing violence or institutionalization, 2) organic brain damage, 3) inadequate coping strategies, 4) social and emotional stress, and 5) poorly developed defense mechanisms. Prevalence figures for children having a dual diagnosis vary widely because of differences in diagnostic criteria, diagnostic instruments, sample size, type of study, and location of residence; however, a conservative estimate would be 20%–30%. Having characteristics such as physical or sensory disabilities and limited communication skills often impair children's performance on tests and contribute to the difficulties of diagnosing mental health problems in children with mental retardation. One of the major problems noted by researchers in this field is that there are no standard diagnostic criteria appropriate for children with mental retardation. Standard classification systems, such as the *Diagnostic and Statistical Manual of Mental Disorders, Fourth Edition, Text Revision* (DSM-IV-TR) (American Psychiatric Association, 2000), have been used to classify mental illness among children with mental retardation, but they can result in inappropriate diagnoses. For example, a child without a disability whose speech is disorganized and out of control and who uses many gestures could be diagnosed with a psychotic disorder but that diagnosis may not be appropriate for a child with severe mental retardation who uses adaptive communication. Furthermore, psychiatric diagnoses are based on a child's reporting of his or her subjective experiences and feelings. This may be difficult or impossible for children with severe communication impairments. Therefore, a separate or modified diagnostic and classification system may be needed for children with severe and multiple disabilities. Groups such as NADD (also known as the National Association for the Dually Diagnosed) and the European Association on Mental Health Aspects of Mental Retardation (MHMR) have developed assessment tools and treatment protocols for this population. Although some of the same psychological diagnostic tools that are used with the general population can also be used with children with severe and multiple disabilities, they need to be carefully adapted and individualized when used with these children (Levitas, Hurley, & Pary, 2001).

Psychiatrists, psychologists, and counselors need to modify the processes of taking a history and examining mental status (Levitas, 2001). Although the presentation of psychiatric symptoms in children with mild mental retardation is generally similar to those in the population without mental retardation, the presentation of psychiatric symptoms usually differs in children with severe and profound mental retardation. Sensory and physical disabilities can compound this problem.

Several screening and diagnostic instruments have been developed for detecting mental illness in children with mental retardation (Aman, 1991; Reiss, 1993). The following instruments have been used in different environments to detect and quantify symptoms of mental illness: The Aberrant Behavior Checklist (Aman, Singh, Stewart, & Field, 1985), Reiss Scales for Children's Dual Diagnosis (Reiss & Valenti-Hein, 1990), Diagnostic Assessment for the Severely Handicapped Scale (Matson, Gardner, Coe, & Sovner, 1990), Child Symptom Inventory (Gadow & Sprafkin, 1994), The Nisonger Child Behavior Rating Form (CBRF) (Aman, Tasse, Rojahn, & Hammer, 1996), and The Behavior Problems Inventory (Rojahn, Matson, Lot, Esbensen, & Smalls, 2001). Teachers have used the Reiss screen (1993) effectively to determine if students with mental retardation need further evaluation for mental disorder. Screening tools designed for use with the general population of children, including the Child Behavior Checklist (CBCL) and the Teacher's Report Form (TRF) (Achenbach & Rescorla, 2001) can also be used with children with disabilities including severe and multiple disabilities, but scores need to be interpreted with caution because elevated scores may be partially related to the child's disability rather than psychopathology (Dekker, Koot, van der Ende, & Verhulst, 2002). Therefore, these checklists can be very useful to identify specific areas of concern, but global scores may be misleading.

Specific to mental illness in mental retardation are some clinical phenomena. When these are properly applied, the behaviors of children with mental retardation can be understood with greater clarity. *Diagnostic overshadowing* (Reiss, 1993) refers to instances in which the presence of mental retardation makes it more difficult to interpret mental health symptoms. In other words, atypical behavior may be attributed to mental retardation rather than to a mental health problem. Sovner (1986) identified four factors that may influence the diagnosis of mental illness in mental retardation: 1) intellectual distortion, 2) psychosocial masking, 3) cognitive disintegration, and 4) baseline exaggeration. Intellectual distortion refers to the increased difficulty that may be experienced in coping with various situations because of limited communication and cognitive skills. Psychosocial masking is the effect of disabilities on the content of psychiatric symptoms. Cognitive disintegration is the tendency of people with mental retardation to become disorganized under emotional stress. Baseline exaggeration refers to the fact that during a period of emotional stress, these behavior problems may significantly increase in severity. In spite of these problems with diagnosis, a clinician may diagnose mental illness in a child with mental retardation if there is

- A sudden change in behavior
- No obvious communicative function for the behavior
- Accompanying biological disturbances such as disturbed sleep, lack of appetite, and lack of interest in activities that the individual usually enjoys
- No physical illness detected that would account for the change in behavior

In children with mental retardation, milder psychiatric disorders can be mistaken for more severe psychotic disorders (Myers, 1999). For example, a child in an intense state of anxiety may be talking to his imaginary friend and those around him might interpret this as a hallucinatory experience typical of a serious psychotic mental disorder. This behavior is not necessarily associated with hallucinations or psychosis when it occurs in children with mental retardation, however. Hence, it is very important to collect information from different sources across different environments and to observe the child with mental retardation repeatedly in different environments (e.g., classroom, playground) before making a diagnosis of a psychotic condition. If clinical diagnosis is made in haste, it can lead to the prescription of unnecessary medication that might have side effects. Children with severe disabilities who are not communicative might react with anxiety, aggression, or self-injury to the medication's side effects. This can lead to additional medication prescription, thereby leading toward a downward spiral in clinical condition. In the classroom environment, teachers should record observable behaviors without adding their interpretation and communicate their observations to the psychiatrist or the treatment team in order to facilitate diagnosis and formulate appropriate treatment.

Studies on clinical symptoms of psychiatric disorders in children with mental retardation show that people with mental retardation requiring limited to intermittent supports have symptoms similar to individuals without mental retardation (Bergman, 1991). Patterns of psychopathology manifested by children with mental retardation who require extensive supports appear to be different in that autism and related pervasive developmental disorders appear to be more common in this group. Stereotypic behaviors (e.g., hand flapping, toe walking) and self-injurious behaviors (discussed later in this chapter) may occur as symptoms of underlying major neuropsychiatric disorder, especially in children with mental retardation requiring extensive supports (Bergman, 1991). More research needs to be done, however, before it will be known whether these actually represent real differences in mental processes between children with mild disabilities and children with more severe disabilities or whether the apparent differences are the result of limited communication with children with disabilities.

Children with mental retardation can experience depression, bipolar disorder, anxiety disorders, obsessive-compulsive disorders, and psychotic disorders. Some individuals with mild mental retardation are likely to abuse drugs and alcohol if they are in the company of persons who abuse drugs. Children with mental retardation may have attention-deficit/hyperactivity disorder and oppositional defiant disorder. Presence of seizures complicates the picture further. Some children have symptoms of an autism spectrum disorder but may not fulfill all the criteria for a diagnosis of autistic disorder. Such children are categorized under the rubric of pervasive developmental disorder-not otherwise specified (PDD-NOS). Whatever the diagnosis, it is the traditional practice in psychiatry to target the maladaptive behaviors. The type of diagnosis determines the type of services children get from the school system and the health system, however. Recently, behavioral phenotypes for certain genetic syndromes such as Down syndrome, fragile X syndrome, Angelman syndrome, Lesch-Nyhan syndrome, Prader-Willi syndrome, and Williams syndrome have been identified (Moldavsky, Lev, & Lerman-Sagie, 2001). Identification of behavioral characteristics of known genetic syndromes helps in planning the type of interventions needed early on and taking preventive measures to avoid certain complications (Dykens, Hodapp, & Finucane, 2000).

The Effects and Risks of Psychoactive Medications

Closely related to the issue of dual diagnosis are concerns about the use of psychoactive medication used with people with mental retardation. Until the mid-1980s, people with severe behavior problems often were given massive doses of tranquilizers to calm them down (Gadow & Poling, 1988). The consequence was inhibition of the person's total functioning, not just a decrease in the target behavior. In addition, these individuals often experienced long-term side effects such as tardive dyskinesia, which is characterized by involuntary movements of the limbs and face, and other conditions that interfere with day-to-day activities. A public outcry arose regarding the indiscriminate use of psychotropic medication in people with developmental disabilities, especially those who were in institutional environments (Arnold, 1993; Baumeister, Todd, & Sevin, 1993). The major tranquilizers such as chlorpromazine, fluphenazine, haloperidol, and thioridazine, also called antipsychotic medications, were traditionally used for management of psychotic disorders and often used with children and adults with mental retardation to suppress undesirable behavior, even when no signs of psychosis were present. They are known to have many problematic, long-term side effects. Since the 1990s, a different category of antipsychotic medication has been developed that is believed to have fewer long-term complications. These atypical or novel antipsychotics include clozepine, risperidone, olanzepine, quiteapine, zyprasadone, and aripiprazole. In addition, other classes of drugs such as the newer antidepressants (e.g., fluoxetine, paroxitine, sertraline) have also been used to treat mental health or behavior problems in children and adults with disabilities. Although these medications appear much safer than major tranquilizers, no medication is free of risk and their relative newness leaves the possibility that some long-term effects remain to be discovered.

Decisions regarding medications must be based on the individual needs of the child, after weighing, as carefully as possible, the potential for harm and benefit to the individual. Medications should never be prescribed primarily for the benefit of others. Past history of the field indicates the need for great caution before prescribing any medication to children with severe and multiple disabilities. For example, the drug fenfluramine, once thought to produce substantial improvements in children with autism, was later found to produce no benefits (e.g., Leventhal et al., 1993) and, in fact, caused severe heart damage (e.g., Hopkins & Polukoff, 2003). The complex health needs of these children, including the fact that they may require other medications for other conditions, suggests a need for even greater caution. Medication should never be used in place of a behavioral or training program; when it must be used, it should be used as a time-limited measure to supplement the effects of teaching, counseling, nonaversive behavioral intervention, or other programs. Decisions should be based on the recommendations of the collaborative team. The American Academy of Child and Adolescent Psychiatry (AACAP, 1999) established practice parameters and guidelines for psychiatrists who help people with mental retardation and comorbid mental illness to manage their mental illness. These guidelines are valuable to psychiatrists and it is hoped that people treating this group will follow the best practice method to improve quality of life.

SELF-INJURIOUS BEHAVIOR

Self-injurious behavior (SIB) is seen in some students with severe or multiple disabilities. These students harm themselves through their own repetitive, stereotypic, or intense episodic behavior. They may bang their heads, poke their eyes, scratch or tear their skin, bite their arms or fingers, or engage in other self-damaging behavior. The effects of this behavior range from mild irritation to severe and permanent injury. In addition, SIB is often very disruptive to activities and demoralizing to parents, staff, classmates, and others. It should be noted that self-injury is not restricted to people with mental retardation and autism.

Deliberate self-injury can occur in people with typical intelligence and may serve multiple functions within a given individual, and the underlying condition can be neurochemical, environmental, or both (Thompson, Axtell, & Schaal, 1993). SIB has been divided into four major categories: 1) stereotypic, 2) psychotic, 3) compulsive, and 4) impulsive (Simeon & Favazza, 2001).

Causes

No single cause appears to explain all SIB among children with disabilities. In some individuals, SIB has a social function, such as gaining attention or escaping from demands, but in others this behavior occurs regardless of social context or response (Saloviita, 2000). A few specific organic conditions, such as Lesch-Nyhan syndrome and Prader-Willi syndrome, appear to predispose individuals to SIB. Some theories suggest that self-inflicted pain helps block other more aversive sensations, may increase the production of natural opiates in the system and thus be reinforced (White & Schultz, 2000), or may be used by the individual to raise the general level of arousal (much in the way that a tired driver sometimes turns up the car radio, opens the window to let in cold air, or even slaps his or her own cheeks to try to stay alert). Other explanations are more behavioral, suggesting that the behavior is developed, maintained, and strengthened as the individual learns that it is associated with reinforcement or escape from aversive stimuli. For example, children may learn that SIB quickly attracts the attention of caregivers or distracts caregivers, thereby providing the individual with the opportunity to escape from demands of a task. Behavioral and organic explanations are not mutually exclusive, and it is likely that these and other factors interact in at least some children (Scotti, Evans, Meyer, & Walker, 1991).

In some cases self-injury can be a sign of a psychiatric condition (Thompson et al., 1993) and in others it may be associated with an affective disorder such as depression (Sovner, Fox, Lowry, & Lowry, 1993). Some efforts have been made at developing models of the locus of SIB. Some of the biological models involve dysfunction of chemical substances in the brain such as dopamine, serotonin, and endorphin (Aman, 1993). SIB can also occur as a symptom of physical or sexual abuse in children with and without developmental disabilities. For example, Mansell, Sobsey, and Moskall (1998) found that SIB occurred in 26% of sexually abused children with developmental disabilities who were receiving treatment for sexual abuse but also was present in 7% of children without disabilities receiving treatment for sexual abuse.

While making decisions on the educational management plan for a child with SIB, three factors should be considered: 1) the temporal pattern and degree of repetitiveness (regularity) of action, 2) the degree to which self-injurious performance is under the control of external environmental consequences, and 3) the degree to which pain maintains self-injury (Thompson et al., 1993). In a few cases, aggressive or disruptive behavior or SIB actually results from seizure activity. When this is the case, appropriate anticonvulsant medication can reduce or eliminate the behavior.

Intervention

A wide variety of drugs is used to reduce or eliminate SIB. Tranquilizers, opiate antagonists, beta blockers, stimulants, antidepressants, and anticonvulsants are sometimes used (Davanzo, Belin, Widawski, & King, 1998; Gadow & Poling, 1988; Long & Miltenberger, 1998). Although many of these drugs have been at least partially successful for certain individuals in achieving some reduction in SIB, they often suppress other, more appropriate behavior to a greater or equal extent; interfere with learning; have deleterious side effects; and create chronic dependency because any improvement achieved typically is reversed when use of the drug ceases. Therefore, drugs should not be considered as a primary resource for treating SIB. They may be considered as a time-limited component of intervention if the behavior puts the individual in immediate danger.

Restraints

Another common approach to managing severe SIB has been use of restraint. Restraint devices have been applied in the form of elbow or knee splints, camisoles (straightjackets), restraint nets, support belts, or a number of other appliances. Restraint has also been used in the form of an adult holding the child and restricting movements.

Although restraints continue to be frequently used in some environments, there are several serious problems that must be considered. First, restraints are dangerous and must be considered high-risk procedures. Serious injuries and significant numbers of deaths have resulted from attempts to use restraints. Although many of these cases involve poorly trained staff and misapplication of procedures, deaths frequently occur even when "model" restraint procedures are used.

Second, the use of restraint has been shown to reinforce the SIB in some individuals (Favell, McGimsey, & Jones, 1978). Even though the immediate effect of restraint may be to make it more difficult for the child to cause an injury, the frequency and intensity of self-injury may increase as soon as the child is released. This can lead to a vicious cycle in which the use of restraint becomes more and more frequent while SIB intensifies.

Third, restraints are socially stigmatizing and make inclusion and normal interaction much more difficult. This increases social isolation and often results in fewer opportunities to take part in desired activities that might help develop more desirable behavioral alternatives.

Fourth, the application of restraint is governed by a long list of professional policies, agency procedures, laws, and court decisions that are rarely considered in the use of these procedures in school environments. Unfortunately, the failure to consider the appropriate regulatory law and policy is commonly identified after restraint results in injury. As a result, schools and individual personnel who employ these procedures may find themselves civilly or even criminally liable for any harm resulting from the use of these procedures.

Finally, restraints always interfere with a much broader class of behavior than the ones they are intended to suppress; for example, restraints that are intended to stop a child from biting his or her fingers may also make self-feeding impossible. As educators, our goal is to enable children, not to incapacitate them. For all of these reasons, restraint is never a desirable procedure. It should be used as infrequently as possible and only to prevent clear and present danger (e.g., stopping a child from running out into traffic).

First Aid

First aid and other forms of treatment are often important elements in a total program for children with SIB. Methods for controlling bleeding and other first aid measures are discussed in the Classroom Emergencies section of this chapter. Other treatments (e.g., sterile dressings, surgery to repair detached retinas) may be required in some cases. The health care team should work closely with the educational team in determining appropriate treatments. Because the care and attention associated with a treatment may reinforce the SIB of some children, it is essential that their treatment be provided in a neutral manner that minimizes reinforcement. Another important caveat is that even the best treatment can only be expected to slow the rate of damage if severe SIB continues. Therefore, treating the injuries should be considered a necessary component of the child's care, but primary emphasis should be placed on eliminating the SIB.

Nonaversive Intervention

In the past, punishment or aversive procedures were commonly used in an attempt to treat SIB as well as other behavior problems. Although some remaining proponents argue that in some extreme cases, aversive procedures are necessary and effective, nonaversive interventions and positive behavioral supports have been increasingly accepted as a better approach in the vast majority of cases (Mathieson & Price, 2002). Positive approaches that do not require inflicting discomfort on children have been demonstrated to be both effective and more humane than using aversives (Donnellan & LaVigna, 1990; Evans, Scotti, & Hawkins, 1999; Scotti et al., 1991).

Nonaversive intervention requires a functional analysis of the behavior along with its temporal, social, and physical contexts. Antecedents and consequences of the behavior are carefully examined to determine the function of the behavior for the child. For example, two children may have episodes of hitting their heads, but one may hit herself when she is left alone whereas the other may do so when he is asked to carry out a difficult task. For the former, hitting herself may function as a means of attracting attention from caregivers. For the latter, hitting himself may function as a means of escaping from task demands. Because the behavior of the two students is almost identical, team members can make and test hypotheses regarding the function only by considering the specific contexts and effects of each behavior. Once the function of the behavior has been identified, intervention can be designed to provide training in a more socially appropriate and less dangerous method of serving the function. It is important to remember that requesting attention or protesting a demand is not the problem. Everyone has a right and a need to carry out these functions at times; rather, it is the method of carrying out these functions that needs to change. Unfortunately, caregivers often ignore appropriate requests for attention and protests but respond to inappropriate behavior that is more difficult to ignore. Effective transfer of the behavioral function to a more appropriate form of behavior requires caregivers to respond to the new form of behavior as quickly and as enthusiastically as they responded to the less appropriate form (Carr et al., 1994). For more information on methods of teaching communication functions, please refer to Chapter 12.

CLASSROOM EMERGENCIES

Efforts to prevent classroom emergencies can greatly reduce the frequency and severity of these episodes. Despite even the best prevention efforts, emergencies sometimes occur, and all staff working with children with severe and multiple disabilities must be prepared to respond to them.

General Strategies

A practical course in safety and first aid with periodic refresher classes should be included in the training of all staff. Most professionals who work with children are required to be periodically certified in basic life support and CPR. Staff working with students with severe and multiple disabilities also need specific training related to the special needs of these children. For example, unless there is a possibility of brain injury, first aid procedures dictate that children who have lost a considerable amount of blood be positioned laying on their backs with their feet raised to reduce shock and ensure a better supply of blood to the brain. Children who do not understand the reason for being asked to assume this position, however, may resist. Forcing children to assume the "shock position" is almost always counterproductive. The physical demands and emotional stress of confrontation typically increase blood loss. Therefore, allowing the child to sit and relax is generally better than forcing a child to lie down.

Special consideration must be made when positioning students with tracheostomies. The education team needs to be familiar with modifications to the resuscitation procedures required for these children in respiratory emergencies (Heller, Forney, Alberto, Schwartzman, & Goeckel, 2000). Similarly, teachers who work with students who are in wheelchairs need to know how resuscitation and procedures to clear the airway can be modified to apply to these children, if necessary.

Every classroom needs a plan for handling emergencies, and it is important that all team members be familiar with the plan in advance. For example, team members need to know whether to call the school nurse, the principal, the parent, or an ambulance in case of a serious emergency, and all of these important telephone numbers should be readily available. For some students, particularly those with highly individualized health care needs, a plan should also be in place (and approved by parents) to contact the child's physician directly. Any health care information that is likely to be relevant in an emergency situation (e.g., current medications, blood type, allergies) should be kept in an easily accessible file that can be taken with the child if he or she needs to be transported to a hospital or other environment for treatment. It may be useful to keep general consent forms for emergency treatment in this file, although the value of this type of consent is questionable. These types of consent are given in advance, not after being informed of a current situation and the specific risks and potential benefits of treatment, so they cannot substitute for the fully informed consent to permit medical treatment unless the child is in grave danger or it is a life-or-death situation. Nevertheless, large areas of uncertainty remain regarding what treatments are essential and how long a delay is justifiable. Schottke's (2001) work, *First Responder: Your First Response in Emergency Care,* is a practical and handy book on first aid and emergency situations for school staff to refer to periodically.

Some Specific Emergencies

The following are some specific emergencies that team members may encounter when working with students with severe and multiple disabilities.

Choking/Airway Obstruction

Preventing and treating airway obstruction are probably the most important emergency health care skills for teachers of students with severe and multiple disabilities. These skills are essential for four important reasons:

1. Airway obstruction is a major cause of accidental death of children (Tarrago, 2000).

2. The risk of airway obstruction is greater for children with disabilities.

3. If complete obstruction of the airway occurs, treatment must be given immediately; there is rarely enough time to obtain outside help to save a child.

4. Simple prevention and treatment methods could save almost every choking victim.

Although the exact extent of the increased risk for children with severe and multiple disabilities is unknown, a number of risk factors have been identified in the general public (Dailey, 1983; Tarrago, 2000) that indicate substantially increased risk for children with disabilities: 1) decreased gag reflex, 2) incomplete chewing, 3) use of medication, 4) missing teeth, and 5) altered consciousness. See Chapter 12 for more on the risk of choking and airway obstruction related to feeding and eating.

Signs and Symptoms   In spite of the best prevention efforts, choking incidents will continue to occur from time to time. Parents, teachers, and other mealtime caregivers must be adequately trained to recognize and treat airway obstruction. Early symptoms of complete airway obstruction are nonspecific. In the first 1–3 minutes, the child is likely to remain conscious but indicate distress through agitated movement and possible clutching of the throat or tears in the eyes. The child attempts to breathe but no air can be felt entering or leaving the nose or mouth. Because no air can enter or leave, the child cannot vocalize. Pulse and blood pressure increase rapidly. Color gradually begins to change to a deep red or purple, the beginning of cyanosis. During the next phase, which lasts approximately 3 minutes, the child loses consciousness. Cyanosis deepens to a mottled blue or purple. Pulse and blood pressure drop rapidly. Attempts at respiration weaken. About 5 minutes (often less) after the initial obstruction, the child enters a third phase, deep coma. Blood pressure, pulse, and attempts at respiration are absent. Pupils become dilated. Brain damage and death will ensue rapidly unless the airway is cleared and pulse and respiration restarted.

Treatment   The rapidity of these events demands immediate action. Available time is often further restricted by failure to notice a problem until the second stage or by the mistaken belief that an epileptic seizure or other problem is the cause. Attempting mouth-to-mouth resuscitation and finding that air will not go in or come out confirms airway obstruction.

The best training requires direct instructor-to-student contact, which can be obtained in first aid courses or specialized training programs, but some general discussion of these procedures is included next. One great procedure that has saved thousands of lives from choking deaths is the subdiaphragmatic thrust (Heimlich maneuver). Heimlich (1982) urged the use of the maneuver as treatment for choking. He stated that back blows are less effective and may convert a partial obstruction into a complete one or a treatable obstruction into an untreatable one. The following describes the procedure for performing the subdiaphragmatic thrust in adults: 1) Place arms around the individual from the rear, 2) grasp one wrist with the other hand, 3) make a fist with the empty hand, 4) press the fist against the individual's upper abdomen just below the tip of the sternum (breastbone), and 5) hug forcefully while pressing the fist upward and into the abdomen (Heimlich & Uhley, 1979; Leiken & Feldman, 2000). This procedure forces the abdomen upward and compresses the air in the lungs, which pushes out the obstruction. (Placement of the rescuer's arms should be slightly higher for a child, as illustrated in Figure 8.2). If the mouth is full, then it is desirable to clear it carefully (so that nothing is pushed further into the throat or airway) before carrying out the subdiaphragmatic thrust. If the rescuer cannot position him- or herself behind the individual, an alternative procedure positions the person supine on the floor or firm surface and the rescuer kneels over the individual, facing his or her head. The rescuer applies the thrust by positioning the hands just below the sternum (as described previously) and leaning rapidly and forcefully forward. Chest thrusts are similar to the subdiaphragmatic thrusts, except that pressure is applied directly to the middle of the sternum (breast bone). This method may be necessary to use if the choking person is quite obese or in the advanced stages of pregnancy. Chest thrusts may be applied with two fingers and the infant-in-supine position for children younger than 1 year old (Leikin & Feldman, 2000; St. John Ambulance, 2001). Although there continues to be some controversy about the best treatment for infants (younger than 1 year old), since 1985, all major first aid groups have endorsed the Heimlich maneuver as treatment in most choking emergencies (American Heart Association, 2002; Leikin & Feldman, 2000).

A finger sweep of the mouth and upper throat also may remove obstructions. This method is sometimes effective when other methods fail but should be used as an initial measure only if the choking victim is unconscious and the obstruction is visible in back of the mouth because of the danger of pushing obstructions farther into the airway or compacting the obstruction. These difficulties are especially likely to occur with a young child with a small oropharyn-

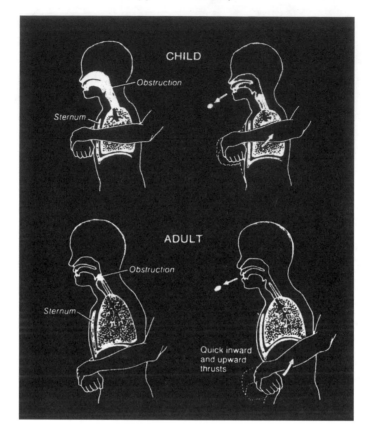

Figure 8.2. Subdiaphragmatic thrust and chest thrust. (From Batshaw, M.L., & Perret, Y.M. [1986]. Children with handicaps: A medical primer [2nd ed., p. 439]. Baltimore: Paul H. Brookes Publishing Co; reprinted by permission of the author.)

geal space in which to work. Performance of a finger sweep involves the rescuer positioning the victim supine (on a sloping surface with head lower than feet if possible) with the head extended back. The rescuer carefully inserts an index finger into the side of the mouth and hooks it around the obstruction, then pulls it out. If part of the obstruction is removed, the procedure is repeated only after a check reveals that the airway remains obstructed.

Brain Injury

Any child can sustain a brain injury. They are the most common causes of death and disability among children. Acquired brain injuries are most frequently the result of a traumatic injury but can also occur as a result of a blockage or rupture of part of the brain's blood supply. Some of the special considerations related to recognizing and treating brain injury in children with severe disabilities are also discussed. Brain injury is frequently classified as *concussion* (i.e., a temporary disturbance in brain function as a result of an impact) or compression (i.e., pressure on some part of the brain caused by a fracture of the skull, swelling, or the collection of fluid in an area of the brain). Table 8.3 lists some of the common signs of concussion and compression and some special considerations for children with severe and multiple disabilities and basic first aid measures. As shown in this table, signs of concussion and compression overlap,

Table 8.3. Common signs and symptoms of concussion and compression

Concussion[a]	**Special considerations for individuals with severe and multiple disabilities**
Partial loss of consciousness	Many of these signs can be masked if they are present prior to injury.
Shallow breathing	Seizures are more common in concussion among people with preexisting seizure disorders.
Weak pulse	
Pale appearance	
Headache	Seizures sometimes produce many of the same signs as brain injury.
Confusion	
Complete loss of consciousness	Medications (e.g., anticonvulsants, tranquilizers) may mask symptoms.
Rapid pulse	
Cool skin	Some individuals may not be able to communicate how they feel.
Vomiting	
Loss of memory (especially for recent events)	
Potentially injurious event (may have been seen)	**First aid treatment and response**
	Assess consciousness, observe for breathing difficulties, and keep under constant observation.
Compression[b]	
Partial loss of consciousness	Maintain open airway and provide assisted breathing, if required.
Seizures (mild to severe)	
Slowing of pulse	Call for medical assistance.
Raised body temperature	Do not give food or fluids.
Dilated pupils	Protect area of injury from any further trauma (and from contamination, if open wound).
Coordination problems	
Confusion	
Complete loss of consciousness	Do not move person, if possible, to avoid further injury.
Irregular breathing	
Flushed face	Keep injured person calm and inactive if possible. (Do not use excessive restraint.)
Unequal pupils	
Weakness (may affect one side more than the other)	Prevent nose blowing if possible.
	Avoid pressure to area of injury.
External injury may or may not be present	Unless bleeding is so severe that is must be stopped, do not use direct pressure to skull injuries.
Potentially injurious event (may have been seen)	

[a]Usually these signs and symptoms begin immediately or shortly after injury.

[b]These signs and symptoms may begin immediately or shortly after injury but may be delayed significantly.

and the distinction between the two is more difficult to make if the individual sustaining the injury has epilepsy, a movement disorder, or communication impairments. Many medications used by people with disabilities can also mask symptoms. Because the rapid diagnosis and treatment of brain injury is essential for the best treatment, and accurate diagnosis may be impossible without careful evaluation by a physician using sophisticated tests and equipment, it is better to err on the side of safety and have the child evaluated if signs of injury are ambiguous.

First aid measures often consist only of keeping the child safe and calm until help arrives (American Red Cross, 2002). No food or fluids should be given because intake may increase swelling in the brain. Eating and drinking also may cause aspiration because swallowing may be difficult and the typical reflexes to close the airway during swallowing will be impaired. The danger of vomiting is also increased, which is particularly problematic because vomiting is likely to increase pressure on the brain and create further risk of aspiration.

Because children sustaining brain injury are likely to lose consciousness or have a seizure, they should be protected against falling. If bleeding from a head wound is not too severe, it is better to allow bleeding than to apply pressure. One should keep the child calm and comfortable, observing continuously for changes, particularly any difficulty with breathing. If the child will lie down quietly, he or she should be encouraged to do so, but it is important that the child avoid restraint or struggling, both of which may aggravate the injury. Do not use shock position or elevate feet above the head because this may increase pressure on the brain.

Poisoning

Schools can be the source for a surprising array of toxic materials. Pesticides and herbicides are frequently used in schools, and attempts to pass federal legislation to regulate their use have been unsuccessful despite strong support from groups such as the National Education Association (NEA) (2001). A new version of the School Environment Protection Act, which includes such measures as requiring that schools notify parents of the pesticides used in their child's classroom, was introduced in April 2003 (Chapman, 2003). Science classes often use highly toxic and sometimes attractive substances such as mercury (Tominack et al., 2002). As a result, chemicals used in science classes account for approximately one third of poisonings in schools (Perry, Dean, & Krenzelok, 1992). Art classes frequently use toxic materials such as many ceramic glazes and some paints (British Columbia Art Teachers Association, 1991). Many cleaning supplies can also be toxic if ingested. Medications used in schools may also be toxic when consumed in large amounts or by the wrong students. Many children are allergic to foods such as peanuts, which can be highly toxic and even fatal, even if ingested in very small amounts. Schools must be careful to check for hidden peanut products, such as peanut oil, when distributing snacks to children, and to ensure that students' peers do not share food with them. Common plants such as mistletoe used in holiday decorating can also be toxic if eaten (see also Batshaw 2001, p. 154). Many children are also severely allergic to bees and other insects. Some materials such as latex can cause a serious allergic reaction in some children, so nonlatex gloves and other products should be used in school.

Children with severe and multiple disabilities may not understand the danger associated with ingestion of these substances and therefore are at greater risk than other students. Often, problems can be prevented, and everyone who works with children who have severe and multiple disabilities should practice vigilance. These efforts include 1) keeping all cleaners, pesticides, drugs, and other dangerous substances safely locked away; 2) being certain that no poisonous plants are kept in areas frequented by children; 3) discarding old or excess medication, pesticides, cleaners, and so forth in a safe manner; 4) keeping all dangerous substances in childproof containers; 5) helping children learn to communicate that they have come in contact with a toxin; and 6) making plans of action in the event that a chld is exposed.

Fortunately, the development of a network of poison control centers across North America has greatly simplified the basic first aid protocol for ingestion of toxic substances. One should contact the poison control center immediately, be prepared to give information about the situation, and follow the instructions provided. Staff of the poison control center will need to know what substance was ingested, how much, and how long ago. They should also be told the child's age, approximate weight, any available information regarding special medical conditions, and what medications, if any, the child normally takes. Poison control staff may recommend immediate first aid measures and will often suggest that the child be brought in for examination.

When the child goes for examination, the container that held the substance, any labeling material available, and any remaining sample of the substance should be brought. If the toxic substance was a plant (e.g., rubber plant, which triggers latex allergy), one should bring it or part of it for identification. If the child vomited, one should try to bring the vomitus or at least a sample of it for examination. It is essential to note the time of the ingestion and bring along any records available regarding health conditions, allergies, and medications. In the rare case that contacting the poison control center is not possible, one should check the label of the substance for directions on how to treat ingestion. Several glasses of water may help to dilute the substance and may induce vomiting. Providing fluids or inducing vomiting is not normally recommended unless instructed by qualified medical personnel or the poison control center, however. This is because vomiting can make things worse in some cases. For example, many cleaning products and paints contain petroleum products that could cause much more harm if aspirated during vomiting than in the stomach. The few seconds or minutes required to check with the appropriate experts can help avoid such situations. In case appropriate medical authorities do instruct the induction of vomiting, however, syrup of ipecac is commonly used for that purpose and should be kept on hand. Inducing vomiting may be difficult in some children with severe and multiple disabilities because of medications that they are receiving or depressed reflexes.

Bleeding

External bleeding is easily recognized and easily treated. Almost all bleeding, including bleeding resulting from severe injuries, can be controlled by direct pressure. If available, a sterile bandage or clean cloth can be pressed over a wound. When those items are unavailable, pressure applied with the bare hand works quite satisfactorily. Whenever possible, and particularly if the individual applying pressure has any broken skin, it is recommended that he or she wear gloves to minimize the risk of transmission of communicable disease. Immediate emergency medical intervention should be sought in all instances of severe bleeding to avoid shock or even death from blood loss.

The child who is injured should be encouraged to rest and stay calm and, if possible, the injured body part should be elevated in relation to the rest of the body. If the injury appears to be severe, medical advice and assistance must be sought. If internal bleeding is suspected, the child who is injured should be at rest. If possible, the child should lie down with the legs slightly elevated. The child who is injured should be kept warm and medical advice and assistance should be sought as quickly as possible.

ABUSE

Sadly, child abuse is a worldwide phenomenon, a terrible reality to many children that transcends race, religion, color, socioeconomic status, and place of residence. Significant proportions of children from all segments of society are subjected to physical, sexual, or emotional abuse or neglect (Hornor, 2002; Spencer, 2002). In 1998, estimates found that approximately 2.9 million children were reported to Child Protective Services as being abused and/or neglected; nearly a third of these cases were confirmed (Children's Defense Fund, 2001). The incidence of child abuse and neglect among children with disabilities appears to be at least twice as high as it is for the general population (Sobsey, 2002).

As diagnostic techniques improve, the role of abuse in causing disability becomes clearer and, unfortunately, abuse appears more extensive than previously believed (Sobsey, 2002). For example, improved brain neuroimaging techniques have helped to identify many cases of shaken baby syndrome, which likely would have been diagnosed only as "brain damage of undetermined origin" in previous years (Sobsey, 2002). In addition, previous understanding of the long-term effects of shaken baby syndrome was based largely on the neurological examination on release from the hospital after an acute injury. It is now well documented that many children released with normal neurological exams develop significant developmental and neurological anomalies as long as 2 years after being released (Sobsey, 2002). Although the direct effects of traumatic injuries due to child abuse can be devastating, the psychological trauma caused by more subtle mechanisms can be equally tragic.

Research has made it clear that physical, sexual, or emotional abuse or severe neglect also affects the development of children's nervous systems by producing biochemical changes related to extreme stress or trauma (Chaffin & Hanson, 2000). These changes can cause disabilities or increase the complexity and severity of existing disabilities. Although any one form of abuse or neglect can produce this effect, it is typically more extreme as the number and types of emotional trauma accumulate (Chaffin & Hanson, 2000). These neurological changes occur whether any direct physical injury results from abuse, but when physical injuries do occur, these injuries compound this effect. Although this effect is now very well demonstrated, much more research will be required to understand some aspects of this process. Some children appear to be more vulnerable to the neurological changes associated with abuse, but the reasons for these differences in vulnerability and the extent of these differences are not fully understood. Existing research suggests that on average, this effect could produce a 15-percentile drop in academic achievement (e.g., Sullivan & Knutson, 2000), including in children with severe and multiple disabilities. This estimate must be considered very tentative, however, because a number of potentially confounding factors (e.g., existing disabilities, other stressors, behavior problems, seizures) would need to be carefully controlled for before drawing a more certain conclusion. Perhaps most importantly, much more needs to be learned about what can be done to minimize the harm done to children who have been traumatized by abuse. Initial work with traumatized children suggests that these children develop exaggerated stress responses as a result of trauma. As a result, even minor stresses produce further biochemical changes. Calm learning environments are essential to any progress toward more normal responses to stress. In some cases, heart-rate monitors signal to teachers when the child is beginning to experience a stress response and the teacher can shift focus to restore calm before attempting to work on anything else.

Increasing awareness of the extent of abuse and neglect among children with disabilities and of the degree of harm experienced by those who have been abused has resulted in the development and implementation of programs to prevent, detect, and respond to abuse. The American Academy of Pediatrics (2001), through its committee on Child Abuse and Neglect and on Children with Disabilities, developed a set of recommendations for assessing maltreatment of children with disabilities. Pediatricians should evaluate children for disabilities when they suspect maltreatment. Teachers should report any suspicion of abuse to the school authorities so that they can check with parents about the reason for any signs of injury in the child. If the parental information is inconsistent and if suspicion remains, then the appropriate social agency (e.g., children and youth services) should be notified. This is generally a tough decision to make.

In addition to experiencing violence, children from abusive families typically grow up in a home that fails to provide appropriate developmental opportunities. The stimulation for the child is inconsistent and disorganized. The experience for each child varies; however, all children from such environments seem to acquire developmental impairments and outcomes across all the studies on abuse (Wolfe, 1999).

Different factors can contribute to both abuse and disability. For example, excessive use of alcohol within families has been found to be associated with physical and sexual abuse of children within these families (e.g., Cyr, Wright, McDuff, & Perron, 2002), and maternal ingestion may cause fetal alcohol syndrome, which causes a myriad of developmental delays and other difficulties throughout life (Jones & Bass, 2003; Streissguth, 1997). Although the cause of disability appears to be unrelated to abuse, children with disabilities are more frequently targets of abuse than are children who do not have disabilities. Furthermore, although children with disabilities are affected by abuse in the same ways as other children, they are often excluded from intervention programs that serve other children. Even when programs are accessible to children with disabilities, the programs are rarely appropriately individualized to meet the needs of children with severe and multiple disabilities.

The Nature and Extent of Abuse

Increased Risk

Since the 1960s, studies have repeatedly linked increased risk for abuse with childhood disability, and recent studies have confirmed this association. The precise extent of increased risk, however, differs from study to study. A large study completed in 1993 and based on a nationally representative sample of abused children in the United States is commonly presented as the most authoritative. It concluded that children with disabilities were 1.67 times as likely to be maltreated as children without disabilities (Crosse, Kaye, & Ratnofsky, 1993). Unfortunately, failure to control for age resulted in significant distortion of the results. For example, the researchers assumed that learning disabilities and mental retardation would be diagnosed in infants and preschool children at the same rates that they are diagnosed in school-age children. Because many disabilities go undiagnosed until children enter school and one third of the sample of abused children were 5 years old or younger, the comparison led to serious underestimation of the relationship between abuse and disability.

Sullivan and Knutson's (2000) study of a cohort of more than 50,000 children in a Midwest city probably presents the best estimate of the association between abuse and disability. It certainly represents the most relevant comparison for educational environments. This study started with all children registered in school programs and then determined which children had been identified as having special needs and which children had a history of abuse. A history of abuse was 3.4 times more common among children identified as having special learning needs as among other children. Almost one quarter (22%) of children with a history of maltreatment had been identified as needing special education, and almost one third (31%) of children in special education had a confirmed history of child maltreatment.

Children with developmental disabilities who were sexually abused were similar to other sexually abused children in that they exhibited the same behavioral symptoms (Mansell et al., 1998). They differed from children without disabilities, however, in that they typically exhibited a larger number of symptoms and were more likely to exhibit symptoms in the areas of aggression, poor self-esteem, inappropriate anger, nightmares, lack of sexual knowledge, inappropriate sexual remarks and unusual comments about family, extreme withdrawal, SIB, and withdrawal into fantasy.

A Multifactorial Model of Abuse

Traditional explanations for the increased abuse of children with disabilities have proven inadequate. Much emphasis has been placed on a model that suggests that with increasing severity of disability, the individual becomes more dependent. As dependency increases, family stress also increases, and this increase in family stress could potentially precipitate abuse. Some children with chronic illnesses or disabilities do place high emotional, physical, economic, and social demands on their families (Botash & Church, 1999). Families with limited social and community support, lack of respite care, increased requirements for special health care, and unmet educational needs may experience greater risk (American Academy of

Pediatrics, 2001). Nevertheless, the severity of disability or level of dependency of a child is a poor predictor of abuse. The willingness of researchers and professionals to accept a model that ultimately places the cause of abuse with the victim not only is ethically worrisome but also shows little potential for producing solutions.

A multifactorial model considers factors within the context of the interaction between the victim and the offender, the environment, and the social and cultural milieu (Sobsey, 2002). For example, excessive compliance has been identified in many individuals who have disabilities and who have been abused, but this may result from an "educational focus" on compliance training for people with disabilities and not from any inherent trait in the individuals. In this model, beliefs about and attitudes toward children with disabilities are important factors in whether children with disabilities will be abused. A much more complete description of this model and other potential models for understanding the association between abuse and disability is given in Petersilia (2001).

Prevention and Intervention

Detecting and Reporting Abuse

Most states require educational and health care professionals to report suspected abuse to police or child protection agencies, and some states require any individual to report suspected abuse (Houry, Sachs, Feldhaus, & Linden, 2002) Nevertheless, abuse frequently goes undetected, and when detected, it often goes unreported (Sobsey, 1994a, 1994b). Several reasons contribute to poor detection and unreported abuse (Sobsey, 1994b).

First, offenders generally hide their abusive behavior well. They select times and places that provide privacy, and they often choose individuals who cannot or will not tell what has happened to them. Offenders also may go to great lengths to construct alternative explanations for unexplained injuries or other signs of abuse. Many children with severe and multiple disabilities cannot communicate clearly about their mistreatment and may not know that they have a right to better treatment (Sobsey, 1994b). They may also view the treatment as "normal" or think that others know about it and are just not saying anything. For example, when one mother asked her 5-year-old daughter why she never told about the frequent sexual assaults she had endured, her daughter replied simply, "I thought you knew." Even when they understand that they are being mistreated and are capable of telling about the abuse, many individuals are intimidated by the offenders. Most signs of abuse are inconclusive and may easily be attributed to other causes. Symptom masking, the attribution of a particular symptom to a known preexisting condition rather than its real cause, often occurs when the person who has been abused has a disability. For example, behavioral changes, withdrawal, fearfulness, and frequent bruises or even fractures that result from abuse may be attributed to a child's disability rather than mistreatment. Finally, team members may be reluctant to accept evidence that their colleagues and co-workers are abusing the children they serve.

In spite of these problems, knowledge of the signs of abuse can be very useful in detecting it. Common signs of child abuse are listed in Table 8.4. Many of these signs are ambiguous, and it is often an overall pattern or impression that is more powerful than any single sign. Each school or agency should have a protocol in place for reporting suspected abuse. Because there is rarely direct or overwhelming evidence at the time of the initial report, it is important that staff understand that they must report suspected abuse and that many of these reports will prove unfounded or lack sufficient evidence for confirmation. In schools and agencies that have protocols requiring internal reporting, provisions should mandate external reporting. No report should be dismissed arbitrarily; thorough investigation is essential.

A Multipronged Approach

Abuse prevention efforts cannot eliminate all risk of abuse, but they can significantly reduce those risks. Effective prevention methods may involve efforts directed toward the child, potential offenders, other program staff and family members, administrative reform, legislative reform, and cultural attitude change. Education is a powerful intervention against abuse. Teaching children that they have a right to be treated decently and how to assert those rights helps to reduce children's risk for abuse. Communication skill training is vital to abuse prevention. Children who can express their feelings and indicate when they believe that they are being mistreated are less likely to be abused or exploited. Appropriate social and sex education is also important to prevent sexual abuse and exploitation (Sobsey, 1994b). Children who do not receive appropriate sex education from parents and teachers are likely to accept inappropriate sex "education" from an abuser. Program staff, parents, and advocates also need to learn to recognize and report abuse. Early recognition and response to problems is an essential element of abuse prevention because most abuse begins in milder forms and escalates to more severe forms.

Learning to recognize and cope with one's own reluctance to respond to a situation may be among the most difficult things to learn. Because stress can lead to abuse, family members and caregivers should learn to recognize early signs of difficulty and stress that they are experiencing in managing their child with a disability and know where they can go for advice or counseling. Although stress may play a smaller part in precipitating abuse, helping individuals through periods of stress may avert some abuse. Even more important,

Table 8.4.　Common signs of child abuse

All forms of abuse	
Direct observation (tangible acts)	Promiscuity
Withdrawal	Threats
Resistance to touch	Sexual precocity
Fear of specific caregivers	Extreme withdrawal
Poor self-esteem	Inappropriate sexual behavior
Victimization of others	Unexplained pregnancy
Disclosure	Sexually transmitted disease
Escape behavior	
Hypervigilance	**Neglect**
Sleep disturbances	Low affect
Passivity	Dehydration
Reenactment	Indifference to other people
Fear of specific environments	Unusual need for attention
Self-abuse	Poor nutritional status
Stoical responses to discomfort	Stoical responses to discomfort
Inappropriate behavior	Untreated illness or injuries
Behavior regression	

All forms of abuse

Direct observation (tangible acts)
Withdrawal
Resistance to touch
Fear of specific caregivers
Poor self-esteem
Victimization of others
Disclosure
Escape behavior
Hypervigilance
Sleep disturbances
Passivity
Reenactment
Fear of specific environments
Self-abuse
Stoical responses to discomfort
Inappropriate behavior
Behavior regression

Physical abuse

Frequent injury
Unexplained coma
Noncompliance
Unexplained injury
Threats
Grab marks
Atypical injury
Aggression
Unreported fractures
Patterned injury
Temporarily dispersed injuries

Sexual abuse

Genital irritation
Aggression
Resistance to touch
Noncompliance
Gender-specific fear

Promiscuity
Threats
Sexual precocity
Extreme withdrawal
Inappropriate sexual behavior
Unexplained pregnancy
Sexually transmitted disease

Neglect

Low affect
Dehydration
Indifference to other people
Unusual need for attention
Poor nutritional status
Stoical responses to discomfort
Untreated illness or injuries

Abusive caregiver traits

Authoritarian behavior
Seeks isolated contact
History of violence or coercion
Dehumanizing attitudes
Difficulty relating to authority
Hostility toward reporters
Abusive counterculture in environment
Fearful of victim
Grooming behavior
Competition with child
Rationalization and euphemism
Unusual concern for privacy
Use of alcohol or disinhibiting drugs
Problems of self-control
Negative evaluation of child
Failure to support abuse control measures
Expression of myths of devaluation
Subverts investigation
Blames victim
Tests limits and boundaries
Self-reports of stress

because family homes generally appear safer than institutional care, support for families in need can go a long way toward reducing abuse.

Administrative reform is also useful in preventing abuse. Careful screening of staff is essential. Individuals with known histories of perpetrating physical or sexual abuse or other violent crimes should not be hired to provide care to children with disabilities. Administrative reform is also essential to demonstrate an unequivocal commitment to protecting the children served by a school or agency. Criminal behavior must be treated as such and not as an employee relations problem or, perhaps worse, as a public relations problem. Agency administration must ensure that employees place a high priority on protecting the children whom they serve. Staff should be periodically trained on the nature of child abuse and its prevention. They should be trained, as well, to provide adequate safeguards in the classroom in order to protect children from each other: Clustering children with disabilities who are vulnerable with children who are aggressive can be considered another form of abuse.

Some specific provisions in legislation that may serve as useful deterrents to abuse include 1) allowing victims of abuse to testify in a manner most appropriate to their communication skills, 2) guaranteeing that employees who report abuse will not be administratively harassed, 3) guaranteeing that victims of abuse who have disabilities and their families will not have services disrupted in retaliation for reporting abuse, and 4) ensuring that all reports of abuse go to an impartial advocate outside of the agency involved.

Attitude change is also essential to preventing abuse. The powerful role of attitudes in facilitating abusive behavior cannot be ignored (Sobsey, 2002). Perceptions that people with disabilities are less than fully human, "damaged merchandise," incapable of suffering, dangerous, or helpless have all been identified as factors in abuse. In the abuser, these myths become full blown and provide the rationale that abusers may use in disinhibiting aggressive and sexual drives (Sobsey & Mansell, 1990).

Intervention for Individuals who Experience Abuse

For the child with severe and/or multiple disabilities who is being abused, as for any child, the best general intervention is ending the abuse and ensuring a supportive environment that can begin to nurture some positive growth in the child. Medical treatment is required for some children. Teaching self-protection skills may reduce the chances for repeated occurrences.

Counseling is typically an important component of the intervention that children receive to minimize or reverse the effects of abuse (Mansell & Sobsey, 2001). Counseling will often require significant modification to be appropriate for children with severe communication impairments. Nevertheless, individualized programs developed through consultation between generic abuse counselors and specialists in areas related to the child's disability are probably the most effective approach to providing services to an abused child with severe and/multiple disabilities.

SUMMARY

This chapter has presented some of the common health care problems experienced by children with severe and multiple disabilities and some basic information about methods of prevention and intervention. Communicable diseases, seizure disorders, associated mental health problems, SIB, classroom emergencies, and abuse are among the health concerns that have particular implications for children with severe and multiple disabilities. The education and health care teams must work together to determine individual needs in these areas and develop individual prevention and intervention strategies.

REFERENCES

Achenbach, T.M., & Rescorla, L.A. (2001). *Manual for ASEBA School-Age Forms and Profiles.* Burlington: University of Vermont, Research Center for Children, Youth, and Families.

Aicardi, J. (1994). *Epilepsy in children* (2nd ed.). New York: Raven Press.

Aman, M.G. (1991). *Assessing psychopathology and behavior problems in persons with mental retardation: A review of available instruments.* DHHS publication No. (ADM) 91–1712. Rockville, MD: U.S. Department of Health and Human Services.

Aman, M.G. (1993). Efficacy of psychotropic drugs for reducing self-injurious behavior in the developmental disabilities. *Annals of Clinical Psychiatry, 5,* 171–188.

Aman, M.G., Singh, N.N., Stewart, A.W., & Field, C.J. (1985). The Aberrant Behavior Checklist: A behavior rating scale for the assessment of treatment effects. *American Journal of Mental Deficiency, 89,* 485–491.

Aman, M.G., Tasse, M.J., Rojahn, J., & Hammer, D. (1996). The Nisonger CBRF: A child behavior rating form for children with developmental disabilities. *Research in Developmental Disabilities, 17,* 41–57.

Amar, A.P., Levy, M.L., McComb, J.G., & Apuzzo, M.L. (2001). Vagus nerve stimulation for control of intractable seizures in childhood. *Pediatric Neurosurgery, 34,* 218–223.

American Academy of Child & Adolescent Psychiatry (AACAP). (1999). Practice parameters for assessment and treatment of children, adolescents and adults with mental retardation and comorbid mental disorders. *Journal of the American Academy of Child & Adolescent Psychiatry, 38,* 5S–31S.

American Academy of Pediatrics. (1999). Emergency preparedness for children with special health care needs. Committee on Pediatric Emergency Medicine. American Academy of Pediatrics. *Pediatrics, 104*(4), e53.

American Academy of Pediatrics. (2000). Education of children with Human Immunodeficiency Virus infection (Committee on Pediatric AIDS). *Pediatrics, 105,* 1358–1360.

American Academy of Pediatrics, Committee on Child Abuse and Neglect and Committee on Children with Disabilities. (2001). Assessment of maltreatment of children with disabilities. *Pediatrics, 108,* 508–512.

American Heart Association. (2002). *Transcript of National Conference on Standards and Guidelines for CPR and Emergency Care* [Cassette recording]. Dallas, TX: Author.

American Psychiatric Association. (2000). *Diagnostic and statistical manual of mental disorders* (4th ed., Text rev.). Washington, DC: Author.

American Red Cross. (2002). *Community first aid and safety.* San Bruno, CA: Staywell.

Annegers, J.F. (2001). The epidemiology of epilepsy. In E. Wyllie (Ed.), *The treatment of epilepsy: Principles & practice* (pp. 131–138). Philadephia: Lippincott Williams & Wilkins.

Appleton, R., Baker, G., Chadwick, D., & Smith, D. (2001). *Epilepsy* (4th ed.). London: Martin Dunitz.

Appleton, R., & Gibbs, J. (1998). *Epilepsy in childhood and adolescence.* London: Martin Dunitz.

Arnold, L.E. (1993). Clinical pharmacological issues in treating psychiatric disorders of patients with mental retardation. *Annals of Clinical Psychiatry, 5,* 189–198.

Batshaw, M.L. (Ed.). (2002). *Children with disabilities* (5th ed.). Baltimore: Paul H. Brookes Publishing Co.

Batshaw, M.L, & Perret, Y.M. (1986). *Children with handicaps: A medical primer* (2nd ed., p. 439). Baltimore: Paul H. Brookes Publishing Co.

Baumeister, A.A., Todd, M.E., & Sevin, J.A. (1993). Efficacy and specificity of pharmacological therapies for behavioral disorders in persons with mental retardation. *Clinical Neuropharmacology, 16,* 271–294.

Bergman, J.D. (1991). Current developments in the understanding of mental retardation. Part II: Psychopathology. *Journal of the American Academy of Child and Adolescent Psychiatry, 30,* 861–872.

Borthwick-Duffy, S.A. (1994). Epidemiology and prevalence of psychopathology in people with mental retardation. *Journal of Consulting and Clinical Psychology, 62,* 17–27.

Bosch, J.J. (2002). Use of directed history and behavioral indicators in the assessment of the child with a developmental disability. *Pediatric Health Care, 17,* 170–179.

Botash, A.S., & Church, C.C. (1999). Child abuse and disabilities: A medical perspective. *APSAC Advisor, 12,* 10–18.

British Columbia Art Teachers Association. (1991). Art safety. *BCATA Journal for Art Teachers, 31*(2) [ERIC Document Reproduction Service No. ED395844]

Caldwell, T.H., Todaro, A.W., & Gates, A.J. (1991). Special health care needs. In J.L. Bigge (Ed.), *Teaching individuals with physical and multiple disabilities* (3rd ed., pp. 50–74). New York: Macmillan.

Camfield, P., & Camfield, C. (2003). Childhood epilepsy: What is the evidence for what we think and what we do? *Journal of Child Neurology, 18,* 272–287.

Campbell, M., & Malone, R.P. (1991). Mental retardation and psychiatric disorders. *Hospital Community Psychiatry, 42,* 374–379.

Carr, E.G., Levin, L., McConnachie, G., Carlson, J.I., Kemp, D.C., & Smith, C.E. (1994). *Communication-based intervention for problem behavior: A user's guide for producing positive change.* Baltimore: Paul H. Brookes Publishing Co.

Caveness, W.F., & Gallup, G.H. (1980). A survey of public attitudes toward epilepsy in 1979 and an indication of trends over the past thirty years. *Epilepsia, 21,* 509–518.

Chabolla, D.R., & Cascino, G.D. (2001). Clinical use of the electroencephalogram in the diagnosis of epilepsy. In E. Wyllie (Ed.), *The treatment of epilepsy: Principles & practice* (pp. 193–208). Philadephia: Lippincott Williams & Wilkins.

Chaffin, M., & Hanson, R.F. (2000). Treatment of multiply traumatized abused children. In R.M. Reece (Ed.), *Treatment of child abuse, common ground for mental health, medical and legal practitioners* (pp. 271–288). Baltimore: Johns Hopkins University Press.

Chapman, S. (2003, May 5). U.S. schools adopt IPM more and more. *Pesticide & Toxic Chemical News, 31*(28), 18.

Children's Defense Fund. (2001). *Yearbook 2001: The state of America's children.* Washington, DC: Author.

Crosse, S.B., Kaye, E., & Ratnofsky, A.C. (1993). *A report on the maltreatment of children with disabilities* (Contract No: 105-89-1630): Washington, DC: National Center on Child Abuse and Neglect.

Cyr, M., Wright, J., McDuff, P., & Perron, A. (2002). Intrafamilial sexual abuse: Brother-sister incest does not differ from father-daughter and stepfather-stepdaughter incest. *Child Abuse & Neglect, 26,* 957–973.

Dailey, R.H. (1983). Acute upper airway obstruction. *Emergency Medicine Clinics of North America, 1,* 261–277.

Dales, L., Hammer, S.J., & Smith, N.J. (2001). Time trends in autism and in MMR immunization coverage in California, *Journal of the American Medical Association, 285,* 1183–1185.

D'Amelio, M., Shinnar, S., & Hauser, W.A. (2002). Epilepsy in children with mental retardation and cerebral palsy. In O. Devinsky & L.E. Westbrook (Eds.), *Epilepsy and developmental disabilities.* Boston: Butterworth-Heinemann.

Davanzo, P.A., Belin, T.R., Widawski, M.H., & King, B.H. (1998). Paroxetine treatment of aggression and self-injury in persons with mental retardation. *American Journal of Mental Retardation, 102,* 427–437.

Dekker, M.C., Koot, H.M., van der Ende, J., & Verhulst, F.C. (2002). Emotional and behavioral problems in children and adolescents with and without intellectual disability. *Journal of Child Psychology and Psychiatry, 43,* 1087–1098.

DePaepe, P., Garrison-Kane, L., & Doelling, J. (2002). Supporting students with health needs in schools: An overview of selected health conditions. *Focus on Exceptional Children, 35*(1) 1–24.

Devinsky, O. (1994). *A guide to understanding and living with epilepsy.* Philadelphia: F.A. Davis.

Devinsky, O., & Westbrook, L.E. (2002). *Epilepsy and developmental disabilities.* Boston: Butterworth-Heinemann.

Donnellan, A.M., & LaVigna, G.W. (1990). Myths about punishment. In A.C. Repp & N.N. Singh (Eds.), *Perspectives on the use of nonaversive and aversive intervention for persons with developmental disabilities* (pp. 33–57). Sycamore, IL: Sycamore Publishing Co.

Dykens, E.M., Hodapp, R.M., & Finucane, B.M. (2000). *Genetics and mental retardation syndromes: A new look at behavior and interventions.* Baltimore: Paul H. Brookes Publishing Co.

Ekvall, S.W., & Iannaccone, S. (1993). Epilepsy. In S.W. Ekvall (Ed.), *Pediatric nutrition in chronic diseases and developmental disorders: Prevention, assessment, and treatment* (pp. 99–102). New York: Oxford University Press.

Englund, J., Baker, C., Rakino, C., et al. (1997). Zidovudine, didanosine, or both as the initial treatment for symptomatic HIV infected children: AIDS Clinical Trials Group (ACTG) Study 152 Team. *New England Journal of Medicine, 336,* 1704–1712.

Ettinger, A.B., & Steinberg, A. (2001). Psychiatric issues in patients with epilepsy and mental retardation. In A.B. Ettinger & A.M. Kanner (Eds.), *Psychiatric issues in epilepsy: A practical guide to diagnosis and treatment* (pp. 181–199). Philadephia: Lippincott Williams & Wilkins.

Evans, I., Scotti, J.R., & Hawkins, R. (1999). Understanding where we are going by looking at where we have been. In Scotti, J.R. & Myer, L.H. (Eds.), *Behavioral intervention: Principles, models, and practices* (pp. 3–23). Baltimore: Paul H. Brookes Publishing Co.

Ewing-Cobbs, L., Kramer, L., Prasad, M., Canales, D.N., Louis, P.T., Fletcher, J.M., Vollero, H., Landry, S.H., & Cheung, K. (1998). Neuroimaging, physical, and developmental findings after inflicted and noninflicted traumatic brain injury in young children. *Pediatrics, 102*(2) Part 1), 300–307.

Farley, J.A., & McEwan, M. (2000). Epilepsy. In P.L. Jackson & J.A. Vessey (Eds.), *Primary care of the child with a chronic condition* (3rd ed.). St. Louis: Mosby.

Favell, J., McGimsey, J., & Jones, M. (1978). The use of physical restraint in the treatment of self-injury and as positive reinforcement. *Journal of Applied Behavior Analysis, 11*, 225–241.

Fischer, J.H. (2000). Guide to antiepileptic agents 2000. *CNS News Special Edition, 2*, 42–47.

Freeman, J.M., Vining, E.P.G., & Pillas, D.J. (2003). *Seizures and epilepsy in childhood: A guide for parents* (3rd ed.). Baltimore: Johns Hopkins University Press.

Gadow, K.D., & Poling, A.G. (1988). *Pharmacotherapy and mental retardation.* Boston: Little, Brown.

Gadow, K.D., & Sprafkin, J. (1994). *Child symptom inventory manual.* Stonybrook, NY: Checkmate Plus.

Glaser, D. (2000). Child abuse and neglect and the brain—a review [In Process Citation]. *Journal of Child Psychology and Psychiatry, 41*, 97–116.

Gordon, N., & Sillanpaa, M. (1997). Epilepsy and prejudice with particular relevance to childhood. *Developmental Medicine and Child Neurology, 39*, 777–781.

Guess, D., Roberts, S., Siegel-Causey, E., Ault, M., Guy, B., Thompson, B., & Rues, J. (1993). Analysis of behavior state conditions and associated environmental variables among students with profound handicaps. *American Journal on Mental Retardation, 97*, 634–653.

Gururaj, A.K., Sztriha, L., Bener, A., Dawodu, A., & Eapen, V. (2003). Epilepsy in children with cerebral palsy. *Seizures: European Journal of Epilepsy, 12*(2), 110–114.

Heimlich, H.J. (1982). First aid for choking children: Back blows and chest thrusts cause complications and death. *Pediatrics, 70*, 120–125.

Heimlich, H.J., & Uhley, M.H. (1979). The Heimlich maneuver. *Clinical Symposia, 3*(3), 1–32.

Heller, K.W., Forney, P.E., Alberto, P.A., Schwartzman, M.N., & Goeckel, T.M. (2000). *Meeting the physical and health needs of children with disabilities: Teaching student participation and management.* Belmont, CA: Wadsworth/Thomson Learning.

Holmes, G.L. (2002). Childhood-specific epilepsies accompanied by developmental disabilities: Causes and effects. In O. Devinsky & L.E. West Brook (Eds.), *Epilepsy and developmental disabilities* (pp. 23–32). Boston: Butterworth-Heinemann.

Holzapfel, S., Strehl, U., Kotchoubey, B., & Birbaumer, N. (1998). Behavioral psychophysiological intervention in a mentally retarded epileptic patient with brain lesion. *Applied Psychophysiology and Biofeedback, 23*(3), 189–202.

Hopkins, P.N., & Polukoff, G.I. (2003). Risk of valvular heart disease associated with use of Fenfluramine. *BMC Cardiovascular Disorders, 3*, 5.

Hornor, G. (2002). Child sexual abuse: Psychosocial risk factors. *Journal of Pediatric Health Care, 16*, 187–192.

Houry, D., Sachs, C.J., Feldhaus, K.M., & Linden, J. (2002). Violence-inflicted injuries: Reporting laws in the fifty states. *Annals of Emergency Medicine, 39*, 56–60.

Jackson, P.L., & Vessey, J.A. (Eds.). (2000). *Primary care of the child with a chronic condition* (3rd ed.). St. Louis: Mosby.

Jacobson, J.W. (1990). Do some mental disorders occur less frequently among persons with mental retardation? *American Journal on Mental Retardation, 94*, 596–602.

Jetdrzejczak, J., Owczarek, K., & Majkowski, J. (1999). Psychogenic pseudoepileptic seizures: Clinical and electroencephalogram (EEG) video-tape recordings. *European Journal of Neurology, 6*, 473–479.

Jones, M.W., & Bass, W.T. (2003). Fetal alcohol syndrome. *Neonatal Network, 22*(3), 63–70.

Kennamer, M. (2002). *Basic infection control for health care providers.* Albany, NY: Delmar Thomson Learning.

Kuhn, L., & Stein, Z.A. (1995). Mother-to-infant HIV transmission: Timing, risk factors and prevention. *Pediatric Perinatal Epidemiology, 9*, 1–29.

Leiken, J.B., & Feldman, B.J. (Eds.).(2000). *American Medical Association handbook of first aid and emergency care* (Rev. ed.). New York: Random House.

Leventhal, B.L., Cook, E.H., Jr., Morford, M., Ravitz, A.J., Heller, W., & Freedman, D. (1993). Clinical and neurochemical effects of fenfluramine in children with autism. *Journal of Neuropsychiatry and Clinical Neurosciences, 5*, 307–315.

Levitas, A. (2001). Introduction to the special issue. *Mental Health Aspects of Developmental Disabilities, 4*, 1.

Levitas, A.S., Hurley, A.D., & Pary, R. (2001). The mental status examination of patients with mental retardation and developmental disabilities. *Mental Health Aspects of Developmental Disabilities, 4*, 2–16.

Lhatoo, S.D., & Sander, J.W. (2002). Sudden unexpected death in epilepsy. *Hong Kong Medical Journal, 8*, 354–358.

Long, E.S., & Miltenberger, R.G. (1998). A review of behavioral and pharmacological treatments for habit disorders in individuals with mental retardation. *Journal of Behavior Therapy and Experimental Psychiatry, 29*, 143–156.

Lucchino, R. (1993). Psychiatric morbidity in older people with moderate and severe learning disability, I: Development and reliability of the patient interview (PAS-ADD). *British Journal of Psychiatry, 163*, 471–480.

Luders, H.O., & Wyllie, E. (2001). Classification of seizures. In E. Wyllie (Ed.), *The treatment of epilepsy: Principles & practice* (pp. 287–290). Philadephia: Lippincott Williams & Wilkins.

MacFaul, R. (1986). Medical care in severe and mental handicap [Editorial]. *Archives of Disease in Childhood, 61*, 533–535.

Mansell, S., & Sobsey, D. (2001). *Counselling people with developmental disabilities who have been sexually abused.* Kingston, NY: NADD Press.

Mansell, S., Sobsey, D., & Moskall, R. (1998). Clinical findings among sexually abused children with and without developmental disabilities. *Mental Retardation, 36*, 12–22.

Marge, M. (1988). Health promotion for persons with disabilities: Moving beyond rehabilitation. *American Journal of Health Promotion, 2*, 29–44.

Mathieson, K., & Price, M. (2002). *Better behaviour in classrooms: A framework for inclusive behaviour management.* New York: Routledge Falmer.

Matoth, I., Taustein, I., Kay, B.S., & Shapira, Y.A. (2002). Overuse of EEG in the evaluation of common neurologic conditions. *Pediatric Neurology, 27*(5), 378–383.

Matson, J.L., Gardner, W.I., Coe, D.A., & Sovner, R. (1990). A scale for evaluating emotional disorders in severely and profoundly mentally retarded persons. *British Journal of Psychiatry, 159,* 404–409.

McCulloch, J. (2000). *Infection control: Science, management and practice.* Philadelphia: Whurr Publishers.

Moldavsky, M., Lev, D., & Lerman-Sagie, T. (2001). Behavioral phenotypes of genetic syndromes: A reference guide for psychiatrists. *Journal of the American Academy of Child and Adolescent Psychiatry, 40,* 749–761.

National Education Association. (2001, July 18). *Testimony on behalf of the National Education Association Submitted to the Committee on Agriculture, U.S. House of Representatives, on The School Environment Protection Act of 2001.* Washington, DC: Author.

National Institute of Neurological Disorders and Stroke (NINDS). (2001). *Seizures and epilepsy—Hope through research.* Bethesda, MD: Author.

Nehring, W.M. (2000). Cerebral palsy. In P.L. Jackson & J.A. Vessey (Eds.), *Primary care of the child with a chronic condition* (3rd ed., pp. 305–330). St. Louis: Mosby.

O'Donohoe, N.V. (1994). *Epilepsies of childhood* (2nd ed.). Boston: Butterworth Heinemann.

Orelove, F.P., Hollahan, D.J., & Myles, K.T. (2000). Maltreatment of children with disabilities: Training needs for a collaborative response. *Child Abuse & Neglect, 24*(2), 185–194.

O'Sullivan, C.M. (1989). Alcoholism and abuse: The twin family secrets. In G.W. Lawson & A.W. Lawson (Eds.), *Alcoholism and substance abuse in special populations* (pp. 273–303). Rockville, MD: Aspen Publishers.

Perrine, K. (1994). Future directions for functional mapping. *Epilepsia, 35*(Suppl. 6), S90–S102.

Perry, P.A., Dean, B.S., & Krenzelok, E.P. (1992). A regional poison center's experience with poisoning exposures occurring in schools. *Veterinary and Human Toxicology, 34,* 148–151.

Petersilia, J. (2001). Crime victims with developmental disabilities: A review essay. *Criminal Justice and Behavior, 28,* 655–694.

Raskin, S.A. (1997). The relationship between sexual abuse and mild traumatic brain injury. *Brain Injury, 11*(8), 587–603.

Reece, R.M., & Sege, R. (2000). Childhood head injuries: Accidental or inflicted? *Archives of Pediatric and Adolescent Medicine, 154,* 11–15.

Reiss, S. (1990). Prevalence of dual diagnosis in community based day programs in Chicago metropolitan area. *American Journal on Mental Retardation, 94,* 578–585.

Reiss, S. (1993). Assessment of psychopathology in persons with mental retardation. In J.L. Matson & R.P. Barrett (Eds.), *Psychopathology in the mentally retarded* (2nd ed., pp. 17–40). Boston: Allyn & Bacon.

Reiss, S., & Valenti-Hein, D. (1990). *Reiss Scales for Children's Dual Diagnosis Test Manual,* Worthington, OH: IDS Publishing Corporation.

Rojahn, J., Matson, J.L., Lot, D., Esbensen, A.J., & Smalls, Y. (2001). The Behavior Problems Inventory: An instrument for the assessment of self-injury, stereotyped behavior, and aggression/destruction in individuals with developmental disabilities. *Journal of Autism and Developmental Disorders, 31,* 577–588.

Saloviita, T. (2000). The structure and correlates of self-injurious behavior in an institutional setting. *Research in Developmental Disabilities, 21,* 501–511.

Schottke, D. (2001). *First responder: Your first response in emergency care.* Boston: Jones & Bartlett.

Scorgie, K., & Sobsey, D. (2000). Transformational outcomes associated with parenting children with disabilities. *Mental Retardation, 38*(3), 195–206.

Scotti, J.R., Evans, I.M., Meyer, L.H., & Walker, P. (1991). A meta-analysis of intervention research with problem behavior: Treatment validity and standards of practice. *American Journal on Mental Retardation, 96*(3), 233–256.

Sedlak, A.J., & Broadhurst, D.D. (1996). *The third national incidence study of child abuse and neglect.* Washington, DC: U.S. Department of Health and Human Services.

Simeon, D., & Favazza, A.R. (2001). Self-injurious behaviors: Phenomenology and assessment. In D. Simeon & E. Hollander (Eds.), *Self-injurious behaviors: Assessment and treatment* (pp. 1–28). Washington, DC: American Psychiatric Publishing.

Sobsey, D. (1994a). Sexual abuse of individuals with intellectual disabilities. In A. Craft (Ed.), *Practice issues in sexuality and learning disabilities* (pp. 93–115). London: Routledge.

Sobsey, D. (1994b). *Violence and abuse in the lives of people with disabilities: The end of silent acceptance?* Baltimore: Paul H. Brookes Publishing Co.

Sobsey, D. (2002). Exceptionality, education, & maltreatment. *Exceptionality, 10*(1), 29–46.

Sobsey, D., Gray, S., Wells, D., Pyper, D., & Reimer-Heck, B. (1991). *Disability, sexuality, and abuse: An annotated bibliography.* Baltimore: Paul H. Brookes Publishing Co.

Sobsey, D., & Mansell, S. (1990). The prevention of sexual abuse of people with developmental disabilities. *Developmental Disabilities Bulletin, 18*(2), 61–73.

Sovner, R. (1986). Limiting factors in the use of DSM-III criteria with mentally ill/mentally retarded persons. *Psychopharmacology Bulletin, 22*(4), 1055–1059.

Sovner, R., Fox, C.J., Lowry, M.J., & Lowry, M.A. (1993). Fluoxetine treatment of depression and associated self-injury in two adults with mental retardation. *Journal of Intellectual Disability Research, 37,* 301–311.

Spencer, D. (2002). Pediatric trauma: When it is not an accident. *Accident & Emergency Nursing, 10,* 143–148.

St. John Ambulance. (2001). *Guide to first aid and CPR.* Toronto: Random House Canada.

Stallard, P., Williams, L., Lenton, S., & Velleman, R. (2001). Pain in cognitively impaired, non-communicating children. *Archives of Disease in Childhood, 85,* 460–462.

Steffenburg, U., Hagberg, G., & Kyllerman, M. (1996). Characteristics of seizures in a population based series of mentally retarded children with active epilepsy. *Epilepsia, 37,* 850–856.

Streissguth, A. (1997). *Fetal alcohol syndrome: A guide for families and communities.* Baltimore: Paul H. Brookes Publishing Co.

Sullivan, P.M., & Knutson, J.F. (1998). The association between child maltreatment and disabilities in a hospital based epidemiological study. *Child Abuse and Neglect, 22,* 271–288.

Sullivan, P.M., & Knutson, J.F. (2000). Maltreatment and disabilities: A population-based epidemiological study. *Child Abuse & Neglect, 24,* 1257–1273.

Sunder, T.R. (1997). Meeting the challenge of epilepsy in persons with multiple handicaps. *Journal of Child Neurology, 12* (Suppl.), S38–S43.

Tarrago, S.B. (2000). Prevention of choking, strangulation, and suffocation in childhood. *WMJ (Official publication of the State Medical Society of Wisconsin), 42*(9), 43–46.

Taylor, B., Miller, E., Farrington, C.P., Petropoulos, M.C., Favot-Mayaud, I., Li, J., & Waight, P.A. (1999). Autism and measles, mumps and rubella vaccine: No epidemiological evidence for a causal association. *Lancet, 353,* 2026–2029.

Thompson, T., Axtell, S., & Schaal, D. (1993). Self-injurious behavior: Mechanisms and intervention. In J.L. Matson & R.P. Barrett (Eds.), *Psychopathology in the mentally retarded* (2nd ed., pp. 179–211). Needham Heights, MA: Allyn & Bacon.

Thuppal, M. (1994). *Health care needs of persons with severe disabilities.* Unpublished master's thesis, University of Alberta, Edmonton, Canada.

Tominack, R., Weber, J., Blume, C., Madhok, M., Murphy, T., Thompson, M., et al. (2002). Elemental mercury as an attractive nuisance: Multiple exposures from a pilfered school supply with severe consequences. *Pediatric Emergency Care, 18,* 97–100.

Traci, M.A., Seekins, T., Szalda-Petree, A., & Ravesloot, C. (2002). Assessing secondary conditions among adults with developmental disabilities: A preliminary study. *Mental Retardation, 40,* 119–131.

Vining, E.P.G., & Freeman, J.M. (1996). Epilepsy and developmental disabilities. In A.J. Capute & P.J. Accardo (Eds.), *Developmental disabilities in infancy and childhood: Vol. II. The spectrum of developmental disabilities* (2nd ed., pp. 511–520). Baltimore: Paul H. Brookes Publishing Co.

Wakefield, A.J., Murch, S.H., Anthony, A., Linnell, J., Casson, D.M., Malik, M., Berelowitz, M., Dhillon, A.P., Thomson, M.A., Harvey, P., Valentine, A., Davies, S.E., & Walker-Smith, J.A. (1998). Ileal-lymphoid-nodular hyperplasia, non-specific colitis, and pervasive developmental disorder in children. *Lancet, 351,* 637–641.

Weinstein, S. (2002). Epilepsy. In M.L. Batshaw (Ed.), *Children with disabilities* (5th ed., pp. 493–523). Baltimore: Paul H. Brookes Publishing Co.

White, T., & Schultz, S.K. (2000). Naltrexone treatment for a 3-year-old boy with self-injurious behavior. *American Journal of Psychiatry, 157*(10), 1574–1582.

Wolfe, D.A. (1999). *Child abuse: Implications for child development and psychopathology.* Thousand Oaks, CA: Sage Publications.

Wolfe, L.C., & Selekman, J. (2002). School nursing: What it was and what it is. *Pediatric Nursing, 28,* 403–407.

Zlutnick, S., Mayville, W.J., & Moffat, S. (1975). Modification of seizure disorders: The interruption of behavioral chains. *Journal of Applied Behavior Analysis, 8,* 1–12.

For More Information

The following are some recommended Internet resources for school personnel serving children with multiple disabilities.

American Academy of Pediatrics: Emergency Preparedness
http://www.aap.org/advocacy/emergprep.htm
Includes the official policy and blank plan forms for emergency preparedness for children with special health care needs.

Bandaids and Blackboards
http://www.faculty.fairfield.edu/flcitas/boards3.html
A mix of practical information and emotional support for students with chronic illnesses and disabilities, families, and others.

Center for Health and Health Care in Schools
http://www.healthinschools.org/home.asp
Good source of general information on health care issues in schools.

Family Village
http://www.familyvillage.wisc.edu/index.htmlx
Great information for teachers and families. The library section has clear and practical information on specific diagnoses and syndromes.

National Center for Chronic
Disease Prevention and Health Promotion
Adolescent & School Health
http://www.cdc.gov/nccdphp/dash/index.htm
Excellent current information on communicable diseases and precautions. Although this site is not as comprehensive as some might expect, it is linked to the entire spectrum of Centers for Disease Control and Prevention (CDC) sites, and you can locate documents throughout the CDC sites using this site.

Med Web Plus
http://www.medwebplus.com/subject/Pediatrics/School_Health
Includes a wide range of information through the search function

Medscape
http://www.medscape.com
When you register, you will be asked to enter an interest area. When you sign in, you will be directed to that area. "Pediatrics" is usually the best choice for school personnel. Use the search function to find information on specific medications, syndromes, communicable diseases, and so forth.

NADD (National Association for the Dually Diagnosed)
http://www.thenadd.org/
Provides excellent information on mental health issues for children and adults with intellectual disabilities

National Center on Birth Defects and Developmental Disabilities
http://www.cdc.gov/ncbddd/default.htm
Another excellent source of information within the CDC sites. Also available in Spanish

National Institutes of Health
Combined Health Information Database Search Page
http://chid.nih.gov/detail/detail.html
Provides a wealth of reliable information on health care issues that affect children with disabilities and school health

National Institute of Neurological Disorders and Stroke
http://www.ninds.nih.gov/
Provides up-to-date information about specific conditions and a few other related topics

Parent Center
http://www.parentcenter.com/health/ills&inj/7875
Provides concise information on emergency procedures, including CPR and Heimlich maneuver

Quality Mall
http://www.qualitymall.org/main/
This noncommercial site lists a wide variety of services, products, and practices that can improve life for people with developmental disabilities.

School Health Resources for
Pediatricians: American Academy of Pediatrics
http://www.schoolhealth.org/
This site covers a wide range of topics. Some are highly technical and written for physicians, but much of the available information is written for a general audience.

CHAPTER 9

Integrating Health Care and Educational Programs

Kathryn Wolff Heiler

All teachers must maintain safe, healthy environments for all of their students to promote health and learning. Teachers who have students with severe and multiple disabilities often need specialized knowledge and skills to address specific health issues. In some instances teachers will need to know how their students' health can affect educational performance, whereas in other situations teachers will need to know what to do if a health problem should occur. Understanding these students' special health care needs can make a significant difference in providing proper health management and appropriate educational adaptations to address health issues.

Students with severe and multiple disabilities have a wide range of medical problems that teachers need to understand so that they can monitor students effectively and intervene should a problem occur. Some of these common medical problems include nutritional problems, anemia, dehydration, skin irritation and pressure sores, respiratory infections, asthma, ear infections, and contractures. Teachers often need to monitor for the occurrence of these in addition to any specific health concerns the students may have due to their disabilities (e.g., conditions with degenerative muscles, seizures). Teachers should also have an understanding of the treatments and medications used to treat common medical problems and disability-specific problems.

Some students with severe and multiple disabilities have conditions that require specialized health care procedures. These include tube feeding, clean intermittent catheterization (CIC), colostomy care, tracheostomy suctioning, and others. Due to advances in medical technology and educational policies supporting the education of all students, students who require health care procedures are often found in the school environment, and their procedures often need to be performed during school hours. Teachers not only need to be familiar with these procedures but they also need to consider if a student can or should be taught to assist with the performance of his or her own procedure.

In order to assist teachers and school staff in addressing students' health needs and integrating health care and educational programs, this chapter provides information on creating a safe, healthy environment for all students. This is followed by information on common medical concerns for students with severe and multiple disabilities and the types of medications often taken by this population of students. Because some conditions are treated by health care procedures, a special section on this is provided. The chapter concludes with a discussion of the impact of severe and multiple disabilities on health and school performance and the importance of the educational team.

MAINTAINING A SAFE, HEALTHY ENVIRONMENT

School personnel should maintain a safe, healthy environment and should have clear plans of action in place to respond to specific problems and emergencies. This includes arranging the environment to prevent injury and the spread of infection and having accessible evacuation procedures. School personnel should also be knowledgeable regarding students' disabilities and related health issues and able to make appropriate accommodations to address student's heath needs in the school environment (DPHD Critical Issues and Leadership Committee, 1999). Teachers, nurses, and the rest of the educational team need to work together and share information to promote a safe, healthy environment for all children.

To prevent injury, teachers should carefully inspect their classrooms for any hazards that could result in an accident or aggravate an existing disorder. For example, aisles should be kept clear to avoid the possibilities of falls for students using mobility devices such as walkers and canes. Students who have tracheostomies (i.e., surgically made hole in the neck through which to breathe) should not use plastic bibs because of the possibility of suffocation. Classrooms should avoid having class pets such as hamsters because they can precipitate some students' asthma attacks. Use of flashing lights in a classroom display should be avoided if students in the class have seizures that are triggered by flashing lights. Understanding each student's specific health condition or disability and discussing needed cautionary measures with the team will help ensure a safe classroom environment.

Teachers need to maintain universal precautions to prevent the spread of infection. Universal precautions refer to a group of standards that were originally developed for hospital use to decrease contact with bodily secretions, transmission of infections, and risk of individuals acquiring infections (Skale, 1992). These procedures include washing hands appropriately, using personal protective equipment (e.g., gloves), following decontamination procedures (e.g., cleaning of environmental surfaces), taking personal hygiene precautions, and disposing of wastes properly (Heller, Forney, Alberto, Schwarztman, & Goeckel, 2000; Medcom Trainex, 1993). These procedures have been adapted by schools and are used routinely with all students.

Students should also be taught universal precautions, especially proper hand washing. Hand washing, like other multistep skills, can be broken down into a series of steps referred to as a task analysis. The task analysis will need to be modified to meet a student's specific disability. For example, if the student has the use of one hand only, the task analysis will need to be modified to allow for changes in the hand-washing procedure, as well as any needed modifications to the soap dispenser. Other types of disabilities may require such adaptations as the use of handle extensions or scrubbing brushes. In some cases, the student will only be able to do some of the steps and will require assistance on the others. Part of the teaching process should include instructing on when hand washing should occur. Hand washing is commonly performed before preparing food, before eating, after using the restroom, before taking medications, and when hands are dirty.

In addition to hand washing, students should be taught proper hygiene to reduce the risk of infection. Proper hygiene includes such skills as brushing teeth and hair and washing one's face. Students should learn to use their personal hygiene items and not share them with others. Students should also be taught to cover any open cuts with a Band-Aid to help protect the wound from infection and prevent the leakage of blood into the environment (Heller, Bigge, & Allgood, 2001).

Another important aspect of keeping a safe, healthy environment is being certain that the classroom emergency evacuation procedures (e.g., in the case of a fire alarm or bomb threat) can be carried out for students who use mobility devices. Often, the plan for assisting a student with a severe and/or multiple disability out of a classroom to a safe area can be accomplished, but little thought is given as to how the student would evacuate the building should he or she be in the cafeteria, gymnasium, or other location at the time of an emergency. Often, several adults are needed to help evacuate these students. Careful planning on how this will be accomplished when students are in various locations throughout the school should occur. Teachers need to try out the various evacuation routes to ascertain if the route will accommodate a mobility device (e.g., wheelchair, walker) and if the route will safely take students away from the school to the designated area.

School personnel should be prepared for a wide range of emergencies. This includes basic first aid and cardiopulmonary resuscitation (CPR). Because of the possibility of choking accidents, for example, personnel should be trained in the Heimlich maneuver (a special procedure used to expel food or items from the person's airway). (See Chapter 8 for an illustration of the Heimlich maneuver and other information on coping with emergencies.) A well-prepared school staff can make a significant difference in the outcome of an emergency.

In order to effectively promote a safe, healthy environment for students with severe and multiple disabilities, teachers need to be knowledgeable about 1) common medical conditions, 2) medications, 3) health care procedures, 4) severe and multiple disabilities and their impact on health and school performance and 5) working as a team. These five areas will be described across major sections of this chapter.

COMMON MEDICAL CONDITIONS

Teachers may encounter several common medical conditions with students with severe and multiple disabilities. Teachers need to know what to look for in order for early detection to occur. Any suspicions should be reported to the parents (and school nurse) so that the student's physician can be contacted. Some of the most common medical problems are nutritional problems and anemia, dehydration, skin irritation and pressure sores, respiratory infections, asthma, ear infections, and contractures.

Nutritional Problems and Anemia

Students with severe and multiple disabilities are at risk for developing nutritional problems, such as malnutrition and anemia.

Causes

Children with neurodevelopmental disabilities, such as cerebral palsy, are particularly at risk for developing malnutrition due to uncoordinated swallowing, gastroesophageal reflux, and constipation (Chong, 2001). Unfortunately, malnutrition may go unnoticed until it becomes severe due to growth reduction and medical issues that are often present with this population of students.

Other nutritional problems may also occur in students with severe and multiple disabilities, such as obesity, food intolerance, food allergies, and drug-nutrient interactions (Gonzalez, Nazario, & Gonzalez, 2000). Nutritional problems may also arise in students who have conditions that interfere with proper hydration and nutritional absorption (e.g., short bowel syndrome).

Anemia is another common problem that can occur in students with severe and multiple disabilities. When students have difficulty chewing or swallowing, they may avoid foods that are more difficult to eat such as meats, poultry, and dried fruits. When certain foods are avoided, such as those high in iron, folic acid, and vitamin B_{12}, anemia can occur.

Treatment and Prevention

The first step in correcting nutritional problems and anemia is to be alert for possible signs that these problems are occurring. Mild deficiencies or mild anemia may not be noticeable initially but will become noticeable as they worsen. For example, a child with anemia will have increased fatigue and become less active. As anemia worsens, other symptoms will emerge such as weakness, drowsiness, irritability, headache, gastrointestinal problems, and vertigo. Eventually, severe anemia can result in heart failure or shock (Beers & Berkow, 1999).

To avoid nutritional problems and anemia, it is important that students eat well-balanced meals. Meals need to be prepared so that students can easily chew and swallow the food. In some cases, meals may need to be pureed. It is important that foods are not mixed together but offered separately to provide students with opportunities for choice making and experiences with different tastes of food. If a student does not like certain foods, foods containing similar nutrients may be offered as substitutes. Because tastes change, it is a good idea to reintroduce foods at different times in a child's life. Vitamins and other supplements may be recommended by the student's physician to supplement missing nutrients. Teaching students to self-feed and choose the foods from the lunch menu are important skills to help to ensure that students eat sufficient quantities of food. If anemia or nutritional problems are suspected, the teacher should notify the school nurse and family. The family should take their child to a physician to determine the underlying cause and obtain appropriate treatment.

Dehydration

Causes

Dehydration occurs when the amount of fluids leaving the body (from urination, defecation, vomiting and/or sweating) exceeds the amount of fluids taken into the body (from drinking and eating). All students are at risk of dehydration from diarrhea or vomiting; however, students with mental retardation and students with severe and multiple disabilities who have mental retardation and neurological disabilities associated with swallowing difficulties are at higher risk for dehydration (Kennedy, McCombie, Dawes, McConnell, & Dunnigan, 1997; Whitehead, Couper, Bourne, & Byard, 1996). This is especially the case if a child is unable to communicate that he or she is thirsty or if a child lacks the mobility skills to obtain a drink of water. School personnel may not realize that a student is not getting enough to drink, and dehydration may occur from insufficient fluid intake.

Treatment and Prevention

It is important to be alert for warning signs of dehydration and to report to the nurse and parents any observed symptoms of dehydration. In mild dehydration, the individual often becomes restless and thirsty. As dehydration worsens and falls into the moderate range, however, the individual may become lethargic and irritable, with respirations becoming deep and sometimes rapid. At this level of dehydration, tears are decreased or absent, and the skin elasticity is reduced. Skin elasticity can be evaluated easily by gently pinching the skin on the back of the hand. Normally, the skin should immediately retract back into position. In moderate dehydration, the skin retracts back into position slowly. If dehydration continues to worsen, the individual becomes more lethargic or comatose and the skin is cold, sweaty, and possibly cyanotic (i.e., having bluish discoloration). In this state of dehydration, the skin of the fingers and toes will become wrinkled, and if the skin is pinched, it will retract back into position very slowly. In severe dehydration, blood pressure drops, the pulse becomes weak, and respirations become deep and rapid (Behrman, Kliegman, & Jenson, 2000). Severe dehydration can result in death if not treated.

The treatment of dehydration will depend on its severity. Mild dehydration may be treated by increasing fluid intake. More moderate or severe dehydration typically require IV fluids. Prevention of dehydration is the best course. Fluids should be given regularly with meals and at regularly scheduled times throughout the day. Students should be taught to request a drink through verbal responses or through augmentative and alternative communication (AAC). Students should also be taught to independently (or through partial participation) drink out of a cup or adapted container. (See Chapter 12 on mealtime skills.)

Skin Irritation and Pressure Sores

Causes

All students can get scrapes and skin irritation from participating in everyday activities. Students with severe and multiple disabilities are especially prone to developing skin irritations that may lead to infection. This can occur from prolonged contact with sweat, urine, or feces. Many of these students may not be fully toilet trained and thus use diapers. Some students may use external urinary catheters (condom catheters) that collect urine in a leg bag. Other students may have colostomies and wear colostomy bags (which collect feces that exit through the colostomy). These situations result in an increased likelihood that urine or feces will come in contact with the skin and result in skin irritation.

To prevent skin irritation from occurring, prompt and thorough cleaning of the area should occur. Students should be taught to perform this skill independently (or with partial participation). If the student does an inadequate job of cleaning, however, the adult needs to assist the student in order to promote skin health and hygiene.

Students with severe and multiple disabilities may also develop pressure sores (i.e., decubitus ulcers). This is especially the case with students who have physical impairments that impede their ability to move around and shift their weight. Pressure sores occur from a combination of intrinsic and extrinsic factors. Intrinsic factors include a loss of pain and pressure sensation; minimal fat and muscle padding between the skin and bony areas; and spasticity, which can compromise circulation. Extrinsic factors include infrequent shifting of the student's position and irritation from poorly fitted braces, wheelchair supports, and wrinkled clothing (Beers & Berkow, 1999).

Treatment and Prevention

Teachers need to be alert for signs of skin irritation and pressure sores and report to the nurse and parents any symptoms they may observe. Skin irritation typically appears as skin redness that may be accompanied by swelling or a rash. Treatment will depend on the cause and severity.

The appearance of pressure sores will vary depending on how long they have been developing and their severity. Initially, all that will be present to indicate the beginning development of a pressure sore is skin redness that lasts more than 30 minutes. Warmth, swelling, blistering, or a dark black area may also occur (Wong, 1995). At this point, keeping weight off of the area may be all that is needed. Without proper treatment, the condition will worsen, resulting in cell death and skin breakdown. When this happens, an opening or ulceration on the skin occurs. The size of the pressure sore varies and is often described as being the size of a dime, quarter, or other coin. Unfortunately, what is seen on the surface of the skin is usually rather small compared with what is happening under the skin, where the injured area is much larger. Pressure sores have been compared with icebergs in that most of the damage occurs under the skin. Without medication and proper treatment, the ulceration can extend to the bone. In extreme cases a systemic infection can result, which can be life threatening. In severe cases, medication and surgery may be necessary (Homma et al., 2001; Thomson, Azhar, & Healy, 2001).

Pressure sores are preventable. Students who use wheelchairs should shift their position or weight every 10–15 minutes (Beers & Berkow, 1999). Students who have impaired lower body movement should not sit continuously in their wheelchairs for more than 2 hours. They can be repositioned in other equipment or take short breaks from their chairs. Students are often taught to request assistance in repositioning themselves or in taking breaks from their wheelchairs. When moving a student, to decrease the risk of tearing his or her skin, it is important that care is taken to avoid sliding the student's skin against any surface.

Maintaining good skin health is another factor important to the prevention of pressure sores. For example, the skin should be kept clean and dry because skin that is wet or sweaty has been linked to pressure sore formation. Harsh soaps or preparations should be avoided; skin softeners may be helpful. Also, maintaining range of motion and good body alignment and posture can help with decreasing the incidence of skin breakdown. Pressure-minimizing devices, such as special cushions, can help maintain good skin health by decreasing pressure on the skin when they are carefully selected for the individual (Ferrarin, Andreoni, & Pedotti, 2000).

It is important that the skin is checked for any signs of pressure sores on a regular basis. This includes skin that is under pressure as well as skin that could be irritated from being in contact with equipment such as orthosis or wheelchair supports. Students with impaired sensation may not sense that they are getting a pressure sore, or they may be unable to communicate with others effectively. Teachers need to check for redness, irritation, or ulceration (in a way that respects the student's privacy) and report any skin problem to the parent, school nurse, or other designated individual. Whenever possible, students should be taught to inspect their skin for problems and to inform an adult. If a student or teacher detects any signs of skin breakdown, the student needs to be positioned so that there is no further pressure on the skin where the breakdown is occurring. For example, if a pressure sore is detected on a student's buttocks, the student may be positioned on his or her side.

Respiratory Infections

Causes

Individuals with severe and multiple disabilities have an increased risk of acquiring respiratory infections. This is because some individuals with severe and multiple disabilities have physical impairments such as cerebral palsy that can result in a weak cough and difficulty clearing the airway due to muscular weakness. Secretions then accumulate in the lungs, which can result in bacterial growth and infection. When ineffective clearing of the airway is combined with poor nutritional status and chest wall (or spine) deformity, there is an increased risk of significant morbidity and mortality from respiratory infections (Toder, 2000).

Treatment and Prevention

Prevention is the best course in decreasing the occurrence of respiratory infections. Students prone to respiratory infections may use aerosol therapy, postural draining (assuming certain prescribed positions to help in the removal of secretions by gravity), percussion (technique of clapping the chest and back over certain lung fields to loosen secretions), or suctioning to decrease secretion accumulation and improve respiratory functioning (Morse & Colatarci, 1994). Teachers may need to adjust a student's activities to include these procedures. Also, it will be important to provide opportunities for students to engage in regular exercise that may help improve respiratory functioning.

Proper infection control is also important to decrease the risk of transmission of a respiratory infection. Students should be taught to cover their mouths and turn their heads when they cough or sneeze. Proper hand washing and tooth brushing techniques should also be taught. School staff should also engage in hand washing and cleaning environmental surfaces. Sick students should be sent home to reduce the spread of infection. If a respiratory infection is detected, school personnel should inform the parents so that they may take their child to the doctor to determine the course of treatment (e.g., medication).

Asthma

Causes

Asthma is the most common childhood pulmonary disease, and it is on the increase (Ladebauche, 1997). Since 1969, it has increased 232%—currently it is estimated that 1.4% of all children in the United States experience some degree of disability due to asthma (Newacheck & Halfon, 2000). Asthma is also the leading chronic condition resulting in school absences, with an average of 5–7 lost school days per year per child (Behrman et al., 2000). Asthma is described as a lung disease with reversible airway obstruction and airway inflammation. An increased responsiveness (or hyperreactivity) to a variety of stimuli is also present.

Each student will vary as to what triggers an asthma attack. Some students have extrinsic asthma in which the asthma attack is triggered by allergies, such as those to pollen, dust mites, or cats. Some students have intrinsic asthma in which there is no identifiable allergen, but asthma attacks may be triggered by viral respiratory infections and environmental stimuli such as air pollution. Some students will have a combination of extrinsic and intrinsic types and be considered to have mixed asthma. Still other students' asthma will be triggered by exercise (exercise-induced asthma) or aspirin (aspirin-induced asthma) (Heller, Alberto, Forney, & Schwartzman, 1996).

Treatment and Prevention

One of the goals of setting up a healthy school environment is to try to avoid the triggers of an asthma attack. If a student is allergic to a pet in the classroom, the animal should be moved to a different location. Students with exercise-induced asthma may need medication prior to exercising and require close monitoring during exercise. In some instances, there may be exercise restrictions. Students who are sensitive to pollution may need to stay indoors on days with high levels of pollution.

Teachers also need to know the signs indicating when a student is having an asthma attack and what to do should one occur. An asthma attack typically consists of episodes of shortness of breath, wheezing, and difficulty breathing due to the narrowing of the airway from inflammation and secretion obstruction. When extreme respiratory distress is present, however, wheezing may be absent. Shortness of breath may be so severe that the student is unable to walk or talk.

In most cases, medication such as an inhaler will need to be given near the onset of an attack. A plan must be in place should the inhaler not relieve the symptoms, however. If a student is having severe difficulty breathing and medication is not working, an ambulance should be called. Although rare, deaths have occurred from asthma (approximately 19 deaths per million people) (Beers & Berkow, 1999). Students should be taught what to do when an attack occurs. This may range from communicating on an AAC device that they are having trouble breathing to learning how to administer the inhaler themselves.

Otitis Media

Causes

Children often acquire otitis media, an infection of the middle ear. Often this bacterial or viral infection occurs when an upper respiratory infection is present. Individuals of all ages can acquire this infection, although it is more common in children age 3 and younger. After 3 years of age, a child's eustachian tubes are better aligned to allow fluid to drain. Students with severe and multiple disabilities who spend a large amount of time in a lying position are more susceptible to acquiring otitis media (Sobsey & Cox, 1996).

Treatment and Prevention

The first sign of an ear infection is typically a persistent earache, which, in young children, may be accompanied by fever, nausea, vomiting, and diarrhea (Beers

& Berkow, 1999). In some instances, children may experience significant hearing loss (up to 40 dB) with otitis media (Zargi & Boltezar, 1992). Students with severe and multiple disabilities may rub their ears, headbang, or engage in other self-injurious behaviors when otitis media is present (O'Reilly, 1997). When these types of behaviors occur, it is always important to rule out a medical basis for the behavior. Also, it is important that students are taught to communicate pain or discomfort. When a student communicates that his or her ear hurts, the school should notify the parents and the parents should take the student to a physician for examination. Medical treatment may include antibiotics, decongestants, or myringotomy tubes placed into the ears. The teacher will need to make appropriate modifications if hearing is decreased (see Chapter 10 on sensory impairments).

Contractures

Causes

When students have conditions resulting in limited movement or high muscle tone, normal stretching and movements of the arms and legs may not occur. When this is the case, the collagen fibers in the joints can change and result in a permanent shortening of the muscles. This shortening is referred to as a contracture (Wong, 1995). Contractures can result in a decrease in range of motion. For example, a contracture of the elbow will result in the inability to straighten the arm. Depending on its location and severity, a contracture can interfere with everyday tasks such as sitting, walking, and eating.

Treatment and Prevention

To help prevent contractures or their progression, the physician may order physical therapy and/or occupational therapy. The therapists may have the student go through range-of-motion exercises that can often be integrated into functional tasks to help decrease the formation or progression of contractures. Bracing equipment (e.g., orthosis) may help maintain alignment and decrease the development of contractures. The physician may also prescribe medications to treat spasticity such as baclofen (which can be delivered using a baclofen pump) or Botulinum toxin type A (Gormley, 2001; Ruiz, Pascual, & Bernardos, 2000). In some instances surgeries may be performed, such as a heel cord release. Often, the physician will prescribe a combination of treatment. The factors that predispose an individual to the development and worsening of contractions are still present even after treatment, however, so it is important that long-term management programs be developed and followed (Farmer & James, 2001).

In the classroom it is important that students are encouraged to be active and to use their arms and legs as much as possible. For example, most students with hemiplegic cerebral palsy will have a tendency to use the arm unaffected by cerebral palsy and not the affected side. This will usually result in the formation of contractures on the affected side. The teacher should encourage the student to use the affected arm in order to help prevent or lessen contractures. Teachers can prompt students to participate in activities that require both arms (e.g., picking up a ball), position desirable material near the affected arm, and provide positive reinforcement.

MEDICATIONS

Students with severe and multiple disabilities often take medications for a wide range of disorders. Teachers need to be familiar with their students' medications in order to help determine the medications' effectiveness and to be able to report any side effects. If teachers are involved in administration of the medications, they also need to be familiar with proper medication guidelines. Teachers may also teach some of their students with severe and multiple disabilities to participate in certain aspects of medication management (e.g., learning when to take their medications, taking their medications, positioning themselves for suppository administration).

Types of Medications

Some of the most common categories of medications prescribed for students with severe and multiple and developmental disabilities are antiepileptics, antispasticity, antireflux, antibiotic, psychotropic, skin preparations, and respiratory (Batshaw et al., 1996; Physicians' Desk Reference, 2002). These medications often play an integral role in the management of a wide variety of conditions common to students with severe and multiple disabilities. In some instances, however, there can be significant side effects, including adverse effects on growth and development (Rempel & Coates, 1999). It is therefore important that teachers understand the reason why the medication was prescribed for each student and what potential side effects can occur. In this way, teachers can monitor the medication properly for effectiveness and adverse effects. A sample of medications under each category and their side effects can be found in Table 9.1. Because of the numerous side effects, contraindications, and drug interactions of these and other medications, teachers should obtain information on side effects of their students' medications from pharmacology books, medication package inserts, information from a pharmacist or nurse, or reliable on-line sources.

Table 9.1. Medications commonly prescribed for students with severe and multiple disabilities

Category	Examples of medications: Generics (and brand names)	Treatment area and/or delivery method	Sample side effects*
Antiepileptic	Carbamazepine (Tegretol)	Tonic-clonic and partial seizures	Dizziness, drowsiness
	Clonazepam (Klonopin)	Absence, myoclonic and atonic	Drowsiness, behavior problems
	Ethosuximide (Zarontin)	Absence	Gastric upset, headache
	Phenobarbital (Luminal)	Tonic-clonic and partial	Sedation, vertigo
	Phenytoin (Dilantin)	Tonic clonic and partial	Decreased coordination, nausea
Antispasticity	Baclofen (Lioresal)	Oral administration	Drowsiness, constipation
	Baclofen, intrathecal	Baclofen pump	Fatigue, headache
	Botulism toxin type A		Headache, nausea
	Dantrolene sodium (Dantrium)	Cerebral or spinal spasticity	Dizziness, diarrhea
	Diazepam (Valium)	Also an anxiolytic and antiepileptic	Drowsiness, ataxia
Antireflux	Cimetidine (Tagamet)	Antireflux and treats ulcers	Headache, diarrhea
	Metoclopramide hydrochloride (Reglan)		Restlessness, fatigue
	Ranitidine hydrochloride (Zantac)		Headache, constipation
Antibiotics	Amoxicillin (Amoxil)		Nausea, rash
	Cephalexin hydrochloride (Keflex)		Diarrhea, rash
	Erythromycin		Nausea, vomiting, diarrhea
Psychotropic	Amitriptyline hydrochloride (Elavil)	Antidepressant	Hypotension, delusions
	Chloral hydrate (Noctec)	Sedative	Sedation
	Diazepam (Valium)	Anxiolytics	Drowsiness, ataxia
	Haloperidol (Haldol)	Antipsychotic	Movement abnormalities
	Methylphenidate (Ritalin)	CNS stimulant	Nervousness, insomnia
	Naltrexone (ReVia)	Opiate antagonist	Nausea, headache

(continued)

391

Table 9.1. *(continued)*

Category	Examples of medications	Treatment area	Sample side effects*
Skin	Duoderm	Decubitus ulcers (sterile dressing)	
	Griseofulvin (Fulvicin)	Skin antifungal	Skin rash
	Hydrocortisone (Caldecort)	Skin steroid	Itching, irritation
	Lanolin (A & D ointment)	Skin diaper rash	Itching
	Mupirocin 2% (Bactroban)	Skin antibiotic	Burning, stinging
	Permethrin 1% (Nix)	Scalp preparation for lice	Burning, itching
Respiratory	Albuterol (Proventil)	Treats acute asthma attacks	Tremors, nervousness
	Cromolyn (Intal)	Prevention of asthma attacks	Cough, nasal congestion
	Methylprednisolone (Medrol)	Reduces airway inflammation	

*Each medication has many different side effects; this table provides only a few examples.

Antiepileptic Drugs

Antiepileptic drugs, also known as antiseizure or anticonvulsant medications, are taken to prevent, decrease, or stop seizures. The choice of antiepiletic medication will depend on the type of seizure. Once the physician has selected the drug of choice for the student's particular seizure, a small dosage is given and then is gradually increased. Blood testing is performed periodically to determine if the medication is within therapeutic levels (McBrien & Bontibius, 2000). Blood testing is important because individual differences in absorption, distribution, metabolism, and excretion affect how much of the medication the student is actually receiving. Because of these differences, one student may take more of the same medication than another student but actually be getting less of it.

If seizure activity has not decreased even when the medication has been steadily increased within a therapeutic level, a second medication is usually added. The second medication should be increased gradually and blood concentrations monitored. Sometimes it can take a while to determine the proper medication (or combination of medications) and dosage. If a medication does not appear to be working, it is important that the parents do not suddenly stop an antiepileptic drug (unless directed by a physician) because this can cause the child to have a seizure. School personnel need to administer these medications when ordered and be careful to administer each dose. It is important to report all seizure activity because this can influence medication changes. If medication is not properly controlling the seizures, the physician may try other treatments such as surgery (e.g., removal of a portion of one lobe of the brain) or a vagus nerve stimulator (McBrien & Bontibius, 2000). (See Chapter 8 for more information.)

Seizure medications, like all medications, have potential side effects. These side effects can range in degree from being very minor (e.g., mild fatigue) to serious (e.g., congestive heart failure). The presence and severity of the side effects will partially depend on the make up of the individual. Teachers should be familiar with the possible side effects of the medication and report them if they are present. For example, many seizure medications cause fatigue as a side effect. It is important that the degree of fatigue be reported to the parent and/or school nurse. If the fatigue is excessive, the physician may change the medication. The presence of other side effects may result in a change of medication as well.

Antispasticity Medications

Students with high muscle tone, such as those who have severe spastic quadriplegic cerebral palsy, may be prescribed medication to decrease muscle tone and gain more functional control. Three oral medications used to treat spasticity are valium, dantrolene, and tizanidene (Gormley, 2001). Although valium has been shown to decrease spasticity, its sedating effect may make it undesirable. The sedating effect often decreases over several days or weeks, however. If the sedating effects do not decrease over time, teachers should report this to the nurse and parents. Besides being given orally, valium may also be administered nasally, rectally, intravenously, or intramuscularly. Dantrolene has been considered a drug of choice for spasticity that originates from brain damage (as in cerebral palsy). Although it is less sedating than valium, it may have a side effect of weakness. Tizanidene is a newer medication that has been used to treat spasticity due to spinal cord injury, but as of 2004 it was used more with adults.

Two other medications that may be used to reduce spasticity are Botulinum toxin type A and baclofen. Botulinum toxin type A is administered by intramuscular injection. Its effect lasts several months and has been shown to be effective in reducing spasticity. In one study, individuals with mild cerebral palsy experienced progressive improvements in walking after using this medication (Ruiz et al., 2000). Baclofen has been found to significantly reduce spasticity. It is often delivered through an implanted computerized pump that has a small catheter (tube) leading from the pump into the spinal column. Small amounts of baclofen are delivered throughout the day from the pump directly into the spinal fluid (Gormley, 2001). Teachers should be familiar with their student's medication (and pump if one is being used). Teachers should observe for changes in spasticity and tone as well as any medication's side effects (e.g., drowsiness, muscle weakness, nausea).

Antireflux Medications

Some students with severe and multiple disabilities may have gastroesophageal reflux (GER). GER is the backward or return flow of stomach contents into the esophagus. This can result in discomfort or aspiration (the inhaling of stomach contents). The most common symptom is heartburn, often severe, which can inflame the esophagus and result in painful or uncoordinated swallowing. When this occurs, students may be inclined to eat less than they should.

When aspiration occurs due to GER, no immediate symptoms may be present, but a respiratory infection or aspiration pneumonia may result. If a large amount of food has traveled into the lungs, the symptoms may be severe and may include a fast heart rate, rapid breathing, shortness of breath, coughing, wheezing, fever, cyanosis, and/or difficulty breathing. If aspiration is suspected, the student's parents should be notified and his or her emergency plan followed. Whenever severe symptoms (or any difficulty breathing) are present, an ambulance should be called.

GER may be treated by medication. Antireflux medications are used to either promote stomach emptying (because stomach distention may contribute to reflux) or decrease stomach acidity, which can help tighten the lower esophageal muscle (sphincter) and decrease irritation (Batshaw et al., 1996). Teachers may be asked to look for signs of reflux and aspiration and monitor the effectiveness of their student's antireflux medication. Teachers may also be asked to modify students' food by adding thickener to liquids or pureeing food to help promote swallowing, for example. In severe cases of GER, medication and food modifications may not be sufficient, and the student may require surgery (fundoplication).

Antibiotics

Antibiotics are commonly prescribed when a person has a bacterial infection. Antibiotics may hasten recovery, decrease the severity of the infection, and avoid complications. Many infections are caused by viruses, however, and antibiotics are not effective in treating viruses. Treatments of infections must then take into account the infection's etiology. Antibiotics should be prescribed only when bacteria are suspected because the indiscriminate use of antibiotics can result in antibiotic-resistant bacteria (Batshaw et al., 1996). Teachers need to be alert to signs of infection, and when the student is taking antibiotics, teachers should observe for improvement of the student's condition.

Psychotropic Drugs

Psychotropic drugs influence mood and behavior and may be used to treat hyperactivity, self-injury, aggression, or other undesirable behaviors in individuals with developmental disabilities (Curtis, 1997). Typically this class of medication can be divided into six different categories: CNS stimulants, antidepressants, antipsychotics, opiate antagonists, anxiolytics, and sedatives. CNS stimulants are often used in children with attention disorders. Antidepressants may be used for clinical depression, but they have also been used for treating attention disorders that co-exist with anxiety or depression. Antipsychotics can be used to treat such disorders as psychosis, aggression, self-injurious behavior (SIB), and anxiety. Opiate antagonists have been used in low doses in the management of SIB. Anxiolytics have been used for the management of anxiety and convulsions and may be used to decrease aggression and muscle tone. Sedatives may be prescribed to treat sleeplessness (Batshaw et al., 1996).

Teachers need to monitor the effects of psychotropic drugs closely. Depending on the underlying condition, the teacher may need to take data on the frequency of the target behavior (e.g., SIB) to help determine if the medication is having an effect. Also, teachers should know about potential side effects and signs of toxicity and report any occurrence of these.

Skin Preparations

As previously discussed, students with severe and multiple disabilities who have impaired mobility are at risk of developing pressure sores and skin irritation. Skin medications may be prescribed to treat skin infections and pressure sores. School personnel may be asked to monitor the effectiveness of the preparation and be sure they utilize proper skin care techniques (e.g., proper cleaning of an area, repositioning the student on a regular basis).

Skin preparations may also be prescribed for a variety of other conditions. Fungal infections, diaper rash, skin infections, and lice are just a few examples. It is important that when skin medications are applied, people administering the medication wear gloves so that none of the medication is absorbed into their skin.

Respiratory Medications

Students with asthma or respiratory conditions typically need medication to increase respiratory functioning, including bronchodilators (that open up the air passages) or anti-inflammatory agents (that reduce airway inflammation). These medications are often delivered through an inhaler or nebulizer, so school personnel will need to know how to use them properly. If medication is to be given on an as-needed basis (typically written by a physician as "p.r.n."), teachers will need to know what to look for to determine if medication is needed. If the medication is ineffective and/or breathing difficulties are severe, a plan should be in place as to what should occur. In many cases this may involve calling 911.

Medication Guidelines

Receiving and Storing Medications

Schools should only accept prescription and over-the-counter (nonprescription) medications when accompanied with a permission form. The medication should be in its original container and have the student's name, dosage, and frequency of administration. The pharmacy and physician's telephone numbers should also accompany the medication in case they need to be contacted.

On receiving the medication, the expiration date should be checked. The month displayed indicates that the medication will expire at the end of the month, not the beginning. The person receiving the medication should also check how the medication is to be stored. Some medications cannot be exposed to light, whereas others need to be stored in the refrigerator. For medications requiring refrigeration, it is important that the medication is never placed in the refrigerator door because that portion of the refrigerator may not be cold enough when the door is frequently opened. All medications should be kept in a secure, locked storage container. The only exceptions to this are medications taken on an as-needed basis that must be close at-hand for emergencies, such as an inhaler for asthma or medication for severe bee sting allergy. These might be kept with the student (e.g., in a closed backpack located on the back of the student's wheelchair).

Administration of Medications

Schools should have policies in place regarding who can administer medications. If non-nursing personnel are allowed to administer such medication, it is important that they be given proper training. Although directions for administering oral medications may seem obvious, situations can arise that necessitate giving the medication to the student when he or she is unwilling to take it, making administration difficult. Also, other routes of administration may not be as familiar to non-nursing personnel, such as nebulizer use.

Several practices should be put in place to prevent errors in medication administration. First, the person who is administering the medication should check the five Rs: 1) right student, 2) right drug, 3) right dose, 4) right route, and 5) right time (Heller, 2002; Skale, 1992). Second, any precautions should be noted, such as if the medication should be taken with food. Third, the person administering the medication should then check it for contamination; this is done by looking for a change in the medication's color, consistency, or odor. Fourth, the medication label should be read three times: 1) when taking it out of storage, 2) before giving it, and 3) before returning it to storage. Finally, a form should be used to document when the medication was administered. A sample form that can be used to report medications and health care procedures is provided in Figure 9.1.

Many possible problems can occur during medication administration. It is important that the person administering the medication and the school staff know what to do if such problems arise. Some of these common problems include side effects, allergic reactions, intolerance, missed dosage, overmedication, incomplete administration, wrong medication or dose, and choking. For each student, a plan should be made for each separate medication that specifies what to do if one of these problems should occur. The time to find out is not when a problem has happened.

Teaching Students to Be Involved in Medication Administration

Some students with severe and multiple disabilities can be taught to take their medication with assistance. Some students are taught the times that they take

Monthly Medication/Procedure Report

Student's name: _Joe Smith_ Month: _February_

Directions: Write the medications/procedures, dates and times for each week. At the beginning of each day, write in the times for that day. When procedure is performed, cross out times and initial. If not done, circle time. If done at different time, circle time and record new time.

Meds/procedure	Dates	Time(s)	Mon.	Tues.	Wed.	Thurs.	Fri.
Dilantin 5 mg oral	2/1-2/5	10	10 KH	10 KH			
Tube feed	2/1-2/5	9 12	8 KH 12 KH	8 KH ⑫ 1:30 KH			
Suction	2/1-2/5	p.r.n.	10 KH 2:30 KH	8 KH 12:45 KH			

Meds/procedure	Dates	Time(s)	Mon.	Tues.	Wed.	Thurs.	Fri.

Meds/procedure	Dates	Time(s)	Mon.	Tues.	Wed.	Thurs.	Fri.

Meds/procedure	Dates	Time(s)	Mon.	Tues.	Wed.	Thurs.	Fri.

Figure 9.1. Sample monthly medication/procedure report. (From *Meeting physical and health needs of children with disabilities: Teaching student participation and management, 1st edition,* by K. Heller, P. Forney, P. Alberto, M. Schwartzman, and T. Goekel © 2000. Reprinted with permission of Wadsworth, an imprint of the Wadsworth Group, a division of Thomson Learning. Fax 800 730-2215.)

their medications and which pill or type they take at which time. Some students may learn this schedule through a picture or object schedule. Some students may be taught to use a compartmentalized dispenser that separates the pills into the different times of the day they are to be administered.

Learning the purposes of the medications is also important. Some students may be able to learn what each medication is for or have information programmed on their AAC device (e.g., "That's my seizure pill," "That's to help me breathe"). Having students able to identify their medications can help decrease errors and promote independence.

HEALTH CARE PROCEDURES

Many students with severe and multiple disabilities require various health care procedures, which often need to be performed during school hours. Procedures such as tube feeding, CIC, suctioning, colostomy care, and ventilator management are often provided in the school environment (Heller, Fredrick, Dykes, Best, & Cohen, 2000). Teachers need to be familiar with these procedures to effectively monitor for problems, assist with implementation, and help to determine if students can learn to self-perform all or part of their own health care procedure as an educational goal. This section begins by discussing policy and procedures regarding health care, then proceeds with an overview of the two common health care procedures (tube feeding and CIC), individualized health (care) plans (IHPs), individualized education programs (IEPs), and instructional considerations.

Policy Guidelines and Role Responsibilities

Although there has been much controversy regarding who is responsible for providing health care procedures, Supreme Court cases have been very clear that it is the schools' responsibility to provide these services. In 1984, a landmark Supreme Court case, *Irving Independent School District v. Tatro,* involved a boy who needed CIC. The Supreme Court's decision obligated the schools to provide health care services as related services if they met three criteria: 1) the child required special education 2) the child was unable to participate in an educational program without the necessary service being performed during the school day, and 3) the procedure did not require a physician but could be performed by a nurse or other qualified person (Rapport, 1996). Similarly, in 1999, the Supreme Court case *Cedar Rapids Community School District v. Garret F.* involved a student with a spinal cord injury who required severe and multiple health care procedures, including ventilator management, tracheostomy suctioning, urinary catheterization, and blood pressure monitoring. The Supreme Court supported its previous ruling in the *Tatro* case that obligated the school system to provide the necessary health care services, thus enabling students with complex health care needs to be provided with necessary supports in the school environment.

Public schools are abiding by these legal rulings, and nurses, teachers, paraprofessionals, and other school personnel are performing health care procedures across the nation. According to one national study (Heller, Fredrick, et al., 2000), high percentages of special education teachers (60.0%) and paraprofessionals (57.8%) who have students requiring tube feeding reported performing the tube feeding procedure with nursing support or by themselves. This is also true of other common health care procedures such as CIC (33.7% of teachers and 45.3% of paraprofessionals reported performing this procedure). Other health care procedures (e.g., colostomy care, tracheostomy suctioning) also have been performed by high percentages of nurses, teachers, and paraprofessionals in the school environment. Sometimes the nurse, teacher, and paraprofessional are all authorized to perform the procedures (which accounts for the percentages equaling over 100%), whereas other times only the nurse or teacher can perform it.

The decision as to who will provide the health care service is based on each state's Nurse Practice Act, state regulations, school policies, and the decision of the nurse and educational team as to whether the procedure should be performed by a nurse or delegated to qualified (and legally sanctioned) personnel (e.g., a trained teacher, a paraprofessional). Due to significant shortages of school nurses, many states' Nurse Practice Acts allow nurses to delegate certain health care procedures. If delegation is determined to be appropriate, nurses will typically provide training and supervision to the unlicensed personnel. This has often resulted in teachers and paraprofessionals being trained to perform health care procedures under the nurse's supervision, with the nurse retaining accountability for the appropriateness of delegating the health care procedure (National Council of State Boards of Nursing, 1995). Some health care procedures may not be delegated because of the health status of the student, the complexity of the health care procedure, or the inability of the unlicensed personnel to adequately master the skills needed to perform the procedure.

Some states have guidelines regarding which health care procedures can be delegated. Other states leave it up to each individual school district to determine who is responsible for performing the health care procedure. This can result in great variability within a state or city. For example, in Atlanta, one school district has nurses perform tube feeding procedures, and in a neighboring school district, the procedures are delegated to teachers and paraprofessionals. When there are no state guidelines, it is critical that each school district develop policies and guidelines to determine who can provide health care procedures and under what circumstances. In situations in which a school system does not have any students requiring health care procedures, it is still important that guidelines be developed so that the school system will be prepared. Guidelines typically include how the decision will be made to determine who will perform these procedures, who can perform the procedures given appropriate training, how the procedures are to be performed (pending doctor approval), who performs the training, training guidelines, and frequency of supervision (Heller, Forney, et al., 2000; Mulligan-Ault, Guess, Struth, & Thompson, 1988). Some school systems use written procedures to guide their decision making as to the responsibility for the procedures; other school systems set up a medical review board to determine who will be performing the procedures for each individual student (Jordan & Weinroth, 1996). Regardless of who performs the procedure, it is important that those school personnel who are in contact with the student understand the procedure and know what to do if a problem occurs.

Training Issues

If a procedure is going to be delegated to unlicensed personnel (e.g., teacher, paraprofessional), then appropriate training must be in place. Training should be provided by the school nurse or other qualified medical personnel who can also provide appropriate supervision and updating. Although other teachers and parents may be familiar with the procedure, a health care professional is needed who has expertise in the area to provide the training. More than one person typically receives the training so that back-up personnel are available should the primary person be absent from school.

Training usually consists of 1) the rationale and correct implementation of each step of the procedure; 2) ability to identify early subtle signs of side effects, problems, or complications; 3) knowledge of appropriate interventions when side effects, problems, or complications occur; 4) knowledge of emergency procedures; 5) knowledge of how to fill out a medication/procedure report; and 6) documentation of training (Heller, Fredrick, et al., 2000). Training should occur with the actual student over several guided sessions. The steps of the procedure should also be provided in written format. Information should be provided on what should be monitored, what problems to look for, and what to do if problems occur. Knowledge of emergency procedures must also be in place.

The person performing the procedures should be shown how to maintain documentation each time the procedure is performed. As discussed under the medication section of this chapter, a simple form with the times checked so as to indicate that the procedure was performed can easily be maintained. If it is determined that the teacher (or other designated person) is not comfortable performing the procedure when training is finished, then further training should be given until the person is comfortable, or someone else should be selected. A health care procedure should not be delegated to someone who is unable to perform the procedure.

Once the teacher or adult has been trained on the procedure and on associated problems and interventions, a form may be used to document that the training took place and that the nurse has verified competency with the procedure with a particular student. It is important to note that health care procedures are considered nongeneralizable across students. If a teacher has demonstrated knowledge and skill in performing tube feeding with Susan, for example, the teacher will need to be taught to tube feed Joe. This is because subtle differences may exist between the two students or the procedure may be slightly different. Training and documentation of the training is student specific, not procedure specific.

Once someone has completed training successfully, he or she should receive periodic supervision. During supervision, several areas may be evaluated through a series of questions:

1. Is the procedure still being performed as trained?
2. Is the procedure being performed in a safe and effective manner?
3. Is the record-keeping system sufficient and not cumbersome?
4. Are staffing needs adequate?
5. Are the parents comfortable with how the procedure is being performed?
6. Is communication between the school and home ongoing and effective?
7. Is the process supportive of the student's educational program?
8. Is there ready access to emergency procedures and the student's health plan? (Sobsey & Cox, 1996)

If any problems are identified, additional training may be needed or modifications may need to be put in place. Ongoing supervision assures that the procedures are being performed correctly and that the necessary supports are in place to assure that the procedure goes smoothly. As mentioned previously, two of the most common procedures that teachers may encounter are tube feeding and CIC.

Tube Feeding (Gastric Gavage)

Some students with severe and multiple disabilities are unable to obtain proper fluids and nutrition orally. This may be due to such conditions as neuromotor impairments (e.g., severe cerebral palsy with oral-motor difficulties), congenital abnormalities (e.g., throat, esophagus, or stomach abnormalities), trauma, and tumors. When these conditions are present and interfere with eating, a tube may be placed into the student's stomach or intestines to provide proper nutritional support. This is referred to as tube feeding or gastric gavage. Tube feeding has been found to promote growth and improve a child's quality of life (Smith, Camfield, & Camfield, 1999; Tawfik, Dickson, Clarke, & Thomas, 1997).

Tube feeding is most commonly delivered via nasogastric (NG) tube, gastrostomy tube (G-tube), and gastrostomy button (also known as a *skin level device*). An NG tube is placed through the nose (naso) and into the stomach (gastric). In some cases, a tube may be placed through the mouth or a tube may end in the small intestine. This type of route is typically temporary and used on a short-term basis. The NG tube may be inserted prior to each feeding or remain in place. In either case, when this type of route is used, the tube must be checked for proper placement every time before the feeding is given. It is possible that the tube can became dislodged and go into the windpipe. If this occurs and placement is not checked prior to feeding, the food will go directly into the lungs and result in an emergency situation.

A G-tube or gastrostomy button is inserted through a surgical incision made through the abdominal wall into the stomach or intestine. A G-tube or gastrostomy button is usually used on a long-term basis. Neither one is necessarily permanent, however, because some children may be able to take sufficient food orally at a future time and have the gastrostomy removed.

When a student has a G-tube, a tube can be seen coming through the skin and it is usually coiled and taped against the skin when not in use. When a student has a gastrostomy button, all that can be seen is a small opening and a small cap that closes off the opening of the gastrostomy button. When feeding occurs with a gastrostomy button, a tube is attached to the button through which liquid nourishment can be delivered.

Tube feedings may be delivered in a number of different ways. Some students are fed using a bolus method in which a syringe barrel is attached to the end of the tube (or the connecting tube of a gastrostomy button). In this method the formula is delivered by gravity over a short period of time. As seen in Figure 9.2, this girl has a gastrostomy button and is participating in performing her own feeding using the bolus method. Another method uses an intermittent gravity drip in which the formula is usually in a bag and drips more slowly over a longer period of time. A third method is a continuous method in which the formula is given continuously throughout the day.

The physician will determine the type of delivery based on what the student can tolerate best. Some students will become nauseated, vomit, and have

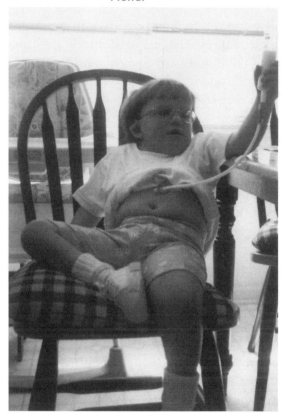

Figure 9.2. A girl feeding herself through her gastrostomy button using the bolus tube-feeding method. (From *Meeting physical and health needs of children with disabilities: Teaching student participation and management, 1st edition,* by K. Heller, P. Forney, P. Alberto, M. Schwartzman, and T. Goekel © 2000. Reprinted with permission of Wadsworth, an imprint of the Wadsworth Group, a division of Thomson Learning. Fax 800 730-2215).

cramping even when the food is delivered at a normal rate or in typical amounts using the bolus method. In these situations, the physician may order a much slower method that delivers small amounts of food over a longer period of time, such as with the intermittent gravity drip method or the continuous method. When a slower delivery method is used, the student may have a mechanical feeding pump to precisely deliver the food at a constant rate.

Tube Feeding Guidelines

Several basic guidelines pertain to all methods of tube feeding. For safe and correct tube feeding management, it is important that school personnel be familiar with them. These guidelines are as follows (Heller, Forney, et. al., 2000; Sobsey & Cox, 1996):

1. School personnel should know if the student can take any food or drink by mouth.

2. Tubing should be checked for placement (if an NG tube) and patency (openness).

3. Students should never be fed flat on their backs; they should be elevated at least 30 degrees. Students may be tube fed sitting upright or on their side.

4. Tube feeding should be given at an appropriate rate because feeding too fast can result in cramping, diarrhea, nausea, and vomiting. The higher the syringe barrel or feeding bag is placed, the faster the rate of delivery.

5. Correct tube feeding procedure involves preventing air from entering the stomach because this can cause cramping, diarrhea, nausea, and vomiting.

6. Usually, the liquid should be given at room temperature. Storage of unused feeding should follow the package insert or physicians' orders. Refrigeration is often necessary.

7. Equipment should be properly cleaned. Often, cleaning with soap and water is all that is needed, but personnel should follow the procedure given by the physician or nurse.

8. Personnel should know what they should do for the common problems associated with this health care procedure: aspiration, tube displacement, nausea, vomiting, cramping, diarrhea, site infection, leaking of stomach contents, and clogged tube.

9. Appropriate training and supervision should occur for school personnel involved with the student.

10. The educational team should determine if the student can or will learn to perform or partially participate in the performance of the health care procedure.

Clean Intermittent Catheterization

Some students with severe and multiple disabilities will require CIC. In this procedure, a catheter (tube) is inserted into the urethra and up into the bladder. The catheter only stays in place long enough for all of the urine to be expelled from the bladder, and then the catheter is removed. The procedure may be used with students who have neurogenic bladders resulting from such conditions as spinal cord injury or spina bifida. A neurogenic bladder refers to an abnormality of the nerves that control the bladder and the sphincter (muscle that allows urine to be released from the bladder). Children with neurogenic bladders cannot feel when their bladders are full and are unable to voluntarily control their sphincters. For some children, the damaged nerves will result in the sphincter muscle being too loose, so urine will dribble continually. This increases the risk of pressure sores and skin irritation. Other children with neurogenic bladders may have sphincters that are too tight and that require a lot of pressure in the bladder to allow the sphincter to open. This can result in complications by the urine being forced backwards toward the kidney (reflux) (Shaer, 1997). Over time, kidney infections and kidney damage can occur. Also, an abnormally tight sphincter may result in the bladder not completely emptying the urine, which increases the risk of infection. One of the ways of treating a neurogenic bladder is through CIC.

Urinary catheterization used to always be a sterile procedure until the 1970s, when Dr. Jack Lapidus introduced the idea that a clean catheter and a clean procedure could be used instead of a sterile one (Lapides, Diokno, Silber, & Lowe, 1972). Studies have shown that using clean rather than sterile supplies and techniques put students at no increased risk of urinary tract infection (Van Hala, Nelson, Hurbitz, Panzi, Bloom, & Ward, 1997). When a physician orders CIC, he or she may decide that the catheter can be reused multiple times as long as it is thoroughly cleaned between uses. In other instances, the physician may decide that a sterile catheter should be used and discarded after a one-time use. In both of these instances, the procedure uses a clean technique in which only clean (not sterile) gloves are worn.

The CIC procedure is typically a time-based procedure. Usually, the physician will order that the procedure must be performed every 3–4 hours; however, new equipment such as the Bladder Manager allows the procedure to be volume based. The Bladder Manager is a portable device in which a sensor is placed on the skin over the bladder and a read-out of the amount of urine in the bladder appears on a monitor. Catheterization then occurs when the volume of urine reaches a certain amount, thus eliminating the possibility of catheterizing too often or too late as can happen with time-based catheterization (Binard, Persky, Lockhart, & Kelley, 1996).

Clean Intermittent Catheterization Guidelines

Several basic guidelines pertain to CIC. It is important that school personnel be familiar with these guidelines for the safety and correct management of students receiving this procedure:

1. Be sure catheterization occurs at the times specified.

2. When assisting a student to catheterize, the student should be treated with dignity and respect at all times.

3. Catheterization should occur in a private location.

4. Adults assisting the student should always wear gloves. Plastic gloves will need to be used rather than latex gloves if a latex allergy is present. Often, plastic gloves will be used if the student has a physical disability in which there is a high incidence of latex allergies (e.g., spina bifida).

5. Personnel should know what to do to address the common problems associated with this health care procedure—infection, inability to pass the catheter, omission of catheterization, no urine on catheterizations, urine between catheterizations, bleeding, swelling, and discharge.

6. Appropriate training and supervision should occur for school personnel involved with the student.

7. The educational team should determine if the student will learn to perform or partially participate in the performance of the health care procedure.

8. If a girl is being taught to perform the procedure, then she should be taught not to rely on a mirror to view the area of catheter insertion because problems can occur should a mirror be unavailable.

Health Care Procedures and the Individualized Health (Care) Plan

Students who require health care procedures should have an individualized health (care) plan (IHP). An IHP is designed to provide vital information regarding a student's medical condition and contains a plan to address the student's health needs. IHPs vary as to the information contained in them. Some students will have IHPs that cover an array of areas such as medical history, current medical condition, type of health care procedures being performed, feeding and diet considerations, special equipment and devices, and transportation needs (Rueve, Robinson, Worthington, & Gargiulo, 2000). If a student has a health care procedure, an IHP specific to that procedure should be in place. If the student has more than one procedure (e.g., tube feeding and CIC), two IHPs should be constructed.

IHPs addressing health care procedures contain general and specialized information. Typically the IHP will include student information, history, diagnosis, assessment data, goals of care, interventions, expected outcomes, and emergency contacts (Haas, 1993; Heller, Forney, et al., 2000). In addition to this information, child-specific information regarding the particular health care procedure is provided. As seen in the sample IHP in Figure 9.3, very specialized information is included such as the tube feeding route, type of delivery, formula, preparation of formula, and tube feeding schedule. This IHP also has a place to indicate if a written procedure is attached. Most important, the IHP has a listing of the typical feeding problems and emergencies and what action to take should

Name: <u>Susie Jones</u>   Date: <u>3/1/02</u>

School: <u>Banks Elementary School</u>   Grade: <u>3rd</u>

Contact person regarding this IHP: <u>Miss Long, R.N. or Mrs. Warnick</u>

Student Information and History

Susie is an 8-year old girl with moderate spastic quadriplegia cerebral palsy. She had a gastrostomy inserted when she was 4 years old due to a severe gag reflex and an inability to take in enough nutrition. Her doctor ordered no oral feedings due to aspiration.

Diagnosis and Assessment Data

Susie has appropriate weight for her height. She is currently tolerating her feedings well and has appropriate bowel elimination. Her diagnosis consists of impaired swallowing resulting in an inability to eat independently. This has resulted in the need for tube feedings.

Goal of Care

Administer tube feedings (via gastrostomy tube) as primary form of nutrition.

Interventions

1. The nurse (Miss Long) will instruct Susie's special education teacher (Mrs. Warnick), paraprofessional (Mrs. Thomson), and one other teacher (Mr. Lennox) on Susie's tube feeding procedure. Included in the instruction is information on how to monitor for common tube feeding problems and what to do should they occur.
2. The nurse will supervise staff administering feedings on a regular basis.
3. The nurse and teacher will collaboratively teach Susie to self-administer tube feedings.

Expected Outcomes

1. Susie will receive adequate nutrition through tube feeding.
2. Staff will demonstrate competence in tube feeding and the actions to take should a problem occur.
3. Susie will learn to partially or fully participate in tube feeding herself.

Emergency information and contacts

Dr. Bove: (678) 651-2222,

Mrs. Jones: work number: (404) 555-1234; home number: (404) 555-9876; cell phone number: (404) 555-5678

Figure 9.3. Sample IHP for tube feeding. (From *Meeting physical and health needs of children with disabilities: Teaching student participation and management, 1st edition,* by K. Heller, P. Forney, P. Alberto, M. Schwartzman, and T. Goekel © 2000. Reprinted with permission of Wadsworth, an imprint of the Wadsworth Group, a division of Thomson Learning. Fax 800 730-2215.)

Figure 9.3. *(continued)*

Specialized information

1. Tube feeding route: gastrostomy tube
2. Type of tube feeding: Bolus method
3. Formula: 1 can Ensure, 1 can dry baby food with water, extra water as needed for flushing tube and providing hydration
4. Preparation of formula: add amount of water specified on baby food box
5. Schedule of feeding: every four hours (9:00 a.m., 1:00 p.m.)
6. Child specific procedure attached: __X__ yes ____ no
7. Directions for feeding problems and emergencies specifically for *Susie Jones*:

   a) Aspiration: Immediately stop feeding at any signs of aspiration and page nurse. Call 911 if any difficulty in breathing is present.

   b) Tube displacement: Immediately stop tube feeding. Call the nurse to come replace the tube. If she can not be reached, contact school administrator to arrange transportation to hospital for replacement. (Important to note that the opening will close within a few hours unless a new tube is inserted.)

   c) Nausea, vomiting, and cramping: Stop tube feeding immediately. Check for the following: spoiled formula, tube feeding being delivered too rapidly, excess air entering the stomach, & formula is at room temperature. Check for signs of illness. Contact school nurse to determine illness and to check your procedure of administering the food.

   d) Diarrhea: Follow directions for nausea, vomiting, and cramping.

   e) Infection: If site is red, swollen, or has suspicious discharge, fill out a health report and send to school nurse and parents. Nurse will follow up regarding appropriate treatment.

   f) Leaking of stomach contents: Check to be sure clamp is securely fastened. If stomach contents are leaking from opening, around the tube, call the nurse.

   g) Clogged tube: Follow proper procedure of first "milking" the tube. If this does not work, introduce small amounts of water with the plunger, slowly pulling forward and back with the plunger until clog is cleared (as demonstrated in initial training). If still clogged, call the school nurse.

they occur. This last section can be invaluable. Before a problem arises, school personnel (including the nurse) and parents must come to an agreement as to what to do if certain problems occur. By having this available on an IHP, everyone knows what to do should a problem arise instead of wasting time determining what to do once something has happened.

Health Care Procedures and the Individualized Education Program

Health care procedures such as tube feeding and CIC are often viewed as self-care skills or independent living skills. A position paper from the Division for Students with Physical and Health Disabilities (DPHD) of the Council for Exceptional Children urges teachers to consider health care procedures as self-care skills (or independent living skills) and to consider teaching students to perform these procedures in order to increase independence (DPHD Critical Issues and Leadership Committee, 1999). Just as students with severe and multiple disabilities may receive instruction on how to use a spoon or the restroom, students may receive instruction on how to tube feed or catheterize themselves. Consider Tony, a 16-year-old student with cerebral palsy, moderate mental retardation, and deafness who requires tube feeding. Tony is preparing for supported employment and participates in community-based vocational training. A teacher and nurse taught Tony to tube feed himself, thus increasing his possibility of gaining supported employment because he can take care of his own nutritional needs. In another example, Demetria assists with her tube feeding procedure by holding a syringe barrel. In both of these examples, the students were taught to independently or partially participate in the functional skill of tube feeding. Teaching them to independently or partially participate in tube feeding decreases learned helplessness, increases independence and attention to the task, and can make it easier for someone to assist with the procedure. Many students have been taught to self-perform their health care procedure, including students with mental retardation (Hannigan, 1979; Neef, Parrish, Hannigan, Pzage, & Iwata, 1989; Robertson, Alper, Schloss, & Wisniewski, 1992). As with other self-help or independent living skills, the team will need to decide if teaching the student to self-perform his or her health care procedure is an appropriate goal to address at this time.

When considering teaching a student a health care procedure, he or she may be taught on four different levels, which can be incorporated into the student's IEP in terms of objectives. These are 1) independent performance of the task, 2) partial performance of the task, 3) directing the task, and 4) knowledge of the task (Heller, Forney, et al., 2000). Independent performance of the task targets the goal of the student learning to do the entire procedure. In some cases, due to physical or cognitive impairments, the student may be unable to perform the entire health care procedure but can do a part of it. In this case, objectives are written with the intent that the student will do part of the procedure, thus promoting some independence. For example, the student may assist with tube feeding by mixing the formula or holding the syringe barrel. (See Table 9.2 for a sample of an IEP listing objectives related to performance in tube feeding.)

For a student who has a severe physical disability and is unable to physically participate in the task, after learning the steps he or she may be taught to

Table 9.2. Sample individualized education program (IEP) objectives

Type of IEP objective	Example of objective
Independent performance of task	The student will self-perform the tube feeding procedure according to the task analysis with 100% accuracy for 1 week.
Partial performance of task	The student will add more food to the syringe barrel during the tube feeding procedure with 100% accuracy for four consecutive sessions.
Directing the task	Using his or her AAC device, the student will direct another person in performing each step of the tube feeding procedure with 100% accuracy for 2 weeks.
Knowledge of the task	The student will tell the teacher when it is time for his or her tube feeding to occur.

direct another person in its performance. For example, students may communicate the steps of the procedure through speech or an AAC device. Another advantage is that the student may also be able to inform the person if he or she is doing it incorrectly. The ability to communicate the steps of the procedure empowers the student.

The last type of objective is one in which the student is taught something about the task. For example, the student may be taught the times that tube feeding occurs and communicate to another person when it is time for his or her feeding. In another example, a student may be taught to signal another person if he or she has nausea or abdominal cramping.

It should be noted that the criteria for IEP objectives on health care procedures should be high (typically 100%). The reason is that there is usually no room for doing these procedures incorrectly. If it is thought that the student cannot reach a high criteria on all parts of the procedure, only those steps in which a high percentage is thought to be obtainable should be targeted. Once those steps are achieved with a high level of success, other parts of the procedure may then be targeted.

Teaching Students to Perform Health Care Procedures

Teaching a student to perform his or her own health care procedure requires a team approach. The nurse provides expertise on the procedure, the teacher provides expertise on instruction, and the parents provide specific information about their child. In some situations a physical therapist (PT) may be needed to provide input on positioning and an occupational therapist (OT) may be needed to provide information on manipulating materials. When communication is involved, a speech-language pathologist (SLP) may provide information on AAC use pertaining to the health care procedure.

Once vital information is communicated among the team members, an instructional plan needs to be designed. First, a task analysis would be performed in which the health care procedure is broken down into small steps. The steps may initially be taken from the written steps of the procedure that are attached to the IHP. An example task analysis for a student with a G-tube is provided in Figure 9.4. After the initial task analysis is written out, the next step is to examine each step of the procedure closely and identify any caution steps or time limited steps (Heller, Forney, et al., 2000). A caution step is any step of a procedure in which the student could injure him- or herself by making a quick, jerking, or incorrect movement. In the tube feeding task analysis, the caution step is connecting and disconnecting the syringe barrel as well as removing and reinserting the plug at the end of the tube. This is because the student may pull on the G-tube when doing these steps, possibly inadvertently pulling out the G-tube. A time-limited step is a step that must be completed within a certain time frame to avoid injury. For tube feeding, a time-limited step occurs when more formula (or water) needs to be added to the syringe barrel before all of the formula (or water) empties, because doing this incorrectly could introduce air in the stomach and result in abdominal cramping.

After the caution steps and time-limited steps are identified, the team needs to decide if they will teach these steps along with the others or teach them at a later time. If they are going to be taught, the teacher must use the instructional procedure of shadowing with these steps in order to prevent injury. Shadowing is a procedure in which the teacher keeps his or her hands within 1 inch of the student's hands. The teacher may use any other instructional strategies with the other steps (e.g., time-delay, system of least prompts, demonstration-guided practice, independence practice), but the teacher must prove either shadowing or a more intrusive prompt (i.e., full physical guidance) on caution steps and time-limited steps so that injury can be avoided.

After an initial task analysis is performed and the caution steps and time-limited steps are identified, the student needs to be assessed as to his or her ability to perform the steps of the procedure. The aim of this assessment phase (also referred to as a discrepancy analysis) is to determine what changes need to occur in regard to adaptations, instructional strategies, or task analysis steps. As the student is guided through each step of the task analysis, the types of errors the student makes on each step are examined to ascertain if the errors are due to physical, sensory, learning, health (e.g., endurance), motivation, or communication problems (Heller, Forney, et al., 2000). For example, the assessment may reveal that there is a learning problem that requires the step of preparing the formula to be further broken down into several smaller steps. On another step, the assessment may reveal that the student has difficulty

Steps of Task Analysis

1. Wash hands

2. Prepare formula

3. Kink the G-tube

CS   4. Remove plug at end of G-tube

CS   5. Attach syringe barrel to end of G-tube

6. Pour prepared formula into barrel

7. Hold barrel 6 inches above stomach

8. Unclamp or unkink tube

9. Wait while food goes through G-tube into the stomach

TLS   10. Add more formula before it completely empties the syringe barrel

11. Wait while food goes through G-tube

TLS   12. Continue adding food until completed (repeating steps 6, 9 and 10)

TLS   13. Add water before food is completely emptied from syringe barrel

TLS   14. Add more water when formula nears bottom of syringe barrel to flush tube

15. Kink G-tube before water completely empties from barrel

CS   16. Take off syringe barrel

CS   17. Put plug in tube

Figure 9.4. Sample task analysis for gastrostomy (G-tube) feeding, bolus method, with caution steps (CS) and time-limited steps (TLS) indicated

pouring the formula due to a physical impairment. A funnel may be used to address this problem. On another step, it may be found that the student has difficulty knowing when to pour more formula, so a red line is placed on the syringe barrel as an antecedent prompt to indicate when more formula needs to be added. When it is determined that adaptations are needed, the teacher and nurse should work together to be sure the adaptations do not compromise the procedure. The reader is referred to Chapter 5 for more information on adaptations.

After the student is assessed on the task analysis and adaptations and adjustments are made to the task analysis based on the results, instruction is ready to begin. A variety of instructional strategies have been used to teach health care procedures, such as prompting strategies, antecedent prompts, learning strategies (e.g., mnemonics, jingle), time-delay, picture prompting systems, simulation practice on a doll (e.g., with doll oriented in same direction as the student for initial teaching of suctioning a tracheostomy), and others. The teacher will select the instructional strategy based on which strategies have been most effective with the student in the past and the student's present performance on the targeted task. (See Chapter 3 for more information on instruction.) Once the instructional strategy is selected, the task analysis should be put on a data sheet. The caution steps and time-limited steps are highlighted on the sheet to remind the teacher to shadow the student during those steps. Also, the adaptations that were determined as being needed during the assessment phase using the discrepancy analysis (e.g., funnel on syringe barrel, red line on syringe barrel) should also be written on the data sheet. Data should be taken on a regular basis to document the student's progress and determine if further adaptations or modifications are needed.

IMPACT OF DISABILITIES ON HEALTH AND SCHOOL PERFORMANCE

Health is not merely the absence of disease or infirmity but also a state of optimal mental, social, and physical well-being *(Dorland's Illustrated Medical Dictionary,* 2000). Given this broader definition, not only do teachers need to monitor students for common health problems and problems involving health care procedures but they also need to have a broader understanding of the student's disability and its impact on health and school performance.

Disability-Specific Monitoring

Although countless conditions compose the category of severe and multiple disabilities, teachers need to be familiar with each of their student's specific medical conditions. By knowing about the student's specific disability, the teacher will have a greater understanding of what health issues can arise and how educational functioning can be affected. Depending on the disability, students may also need to be taught certain activities that will address some of their health issues.

Students with severe and multiple disabilities will typically have conditions that require monitoring during the school day. For example, teachers will often need to monitor for malnutrition, dehydration, pressure sores, infections, and contractures. Students will often need to be monitored for very specific problems depending on the students' disability, however. For example, students with seizure disorders will need to be monitored for seizures, and students with asthma will need to be monitored for asthma attacks. In each instance, teachers will need to know what to look for and what to do if a problem is detected. The nurse, family, and teacher will need to work together to be sure they are accurately monitoring each student's specific condition and have a plan in place of what to do should problems arise.

General Impact of Severe and Multiple Disabilities

Students with severe and multiple disabilities will often have impairments affecting several major functioning areas. Impairments in these areas typically affect performance in school and the student's optimum well-being. These impaired functioning areas are 1) motor or sensory limitations, 2) restricted communication, 3) fatigue and endurance limitations, 4) general health issues, 5) experiential deficits, 6) neurocognitive impairments, and 7) psychosocial and environmental factors (Heller, 2002; Heller et al., 1996).

Motor or Sensory Limitations

Many students with severe and multiple disabilities have impairments affecting their motor movements, vision, or hearing. It is important that teachers closely monitor the students' motoric, visual, and auditory functioning because changes can occur over time. In order to promote optimal functioning, these physical and sensory impairments should be addressed with appropriate adaptations.

When physical disabilities are present, proper positioning is needed to allow for stability and improved movement of the extremities (i.e., arms and legs). Also, adaptive equipment and assistive technology is needed to allow these students to independently or partially participate in a variety of school tasks (e.g., adapted spoons, adapted toothbrush, stabilized paper, alternate computer access). Students with limited mobility will need specialized equipment such as wheelchairs, walkers, or canes. In addition to learning how to use the equipment, some students will also need to learn how to care for the equipment, such as learning how to check their wheelchair for proper functioning. Because of frequent changes that can occur in a student's motoric abilities over time, the teacher should monitor for any changes and report any worsening or improvement of the condition. Equally important is for the teacher to examine the effectiveness of the adaptations, assistive technology, and equipment over time to determine if further changes are needed (e.g., different type of switch to use a device due to worsening of contractures, a new wheelchair because a student has outgrown the old one). (For information on sensory adaptations and assistive technology, refer to Chapter 10.)

Restricted Communication

When restricted communication is present, students may lack the ability to communicate simple wants or to socially interact with others with more complex communicative messages. Students will need to be taught to communicate through one or more forms of AAC (e.g., gestures, communication boards, electronic devices). Without an effective form of communication, students will be severely restricted in their ability to interact across various environments. In some cases, these students who lack an effective communication system may withdraw or display severe behavior problems (e.g., SIB) that can jeopardize their health. As discussed in the communication chapter, students who are nonverbal or who have restricted communication abilities will need to be systematically taught communication skills.

When determining the content of the communication system, it is important to consider vocabulary addressing health needs. Whenever possible, students should be taught to communicate that they do not feel well. Some students will be able to learn to communicate a variety of health problems such as "sick," "nausea," and "pain." Some communication systems will have a picture of a person so that the child can point to where the pain is located, whereas others will have symbols for different parts of the body. For example, a picture of an ear may be used, because otitis media occurs more frequently in individuals with severe and multiple disabilities. Having a way to indicate what hurts is especially important when students have physical disabilities that prevent them from reaching for their ear or other body part to indicate pain.

Some students will also be taught vocabulary specifically addressing needs that they may have when hospitalized. Due to increased hospitalizations that many students with severe and multiple disabilities experience, teaching students simple messages can ease the anxiety, fear, and confusion that can occur with hospitalizations.

Some students will have information about their health needs on their communication systems. Some students will be taught the time that medications or health care procedures occur. They may have a message on their communication system, "It's time for my medication" or "I need a restroom break" (for students requiring CIC who do not want everyone to hear an explicit message about needing this procedure.) Sometimes, students who are physically unable to perform their health care procedures have the steps of the procedure on their communication device to direct someone else in performing the procedure (Heller, Forney, et al., 2000). Being able to direct another person can increase student independence as well as minimize errors. Some students have additional messages such as "You are doing it wrong" on their devices.

Fatigue and Endurance Limitations

Many students with severe and multiple disabilities have fatigue and endurance problems. When a physical disability is present, repeated motor movement may tire the individual. For example, a student with cerebral palsy may experience fatigue from using a communication device or hitting a switch if a great deal of effort is needed. Other students may experience fatigue due to the type of disability they have, such as those with sickle cell anemia who may become tired during school activities and need a break. In other cases, the medication the student is taking may result in fatigue problems.

Teachers need to monitor for fatigue and endurance problems and make appropriate modifications. One possible modification is adjusting students' schedules so that the more demanding activities are scheduled when the students are the most alert. In some instances, a change of activities or a short break will help decrease fatigue. Students may also be taught to indicate when they are tired and need a short break.

General Health Issues

Students who have health issues may be at risk of not performing optimally. Some students may not feel well because of health problems or they may experience discomfort. In these instances, the student's attention will be drawn away from the task. Teachers need to monitor for health problems and make appropriate accommodations (e.g., alleviate discomfort as indicated, provide breaks). Also, teachers need to remember that classroom performance may be erratic when the student is feeling poorly. Most students will need more repetition of the classroom material when feeling ill or having discomfort than they would require when feeling healthy.

Students with severe and multiple disabilities often have increased absenteeism due to illness or surgeries. Some students also miss classroom time because they need to leave classes early due to slower mobility or to have health care procedures performed. Teachers will need to be prepared to accommodate student absences, whether they are for a few months or a few minutes. They may need to reteach skills because of prolonged absences, modify the length of a student's lesson, or build in more repetition when more time is available, for example.

Experiential Deficits

Students may have experiential deficits that affect school performance and health. When a student has a physical or sensory impairment, the student may acquire incomplete or inaccurate information. For example, a student who has never felt a cotton ball because he or she has limited arm movement may think the cotton ball will be hard or a student who is blind may not realize that the tube-feeding formula is mixed and poured into the syringe barrel. Teachers must give students meaningful experiences and not make assumptions about what they already know. For example, students with physical limitations need items (e.g., leaves for a discussion on tree types) brought to them to touch and manipulate with assistance.

Students with physical or health impairments who are learning to partially or completely perform their health care procedures should be introduced to the materials systematically. It is important that assumptions are not made regarding what the student already knows about the materials or equipment when he or she has never participated in performing a procedure. Often, children with severe and multiple disabilities learn little about the procedure prior to being taught. Although a student may have repeated exposure to the health care procedure, the child is often inadvertently taught a very passive role in which the procedures are "done to" the student (Heller, Forney, et al., 2000; Tarnowski & Drabman, 1987).

A lack of experience may also create false assumptions on the part of school personnel. Some students minimize the amount of pain they are feeling. This is because they lack experience with pain or comparison with different levels of pain. Teachers should not assume that the amount of pain being reported is accurate. Also, some nonverbal students will be unable to report feeling pain, but will nonverbally indicate that they are in pain. Teachers should be alert for nonverbal signs of pain such a lack of movement, grasping an area, crying, or even behaviors such as head banging. If pain is suspected, the appropriate person should be notified (e.g., parent, nurse, physician) so that the student can receive proper treatment.

Neurocognitive Impairments

Students with severe and multiple disabilities range in their neurocognitive functioning. Some students will have mental retardation, whereas others will have learning disabilities, distractibility, disorganization, visual-motor impairments, and other difficulties. Some students with severe and multiple disabilities may not have any cognitive impairments, although for the purposes of this book, students have been defined as having mental retardation as one of their multiple disabilities. The type and extent of cognitive impairment will influence how well the student will be able to take care of his or her own health care needs. The educational team will need to examine the student's cognitive functioning to determine the student's level of participation in his or her own health care. Often, the student's abilities are underestimated when physical disabilities are involved along with restricted speech. The educational team will need to be sure that decisions are based on student's demonstrated abilities rather than false assumptions or inaccurate assessments.

Psychosocial and Environmental Factors

Psychosocial and environmental factors can also affect school performance. Three of the major areas under this category are behavioral functioning, learned helplessness, and ineffective learning environment (Heller, 2002). Students with severe and multiple disabilities may have several behaviors that interfere with learning and health. In some instances, severe behavior problems can be present, such as aggression and SIB (Westling & Fox, 2000). It is important that teachers carry out a functional behavioral analysis and an appropriate course of action (e.g., behavior management plan, more appropriate ways to communicate) to decrease the possibility of a student's being injured (e.g., eye-gouging resulting in loss of vision, head banging resulting in brain damage.) As discussed under otitis media, student's health should be ruled out first as a causative factor because the behavior may be due to pain, infection, or other medical problems.

Some students develop learned helplessness, which is lack of persistence at tasks that the student is capable of performing. This typically occurs from adults doing tasks for the student instead of assisting the student in performing them. For example, if an adult feeds the student, the student will not learn to feed him- or herself, but will wait passively for someone to do it. This can increase the risk of malnutrition and dehydration. A student who does not learn how to catheterize him- or herself is vulnerable to being sexually abused. It is important that teachers assist students to learn to do as much for themselves as possible to increase independence. Teachers must be careful not to create an ineffective learning environment in which there are low expectations and minimal demands placed on the student.

WORKING AS A TEAM

To successfully integrate health care and educational programs, it is important that school, home, and medical personnel work closely together. Each has a vital role to help promote a student's health and education. Without a collaborative process, the well-being of the student is at risk.

Sharing of Information

Students with health care needs require clear communication among parents, school nurses, physicians, teachers (e.g., general education teacher, special education teacher) and other school personnel. For example, it is important that everyone understands how to recognize a student's medical problems (e.g., asthma) and what to do should one occur. Parents can provide helpful information regarding the signs and symptoms their child exhibits when an asthma attack occurs, and this needs to be communicated to the child's teachers and other relevant school personnel (e.g., physical therapist). For example, one child may wheeze and be short of breath, whereas another child may be unable to talk due to severe airway constriction (and wheezing is only audible with a stethoscope or on movement).

The school nurse and parents need to communicate to teachers and other school personnel about the student's specific condition and the course of treatment that has been prescribed by the physician. For example, an inhaler or nebulizer is often prescribed for an asthma attack. The school nurse will need to demonstrate how to administer medication using an inhaler or nebulizer to school personnel. Should medication not stop an asthma attack, it will be important that a plan of action be put in place that the entire educational team is aware of and knows how to implement. Having a written plan to follow in these situations will be important, and everyone should be clear as to what is to be done. Any signs or symptoms that school personnel should look out for and any restrictions that need to be followed should also be included in this plan.

Having and discussing written guidelines for the student's treatments can promote good communication among team members. For example, if the physician prescribes tube feeding, it is important that those performing the procedure have a clear understanding of how the physician wants that to be carried out. Some school systems have the school nurse send a written tube feeding procedure to the physician's office for the physician to approve or make changes so as to be sure that it is being implemented correctly. The written procedure is then shared and discussed with the team.

When planning health-related goals for students, it is important to utilize each team member's unique knowledge and skills. For example, decisions need to be made regarding whether a student can participate in the implementation of his or her own health care procedures. The nurse can provide important information regarding the procedures and appropriateness of any adaptations. The teacher can provide important information on instructional strategies and adaptations to promote learning. Related services staff (e.g., physical therapist, occupational therapist, speech-language pathologist) may contribute information on positioning, motor control, and communication. Parents may also give valuable input regarding their child. Together, the team can make decisions regarding the feasibility of teaching the student to self-perform his or her own procedure.

Nursing Roles and Collaborative Teaming

As discussed previously in this chapter, some roles traditionally performed by the nurse, such as tube feeding, may be delegated to a teacher or paraprofessional. In this role-sharing situation, the nurse still retains accountability and is an important resource to the person performing the procedure. This type of role sharing found in collaborative teaming may not be possible or desirable in certain situations, however. In some instances, a nurse may determine that it is unsafe to delegate a procedure. Nurses may also be prohibited in delegating certain procedures based on their state's Nurse Practice Act. Noncompliance with their Nurse Practice Act can jeopardize their nursing license.

Nurses are an important component of the team, especially for students with health care needs. The health care needs of the student cannot be met without a collaborative team approach, however. Each team member, whether he or she is the nurse, teacher, parent, or other school personnel, has important information and skills that are needed across assessment, implementation, and evaluation. Only by working together will there be successful integration of health care within the student's educational programs.

SUMMARY

School personnel should maintain a safe, healthy environment for all of their students. This includes arranging the environment to prevent injury, maintaining universal precautions, ensuring that evacuation procedures are accessible, and knowing how to respond to an emergency. For students with severe and multiple disabilities, teachers should be familiar with common medical problems such as nutritional problems and anemia, dehydration, skin irritation and pressure sores, respiratory infections, asthma, otitis media, and contractures. Because students with severe and multiple disabilities often take a range of medications, teachers should be familiar with these medications and their side effects and the proper procedures for administration. Types of medications may include antiepileptic, antispasticity, antireflux, antibiotic, psychotropic, skin, and respiratory. Teachers also need to be familiar with students' health care procedures so that they know what to do if something should go wrong. Utilizing an IHP that specifies what steps to take should a problem arise will assist school personnel in taking the proper steps. Health care procedures are often viewed as forms of self-help or independent living skills. The educational team needs to decide if the student will learn to independently or partially participate in self-performing these procedures and have IEP goals in place. Other goal options are to have the student direct the task or increase knowledge of the task. Finally, teachers need to be aware of the impact of severe and multiple disabilities on health and school performance and to utilize effective teamwork strategies to address school and health needs.

REFERENCES

Batshaw, M.L., Blum, N.J., Borda, C., DaCosta, N., Georga, S.V., Mars, A.E., Starr, H.L., & Want, P.P. (1996). Medications. In L.A. Kurtz, P.W. Dowrick, S.E. Levy, & M.L. Batshaw (Eds.), *Handbook of developmental disabilities: Resources for interdisciplinary care* (pp. 400–426). Gaithersburg, MD: Aspen Publishers.

Beers, M.H., & Berkow, R. (1999). *The Merck manual of diagnosis and therapy.* Whitehouse Station, NJ: Merck Research Laboratories.

Behrman, R.E., Kliegman, R.M., & Jenson, H.B. (2000). *Nelson textbook of pediatrics* (16th ed.). Philadelphia: W.B. Saunders Company.

Binard, J.E., Persky, L., Lockhart, J., & Kelley, B. (1996). Intermittent catheterization the right way! (Volume vs. time-directed). *Journal of Spinal Cord Medicine, 19,* 194–196.

Cedar Rapids Community School District v. Garret F., 106 F. 3d 822 (526 U.S. 66, 1999).

Chong, S.K. (2001). Gastrointestinal problems in the handicapped child. *Current Opinions in Pediatrics, 13,* 441–446.

Curtis, J.L. (1997). Psychotropic medication use in people with developmental disabilities. *Maryland Medical Journal, 46,* 481–485.

Dorland's illustrated medical dictionary (29th ed.). (2000). Philadelphia: W.B. Saunders.

DPHD Critical Issues and Leadership Committee. (1999). Special report: Position statement on specialized health care procedures. *Physical Disabilities: Education and Related Service, 18*(1), 1–2.

Farmer, S.E., & James, M. (2001). Contractures in orthopaedic and neurological conditions: A review of causes and treatment. *Disability Rehabilitation, 23,* 549–558.

Ferrarin, M., Andreoni, G., & Pedotti, A. (2000). Comparative biomechanical evaluation of different wheelchair seat cushions. *Journal of Rehabilitation Research and Development, 37,* 315–325.

Gonzalez, L., Nazario, C.M., & Gonzalez, M.J. (2000). Nutrition-related problems of pediatric patients with neuromuscular disorders. *PR Health Science Journal, 19,* 35–38.

Gormley, M.E. (2001). Treatment of neuromuscular and musculoskeletal problems in cerebral palsy. *Pediatric Rehabilitation, 4,* 5–16.

Haas, M.B. (1993). Individualized healthcare plans. In M.B. Haas, M.J. Gerber, K.M. Kalb, R.E. Luehr, W.R. Miller, C.K. Silkworth, & S.I. Will (Eds.), *The school nurse's source book of individualized healthcare plans* (pp. 41–44). North Branch, MN: Sunrise River.

Hannigan, K.F. (1979). Teaching intermittent self-catheterization to young children with myelodysplasia. *Developmental Medicine and Child Neurology, 21,* 365–368.

Heller, K.W. (2002). Physical and health disabilities. In R. Gargiulo (Ed.), *Special education in contemporary society: An introduction to exceptionality* (pp. 532–599). Belmont, CA: Wadsworth Publishing Company.

Heller, K.W., Alberto, P.A., Forney, P.E., & Schwartzman, M.N. (1996). *Understanding physical, sensory, and health impairments: Characteristics and educational implications.* Pacific Grove, CA: Brooks/Cole Publishers.

Heller, K.W., Bigge, J., & Allgood, P. (2001). Adaptations for personal independence. In J. Bigge, S. Best, & K.W. Heller (Eds.), *Teaching individuals with physical, health, or multiple disabilities* (4th ed., pp. 536–565). Upper Saddle River, NJ: Merrill/Prentice Hall.

Heller, K.W., Forney, P.E., Alberto, P.A., Schwartzman, M.N., & Goeckel, T. (2000). *Meeting physical and health needs of children with disabilities: Teaching student participation and management.* Belmont, CA: Wadsworth.

Heller, K.W., Fredrick, L., Dykes, M.K., Best, S., & Cohen, E. (2000). Specialized health care procedures in schools: Training and service delivery. *Exceptional Children, 66,* 173–186.

Homma, K., Murakami, G., Fujioka, H., Fujita, T., Imai, A., & Ezoe, K. (2001). Treatment of ischial pressure ulcers with a posteromedial thigh fasciocutaneous flap. *Plastic Reconstruction Surgery, 108,* 1990–1996.

Irving Independent School District v. Tatro. (408 U.S. 883, 1984).

Jordan, A., & Weinroth, M.D. (1996). A school system's model for meeting special health care needs. *Physical Disabilities: Education and Related Services, 15,* 27–32.

Kennedy, M., McCombie, L., Dawes, P., McConnell, K.N., & Dunnigan, M.G. (1997). Nutritional support for patients with intellectual disability and nutrition/dysphagia disorders in community care. *Journal of Intellectual Disability and Research, 41,* 430–436.

Ladebauche, P. (1997). Managing asthma: A growth and development approach. *Pediatric Nursing, 23,* 37–44.

Lapides, L., Diokno, A.C., Silber, S.L., & Lowe, B.S. (1972). Clean, intermittent self-catheterization in the treatment of urinary tract disease. *Journal of Urology, 107,* 458–461.

Medcom Trainex. (1993). *Universal precautions: AIDS and hepatitis B prevention for health-care workers.* Arden Grove, CA: Medcom.

McBrien, D.M., & Bontibius, D.J. (2000). Seizures in infants and young children. *Infants and Young Children, 13,* 21–31.

Morse, J.S., & Colatarci, S.L. (1994). The impact of technology. In S.P Roth & J.S. Morse (Eds.), *A life-span approach to nursing care of individuals with developmental disabilities* (pp. 351–383). Baltimore: Paul H. Brookes Publishing Co.

Mulligan-Ault, M., Guess, D., Struth, L., & Thompson, B. (1988). The implementation of health-related procedures in classrooms for students with severe multiple impairments. *Journal of The Association of Persons with Severe Handicaps, 13,* 100–109.

National Council of State Boards of Nursing. (1995). *Delegation: Concepts and decision-making process.* Available on-line at http://www.ncshn.org/pfiles/delefati.html

Neef, N., Parrish, J.M., Hannigan, K.F., Pzage, T., & Iwata, B. (1989). Teaching self-catheterization skills to children with neurogenic bladder complications. *Journal of Applied Behavior Analysis, 22,* 237–243.

Newacheck, P.W., & Halfon, N. (2000). Prevalence, impact, and trends in childhood disability due to asthma. *Archives of Pediatric Adolescent Medicine, 154,* 287–293.

O'Reilly, M.F. (1997). Functional analysis of episodic self-injury correlated with recurrent otitis media. *Journal of Applied Behavior Analysis, 30,* 165–167.

Physicians' Desk Reference. (56th ed.). (2002). Montvale, NJ: Medical Economics.

Rapport, M.J. (1996). Legal guidelines for the delivery of special health care services in schools. *Exceptional Children, 62*, 537–549.

Rempel, G., & Coates, J. (1999). Special considerations for medication use in children with developmental disabilities. *Physical Medical Rehabilitation Clinics of North America, 10*, 493–509.

Robertson, J., Alper, S., Schloss, P.J., & Wisniewski, L. (1992). Teaching self-catheterization skills to a child with myelomeningocele in a preschool setting. *Journal of Early Intervention, 16*, 20–30.

Rueve, B.A., Robinson, M.J., Worthington, L.A., & Gargiulo, R.M. (2000). Children with special health needs in inclusive settings: Writing health care plans. *Physical Disabilities: Education and Related Services, 19*, 17–18.

Ruiz, P.J., Pascual, P., & Bernardos, V. (2000). Progressive response to botulinum A toxin in cerebral palsy. *European Journal of Neurology, 7*, 191–193.

Shaer, C.M. (1997). The infant and young child with spina bifida: Major medical concerns. *Infants and Young Children, 9*, 13–25.

Skale, N. (1992). *Manual of pediatric nursing procedures*. Philadelphia: J.B. Lippincott.

Smith, S.W., Camfield, C., & Camfield, P. (1999). Living with cerebral palsy and tube feeding: A population-based follow-up. *Journal of Pediatrics, 135*, 307–310.

Sobsey, D., & Cox, A. (1996). Integrating health care and educational programs. In F.P. Orelove & D. Sobsey, *Educating children with multiple disabilities: A transdisciplinary approach* (3rd ed., pp. 217–251). Baltimore: Paul H. Brookes Publishing Co.

Tarnowski, K., & Drabman, R.S. (1987). Teaching intermittent self-catheterization skills to mentally retarded children. *Research in Developmental Disabilities, 8*, 521–529.

Tawfik, R., Dickson, A., Clarke, M., & Thomas, A.G. (1997). Caregivers' perceptions following gastrostomy in severely disabled children with feeding problems. *Developmental Medicine and Child Neurology, 39*, 746–751.

Thomson, H.G., Azhar, A.M., & Healy, H. (2001). The recurrent neurotrophic buttock ulcer in the meningomyelocele paraplegic: A sensate flap solution. *Plastic Reconstructive Surgery, 108*, 1192–1196.

Toder, D.S. (2000). Respiratory problems in the adolescent with developmental delay. *Adolescent Medicine, 11*, 617–631.

Van Hala, S., Nelson, V.S., Hurbitz, E.A., Panzi, A., Bloom, D.A., & Ward, M.J. (1997). Bladder management in patients with pediatric onset neurogenic bladders. *Journal Spinal Cord Medicine, 29*, 410–415.

Westling, D.L., & Fox, L. (2000). *Teaching students with severe disabilities* (2nd ed.). Upper Saddle River, NJ: Merrill.

Whitehead, F.J., Couper, R.T., Bourne, A.J., & Byard, R.W. (1996). Dehydration deaths in infants and young children. *American Journal of Forensic Medicine and Pathology, 17*, 73–78.

Wong, D.L. (1995). *Whaley and Wong's nursing care of infants and children*. St. Louis: Mosby.

Zargi, M., & Boltezar, I.H. (1992). Effects of recurrent otitis media in infancy on auditory perception and speech. *American Journal of Otolaryngology, 13*, 366–372.

CHAPTER 10

Children with
Sensory Impairments

Rosanne K. Silberman, Susan M. Bruce, and Catherine Nelson

Many students with severe and multiple disabilities have a sensory impairment as one of their disabilities. Some students may have a visual impairment, hearing loss, or a combination of these impairments. This chapter provides content on definitions, prevalence, etiologies, and the impact of vision and hearing loss on development and learning. Unique characteristics of students with sensory impairments and multiple disabilities, along with specific adaptations, accommodations, and instructional strategies are provided.

STUDENTS WHO HAVE VISUAL IMPAIRMENTS AND OTHER DISABILITIES

Teachers and other members of a collaborative team who work with students with visual impairments and other disabilities need to have knowledge of the common terms used in the field. Legal definitions and terms related to blindness and visual impairment are used in determining eligibility for specialized educational services and adaptive aids and devices. These definitions and terms also are used as criteria for receiving such benefits as books and audiotapes mailed free of charge, transportation and social security benefits, rehabilitation services, tax exemptions, and free telephone directory assistance (Dowse, 2003; Huebner, 2000).

Legal Definitions

Legal Blindness

A person who is *legally blind* has central visual acuity for distance vision of 20/200 or less in the better eye with correction. This means that if an individual wearing eyeglasses or contact lenses has 20/200 vision, he or she can see an object at 20 feet that a person with normal vision can see from 200 feet away. A person can also be considered legally blind if the visual field is restricted to 20 degrees or less. An individual with a normal visual field can look straight ahead at a target and see objects within a range of 160–180 degrees without turning his or her head or eyes. If a person has normal visual acuity and a field of vision of 20 degrees, he or she has tunnel vision and can see clearly at a distance, but only what a person with a normal visual field can see looking through a long tube. He or she has no peripheral vision and cannot see objects located to the side or above or below him- or herself.

Low Vision

An individual who is considered to have *low vision* has central visual acuity of 20/70 to 20/200 in the better eye with correction, or a visual field restricted to 20–40 degrees or less in the better eye with correction (Brilliant & Graboyes, 1999). Corn and Koenig define someone with low vision as

> A person who has difficulty accomplishing visual tasks, even with prescribed corrective lenses, but who can enhance his or her ability to accomplish these tasks with the use of compensatory visual strategies, low vision and other devices, and environmental modifications. (1996, p. 4)

Although these students have a significant visual impairment, they do use their vision as their primary means of learning and performing a variety of visual tasks in the classroom using optical and nonoptical devices, such as a wide black felt tip marker. They also may use their auditory and tactile senses in combination with receiving visual input.

Partially Sighted

Partially sighted is a historical term that referred to visual acuity between 20/70 and 20/200. This term is rarely used in the educational literature today. It has been replaced by the term *low vision*.

Educationally Meaningful (Functional) Definitions

Legal definitions of blindness and visual impairment based on clinical measurements have limited educational value because they do not provide any information regarding how a student uses his or her vision. According to Deitz and Ferrell (1993), the definition of visual impairment does not consider fluctuating visual abilities as seen in children with cortical visual impairment, environmental factors that affect vision in specific situations, or deteriorating visual loss. Two children with the same acuity may use their vision very differently in home, school, and community environments. For example, one might see a symbol easily on the vending machine, whereas another student may need a magnifier to see the same symbol.

Blind

Blind is a term used by many educators to refer to children and youth who are totally blind or have light perception only. These students use tactual and auditory senses as their primary avenues for learning and gathering information (Corn & Koenig, 1996; Hatlen, 2000; Huebner, 2000).

Visual Impairment *Visual impairment* is a general term that refers to all individuals who have a visual loss that affects learning in school environments. According to the Individuals with Disabilities Education Act (IDEA) Amendments of 1997 (PL 105-17), "visual impairment (including blindness)" is described as "an impairment in vision that, even with correction, adversely affects a child's educational performance. The term includes both partial sight and blindness" (34 C.F.R. § 300.7[c][13]).

Congenital Loss of Vision

Children born with a visual impairment at birth or before visual memory is established are *congenitally* blind or visually impaired. It is important for a teacher or any member of the collaborative team to know the age of onset of the visual impairment for each student. Those who are totally blind rely on senses other than vision for learning and have to be taught using nonvisual instructional strategies.

Adventitious Loss of Vision

Children who acquire a visual impairment after birth and after establishing visual memory (around 5 years of age) are regarded as *adventitiously* blind or visually impaired. These children have a repertoire of visual experiences and concepts that they will be able to use in acquiring new information about the world.

Visual Efficiency

Visual efficiency refers to "the degree to which the student can perform specific visual tasks with ease, comfort, and minimum time. It is unique to each child and cannot be measured or predicted clinically with any accuracy by medical, psychological, or educational personnel" (Barraga & Erin, 2001, p. 23). Some students appear to be visual learners, whereas others with similar visual potential are not as responsive to visual stimuli and perform as if they are unable to see. How one learns to use his or her vision and become visually efficient depends on such factors as visual skills, neuromotor integrity, cognitive abilities, experiences, personality, and attention and organizational behaviors (Corn & Koenig, 1996; Langley, 2004).

Professionals in the Field of Visual Impairment

A variety of professionals in the field of visual impairment provide clinical or educational services to children and youth who are blind or who have low vision, including those with additional disabilities. Some professionals are certified in more than one area and can provide multiple services.

Ophthalmologist

An ophthalmologist is a physician (M.D.) who specializes in the diagnosis and treatment of defects and diseases of the eye. This professional is qualified to perform eye surgery and prescribe drugs and corrective lenses.

Optometrist

An optometrist is a licensed eye care provider (O.D.) who specializes in the measurement and treatment of refractive errors, prescribes eyeglasses or contact lenses, and diagnoses and manages medical eye conditions as regulated by state laws. Some optometrists specialize in low vision.

Optician

An optician is a technician who grinds lenses, fits them into frames, and adjusts frames to the wearer. An optician also fills prescriptions for optical devices such as spectacle-mounted telescopes used for distance vision.

Clinical Low Vision Specialists

A clinical low vision specialist is either an ophthalmologist or optometrist with additional expertise in low vision. He or she conducts clinical low vision evaluations, prescribes optical and nonoptical low vision devices, and provides follow-up services to maximize the use of vision in children and adults with low vision (Pugh & Erin, 1999).

Education/Rehabilitation Professionals

Teacher of Students with Visual Impairments

A teacher of students with visual impairments (TVI) is a certified teacher with knowledge and skills in the education of students who are blind or who have low vision. TVIs provide instruction in the

> Areas of communication, literacy, daily living skills and social-emotional skills, academic support, and career education. In addition, they provide skills to help students with visual impairments access the common core curriculum provided to all students without disabilities. (Pugh & Erin, 1999, p. 82)

TVIs usually earn specialized state teacher certification in blindness and visual impairment from the state in which they live. A TVI is one member of the collaborative team that serves students with visual impairments and multiple disabilities.

Orientation and Mobility Specialist

A certified orientation and mobility specialist (COMS) has completed an undergraduate or graduate university program and has received national certification through the Academy of Certification of Vision Rehabilitation and Education Professionals (ACVREP). COMSs work with children and adults with visual impairments, including those with multiple impairments, to help them learn to orient themselves and maneuver safely, efficiently, and gracefully in home, school, and community environments (Koenig & Holbrook, 2000b, p. 265).

Rehabilitation Teacher

A rehabilitation teacher is a specialist who has the knowledge and skills to help children and adults with visual impairments to develop competence in carrying out daily activities. Specific instructional areas include development or enhancement of personal management skills, communication skills, indoor orientation, low vision utilization, and home management skills. If requested, a rehabilitation teacher can work in a public school environment to provide instruction in daily living skills to children with visual impairments, including those with multiple disabilities. A trained rehabilitation teacher can obtain national certification from ACVREP.

Low Vision Therapist

A low vision therapist (LVT) is a professional who might be trained as a TVI, COMS, or rehabilitation teacher. An LVT is usually employed in a low vision clinic and participates in low vision evaluations of children and adults. The LVT is responsible for providing instruction in the functional use of vision and for helping to select appropriate low vision devices and provide training in the use of these devices. The LVT works closely with other professionals on the collaborative team, such as eye care specialists, TVIs, COMSs, and rehabilitation teachers. An LVT can obtain national certification through ACVREP (Koenig & Holbrook, 2000b, p. 267).

Prevalence of Visual Impairments

Children with visual impairments represent a low-incidence disability and make up a very small percentage of the school population: approximately .04% of the school-age population and .5% of the students served under IDEA (U.S. Department of Education, 2001). Estimates of the number of students who have visual impairments with other disabilities vary depending on the source. However, child count data are frequently inaccurate because students with visual impairments sometimes are counted in other disability areas such as mental retardation, multiple disabilities, learning disabilities, autism, or speech or language impairments (Huebner, 2000; Silberman, 2000). According to the *Twenty-Fourth Annual Report to Congress* (U.S. Department of Education, 2002), the percentage of students ages 6–21 with visual impairments served under IDEA increased by 7.9% from 1992 to 2002. According to the same source, the percentage of children classified as having multiple disabilities, in which students with visual impairments are sometimes counted, increased 24.5% during the same time period.

Miller, Menacker, and Batshaw (2002) cited that one half to two thirds of individuals with developmental disabilities have a visual impairment. Various studies conducted since the 1990s have reported that estimates of the percentage of children with visual impairments who also have multiple disabilities have ranged from 40% to 70% (Deitz & Ferrell, 1993; Teplin, 1995; Wesson & Maino, 1995). Data obtained from specialized agencies in nine states providing services to infants and toddlers with visual impairments during the first year of the Model Registry of Early Childhood Visual Impairment Consortium revealed that 55% of 406 children from birth to 3 years of age had additional disabilities (Hatton, 2001). The five most prevalent additional disabilities were developmental delay, cerebral palsy, deafness and hard of hearing, brain dysfunction, and various syndromes associated with mental retardation. Hatton also reported that additional disabilities were more prevalent in children with cortical visual impairment and retinopathy of prematurity (ROP). (Additional relevant prevalence data can be found in Barraga & Erin, 2001, and Langley, 2004.)

The Structure of the Eye and How We See

Knowledge of the visual system will help educational team members communicate more effectively with medical specialists about their children's eye conditions.

The parts of the eye include the outer protective layer, consisting of the *sclera*, the white part of the eye that forms a protective coating for the eyeball—and the *cornea*, the clear, transparent membrane that also protects the eye. The middle vascular layer between the sclera and the retina consists of the *choroid,* which nourishes the retina; the *ciliary body,* tissues composed of the ciliary processes that secrete aqueous humor (see below); the *ciliary muscle* that controls the shape of the lens; and the *iris,* the colored, circular membrane of the eye that is suspended between the cornea and lens and that expands and contracts to control the amount of light entering the eye. The innermost nerve layer consists of the *retina,* which contains light-sensitive nerve cells and fibers connecting with the brain through the optic nerve (Corn & Koenig, 1996; Levack, Stone, & Bishop, 1994). As light hits an object in a child's field of vision, the light rays are reflected and enter the eye through the cornea and then pass through the *aqueous humor,* the clear fluid that bathes the lens and provides nutrients to the iris and cornea. Then, the light rays pass through the *pupil,* the circular opening in the center of the colored iris. The muscles of the iris control the amount of light entering the eye by expanding or contracting the size of the pupil. The light rays then pass through the crystalline *lens,* the transparent oval structure that is held in place by suspensory ligaments, through the *vitreous humor,* the transparent gel that helps the eye to maintain its shape, and finally to the *retina.* The retina contains light-sensitive nerve cells (neuroreceptors) and fibers. The *macula,* in the central portion of the retina, consists mainly of *cones,* the receptor cells responsible for central visual acuity, fine detail tasks such as reading and seeing distant objects, and color discrimination. The cones function best in bright light. The peripheral portion of the retina contains *rods,* the photoreceptors responsible for vision in dim light, peripheral vision, and motion detection. The retina is responsible for changing an upside-down image it receives to electrical impulses that are carried to the optic nerve and then to the occipital lobe of the visual cortex of the brain, where they are transformed to correct visual images (Sacks, 1998). Damage to any of these structures results in visual disorders. Figure 10.1 illustrates the parts of the eye.

Each eye has six ocular muscles that are responsible for controlling the eye's movements and coordination. Binocular vision (i.e., when both eyes focus on the same object and the brain fuses two images into one single image) can only occur when the eyes move together in a smooth, coordinated manner. These ocular muscles also are responsible for enabling both eyes to move together in different directions and to focus on distant and near ranges (i.e., accommodation).

Causes of Visual Impairments

Many of the causes of developmental disabilities also are the same causes of visual impairments (Mervis, Yeargin-Allsopp, Winter, et al., 2000). The etiologies of the visual impairments that also result in multiple disabilities may be caused by prenatal factors such as congenital infections and abnormalities,

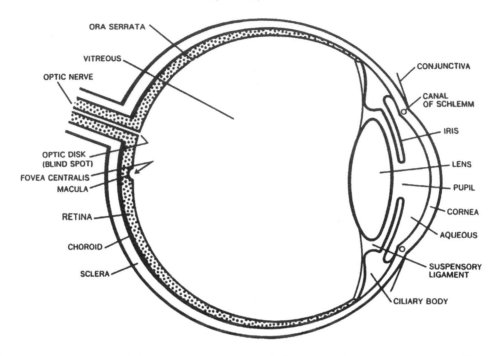

Figure 10.1. Anatomy of the eye. (From Prevent Blindness America. [1994]. *Vision problems in the U.S.* [Pamphlet]. Schaumburg, IL: Author; reprinted with permission of Prevent Blindness America®.)

hypoxia, chromosomal and genetic defects, and parental alcohol and drug abuse. During both the perinatal and the postnatal period, causes of visual impairments may include trauma, hypoxia, infection, and prematurity (Batshaw, 2002; Heller, Alberto, Forney, & Schwartzman, 1996; Orel-Bixler, 1999; Sacks, 1998; Silberman, 2000).

Vision problems in children with severe and multiple disabilities can be classified into three types: refractive (i.e., problems with the focusing mechanism), disorders of the visual pathways (i.e., problems with the transmission of light through the eye or inability of the retina to receive or change light rays to electrical impulses), and disorders of the visual cortex (i.e., problems transmitting impulses from the retina to the brain or the inability of the brain to interpret the images) (Sacks, 1998).

Results of a longitudinal study of 202 infants and toddlers with visual impairments indicated that the frequency of visual disorders differed according to the severity of additional disabilities. ROP and optic nerve hypoplasia were the most frequent in children with mild additional impairments, and cortical visual impairment and ROP occurred most frequently in children with severe additional impairments (Ferrell, 1998).

Eyeglasses or contact lenses usually can correct refractive errors. Those with severe refractive errors, even with the best correction, may still be visually impaired, however. One type of refractive error found in children with visual impairments is myopia or nearsightedness. In this condition, the eyeball is too long and the light rays focus in front of the retina. Students can see near objects clearly, but they have difficulty seeing distant objects. Concave or minus lenses are used to correct myopia. In hyperopia or farsightedness, the eyeball is too short and light rays come to a point of focus behind the retina. Students with this condition are unable to see near objects clearly and might have difficulty seeing tangible symbols on their desk, but they can see distant objects easily. Convex or plus lenses are used to correct hyperopia. In astigmatism, the cornea has an unequal curvature that prevents light rays from focusing on a single point on the retina; students with this condition have difficulty seeing at both near and far distances. Cylindrical lenses are used to correct astigmatism.

Two of the most common disorders of the visual pathways that affect children with multiple impairments are cataracts and ROP. A cataract is a lens that is opaque and appears as a white spot in the pupil. Light rays are unable to pass through it into the vitreous and then to the retina. Congenital cataracts can be caused by inborn errors of metabolism, maternal infections (e.g., rubella, cytomegalovirus), hereditary factors, syndromes, or systemic diseases (Miller et al., 2002; Ward, 2000). Surgery to remove the cataracts should be performed as early as possible (even in a 2-week-old infant) in order to prevent amblyopia, caused by lack of stimulation of the retina. Glasses or contact lenses are used to replace the natural lens. Specific strategies for encouraging their use in children with multiple impairments will be presented later in this chapter.

ROP is a condition related to prematurity and low birth weight (LBW) of infants. Infants weighing less than 1,500 grams, or 3.5 pounds, are at risk for developing ROP (Ward, 2000); the number of affected infants is increasing because many more LBW infants survive due to advances in medical technology (Miller et al., 2002). When an LBW infant is born, blood vessel growth in the underdeveloped retina is incomplete, sometimes causing these fragile and tiny vessels to grow in the wrong direction into the vitreous. They ultimately die and cause scar tissue to develop, which can constrict and pull on the retina, resulting in retinal detachment and loss of vision. Pediatric ophthalmologists have to track the development of the blood vessels in the retina and surrounding tissue in premature infants until after about 40 weeks from conception. Treatments to stop the overgrowth of blood vessels or to reattach the retina are cryotherapy or laser therapy. However, many infants with ROP, even after having treatment, will develop visual impairments that include myopia, cataracts, strabismus, glaucoma, and total blindness (Miller et al., 2002; Ward, 2000). (Detailed information related to causes of ROP and visual behaviors associated with the condition can be found in Hatton, Topor, & Rosenblum, 2004.)

One major cause of visual impairment in children with severe and multiple disabilities due to defects in the brain is cortical visual impairment (CVI). This condition, reported as the most prevalent condition in large samples of young children with visual impairments (Ferrell, 1998; Hatton, 2001), results from injury to the central nervous system rather than to ocular structures (Hatton et al., 2004). CVI is associated with prematurity and may co-occur with ROP and/or periventricular leukomalacia (PKL), a condition that results from damage to the brain in the ventricular area associated with oxygen deprivation (Brodsky, Fray, & Glasier, 2002; Carden & Good, 2003). Brodsky and colleagues (2002), as reported in Hatton and colleagues (2004), described the results of a study of 100 children with CVI in which there were two distinct groups of children who, for the purposes of the study, were divided by the location of the damage to their brains. One group of children was born at full term and had damage to the striate and peristriate cortex; the other group was born prematurely and had damage to the subcortical white matter and/or the optic radiations. Detailed descriptions of the visual behaviors of both groups can be found in Brodsky and colleagues (2002), and Hatton and colleagues (2004). Additional causes of CVI include trauma, meningitis, congenital brain malformations, head trauma, infections, and shunt failure (Barraga & Erin, 2001; Langley, 1998).

Students with CVI represent a heterogeneous group that exhibits a range of neurological impairments and ocular disorders (Carden & Good, 2003; Good, Jan, DeSa, Barkovich, Groenveld, & Hoyt, 1994; Zambone, Ciner, Appel, & Graboyes, 2000). Their eyes, eye movements, and pupillary reactions to light appear normal; however, their visual functioning can fluctuate from hour to hour or from day to day depending on fatigue and levels of sensory input. These students usually do not like to make eye contact or look at faces. They prefer colored objects, tend to light gaze, turn head and eyes away from objects when reaching, use touch rather than vision to identify objects, and prefer familiar environments that are quiet. Specific strategies for working with these students are presented later in this chapter.

Ocular disorders resulting from brain dysfunction also have been reported in students with autism. Some of these visual problems are atypical gaze, limited eye contact, visual avoidance, use of lateral gaze to observe visual objects, and inefficient voluntary visual pursuit of moving objects (Gense & Gense,

2002). Table 10.1 highlights characteristics in typical children, those with visual impairments, and those with autism spectrum disorder (ASD) in areas of communication, social interactions, and responses to sensory information. According to the authors, the information is "not meant to be exhaustive, nor meant to be used for identification. It can, however, be used to inform and direct the family and the rest of the team for an in-depth look at the possible identification of ASD in children who have a vision impairment" (Gense & Gense, 2002, p. 1).

Table 10.2 is a matrix of the characteristics of many specific eye conditions found in children with severe and multiple disabilities, the effects of the eye conditions on vision, and suggested adaptations and educational considerations (Levack et al., 1994). (Additional resources on eye diseases in children can be found in Bishop, 1996; Miller et al., 2002; and Ward, 2000.)

Impact of Visual Impairment and Multiple Disabilities on Development and Learning

Children who are blind, including those with multiple disabilities, are dependent on their remaining senses, particularly hearing and touch, for their acquisition of knowledge about the world. Lowenfeld (1981), considered to be the "father" of this field, stated that blindness imposes three basic limitations on an individual.

Range and Variety of Experiences

One limitation is in the range and variety of experiences. Children who have vision are able to see an actual object or photograph and can understand the properties of that object, whereas students who are blind have to rely on touch to gain information about the size, texture, weight, hardness, surface qualities, pliability, and temperature of objects around them. However, they are unable to use their tactile sense to have direct contact with whole objects that are too large such as mountains, tall buildings, or rivers; nor can they touch objects that are too small or fragile such as butterflies, spider webs, or soap bubbles (Lowenfeld, 1981). Furthermore, they are unable to have direct tactile contact with objects under certain conditions such as burning coal or boiling water.

Mobility, or the Ability to "Get About"

The second limitation is the ability to "get about"; for example, a boy who is blind does not know how to get to his cubby or to the teacher's desk without individuals orienting him to the classroom. Outside of the classroom, he does not know how to go to the lunchroom or gym, and on field trips, obstacles are not apparent to him, so he is not free to explore the environment without another person going with him. Therefore, mobility instruction is essential.

Table 10.1.   Austism spectrum disorder in learners with blindness/vision impairments: Comparison of characteristics

Typical development	Blind/vision impaired	Autism spectrum disorder and blind/vision impairment (ASDVI)
Impairments in Communication		
Makes cooing and gurgling sounds (3–6 months) Copies speech sounds (6–12 months)	Process of acquiring speech and language seems to be the same for children with visual impairment as it is with typical children, but the slower physical development, more restricted range of experiences, and lack of visual stimulation may cause the child to be slower in language development (Scholl, 1986)	Language develops slowly or not at all Development is frequently "splintered"; language development may or may not be consistent with typical developmental norms or sequences May show no interest in communicating
Much jargon with emotional content Able to follow simple commands (18 months) Vocabulary of 150–300 words (24 months)	Echolalic—short duration If experiences are limited, language may be delayed but is not distorted Responds appropriately to language requests; enjoys communication "give and take"	Exhibits concrete understanding and use of language; experiences difficulty with generalizations Echolalic; difficulty breaking this pattern is common. The echolalia often leads to patterns of verbal perseveration with idiosyncratic meanings Experiences difficulties initiating and engaging in meaningful conversations. The range of "topics of interest" is narrow. Has difficulty maintaining a topic chosen by others; exhibits limited or no conversational reciprocity
Understands most simple questions dealing with own environment and activities (36 months) Relates experiences so that they can be followed with reason May briefly exhibit pronoun reversals Takes part in simple conversations (2–3 years)	Vocabulary is built through concrete experiences Can experience difficulty with abstract language because of limited concrete experiences May have pronoun reversals, but they are brief in duration Concept difficulties are common because of lack of visual model; once understood, concepts can be generalized Language development usually follows developmental norms	Exhibits use of words without attaching the usual meanings. Uses nonconventional or nontraditional behaviors as a form of communication (gestures, pulling) Long-term difficulties in using pronouns appropriately Apparent lack of common sense, may be overly active or very passive Experiences difficulties with abstract concepts, often focuses on "irrelevant" information; has literal translation of language; literal/concrete understanding of concepts makes generalization difficult If verbal, converses but focuses on topic of perseverative interest

Typical development	Blind/vision impaired	Autism spectrum disorder and blind/vision impairment (ASDVI)
Impairments in Social Interactions		
Responds to name (6–9 months)	Needs to learn a world exists beyond reach; may exhibit social interest through changing or shifting posture (leaning, turning)	Appears not to hear, does not orient toward sound
Takes turns while playing with adult (e.g.; actions, sounds, facial expressions) (6–12 months)	Engages in social give and take; seeks to share information/experiences with others	Limited social interests, if any Limited understanding of social give and take
Makes simple choices among toys Mimics another child's play (18–24 months)	Play is sometimes observed to be less "imaginative" and more concrete because of the lack of visual model. Redirection of an activity is possible.	Plays repetitively; toys often are not used for intended purpose
Often indulges in make-believe (48 months)	Because of limited visual references, may have difficulty in observing, organizing, and synthesizing the environment; imitative and make-believe play may be delayed but can be specifically "taught" Requires a variety of opportunities to learn and to generalize; needs feedback to understand and comprehend some social situations	Lack of spontaneous or imaginative play; does not initiate pretend play Perseverative behavior is a problem, and redirection of activities can be difficult
Enjoys playing with other children (3–4 years)	Enjoys playing with other children Initiates interactions with adults and children Shows social curiosity; is curious about environment (e.g., may ask about who may be in the room, where a peer may be)	Prefers to spend time alone rather than with others; peer relationships are often distorted Difficulty initiating interaction Exhibits little social curiosity; may find interactions with others to be unpleasant
Able to occasionally use feelings to explain reasons (48 months)	Demonstrates empathy; able to comprehend another's feelings	May treat others as objects; limited ability to understand another's feelings/emotions

(continued)

Table 10.1   *(continued)*

Typical development	Blind/vision impaired	Autism spectrum disorder and blind/vision impairment (ASDVI)
Enjoys playing organized games with other children (5–6 years)	Enjoys playing organized games with other children Has difficulty in observing, organizing, and synthesizing the environment; requires a variety of opportunities	Often is anxious and uncomfortable in social situations; prefers to follow routines and rituals. Experiences difficulties in adapting to change
Demonstrates empathy toward others	Demonstrates empathy; is able to comprehend another's perspective	Not aware of other person's feelings; has difficulty with perspective taking

Restricted, Repetitive, and Stereotyped Patterns of Behavior

Reaches for a toy (3–6 months) Puts in and dumps from containers (12–18 months) Looks at storybook pictures with an adult (18–24 months) Helps with simple tasks (2–3 years) Follows two–step directions Uses materials and toys to make things (3–4 years)	Stereotypic behaviors (rocking, eye-poke) may occur in novel and unfamiliar situations; management of these behaviors can be accomplished with redirection into meaningful activities that provide sensory feedback; child learns to control these behaviors when older Interests may be limited due to exposure; demonstrates an interest in a variety of toys/objects once they are experienced Historically, stereotypic behaviors have been attributed to lack of stimulation of the vestibular system. These behaviors occur more in young children and lessen as the child learns to interact with the environment Interest may be limited to toys/tasks/objects previously experienced; able to engage in a variety of activities with adults and peers Redirection of an activity is possible; response to changes is more easily possible as experiences occur	Plays repetitively; toys are not used as intended May perseverate on specific feature of toy (spinning wheel on car) or engage in a repetitive action with toys/objects; Interruption of a favorite activity, or of a stimulatory motor behavior (hand flapping, rocking from one foot to another) is often met with extreme resistance Highly restricted interests; experience difficulties in being redirected from high interest toys/objects Exhibits extreme interest with one part of an object or one type of object

(continued)

Typical development	Blind/vision impairment	Autism spectrum disorder and blind/vision impairment (ASDVI)
Impairments in Social Interactions		
Shifts attention from one person/item/activity to another	Exhibits typical flexibility in managing changes in routine	Challenging behaviors escalate when experiencing changes in routine or structure; demonstrate inflexibility when transitioning between activities
		Stereotypic behaviors occur throughout life and are difficult to break
		Behaviors increase with anxiety and with stressful situations; they can be very difficult to redirect
		May perseverate on a single item, idea, or person; may demonstrate rigid performance of seemingly nonfunction routine
		May show aggressive or violent behavior or injure self; may throw frequent tantrums for no apparent reason
Responses to Sensory Information		
Turns head toward sounds (3–6 months)	Poor posture often seems due to lack of visual model	Unusual reactions to physical sensations, such as being overly sensitive to touch or underresponsive to pain; sight, hearing, touch, pain, smell, taste may be affected to a lesser or greater degree
Feeds self with spoon, drinks from a cup (12–18 months)	Interests may be restricted due to lack of vision; interests expand with experiences	
Moves body in time to music (18–24 months)		
Puts on clothing with a little help (4–5 years)	Little delay in motor development until the onset of locomotion	Unusual postures and hand movements are common; they can be very difficult to redirect
Jumps, runs, throws, climbs using good balance (3–4 years)	Can be easily engaged	Perseveration on various sensory stimuli is common
	Lack of visual stimulation, so child often creates own; usually can "redirect" the stimulatory behavior	Tactile defensiveness is common and usually not overcome with time
Tolerates normal range of touch, movement, sounds, smells		
Attends to relevant stimuli	Uses residual senses to gain information	Often appears not to hear or focus

From Gense, D., & Gense, M. (2002). *Autism spectrum disorder in learners with blindness/vision impairments: Comparison of characteristics* (Rev. ed.). Washington, DC: Heldref Publications; originally published by RE:view (1994, Summer); adapted by permission.

Control of the Environment and the Self in Relation to It

The third limitation is in the control of the environment and the self in relation to it. A child who is blind cannot glance and see the players on the baseball field; he or she cannot imitate behaviors that typical children with vision learn incidentally, such as learning to walk or using facial or gestural expressions. Visual impairment reduces one's control over knowledge about the reactions of others, and subsequently, students who are blind may become anxious in cooperative learning groups because they feel they are always being observed (Lowenfeld, 1981).

Students with visual impairments and cognitive disabilities, because of their inability to observe stimuli visually, find it especially difficult to imitate others and to synthesize separate skills into meaningful wholes. They also lack the ability to confirm or recall and replicate similar experiences. They are unable to generalize from one environment to another (Barraga & Erin, 2001; Ferrell, 2000; Silberman, 2000; Silberman, Sacks, & Wolfe, 1998). Furthermore, because they are limited in their access to information in the environment, they are less motivated to explore, initiate interactions, or actively participate in daily situations (Chen, 1995). These students learn at slower rates, need more time to acquire new skills, and acquire fewer skills than their peers who have a visual impairment without any additional disabilities (Sacks, 1998).

Impact on Motor Development

Frequently, students with visual loss and cognitive impairments are delayed in their development of gross motor skills because of the combination of their impairments. Many have difficulty rotating parts of their bodies such as their heads and trunks; for example, a student who only has peripheral vision and no central vision may be unable to see an object that the teacher places on the left side of his food tray or desk because he cannot rotate his head. Some students are unable to walk from the desk to the cubby in the classroom. A review of research related to delays in gross motor development in infants with visual impairments has shown that it is the combination of vision loss and the lack of sufficient opportunities, motivation, and encouragement that interferes with the onset of locomotor activities such as crawling and walking (Adelson & Fraiberg, 1974; Fraiberg, 1968; Hart, 1983; Warren, 2000).

Many students with visual impairments and physical disabilities such as cerebral palsy also have difficulties with motor movements, resulting in abnormal movement patterns and problems with balance and coordination. Because of their limited range of motion and abnormal movement patterns, these students may have difficulty moving their heads and/or eyes to visually track across midline and also to scan what is happening in their environment, including the gym, cafeteria,

Table 10.2. Specific eye conditions and diseases with corresponding adaptations

Eye condition	Physical characteristics,[1] medical treatment,[2] and/or cause[3]	Possible resulting effect on vision	Adaptations	Educational considerations
Albinism	[1]Total or partial lack of pigment causing abnormal optic nerve development, may or may not affect the skin color. Can be complete or partial albinism or ocular albinism. May be sensitive to exposure to the sun. [3]Hereditary: May be autosomal recessive or X-linked.	Decreased visual acuity, photophobia, high refractive error, astigmatism, nystagmus, central scotomas, and strabismus.	Magnification, moving close to the object viewed, high contrast, tinted lenses, sunglasses and eyeshades or a cap with a brim, diffused lighting coming from behind the student, reduction of glare, enhanced print, corrective lenses, magnifiers/telescopes for distant vision.	Lighting conditions will need to be controlled to ensure optimal classroom performance. Teacher should not stand in front of the window or the light source when teaching or speaking to the student. High-contrast line markers or templates may be helpful for reading, finding math problems, or locating other important information. Print copies of overheads may need to be provided. Eye fatigue may occur, especially when doing close work. Difficulty with depth perception may occur.
Amblyopia ex anopsia (Lazy eye)	[1]Reduced visual functioning in one eye that causes the student to use only one eye instead of both. [2]With young children, eye exercises, occlusion, or patching of one eye and surgery may help. [3]Caused by disease, strabismus, unequal	Monocularity, some field loss, poor or absent depth perception, may develop blindness in one eye.	Good contrast and glare reduction.	Close work may result in loss of place, eye fatigue, blurring of print, poor concentration. Frequent rest periods may be needed when doing close work. Classroom seating should favor the student's functional eye.

(continued)

Table 10.2. *(continued)*

Eye condition	Physical characteristics,[1] medical treatment,[2] and/or cause[3]	Possible resulting effect on vision	Adaptations	Educational considerations
Amblyopia ex anopsia (Lazy eye) *(continued)*	refractive errors (anisometropia), or opacities of the lens or cornea.			The student may have difficulty with inaccurate reach with steps and drop-offs and other physical activities, and may need more time to adjust to new situations. Familiarization with the environment can ease the awkwardness and help to anticipate distances and heights.
Aniridia	[1]Total or partial absence of the iris. Often patients with aniridia have Wilms' Tumor. [3]Hereditary: Usually is autosomal dominant, but could be autosomal recessive as well.	Decreased visual acuity, photophobia, and field loss that corresponds to the areas where the iris is absent. Cataracts and glaucoma are frequently present. Vision may fluctuate depending on lighting conditions and glare.	Cosmetic contact lenses that create an artificial pupil, tinted lenses, sunglasses and eyeshades, dim lighting, rheostats and lighting controls, magnification.	Lighting conditions will need to be controlled to ensure optimal classroom performance. Teacher should not stand in front of the window or the light source when teaching or speaking to the student. Print copies of overhead transparencies can be helpful. Give extra time to adapt to change in lighting. Be sensitive to eye fatigue.
Anophthalmos, Anophthalmia	[1]Absence of one or both eyeballs. [3]Hereditary, associated with chromosomal variation.	Total blindness, if both eyes are affected.	Prosthetic eyes.	If both eyes are affected, tactual and auditory modes will be used.

(continued)

442

Aphakia	[1]Absence of the lens [3]Usually caused when the lens is surgically removed due to cataracts	Inability to accommodate, may have depth perception problems	Contact lenses, good contrast and lighting, magnification, enlargement, or bringing items closer to the eye	Lights with rheostats and adjustable arms are helpful for close work. Sunvisors can be worn indoors. If contact lenses or glasses are prescribed, they should be worn.
Cataracts	[1]Opacity or cloudiness of the lens, which restricts the passage of light, usually bilateral. Immature or incipient cataracts are only slightly opaque, while mature cataracts are so opaque that the fundus cannot be seen and the pupil may be white. [2]Surgical removal is usually recommended when the cataract becomes mature. Intraocular lens implants or corneal contact lenses may be used after surgery. [3]Caused by injury or trauma, drugs, malnutrition or rubella during pregnancy; aging, some eye diseases (e.g., uveitis, glaucoma, retinitis pigmentosa, retinal detachment) and heredity. May be autosomal dominant or X-linked.	Reduced acuity, blurred vision, poor color vision, photophobia, and sometimes nystagmus. Visual ability fluctuates according to light. Squint or strabismus may be early manifestations of congenital cataracts. Amblyopia may result if not corrected. After surgery the eye(s) cannot accommodate without lens prescriptions.	Magnification, enlargement or bringing the materials closer to the eyes. Eccentric viewing may be helpful. Lighting should come from behind the student and glare should be avoided. If cataracts are centrally located, near vision will be affected and bright light may be a major problem. Low level of illumination may be preferred. If cataracts are in the peripheral area, bright light may be needed to close the pupil and allow the iris to cover most of the cataract area.	Teacher should not stand in front of the window or the light source when teaching or speaking to the student. Lights with rheostats and adjustable arms are helpful for close work. If contact lenses or glasses are prescribed, they should be worn. Time may be needed for adjustment to different lighting situations. Rest periods may be needed when doing close work and variation of near and distant tasks can prevent tiring.

(continued)

443

Table 10.2. *(continued)*

Eye condition	Physical characteristics,[1] medical treatment,[2] and/or cause[3]	Possible resulting effect on vision	Adaptations	Educational considerations
Coloboma	[1]A birth defect that causes a notch or cleft in the pupil, iris, ciliary body, lens, retina, choroid or optic nerve that occurs during fetal development. A "keyhole pupil" often occurs. [3]Hereditary: autosomal dominant.	Decreased acuity, photophobia, nystagmus, strabismus; field loss occurs if it extends to the retina. Cataracts, refractive errors and problems with depth perception may occur. Glaucoma can develop in later life.	Magnification, average or bright light with no glare, cosmetic contact lenses which create an artificial pupil, telescopes for distance viewing, sunglasses and eyeshades if the coloboma is in the iris.	High-contrast line markers or templates may be helpful for reading, finding math problems or locating other important information.
Color Deficiency or Color Blindness	[1]Cone malformation, macular deficiency, partial or total absence of cones. [3]Hereditary: X-linked or caused by retinal disease or poisoning.	Difficulty or inability to see colors and detail, photophobia, nystagmus, macular deficiencies, central field scotomas, normal peripheral fields.	High contrast, tinted lenses, sunglasses or eyeshades, diffused illumination without glare.	Avoid activities dependent on color or discrimination. Alternative techniques for interpreting color will need to be taught (e.g., the position of the red and green lights in a traffic signal, using color identification tags on clothing).
Corneal Ulcers	[1]An open sore or scarring on the cornea. [2]Medication and sometimes scraping or removing the ulcer. If scarring is extensive, a corneal transplant may be necessary. [3]Caused by bacteria, viruses, fungi, vitamin deficiency, a hypersensitive reaction, or lack of tears.	Can appear on any part of the cornea with resulting impairment, blurred vision, and reduced central acuity and can lead to blindness.	Eccentric viewing, good lighting and contrast, magnification.	Lights with rheostats and adjustable arms are helpful for close work.

(continued)

444

(continued)

Cortical Visual Impairment	[1] Damage to the visual cortex or the posterior visual pathways. Pervasive neurological disorders such as cerebral palsy, epilepsy, hydrocephalus, learning disabilities, or deafness may be present. Occasionally optic nerve atrophy, optic nerve hypoplasia, retinal abnormalities and other ocular lesions occur. Spatial confusion is common. [3] Caused by anoxia at birth, a head injury, infections of the central nervous system (e.g., encephalitis and meningitis), shunt failure, or a genetic malformation.	Fluctuation in visual functioning, eye structure may be healthy and intact, sometimes absence of nystagmus, inattention to visual stimuli, preference of touch over vision as the primary exploratory sense, difficulty seeing objects or pictures which are placed close together, difficulty discriminating figure-ground, may have more peripheral than central vision or vice versa. Color perception is generally intact. Visual improvement sometimes occurs over a period of time after the initial insult to the brain. Light gazing frequently occurs. Students may bring objects close to their eyes to block out the extraneous visual clutter in order to concentrate more easily on the object.	High illumination, bright contrast in materials, using consistent visual cues throughout different settings such as school, home and the community. A combination of reading media may be necessary.	Most students who have a cortical visual impairment also have multiple impairments. It is necessary to determine which sensory system gives most accurate information to the student and then pair visual skills with that system. Visual input must be controlled to prevent "visual overloading." Visual images should be simple and presented in isolation. Repetition and routines are very helpful. Tell students what they are seeing and encourage them to feel it and explore it while learning about it. Color coding simple pictures or shapes gives an additional cue for recognition. Restrict the number of people who are directly involved in intervention. When preparing reading materials, use a contrasting paper, template, or marker to block out some of the visual information, or space objects farther apart on a page. Demonstrate how to use a finger to

Table 10.2. *(continued)*

Eye condition	Physical characteristics,[1] medical treatment,[2] and/or cause,[3]	Possible resulting effect on vision	Adaptations	Educational considerations
Cortical Visual Impairment *(continued)*				move from one object to the next on a page. Simplify illustrations. Fluctuations in visual performance may be reduced by eliminating tiredness, extraneous noise and other distractors. It may be necessary to turn off a light or use diffused lighting to get students to focus on a task.
Diabetic Retinopathy	[1]Both juvenile onset and maturity onset diabetes can cause changes in the blood vessels of the retina, causing hemorrhaging in the retina and vitreous, sensory loss in the feet and hands, and possible retinal detachment and blindness. [2]Caused by diabetes mellitus. Dietary controls and insulin treatments may be needed to control the diabetes. [3]Can be hereditary: multifactorial.	Sensitivity to glare, double vision, lack of accommodation, fluctuating acuity, diminished color vision, defective visual fields, floating obstructions in the vitreous, retinal detachment. If hemorrhages recur, vision may fluctuate.	Good lighting and contrast, magnification, closed-circuit television.	Stress and pressure to perform can negatively affect stabilization of blood glucose. Tactual sensation is often poor and reflexes can be slow. Diet can influence attentiveness. Students with advanced sensory loss in their hands and feet may not be able to read braille and may not sense drop-offs.

Enucleation	[1] The anterior chamber or the entire globe of the eye is surgically removed from the orbit. [2] Prosthetic eyes or scleral shells are usually recommended. [3] Caused by accident or trauma, malignancy, or severe pain or disfigurement in a blind eye	If one eye is removed, there is no depth perception. If the remaining eye is impaired, the condition is more serious.	Prosthetic eyes. If one eye remains, good contrast and reduction of glare may help. More time may be needed to adjust to new situations.	Lack of depth perception may result in inaccurate reach, and difficulty with steps and drop-offs. Familiarization with the environment can ease awkwardness and help to anticipate distances and heights. Classroom seating should favor the student's functional eye.
Glaucoma	[1] An eye disease that causes increased pressure in the eye because of blockage in the normal flow of the fluid in the aqueous humor. [2] Eye drops are prescribed and must be used regularly to reduce pressure. Surgery may be needed. [3] Caused by changes in the lens or uveal tract, trauma, reaction to certain medications, surgical procedures or heredity. If inherited: autosomal recessive, autosomal dominant, or multifactorial.	May cause fluctuating visual functioning, peripheral field loss, poor night vision, photophobia, difficulty reading or seeing large objects at close range, decreased sensitivity to contrast, pain or headaches, eye redness, hazy cornea, or wide open pupil. Can lead to degeneration of the optic disc and blindness if untreated.	Sunglasses and eyeshades, lamps with rheostats or adjustable lighting to provide good quality lighting with no glare, good contrast, magnifiers, closed-circuit television, absorptive lenses.	Fluctuations in visual performance can be frustrating to the student. Expectations may need to be adjusted accordingly. Stress and fatigue have a negative effect on visual performance. Teachers should be alert to symptoms of pain and increased pressure. If medication is prescribed, it should be taken regularly. Travel in unfamiliar places may be difficult.
Keratoconus	[1] The cornea becomes cone shaped. Can be found with retinitis pigmentosa, Down syndrome, Marfan syndrome, and aniridia. Seems to be congenital	Decreased distance vision, astigmatism, sensitivity to glare, distortion of entire visual field, possible corneal rupture and can lead to blindness.	Contact lenses are used to retard the bulging of the cornea in the early stages. Good contrast and lighting; avoid glare.	Avoid activities that could cause corneal damage such as contact sports and swimming in heavily chlorinated water.

(continued)

Table 10.2. *(continued)*

Eye condition	Physical characteristics,[1] medical treatment,[2] and/or cause,[3]	Possible resulting effect on vision	Adaptations	Educational considerations
Keratoconus *(continued)*	and bilateral. Usually has onset in young adulthood. [2]Corneal transplants are often necessary. [3]Seems to be inherited (autosomal recessive) but most cases do not show a definite genetic pattern.			
Leber's Congenital Amaurosis	[1]A form of retinitis pigmentosa causing degeneration of the macula occurring at or shortly after birth and progressive central field loss; abnormal corneas and cataracts may be present. [3]Hereditary: autosomal recessive.	Central and peripheral vision can be affected; loss of color vision and detail, nystagmus is present. Excessive rubbing of eyes is characteristic.	Eccentric viewing using peripheral vision, magnification to enlarge the image beyond the scotoma, enlargement of materials or bringing materials closer to the eye, diffused less intense light may permit the eyes to enlarge the pupil so more area can be viewed, telescopes for distance vision, tinted glasses, sunglasses and eyeshades, closed-circuit television with reversed polarity, adjustable lighting without glare.	High contrast line markers or templates may be helpful for reading, finding math problems or locating other important information. Teachers should not stand in front of a window or light source when teaching or speaking to the student. Lights with rheostats and adjustable arms are helpful for close work. Fatigue can become a problem.
Leber's Optic Atrophy	[1]A rare disease characterized by rapidly progressive optic atrophy,	Reduced central acuity, fluctuating visual performance, blurred	High illumination, enlarged print, magnification, high contrast.	Avoid visual clutter; images should be simple and presented in

448

Condition	Description	Effect on Vision		
	which occurs in young men and rarely in women and may include other types of central nervous system involvement. [3]Hereditary: X-linked recessive.	vision, color vision may be impaired; visual perception may be impaired.		isolation. When teaching, avoid standing in front of a busy background and wearing busy patterns. Modify expectations to accommodate fluctuating visual performance.
Macular Disease, Macular Degeneration (Age-Related Macular Degeneration), Congenital Macular Disease	[1]Progressive or degenerating damage to the central part of the retinal cones. Can be "juvenile" (occurring before the age of 7) or "senile." [3]Hereditary: multifactorial.	Affects central vision, photophobia, poor color vision, normal peripheral vision.	Eccentric viewing using peripheral vision, magnification to enlarge the image beyond the scotoma, enlargement of materials or bringing materials closer to the eye, diffused less intense light may permit the eyes to enlarge the pupil so more area can be viewed, telescopes for distance vision, tinted glasses, sunglasses and eyeshades, closed-circuit television with reversed polarity, adjustable lighting without glare.	High-contrast line markers or templates may be helpful for reading, finding math problems or locating other important information. Teachers should not stand in front of a window or light source when teaching or speaking to the student. Lights with rheostats and adjustable arms are helpful for close work. Fatigue can become a problem. Students may need to be seated near the chalkboard.
Microphthalmos, Microphthalmia	[1]A congenital birth defect that causes one or both eyes to be abnormally small. May occur with other congenital abnormalities such as club foot, additional fingers or toes, webbed fingers or toes, polycystic kidneys, and cystic liver.	Decreased visual acuity, photophobia, may have fluctuating visual abilities. May result in cataracts, glaucoma, aniridia, and coloboma.	Average or bright light with no glare, good contrast, may need magnification.	Fluctuations in visual performance can be frustrating to the student and expectations may need to be adjusted accordingly. Be alert for stress and fatigue.

(continued)

Table 10.2. *(continued)*

Eye condition	Physical characteristics,[1] medical treatment,[2] and/or cause[3]	Possible resulting effect on vision	Adaptations	Educational considerations
Microphthalmos, Microphthalmia *(continued)*	[3]Hereditary: most frequently recessive, sometimes dominant.			
Nystagmus	[1]Involuntary eye movements that can be horizontal, vertical, circular, or mixed. Can be elicited when someone watches certain kind of moving objects. [2]Muscle surgery may be helpful. [3]Causes are often unknown but can be hereditary (autosomal recessive) or caused by neurological or inner ear disturbances.	Inability to maintain steady fixation, reduced visual acuity, fatigue, vertigo.	Shifting gaze or head tilting may help to find the "null point" that shows the nystagmus.	Stress and spinning or other rhythmic movements increase nystagmus, and should be avoided when visual functioning needs to be maximized. Close work causes fatigue and visual tasks should be varied to provide rest for the eyes. Line markers, rulers, typoscopes, and other templates may be helpful to keep the place on the page. Good lighting and contrast are helpful.
Optic Atrophy, Optic Nerve Atrophy	[1]Dysfunction of the optic nerve resulting in the inability to conduct electrical impulses to the brain causing loss of vision. The optic disc becomes pale, and there is a loss of pupillary reaction. [3]Caused by disease, pressure on the optic nerve, trauma, glaucoma, toxi-	Fluctuating visual performance, blurred vision, color vision may be impaired, visual perception may be impaired.	High illumination, enlarged print, magnification, high contrast; braille and tactual materials may be needed.	Avoid visual clutter; images should be simple and presented in isolation. When teaching avoid standing in front of a busy background and wearing busy patterns. Modify expectations to accommodate fluctuating visual performance. Vision stimulation pro-

Optic Atrophy, Optic Nerve Atrophy *(continued)*	city or heredity; if inherited: dominant.		gramming is essential for young children to help them learn how to interpret what they see.
Optic Nerve Hypoplasia	[1] A congenital nonprogressive anomaly in which the optic nerve head appears small and gray or pale and is often surrounded by a mottled yellow halo bordered by a dark ring of pigment, called the "double ring sign." There is often indication of abnormalities of the midline structures of the visual system, such as the corpus callosum, causing midline deficiencies. There is often a dramatic asymmetry between the two optic heads. Central nervous system and endocrine anomalies, cerebral palsy and mental retardation also can occur. [3] An insult to the prenatal central nervous system. Commonly found with fetal alcohol syndrome, frequently found in first-born children of very young mothers. May be genetic and can be caused by trauma.	Decreased visual acuity which may vary from light perception to normal acuity, variable field defects, nystagmus.	Avoid visual clutter, images should be simple and presented in isolation. When teaching, avoid stancing in front of a busy background and wearing busy patterns. Modify expectations to accommodate fluctuating visual performance. Vision stimulation programming is essential for young children to help them learn how to interpret what they see.

(continued)

451

Table 10.2. (continued)

Eye condition	Physical characteristics,[1] medical treatment,[2] and/or cause[3]	Possible resulting effect on vision	Adaptations	Educational considerations
Papilledema	[1]A swelling of the optic disk caused by pressure in the skull; optic atrophy may occur. [3]Caused by cerebral tumors, reaction to drugs, abscesses, subdural hematoma, or hydrocephalus.	The blind spot is enlarged, but visual fields and visual acuity are otherwise normal. If optic atrophy occurs, slight to total loss of vision can result.	If optic atrophy occurs, high illumination, enlarged print, magnification, high contrast.	If optic atrophy occurs, avoid visual clutter; images should be simple and presented in isolation. When teaching, avoid standing in front of a busy background and wearing busy patterns. Modify expectations to accommodate fluctuating visual performance.
Ptosis	[1]Drooping of the eyelid; may be unilateral or bilateral, constant or intermittent. [2]Medication may be called for with myasthenia gravis; surgery may be needed if the condition is severe. [3]Caused by heredity, damages to the muscle or nerves, swelling, or tumors.	Reduced visual field may cause amblyopia	Frames can be worn that have a wire crutch that elevates the lid	Position and placement for activities may affect visual efficiency.
Retinal Detachment	[1]Parts of the retina pull away from the supporting structure of the eye and atrophy. [2]The retina may be reattached if little time has transpired. [3]Caused by diabetes, a	Field loss, blurred vision, scotomas or blind spots, possibly loss of central vision; myopia and strabismus often occur when there is remaining vision. When the retinal	Magnification for close work, telescopes for distance viewing, eccentric viewing, high illumination. Eliminate glare.	Avoid contact sports and any physical activity that may result in a sudden jar of the head to prevent further detachment.

452

(continued)

Retinal Detachment *(continued)*	blow to the head, trauma, or degenerative myopia.	detachment is in the central area, see the adaptations and educational considerations in macular disease. When the detachment is in the periphery, see the adaptations and educational considerations in retinitis pigmentosa.		
Retinitis pigmentosa	[1]A progressive disorder that causes degeneration primarily of the light sensitive cells in the periphery of the retina. There are numerous diseases grouped together which damage the retina in this way but manifest additional different characteristics. These include: Usher syndrome, Leber's congenital amaurosis, Laurence-Moon-Biedl syndrome, and Bassen-Kornzweig syndrome. [3]Usually hereditary: autosomal dominant, autosomal recessive, or X-linked.	Loss of peripheral vision, night blindness, tunnel vision, decreased acuity and depth perception, spotty vision because of retinal scarring, and photophobia. Cataracts can develop. May be accompanied by myopia, vitreous opacities, cataracts, or keratoconus. Total blindness occurs in some cases.	High illumination with no glare, absorptive lenses, infrared viewing devices, prism glasses to increase visual field, closed-circuit television for maximum contrast.	Physical activities and mobility may be restricted by low light situations such as bad weather and nighttime. Teach organized search patterns using a "grid" pattern to aid the student in locating objects or visual targets. Students may need to be seated farther away to increase their visual field. Precautions should be taken to prevent retinal detachment.
Retinoblastoma	[1]A malignancy of the retina in early childhood which usually requires enucleation and can occur in one or both eyes.	If one eye is removed, there is no depth perception. If the remaining eye is impaired, the condition is more serious. The first sign of the disease may be strabis-	Prosthetic eyes.	The absence of depth perception may result in inaccurate reach, and difficulty with steps and drop-offs. Students may

Table 10.2. *(continued)*

Eye condition	Physical characteristics,[1] medical treatment,[2] and/or cause,[3]	Possible resulting effect on vision	Adaptations	Educational considerations
Retinoblastoma *(continued)*	[2]Surgery, radiotherapy, chemotherapy, cryotherapy, or photocoagulation may be helpful. Bilateral retinoblastoma has increased risk of developing other tumors. Regular physical examinations are encouraged. [3]Hereditary: autosomal dominant.	mus (esotropia or exotropia).		have good spatial awareness due to early vision. Many have cognitive and academic abilities at the high and low extremes.
Retinopathy of Prematurity (Retrolental fibroplasia)	[1]A curtailment of retinal blood vessel development in premature infants that can lead to bleeding, scarring, and retinal detachment. Can range from minimal damage to complete blindness. [2]Treatments include vitamin E therapy, photocoagulation procedures, cryotherapy, scleral buckling procedures, and vitrectomy, but none are totally successful. Some cases resolve themselves without intervention.	Decreased visual acuity, severe myopia, possible retinal detachment, spotty vision strabismus, retinal scarring, field loss, possible glaucoma.	High illumination, magnification for close work, telescopes for distance viewing, closed-circuit television.	Students may have brain damage resulting in behavior problems and/or developmental delays. Precautions should be taken to prevent retinal detachment. Early intervention and sensory stimulation are important.

Condition	Characteristics	Effects on Vision	Aids/Devices	Educational Implications
Retinopathy of Prematurity (Retrolental fibroplasia) (continued)	[3]Primary contributors are low birthweight, early gestational age, and duration and administration of oxygen.			
Rod Monochromacy (Achromatopsia)	[1]Cones are absent or abnormal, resulting in the absence of color vision. [3]Hereditary: autosomal recessive or X-linked.	Poor visual acuity but near vision is usually better than distance vision. Nystagmus and photophobia improve with age. Colors are seen as shades of gray.	Tinted lenses, reduced lighting.	Students will not be able to perceive colors but may learn to make color judgments based on brightness. Alternative techniques for interpreting color will need to be taught (e.g., the position of the red and green lights in a traffic signal using color identification tags on clothing).
Strabismus	[1]The inability of both eyes to look directly at an object at the same time, a muscle imbalance, often secondary to other visual impairments. [2]With young children, eye exercises, occlusion or patching of the good eye or surgery may help. [3]Hereditary: multifactorial.	Affects binocular vision, depth perception and eye–hand coordination. There are different types of strabismus: **esophoria**—a tendency for one or both eyes to turn inward, **esotropia** or "crossed eyes"—an inward deviation of one eye in relation to the other, **exophoria**—a tendency for one or both eyes to turn outward, **exotropia** or "walled eyes"—an outward deviation of one eye in relation to the other, **hypertropia**—a tendency for one or	Prismatic glasses, eccentric viewing, some students may use one eye for distance tasks and one eye for near tasks.	Close work may result in loss of place, eyestrain, blurring of print, poor concentration. Frequent rest periods may be needed when doing close work. Students may have difficulties in physical activities and may need more time to adjust to unfamiliar visual tasks. Classroom seating should favor the student's stronger eye.

(continued)

Table 10.2. (continued)

Eye condition	Physical characteristics,[1] medical treatment,[2] and/or cause,[3]	Possible resulting effect on vision	Adaptations	Educational considerations
Strabismus (continued)		both eyes to turn upward, **hyperopheria**—a deviation of one eye upward, **hypophoria**—a tendency for one or both eyes to turn downward, and **hypotropia**—a tendency for one eye to turn downward lower than the other. May cause eyestrain and difficulty following fast moving objects, tracking, fixating, and scanning.		
Toxoplasmosis	[1]Inflammation of the retina and choroid which causes scarring. Congenital toxoplasmosis infects the fetus in utero; acquired toxoplasmosis can develop any time. [2]Anti-inflammatory medications, photocoagulation, cryotherapy. [3]Caused by microorganisms found in animal feces and raw meat.	Field loss, scotomas or blind spots, possibly loss of central vision, and squint. When the retinal damage is to the central area, see the adaptations and educational considerations in macular disease. When the damage is in the periphery, see the adaptations and educational considerations in retinitis pigmentosa.	Microscopes, telescopes, eccentric viewing.	High-contrast line markers or templates may be helpful for reading, finding math problems, or locating other important information.

This is a partial listing of eye conditions and diseases, which can be found in its entirety on pages 123–150 in *Low Vision: A Resource Guide with Adaptations for Students with Visual Impairments* (2nd ed.) by N. Levack, G. Stone, and V. Bishop (1994). Adapted with permission of the Texas School for the Blind and Visually Impaired, Austin, Texas.

or classroom. These children also have delays in fine motor skills in using their arms, hands, and fingers.

Vision plays an important role in encouraging infants and young children to have physical contact with objects in close range. Because of their lack of vision, many children with visual impairments and other disabilities have poor motor coordination, are not motivated, and might have limited opportunities to reach for, grasp, and release objects (Silberman, 2000). These delays in fine motor development also hinder development of daily living skills such as eating, dressing, and grooming. Furthermore, children with such delays may have difficulty grasping and releasing their book bags and materials used in the classroom.

Impact on Social Interactions

Children and youth with visual impairments and cognitive impairments have difficulties with social interactions. Vision plays an important role in perceiving and generating responses to a smile or a grimace, and infants who are blind may not smile or laugh readily without specific interventions (Sacks & Silberman, 2000a; Warren, 2000). A variety of gaze behaviors, such as eye-to-eye contact, guides parents in responding appropriately to their infants and engaging in interactive routines. Without eye contact, children and youth with visual impairments are unable to respond to social signals of others and therefore, opportunities for reciprocal interactions are either nonexistent or limited (Frame, 2000; Kirkwood, 1997). They often are isolated and require specific interventions in areas such as initiating and sustaining interactions, turn taking, and making choices in order to interact with other peers with and without disabilities in their classroom (Silberman, 2000).

Some children with visual impairment, including those with multiple impairments, engage in stereotypic or self-stimulatory behaviors such as repetitive body movements, rocking, eye rubbing and pressing, hand flapping, and side-to-side head turning. One theory as to why these children exhibit more of these behaviors than children who are sighted, particularly those behaviors that are directed more to the eyes, is that they increase or decrease levels of stimulation (Bambring & Troster, 1992; Jan, Good, Freeman, & Espezel, 1994); others exhibit such behaviors to alleviate boredom and keep amused (Downing, 1999). When self-stimulatory behaviors are so persistent that they interfere with functional activities throughout the day, formal interventions using applied behavioral analysis may be necessary (Mar & Cohen, 1998).

Impact on Communication Skills

With regard to the development of communication skills, vision plays an important role in facilitating communication. As indicated, eye contact facilitates contact with the environment and communicative interchanges between parent and child. Parents and other caregivers do not receive the communicative signals necessary for beginning communicative interactions and exchanges. Language is a critical connector to other people; it is a means of building social relationships (Barraga & Erin, 2001). A study conducted in the Netherlands has confirmed difficulties with communicative exchanges between children with both visual and auditory impairments and their teachers and caregivers (Janssen, Riksen-Walraven, & Van Dijk, 2003).

Children with visual impairments and cerebral palsy have more difficulties with expressive and nonverbal forms of communication. Some who retain primitive reflexes have difficulty with the muscles that control the mouth and are unable to develop speech, or they have difficulty articulating and slur their words. Their lack of eye contact combined with their inability to move facial muscles makes it difficult to develop appropriate social interactions (Heller, Alberto, Forney, & Schwartzman, 1996; Silberman, 2000).

Symptoms of Possible Visual Impairments

Parents are the primary individuals who will note symptoms that might be indicative of possible visual problems in infants and young children. Some of these symptoms include visual inattention, inconsistent or lack of responses to familiar faces, failure to fixate and follow objects or faces, and presence of abnormalities such as nystagmus or unusual eye movements (Langley, 2004). Teplin (1995) noted additional specific symptoms that, if observed, should be followed up with evaluation by a pediatric ophthalmologist or optometrist.

- Lack of eye contact by 3 months of age with conversational partners
- Lack of visual fixation or following by 3 months of age
- Overreaching or underreaching for objects by 6 months of age
- Persistent lack of coordinated eye movements or sustained crossing of one eye after 4–6 months
- Frequent horizontal or vertical "jerky" eye movements
- Lack of a clear black pupil
- Persistent tearing when not crying
- Sensitivity to bright light
- Drooping of an eyelid that results in an inability to see the pupil
- Any asymmetry of pupillary size
- Obvious abnormality of the shape or structure of the eye

Observable characteristics in school-age children with and without disabilities besides those listed that might also indicate a visual impairment include

- Red-rimmed, swollen, or encrusted eyes

- Excessive blinking

- Itchy eyes

- Tilting or turning the head to one side to see an object

- Squinting or closing one eye to see an object

- Thrusting the head forward to see an object

- Tripping, bumping into objects, or appearing disoriented (Vaughn, Bos, & Schumm, 2003, pp. 156–157)

It is important to note that there are other behavioral characteristics that are unique in students with multiple disabilities that might make a teacher or any member of the collaborative team suspect that the student has a visual impairment. These include finger flicking in front of the eyes; bringing objects to the mouth for exploration; locating objects on sound cues rather than on visual cues; poking, pressing, or rubbing the eyes; or becoming quiet when sounds are presented (Westling & Fox, 2004).

When any of the previously mentioned symptoms appear, students should be referred to eye care specialists for a clinical examination that includes a history, reason for referral, and physical examination of the eyes. This examination should be conducted in an ophthalmologist's or optometrist's office. The results provide information that can be used for diagnosis and treatment of the student's eye condition, but the outcomes of a clinical examination do not provide information on how the student will perform visually in other environments in which variables such as lighting and contrast cannot be controlled (Anthony, 2000).

Vision Screening of Infants and Children with Multiple Disabilities

Several clinical vision screening tests can be administered to infants and children with multiple impairments that do not require a verbal response or character recognition. These tests are the optokinetic nystagmus (OKN), the preferential looking (PL), and electrophysiological testing. The electroretinogram (ERG) and the visual evoked potential (VEP), two electrophysiological tests, are used to determine if the source of the visual problem is in the eyes or in the brain. (Descriptions and purposes of these techniques can be found in Miller et al., 2002, and Orel-Bixler, 1999.)

Functional Vision Assessment

The functional vision assessment (FVA) is usually conducted by certified TVIs and/or COMSs in collaboration with the family and other members of the collaborative team who have an impact on the student's daily life. The FVA supplements the results of a clinical eye examination that is conducted in the office of an ophthalmologist or optometrist. The major purposes of the FVA for students with visual impairments and multiple disabilities are to determine the students' visual performance in a variety of formal and informal environments and to find appropriate strategies that would help to engage students visually during their daily routines in the home and school (Anthony, 2000; Topor & Erin, 2000; Topor, Rosenblum, & Hatton, 2004). Standard screening instruments and procedures are inappropriate for use with children with visual impairments and multiple disabilities who are unable to indicate preferences or make choices. Responses such as blinking, turning one's head, or widening the eyes may be the only verification that a child is aware of changes in the visual environment (Barraga & Erin, 2001). The FVA should be done in different environments, by different members of the collaborative team, and over a period of time. A COMS may want to find out more about the student's vision in the indoor gym and on the outside playground; a TVI might want to evaluate the student's vision in the classroom in order to determine the optimum size and preferred colors of a planned pictorial communication system. The results of the FVA should be presented in concrete terms that are helpful to the team in designing instructional programs with a student with a visual impairment. For example, a report might state, "The student, using a pincer grasp, can pick up the brown raisin on the white table when placed 6 inches away" (Lewis, 2004, p. 465).

Considerations When Conducting Visual Functioning Assessments

A child with a visual impairment and multiple disabilities may need instruction in how to respond to specific visual activities or stimuli before an actual assessment of visual function is administered and recorded. The child may see the target, but he or she may not know how to respond to the teacher's request. For example, a girl with a visual impairment and multiple disabilities may see the pictorial symbols at near distance; however, she does not respond correctly to the direction, "Find the two animals that are the same" because she does not have the concepts of same and different, not because she cannot see the symbols. Knowing how a child learns, communicates, and uses objects is critical to interpreting responses (Zambone et al., 2000).

Sensory functioning is another consideration that needs to be addressed during assessment activities. Some children with visual impairments and multiple disabilities may be able to attend to only one sensory channel at a time; others may require a combination of sensory channels (e.g., visual, auditory, and/or tactile) in order to respond to a visual stimulus (Zambone et al., 2000). One child may visually track a peer walking across the room only if he or she is positioned appropriately and has head control; another child may need sound paired with the visual stimulus in order to visually follow the same peer.

A third consideration relates to 1) recognizing and using the child's communication mode and 2) using appropriate pacing during interactions with the child when conducting an assessment of visual skills. Some students with visual impairments and multiple disabilities are unable to respond verbally and may use alternate modes such as gestures or sounds. Some students may respond immediately; others may need more time to process the directions before responding. In addition, evaluators need expertise in understanding and interpreting the behavioral responses of students who cannot express themselves. For example, a child presented with a brightly colored visual object 14 inches away may become still, move his or her limbs in an excited manner, or vocalize to indicate a visual response to the stimulus (Topor, 1999; Zambone et al., 2000).

Components of a Functional Vision Assessment The FVA usually consists of systematically observing and assessing a student in a variety of familiar and unfamiliar age-appropriate and motivating activities over a period of time in order to obtain the student's best visual capabilities (Erin, 1996). One important area that needs to be included in the FVA assessment report is the background information regarding the student's 1) medical and developmental history that affects his or her use of vision (e.g., medications taken, seizures and seizure patterns), 2) optimum positions (e.g., supine, prone, sidelying) for indicating visual responses, and 3) temperament and biobehavioral states during different activities.

The components of the observational FVA include the following: observation of the eyes; ocular reflexes; oculomotor skills; repetitive behaviors; use of eyeglasses; ability to navigate physical obstacles; near, intermediate, and distance vision; and visual field (Topor et al., 2004). Although a description of each of these components is beyond the purview of this chapter, assessment of several oculomotor skills, adapted from Anthony (2000), that are important for visually attending to routines are presented and described next.

- *Fixation:* The ability to establish and maintain eye gaze on an object (e.g., when a student is looking at a photograph of her brother in a family photo album on the desk). Factors to observe include eye widening or squinting; eye, head, and/or body positioning; and eccentric viewing patterns (e.g., instead of looking directly using central vision at the photograph of her brother, the student turns her head and uses peripheral vision to see the photograph).

- *Tracking:* The ability to visually follow a moving target (e.g., watching a peer walk to the door). Factors to observe include the student's head and body position, the quality of the eye movements (whether they move smoothly and whether the head also moves), and the movement pattern (crossing midline to follow the peer).

- *Shift of gaze:* The ability of the eyes to stop looking at one object and move to a second one at the same or differing distance (e.g., using shift of gaze to make a choice on a communication board of a preferred picture book to read with a peer). Factors to consider include spacing of the objects used, amount of visual clutter, and presence of head movement during shift of gaze.

- *Scanning:* The ability to move one's head and eyes to search for and find a target. The student uses shift of gaze from one object to another in a systematic visual search pattern (e.g., locating one's backpack among several located in the back of classroom). Factors to consider include the breadth of the visual field in searching, amount of visual clutter, and positioning of body in relation to objects.

See Figure 10.2, which describes components of the FVA appropriate for a student with multiple disabilities.

One formal instrument to assess the FVA is the *Individualized Systematic Assessment of Visual Efficiency (ISAVE)*. ISAVE is a comprehensive process for screening and assessing visual behaviors of children with multiple disabilities functioning within the birth to 5-year developmental range (Langley, 1998). Qualified TVIs or members of the collaborative team who are skilled in observing visual behaviors can administer it. ISAVE consists of checklists for each of the components that can be completed during daily routines. It provides strategies for assessing environmental, sensory, perceptual, and physical influences related to the use of vision. The unique features include 1) an ecological assessment of visual behaviors; 2) a component that addresses critical postural, movement, and transitional behaviors that support and contribute to the development of specific visual skills; 3) a component that ascertains whether the child displays the characteristics of CVI, and 4) a component that assists in evaluating and managing the vision in children who only have light perception in both eyes. (Several additional valuable resources that provide comprehensive strategies for conducting the FVA with children with multiple disabilities can be found in Anthony, 1996; Erin, 1996; Topor et al., 2004; and Zambone, 2000.)

Learning Media Assessment

After completing the FVA, TVIs should conduct a learning media assessment (LMA) with students who are blind or visually impaired and have additional dis-

Visual Conditions and Functional Vision:
Issues for Early Intervention

Session 4: Functional Vision Assessment and Age-Appropriate Learning Media Assessment

Handout J: Individual Sensory Learning Profile

Individual Sensory Learning Profile Interview

Child's name: _____ DOB: _____

Current age: _____ Date: _____

Completed by: _____

Please complete with the child's primary caregiver and/or the child's early interventionist, teacher, and/or therapist.

Background Information

Medical diagnoses:

Current medications and their purpose:

Sensory Profile Questions

Vision

Does the child have a diagnosis as being blind or visually impaired?

Yes _____   No _____

Has the child been diagnosed as legally blind?

Yes _____   No _____

If so, what is the medical diagnosis?

Does the child wear glasses or use other optical devices? If so, please give the prescription and/or details about the devices.

Right _____ Left _____ Both _____

Does the child respond visually to a human face?

Yes _____   No _____

Does the child respond to other visual stimuli?

Yes _____   No _____

If so, what are the characteristics of the visual stimuli?

Illuminating _____   Shiny/light reflective _____   High contrast _____

Pastel colored _____   Brightly colored _____   Familiar _____

Other characteristics or details about visual stimuli: _____

_____

Figure 10.2. Components of the Functional Vision Assessment (FVA) for a student with multiple disabilities. (From Anthony, T.L. [1997]. *Individual sensory learning profile interview.* Unpublished document; used by permission.)

Figure 10.2. *(continued)*

Is there an immediate or delayed response to visual stimulus? Please describe:

What type of environment seems to best support visual responsiveness?

Presentation to midline, left, right, top, bottom of visual field (circle all that apply)

Focal distance (describe in inches or feet) _____

Illumination preferences _____

Familiar settings/items _____   *Quiet* _____   *Low visual clutter* _____

Accompaniment of other sensory stimuli _____

Other environmental preferences including positioning needs for visual attending:

Items that child shows a visual response/preference to

Hearing

Does the child have a diagnosis of being deaf/hard of hearing or having a central auditory processing disorder?

Yes _____   No _____

Does the child wear hearing aids or use other sound amplification devices?

Yes _____   No _____

If yes, please list the listening devices used:

Is there a history of ear infections?

Yes _____   No _____

Does the child attend to auditory stimuli?

Yes _____   No _____

If so, what are the characteristics of the auditory stimuli?

Human voice   *Yes* _____   *No* _____

Environmental sounds   *Yes* _____   *No* _____

Sound volume   *Low* _____   *Moderate* _____   *High* _____

Other characteristics or details about auditory stimuli:

Is there an immediate or delayed response to auditory information? Please describe.

Figure 10.2. *(continued)*

What type of environment seems to best support auditory responsiveness?

   Sound presentation distance (describe in inches or feet) _____

     Quiet _____   *Low noise clutter* _____   *Echolocation boundaries* _____

     Accompaniment of other sensory stimuli _____

Other environmental preferences for auditory responsiveness:

Items that child shows an auditory response/preference to:

Touch/kinesthetic/vestibular

Does the child have a diagnosis of cerebral palsy or other disorder affecting movement?

Yes _____   No _____

Does the child benefit from any orthopedic or special positioning/ambulation/mobility device?

Yes _____   No _____

If yes, please list:

Does the child respond positively or negatively to being touched?

Positively _____   Negatively _____

Please explain preferences or aversions for being touched (e.g., soft, firm, predictable).

Does the child respond positively or negatively to touching people/objects?

Positively _____   Negatively _____

Please explain preferences or aversions for touching people/objects.

Does the child respond positively or negatively to movement?

Positively _____   Negatively _____

abilities to evaluate students' efficiency in visual, tactile, and auditory sensory channels and to assess their potential for and use of literacy skills. It is reasonable to expect that some students who have cognitive impairments might be able to meet a state standard of using reading and writing to accomplish daily practical tasks by reading a tactile label on a can of soup or using a visual symbol to identify one's cubby (Koenig, Holbrook, Corn, DePriest, Erin, & Presley, 2000).

Several factors should be considered when conducting an LMA with this population. First is to have an open mind and consider all literacy options without prejudging a student's abilities. Second is to regard each student as having unique needs and abilities. The third relates to determining each student's literacy goals. One student's goal might be to use a communication board, for which he or she would need to learn either tactile or visual symbols; a goal for another student might be to use a monocular device and read environmental signs to obtain information visually, such as the name of a restaurant or the signs for ladies' or men's room entrances (Koenig et al., 2000).

The TVI and other members of the team should begin doing the LMA by observing and recording information related to the student's use of sensory channels in completing tasks during daily routines. The LMA should pose questions to obtain information on how the student demonstrates the following:

- Recognition of others
- Initiation of reaching response to a person or object
- Exploration, discrimination, and identification of objects
- Use of visual-motor and fine motor skills
- Interest in pictures and books
- Interest in writing tasks
- Identification of names or simple words

Comprehensive procedures for conducting LMAs can be found in Koenig and Holbrook (1995), and Koenig and colleagues (2000).

Environmental Considerations

Several environmental factors affect the visual efficiency of children with visual impairments and other disabilities. It is important for the TVI, COMS, and other members of the collaborative team to observe children in their daily routines in the classroom or home to determine the environmental conditions that either enhance or reduce their visual skills. By modifying the environment, many students are able to participate in activities without becoming visually fatigued and, subsequently, they perform more competently.

Lighting

Some students with visual impairments and multiple disabilities may not be able to express their preferences for lighting conditions, nor can they move to where they might see best. The type, amount, and position of lighting that is appropriate for each student should be noted during visual activities (Anthony, 2000; Utley, Roman, & Nelson, 1998). It is important to observe whether students with visual impairments and other disabilities prefer natural light, incandescent lighting, or fluorescent lighting when performing visual tasks. Some might show fatigue in rooms in which fluorescent lighting is used. A TVI or COMS should observe whether a student with a visual impairment moves slower or quicker when moving through a dimly or brightly lit corridor from the classroom to the lunchroom. Also, he or she should note whether the student performs differently on visual tasks during morning or afternoon sunlight. Students should always face away from the window when looking at people or objects. Some students with visual impairments and multiple disabilities may see better when overhead illumination in the room is reduced, either by using a personal desk lamp or by having a teacher or peer shine a light on the objects on their desks. The use of window shades or blinds and rheostats on overhead lights also may increase visual efficiency for some students (Anthony, 2000; Corn, DePriest, & Erin, 2000; Levack et al., 1994).

Color and Contrast

One of the most effective techniques for increasing visual efficiency is to integrate enhanced contrast into daily routines by making the environment more visible (Utley et al., 1998). For example, during mealtime routines, black non-gloss placemats can be used under yellow dishes. During a leisure time activity incorporating O&M skills, dark brown-colored furniture in the play room can be contrasted with lightly stained floor color or beige carpeting to make them each more noticeable, which will help students orient and navigate more easily.

Glare

Some students with visual impairments and other disabilities have difficulty with visual tasks because of glare. Environmental modifications and modifications to materials and work surfaces can be made to reduce interference from glare on a student's visual activities. For example, students should sit with their backs to windows; walls should have a matte finish; monitors on closed-circuit televisions (CCTVs, see Assistive Technology Devices section) or computers should be in positions that are free from glare; and desks or clear acrylic wheelchair trays that have shiny surfaces should be replaced with solid color, light-absorbing cloth. Utley and colleagues (1998, p. 383) presented several excellent examples of routines with suggestions to increase contrast and reduce glare.

Visual Clutter

The classroom and particularly the area around a student's desk should be kept simple. Visual clutter, such as unnecessary materials on the desk, causes confusion and lowers visual efficiency. Furniture should be arranged so that there are wide passageways for wheelchairs; extra pieces of furniture need to be removed. Students with CVI particularly have a difficult time with irrelevant visual materials and are unable to focus on the activity (Levack et al., 1994).

Size and Distance

A consideration related to the environment is the size of objects presented and the distance from the teacher or chalkboard in the classroom. Depending on the etiology of the visual impairment and whether central or peripheral vision is affected, some students will need to be close to the teacher and others will need to be farther back or to one side.

Ambient Noise

The noise level in the classroom or other parts of the school may be unsettling for students with visual impairments and multiple disabilities. The team should observe whether students need a quiet environment in which to perform activities efficiently.

Optical and Nonoptical Devices to Enhance Sensory Functioning

In addition to modifying the learning environment to increase visual efficiency, members of the team can help students with visual impairments, including those with multiple disabilities, to use optical and nonoptical devices to assist them with educational and everyday tasks. Optical devices use lenses to make a visual image larger or smaller or to change its position. Ophthalmologists or optometrists prescribe them, and a TVI or COMS needs to provide instruction in their use. Common devices include various types of magnifiers that are used for near vision tasks, such as reading a picture on a schedule system, and telescopes that are used for obtaining distance information, such as reading a street sign. Corn and colleagues (2000) presented a list of typically prescribed optical devices.

Nonoptical devices to enhance visual functioning are not prescribed by low vision specialists. Many are commercially available and easy to obtain. They include book stands, wide felt-tipped pens and markers, yellow acetate that is placed over a printed page, large-print books, bold-line paper, line markers and reading windows, sun visors, adapted measurement tools, and calculators with large print displays (Spungin, McNear, & Torres, 2002).

Students who are blind or visually impaired with additional disabilities can benefit from devices that enhance other sensory functioning. Devices that enhance auditory functioning include cassette tape and compact disc players, recorded books, talking calculators, voice recorders, audible gym equipment such as beeper balls and goal locators, and other low-tech devices such as talking watches and alarm clocks. Aids that enhance tactile functioning include braille, tactile graphic images, raised-line paper, raised-line drawing boards, tactile markers, braille labelers for tapes and CDs, measurement tools with raised markings, and teacher-made materials using puff paint and tactile stickers. In addition, board games and playing cards in tactile format are available (Spungin et al., 2002).

Assistive Technology Devices

Students with visual impairments, including those with multiple impairments, may benefit from specialized equipment and assistive technology in their classroom, such as the following:

- Braillewriter: This is a mechanical device that is used to produce braille. Some students who are blind may enjoy using the braillewriter to make tactual braille characters simultaneously with their sighted peers who are writing stories with their pens and pencils. The braillewriter has six keys, a space bar, and a carriage return. The student simultaneously presses down combinations of keys to produce tactile symbols.

- Closed-circuit television: CCTV consists of a television camera mounted on a stand to input graphic or print material, and the student can see the enlarged graphic or enlarged print from a monitor. The font size can be modified and students can choose to have a white background with black letters or illustrations or a black background with white letters.

- Computers: Computers are available that are equipped with software and devices for users who are blind or who have low vision. Students who have additional disabilities may also benefit from state-of-the art technology. Screen-reading software with voice output enables students to listen to information that is presented on the screen. Braille translation software and a braille embosser (printer) enables the student, a peer, or a member of the collaborative team to convert information presented on the screen to braille and then print it. Screen enlargement software can modify the size of the images projected on the monitor (Friend & Bursick, 2002).

Classroom Adaptations

The following adaptations and strategies are helpful to teachers in any environment, but they are particularly useful in inclusive classrooms when students with visual impairments and additional disabilities are with their peers without disabilities:

- For safety reasons, keep cabinet doors closed and encourage all students to keep their belongings (e.g., backpacks) under a table so that no one will trip over them.

- Orient students with visual impairments and multiple disabilities to the physical arrangement of the room and, if changes are made, inform these students.

- Teachers or peers should avoid standing with their backs to windows because the glare will prevent the student with low vision from seeing clearly or focusing on them.

- Feel comfortable using words commonly used such as *see* and *look* with a student who is blind. The student sees and looks with his or her hands.

- When approaching a student who is blind, always state one's name and encourage peers in the class to do the same. It is sometimes difficult for these students to identify voices.

- Use verbal cues with the student with a visual impairment such as calling the student by name; he or she may not be aware of facial expressions or body language from those around him or her.

- When praising a student, use a pat on the back or shoulder or a verbal phrase instead of a smile of approval.

- Encourage students with visual impairments and additional disabilities to have good posture and to have eye contact or face-to-face contact with a peer or adult.

- Using a positive manner, discourage mannerisms such as eye-poking, which can damage the student's eye. All members of the collaborative team should do this consistently and as early as possible in order to prevent habits that become difficult to break.

- Modify or replace mannerisms such as rocking with other behaviors that might appear more appropriate to others.

- Students with visual impairments and multiple disabilities should be provided with three-dimensional concrete objects or models during demonstrations and should be positioned near the teacher in order to touch the materials that are being described to the class (Spungin et al., 2002; Torres & Corn, 1990).

The following considerations are important when selecting materials for children with CVI:

- Use high-contrast and primary colors

- Add verbal and tactile clues to visual presentations

- Simplify the environment and avoid crowding

- Use repetition and constancy when presenting objects

- Use movement when presenting objects (Orel-Bixler, 1999)

Expanded Core Curriculum

The expanded core curriculum for students with visual impairments, including those who have severe and multiple disabilities, was introduced by Hatlen (2000). This curriculum encompasses those unique skill areas that need to be systematically and sequentially taught to this population because of the nature of blindness and visual impairment. The eight goal areas of the expanded core curriculum, with examples of specific skills applicable to students with visual impairments and multiple disabilities, are described in the following sections.

Goal Statement 1: Compensatory Skills or Functional Academic Skills Including Communication Modes

Compensatory skills or functional academic skills include maintaining interaction at eye level, using touch cues to initiate or terminate interactions, using universal modes of communication, adapting communication to learner's pace, establishing trust with the learner, and interpreting what is going on in the environment.

Goal Statement 2: Orientation and Mobility

Instruction in O&M focuses on developing body image, mastering spatial and positional concepts and environmental awareness, learning layout of classroom and rooms at home, maintaining contact with the physical environment (e.g., landmarks), moving independently, and using adaptive mobility devices (Lewis, 2004). Students with visual impairments and multiple disabilities should be provided with O&M instruction to help them to become as independent as possible. Even students who are nonambulatory and have difficulty expressing themselves can gain a variety of skills in orienting to their environment and controlling how others move them (Erin, 2000). Because O&M is integrated into almost all daily activities and environments, it is important for the COMS to provide direct training to students, as well as strategies to teachers and other members of the team who work more directly with the students. Classroom teachers can help the team by providing information about the student's preferences for activities and places and by incorporating these preferences into motivating the student to move (Perla & Ducret, 1999).

When determining priority O&M skills to teach, the COMS should become familiar with all of the other assessment records (e.g., medical, psychological, low vision, and hearing evaluations). Because of the emphasis on acquiring practical skills within natural environments, a functional approach to assessment and programming should be implemented that would lead to positive student outcomes in natural environments (Mar, 2002). The team should do an ecological inventory to identify all of the travel environments in the student's daily routine with the steps of each routine recorded. Through discrepancy analysis, the student's performance of each step will be observed to determine which steps the student can do independently, which ones need to be adapted, and which ones should be taught. Instruction needs to be broken down into task-analyzed, meaningful units, and skills should be taught in natural environments at appropriate times of the day; for example, the student should learn the route of traveling to the lunchroom at the end of each morning and not at the end of the day or on arrival at school (Fazzi, 1998). Several students may be using the same route to the lunchroom but each may be learning a different skill. For example, one ambulatory student may be practicing identifying landmarks along the way; one student in a wheelchair may be learning to follow directions given by a peer and to move faster; and another student, moved in the wheelchair by a peer, may be learning to trail the wall with her hand (Barraga & Erin, 2001; Erin, 2000).

An excellent functional assessment tool for recording student skill levels in different travel environments is Teaching Age-Appropriate Purposeful Skills (TAPS) (Pogrund et al., 1993). Each of the five sections of TAPS begins with a list of functional O&M tasks in a particular environment, and then the tasks progress from easy to complex. TAPS is valuable to the COMS in that it provides current levels of performance and guidelines for progress in a variety of natural environments.

Students with visual and motoric impairments should be provided with O&M instruction using such devices as wheelchairs, walkers, adapted canes, or other mobility aids. The COMS, in collaboration with the physical therapist and other members of the team, needs to develop realistic goals to ensure that these students are actively involved in traveling as independently as possible from place to place in familiar environments, using the principles of partial participation. Some steps of a daily activity that a student can achieve through partial participation include locking and unlocking brakes, pointing in the direction of where he or she wants the teacher to turn the wheelchair to go in a certain direction, and assisting in pushing a door open (Smith & Levack, 1999).

It is important for students to be in contact with the physical environment when moving. Some students with visual impairments and multiple disabilities may refuse to use their hands for exploration but will accept holding a long-shaped toy or stick to use to stay in contact with the wall when trailing from the lunchroom to the bathroom. The student can explore doors, openings, corners, and other environmental landmarks. (See also Pogrund et al., 1993, for additional specific techniques for teaching O&M to students using a wheelchair.)

Children with visual impairments and multiple disabilities who are unable to move independently should learn to communicate choices as to where they want to go, learn safety measures, and learn some directionality concepts that enhance knowledge of their own body movement (e.g., turn left toward the voice of the teacher) (Barraga & Erin, 2001).

Some environmental adaptations that are helpful with O&M for students with visual impairments and multiple disabilities include the following:

- Place an identifiable material at level of the student's hand by the doors of rooms such as the classroom, lunchroom, and cafeteria to help students identify these rooms.

- Mark different areas of the classroom with varied textured floor coverings to help the student recognize these areas immediately.

- Mark stair treads, poles, and classroom doors with a contrasting color.

- Keep hall doors closed all the way to prevent injury.

- Provide a storage area for canes and other mobility devices.

Goal Statement 3: Social Interaction Skills

Promoting social interaction skills involves providing opportunities for positive interaction; establishing areas of interest; sharing and providing support; teaching conflict resolution; and fostering skills involving social norms such as facing a peer or teacher when speaking, taking turns, and standing at appropriate distances from peers. Instruction should involve modeling, peer buddies, and peer tutors (Barclay, 1999; Sacks & Silberman 2000b; Sacks, Wolffe, & Tierney, 1998).

Goal Statement 4: Independent Living Skills

Independent living skills include self-care skills (e.g., bathing, toileting) and skills performed in the community (e.g., shopping skills and restaurant skills that include waiting, ordering, and paying a cashier) (Koenig & Holbrook, 2000a). Independent living skills promote independence, are age-appropriate, require active participation to avoid learned helplessness, and are taught only in natural environments in the home and school. Effective strategies in teaching daily living skills involve repeated visual or hand-under-hand kinesthetic demonstrations for systematic instruction, gradual fading of assistance and prompts, and significant periods of practice. (See Chapter 13 for adaptations and strategies related to self-care skills.)

Goal Statement 5: Recreation and Leisure

The component of recreation and leisure includes selecting age-appropriate activities that are incorporated into weekly routines and based on student and family preferences. Considerations include communication modes, appropriate time of day, and orientation to play area. Team members should provide physical guidance as needed, provide immediate feedback, and encourage peer and/or sibling participation. Adapting activities can be done through modifications to 1) the environment (e.g., creating visible/tactual boundaries, lowering height of goals/baskets, orienting student to area); 2) playing object (e.g., modify size, make it softer/harder, use sound/bright color, change the texture or make object heavier/lighter), and 3) game (e.g., modify rules and/or objectives, increase tactile/visual cues) (Lieberman, 1998; Lieberman & Stuart, 2002).

Goal Statement 6: Career Education

Instruction in career education skills begins at the preschool level and continues throughout children's school years. Skills at the preschool level include orienting and attending to a speaker, following one-word directions, taking turns, and using a cubby to store tools. Elementary school students can be taught skills including exchanging pleasantries (e.g., saying "hello" and "thank you" to the bus driver and lunchroom workers), bringing low-vision and assistive devices to classroom, demonstrating socially acceptable behavior such as covering one's mouth when coughing, and helping with household and school chores (e.g., handing out snacks or papers to take home). Career education skills at the middle school level can include identifying major community workers and their roles and making choices about job preferences. High school students can be taught skills such as cleaning up and washing dishes at a restaurant, shredding paper in an office, putting books on shelves, rewinding videotapes and audiotapes in a library, and packaging food in a grocery store (Wolffe, 2000).

Students with visual impairments and multiple disabilities can partially participate with and without assistive devices in many career education activities that result in vocational opportunities. Some of these activities could be in volunteer positions such as greeters at social functions or accepters of funds at charity functions or religious institutions, ushers at movie theatres, and animal feeders at local animal shelters. Students can participate in cooperative assembly-line jobs that provide them with socialization skills and pride in having self-worth. (See Langley, 2000, for additional creative suggestions.)

Goal Statement 7: Assistive Technology

Assistive technology used with students with visual impairments and multiple disabilities ranges from devices as simple as a button or lever switch to more complex devices such as a computer. Through the use of assistive technology, students can acquire developmental milestones such as an understanding of cause and effect. They can also use assistive technology to communicate their choices and requests and to comment on something of interest in their daily routines. Alternative keyboards are used to enhance concept development, picture, and tactual discrimination, and beginning letter and number identification. Some keyboard adaptations are keyboard labels, slant boards, and expanded keyboards with overlays (e.g., IntelliKeys).

Goal Statement 8: Visual Efficiency

Visual efficiency, the extent to which students use their remaining vision in classroom activities and routines, needs to be emphasized in instructional programs. The visual behaviors that need to be enhanced and embedded throughout the students' school day include localizing, fixating, scanning, tracking, shifting gaze, and eye-hand coordination.

STUDENTS WHO ARE DEAF OR HARD OF HEARING WITH ADDITIONAL DISABILITIES

Students who are deaf or hard of hearing with additional disabilities are a diverse group of learners. All of these students have limited access to information that is usually gained through the sense of hearing and fewer opportunities to experience communication and language with others. This section addresses the causes, educational needs, and instructional strategies that will support the classroom teacher to ensure that students who are deaf or hard of hearing with additional disabilities will participate fully in educational programs and, more important, be prepared to participate fully in their future communities.

Definitions

IDEA '97 uses the term *deafness* to mean a

> Hearing loss that is so severe that the child is impaired in processing linguistic information through hearing, with or without amplification, and that

adversely affects a child's educational performance. (34 C.F.R. § 300.7 [c][3] of IDEA 1997).

Hearing impairment is defined as impairment in hearing, whether permanent or fluctuating, that adversely affects a child's educational performance but that is not included under the definition of deafness in this section. (c) (5)

The terms *deaf* and *hard of hearing* are the preferred terms of the Deaf community and are used throughout this section. Each is described more in depth next.

Deaf

Children who are deaf have a hearing loss that is significant enough to interfere with processing linguistic information received through the auditory channel, regardless of whether a hearing aid is worn (Kuder, 2003; McCormick, Loeb, & Schiefelbusch, 2003).

Hard of Hearing

Children who are hard of hearing are able to process linguistic (language) information that they receive though the auditory channel, usually with hearing aids.

Children who are born with a hearing loss are said to be *congenitally deaf or hard of hearing.* Children who develop hearing loss later are said to be *adventitiously deaf* or *hard of hearing.* Children with *prelingual deafness* lost hearing prior to acquiring language, generally regarded as occurring prior to the age of 2 years old. Children with *postlingual deafness* acquire deafness after language is achieved. Some children have a progressive loss, which means that they lose hearing over time. Hearing losses may be *unilateral* (existing in only one ear) or *bilateral* (involving both ears).

Professionals Who Serve Children Who Are Deaf or Hard of Hearing

Students who are deaf or hard of hearing with additional disabilities need the services of professionals associated with the field of deafness. Several are listed next.

Teacher of the Deaf or Hard of Hearing

A teacher of the deaf or hard of hearing may be a classroom teacher or a consultant who serves children who are deaf or hard of hearing, including those who have additional disabilities. In the classroom teacher role, the specialist is responsible for planning and delivering the educational curriculum as well as for providing specific instruction in communication, speech, and audition or listening skills.

In the role of a consultant, this specialist can be expected to explain student audiograms; train the teacher in hearing aid care; coordinate routines for checking and charging hearing aid batteries with the family; check and troubleshoot hearing aids, FM systems, and cochlear implants; make recommendations about communication intervention; and make referrals to the audiologist when needed. The consultant should assist the classroom teacher in providing the child with necessary adaptations and accommodations.

Classroom Teacher

The classroom teacher may be a general education teacher or a teacher prepared in special education but not necessarily in the area of deafness. The classroom teacher is responsible for the provision of the educational curriculum as well as for meeting the child's day-to-day needs such as hearing aid and cochlear implant management. The classroom teacher may not have sufficient skills or training to address all of the needs of a child who is deaf or hard of hearing with additional disabilities. Assistance and support may be needed in order to provide the accommodations and adaptations that are recommended by specialists in sensory areas.

Otologist

The otologist is a physician who specializes in the ear and diseases of the ear. Otologists screen for hearing loss (and then make referrals to the audiologist). They may perform surgical procedures on the ear, including the implantation of cochlear implants (Hardman, Drew, & Egan, 2002).

Audiologist

The educational audiologist can be expected to perform auditory assessment; make medical referrals; ensure appropriate fit of hearing aids; provide auditory training (i.e., teach the child to make maximum use of hearing); teach speech reading (i.e., teach the child to understand the speech of others through visual and tactile input); and offer hearing loss prevention programs, counseling, and guidance for students, teachers, and families (Martin & Clark, 2003). Educational audiologists are often called in to troubleshoot problems with hearing aids (e.g., analyze the cause of feedback, a high-pitched noise that is sometimes emitted from a hearing aid).

Speech and Language Pathologist

The speech and language pathologist (SLP) provides support for the development of communication and language. This specialist works closely with the teacher of the deaf or hard of hearing and the audiologist. This speech or language specialist may provide one-to-one communication instruction with students, group lessons within the classroom, and consultation in communication and language with the classroom teacher. This professional can also be expected to provide information on low and high-tech communication devices and software appropriate for a student who is deaf or hard of hearing.

Sign Language Interpreter

Although this team member is commonly needed for students who are deaf, the sign language interpreter is also needed for some students with additional disabilities. The need for an interpreter hinges on a student's level of language development and the communication skills of professionals in the school environment. Interpreters are beneficial to students who are able to gain information through the process of interpretation. Interpreters serving students who are deaf or hard of hearing with additional disabilities are responsible for adapting to the needs of each student. For example, if the student has a cognitive impairment, the interpreter might need to sign more slowly and reduce or eliminate the use of fingerspelling (hand shapes used to express the letters of the alphabet).

Prevalence of Hearing Loss

Martin and Clark (2003) reported the prevalence of hearing loss in children to be as high as 6 in 1,000. Twenty-five percent of children who are deaf or hard of hearing have one additional disability (Schirmer, 2001), with 9% having a cognitive disability (Heward, 2003).

In addition, neurological disability, physical disability (usually due to cerebral palsy or seizures), and visual impairment are common co-occurring disabilities with hearing loss (Gallaudet Research Institute, 2003).

More than one quarter of the children with mild cognitive impairments also have a sensory loss (either vision or hearing) and more than half with severe cognitive impairments have a sensory loss (Batshaw & Shapiro, 2002; Westling & Fox, 2004).

The Structure of the Ear and How We Hear

The process of hearing is known as *audition*. A sound occurs in the environment and is transmitted as sound waves, which are vibrations in the air. The outer ear gathers the sound waves and sends them down the auditory canal. The sound waves then enter the middle ear and cause the tympanic membrane (eardrum) to move. The malleus (hammer), incus (anvil), and stapes (stirrup) are three tiny bones between the eardrum and the oval window. They are known as the *ossicles* and are set into motion, which results in sound being carried through the

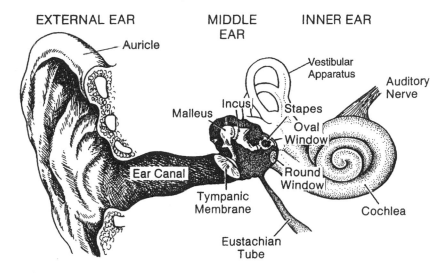

Figure 10.3. Structure of the ear. (From Herer, G.R., Knightly, C.A., & Steinberg, A.G. [2002]. Hearing: Sounds and silences. In M.L. Batshaw (Ed.), *Children with disabilities* [5th ed., p. 196]. Baltimore: Paul H. Brookes Publishing Co.; reprinted by permission.)

oval window into the inner ear. The inner ear includes the cochlea and the semicircular canals. The cochlea is snail shaped and contains fluid that moves in response to the mechanical energy that is generated by the ossicles. The cochlea also contains tiny hair cells that convert mechanical energy to electrical impulses that are moved along by neurons on the auditory nerve to the brain. The brain then interprets the sound waves to give meaning to auditory input (Schirmer, 2001). Figure 10.3 presents the physical structure of the ear (Herer, Knightly, & Steinberg, 2002).

Categorizations of Hearing Loss

Hearing loss is categorized in two ways, by type of loss and by severity of loss. The four types of hearing loss include sensorineural, conductive, mixed, and central hearing loss or central auditory processing disorder. Severity or level of hearing loss can be categorized as mild, moderate, moderate-severe, severe, and profound.

Types of Hearing Loss

The four types of hearing loss are described in more detail here.

1. *Sensorineural loss* occurs when there is damage to the inner ear, auditory nerve, or neural pathways (McCormick et al., 2003; Peterson & Hittie, 2003).

2. *Conductive loss* occurs when there is interference with the movement of sound from the ear canal to the inner ear. Such losses are associated with obstructions or malformations in the outer or middle ear. These might include ear wax, infections, fluid, or problems with the middle ear bones or membranes (Peterson & Hittie, 2003).

3. *Mixed* or *combined hearing loss* describes losses that are both sensorineural and conductive.

4. *Central hearing loss* or *central auditory processing disorder* are terms used to describe the experience of children who appear to hear normally (as evidenced by their physical responses to sound) but struggle with interpreting the meaning of sounds (Kuder, 2003). No physiological cause has been identified within the ear that explains what is described as an *auditory processing problem*. This type of loss is caused by damage to the brain, often from stroke or disease.

Characteristics of children with central hearing loss include poor auditory attention, difficulty listening in the presence of background noise, impaired short-term memory, poor auditory integration, poor auditory sequencing, difficulty understanding rapid speech and other forms of auditory stimuli that have reduced redundancy, and difficulty associating auditory with visual symbols (Hood & Berlin, 1996).

Levels of Hearing Loss

The second way to describe hearing loss is by the severity or level of loss. Levels of hearing loss are defined as mild, moderate, moderate-severe, severe, and profound (Schirmer, 2001). Some texts also describe a slight hearing loss, whereas others do not include the moderate-severe level.

Levels of hearing loss can be depicted on an audiogram, a graph that displays the results of audiological testing. Decibels (dB) represent the relative intensity or loudness of a sound and are recorded along the vertical axis of the audiogram. Children with normal hearing will hear sounds from 0 dB to 130 dB. Frequency, or pitch, is measured by cycles of sound per second, expressed in hertz, and are located along the horizontal axis of the audiogram. Humans hear sounds from 20 Hz to 20,000 Hz (Bowe, 2000). The intensity level at which a student responds to a sound is called the threshold. When a student has a 55 dB loss, he or she is able to hear sounds at 55 decibels of intensity of loudness and above. The audiogram displays the level of loudness needed for different frequencies to be heard. Therefore, a child may have a severe loss in the higher frequencies but a moderate loss in the lower frequencies.

Children with severe and profound losses are said to be deaf. Children with mild to moderate-severe losses are said to be hard of hearing. It is important to distinguish between the child's unamplified level of hearing loss (what is heard *without* hearing aids) and his or her amplified level (what is heard *with* hearing aids).

Other Important Characteristics of Hearing Loss

In addition to knowing the type and level of hearing loss, it is also important to know the age of onset at which the hearing loss occurred. Children who have hearing when they are young are able to benefit from auditory experiences. In general, the earlier the age of onset and the more severe the hearing loss, the more dramatic the impact of hearing loss on development.

Age of identification is the age of the child when the hearing loss is identified. This should be closely associated with the age of amplification, although some children may require training to wear hearing aids. Early identification and immediate amplification are of great benefit to the child.

In some cases, hearing loss may be progressive in nature, which means that the child's hearing loss is increasing. Some children who are hard of hearing may become deaf due to progressive hearing loss. Children with progressive hearing loss need more frequent auditory assessments, and the educational interventions they require will change over time. Students with progressive losses will likely need emotional support as their hearing loss increases.

Causes of Hearing Loss

Genetic Causes

Approximately 50% of the incidence of deafness is believed to be due to genetic causes (Heward, 2003). More than 200 genetic causes of hearing loss have been identified (Peterson & Hittie, 2003), although many are *not* associated with the occurrence of additional disabilities.

Down syndrome is one of the most common genetic causes of mental retardation (Heward, 2003) and is also associated with hearing loss. Approximately two thirds of children with Down syndrome have hearing loss (Roizen, 2002). Usually, these children are considered hard of hearing due to unilateral or bilateral loss that is sensorineural, conductive, or mixed. Some children with Down syndrome are prone to ear infections, resulting in hearing that fluctuates, which is especially important for a teacher to know about. Hearing loss plays a significant role in the language delays of about 10% of these children (Chapman, Seung, Schwartz, & Bird, 1998). In addition, some have heart anomalies and other health issues. Classroom teachers of students with Down syndrome will need to know about the status of the child's health, vision, and hearing.

Infectious Causes

Prenatal Infections   One infectious cause of hearing loss is prenatal infection, also known as *intrauterine* or *maternal* infection. In prenatal infections, the pregnant mother contracts the infection and passes it to the fetus. The acronym STORCH has been used as an umbrella term to describe the most common intrauterine infections including syphillis (S), toxoplasmosis (T), other interuterine infections such as varicella (O), rubella virus (R), cytomegalovirus (C), and herpes simplex virus (H) (Silberman, 2000). These infections are also associated with vision loss, mental retardation, and ongoing health concerns. Two of these include

- *Cytomegalovirus:* When this book was published, cytomegalovirus (CMV) was the most common prenatal cause of sensorineural hearing loss worldwide (Leung, Sauve, & Davies, 2003). CMV infection occurs in approximately 0.2%–2.5% of all live births. Although most congenitally infected infants (90%) are asymptomatic at birth, CMV is a major cause of sensorineural hearing loss, mental retardation, and neurologic deficits (Barbi, Binda, Caroppi, Ambrosetti, Corbetta, & Serch, 2003; Pess, 2002). Seven to fifteen percent of asymptomatic infants will have a sensorineural hearing loss (Fowler, Dahle, Boppana, & Pass, 1999). Of those infants born with symptoms of CMV, 30%–50% will develop sensorineural hearing loss (Dahle et al., 2000), and 80% of them will develop late-onset or progressive hearing loss (Dahle et al., 2000; Leung et al., 2003). Therefore, children with congenital CMV infections should have long-term audiological follow-up for early identification of hearing problems (Leung et al., 2003). CMV may also cause jaundice, microcephaly, hemolytic anemia, and enlargement of the liver and spleen (Hardman et al., 2002).

  It is important to note that children with congenital CMV can continue to shed the virus up to the age of 3 years and even beyond; as a result, teachers of childbearing age need to take universal precautions with these children and other children who might also have undiagnosed infectious CMV. (Leung et al., 2003; Schirmer, 2001).

- *Toxoplasmosis:* Toxoplasmosis is a form of parasitic infection that can cause hearing loss, vision loss, jaundice, anemia, microcephaly (unusually small head), hydrocephalus (a condition that results in the accumulation of spinal fluid in the brain), and central nervous system disorders such as seizures (Leung et al., 2003). Toxoplasmosis is transmitted through direct contact with infected animal feces or undercooked meats.

Postnatal Infections   Postnatal infections—also called childhood infections—that result in high fevers occasionally cause loss of hearing. Such infections include bacterial meningitis, mumps, measles, and chickenpox. The most common postnatal infection that causes hearing loss in children is otitis media, an infection that spreads from the eustachian tube to the middle ear and is commonly called an "ear infection." When the onset of infection is recent, the condition is called *acute otitis media*. Symptoms include fever, pain, and tugging on the ear. Chronic otitis media is said to occur when otitis media lasts for 3 or more months. Otitis media with effusion (OME) may occur with or without infection. In OME, the normally air-filled middle ear space is filled with fluid that may be either sterile or infected. It is often symptomless because an active infection may not be present; however, it almost always affects hearing. The hearing loss may be temporary, fluctuating, or permanent (Flexer, 1999). Some populations of children are particularly prone to otitis media, including children who have Down syndrome, children born with cleft palates (even after repair), and children who were in neonatal intensive care units as infants and had naso-tracheal intubation (a small tube inserted through the nose into the trachea to help the infant breathe) (Flexer, 1999). Children who have frequent or chronic otitis media before the age of 3 may have difficulties with attention and language learning (Cranford, Thompson, Hoyer, & Faires, 1997; Northern & Downs, 2002).

Prematurity

Prematurity has been shown to be correlated with hearing loss. The incidence of hearing loss identified in full-term newborn babies is 4 in 10,000. The incidence of hearing loss among infants who are very low birth weight (less than $3\frac{1}{3}$ pounds) is 51 in 10,000. This great disparity reinforces the importance of hearing screening for this group (Rais-Bahrami, Short, & Batshaw, 2002). Such infants are more likely to develop sensorineural hearing loss due to complications of prematurity, such as brain hemorrhage and reduced oxygen to the inner ear (Schirmer, 2001), and from the use of medications that become ototoxic (Rais-Bahrami et al., 2002).

Structural Differences

Structural differences, such as congenital aural atresia (congenital malformation or absence of the auditory canal), may also cause hearing loss. Congenital aural atresia causes a build-up of cerumen (ear wax) and is a major cause of congenital, conductive hearing loss. Cleft palate, which occurs when the roof of the mouth does not close, may also cause hearing loss (Herer et al., 2002).

Trauma

Trauma is another cause of adventitious hearing loss. Trauma may occur as the result of an accident (e.g., automobile accidents, falls) or from child abuse.

Trauma may also cause vision loss, mental disability, and behavioral changes. Children who have become deaf or hard of hearing from trauma are likely to experience the loss of hearing emotionally as well physically. The classroom teacher needs to gain understanding about how the child has changed as a result of the trauma. The child will look to the classroom teacher for emotional support.

Ototoxic Medications

Ototoxic medications (those that are potentially damaging to hearing) may also cause hearing loss. Some antibiotics fall into this category of medications, but dosages can be monitored to prevent toxicity.

Other Causes

Rarer causes of hearing loss include anoxia (lack of oxygen to the infant during the birth process) and incompatibility of mother and infant blood (rH factor) (Peterson & Hittie, 2003). These causes are associated with additional disabilities.

Recognizing Hearing Loss

The following may be signs of hearing loss in infants and children with multiple disabilities. The existence of these signs should warrant at least medical evaluation and possibly a full audiological evaluation:

- Frequent earaches or colds
- Discharge from the ears
- Does not awaken or startle to loud sounds
- Lack of babbling or cooing, or persistence of such vocalizations in older child
- Failure to localize sounds
- Failure to imitate vocalization
- Difficulty understanding directions
- Lack of response to questions
- Requests to repeat what was said
- Distractibility
- Inattention
- Avoidance of tasks with auditory demands
- Demonstration of better responses to low- or high-pitched sounds
- Disorientation or confusion when noise levels are high
- Poor articulation (McCormick et al., 2003; Newton & Moss, 2001; Westling & Fox, 2004).

When such characteristics are observed in school, they should be reported to the parents, the school nurse, and the teacher of deaf and hard of hearing students.

Assessment of Hearing Loss

The age of hearing loss identification and subsequent amplification is critical to the child's development. When denied early opportunities to use residual hearing, the child's long-term ability to use audition for learning is affected because of both physiological reasons (deterioration of the auditory pathways) and psychosocial reasons (lack of development of auditory attention, practice, and auditory-based learning). Therefore, infant hearing screening is a necessity.

Infant screening efforts have improved markedly in recent years, from 11 states conducting hearing screening in 1999 (White, 2002) to all 50 states and the District of Columbia screening today. The percentage of children screened in 2003 varied from state to state, ranging from 22%–99.5% of infants (National Center for Hearing Assessment and Management, 2003), with a national rate of 86.5% (http://www.infanthearing.org/newsletter/index.html). The most common screening test is the Otoacoustic Emissions Screening (OAE) (also known as Transient Evoked Otoacoustic Emissions), which measures emissions sent by the inner ear in response to sound. This test can be administered to every newborn (Bowe, 2000; Martin & Clark, 2003), although it is particularly important to screen higher risk infants, such as those in neonatal intensive care units and those with very low birth weight. Such infants are at higher risk for both hearing loss and additional disabilities.

Audiological assessment of children with multiple disabilities can be more challenging because these children may have difficulty following the directions presented during conventional audiometric testing (Schirmer, 2001). In addition, their motor and visual impairments may limit the type of assessment that can be performed. Common audiological testing methods used to evaluate the hearing of children with multiple disabilities follow. The OAE is also used as a screening test with children with multiple disabilities. The final two tests discussed subsequently, Auditory Brain Stem Response (ABR) and Impedance (immittance) measures, are additional passive forms of testing, which means that the child does not have to demonstrate a specific action in response to sound. Such passive measures can be useful for children with either limited deliberate movements or more severe developmental delays.

- *Behavior Observation Audiometry (BOA)* involves observing changes in the child's actions in reponse to sounds. For example, the child may suck more vigorously as the sound level increases.

- *Visual Reinforcer Audiometry (VRA)* involves the use of a visual stimulus paired with auditory input. When a sound is presented and the child looks toward the toy, the activation of the mechanical toy serves as reinforcement for a correct response. The toy is not activated if the child looks when sounds are not presented. The child must be able to visually locate the toy and turn his or her head toward it in order to utilize this approach (Westling & Fox, 2004).

- *Tangible Reinforcer Operant-Conditioning (TROCA)* is similar to VRA, but the child is expected to press a button or bar when the sound is emitted. A tangible reinforcement, such as a small edible, is provided when the child pushes the button. The child must be able to learn the association between the sound and the desired response of pushing the button.

- *Play Audiometry* requires the child to perform a specific action (that is taught), such as dropping a block into a bucket, when a sound is heard. The classroom teacher may play an important role in teaching such a response so that more accurate testing results can be obtained.

- *Auditory Brain Stem Response (ABR)* can be used to assess children who are unable to demonstrate a deliberate motor or visual response to sound. This is a physiological measure of hearing that uses electrodes that are placed on the child's head to measure brain wave responses to sound.

- *Impedance (Immittance) Testing* can be used to assess the functioning of middle ear, eardrum, and eustachian tubes. A probe is inserted into the ear and a tone is emitted. This tone is reflected from the middle ear to a microphone connected to the probe tip, allowing detection of malfunctioning parts within the ear. Impedance testing is not a measure of hearing sensitivity and as such, must be included as part of a battery of tests (Flexer 1999).

In addition, the teacher of the deaf or hard of hearing may perform a functional hearing screening or evaluation. The screening process includes gathering medical information, interviewing the family, and observing the child's reactions to sounds and voices (Chen, 1999). The screening process may result in referral to the audiologist for a complete clinical hearing assessment. Functional hearing evaluations are also done to determine how children use the hearing reported on the audiogram in their natural environments. This form of assessment is important because children with the same audiograms will function differently in school, home, and community environments. Functional hearing assessment provides information about how children use their hearing in the context of background noise across environments. This information may be used to plan auditory training programs that may be formal or embedded in ongoing activities and routines.

Amplification

Once hearing loss is identified, appropriate amplification must be provided. Amplification may include hearing aids that are available in body-type aids, behind-the-ear, in-the-ear, or in-the-ear canal models. Digital hearing aids are also available that may be programmed and fined-tuned for different environmental conditions.

Body-type aids use a case that holds the microphone, amplifier, circuit modifiers, and battery. The aid is clipped to the child's clothing. This type of hearing aid has been popular in the past due to its higher level of amplification. The sounds produced by clothing, cords, and movement may create interference, however. Most children use behind-the-ear models that are available in a variety of colors. Body-type aids are the best choice for children who have malformed external ears that prohibit the fitting of behind-the-ear models.

Once the appropriate hearing aid has been selected, the home and school will need to coordinate a plan to teach the child to tolerate the aids (Martin & Clark, 2003). In many cases, children are willing to wear the aids immediately, possibly because the benefits seem evident to them. In other cases, the child will need a collaborative effort and ample social reinforcement to achieve daily use of the aids. Very young children can benefit from having the hearing aids attached to safety straps and clipped to their clothing. In this way, if they remove their aids, they will not lose them. It may be necessary to gradually build up the child's tolerance for the hearing aids by increasing the amount of time they are worn each day. Team members may start with using the hearing aids for periods of time that offer opportunities for socialization and motivating auditory input, such as favorite songs and stories. The teacher and family will also need to collaborate on hearing aid care, charging and replacing batteries, and cleansing the ear molds. Batteries are best charged when the child is asleep so that they will be ready for the child's waking hours and the school day. Auditory training may also be recommended to support the child to make maximal use of functional hearing.

Most students, including those with severe and profound hearing losses, will wear hearing aids in school. Amplification is of less help to students with profound losses because amplification makes sounds louder, not clearer. However, even if the hearing aid does not improve access to speech, it may improve auditory access to environmental sounds. Being able to hear car horns and school alarms may increase the child's level of safety and allow for greater independence.

FM systems can be used to make sound more accessible to students with hearing loss. Teachers are able to manipulate the settings on the system to occlude background noise that may interfere with hearing (Kuder, 2003). This allows the teacher to "tune out" interfering sounds during instruction. FM systems may be personal systems worn by the student or sound-field systems that amplify the teacher's voice to the entire classroom (Flexer, 1999). In addition to benefiting students with hearing loss and additional disabilities, the FM sound-field systems benefit classmates with milder disabilities, such as those who have attention challenges.

Other Assistive Devices

The cochlear implant is a device that is implanted into the inner ear. A microphone receives sound, and then the cochlear implant stimulates the auditory nerve fibers in the cochlea. The implant does not amplify sound; it supports the individual to perceive sound (McCormick et al., 2003; Schirmer, 2001). This device may be recommended for some children who are deaf and do not respond to amplification attempts and may improve the child's access to both environmental and speech sounds (Westling & Fox, 2004). Even having increased access to environmental sounds may improve the child's ability to use audition in learning. Successful use of a cochlear implant requires a significant amount of training, and the recipient of the implant must have the motivation to participate in and benefit from the training.

Tactile communication devices that analyze sound into frequency bands and convert the frequency bands into signals that are felt on the skin as vibrations are also available. Children with the most profound hearing losses may receive more benefit from the tactile devices than from conventional hearing aids (Flexer, 1999).

Impact of Hearing Loss and Additional Disabilities

The impact of hearing loss on the child's development will vary greatly, depending on the age of onset, age of the child when the hearing loss is identified, age of child at amplification, type of hearing loss, severity of the hearing loss, and the presence or absence of effective early intervention (Bowe, 2002; Herer et al., 2002). Having other disabilities that interact with hearing loss will affect a child's development. Thus, early identification and amplification, coupled with effective early intervention, will best support the child's development.

Students who are deaf or hard of hearing with additional disabilities have more limited access to information. It is impossible for a hearing person to identify the many things that were learned quite accidentally by listening in or simply passing by a conversation. Much of what is learned incidentally through hearing will not be available to the child with severe hearing loss. In addition, social cues such as those expressed through voice volume and intonation will be less accessible to students who are deaf or hard of hearing.

For most individuals, the primary impact of deafness is on communication and language development. Often, hearing people associate this concern with the need to master speech. However, the greater concern is that the child be provided with a context that supports the development of communication and language. An important first step is for others to communicate in a method that is accessible to the child. The hearing child has countless opportunities to listen to speech before producing it. The child who is deaf with additional disabilities needs opportunities to experience communication receptively in his or her preferred expressive form (which may include the use of signs or sign language, gestures, pictures, and photographs). The strategies presented in the deafblind section of this chapter will also support many of the students with hearing loss and additional disabilities.

Educational Assessment

Assessment of students who are deaf or hard of hearing with additional disabilities may be challenging to the collaborative team because of communication difficulties. In addition, many of the available instruments lack suggested accommodations for children with hearing loss. Relevant tests must be selected to meet the individual child's needs. Some students who are deaf or hard of hearing with additional disabilities may be assessed using tools developed for students who are deaf, although additional accommodations will be required. Some of these additional accommodations may include proper positioning, use of augmentative and alternative communication (AAC) devices, use of pauses to provide time for child to process information, and/or assessment over multiple sessions (in response to the child's attention span and stamina). Other individuals will be best served by the assessments developed for students with multiple disabilities who are in their same age group, providing that accommodations are addressed.

Because oral and written language limitations are often present in children who are deaf and hard of hearing with multiple disabilities, nonverbal assessment scales or performance sections of assessments will be used. Such children who also have physical disabilities may not also be able to demonstrate their knowledge through nonverbal tests due to their motor limitations. Therefore, it is important that classroom teachers and family members who know the child well participate with psychologists in the assessment process.

Curriculum-based assessments, both commercially produced and teacher made, sometimes offer a link between what is assessed and what should be taught. The Behavioral Characteristics Progression (BCP) (Vort Corporation, 1997) is a particularly strong curriculum-based assessment tool for students with multiple disabilities. This assessment is appropriate for any child with a developmental age of 1 year through young adult. It samples more than 2,300 skills and has components that are particularly appropriate for students who are deaf or hard of hearing with additional disabilities. For example, it includes sections on auditory perception, sign language, fingerspelling, speech reading, and articulation. This assessment is teacher friendly because it includes an activity guide that provides task-analyzed activities that correlate to the assessment items. Therefore, it supports the classroom teacher in making the transition from assessment to instruction. Assessments discussed in the deafblind section of this chapter are also appropriate for some children who are deaf or hard of hearing with additional disabilities.

Informal assessment is the most common form of assessment performed by teachers. This includes the use of teacher-developed assessment formats. It also includes the careful observation of the impact of teaching on student learning. Such ongoing assessment should result in immediate adjustments to teaching.

Informal assessment of communication is critical because communication is the developmental area most affected by hearing loss. Children with multiple disabilities may have difficulty expressing themselves through verbalization or sign language because motor impairments and cognitive delays may impede communication in these forms. A complete evaluation of the child's expressive and receptive forms of communication (body language, facial expressions, gestures, vocalizations, and verbalizations), intents of communication (purpose of communication, such as protest and requests), and messages (content) should be performed. This, coupled with information obtained from formal assessment tools, can become the basis of program planning in the area of communication.

Communication assessment should examine the child's communication, both expressive and receptive, across environments and contexts. At the same time, it is important that the communication environment also be analyzed including the communications used by all communication partners (Rowland & Schweigert, 2003). Communication intervention should then occur across contexts and communication environments and should be modified as indicated by the environmental assessment. This may involve ensuring that others in the child's life know how to communicate with the child using his or her communication system. For example, if a child who has multiple disabilities is learning some basic signs, adults must be able recognize those signs and have a sign repertoire that far exceeds the child's.

The emphasis on formal and standardized testing under such federal laws such as the No Child Left Behind Act of 2001 (PL 107-110) has resulted in an increase in alternate assessment measures for children with multiple disabilities, such as portfolio assessment. See Chapter 4 for more content related to alternate assessment.

Teaching Approaches and Strategies

Instruction should be based on results from a variety of formal and informal assessments. The results of such assessments will help collaborative team members develop a student's IEP that articulates the goals and objectives selected for an individual child for the period of 1 year. The IEP process ensures that parental concerns are addressed through the child's educational program. One important consideration is the child's use of hearing, which can be strengthened through auditory training.

Auditory Training

The purpose of auditory training, also known as auditory learning (Heward, 2003), is to support the child to improve his or her use of hearing. Even if the child's hearing loss prohibits understanding speech sounds, auditory training may have the following benefits:

- Awareness of environmental sounds that may signal danger

- Awareness of sounds that occur before tactual contact (such as the teacher's voice before the teacher's touch)

- Awareness of sound for pleasure

- Awareness of sound for greater involvement in the environment

- Awareness of pauses, intonations, or patterns of speech as clues to the meaning of oral communication

Children who are typically developing hear something of interest and then turn their head to see the source of sound. Children who are deaf or hard of hearing with multiple disabilities will demonstrate response to sounds in unique ways. Examples of such responses include leaning toward the sound source (especially when reach is not physically possible), a widening or blinking of the eye, or a change in breathing or alertness patterns. Therefore, adults who provide auditory training must be able to recognize each child's responses to sound.

The purpose of auditory training programs is to help children who are deaf or hard of hearing develop the following skills (Flexer, 1999):

- Detection (knowing when sound is present)

- Attention (focus on a particular sound)

- Localization (identifying the location of sound)

- Tracking (identifying changing locations and movement of sound source)

- Discrimination (recognizing differences in sound qualities, intensities, duration, and pitch)

- Identification (the ability to recognize a stimulus and label or repeat it. This process is the recognition of duration, rate, intensity, and emphasis of various sounds including speech. It also involves the recognition of individual speech sounds or phonemes such as /b/, /m/, /s/.)

- Comprehension (the ability to attach specific meaning to auditory input).

The teacher of the deaf or hard of hearing may assist the classroom teacher to implement an individualized auditory training program that addresses these skills. One technique used in an auditory training program is the use of polar opposites or contrasting experiences. When a child is becoming aware of sound (detection) he or she must learn to distinguish between the presence of sound and its opposite, absence of sound. So the two conditions are presented in contrast. Loud and soft sounds are contrasted when a child is learning to discriminate among sounds. When the child is learning to identify sound, high sounds and low sounds as well as long and short sounds and contrasting speech sounds or phonemes are presented.

Another technique is to use an auditory training program to help a child localize and attach meaning to specific sounds (Flexer, 1999). For instance, when a dog barks, the teacher or parent might say, "Listen, did you hear that? I think I heard a dog, let's go see." The adult would then assist the child to go where he or she could watch the dog bark.

Classroom teachers and parents can use vibratory experiences paired with auditory input to build awareness of sound in children who are deaf with additional disabilities. For example, an adult can hold an infant close to his or her chest while talking or singing, providing auditory input and tactile feedback from chest movements. Students will also benefit from pairing sound and movement experiences. Clapping and shaking of toys and instruments may be paired with verbal games and singing. Some musical instruments also produce both sound and vibration. Examples include tambourines, piano, tone bars, and drums.

Language Approaches

The primary emphasis in educating children who are deaf and hard of hearing, including those with multiple disabilities, is to encourage the development of communication and language. The most common approaches to educating children who are deaf and hard of hearing (and those with additional disabilities) are auditory-oral, auditory-aural (also known as auditory-verbal [AV]), manual, and total communication (TC). Both the auditory-oral and the auditory-aural approach emphasize the importance of listening to speech and the mastery of verbal skills. Auditory-oral training utilizes speech reading and contextual cues in addition to auditory training. Auditory-aural emphasizes reliance on hearing and is frequently used with children who have had cochlear implants (Zapien, 1998).

The manual approach emphasizes the use of sign language as the primary form of receptive and expressive communication. Sign systems include American Sign Language (ASL) (accepted as the language of the deaf in the United States) and other systems that are translations of English, including Seeing Essential English, Pidgin Signed English, and Signing Exact English (Hardman et al., 2002). Fingerspelling is used with all of the sign systems.

The TC approach incorporates all of the elements of each of the approaches described previously. The philosophy of TC is that anything and everything that supports receptive and expressive communication will be employed to support the child. This may include the use of cued speech, an approach that pairs the use of hand signals to support the learning of speech reading. The TC approach includes the use of all forms of communication and in doing so, it addresses the needs of children who do not express verbally or in sign language due to additional disabilities such as motor challenges. Pictures, photographs, and augmentative communication devices will be the best forms for some children who are deaf with additional disabilities The goal of the team, including the family, is to select the approach that most closely meets the needs of the individual child.

Additional Instructional Strategies

The four aspects of communication can be a useful structure for both informal assessment and intervention with students who are deaf or hard of hearing and have multiple disabilities:

1. Form: The methods used to communicate expressively and receptively

2. Function: The purpose of communication

3. Content: The message

4. Context: The physical arrangement of environments, child characteristics (including those that are related to the disability and those that are not), activities and routines, communication partners, and the process of communication (i.e., initiating, sustaining, and terminating conversations) (Bruce, 2002)

See Chapter 11 for specific communication strategies associated with each of these aspects. Strategies suggested in the deafblind section of this chapter will also be helpful when working with most students who are deaf or hard of hearing with additional disabilities.

Intervention may include teaching members of the collaborative team new skills. Team members will need to understand the meaning of the child's expressive communication and how to provide receptive opportunities in the child's preferred communication form(s). Perhaps of greatest initial importance is how responsive potential communication partners are to the child's communication attempts. When peers and adults become more responsive, the child who is deaf or hard of hearing is likely to increase the frequency and persistence of his or her expressive communication.

The following suggestions will enhance interaction skills between students who are deaf or hard or hearing with various communication partners including peers in the general education classroom (Downing & Demchak, 2002; Heward, 2003):

- No more than one person should speak at a time.
- Speak within a 3- to 4-foot distance from the child.
- Establish eye contact prior to speaking or signing.
- Avoid exaggerating movements of speech.
- Avoid speaking more loudly or more slowly.
- Learn the expressions in all forms (gestures, signs, picture symbols, vocalizations)
- Avoid having the child who is deaf or hard of hearing face the window.
- The communication partner should not have his or her back to the window.

Environmental adaptations in the classroom will help students who are deaf or hard of hearing, including those with mild losses, to use their hearing. One way is through preferential seating, by positioning the child with his or her better ear toward the speaker while also positioning him or her away from interfering background noises. Background noises such as fans, blowers, hallway traffic, and sounds from lights should be reduced. Carpet can be used to muffle noise from movement within the classroom. Tennis balls can be placed on the chair legs to eliminate sounds that occur when chairs are moved. Such accommodations may improve the concentration of all of the children in the classroom.

The Role of Technology

Some children who are deaf or hard of hearing with additional disabilities will learn to read and write (or type). Such children will benefit from instruction on the use of text telephones (TT) (Peterson & Hittie, 2003) in order to communicate with others by telephone. TTs (also known as teletypewriters or TTYs) allow an individual to type in a message that appears on a small screen on the receiver's TT. In addition, a hard copy is produced. If the individual who is deaf wants to communicate via the telephone with a hearing person who does not own a TT, the relay system is also available. The deaf or hard of hearing individual can use his TT to type a message that is received by the relay operator, who then reads the message to the hearing person, converts the hearing person's response to a text message, and sends that response back to the individual who is deaf. Some individuals who are hard of hearing may be able to use the telephone with the use of amplification.

Computer technology, software programs, and the Internet have greatly expanded the world of individuals who are deaf or hard of hearing, including those with additional disabilities. One application of particular relevance is the use of computer aided speech-to-text translation. A trained captionist types in a short hand code to represent what is said. A software program translates this abbreviated code into full text that instantly appears on the screen to be read by the individual who is deaf or hard of hearing. This form of translation provides the individual with the closest version of what was said (Heward, 2003). As a result of the Television Decoder Circuitry Act of 1990 (PL 101-431), all televisions made today are equipped with a decoder to allow the individual who is deaf or hard of hearing to gain access to the printed word to represent the dialogue that occurs in television programs, which is called *closed captioning* (Heward, 2003). *Open captioning* is a term used to describe captioning that appears for live television programs and events.

Alerting devices, such as lights that flash for the doorbell or smoke alarm, may be important safety considerations for the school and home (Heward, 2003). Vibrating alarm clocks and timers can also enhance independence.

STUDENTS WITH DEAFBLINDNESS

Children who are congenitally deafblind have significant vision and hearing losses at birth or before the age of 2 years. These children use touch as their main avenue of learning. They also rely on taste, smell, and movement in order to gain access to people and objects in their environment (Prickett & Welch, 1998). Many children who are congenitally deafblind have some useful vision, hearing, or both. They are able to use their distance senses of vision and hearing for learning at close ranges when provided with appropriate assistive devices and adaptations. It should be noted that having the use of these distance senses, even minimally, is a tremendous support to the development of concepts and communication (Prickett & Welch, 1998).

Some children are born with or acquire a loss of one distance sense as an infant or preschooler and acquire the loss of another distance sense adventitiously after major concepts are learned. If a child is deaf or hard of hearing first, he or she is able to use vision as a major sense for learning and orienting to people, events, and objects in the environment. Losing vision in childhood or adolescence will require the student to be provided with tactile and possibly visual adaptations if any useful vision remains (Prickett & Welch, 1998). If a child is blind or visually impaired first, he or she uses hearing and touch as major senses for learning. Many will learn to read using braille or regular print with optical devices. The loss of hearing later will require the student to acquire new techniques for spoken and written communication. Specific strategies and devices are described later in this section.

Definition

The federal definition of deafblindness stated in IDEA '97 is "concomitant hearing and visual impairments, the combination of which causes such severe communication and other developmental and educational needs that they cannot be accommodated in special education programs for children with deafness or children with blindness" (34CFR300.7[c][2] of IDEA). This definition provides no specific levels of acuity or field loss or hearing loss, and most students will have some vision or hearing that can be used to foster learning.

Professionals in the Field of Deafblindness

All of the professionals discussed in previous sections of this chapter may be part of the collaborative team who ensure appropriate programming for students who are deafblind. The type of services they offer should be adapted to each child's unique needs.

Team Members Unique to Deafblindness

Team members who are unique to the collaborative team serving learners who are deafblind are interpreters for the deafblind, intervenors, and deafblind specialists.

Interpreters for the Deafblind Interpreters for the deafblind perform a different role from interpreters for the deaf or hard of hearing who have normal vision. They convey visual information such as printed content on a handout or on the chalkboard and may assist as a sighted guide when the student travels in familiar and unfamiliar environments. Interpreters may be certified through the national Registry of Interpreters for the Deaf, Inc. However, some interpreters who work in elementary and secondary school environments may lack full national certification and provide tutoring and other instructional assistance to students who are deafblind. They may be referred to as "educational interpreters" or "interpreter-tutors" (Prickett & Welch, 1995, 1998).

Intervenors Intervenors provide one-to-one service to students who are deafblind. Their primary responsibilities are to ensure that the students can obtain information that is available to students who are hearing and sighted and to support the development of students' receptive and expressive communication skills. Intervenors are also responsible for interpreting in the student's preferred forms, translating written communication into an accessible form for the student, providing an experiential base for conceptual understanding, and assisting others including peers to interact with the student who is deafblind (Alsop, Blaha, & Kloos, 2000).

Deafblind Specialists   Deafblind specialists support the team by providing instructional suggestions that are specific to children with deafblindness. Deafblind specialists should have expertise in hearing impairments, visual impairments, and severe disabilities. The role of the deafblind specialist may be to provide direct support to individual children's teams or to provide technical assistance and resource provision related to the unique assessment and programming needs of children and youth who are deafblind. Technical assistance usually does not entail long-term, direct support to individual children. Federally funded deafblind projects provide such technical assistance to individual states or multistate areas. The deafblind project for state or multistate areas can be located by first going to the DB-LINK web site at http://www.tr.wou.edu/dblink then clicking on "State Resource" and then "State Deafblind Projects."

Prevalence of Deafblindness

According to the most recent National Deaf-Blind Child Count Summary (based on preliminary data), 10,578 children were reported as deafblind in the United States in 2002. The summary is a compilation of the most accurate source of data reported by the state deaf-blind projects funded through the U.S. Department of Education (2001). Complete national count data can be located at the DB-LINK web site. The prevalence of deafblindness is difficult to pinpoint because children who are deafblind are typically reported under several of the 13 different disability categories for Part B of IDEA '97, and thus their deafblindness may be unidentified or categorized under another disability. This results in an underreporting of the incidence of deafblindness. In addition, school personnel and families may not consider a child to be deafblind because the child has some functional hearing and/or vision. Thus, many children are not reported as deafblind. Similar problems exist with reporting child count data related to children with visual impairments, as indicated previously in this chapter.

Causes of Deafblindness

The incidence of children who are deafblind due to unknown causes is higher than the incidence attributed to any single identifiable cause; however, the more common causes are discussed here:

- *Prematurity* is one of the leading causes of deafblindness. The sensorineural hearing loss associated with prematurity is due to complications such as ventricular hemorrhages in the infant's brain. The most common vision loss is ROP, discussed in the visual impairment section of this chapter. In addition to having sensory issues, children who are born prematurely may face a multitude of health and learning challenges.

- *CMV* (discussed previously) is also a major cause of deafblindness. The visual complications of CMV include small eyeballs and inflammation of the choroid and retina that can result in optic atrophy, a condition associated with severe vision loss. CMV may also result in a progressive or later onset hearing loss (Herer et al., 2002).

Genetic Causes

Many different genetic syndromes are associated with deafblindness. CHARGE syndrome, Usher syndrome, and Down syndrome are among the most common genetic causes of deafblindness in the United States.

The associated anomalies of CHARGE syndrome include

- Coloboma (C) (a cleft or opening in the eyeball). The severity of the impairment will depend on which part of the eye is affected. Colobomas of the iris may result in problems adjusting to bright light; colobomas of the retina or optic nerve may result in significant visual impairments including visual loss in the upper half of the visual field)

- Heart anomalies (H) (includes any type of heart anomaly)

- Atresia choanae (A) (narrowing or blockage of nasal passages)

- Retarded growth or development (R)

- Genital hypoplasia (G) (incomplete or underdevelopment of genitals)

- Ear anomalies (E), including unusually shaped ears, mild to severe sensorineural loss, and chronic ear infections

Four of these six characteristics must be evident for a diagnosis of CHARGE to be made. In addition, the following characteristics are common, although they are not represented by the CHARGE acronym: cranial nerve anomalies (including olfactory, ocular, facial, or acoustic) and genitorurinary problems (including malformation of the kidney and ureter) (Blake et al., 1998; Brown, 1997; Lewis & Lowther, 2001). Problems with balance have also been identified as particularly significant in individuals with CHARGE (Brown, 2003; van Dijk & de Kort, 2003).

Many children with CHARGE syndrome display compulsive behaviors. Almost all children with CHARGE syndrome experience high levels of anxiety. Therefore, the student's collaborative team will need to work closely to provide the best services for the student. For example, the classroom teacher will be responsible for noticing features of the environment that cause stress for the student and then will need to plan accordingly, reducing anxiety-evoking situations as much as possible. Classroom teachers will need to know the impact of the colobomas on the child's visual field; for example, colobomas often cause vision loss in the upper field of vision, so this will affect the best location to place materials. Namely, materials must be low enough so that the child with a coloboma can see them. Care must also be taken so that sign language is presented within the child's functional field of vision. A child with a coloboma who is shorter than the person doing the signing will not be able to see the signs. When a child communicating with a signer gives fluctuating responses, this may be a clue that visual accessibility is an issue.

Usher syndrome is the most common form of adventitious deafblindness in the United States. It is an autosomal recessive disorder associated with visual impairments due to retinitis pigmentosa (RP) and hearing impairment. Three major types of the syndrome have been identified, I, II, and III. Children with Usher syndrome I have congenital profound deafness and progressive visual impairments. Night blindness due to RP may be present in individuals with Usher syndrome I in infancy or early childhood and they may be legally blind by adulthood. They also often have delayed gross motor development due to a lack of vestibular function (which affects balance).

Children with type II are usually hard of hearing. Audiograms performed on individuals with this syndrome depict varying levels of hearing loss in the lower frequencies and profound loss in the higher frequencies. Blind spots due to RP may be present by late childhood or early teens and they may be legally blind by early adulthood. Vestibular function is normal. Children with Usher syndrome III have a mild to moderate hearing loss that progresses to a profound loss in adulthood. Night blindness appears in childhood or teens and legal blindness might be present by early to mid-adulthood. Progressive vestibular involvement develops with age (Kimberling, Orten, & Pieke-Dahl, 2000).

Children who are deaf or hard of hearing should be assessed as early as possible by ophthalmologists because 3%–6% of the deaf and perhaps as many in the hard of hearing population have Usher syndrome Type I or II (Davenport, 1994). Early identification will help them to receive interventions they will need to ensure that their unique needs are met.

Because the three types of Usher syndrome have different symptoms and effects that will have an impact on learning, classroom teachers and other members of the collaborative team will need to know which type of Usher syndrome their students have. For example, they will want to know about the child's mobility in dimly lit and differently lit areas within the school environment. The TVI and the O&M instructor can teach sighted guide techniques to the classroom teacher, peers, and other members of the team. The classroom teacher will also want to understand the implications that Usher syndrome has on literacy, including the potential need for braille instruction, socialization, and career education. Perhaps of greatest importance is the role of the teacher in emotionally supporting the student whose sense of self is changing in response to progressive visual impairment.

Less Common Genetic Causes of Deafblindness   Cornelia de Lange syndrome (CdLS) is associated with the following characteristics in addition to vision and hearing loss: microcephaly (small head), short stature, missing or partially formed limbs, small hands, heart anomalies, seizures, small and tilted nose (which makes the nostrils more evident), excessive hair all over the body (often including thin eyebrows that meet each other in the middle), varying levels of cognitive function, a susceptibility to infection, and hypotonicity (Gilbert, 1996). Visual conditions include retinal detachment due to severe myopia or self-inflicted trauma and cortical visual impairment. More than 90% of the children with CdLS have hearing loss that is sensorinueral and is usually bilateral. In addition, they may have otitis media and middle ear malformations (Ireland, 2001).

Dandy-Walker syndrome is a congenital condition that is marked by brain malformation that involves the cerebellum (the area of the back of the brain that governs movement) and blockage of the fourth ventricle of the heart that results in hydrocephalus. Conditions associated with this syndrome in addition to vision and hearing problems include cleft palate, kidney problems, abnormal vertebrae in the lumbar region of the spine, polydactyly, and syndactyly. Motor delays are common. Vision loss is due to retina dysgenesis, nystagmus, colobomas of the choroid, and the formation of cataracts. Hydrocephalus may put pressure on neural pathways, causing both visual and hearing loss (Greenspan, 1998).

Goldenhar syndrome, also known as oculo-auriculo-vertebral or OAV spectrum, is part of a cluster of syndromes that include craniofacial (head and face) malformations. Often, children with Goldenhar have faces that are smaller on one side or the two sides are quite asymmetrical. They may have incomplete development or malformations of facial muscles, lip, palate, and teeth. In addition, they may experience heart, lung, kidney, or gastrointestinal issues. This syndrome is not associated with cognitive impairments. Vision conditions include cysts on the eyeballs, missing portions of eyelids, strabismus, abnormalities of the retina, and ptosis. Hearing loss results from missing or malformed outer ear, narrow or missing ear canals, abnormal skin or cartilage on or in front of the ear, and structural malformations of the middle or inner ear. These structural abnormalities may prohibit the use of hearing aids. In addition to hearing loss, malformation of the facial and jaw muscles may interfere with speech development (Moss, 2002).

Patau syndrome (trisomy 13) is associated with microcephaly and malformation of skull bones and severe intellectual disability. Cleft palate or lip and extra fingers or single palmar crease are common features of this syndrome. Other associated characteristics are small lower jaw, short neck, heart anomalies, and severe renal malformations that may even be fatal. Approximately 95% of the children with Patau syndrome die before the age of 3, and those who survive usually have severe physical and cognitive disabilities. Anophthalmia and microphthalmia are the usual causes of visual loss (http://author.emedicine. com/ped/topic1745.htm). Hearing loss is due to structural malformations and is usually sensorineural.

Infectious Causes

The most common infectious causes of deafblindness are meningitis, encephalitis, and rubella.

Meningitis is an infection of the meninges, the membranes covering the spinal column. Meningitis infections may be bacterial or viral, though the bacterial forms are more serious. Hearing loss is sensorineural due to damage to the cochlea and vision loss is due to optic atrophy (Herer et al., 2002).

Encephalitis is an infection that affects the brain. More than 100 germs may cause encephalitis, including measles, mumps, herpes simplex virus, and aboviruses (infections spread by insects). Hearing loss from encephalitis is sensorineural and may occur in one or both ears. Vision loss is often due to optic atrophy or neurological damage. Encephalitis may cause significant central nervous system damage.

Rubella, one of the STORCH infections, is generally harmless to children and adults; however, it poses an extreme threat to the unborn fetus. When a pregnant woman contracts the rubella virus she may not be particularly ill; however, the child may be born with deafness or deafblindness. In addition, these children often have balance problems, heart disorders, and other health problems including late-onset conditions such as diabetes and thyroid dysfunction (Schirmer, 2001). It is common for children infected with the rubella virus prenatally to have sensorineural hearing loss in both ears and also mild conductive losses for a combined form of hearing loss. Visual conditions include cataracts, glaucoma, keratoconus, pigmentary retinopathy, microophthalmia, strabismus, and optic nerve atrophy.

Other Causes

Additional causes of deafblindness include asphyxia, trauma, and fetal alcohol syndrome (FAS). Asphyxia occurs when oxygen levels in the blood are severely reduced. It may occur in utero, during birth, or after birth. Oxygen supply may be cut off by twisted umbilical cords, obstructed airway, and prolonged labor, among other causes. Asphyxia may have a dire effect on multiple systems, and more than half of the children who experience asphyxia do not survive. Asphyxia may cause sensorineural hearing loss in survivors if the cochlea is damaged. Children who experience vision loss due to asphyxia are most likely to experience cortical blindness and/or conditions associated with muscle imbalances, such as strabismus and nystagmus (Edwards, Goehl, & Gordon, 1992).

Deafblindness may occur as the result of trauma in the form of direct impact to the eye and inner ear or from indirect damage from brain swelling or stroke. Such trauma is most likely to cause cortical visual impairment (CVI), nystagmus, and diplopia (Bigge, Best, & Heller, 2001).

FAS causes visual issues such as strabismus, nystagmus, astigmatism, and myopia. Hearing loss is usually caused by malformations in the middle ear (Wunsch, Conlon, & Scheidt, 2002).

Impact of Deafblindness on Development and Learning

The sections on visual impairment and deafness describe the impact of each of the distance senses on development and learning. The impact of deafblindness is even more remarkable in children because they have experienced losses in both of their distance senses. The impact of deafblindness cannot be understood by simply adding up the effects of the vision and hearing loss, because the two distance senses support each other. The following section describes some of the areas of development that are affected by deafblindness.

Attachment

Vision and hearing play an important role in the formation of attachment between mother and child. The presence of sensory impairments interferes with interactive dialogues that occur between an infant and his or her parents. Unlike infants who can see and hear, the infant who is congenitally deafblind is unable to have eye contact or recognize and respond to other's voices or facial expressions. This interference affects the development of communication, trust, security, and social relationships that extend beyond the child into the outside world (Prickett & Welch, 1995, 1998).

Motor Skills

As indicated in the previous sections, at the very earliest stages of life, vision and hearing encourage the infant to explore and learn about the world. Infants who have vision see something of interest and try to move toward it. Similarly, infants with normal hearing listen to something that makes an interesting sound and then try to explore and move toward those sounds. This type of motivation is reduced in most children who are congenitally deafblind. Without early intervention, their experience of the world is limited to what is within reach.

Communication

Reduced movement and exploration delays the child's experiences in using actions with people and objects, a form of early communication. Delays in moving within the environment also result in reduced opportunities for a child to associate experiences in daily routines with symbols, words, and concepts, also part of communication. Thus, the development of infants with deafblindness is most significantly affected by this lack of communication linked with movement (Miles & Riggio, 1999; Prickett & Welch, 1995, 1998).

Children who are deafblind have fewer communication partners, which reduces both the frequency of modeling in their preferred expressive form(s) and opportunities to practice interaction skills. Others may not understand these children's communication, resulting in fewer and less-appropriate responses to the children's expressive communication.

Access to Sensory Information

As mentioned previously, some information acquired through vision cannot be obtained through other senses (e.g., obtaining sensory information about things that are too distant, such as clouds, or too dangerous, such as fire). Hearing also has unique features that are not experienced through other senses (e.g., attending to different types of input at the same time, such as listening to someone on the telephone while being aware of a speaker announcing the news on the television). Children who are deafblind are unable to receive complete and accurate information from the distance senses, and thus they acquire incomplete and distorted concepts about the world (Prickett & Welch, 1995).

Isolation and Limitations in Experiences

Vision and hearing, the two distance senses, connect an individual with people, actions, objects, and the world that extends beyond his or her personal body space. Someone who is deafblind is basically isolated unless he or she is in close proximity or in direct physical contact with another person. This sense of isolation creates the greatest barrier in the life of someone who is deafblind because of the limitation in opportunities to communicate or interact with people and objects in the environment. Whereas students who are deaf or hard or hearing can see someone signing to them at a distance, students who are deafblind are unable to do so. In addition, someone who is deafblind cannot observe others in a room or overhear conversations. Students who are blind and have some useful hearing also feel isolated when conversations end or shift from one peer to another in a group situation (Miles & Riggio, 1999).

Lack of Incidental Learning

The loss of both distance senses results in a lack of incidental learning, which typically occurs through visual and auditory observation. For example, when a student with vision enters a new classroom at the beginning of the school year, he or she can see how many people are in the room, how many children he or she knows, what types of clothing they are wearing, and the size and physical arrangement of the room. When a student with hearing enters a new classroom, he or she can detect familiar voices and realize friends are there; he or she can detect the mood of the room by hearing the types of conversations taking place. Incidental learning is effortless and it enhances the knowledge and experience base of children who see and hear without any special interventions. A child who is deafblind is unable to benefit from such incidental learning. Even with the assistance of an interpreter, it is impossible to transmit detailed information that can be captured immediately. Therefore, children who are deafblind have to be intentionally and systematically taught to formulate concepts and learn about elements of the environment that are not accessible to them such as that acquired by sighted and hearing children incidentally (Miles & Riggio, 1999; Prickett & Welch, 1995).

Concept Development

Certain concepts such as cause and effect, body image, and a stable self-concept are dependent on vision. A child who is blind has a difficult time learning that objects exist even when he or she is not in direct contact with them (object permanence); the task becomes even more immense for a child who is deafblind. Because the child may not be able to gain access to both visual and auditory features of objects, it is more difficult for the child to learn object concepts and to develop skills such as categorization.

Impact of Progressive Sensory Losses

Usher syndrome and other progressive losses pose unique challenges to students, including threats to self-image and community participation. Individuals who lose vision or hearing experience grief and a reduced sense of independence. Adventitious and progressive losses may result in the need to shift instructional approaches from oral or auditory to other means, because the student may no longer have sufficient hearing to gain meaning from speech and may not have sufficient vision to lipread. Literacy transitions may include the shift from visual presentation of sign to tactile sign and from large print to braille. Students with deafblindness might have difficulty in school or in adult life if they are not transitioned to the appropriate reading medium when it is needed; this underscores the need for ongoing functional vision evaluations. Vocational counseling is important because a student's vision and/or hearing may continue to deteriorate after school graduation. Students who are adventitiously deafblind will need ample support to maintain socialization within the school and larger communities. Most will need high levels of emotional support as they cope with these life-altering changes.

Assessment of Students with Deafblindness

The low-incidence nature of deafblindness coupled with the paucity of appropriate assessment tools creates unique challenges for school professionals called on to assess students who are deafblind. Valid assessment requires collaboration of families and professionals to gather essential information that provides a representative appraisal of the whole child without presenting a fragmented perspective (Barraga & Erin, 2001). In most cases, the use of standardized instruments is inappropriate because of individualized patterns of development in children with deafblindness. Although one purpose of psychological assessment may be to estimate intelligence potential, it is not possible to do so for students who are congenitally deafblind. Even assessments that were normed on this group only measure achievement that was accomplished without language (Geenens, 1999). Therefore, it is appropriate to use tools to determine what the child has learned and needs to learn. Some assessment tools are based on the sequence of development experienced by children without disabilities. Such tools are useful for young children but are not appropriate for assessing students who are more than approximately 8 years old.

The Callier-Azusa Scale, Edition G (Stillman, 1978), is a developmentally based tool that contains 18 subscales in the following six areas of development: motor, perceptual, daily living skills, cognition, communication and language, and social development. The Callier-Azusa Scale also offers a scale that assesses early communication skills.

The INSITE Developmental Checklist (Morgan, 1989) was developed to assess children ages birth to 6 years with multiple disabilities, including sensory loss. It assesses gross motor, fine motor, self-help, cognition, socioemotional, communication, and tactile skills. INSITE is a curriculum-based assessment tool that includes task-analyzed activities for the classroom and the home.

Older students should be assessed using tools that are focused on the desired outcomes of adulthood. Such tools are often called functional or outcomes-based assessments. The Functional Skills Screening Inventory (FSSI) is an example of an assessment instrument founded on the functional outcomes perspective and is appropriate for individuals ages 8 through adult. The FSSI evaluates performance in the following areas: basic skills and concepts, communication, personal care, homemaking, work skills and concepts, community living, and behaviors.

In addition to formal assessment tools, there are a few noteworthy informal assessment structures. Nelson, van Dijk, McDonnell, and Thompson (2002) delineated an assessment framework that uses child-guided strategies to examine a child's biobehavioral or alertness states, orienting responses to outside stimuli, preferred sensory learning channels, likes and dislikes, memory, social interactions, and communication. Intervention strategies are provided for each of the assessed areas. The assessment is further illustrated in the CD-ROM *Child-Guided Strategies for Assessing Children who are Deafblind or have Multiple Disabilities* (Nelson & van Dijk, 2002) in which Dr. Jan van Dijk demonstrates the assessment process and guides viewers as they interpret the results.

Mar and Sall's (1999a) *Dimensions of Communication* was specifically designed to address the needs of children with multiple disabilities (including children who are deafblind) who communicate at the nonsymbolic level, although it can be used with children who can communicate on a symbolic level. The tool development was based on a research study of 103 children and adolescents (Mar & Sall, 1999b). Part I is the assessment, and Part II instructs the collaborative team on translating data into an intervention plan. The assessed areas of communication are symbol use, intent, complexity, social action, vocabulary use, and comprehension.

Interventions

Many children who are deafblind learn primarily through the sense of touch. Their hands become their eyes. It is for this reason that many are adverse to having their hands held and will express this by withdrawing from hand-over-hand assistance. A preferred and more effective strategy is to use hand-under-hand touch (teacher's hand under the hands of the student) when exploring and introducing objects or topics. This technique reduces passivity on the part of the student, is noncontrolling, and enhances the student's tactile experience. It becomes the tactile equivalent of the pointing gesture (Miles, 1998; Miles & Riggio, 1999).

Although instruction will address all domains of learning, communication and language development is a priority for students who are deafblind. The results from formal and informal assessment will be used to establish instructional emphasis and strategies.

Many of the current intervention strategies that are used to support the development of children who are deafblind evolved from the child-centered methods developed by van Dijk and colleagues in the Netherlands in the mid-1960s. The van Dijk approach emphasizes following the child's lead and interests as a mutual relationship between child and partner is established and the child learns that he or she can influence the environment (Janssen et al., 2003; MacFarland, 1995; van Dijk & Nelson, 1997). The approach is conversational in nature as the child and partner (e.g., parent, educator, peer) take turns following each other's movements and actions in a give-and-take format. The resulting conversational dialogue gradually becomes more symbolic as the child's communication and language develop. Each of the child's communicative behaviors, no matter how subtle or atypical, is responded to as a communication initiation. MacFarland (1995) delineated several strategies that form the basis of the van Dijk approach; briefly, these include the following:

- *Resonance:* The conversation partner joins in the child's behavior and develops turn-taking within an activity. The child determines the course of the activity and all of the child's actions are responded to as communication. Through resonance, familiar movements are used to help the child respond to the environment. Self-stimulatory behaviors may be used as the basis for early conversations as the communication partner follows the child's movements. In this manner, self-stimulatory behaviors become more interactive in nature. For example, a child might be flicking his fingers in front of his face; his teacher then imitates his flicking behavior and pauses to allow the child to take a turn doing the same movement. As each takes a turn, an interactive conversation develops from what began as a solitary behavior.

- *Co-active movement:* In this extension of resonance, the partner follows the child's movements and the child is encouraged, in turn, to imitate and follow the partner's movements. The movements are then expanded on to become sequences or chains. Once a pleasurable routine has been established, the partner might stop the routine and wait for the child to communicate that he or she wants the routine to continue. As the child becomes comfortable and familiar with the routine or chain of routines, distance between the child and partner is gradually increased. Co-active movement sequences may be carried out within the context of daily routines. Imitation is encouraged as the child learns to follow the actions of the teacher.

- *Objects of reference:* An object or picture from an activity is used as a common frame of reference so that both the child and the communication partner can know the subject of a conversation even when words or signs are not used. For instance, "water wings" that a child uses in a swimming pool might be an object of reference or tangible symbol for swimming. The partner might point to the wings and make swimming motions and then pause to encourage the child to also make the motions. They can then go over to a container of water and mutually splash in the water as they continue the "swimming" conversation.

- *Characterization:* A referent is chosen based on what in an activity is most meaningful to the child. The characterizations can include gestures; objects; parts of objects; textures; sounds; pictures; three-dimensional models; and/ or spoken, written, or signed words. Activities, people, animals, objects, time, and emotion can all be characterized as a repertoire of referents is built and the child begins to develop symbolic language. Examples of characterizing referents include a piece of a mat used to represent physical therapy and a unique bracelet used to characterize the child's teacher. In the swimming example just presented, water wings become a characterizing referent or tangible symbol for swimming. As the child learns that water wings represent swimming, the symbol can be made more portable by cutting out a small section of the water wings or finding a similar piece of plastic. The child should be involved in this process, and initially the comparison between the actual object and the symbol should occur frequently. The referent or symbol should continue to be the joint focus for conversation but can also be used in choice making. As a word of caution, miniature objects may be especially abstract to children who are deafblind as they cannot see the larger referent and may not make the connection between the two (Rowland & Schweigert, 2000a, 2003). More information on tangible symbols can be found in Chapter 11.

- *Sequential Memory Strategies:* To help the child understand and remember time sequences, two major strategies are used. In the first of the strategies, schedules or calendars are used to help a child understand the beginning and ending of activities as well as the schedule of events of the day. Schedule systems use objects or pictures that are arranged sequentially to represent activities in a child's life. Through the use of schedule systems, a child can understand what is coming up and what has already occurred. The child is encouraged to be an active participant in the calendar system by choosing some of the activities or selecting the order in which they occur. When activities are finished, the symbol can go into a "finished" box to be reviewed at a later time. Using the symbol as a joint focal point, conversations between the child and communication partner should occur before the activity, during it, at completion, and then again when the contents of the finished box are reviewed. The choice of symbols used is individual and should be based on what in an activity is most meaningful to a particular child. Whenever possible, the child should be involved in the construction of symbols. Rowland & Schweigert (2000b), in their study of 41 children that included many with deafblindness, documented the effectiveness of tangible symbols when taught in combination with systematic and flexible instructional strategies. Concrete examples of the use of tangible symbols and schedules are available in a video, *Tangible Symbol Systems* (Rowland & Schweigert, 2000a).

The second strategy is the experience or memory book. This strategy provides a means for the child to record both past and upcoming events as well as to share and reminisce about experiences with others. Experience books may be composed of drawings, photos, objects, and/or parts of objects from activities. For example, if a child has been working in the garden with his grandmother, flowers from the garden may be gathered and placed in a plastic bag that is attached to a piece of sturdy paper. Some soil and few seeds might be glued on the paper and together, the child and his grandmother might draw pictures of themselves working in the garden. The picture could then labeled to promote emerging literacy and allow others in the child's life to understand and share the experience with the child. In this example, the child is actively involved in selecting what will go on a memory page and in its construction. Throughout the process, the experience is discussed and re-enacted as memory is built. The pages of the book should be reviewed frequently and shared with others.

Experience book pages might be used to facilitate choice making about participation in future activities and can be used within schedule systems. It is important that both the schedule systems and experience books be used to form topics of conversations between the child and partner as they converse about activities the child has already experienced or will experience in the future.

- *Drawing:* In this strategy, the child actively participates in creating drawings of experienced activities or objects. The drawings may be used in experience books or in daily schedule systems. The two-dimensional or textured drawings promote the use of residual vision and serve as communication referents for conversations.

- *Anticipatory Strategies:* Familiar routines form the basis for anticipatory communication. A familiar routine allows the child to predict what the next step in an activity will be. Once a routine has become very familiar to a child, a mismatch or change in the activity is added and the child is given the opportunity to acknowledge or express surprise at the change.

- *Symbolic Communication Strategies:* Fading and shaping are used to gradually move from natural (invented) symbols to true symbolic communication. Within natural and interesting routines, symbolic language is used in conjunction with natural symbols, and gradually, use of the natural symbols is faded.

Unique Aspects of Orientation and Mobility Instruction for Students with Deafblindness

Strategies related to O&M, included previously in this chapter in the section on the expanded core curriculum for students with visual impairments and multiple disabilities, are also relevant to students with deafblindness. This section describes only the unique aspects of O&M that relate to students with deafblindness.

Although communication and O&M are often seen as separate domains of learning, they must be deeply integrated for students who are congenitally deafblind. Communication is the most important adaptation that needs to be incorporated into all O&M instruction for this population. When teams plan and implement O&M programs for students with deafblindness, they need to know the student's level of communication skills and the individual systems, modes, and devices that the student uses (Gense & Gense, 2000; Joffee, 1995). SLPs, TVIs, and teachers of the deafblind may provide input to the COMS regarding communication strategies that are effective and appropriate for each student. The following adapted case study describes how an O&M program was developed that accommodated and integrated a student's communication needs.

After conducting functional assessments, Toni's collaborative team, including the communication specialist, the TVI, and the O&M specialist, concluded that Toni's hearing was essentially not functional for her and that she was communicating both expressively and receptively on a nonsymbolic level. Visually, she was able to recognize common objects and pictures. Therefore, the team recommended that she use a system for learning O&M that included touch cues to provide information about body position and movement, such as cues asking Toni to stand, sit, turn left, turn right, and stop. Object and picture cues to identify landmarks and destinations, such as the classroom, lunchroom, bathroom, gym, and bus area were developed based on her interests and preferences. A bulletin board was set up to display all of the cues and all team members used the cues with Toni. The physical learning environments in the classroom and school were structured both to motivate her to move and to be conducive to the teaching of O&M skills and techniques. (adapted from Joffee, 1995, pp. 589–590)

Some students with deafblindness have developed a high level of symbolic communication and are competent in sign language and lipreading. Nevertheless, an interpreter might be needed during O&M lessons. The COMS retains his or her teaching role; however, he or she has to teach the interpreter the concepts and techniques so that the interpreter can help to make the directions clear. Working with an interpreter slows the teaching process, and goals and techniques may need to be modified to ensure that all members of the team are communicating with the student successfully (Miller, 1995). Even when an interpreter is not considered necessary, more time will be required to practice a skill or route because the COMS has to stop and communicate with the student throughout the lesson. For example, it is not realistic to expect the student to acquire cane travel skills on the way to the school bus and sign or lip read at the same time.

Families, teachers, and students typically are concerned about safety issues with regard to O&M instruction, particularly for students who are deafblind. All travel involves risks to some extent, and all members of the team have to weigh these risks in deciding when and how specific skills and techniques will be used. Overprotection is harmful; according to Joffee, students who are not permitted to participate in O&M instruction have "limited opportunities to learn about their environment and develop concepts about movement, time, and position; and to achieve self-esteem" that accompanies the ability to move about and perform real life skills (1995, p. 609).

Certain strategies will help students who are deafblind realize dangerous situations and protect themselves while learning from experience. Students can be allowed to bump into an obstacle (with buffers to avoid injury), for example. Students who are deafblind should also be instructed on how to recognize guides who behave inappropriately and learn to separate physically from a guide who is leading them in an unsafe manner (Joffee, 1995). When in public areas, students can learn to use cards with preprinted messages to obtain assistance from human guides and avoid being led to an incorrect place.

Positive Behavioral Support

It is common for children who are deafblind to exhibit behaviors that are regarded as inappropriate by others. Their lack of vision and hearing makes the world a very unpredictable place, and without appropriate accommodations and intervention, many children act out because they are frightened or confused about expectations and experiences. Many children who are deafblind are also unable to effectively communicate with others and their resulting frustration may be communicated through challenging or self-injurious behaviors. In addition, a significant number of the children with deafblindness are plagued with health problems and physical discomfort. Treatment for behavior problems must be based on an assessment of their underlying causes (Durand & Tanner, 1999). A functional behavioral assessment is required by IDEA '97 for individuals with significant behavior problems. Two methods to systematically accomplish this assessment and support appropriate behavioral intervention are the Motivation Assessment Scale (MAS) (Durand & Crimmins, 1992) and positive behavioral support (PBS), an approach that modifies behavioral management principles to both prevent problem behaviors and support the instruction of alternative behaviors. When used with children who are deafblind, the assessments must begin with an examination of visual and hearing impairments and their possible implications for behavior. In addition, the student's etiology, medication, general health, and communicative methods and abilities must be considered.

The MAS is a questionnaire about where, when, and under what conditions problem behaviors occur that can be given to teachers, paraprofessionals, and family members in order to determine what is motivating a given behavior. Each question is scored using a rating scale and total scores are computed to determine if the motivation for the behavior is to get more or less sensory stimulation, to escape from an activity or individual, to obtain attention, and/or to obtain something tangible. A given behavior may serve more than one purpose. A relative ranking is then computed and, in combination with information gathered from other sources, a hypothesis is generated and an intervention plan developed (Durand & Tanner, 1999; Jackson & Panyan, 2002). The following example demonstrates how the MAS can be used to develop an intervention plan for a young girl who is deafblind.

———————————

Meredith, a young girl with Cornelia de Lange syndrome, frequently engaged in behaviors that included screaming, kicking, biting her own arm, and attempting to bite her caregivers. Scores on the MAS indicated that her behavior was due to her desire to escape activities. A further analysis revealed that the behaviors occurred most often during transitions from activity to activity. It was hypothesized that because of her visual and hearing impairments, she was not able to quickly understand what was being asked of her and where she was being asked to go. Because she did not see and hear the environmental cues that would have told her that a transition was imminent, she was unable to prepare herself to move on to something else. An intervention plan was developed that involved providing extra time to allow Meredith to prepare for the transition and the use of a schedule or calendar system that graphically explained the transition and upcoming activity to her. Because of the careful analysis of the motivations behind the behaviors and the development of an appropriate intervention plan based on the assessment, Meredith's problematic behaviors showed a rapid and dramatic decrease.

The process of PBS is similar to the MAS in that the focus is on determining the purposes of the child's behavior from the perspective of the child and focuses on skill development rather than behavior reduction (Jackson & Panyan 2002). After the analysis is complete, a PBS plan is developed based on the team's hypothesis about the behavior. The decision-making protocol of the PBS plan includes the following: 1) a precise description of the behavior, 2) functional assessment and analysis, 3) hypothesis, 4) lifestyle enhancements, 5) needed environmental changes, 6) specific positive intervention procedures that are respectful and dignified, 7) alternative instruction procedures, 8) incident response and crisis procedures, and 9) reevaluation of the plan (Jackson & Panyan, 2002; McDonnell, Hardman, & McDonnell, 2003; Westling & Fox, 2004).

The following example illustrates the role played by both etiological and environmental factors and the need for both to be addressed in the formulation of intervention plans.

Jeremy was a 12-year-old boy with CHARGE syndrome who engaged in aggression toward other students and teachers. The other children in the classroom were able to sign more fluently than Jeremy could, and because of his colobomas, he was unable to track the rapid signing used in the classroom. The staff did not adjust their sign vocabulary or speed of signing for Jeremy, and he was unable to understand what they were attempting to communicate or what was expected of him. He exhibited multiple signs of anxiety including fidgeting, hand play, moving away, turning his head to avoid visual contact, and angry vocalizations. These behaviors were often followed by acts of aggression including slapping others. Although it was determined that Jeremy could benefit from learning more signs to express his frustrations as prescribed by "teaching alternative behaviors" in the PBS, etiological concerns were important to consider in developing hypotheses for his behavior and a subsequent positive behavioral support plan. Children with CHARGE syndrome very often have high anxiety levels. Therefore, an environment that supports high levels of success is very important. Effective instruction included teaching at the level just above what Jeremy could do independently. This allowed Jeremy to have a model of the next step while not unduly frustrating him. Consistent with "environmental change" in the PBS, communication was altered to include more of the vocabulary signs that Jeremy knew, and signs were presented in Jeremy's best visual field and at a speed that was accessible to him.

Assistive Technology Devices for Deafblind Students

In addition to the assistive technology devices described in the sections on visual impairments and deafness that provide print, speech, or braille access, several additional devices are specifically designed for use by individuals who are deafblind, particularly those with Usher syndrome. They are listed next:

- *Vibrotactile devices* are helpful to individuals who are unable to detect environmental sounds. These devices can translate sounds into vibrations and can help with detecting a variety of objects and people in the environment. Examples of vibrating alerting systems are a knock sensor that can be attached to the inside of a door that activates the receiver when someone knocks, and a vibrating doorbell that transmits signals to a vibrating and audible alarm worn by the user. Other personal alert-vibrating systems are available that can be connected with as many as five sound sources such as the telephone, a pager, a smoke detector, or an alarm clock. Some of the personal alert systems have a row of buttons labeled in braille, each of which corresponds with a different transmitter. When the receiver vibrates, the person can push each button until it vibrates again, indicating which sound source was activated (Sauerburger, 1993; http://www.deafblind.co.uk/equipment.html).

- *Telebraille* is a device that can be used for telephone and face-to-face communication to spell out braille and print messages. The device is connected to a special TDD to provide a row of refreshable braille cells. Messages are typed on the TDD keyboard or are received over the telephone from another TDD; they are then converted into braille and are seen in small print on the TDD screen (Sauerburger, 1993; http://www.deafblind.co.uk/equipment.html).

- *Text telephones* (TTs or TTYs) with large visual displays can be used by individuals who are deafblind and have some functional vision. The color of the foreground and background on the displays can be changed to achieve maximum contrast.

- *Braillephone* can be used as a notebook, calendar, calculator, and phonebook. It comes with cables and works with most available Microsoft Windows screen-reading software. It may be interfaced with a computer that has braille output. It also can be used for face-to-face communication.

ADDITIONAL CONSIDERATIONS IN SENSORY IMPAIRMENT

Placement Decisions for Children and Youth with Sensory Impairments

The collaborative team must consider the unique abilities and needs of each student when making decisions on the placement of students who are blind or visually impaired, deaf or hard of hearing, or deafblind. As indicated in the IDEA '97 amendments, placements of blind and visually impaired students, including those with other disabilities, may not be based solely on factors such as category of disability, significance of disability, availability of special education and related services, availability of space, the configuration of the service delivery system, or administrative convenience (Appendix A, question 1, 64 FR 12406 at 12471, March 12, 1999). The full range of placement options must be considered in determining an appropriate educational environment. Some examples include

- A regular classroom with necessary support services by an itinerant teacher or special teacher assigned to that school

- A regular classroom with services outside the classroom with an itinerant teacher or by a special education teacher assigned to that school

- A self-contained classroom in a general school

- A special school with residential option (Heumann & Hehir, 2000)

Collaborative Education Teams for Children and Youth with Sensory Impairments

Although individual team member roles have been defined and embedded within each section of this chapter, it is important to close by revisiting the importance of the collaborative team approach. The needs of children with sensory and other multiple disabilities far exceed the knowledge and skills of any one profession. It is crucial that occupational and physical therapists, medical personnel, social workers, psychologists, and classroom teachers work together with specialists in the sensory areas to ensure that all of the needs of the child are met in a coordinated manner. The goals and intervention plans that are developed for an individual child must be based on the priorities of the child and his or her family, not the goals of any one specialist. Collective team member expertise should be geared toward helping the child to achieve meaningful life outcomes without overwhelming either the child or the family. The collaborative team model supports the identification of key professionals who provide primary intervention. Because of the tremendous impact of sensory impairments on development and learning, individuals with specialized training in sensory issues must use their expertise to assist other team members in developing and implementing instructional strategies and adaptations that address and accommodate for the student's lack of vision, hearing, or both. At the same time, it must be recognized that parents and other primary caregivers are the core of collaborative teams. These individuals have much to offer as they inform other team members about unique child characteristics as well as their hopes and priorities for the child's learning. Family members can also help ensure that learned skills are generalized to life outside of the classroom.

REFERENCES

Adelson, E., & Fraiberg, S. (1974). Gross motor development in infants blind from birth. *Child Development, 45,* 114–126.

Alsop, L., Blaha, R., & Kloos, E. (2000). *The intervener in early intervention and educational settings for children and youth with deaf-blindness* (Briefing Paper). Monmouth, OR: The National Technical Assistance Consortium for Children and Young Adults Who Are Deaf-Blind.

Anthony, T.L. (1997). *Individual sensory learning profile interview.* Unpublished document.

Anthony, T.L. (2000). Performing a functional low vision assessment. In F.M. D'Andrea & C. Farrenkopf (Eds.), *Looking to learn: Promoting literacy for students with low vision* (pp. 32–83). New York: AFB Press.

Bak, S. (1999). Relationships between inappropriate behaviors and other factors in young children with visual impairments. *RE:view, 31,* 84–91.

Bambring, M., & Troster, H. (1992). On the stability of stereotyped behaviors in blind infants and preschoolers. *Journal of Visual Impairment and Blindness, 86,* 105–110.

Barbi, M., Binda, S., Caroppi, S., Ambrosetti, U., Corbetta, C., & Serch, P. (2003). A wider role in congenital cytomegalovirus infection in sensorineural hearing loss. *Pediatric Infectious Disease Journal, 22*(1), 39–42.

Barclay, L. (1999). Yo-Yo magic or a teacher of the visually impaired learns another lesson in social skills. *RE:view, 31*(3), 126–128.

Barraga, N., & Erin, J. (2001). *Visual impairments and learning* (4th ed.). Austin, TX: PRO-ED.

Batshaw, M.L. (Ed.). (2002). *Children with disabilities* (5th ed.). Baltimore: Paul H. Brookes Publishing Co.

Batshaw, M.L., & Shapiro, B. (2002). Mental retardation. In M.L. Batshaw (Ed.), *Children with disabilities* (5th ed., p. 287–305). Baltimore: Paul H. Brookes Publishing Co.

Becker, H., Schur, S., Paoletti-Schelp, M., & Hammer, E. (1983). *Functional Skills Screening Inventory.* Amarillo, TX: Functional Resources.

Bigge, J., Best, S., & Heller, K. (2001). *Teaching individuals with physical, health, or multiple disabilities.* Upper Saddle River, NJ: Merrill Prentice Hall.

Bishop, V.E. (1996). Causes and functional implications of visual impairment. In A.L. Corn & A.J. Koenig (Eds.), *Foundations of low vision: Clinical and functional perspectives* (pp. 86–114). New York: AFB Press.

Blake, K.D., Davenport, S.L.H.D., & Hall, B.D., Hefner, M.A., Pagon, R.A., Williams, M.S., Lin, A.E., & Graham, J.M. (1998). CHARGE association: An update and review for the primary pediatrician. *Clinical Pediatrics, 37,* 159–174.

Blind Babies Foundation. (1998). Cortical visual impairment. In: *The pediatric visual diagnosis fact sheet.* San Francisco: Author.

Bowe, F. (2000). *Physical, sensory, and health impairments: An introduction.* Upper Saddle River, NJ: Merrill Prentice Hall.

Brilliant, R.L., & Graboyes, M. (1999). Historical overview of low vision: Classifications and perception. In R.L. Brilliant (Ed.), *Essentials of low vision practice* (pp. 2–9). Boston: Butterworth Heinemann.

Brodsky, M.C., Fray, K.J., & Glasier, C.M. (2002). Perinatal and subcortical vision loss: Mechanisms of injury and associated ophthalmologic signs. *Ophthalmology, 109*(1), 85–94.

Brown, D. (1997). CHARGE association. *Talking Sense 43*(2), 1–4.

Brown, D. (2003). Educational and behavioral implications of missing balance sense in CHARGE syndrome. *ReSources, 10*(15), 1–4.

Bruce, S. (2002). Impact of a communication intervention model on teachers' practice with children who are congenitally deafblind. *Journal of Visual Impairment and Blindness, 96*(3), 154–168.

Carden, S.M., & Good, W.V. (2003). Cortical visual impairment. In K.W. Wright & P. H. Spiegel (Eds.), *Pediatric ophthalmology and strabismus* (pp. 936–939). New York: Springer.

Chapman, R.S., Seung, H.-K., Schwartz, S.E., Bird, E.K-R. (1998). Language skills of children and adolescents with Down Syndrome: II. Production deficits. *Journal of Speech, Language, and Hearing Research, 41,* 861–873.

Chen, D. (1995). The beginnings of communication: Early childhood. In K.M. Huebner, J.G. Prickett, T.R. Welch, & E. Joffee (Eds.), *Hand in hand: Essentials of communication and orientation and mobility for your students who are deaf-blind* (pp. 159–184). New York: AFB Press.

Chen, D. (1999). Understanding hearing loss. In D. Chen (Ed.), *Essential elements in early intervention: Visual impairment and multiple disabilities* (pp. 207–245) New York: AFB Press.

Corn, A.L., DePriest, L.B., & Erin, J.N. (2000). Visual efficiency. In A.J. Koenig & M.C. Holbrook (Eds.), *Foundations of education: Instructional strategies for teaching children and youths with visual impairments* (Vol. 2, pp. 464–499). New York: AFB Press.

Corn, A.L., & Koenig, A.J. (1996). Perspectives on low vision. In A.L. Corn & A.J. Koenig (Eds.), *Foundations of low vision: Clinical and functional perspectives* (pp. 3–25). New York: AFB Press.

Cranford, J.L., Thompson, N., Hoyer, E., & Faires, W. (1997). Brief tone discrimination by children with histories of early otitis media. *Journal of the American Academy of Audiology, 8,* 137–141.

Dahle, A.J., Fowler, K.B., Wright, J.D., Boppana, S.B., et al. (2000). Longitudinal investigation of hearing disorders in children with congenital cytomegalovirus. *Journal of American Academy of Audiology, 11,* 283–290.

Davenport, S.L.H. (1994). Spotlight on Usher syndrome: Vision and hearing loss. *Hereditary Deafness Newsletter of America, 4*(1), 1–4.

Deitz, S.J., & Ferrell, K.A. (1993). Early services for young children with visual impairment: From diagnosis to comprehensive services. *Infants and Young Children: An Interdisciplinary Journal of Special Care Practices, 6*(1), 68–76.

Downing, J.E. (1999). *Teaching communication skills to students with severe disabilities.* Baltimore: Paul H. Brookes Publishing Co.

Downing, J., & Demchak, M. (2002). First steps: Determining individual abilities and how best to support students. In J. Downing (Ed.), *Including students with severe and multiple disabilities in typical classrooms* (pp. 37–70) Baltimore: Paul H. Brookes Publishing Co.

Dowse, J.M. (2003). Blindness and low vision. In W.L. Heward (Ed.), *Exceptional children: An introduction to special education* (7th ed., pp. 400–437). Upper Saddle River, NJ: Merrill Prentice Hall.

Durand, V.M., & Crimmins, D. (1992). *The motivation assesssment scale administration guide.* Topeka, KS: Monaco & Associates.

Durand, V.M., & Tanner, C. (1999). Research-to-practice: Reducing behavior problems in students who are deaf-blind. *Deaf-blind Perspectives, 6*(3), 4–6.

Edwards, L.E., Goehl, K.S., Gordon, L.A. (1992). *Profiles: Individuals with deaf-blindness.* Terre Haute: Indiana Deaf-Blind Service Project.

Encephalitis. Retrieved October 8, 2003, from www.yourmedicalsource.com/library/encephalitis/ENC)_whatis.htm/

Erin, J.N. (1996). Functional vision assessment and instruction of children and youths with multiple disabilities. In A.L. Corn & A.J. Koenig (Eds.), *Foundations of low vision: Clinical and functional perspectives* (pp. 221–245). New York: AFB Press.

Erin, J.N. (2002). Students with visual impairments and additional disabilities. In A.J. Koenig & M.C. Holbrook (Eds.), *Foundations of education: Instructional strategies for teaching children and youths with visual impairments* (Vol. 2, pp. 720–752). New York: AFB Press.

Fazzi, D. (1998). Facilitating independent travel for students who have visual impairments with other disabilities. In S.Z. Sacks & R.K. Silberman, *Educating students who have visual impairments with other disabilities* (pp. 441–468). Baltimore: Paul H. Brookes Publishing Co.

Ferrell, K.A. (1998). *Project PRISM: A longitudinal study of the developmental patterns of children who are visually impaired. Final Report.* CFDA 84.0203C (field-initiated research H023C10188). Greeley: University of Northern Colorado.

Ferrell, K.A. (2000). Growth and development of young children. In M.C. Holbrook & A.J. Koenig (Eds.), *Foundations of education: History and theory of teaching children and youths with visual impairments* (2nd ed., Vol. 1, pp. 111–134). New York: AFB Press.

Flexer, C. (1999). *Facilitating hearing and listening in young children.* San Diego: Singular Publishing Group.

Fowler, K.B., Dahle, A.J., Boppana, S.B., & Pass, R.F. (1999). Newborn hearing screening: Will children with hearing loss caused by congenital cytomegalovirus infection be missed? *Journal of Pediatrics, 135,* 60–64.

Fraiberg, S. (1968). Parallel and divergent patterns in blind and sighted infants. *Psychoanalytic Study of the Child, 23,* 264–300.

Frame, M.J. (2000). The relationship between visual impairment and gestures. *Journal of Visual Impairment and Blindness, 86,* 155–171.

Friend, M., & Bursick, W. (2002). *Including students with special needs: A practical guide for classroom teachers.* Needham Heights, MA: Allyn & Bacon.

Gallaudet Research Institute. (2003). *2001–2002 Regional and National Survey,* Washington, DC. Retrieved from http://www.gri.gallaudet.edu/Demographics/

Geenens, D. (1999). Neurobiological development and cognition in the deafblind. In J. McInnes (Ed.), *A guide to planning and support for individuals who are deafblind* (pp. 150–174). Canada: University of Toronto Press.

Gense, D., & Gense, M. (July, 2000). *The importance of orientation and mobility skills for students who are deaf-blind.* Monmouth, OR: DB-LINK: The National Clearinghouse on Children Who Are Deaf-Blind.

Gense, D., & Gense, M. (2002). *Autism spectrum disorder in learners with blindness/vision impairments: Comparison of characteristics.* Washington, DC: Heldref Publications.

Gense, M.A., & Gense, D.J. (1994). Identifying autism in children with blindness and visual impairments. *RE:view, 26*(2), 55–62.

Gilbert, P. (1996). *The A–Z reference book of syndromes and inherited disorders.* Cheltenham, UK: Stanley Thornes Publishers Ltd.

Good, W.V., Jan, J.E., DeSa, L., Berkovich, A.J., Groenveld, M., & Hoyt, C.S. (1994). Cortical visual impairment in children. *Survey of Ophthalmology, 38*(4), 351–364.

Greenspan, S. (1998). Dandy-Walker syndrome. In L. Phelps (Ed.), *Health-related disorders in children and adolescents.* Washington, DC: American Psychological Association.

Hardman, M., Drew, C., & Egan, M. (2002). *Human exceptionality: Society, school, and family* (7th ed.). Needham Heights, MA: Allyn & Bacon.

Hart, V. (1983). *Characteristics of young blind children.* Paper presented at the Second International Symposium of Visually Handicapped Infants and Young Children: Birth to 7. Aruba.

Hatlen, P. (2000). Historical perspectives. In M.C. Holbrook & A.J. Koenig (Eds.), *Foundations of education: History and theory of teaching children and youths with visual impairments* (2nd ed., Vol. 1, pp. 1–54). New York: AFB Press.

Hatton, D.D. (2001). Model registry of early childhood visual impairment: First-Year results. *Journal of Visual Impairment and Blindness, 95*(7), 418–433.

Hatton, D.D., Topor, I., & Rosenblum, L.P. (2004). Visual conditions in infants and toddlers. In D.D. Hatton, I. Topor, & L.P. Rosenblum (Eds.), *Visual conditions and functional vision: Early intervention issues.* Chapel Hill, NC: Early Intervention Training Center for Infants and Toddlers with Visual Impairments.

Heller, K.W., Alberto, P.A., Forney, P.E., & Schwartzman, M.N. (1996). *Understanding physical, sensory, and health impairments.* Pacific Grove, CA: Brooks/Cole.

Herer, G.R., Knightly, C.A., & Steinberg, A.G. (2002). Hearing: Sounds and silences. In M.L. Batshaw (Ed.), *Children with disabilities* (5th ed., pp. 196, 202). Baltimore: Paul H. Brookes Publishing Co.

Heumann, J.E., & Hehir, T. (2000, June 5). *Educating blind and visually impaired students: Policy guidance from OSERS.* 20 U.S.C. 1411-1420; 29 U.S.C. 794. Available online from http://www.tsbvi.edu/agenda/osers-policy.htm.

Heward, W. (2003). *Exceptional children: An introduction to special education.* Upper Saddle River, NJ: Merrill Prentice Hall.

Hood, L., & Berlin, C. (1996). Central auditory function and disorders. In J.L. Northern (Ed.), *Hearing disorders* (pp. 235–236). Needham Heights, MA: Allyn & Bacon.

Huebner, K.M. (2000). Visual impairment. In M.C. Holbrook & A.J. Koenig (Eds.), *Foundations of education: History and theory of teaching children and youths with visual impairments* (2nd ed., Vol. 1, pp. 55–76). New York: AFB Press.

Individuals with Disabilities Education Act Amendments of 1997, PL 105-17, 20 U.S.C. §§ 1400 *et seq*. IDEA '97 Regs: Definitions of Term and Acronyms. Retrieved August 7, 2003, from http://www.ideapractices.org/law/regulations/regs/definitions.

Ireland, M. (2001). Cornelia DeLange syndrome. In S. Cassidy & J. Allanson (Eds.), *Management of genetic syndromes*. New York: Wiley-Liss.

Jackson, L., & Panyan, M.V. (2002). *Positive behavioral support in the classroom: Principles and practices*. Baltimore: Paul H. Brookes Publishing Co.

Jan, J.E., Good, W.V., Freeman, R.D., & Espezel, H. (1994). Eye-poking. *Developmental Medicine and Child Neurology, 25*, 755–762.

Janssen, M.J., Riksen-Walraven, & Van Dijk, J.P.M. (2003). Toward a diagnostic intervention model for fostering harmonious interactions between deaf-blind children and their educators. *Journal of Visual Impairment and Blindness, 97*(4), 197–214.

Joffee, E. (1995). Approaches to teaching orientation and mobility. In K.M. Huebner, J. G. Prickett, T.R. Welch, & E. Joffee (Eds.), *Hand in hand: Essentials of communication and orientation and mobility for your students who are deaf-blind* (pp. 575–611). New York: AFB Press.

Kimberling, W.J., Orten, D., & Pieke-Dahl, S. (2000). Genetic heterogeneity of Usher Syndrome. *Advances in Oto-Rhino-Laryngology, 56*, 11–18.

Kirkwood, R. (1997). The adolescent. In H. Mason & S. McCall (Eds.), *Visual impairment: Access to education for children and young people* (pp. 23–29). London: Fulton.

Koenig, A.J., & Holbrook, M.C. (1995). *Learning media assessment of students with visual impairments*. Austin: Texas School for the Blind and Visually Impaired.

Koenig, A.J., & Holbrook, M.C. (2000a). Planning instruction in unique skills. In A.J. Koenig & M.C. Holbrook (Eds.), *Foundations of education instructional strategies for teaching children and youths with visual impairments* (2nd ed., Vol. 2, pp. 196–220). New York: AFB Press.

Koenig, A.J., & Holbrook, M.C. (2000b). Professional practice. In M.C. Holbrook & A.J. Koenig (Eds.), *Foundations of education: History and theory of teaching children and youths with visual impairments* (2nd ed., Vol. 1, pp. 55–76, 260–276). New York: AFB Press.

Koenig, A.J., Holbrook, M.C., Corn, A.L., DePriest, L.B., Erin, J.N., & Presley, I. (2000). Specialized assessments for students with visual impairments. In A.J. Koenig & M.C. Holbrook (Eds.), *Foundations of education: Instructional strategies for teaching children and youths with visual impairments* (2nd ed., Vol. II., pp. 103–172). New York: AFB Press.

Kuder, S. (2003). *Teaching students with language and communication disabilities* (2nd ed.). Boston: Pearson Education.

Langley, M.B. (1998). *Individualized, systematic assessment of visual efficiency* (ISAVE). Louisville, KY: American Printing House for the Blind.

Langley, M.B. (2000). Strategies for teaching career education skills to students with visual impairments and additional disabilities. In A.J. Koenig & M.C. Holbrook (Eds.), *Instructional strategies for teaching children and youths with visual impairments* (2nd ed., Vol. 2, pp. 715–716). New York: AFB Press.

Langley, M.B. (2004). Screening and assessment of sensory functions. In M. McLean, M. Wolery, & D. Bailey (Eds.), *Assessing infants and preschoolers with special needs* (3rd ed., pp. 123–171). Upper Saddle River, NJ: Pearson/Merrill Prentice Hall.

Leung, A., Sauve, R., & Davies, D. (2003). Congenital cytomegalovirus infection, *Journal of the National Medical Association, 95*(3), 213–217.

Levack, N., Stone, G., & Bishop, V. (1994). *Low vision: A resource guide with adaptations for students with visual impairments* (2nd ed.). Austin: Texas School for the Blind.

Lewis, C., & Lowther, J. (2001). CHARGE association: Symptoms, behaviour, and intervention. *Educational Psychology in Practice, 17*(1), 69–77.

Lewis, S. (2004). Visual impairments. In R. Turnbull, A. Turnbull, M. Shank, & S.J. Smith (Eds.), *Exceptional lives: Special education in today's schools* (4th ed., pp. 456–486). Upper Saddle River, NJ: Pearson/Merrill Prentice Hall.

Lieberman, L. (2002). Fitness for individuals who are visually impaired or deafblind. *RE:view, 34*(1), 13–23.

Lieberman, L., & Stuart, M. (2002). Self-determined recreational and leisure choices of individuals with deaf-blindness, *Journal of Visual Impairment and Blindness, 96*(10), 724–735.

Lowenfeld, B. (1981). *Berthold Lowenfeld on blindness and blind people: Selected papers by Berthold Lowenfeld.* New York: AFB Press.

MacFarland, S.Z.C. (1995). Teaching strategies of the van Dijk curricular approach. *Journal of Visual Impairment and Blindness, 89*(3), 222–228.

Mar, H. (2002). Phases: Psychologists helping to assess students' educational strengths. *Deaf-Blind Perspectives, 10*(1), 1–4.

Mar, H., & Sall, N. (1999a). *Dimensions of communication.* Paterson, NJ: Authors.

Mar, H., & Sall, N. (1999b). Profiles of the expressive communication skills of children and adolescents with severe cognitive disabilities. *Education and Training in Mental Retardation and Developmental Disabilities, 34*(1), 77–89.

Mar, H.H., & Cohen, E.J. (1998). Educating students with visual impairments who exhibit emotional and behavior problems. In S.Z. Sacks & R.K. Silberman (Eds.), *Educating students who have visual impairments with other disabilities* (pp. 262–302). Baltimore: Paul H. Brookes Publishing Co.

Martin, F., & Clark, J. (2003). *Introduction to audiology* (8th ed.). Needham Heights, MA: Allyn & Bacon.

McCormick, L., Loeb, D.F., & Schiefelbusch, R.L. (2003). *Supporting children with communication difficulties in inclusive settings: School-based language intervention* (2nd ed.). Boston: Pearson Education.

McDonnell, J., Hardman, M., & McDonnell, A. (2003). *An introduction to persons with moderate and severe disabilities: Emotional and social issues* (2nd ed.). Needham Heights, MA: Allyn & Bacon.

Mervis, C.A., Yeargin-Allsopp, M., Winter, S., et al. (2000). Aetiology of childhood vision impairment, Metropolitan Atlanta, 1991–1993. *Paediatric and Perinatal Epidemiology, 14,* 70–77.

Miles, B. (1998). Talking the language of the hands to the hands. *DB Link Fact Sheet: The National Clearinghouse on Children Who are Deaf-Blind.* Retrieved September 2, 2003 from http://www.tr.wou.edu/dblink/hands2.htm.

Miles, B., & Riggio, M. (1999). *Remarkable conversations: A guide to meaningful communication with children and young adults who are deafblind.* Watertown, MA: Perkins School for the Blind.

Miller, D. (1995). Working with interpreters. In K.M. Huebner, J.G. Prickett, T.R. Welch, & E. Joffee (Eds.), *Hand in hand: Essentials of communication and orientation and mobility for your students who are deaf-blind* (Vol. 1, p. 590). New York: AFB Press.

Miller, M.M., Menacker, S.J., & Batshaw, M.L. (2002). Vision: Our window to the world. In M.L. Batshaw (Ed.), *Children with disabilities* (5th ed., pp. 165–192). Baltimore: Paul H. Brookes Publishing Co.

Morgan, E. (1989). *INSITE Developmental Checklist: 0–6 years.* Logan: Utah State University.

Morse, M.T. (1999). Cortical visual impairment: Some words of caution. *RE:view, 31*(1), 21–26.

Moss, K. (2002). Vision and hearing loss associated with Goldenhar Syndrome. *See/Hear, 7*(1), 22–23.

National Center for Hearing Assessment and Management. (2003). *Universal newborn hearing screening: Summary statistics of UNHS in the United States.* Retrieved October 7, 2003 from (http://www.infanthearing.org/status/unhsstate.html. Logan: Utah State University.

Nelson, C., & van Dijk, J. (2002). *Child-guided strategies for assessing children who are deaf-blind or have multiple disabilities* [CD-ROM]. The Netherlands: Aapnootmuis.

Nelson, C., van Dijk, J., McDonnell, A., & Thompson, K. (2002). A framework for understanding young children with severe disabilities: The van Dijk approach to assessment. *Research and Practice for Persons with Severe Disabilities, 27*(2), 97–111.

Newton, G., & Moss, K. (2001). Early identification of hearing and vision loss is critical to a child's development. *See/Hear, 6*(3), 27–30.

No Child Left Behind Act of 2001, PL 107-110, 115 Stat. 1425, 20 U.S.C. §§ 6301 *et seq.*

Northern, J.L., & Downs, M.P. (2002). *Hearing in children* (5th ed.). Needham Heights, MA: Allyn & Bacon.

Orel-Bixler, D. (1999). Clinical vision assessments for infants. In D. Chen (Ed.), *Essential elements in early intervention: Visual impairments and multiple disabilities* (pp. 107–156). New York: AFB Press.

Perla, F., & Ducret, W. (1999). Guidelines for teaching orientation and mobility to children with multiple disabilities. *RE:view, 31*(3), 113–119.

Pess, R.F. (2002). Cytomegalovirus infection. *Pediatric Review, 23,* 163–169.

Peterson, J., & Hittie, M. (2003). *Inclusive teaching: Creating effective schools for all learners.* Boston: Pearson Education.

Pogrund, R., Healy, G., Jones, K., Levack, N., Martin-Curry, S., Martinez, C., Marz, J., Roberson-Smith, B., & Vrba, A. (1993). *Teaching age-appropriate purposeful skills: An orientation and mobility curriculum for students with visual impairments.* Austin: Texas School for the Blind and Visually Impaired.

Prevent Blindness America (1994). *Vision problems in the U.S.* Schaumburg, IL: Author.

Prickett, J.G., & Welch, T.R. (1995). Adapting environments to support the inclusion of students who are deaf-blind. In N. Haring & L. Romer (Eds.), *Welcoming students who are deaf-blind into typical classrooms: Facilitating school participation, learning, and friendships* (pp. 171–193). Baltimore: Paul H. Brookes Publishing Co.

Prickett, J., & Welch, T. (1998). Educating students who are deafblind. In S.Z. Sacks & R.K. Silberman (Eds.), *Educating students who have visual impairments with other disabilities* (pp. 139–159). Baltimore: Paul H. Brookes Publishing Co.

Pugh, G., & Erin, J. (Eds.). (1999). *Blind and visually impaired students: Educational service guidelines.* National Association of State Directors of Special Education and the Hilton-Perkins Program. Watertown, MA: Perkins School for the Blind.

Rais-Bahrami, K., Short, B.L., & Batshaw, M.L. (2002). Premature and small-for-date infants. In M.L. Batshaw (Ed.), *Children with disabilities* (5th ed., p. 93) Baltimore: Paul H. Brookes Publishing Co.

Roizen, N.J. (2002). Down syndrome. In M.L. Batshaw (Ed.), *Children with disabilities* (5th ed., pp. 307–320). Baltimore: Paul H. Brookes Publishing Co.

Rowland, C., & Schweigert, P. (1993). *Analyzing the communication environment: An inventory of ways to encourage communication in functional activities.* Tucson, AZ: Communication Skill Builders.

Rowland, C., & Schweigert, P. (2000a). *Tangible symbol systems* (2nd ed.). Portland: Oregon Health Sciences University.

Rowland, C., & Schweigert, P. (2000b). Tangible symbols, tangible outcomes. *Augmentative and Alternative Communication, 16,* 61–78.

Rowland, C., & Schweigert, P. (2003). Cognitive skills and AAC. In D.R. Beukelman & J. Reichle (Series Eds.) & J.C. Light, D.R. Beukelman, & J. Reichle (Vol. Eds.), *Augmentative and alternative communication series: Communicative competence for individuals who use AAC: From research to effective practice* (pp. 241–275). Baltimore: Paul H. Brookes Publishing Co.

Sacks, S.Z. (1998). Educating students who have visual impairments with other disabilities: An overview. In S.Z. Sacks & R.K. Silberman (Eds.), *Educating students who have visual impairments and other disabilities* (pp. 3–38). Baltimore: Paul H. Brookes Publishing Co.

Sacks, S.Z., & Silberman, R.K. (2000a). Social skills issues in vision impairment. In B. Silverstone, M.A. Lang, B.P. Rosenthal, & E.E. Faye (Eds.), *The lighthouse handbook on vision impairment and vision rehabilitation* (Vol. 1, pp. 377–393). New York: Oxford University Press.

Sacks, S.Z., & Silberman, R.K. (2000b). Social skills. In A.J. Koenig & M.C. Holbrook (Eds.), *Foundations of education: Instructional strategies for teaching children and youths with visual impairments* (Vol. 2, 2nd ed., pp. 616–652). New York: AFB Press.

Sacks, S.Z., Wolffe, K.E., & Tierney, D. (1998). Lifestyles of students with visual impairments: Preliminary studies of social networks. *Exceptional Children, 64,* 463–478.

Sauerburger, D. (1993). *Independence without sight or sound: Suggestions for practitioners working with deaf-blind adults.* New York: AFB Press.

Schirmer, B.R. (2001). Deafness. *Psychological, social, and educational dimensions of deafness.* Needham Heights, MA: Allyn & Bacon.

Scholl, G.T. (1986). What does it mean to be blind? In G.T. Scholl (Ed.), *Foundations of education for blind and visually handicapped children and youth: Theory and practice* (pp. 23–33). New York: AFB Press.

Silberman, R.K. (2000). Children and youth with visual impairments and other exceptionalities. In M.C. Holbrook & A. Koenig (Eds.), *Foundations of education: History and theory for teaching children and youths with visual impairments* (2nd ed., Vol. 1, pp. 173–196). New York: AFB Press.

Silberman, R.K., Sacks, S.Z., & Wolfe, J. (1998). Instuctional strategies for educating students who have visual impairments with other disabilities in classroom and community environments. In S.Z. Sacks & R.K. Silberman (Eds.), *Educating students who have visual impairments with other disabilities* (pp. 101–138). Baltimore: Paul H. Brookes Publishing Co.

Smith, M., & Levack, N. (1999). *Teaching students with visual and multiple impairments* (2nd ed.). Austin: Texas School for the Blind and Visually Impaired.

Spungin, S.J., McNear, D., & Torres, I. (2002). *When you have a visually impaired student in your classroom: A guide for teachers.* New York: AFB Press.

Stillman, R. (1978). *The Callier-Azusa Scale.* Dallas: The University of Texas.

Television Decoder Circuitry Act of 1990, PL 101-431, 47 U.S.C. §§ 303 *et seq.*

Teplin, S.W. (1995). Visual impairment in infants and young children. *Infants and Young Children: An Interdisciplinary Journal of Special Care Practices, 8*(1), 18–51.

Topor, I.L. (1999). Functional vision assessments and early interventions. In D. Chen (Ed.), *Essential elements in early intervention: Visual impairment and multiple disabilities* (pp. 157–206). New York: AFB Press.

Topor, I.L., & Erin, J. (2000). Educational assessment of vision function in infants and children. In B. Silverstone, M. Lang, B. Rosenthal, & E. Faye (Eds.), *The Lighthouse handbook on vision impairment and vision rehabilitation* (Vol. 2, pp. 821–833). New York: Oxford University Press.

Topor, I.L., Rosenblum, L.P., & Hatton, D.D. (2004). *Functional vision assessment and age-appropriate learning media assessment.* Chapel Hill: Early Intervention Training Center for Infants and Toddlers with Visual Impairments, FPG Child Development Institute, University of North Carolina.

Torres, I., & Corn, A.L. (1990). *When you have a visually handicapped child in your classroom: Suggestions for teachers.* New York: AFB Press.

U.S. Department of Education. (2001). *Twenty-third annual report to Congress on the implementation of the Individuals with Disabilities Education Act.* Washington, DC: Author.

U.S. Department of Education. (2002). *Twenty-fourth annual report to Congress on the implementation of the Individuals with Disabilities Education Act.* Washington, DC: Author.

Utley, B.L., Roman, C., & Nelson, G.L. (1998). Functional vision. In S.Z. Sacks & R.K. Silberman (Eds.), *Educating students who have visual impairments and other disabilities* (pp. 371–412). Baltimore: Paul H. Brookes Publishing Co.

van Dijk, J., & de Kort, A. (2003). *Living with CHARGE: Assessment, prevention, and intervention of challenging behavior* [CD-ROM]. The Netherlands: AapNootMuis.

van Dijk, J., & Nelson, C. (1997). History and change in the education of children who are deaf-blind since the rubella epidemic of the 1960s: Influence of methods developed in the Netherlands. *Deaf-Blind Perspectives, 5,* 1–5.

Vaughn, S., Bos, C., & Schumm, J. (2003). *Teaching exceptional, diverse, and at-risk students.* Boston: Pearson Education.

Vort Corporation. (1997). *Behavioral Characteristics Progression (BCP).* Palo Alto, CA: Author.

Ward, M.E. (2000). The visual system. In M.C. Holbrook & A.J. Koenig (Eds.), *Foundations of education: History and theory of teaching children and youths with visual impairments* (2nd ed., Vol. 1, pp. 77–110). New York: AFB Press.

Warren, D.H. (2000). Developmental perspectives. In B. Silverstone, M.A. Lang, B.P. Rosenthal, & E.E. Faye (Eds.), *The Lighthouse handbook on vision impairment and vision rehabilitation* (Vol. 1, pp. 325–337). New York: Oxford University Press.

Wesson, M.D., & Maino, D.M. (1995). Oculovisual findings in children with Down syndrome, cerebral palsy, and mental retardation without specific etiology. In D.M. Maino (Ed.), *Diagnosis and management of special populations* (pp. 17–54). St. Louis: Mosby Year Book.

Westling, D., & Fox, L. (2004). *Teaching students with severe disabilities* (3rd ed.). Upper Saddle River, NJ: Pearson.

White, K. (2002). Early hearing detection and intervention. *See/Hear, 7*(2), 24–27.

Wolffe, K. (2000). Career education. In A.J. Koenig & M.C. Holbrook (Eds.), *Instructional strategies for teaching children and youths with visual impairments* (2nd ed., Vol. 2, pp. 679–719). New York: AFB Press.

Wunsch, M.J., Conlon, C.J., & Scheidt, P.C. (2002). Substance abuse: A preventable threat to development. In M.L. Batshaw (Ed.), *Children with disabilities* (5th ed., p. 112) Baltimore: Paul H. Brookes Publishing Co.

Zambone, A.M., Ciner, E., Appel, S., & Graboyes, M. (2000). Children with multiple impairments. In B. Silverstone, M.A. Lang, B.P. Rosenthal, & E.E. Faye (Eds.), *The Lighthouse handbook on vision impairment and vision rehabilitation* (Vol. 1, pp. 451–468). New York: Oxford University Press.

Zapien, C. (1998). Options in deaf education: History methodologies, and strategies for surviving the system. *Exceptional Parent 28*(9), 40–50.

For More Information

National organizations that are involved with advocacy and educational issues related to students with sensory impairments are listed below.

ORGANIZATIONS ON BLIND AND VISUALLY IMPAIRED

American Council of the Blind
1155 15 Street, NW
Washington, DC 20005
800-424-8666, 202-467-5081
http://www.acb.org

American Foundation for the Blind
11 Penn Plaza, Suite 300
New York, NY 10011
1-800-232-5463, 212-502-7600
http://www.afb.org

American Printing House for the Blind
1839 Frankfort Avenue
Post Office Box 6085
Louisville, KY 40206
1-800-223-1839, 502-899-2274
http://www.aph.org

Association for Education and Rehabilitation of the Blind and Visually Impaired (AER)
1703 North Beauregard Street
Suite 440
Alexandria, VA 22311
703-671-4500
http://www.aerbvi.org/welcome.htm

National Association for Parents of Children with Visual Impairments (NAPVI)
Post Office Box 317
Watertown, MA 02471
800-562-6265, 617-972-7441
http://www.napvi.org

National Federation of the Blind
1800 Johnson Street
Baltimore, MD 21230
410-659-9314
http://www.nfb.org/

Recording for the Blind and Dyslexic
National Headquarters
20 Roszel Road
Princeton, NJ 08540
800-221-4792, 609-520-8031
http://www.rfbd.org

ORGANIZATIONS ON DEAF AND HARD OF HEARING

Alexander Graham Bell Association for the Deaf
3417 Volta Place NW
Washington DC 20007
202-337-5220 (voice), 202-337-5221 (TTY)
http://www.agbell.org

American Society for Deaf Children
Post Office Box 3355
Gettysburg, PA 17325
800-942-ASDC (parent hotline), 717-334-7922 (voice/TTY)
http://www.deafchildren.org

Boys Town National Research Hospital
555 North 30th Street
Omaha, NE 68131
402-498-6631
http://www.boystownhospital.org

Gallaudet University
800 Florida Avenue NE
Washington, DC 20002
202-651-5258 (voice/TDD)
http://www.gallaudet.edu

National Association of the Deaf
814 Thayer Avenue
Silver Spring MD 20910
301-587-1788 (voice), 301-587-1788 (TTY)
(includes a juniors chapter)
http://www.nad.org

ORGANIZATIONS ON DEAFBLINDNESS

American Association of the Deaf-Blind
814 Thayer Avenue
Silver Spring, MD 20910
301-495-4403 (voice), 301-495-4402 (TTY)
http://www.aadb.org

Helen Keller National Center for Deaf-Blind Youths and Adults
141 Middle Neck Road
Sands Point, NY 11050
516-944-8900
http://www.hknc.org

National Clearinghouse on Children Who Are Deaf-Blind (DB-LINK)
345 North Monmouth Avenue
Monmouth, OR 97361
800-438-9376
http://www.tr.wou.edu/dblink

National Coalition on Deaf-Blindness
175 North Beacon Street
Watertown, MA 02172
617-972-7347

National Family Association for the Deaf-Blind
111 Middle Neck Road
Sand Point, NY 11050
800-255-0411

National Organization for Rare Disorders (NORD)
55 Kenosia Avenue
Post Office Box 1968
Danbury, CT 06813-1968
800-999-6673 (voice), 203-797-9590 (TDD)

National Technical Assistance Consortium for Children and Young Adults Who Are Deaf-Blind (NTAC)
Western Oregon University
345 North Monmouth
Monmouth, Oregon 97361
http://www.tr.wou.edu/ntac

CHAPTER 11

Communication Skills

June E. Downing

Communication is a critical life skill that empowers all of us to make our needs known and establish our relationship with others (Warren, 2000). As Mirenda (1993) contended, communication has no prerequisites other than breathing and having a desire to express something. Despite the challenges that individuals with severe and multiple disabilities encounter, communication is one skill of which everyone is capable. The manner, amount, and sophistication of the communication may vary from individual to individual or situation to situation; however, all people communicate. This fact is particularly important for those individuals who have considerable difficulty completing tasks on their own. When someone is unable to perform the action by him- or herself, knowing how to request assistance when needed and maintain control over the type and quality of that assistance is essential.

COMPONENTS OF COMMUNICATION

Communication does have certain inherent components. Communication skills involve *form* (a way to communicate), *function* (a purpose or reason to communicate), *content* (something to communicate about), and a *social component* (someone to communicate with). These components are described in the following paragraphs.

Form

Speech is the most common means of communication, but it is not a necessary means. Communication can occur without speech and can take many different forms. A raised eyebrow, a sigh, a smile, and hands on hips can all convey different messages. Individuals without disabilities use speech, facial expressions, body language, objects, vocalizations, conventional gestures (e.g., pointing), and other means to express themselves. Individuals with severe and multiple disabilities who may not be able to use speech to communicate effectively will use other modes depending on these individuals' physical, sensory, and cognitive abilities (Beukelman & Mirenda, 1998; Downing, 1999; Orelove & Sobsey, 1996). For someone who cannot easily use speech, no one mode of communication needs to be determined, but rather, multiple means of communication are recommended (Blischak & Lloyd, 1996; Iacono, Mirenda, & Beukelman, 1993; Mirenda, 1999; Sigafoos & Drasgow, 2001). The benefits of multimodal communication are that all individuals, no matter the severity of their disabilities, can and do communicate. Some of these means can be unaided (i.e., nothing added to the individual), such as manual sign, gestures, or facial expressions, whereas others are aided, using either low or high technology, such as pictorial systems, parts of objects, or an array of augmentative and alternative communication (AAC) methods including complex voice-output communication aids (VOCAs) (see Table 11.1 for examples of aided and unaided AAC communication types). The advantage of unaided communication is that the individual can communicate at any time, anywhere, and with anyone without needing any adaptive equipment—the individual always has the means of communication at his or her disposal. Unaided communication can be highly symbolic (e.g., speech, American Sign Language [ASL])—to convey any message—or very concrete (e.g., nodding the head, pointing to an item) to convey a more limited and contextually bound message. Unaided communication also can be complex to

Table 11.1.   Types of augmentative and alternative communication

Type of communication	Aided	Unaided
Symbolic	Picture device (e.g., a CD holder with photographs to tell about the student's interests)	Speech
		Sign (e.g., vocabulary from American Sign Language or adapted sign systems)
	Texture device (e.g., a choice board of different textures to make specific requests)	
	Voice output device (e.g., Tech Talk for greetings, requests, comments)	
Nonsymbolic	Actual object (e.g., an empty can of soda to request a soda)	Facial expressions (e.g., wide eyes to show surprise)
		Body movements (e.g., a shrug, pointing)
		Vocalizations (e.g., grunt, squeal to gain attention)

produce (e.g., speech) or very simple (e.g., facial expressions). Aided communication bypasses difficulties that may be encountered when producing complex forms of communication such as speech and ASL. Aided communication requires a relatively simple physical behavior (e.g., pointing, switch use) to convey messages and provides visual auditory, or tactile reminders of the messages that can be made. High technological communication devices allow the individual to express almost any message. Less technologically complex devices may severely limit the number and types of messages possible. The greatest disadvantage to any form of aided communication is that it requires the individual to rely on something external to the person. As a result, access and portability become critical considerations.

Several experts in the field have described the diversity of communication modes (Beukelman & Mirenda, 1998; Cress, 2002; Mirenda, 1999). Individuals who do not use speech typically use a variety of communicative modes in all of their interactions. How they communicate will depend on individual factors such as physical abilities, sensory limitations, cultural preferences, and demands of the environment. Whereas some students may benefit from using manual signs along with some speech and gestures, other students may not have the physical ability to make effective use of manual signs expressively but use facial expressions, vocalizations, and pictorial information instead. Consider the following example.

Natasha, a 7-year-old student, uses facial expressions; some vocalization; a few body gestures; a BIGmack or VOCA; color photographs; objects; and a few signs such as EAT, CRACKER, and MORE for both expressive and receptive communication. When offered something to eat that she does not want, she whines, tightens her face in dislike, and turns her head away from the offered food. When offered different toys to play with, she will grab the one she prefers. When asked if she would like to continue in different activities that she enjoys, she will smile and make a giggly sound. To explain what activity is next, Natasha will be told and shown the colored photograph of that activity. Natasha does not need to rely on only one form of communication but uses all that have meaning for her and her communication partners.

Although an individual's expressive communication is typically considered when recommending AAC, various forms of communication also are used for receptive communication. People who serve as conversation partners with the student with severe and multiple disabilities should make use of several modes of communication to make the message as clear as possible. For example, a fifth grader may ask her classmate who has severe and multiple disabilities if she would like to go for a walk at break or have a drink of water. She does this by using speech as well as pointing to the picture symbols that her classmate uses and gestures as indicated to make her message easily understood. This use of multiple modes of communication for receptive purposes not only clarifies the message but also models the expressive communication that is desired. Furthermore, the means of communication used for expressive purposes may differ from those used receptively. For example, Mason, who has severe physical and cognitive impairments, relies on speech, manual signs, facial expressions, pictures, and gestures for receptive communication. He uses facial expressions, pictures, some vocalizations, and body movements expressively.

Function

Communication is fostered by multiple reasons or functions (Beukelman & Mirenda, 1998; Downing, 1999). We all need to request objects and activities that we need or desire. We need to reject what we do not wish to have or do. We may need to confirm when something is right and deny something that is wrong. We may want to share information about others or ourselves or simply engage in an interaction for the purely social benefit (Light, 1997). We may need to ask for information to make things clearer. Whatever the reason for the communication, it is clear that without a reason, there will be no communication.

For beginning communicators, the function or pragmatic nature of the communication typically exceeds in importance the form or manner in which the message is produced. In other words, a student may have a strong need to get out of his or her wheelchair but does not have a conventional means of expressing this need. However, he can flail his arms a bit, whine, and show irritation on his face, which conveys this message to a familiar support person. Giving this student a clearer and more conventional means to request an alternative position is necessary so that all communication partners (familiar and unfamiliar) can respond accordingly; however, what is even more important is responding quickly to this request in its present form to acknowledge that the message has been received and understood.

Content

All communication exchanges must be based on having something to say. When individuals desire to express themselves, it implies that they have things they do, activities they engage in that give them substance to share with one another. Although having something to talk about may not be difficult for those without disabilities (although sometimes it can be), individuals who have severe and multiple disabilities may have such limited experiences and interactions with others that finding something to share, other than requesting basic needs, may be challenging. Durand, Mapstone, and Youngblade (1999) emphasized the importance of students with and without severe disabilities sharing experiences on a regular basis for communication exchanges to occur. Besides shared experiences with individuals without disabilities, we need to ensure that individuals with severe and multiple disabilities have ongoing opportunities to experience all of life's activities just as anyone would. The next step is to devise a means for these individuals to share their experiences with others.

Social Component

Communication, by definition, requires at least two people: a sender and a receiver of the message. For individuals with severe and multiple disabilities, who struggle to convey their messages, communication partners must be particularly sensitive and responsive to their efforts. Unfortunately, the communication attempts made by individuals with severe and multiple disabilities often go undetected by those around them (Houghton, Bronicki, & Guess, 1987; Iacono, Carter, & Hook, 1998). Therefore, it is essential that competent communication partners be encouraged to interact frequently with individuals having severe and multiple disabilities. Classmates without disabilities represent a useful resource for this social element of communication. Typically, several classmates are available at any one point in time, and they can be taught how to be effective communication partners if needed.

ASSESSING COMMUNICATION SKILLS

Numerous assessment tools are available to assess both expressive and receptive communication skills. Many of these tools specifically are designed for children and adults with severe disabilities (cf., Bzoch & League, 1991; Connard & Bradley-Johnson, 1998; Hedrick, Prather, & Tobin, 1984; Huer, 1988). Although these assessment tools may provide a very general idea of the communication skills of a particular individual, they may not specifically address the exact communication needs experienced by that individual in typical environments. Also, standardized assessments may be normed on an inappropriate age range (e.g., normed on very young children and inappropriately used with older students having severe and multiple disabilities). The resulting scores in terms of mental and developmental age will not paint a true picture of individual ability and need (Mar & Sall, 1999). Furthermore, many standardized assessments provide only a static determination of a student's communication skills without contextual information (Cole, Dale, & Thal, 1996).

Instead of a standard score for a student's communicative performance as obtained from a specific assessment tool, a more practical approach is recommended. Information is needed as to the communicative abilities of the student under more optimal conditions, such as when the student is motivated and assisted to interact. Dynamic assessment captures what the child needs to do within a meaningful context with the guidance and support of an adult (Kublin, Wetherby, Crais, & Prizant, 1998). Unlike traditional assessments, which measure independent performance in an out-of-context situation, dynamic assessment provides meaningful information on a child's communicative efforts and potential ways to facilitate the child's skill level. Through this approach there is a direct link between assessment and effective intervention (Beck, 1996).

Ecological Assessment

Whereas standardized assessments assume a specified progression of skills needed by all people, an ecological approach targets the skills needed in a given environment and activity. Highly individualized, an ecological assessment analyzes the communicative requirements of the natural environment for a given student, determines what the student is currently doing in this environment and identifies what skills are lacking. This type of assessment also encourages the assessor to arrive at initial considerations for what might be supportive of enhanced communicative skills. In Figure 11.1, the third-grade science activity of learning about solids and liquids has been analyzed to identify the behavioral and communicative expectations for Neil, a young boy with severe and multiple disabilities.

Unlike standardized assessment tools that target skills at one point in time and without a meaningful context, an ecological assessment involves observational data collected while an individual is communicating within natural routines and environments. By observing how the individual with severe and multiple disabilities communicates when in familiar and comfortable environments, with familiar communication partners, and preferably, when most motivated, a more realistic picture of the individual's abilities in this area can be obtained (Downing, 1999; Reichle, York, & Sigafoos, 1991). Careful and repeated observations over time provide information on how the individual communicates (form) and for what reasons (function), vocabulary used (content), and the most frequent communication partners. The observation form in Figure 11.2 depicts an analysis of interactions among children on a playground at recess. The analysis captures the various forms of communicative behavior used by the

Student: Neal is an 8-year-old with lots of energy, very specific likes and dislikes, a mild bilateral hearing loss, and mild cerebral palsy. He has been labeled as having severe intellectual impairments.

Activity: Science: The study of liquids and solids   Level: 3rd grade

Steps in activity (peers without disabilities)	Natural cues (all children)	Student performance	Communication skills in steps (receptive and expressive)	Discussing analysis	Intervention plan (initial ideas)
1. Attend to teacher demonstration	Teacher instructing	P	*Receptive:* Understand teacher	May not understand topic	Make sure Neal sits close to teacher. Provide pictorial instructions/examples.
2. Respond to teacher questions	Teacher asking questions Knowledge of answer	P	*Receptive:* Understand teacher's questions *Expressive:* Answer questions	Nonverbal May not understand	Make sure teacher asks Neal one very simple question (e.g., to find a certain picture by matching). Move correct picture closer to him.
3. Get with a partner	Teacher direction Not having a partner	−	*Receptive:* Understand teacher direction and request of peer *Expressive:* Ask a peer to be a partner	Nonverbal May not understand Prefers to be alone	Offer him two photo choices of peers to choose from. Teach him to use his "Do you want to work with me?" pictorial card with peer he chooses.
4. Complete worksheet on topic	Teacher direction Worksheet not completed Knowledge of what to do	P	*Receptive:* Understand teacher direction and peer's comments *Expressive:* Comment on question on worksheet	Nonverbal Difficulty understanding Does not write	Adapt worksheet with more spaces. Neal puts a mark on the picture of an item as asked for by the peer who labels it solid or liquid. Neal uses a special grip on a marker.
5. Sign name to worksheet and hand in	Teacher direction Others turning worksheet in	+	*Receptive:* Understand teacher	May not understand Does not write	Peer draws a thick black line on the paper and offers Neal three signature stamps to choose from to write his name. Let Neal collect all worksheets.

Figure 11.1. Ecological inventory of communication skills. (Key: + Independent performance; P Required some assistance; − Did not perform the skill)

535

Student: Alan
Activity: Recess
Observer: JD

Date: Feb. 18, 2004
Grade: 2nd

BEHAVIOR (Form) / INTENT (Function)

Conversational partners	Gross vocalization	Simple body movements	Simple action on people	Simple action on objects	Point	Facial expressions	Extend hand(s)	Nod/shake head	Other conventional gestures	Object symbols	Picture symbols	Manual signs	Speech	Initiation or response	Protest/reject	Make request	Gain attention	Direct attention	Social interaction	Confirm/deny	Label/comment	Other intents	Content
Anthony (peer)	✓				✓																		"Alan, wanna see my baseball cards?"
Alan	✓												R							✓			"I don't know."*
Anthony	✓	✓			✓																		"Here, look at this one!"
Alan	✓	✓											R	✓									"No."*
Anthony				✓	✓	✓																	"OK. How about this one?"
Alan													R						✓				"OK."*
Alan		✓				✓							I		✓								"I want to do something else."*
Anthony																							"Alan, where do you want to go?"
Alan			✓										R							✓			"I'm going to the sand."*
Anthony	✓																						OK. I'll come too."
Alan	✓												R	✓									"OK. Just don't touch me."*

536

Anthony (peer)									"Alright. Do you want to play by Mason & Daniel, or over by Chris?"
Alan	√				R			√	"Mason & Daniel."*
Anthony	√								"Hey guys, can Alan play here?"
Mason									"OK. Hi Alan."
Alan	√	√			R		√		"Hi."*
Alan	√	√	√		I			√	"What's this?*"

Figure 11.2. Communication observation form for Alan. (*Key:* I = Initiation; R = Response; * = Interpretation of Alan's communicative behavior; adapted from Rowland C., Schweigert P., & Stremel, K. [1992]. *Observing and enhancing communication skills.* Copyright © 1992 by Communication Skill Builders, a division of The Psychological Corporation. Adapted by permission. All rights reserved.)

537

target student (Alan in Figure 11.2), whether the communication is an initiation or a response, the function of the behavior, and what the interaction might sound like if the target student had speech. With this approach, even seemingly unintentional forms of communication can be documented and recorded within the interaction. The advantage of such an assessment procedure is that the assessment information applies directly to intervention strategies.

An ecological assessment of communication recognizes the dynamic nature of the communication environment and can be helpful in recognizing the different communicative demands that can change depending on the social situation. In addition to obtaining observational information on the student's current communication skills within meaningful environments and activities, an ecological assessment identifies how others communicate and what expectations for communication exist (Reichle et al., 1991). Assessment findings do not result in a prediction of mental age or developmental level, but rather, in a documentation of what the student can do and where needs exist in order to make interactions most effective.

Significant Other Input

The most logical starting point for any meaningful assessment of a student's communication skills is an interview with those who know the student best (Downing, 1999; Giangreco, Cloninger, & Iverson, 1998). Family members can provide critical information on how their child communicates most effectively, when and where this occurs, the frequency of interactions, and the communication breakdowns. They also know the child's favorite communication topics and partners. They are familiar with past communication intervention efforts and their effectiveness. Perhaps most important, they can share information on their preferences for their child's communication skills and their hopes for the future. The needs and desires of those significant in the student's life should guide the direction of the communication intervention because these individuals will be providing the most direct and long-term support. Sometimes, in the field of augmentative and alternative communication, what is *possible* to attain may not be what is *best* for an individual student or his or her family. Listening to the family and other significant individuals will determine what to assess and where to assess as well as how to make best use of the assessment information.

RECOMMENDED PRACTICE IN COMMUNICATION INTERVENTION

Considerable research exists on specific strategies shown to have some effectiveness in improving the communication skills of students with severe and multiple disabilities (Granlund & Olsson, 1999: Reichle, 1997; Schlosser, 1999).

Such strategies include 1) teaching within natural environments and routines (Beukelman & Mirenda, 1998; Sigafoos, 1999), 2) providing multiple opportunities to practice communication skills (Downing, 1999; Schwartz, Carta, & Grant, 1996), 3) ensuring responsive partners (Higginbotham & Wilkins, 1999; Warren, 2000), and 4) systematic instruction (Drasgow, Halle, Ostrosky, & Harbers, 1996; Sigafoos, 1999).

Teaching within Natural Environments

Teaching within natural environments is a recommended practice that cuts across several different intervention approaches (Beukelman & Mirenda, 1998; Romski, Sevcik, & Adamson, 1997; Sigafoos, 1999). Instead of removing the student from typical and daily activities, with this approach, the intervention occurs in natural environments and activities in which the student needs to communicate. In this way, no demand is made on the student to learn important communication skills in one environment and then transfer or generalize that skill to where it is most likely to be needed.

As opportunities naturally emerge that require communication interactions, the teacher intervenes as needed to support and enhance the student's communication skills. Various team members analyze the environment to determine the most optimal times for intervention as well as when communicative behavior could enhance the social situation.

Enhancing Communicative Opportunities

Students with severe and multiple disabilities often need several opportunities to practice skills. Although, in most typical activities, many opportunities naturally exist for communication interactions, the need for repetition to practice skills makes it necessary to create additional opportunities. Unfortunately, many environments for students who use AAC do not provide the necessary amount of opportunities for desired communication skill development (Beck et al., 2001; Rowland & Schweigert, 1993; Sigafoos, 1999).

Several strategies can be employed to increase the number of opportunities in a given day for a student to engage in communicative interactions. One critical strategy that is relatively easy to implement concerns the act of offering choices.

Offering Choices

The value of choice making to enhance communication skills has been well supported in the field (Beukelman & Mirenda, 1998; Downing, 1999; Sigafoos, 1999). Instead of giving a student a particular item (e.g., food, drink, toy, work), allowing the student to make a choice creates an opportunity for the student to communicate. The choice can be offered using speech, the items themselves, representative pictures of the items, parts of the items, or signs. Different modes of input should enhance the student's understanding of the choice and offer the student multiple means of expressing a preference (e.g., signing, looking, pointing to a picture, grabbing an item). Even if the communication partner is fairly convinced of the student's preference (e.g., juice and not water), the choice should still be offered. Preferences change, and the student needs to learn that he or she is in control of the interaction. Making choices throughout the day (even simple ones) can lead to the development of self-determination, and all individuals need practice to develop the lifelong skills of self-determination (Agran, King-Sears, Wehmeyer, & Copeland, 2003; Brown, Gothelf, Guess, & Lehr, 1998; Taylor, 2001; Wehmeyer, 1997). Choices could include what clothes to wear, food to eat, activities to engage in, items to play or work with, other individuals to interact with, places to go, items to purchase, and so forth. The opportunities are readily available but must be recognized and used. Multiple choices may be presented at once, although with the beginning communicator, choices may need to be limited initially, or they could be presented one at a time with the student's response to each option used as an indication of preference. Table 11.2 provides an abbreviated list of potential choices that may be relevant across a student's day, regardless of the student's age.

Creating the Need to Communicate

Another strategy to enhance communication opportunities involves identifying and/or creating the need to interact. For example, offering a student items or activities that he or she is known to dislike allows the student to reject (or "say" no). Not giving a student a sufficient amount of a favorite item (e.g., food, drink, time with a toy) encourages the student to request more. Encouraging peers to greet a classmate with severe disabilities provides the opportunity for this student to respond to each greeting. Showing interest in a student's photographs

Table 11.2.   Choices for students of all ages throughout the school day

- Choosing a partner to work with or sit by
- Choosing materials to use in an activity
- Choosing food or drink for snack and lunch
- Choosing rhythm instrument for music/band
- Choosing activity at nutrition break/recess
- Choosing a position to work in (wheelchair, wedge, or stander)
- Choosing a book to read or have read
- Choosing colors of markers, pens, or paper to use
- Choosing a software program

and/or items provides the student with the opportunity to comment about them. Table 11.3 includes examples of different communication skills demonstrated in various classrooms from kindergarten through high school. Variations of any of these examples could be supported throughout each day to provide multiple opportunities to practice emerging skills. Communication partners must identify all opportunities for enhancing communication and make good use of them as often as possible.

Responsive Communication Partners

An effective way to enhance communication opportunities is to ensure the presence of responsive communication partners (Siegel & Cress, 2002; Warren, 2000). Unfortunately, studies have demonstrated that communication partners,

Table 11.3   Examples of communication skills across classes and grade levels

Communicative function (purpose)	Kindergarten	Fourth grade	Tenth grade
Rejecting	Pushes away crayon to do worksheet	Clenches teeth when a certain food is offered	Points to "No" symbol (unhappy face) when asked to start math assignment
Making comments	Uses voice output device to say, "You're funny!" when peer does something silly at play time	Points to "Wow! That's cool" pictorial symbol on device when shown a peer's science model	Points to newspaper ad of a movie in a conversation book that states the movie and if he liked it or not
Requesting information	Uses a quizzical look on face and looks at a new volunteer in the room	Grabs an item in social studies class, brings close to eyes, looks up at peer	Signs WHAT? and points to a cassette tape during study hall
Requesting items/actions	Reaches for a cookie at snack time	Vocalizes "ba" for ball during recess to play with peers	Points to one of three peers' photographs to ask that peer to work with him
Confirming/ denying	Smiles when asked if he wants the red marker to draw with	Nods head when asked if a photo in her conversation book is her mother.	Looks away when asked if he was asking for help

even when they are trained teachers, may miss communicative efforts of students with severe and multiple disabilities (Blackstone, 1997; Houghton et al., 1987; Rowland, 1990). Responsive partners who can recognize communicative efforts of students with severe and multiple disabilities, regardless of the unconventionality of their communicative behaviors, and then respond in a positive and appropriate way to these behaviors, are critical to the development of communication skills for students with severe and multiple disabilities. Helping those individuals working closely with students who are just beginning to develop communication skills to recognize the importance of being sensitive (nondirective) and responsive to initial communication can create a more positive social environment (Yoder & Warren, 1999; Yoder, Warren, McCathren, & Leew, 1998).

_____

Carrie, a first grader, has limited movement, low affect, and is blind. When she lifts her head up and smiles, her classmates know to quickly respond and ask what she would like. They offer her two tactile choices representing activities that are feasible at that time (e.g., a computer disk to represent computer time and a tape to represent listening to a book). In this way, Carrie learns how to bring others to her to make her request.

_____

Strategies to enhance sensitivity and responsiveness to unique and conventional communicative behavior include training communication partners to recognize the potential communicative value of unique behaviors, responding quickly and appropriately, and following the individual's lead. Essentially, the goal is to help the student with disabilities recognize that circumstances change contingent on producing certain behaviors that are recognized by others (Harwood, Warren, & Yoder, 2002). Being responsive to early communicative efforts helps these beginning communicators to recognize the impact they can have. Communication dictionaries (Beukelman & Mirenda, 1998; Mirenda, 1999; Siegel & Wetherby, 2000) help familiar and unfamiliar communication partners consistently recognize specific behaviors for their communicative intent by stating the observable behavior, the intent of the behavior, and the desired response. Table 11.4 provides examples of entries in such a custom communication dictionary for Kyra, a student. Once behaviors can be identified as communicative, or potentially so, others can respond faster, more appropriately, and consistently.

When students with severe and multiple disabilities are grouped homogeneously by ability level, interacting with one another becomes very difficult. All students struggle with the same limited—and oftentimes unconventional—communication skills. When given the opportunity to be placed with their age-

Table 11.4.   Sample communication dictionary for Kyra

What Kyra does	What it means	How to respond
Vocalizes loudly	She wants attention.	Come to her immediately, show her how to use her BIGmack to request attention. Then offer her choices of what to do.
Cries and thrashes around	She is uncomfortable in her wheelchair (or other position).	Quickly change her position, offering her choices of alternative positions. Check for redness or sores.
Thrusts her head back hard	She is rejecting whatever is happening.	Stop what is happening and offer her alternatives if at all possible. Follow up the activity with something she really enjoys doing.

appropriate peers in typical classrooms, students with severe and multiple dis-abilities have a relatively large number of communication partners who have considerable skills in interactive behavior.

Peers without disabilities model communication skills, demonstrate inter-active behaviors typical of their age group, and can serve as responsive commu-nication partners. To help peers interact most effectively with their classmates who have severe and multiple disabilities, it may be necessary to teach them specific interaction strategies (Carter & Maxwell, 1998). Peers can be taught to get at eye level, wait for their classmate to interact, ask yes/no questions, and use some signs for interacting with their classmates who use sign receptively and/or expressively. Peers should know how to use an AAC device(s), make sure that the device is available to the student, and encourage the student to interact. If the student with severe and multiple disabilities has particularly unique communicative behaviors or behaviors that are difficult to discern, some training should be provided to peers in recognizing these behaviors and their intent and knowing ways to respond. For example, a student may have a high-pitched squeal that sounds as if she might be in pain or frightened; however, this sound actually conveys her happiness and excitement when engaged in certain activities. Teaching her classmates the correct intent of this vocalization helps them to respond appropriately and encourage her to interact more.

Recognizing Reasons to Communicate Other than Requesting

Although offering the student choices throughout each day is a recommended practice designed to increase the number of communication interactions, limit-ing the student to requests only (e.g., "I want this") can make it difficult for the student to experience other reasons to communicate. Teaching the student to engage in different kinds of communication interactions increases the number of opportunities to practice critical skills and recognize the power of communicating. One of the most meaningful reasons to communicate is to establish social closeness (Light, 1997). This is somewhat difficult to achieve if the student is only provided opportunities to make requests. Students need to be provided with a means of sharing information about themselves, teasing, joking, and responding to others' social interactions. A variety of different communicative functions are delineated in Table 11.5.

Although teaching students to make requests is relatively straightforward and leads to a clearly observable outcome (e.g., the student gets what is desired), encouraging the student to engage in communicative exchanges for establishing social relationships with others may ultimately be more reinforcing (Light, Parsons, & Drager, 2002). For instance, April, a beginning communicator, may enjoy using a VOCA to say, "That's silly!" because of the reaction it gets from her peers during different activities of the day. When she makes this statement, her classmates respond by giggling, coming closer to her, and interacting with her. This can be very reinforcing for a child who may have extreme difficulties initiating interactions with others. However, this particular girl will be severely limited in her ability to draw others to herself if those supporting her needs fail to recognize social closeness as a valid need and only provide her with means to request objects or actions.

Although it is relatively easy to develop means of requesting things—whether using objects, parts of objects, pictures, signs, and so forth—creating the means for a student to engage in developing close social relationships with friends is much more difficult. Those supporting the student must find ways to allow the student to "talk" about his or her life, what interests him or her, and what he or she finds amusing. This can be done with photographs, pictures, and parts of realia from various events with prewritten messages for the conversation

Table 11.5.   Functions of communication

Function	Example
Request	"I want to get on the computer."
Reject	"I don't want to do that worksheet."
Confirm/deny	"Yes, that's what I wanted," or "No, not that one."
Gain attention	"Hey, can anyone come over here?"
Direct attention	"Wow! Look at that garbage truck!"
Comment	"I love watching MTV!"
Label	"That's red."
Social closeness	"You are so silly. Come sit here."
Ask for information	"What do you want me to do?"

partner to read. Conversation books have been developed and designed to address the social needs of students with severe and multiple disabilities. Hunt, Alwell, and Goetz (1991) found that using conversation books with students with severe and multiple disabilities improved their ability to interact with their classmates without disabilities. Conversation books may not contain requests, but they use pictures, photographs, tactile items, parts of items, and so forth with written messages and questions regarding these symbols to encourage interactions among students of vastly different abilities. See Figure 11.3 for an example of a conversation book used by a fourth grader with his classmates who do not have disabilities.

SYSTEMATIC INSTRUCTION

Beginning communicators, especially those with complex and multiple impairments, probably will benefit from direct and systematic instruction. Given an

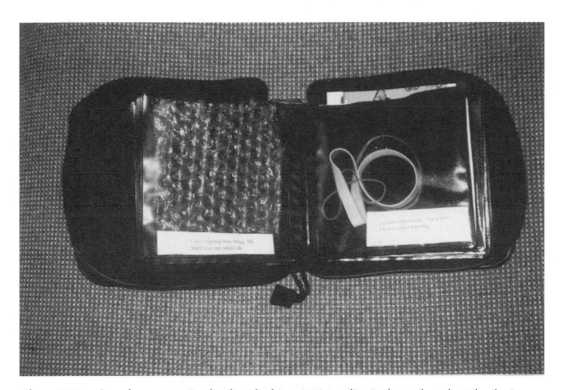

Figure 11.3. Sample conversation book with object. Written slips in the pockets describe the items that convey personal information about the student. In this photograph, the message on the right says, "I love popping these things. My Mom goes ape when I do," and the message on the right says, "I collect rubber bands. I have tons! Do you collect anything?"

array of instructional techniques, such as prompts, cues, wait time, modeling, positive reinforcement, and corrective feedback, beginning communicators are taught to use specific communication skills for different communication purposes (Sigafoos, 1999). The intervention strategy chosen for a given student will depend on a number of variables, including the current ability level, the desired communicative skill, the intent of the interaction, the social situation, conversational partners, and learner preferences, to name a few. Communicative interactions requiring a prompt response, such as returning a greeting or indicating one's presence to a roll call, initially may require the teacher to employ considerable physical guidance. Fading physical support would occur as students begin to demonstrate the desired behavior. For example, when one student, Robyn, is greeted by her peer with a high-five, the teaching assistant will quickly prompt Robyn at the forearm and elbow to return the high-five. As Robyn starts to indicate her understanding of the greeting, the teaching assistant fades her prompt to touching the back of Robyn's upper arm, then to tapping her shoulder, and finally to a giving her a verbal cue: "How do you say hi?" Such a procedure is termed a *most-to-least prompting strategy.*

Other communicative interactions allow more time to shape the desired behavior. For example, when asking a student what activity he or she would like to do first, a wait period can be employed to allow the student a chance to physically explore all options tactilely before making a selection. If no selection is made, the teacher can tap the student's elbow and wait a few seconds to see if that prompt was effective. If not, the teacher may guide the student's hands to feel each item. If no response is given after a few seconds delay (e.g., 3 seconds), the teacher might reduce the choices to two and ask the student to choose. If no response is given after the specified wait time, the teacher may move one of the items under the student's hand, help the student to grasp the item, and then begin to use the item in the activity. This process of increasing prompts is termed a *least-to-most prompting strategy.*

Systematic teaching procedures should not be intrusive but should provide sufficient support and direction to assist the student in acquiring the behavior. Modeling the use of an AAC system, for example, may provide sufficient support in a given situation for a student to demonstrate the desired behavior. Other times, a series of prompts may need to be employed. Ultimately, the goal is for the student to engage in spontaneous communicative behavior without instructional support.

Enhancing the Social and Physical Environment

Regardless of the teaching strategy used, the environment within which interactions occur must be carefully considered. As stated previously, the natural environment is the preferred location for communication intervention; however, accommodations can be made to natural environments to heighten communication skill development. Teachers and care providers need to pay careful attention to potential environmental accommodations that can be made to further support the communicative efforts of children with severe and multiple disabilities.

Social Environment Accommodations

Beginning communicators of any age need many opportunities within any given day to engage in and practice communication skills. Efforts can and should be made to physically place the student close to responsive and interactive partners (typically their peers without disabilities). Adults can monitor their own position in regard to the student and ensure that while providing support, they (the adults) are not interfering with potential social interactions (Giangreco, Edelman, Luiselli, & MacFarland, 1997). Instead of positioning him- or herself between the target student and a nearby peer, for example, the supporting adult can sit behind both students or offer assistance from across a table or desk. Increasing the time students work in pairs or groups supports the potential for student interactions, so when possible, opportunities for encouraging students to work together versus independently should be expanded. Hughes, Carter, Hughes, Bradford, and Copeland (2002) cautioned against always placing students with disabilities in the role of being instructed by a classmate or peer tutor without disabilities, however. Such unequal relationships can hinder social interactions. Therefore, students should also be given time to interact on a more equal basis during unstructured times throughout the day (e.g., passing in the hall, lunch, recess, before and after school). Students with disabilities can be offered choices in terms of which students without disabilities they would like to spend time with.

Physical Environment Accommodations

Certain accommodations and adjustments to the physical environment can help increase the number of opportunities for communication. Teachers and family members can create reasons for students to communicate by not always anticipating needs and providing students with what they may want. This general strategy has been effective with a number of students with various abilities (Schwartz et al., 1996; Sigafoos, 1999). Keeping items desired by the student just beyond the student's reach creates a need for the student to request them. Giving a student an insufficient amount of an item (e.g., food, drink, time to play) creates a need for the student to request more of the item. To provide the opportu-

nity for a student to reject something, teachers can purposefully provide an item
or task that they know the student does not want. Then, when the student
expresses his or her rejection of the item, the teacher can very quickly and positively respond by producing an alternative. Sigafoos and Roberts-Pennell (1999)
found a positive impact of offering students with severe and multiple disabilities
the incorrect item to teach them the communicative function of rejecting.

Ensuring rich, interesting learning environments with pictures, books, and
items to explore provides all students with opportunities to direct the attention
of others to these items and to comment on these artifacts. Books with photographs of students engaged in favorite activities at home or at school, complete
with captions and questions, allow students to discuss their day with classmates
without disabilities, teachers, family members, and neighborhood friends. Books
with collected items representing a student's interests and accompanying statements can be used for those students with no vision or for students not at a
more symbolic level of representation.

Physical position needs to be considered for students with severe physical
impairments as well as for those students who have hearing and/or visual impairments. Physical and occupational therapists can help the team to determine the
best physical position for a student to be in so that he or she can most effectively
communicate. The student needs to be physically supported and comfortable; be
able to see, hear, and/or touch conversational partners and any AAC being used;
and be able to physically engage in different communicative behaviors without
considerable effort. Considerations for effective communication skills intervention are stated in Table 11.6.

Ensuring Access to Augmentative and Alternative Communication Devices

Students with severe and multiple disabilities often struggle to understand what
others are saying and often have great difficulty conveying their own thoughts
(Hughes, Pitkin, & Lorden, 1998; Iacono et al., 1998). Ensuring that these students have ready access to various means of communication (both receptively
and expressively) is a critical consideration for all care providers, friends, teachers, and others. As of 2004, numerous low and high technological devices
existed to support the communicative needs of most students. Furthermore, legislation and advocacy efforts have changed how these devices are funded, making it much easier for families to obtain the appropriate device(s) (Blackstone,
2001). The necessity of ensuring assistive technology for students requiring this
support in order to benefit from their special education program was included
as a mandate in the 1997 reauthorization (PL 105-17) of the Individuals with

Table 11.6. Considerations for effective communication skills intervention

Is the student in the best physical position to communicate effectively?	Is the student in the best physical position to use augmentative and alternative communication? Is the student at eye level and close to other students with whom to communicate? Is the student physically close to see, hear, and/or touch conversational partners?
Does the student have easy access to needed augmentative and alternative communication devices?	Have different communication devices been obtained or developed for different social situations?
Is the student a part of different social groups throughout the day?	Are students encouraged to work as partners or in small groups? Are students encouraged to interact at lunch and recess?
Does the student have a need or desire to communicate?	Has the environment been arranged so that the student needs to communicate for different purposes?

Disabilities Education Act. This addition to the law made it much easier for team members to recommend augmentative communication devices (ACDs), also referred to as augmentative and alternative communication (AAC) devices, and other assistive technology for a particular student. Another major support for obtaining the necessary equipment occurred when Medicare, the largest health care program in the United States, revised its policies concerning the coverage of ACDs. Prior to January 1, 2001, ACDs were considered "convenience items," which were not eligible for funding. With considerable advocacy support from a number of professional and consumer organizations, Medicare changed its policy to consider ACDs "durable medical equipment," making them a fundable item (Blackstone, 2001). In addition, considerable support exists to demonstrate that the use of ACDs does not hinder the development of speech (a common concern) and, in fact, facilitates its development (Brady, 2000; Schwartz, Garfinkle, & Bauer, 1998; Sevcik, Romski, & Adamson, 1999).

Augmentative and Alternative Communication Devices

ACDs can range from a simple, low-technology Velcro board holding two items at a time to highly complex and technological electronic devices with dynamic displays and speech output (see Table 11.7) (Downing, 2000). Any one individual could make use of a wide variety of such devices from simple to complex, depending on individual needs, preferences, communication partners, and the communication situation. Although the more complex devices often are believed to be better suited to those with considerable cognitive ability, preventing

Table 11.7.   Examples of low- and high-tech augmentative and alternative communication devices

Low-technological devices	High-technological devices
Object boards/books	Tech Talk—8 messages at 12 levels (from AMDI)
Pictorial symbols in wallets, books, on boards, CD holders, and wristbands	Go Talk—36 messages at 4 levels (from Attainment Co.)
Pictorial display in a photograph album; frame with voice output (4 messages)	Springboard—4 to 32 messages (from Prentke Romich)
Rotary scanner and switch with pictures or objects	Voice Pal™—5 messages (from Adaptivation)

the use of such devices over concerns that the individual with severe and/or multiple disabilities will not make effective use of them could be even more limiting. Students can learn increased communication skills through the use of different devices (Romski, Sevcik, Hyatt, & Cheslock, 2002). All students deserve the right to have the best means to communicate. Even if they are unable to use all aspects of a given device, the device may still address a specific need. For example, not everyone who uses a computer is capable of maximizing its full potential; however, that does not mean that the individual should not benefit from what can be gained by using the computer even minimally.

Purchasing expensive equipment that will not be used by the individual should also be avoided, however. It is important to remember that individuals with physical disabilities who are of average or even gifted intelligence do not rely solely on expensive and complex AAC devices. These individuals use a variety of high- and low-technology devices as well as facial expressions, vocalizations, and body gestures, depending on the situation (Beukelman & Mirenda, 1998). In fact, individuals using communication devices often report preferring low technological to high technological communication systems because they seem to enhance the interactions with others (Muller & Soto, 2000). The focus truly is on effective communication, not on how the message is produced.

Different types of symbols can be used to convey messages as part of an augmentative and alternative communication system. The individual's abilities, needs, interests, and preferences determine the types of symbols used, how they are displayed, and how they are selected to convey messages. For students with additional visual impairments, communication symbols will need to be clear, visually uncluttered, and with good contrast. Depending on the student's visual abilities, symbols may need to be enlarged and/or outlined in bold. Use of color to increase the resemblance to the actual referent should be considered. If a child's blue cup is used to represent *drink,* for example, then the pictorial representation for *drink* should be blue as well. Symbols can very closely resemble what they are to represent, such as a part of the actual item (e.g., an empty snack wrapper to mean snack time, a photograph of a computer to represent time on the computer), or can be quite abstract symbols (e.g., unrelated textures, print). Types of symbols can include a wide array of graphics (commercially or handmade) or tangible items, depending on cognitive, visual, and physical abilities of the individual. Regardless of the symbols used or reading ability of the student, a written message should be paired with all symbols to make the communicative intent clear to the conversational partner.

Cultural and familial influences also must be considered when making decisions concerning AAC development or purchase. Depending on such influences, the text message may be in English as well as the family's native language. In addition, families may have preferences for certain symbols used, the outward appearance of the device, and whether voice output is desired. Symbols may be perceived differently depending on one's cultural background and experiences, making it imperative that families be involved in symbol selection (Huer, 2000). Parette, Brotherson, and Huer (2000) stressed the critical importance of involving the family in all AAC decision making, given differences in culture, values, and desired goals.

To create a message, the student can directly select the appropriate symbols by pointing, looking at, reaching toward, grasping, or handing them to another person. Such a method of selecting a message is called direct selection and is the preferred method because it tends to be the clearest and most efficient (Beukelman & Mirenda, 1998; Romski et al., 2002). When the student is physically unable to select the message directly, then a scanning system can be used. Symbols can be systematically lighted electronically or pointed to by another until the student indicates the desired symbol(s) with a switch, a vocalization, or other physical means. Greater time is required in the creation of the message using scanning to select, and sufficient wait time must be provided.

Facilitated Communication

Facilitated communication (FC), a controversial approach to teaching and helping some students to communicate, combines physical and emotional support with the use of an AAC device (Biklen, 1993; Crossley, 1994). Although this approach uses several strategies of direct instruction (e.g., prompts, reinforcement, fading), the controversy surrounding it focuses on the authorship of the created message (Green & Shane, 1994; Kaiser, 1994). The major concern with the technique is that the person supporting the student (the facilitator) will consciously or unconsciously take a primary role in developing messages that are then said to come from the student. Such influence is present in any use of ACDs when the person using the device requires substantial assistance to do so, however. Obviously, with any intervention strategy, the critical goal is to fade support to allow the student maximum independent performance. When FC is done correctly, the facilitator does not move the student's hand to create the message but instead, follows the student's lead and only provides support as needed to allow the student access to the device (Crossley, 1994). The facilitator steadies the individual's arm but does not direct it in the development of a message.

The ACD used in FC can be a simple letter board, a complex electronic device, a picture-based system, objects, or essentially any device that requires direct selection of the message. When performed correctly, authorship of the message by the individual with severe disabilities can be ascertained (Biklen, Saha, & Kliewer, 1995; Cardinal, Hanson, & Wakeham, 1996). FC thus offers some individuals with severe and multiple disabilities an opportunity to express themselves and should be considered as a viable intervention option.

Importance of Early Intervention

Because all individuals can acquire and improve communication abilities and there are no prerequisite skills, early intervention to help young children as soon as possible is strongly recommended (Romski et al., 2002; Warren, 2000). A young child may develop unconventional means of communicating needs and desires and will need systematic support and guidance to acquire more conventional modes that are more universally recognized and, therefore, efficient. When communication intervention is delayed, the child may grow up relying on unacceptable modes of communication such as yelling, kicking, hitting, biting, or scratching to meet his or her needs. The more such forms of communication are effective (i.e., meet needs) over a long period of time, the more difficult the process to teach more acceptable behaviors that could be exchanged for these.

Unconventional Behaviors

Everyone needs to communicate. When limitations exist that prevent clear and accepted forms of communication, individuals will resort to developing an alternative system that serves a purpose. Without access to conventional means of communication that are effective, the student will likely develop a system of communication that may be effective—but not preferred by others. Sigafoos (2000) found a strong inverse relationship between insufficient communication skills and amount of aberrant behavior in 13 young children with developmental disabilities. For instance, if a child learns that banging his or her head against a wall and screaming quickly brings someone and provides him or her with the attention he or she needs, the child may continue to use this form of communication because of its effectiveness. The development of such communicative behaviors may be most prominent in children and youth who cannot see or hear how others are communicating to have their needs met or in those who may be unable to act in a more conventional manner physically. For example, a child who uses a wheelchair and cannot use speech or move well at all may need to rely on crying and banging on his wheelchair to request attention, to get out of the chair, or to move. Considerable research in this field strongly recommends that those interacting with the individual regard the "unacceptable" behavior as communicative, not "bad," and provide the individual with alternative ways to communicate that are more acceptable and less harmful to self and others, yet equally effective (O'Neill, Horner, Albin, Sprague, Storey, & Newton, 1997; Sigafoos, O'Reilly, Drasgow, & Reichle, 2002; Wacker, Berg, & Harding, 2002). The alternative method of communication must be efficient (meet the same needs as the less-acceptable behavior) and require the same or less energy output. A functional analysis of the behavior and situation is needed to determine how the student communicates, what happens as a result, alternative ways for the student to communicate if needed, and ways to alter the situation so that the alternative means of communication will be more readily available. Functional communication training (FCT) refers to the specific teaching of alternative and more acceptable means of communication to meet the student's needs, thus reducing the need to behave in a less acceptable manner (Carr, Levin, McConnachie, Carlson, Kemp, & Smith, 1994; Mirenda, 1997; Ostrosky, Drasgow, & Halle, 1999). The student must be taught alternative strategies to have needs met in ways described earlier as recommended practices (e.g., responding immediately, ensuring the availability of the alternative mode, following the student's lead, recognizing the need to direct the student's attention to the alternative strategy).

———————

When Tia became frustrated and desired a break from her math work, she bit her wrist and squealed. Tia has been provided with a small wristband that bears the pictorial symbol and message ("I really need a break"), which she wears most of her day. This device was chosen because it is simple to use, always available, does not take up any room, and fits with the pattern of behavior that Tia was used to demonstrating. Careful observation of Tia during math made it clear that Tia usually became frustrated within 10 minutes of this activity. Knowing this time limit, those working with Tia were able to detect her growing frustration and direct her attention to the symbol on her wrist before she felt the need to squeal or bite herself. Of course, effort was also made to offer Tia several choices of materials to use, order of tasks, and peers to work with; and to give her considerable support to help her to be successful.

Early efforts to assist children to communicate effectively and in the most conventional means possible not only stymie the potential development of inappropriate communication skills but also can help children meet their social needs. The challenge for the field is to find the most effective strategies for each individual child to support that child's receptive and expressive communication needs.

A COLLABORATIVE APPROACH TO COMMUNICATION

To ensure consistency across team members in supporting the communication skill development of students with severe and multiple disabilities, a collaborative approach is recommended (see Chapter 1). In this model, team members readily share information, engage in role release, and cooperate in all aspects of assessment and intervention. Because no one family member or service provider can (or should) be with a student with challenging needs all of the time, everyone supporting the student will need to know how the student communicates and how to build on these communication efforts. The importance of true collaborative teaming to ensure effective instruction is considered a best practice with students who have disabilities, especially those students in inclusive classrooms (Giangreco, 2000; Orelove & Sobsey, 1996; Soto, Muller, Hunt, & Goetz, 2001).

As an alternative to relegating communication skills development to one person (e.g., the speech-language pathologist [SLP]), sharing the responsibility among teachers, family members, related services providers, friends, and others close to the individual ensures more consistent support throughout the day, whether at home or school. Not only do team members need to share responsibility for intervention but also they need to respect each person's input regardless of roles, degree, and years of expertise. Each person will have a unique and valid perspective that needs to be heard and considered. Everyone on the team can contribute different information that may be particularly beneficial to meeting the student's communication needs. Family members are much more familiar with what their child needs to say and understand at home and in the neighborhood. Teachers and paraprofessionals will have a clear idea of interaction needs during school activities whereas peers can be very helpful in determining what is necessary for social interactions. Because different people see the student with severe and multiple disabilities in different situations throughout each day, collaboration is logical.

Integrative Service Delivery

Using a collaborative approach and adhering to the recommended practice of teaching within natural contexts, all service providers contribute to the student's educational program by infusing or embedding their expertise into the student's customary activities of the day. In contrast to a pull-out model of service delivery in which related service providers remove students from their classes to work with them individually or in small groups on discipline-related skills, in an integrative service delivery model, specialists bring their expertise to the student (Craig, Haggart, & Hull, 1999; McWilliam, 1996).

Following a pull-in integrative therapy services model, an SLP enters an eleventh-grade drama class in which she supports Shane, who has a winning smile and a love of hard rock music and the outdoors. Shane also has severe cognitive impairments, quadriplegia cerebral palsy, and is nonverbal. In this class, students participate in considerable group work, which makes it ideal for addressing communication skills that Shane is learning. Once a week, the SLP monitors Shane's use of his AAC devices, facilitates interactions with peers, and shapes Shane's responses and initiations. This SLP also works with Shane once a week at lunch to support his requests for food and assistance, and she facilitates his social interactions with peers through the use of a personalized conversation book. By infusing her skills and knowledge into Shane's drama class and lunch, the SLP is able to demonstrate to others who support Shane how she delivers her services. As a result, they can replicate the techniques she uses to support this student.

Several benefits result from an integrative therapy services model. Students do not have to miss classroom activities while they receive therapy elsewhere. Pulling the student out intermittently for services can be disruptive not only for the student but also for other students and the teacher (Giangreco, 2000; Giangreco, Edelman, & Nelson, 1998). The communication demands of the typical environment are addressed as they naturally occur; therefore, the potential problem of generalization of skills from the learned to applied environment is eased. The SLP is able to observe the communication opportunities and expectations of others and make recommendations accordingly. In addition, others in the classroom can benefit from seeing how this specialist supports a particular student so that they can best replicate techniques. Finally, the SLP can provide additional support to the classroom teacher by helping other students as needed on whatever topic is being studied. Such an arrangement makes efficient use of limited resources.

SUMMARY

This chapter highlights the communication skills and needs of students who have severe and multiple disabilities. Recognizing the communicative potential of these individuals and helping them to expand their abilities in this area are addressed as critical service provider responsibilities.

The multimodal nature of communication and the multiple reasons underlying the communication of students with severe and multiple disabilities to communicate has been emphasized. Because no one device or method will suffice, students need to be encouraged to use a variety of different modes for both receptive and expressive purposes. Students also need support to engage in communicative interactions for multiple reasons (not just for making requests). Helping students be at their communicative best is the responsibility of all involved stakeholders at school and home who work collaboratively and cooperatively to this end.

REFERENCES

Agran, M., King-Sears, M.E., Wehmeyer, M.L., & Copeland, S.R. (2003). *Teachers' guides to inclusive practices: Student-directed learning.* Baltimore: Paul H. Brookes Publishing Co.

Beck, A.R. (1996). Language assessment methods for three age groups of children. *Journal of Children's Communication Development, 17*(2), 31–66.

Beck, A.R., Thompson, J.R., Clay, S.I., Hutchins, M., Vogt, W.P., Romaniak, B., & Sokolowski, B. (2001). Preservice professionals' attitudes toward children who use augmentative and alternative communication. *Education and Training in Mental Retardation and Developmental Disabilities, 36,* 255–271.

Beukelman, D.R., & Mirenda, P. (1998). *Augmentative and alternative communication: Management of severe communication disorders in children and adults* (2nd ed.). Baltimore: Paul H. Brookes Publishing Co.

Biklen, D. (1993). *Communication unbound: How facilitated communication is challenging traditional views of autism and ability/disability.* New York: Teachers College Press.

Biklen, D., Saha, N., & Kliewer, C. (1995). How teachers confirm the authorship of facilitated communication. *Journal of The Association for Persons with Severe Handicaps, 20,* 45–56.

Blackstone, S.W. (1997, January–February). The intake's connected to the input. *Augmentative Communication News, 10*(1), 1–6.

Blackstone, S.W. (2001, October). Medicare reimbursement for SGDs. *Augmentative Communication News, 13*(6), 6–7.

Blischak, D.M., & Lloyd, L.L. (1996). Multimodal augmentative and alternative communication: Case study. *Augmentative and Alternative Communication, 12,* 37–46.

Brady, N.C. (2000). Improved comprehension of object names following voice output communication aid use: Two case studies. *Augmentative and Alternative Communication, 16,* 197–204.

Brown, F., Gothelf, C.R., Guess, D., & Lehr, D.H. (1998). Self-determination for individuals with the most severe disabilities: Moving beyond chimera. *Journal of The Association for Persons with Severe Handicaps, 23,* 17–26.

Bzoch, K.R., & League, R. (1991). *REEL–2. (Receptive and Expressive Emergent Language Test–2nd ed.).* Austin, TX: PRO-ED.

Cardinal, D.N., Hanson, D., & Wakeham, J. (1996). Investigation of authorship in facilitated communication. *Mental Retardation, 34,* 231–242.

Carr, E.G., Levin, L., McConnachie, G., Carlson, J.I., Kemp, D.C., & Smith, C.E. (1994). *Communication-based intervention for problem behavior: A user's guide for producing positive change.* Baltimore: Paul H. Brookes Publishing Co.

Carter, M., & Maxwell, K. (1998). Promoting interaction with children using augmentative communication through a peer-directed intervention. *International Journal of Disability, Development and Education, 45,* 75–96.

Cole, K.N., Dale, P.S., & Thal, D.J. (Vol. Eds.) & Warren, S.F., & Reichle, J. (Series Eds.). (1996). *Communication and language intervention series: Vol. 6. Assessment of Communication and language.* Baltimore: Paul H. Brookes Publishing Co.

Connard, P., & Bradley-Johnson, S. (1998). *APPSI: Assessment for persons profoundly or severely impaired.* Austin, TX: PRO-ED.

Craig, S.E., Haggart, A.G., & Hull, K.M. (1999). Integrating therapies into the educational setting: Strategies for supporting children with severe disabilities. *Physical Disabilities: Education and Related Services, XVII,* 91–109.

Cress, C.J. (2002). Expanding children's early augmented behaviors to support symbolic development. In J. Reichle & D.R. Beukelman (Series Eds.) & J. Reichle, D.R. Beukelman, & J.C. Light (Vol. Eds.), *Augmentative and alternative communication series. Exemplary practices for beginning communicators: Implications for AAC* (pp. 219–272). Baltimore: Paul H. Brookes Publishing Co.

Crossley, R. (1994). *Facilitated communication training.* New York: Teachers College Press.

Downing, J.E. (1999). *Teaching communication skills to students with severe disabilities.* Baltimore: Paul H. Brookes Publishing Co.

Downing, J.E. (2000). Augmentative communication devices: A critical aspect of assistive technology. *Journal of Special Education Technology, 15*(3), 35–40.

Drasgow, E., Halle, J.W., Ostrosky, M.M., & Harbers, H.M. (1996). Using behavioral indication and functional communication training to establish an initial sign repertoire with a child with severe disabilities. *Topics in Early Childhood Special Education, 16,* 500–521.

Durand, V.M., Mapstone, E., & Youngblade, L. (1999). The role of communicative partners. In J.E. Downing, *Teaching communication skills to students with severe disabilities* (pp. 139–156). Baltimore: Paul H. Brookes Publishing Co.

Giangreco, M.F. (2000). Related services research for students with low-incidence disabilities: Implications for speech-language pathologists in inclusive classrooms. *Language, Speech, and Hearing Services, 31,* 230–239.

Giangreco, M.F., Cloninger, C.J., & Iverson, V.S. (1998). *Choosing outcomes and accommodations for children (COACH): A guide to educational planning for students with disabilities.* (2nd ed). Baltimore: Paul H. Brookes Publishing Co.

Giangreco, M.F., Edelman, S.W., Luiselli, T.E., & MacFarland, S.Z.C. (1997). Helping or hovering? Effects of instructional assistant proximity on students with disabilities. *Exceptional Children, 64,* 7–18.

Giangreco, M.F., Edelman, S.W., & Nelson, C. (1998). Impact of planning for support services on students who are deaf-blind. *Journal of Visual Impairments and Blindness, 92*(1), 18–29.

Granlund, M., & Olsson, C. (1999). Efficacy of communication intervention for pressymbolic communicators. *Augmentative and Alternative Communication, 15,* 25–37.

Green, G., & Shane, H.C. (1994). Science, reason, and facilitated communication. *Journal of The Association for Persons with Severe Handicaps, 19,* 157–172.

Harwood, K., Warren, S.F., & Yoder, P. (2002). The importance of responsivity in developing contingent exchanges with beginning communicators. In J. Reichle & D.R. Beukelman (Series Eds.) & J. Reichle, D.R. Beukelman, & J.C. Light (Vol. Eds.), *Augmentative and alternative communication series. Exemplary practices for beginning communicators: Implications for AAC* (pp. 59–96). Baltimore: Paul H. Brookes Publishing Co.

Hedrick, D.L., Prather, E.M., & Tobin, A.R. (1984). *SICD-R: Sequenced Inventory of Communication Development–revised.* Austin, TX: PRO-ED.

Higginbotham, J., & Wilkins, D. (1999). Slipping through the timestream: Social issues of time and timing in augmented interactions. In D. Kovarsky, J. Duchan, & M. Maxwell (Eds.), *Constructing (in)competence: Disabling evaluations in clinical and social interaction* (pp. 49–82). Mahwah, NJ: Lawrence Erlbaum Associates.

Houghton, J., Bronicki, G., & Guess, D. (1987). Opportunities to express preferences and make choices among students with severe disabilities in classroom settings. *Journal of The Association for Persons with Severe Handicaps, 12,* 18–27.

Huer, M.B. (1988). *Nonspeech test for receptive/expressive language.* Wauconda, IL: Don Johnston Co.

Huer, M.B. (2000). Examining perceptions of graphic symbols across cultures: Preliminary study of the impact of culture/ethnicity. *Augmentative and Alternative Communication, 16,* 180–185.

Hughes, C., Carter, E.W., Hughes, T., Bradford, E., & Copeland, S.R. (2002). Effects of instructional versus non-instructional roles on the social interactions of high school students. *Education and Training in Mental Retardation and Developmental Disabilities, 37,* 146–162.

Hughes, C., Pitkin, S.E., & Lorden, S.W. (1998). Assessing preferences and choices of persons with severe and profound mental retardation. *Education and Training in Mental Retardation and Developmental Disabilities, 33,* 299–316.

Hunt, P., Alwell, M., & Goetz, L. (1991). Interacting with peers through conversation turn taking with a communication book adaptation. *Augmentative and Alternative Communication, 7,* 117–126.

Iacono, T., Carter, M., & Hook, J. (1998). Identification of intentional communication in students with severe multiple disabilities. *Augmentative and Alternative Communication, 14,* 102–114.

Iacono, T.A., Mirenda, P., & Beukelman, D. (1993). Comparison of unimodal and multimodal AAC techniques for children with intellectual disabilities. *Augmentative and Alternative Communication, 9,* 83–94.

Individuals with Disabilities Education Act Amendments of 1997, PL 105-17, 20 U.S.C. §§ 1400 *et seq.*

Kaiser, A.P. (1994). The controversy surrounding facilitated communication: Some alternative meanings. *Journal of The Association for Persons with Severe Handicaps, 19,* 187–190.

Kublin, K.S., Wetherby, A.M., Crais, E.R., & Prizant, B.M. (1998). Prelinguistic dynamic assessment: A transactional perspective. In A.M. Wetherby, S.F. Warren, & J. Reichle (Eds.), *Transitions in prelinguistic communication* (pp. 285–312). Baltimore: Paul H. Brookes Publishing Co.

Light, J. (1997). "Communication is the essence of human life": Reflections on communicative competence. *Augmentative and Alternative Communication, 13,* 61–70.

Light, J.C., Parsons, A.R., & Drager, K. (2002). "There's more to life than cookies": Developing interactions for social closeness with beginning communicators who use AAC. In J. Reichle, D.R. Beukelman, & J.C. Light (Eds.), *Exemplary practices for beginning communicators: Implications for AAC* (pp. 187–218). Baltimore: Paul H. Brookes Publishing Co.

Mar, H.H., & Sall, N. (1999). Profiles of the expressive communication skills of children and adolescents with severe cognitive disabilities. *Education and Training in Mental Retardation and Developmental Disabilities, 34,* 77–89.

McWilliam, R.A. (1996). *Rethinking pull-out services in early intervention.* Baltimore: Paul H. Brookes Publishing Co.

Mirenda, P. (1993). AAC: Bonding the uncertain mosaic. *Augmentative and Alternative Communication, 9,* 3–9.

Mirenda, P. (1997). Supporting individuals with challenging behavior through functional communication training and AAC: Research review. *Augmentative and Alternative Communication, 13,* 207–225.

Mirenda, P. (1999). Augmentative and alternative communication techniques. In J.E. Downing, *Teaching communication skills to students with severe disabilities* (pp. 119–138). Baltimore: Paul H. Brookes Publishing Co.

Muller, E., & Soto, G. (2000, August). *Communication in context: An ethnographic approach in understanding the dynamics of AAC.* Poster presented at the International Society for Augmentative and Alternative Communication, Washington, DC.

O'Neill, R.E., Horner, R.H., Albin, R., Sprague, J., Storey, K., & Newton, J.S. (1997). *Functional assessment and program development of problem behaviors: A practical handbook.* Pacific Grove, CA: Brooks/Cole Thomson Learning.

Orelove, F.P., & Sobsey, D. (1996). *Educating children with multiple disabilities: A transdisciplinary approach* (3rd ed.). Baltimore: Paul H. Brookes Publishing Co.

Ostrosky, M.M., Drasgow, E., & Halle, J.W. (1999). "How can I help you get what you want?" A communication strategy for students with severe disabilities. *TEACHING Exceptional Children, 31*(4), 56–61.

Parette, H.P., Brotherson, M.J., & Huer, M.B. (2000). Giving families a voice in augmentative and alternative communication decision-making. *Education and Training in Mental Retardation and Developmental Disabilities, 35,* 177–190.

Reichle, J. (1997). Communication intervention with persons who have severe disabilities. *Journal of Special Education, 31,* 110–134.

Reichle, J., York, J., & Sigafoos, J. (1991). *Implementing augmentative and alternative communication: Strategies for learners with severe disabilities.* Baltimore: Paul H. Brookes Publishing Co.

Romski, M.A., Sevcik, R.A., & Adamson, L.B. (1997). Framework for studying how children with developmental disabilities develop language through augmented means. *Augmentative and Alternative Communication, 13,* 172–178.

Romski, M.A., Sevcik, R.A., Hyatt, A.M., & Cheslock, M. (2002). A continuum of AAC language intervention strategies for beginning communicators. In J. Reichle, D.R. Beukelman, & J.C. Light (Eds.), *Exemplary practices for beginning communicators: Implications for AAC* (pp. 1–23). Baltimore: Paul H. Brookes Publishing Co.

Rowland, C. (1990). Communication in the classroom for children with dual sensory impairments: Studies of teacher and child behavior. *Augmentative and Alternative Communication, 6,* 262–274.

Rowland, C., & Schweigert, P. (1993). Analyzing the communication environment to increase functional communication. *Journal of The Association for Persons with Severe Handicaps, 18,* 161–176.

Rowland, C., Schweigert, P., & Stremel, K. (1992). *Observing and enhancing communication skills.* New York: Communication Skill Builders.

Schlosser, R.W. (1999). Comparative efficacy of intervention in augmentative and alternative communication. *Augmentative and Alternative Communication, 15,* 56–68.

Schwartz, I.S., Carta, J.J., & Grant, S. (1996). Examining the use of recommended language intervention practices in early childhood special education classrooms. *Topics in Early Childhood Special Education, 6,* 251–272.

Schwartz, I.S., Garfinkle, A.N., & Bauer, J. (1998). The picture exchange communication system: Communication outcomes for young children with disabilities. *Topics in Early Childhood Special Education, 18,* 144–159.

Sevcik, R.A., Romski, M.A., & Adamson, L.B. (1999). Measuring AAC intervention for individuals with severe developmental disabilities. *Augmentative and Alternative Communication, 15,* 38–44.

Siegel, E., & Cress, P. (2002). Overview of the emergence of early AAC behaviors: Progression from communicative to symbolic skills. In J. Reichle & D.R. Beukelman (Series Eds.) & J. Reichle, D.R. Beukelman, & J.C. Light (Vol. Eds.), *Augmentative and alternative communication series. Exemplary practices for beginning communicators: Implications for AAC* (pp. 2–8). Baltimore: Paul H. Brookes Publishing Co.

Siegel, E., & Wetherby, A. (2000). Nonsymbolic communication. In M. Snell & F. Brown (Eds.), *Instruction of students with severe disabilities* (5th ed., pp. 409–451). Upper Saddle River, NJ: Prentice-Hall.

Sigafoos, J. (1999). Creating opportunities for augmentative and alternative communication strategies for involving people with developmental disabilities. *Augmentative and Alternative Communication, 15,* 183–190.

Sigafoos, J. (2000). Communication development and aberrant behavior in children with developmental disabilities. *Education and Training in Mental Retardation and Developmental Disabilities, 35,* 168–176.

Sigafoos, J., & Drasgow, E. (2001). Conditional use of aided and unaided AAC: A review and clinical case demonstration. *Focus on Autism and Other Developmental Disabilities, 16,* 152–161.

Sigafoos, J., O'Reilly, M.F., Drasgow, E., & Reichle, J. (2002). Strategies to achieve socially acceptable escape and avoidance. In J. Reichle & D.R. Beukelman (Series Eds.) & J. Reichle, D.R. Beukelman, & J.C. Light (Vol. Eds.), *Augmentative and alternative com-*

munication series: Exemplary practices for beginning communicators: Implications for AAC (pp. 157–186). Baltimore: Paul H. Brookes Publishing Co.

Sigafoos, J., & Roberts-Pennell, D. (1999). Wrong-item format: A promising intervention for teaching socially appropriate forms of rejecting to children with developmental disabilities. *Augmentative and Alternative Communication, 15,* 135–140.

Soto, G., Muller, E., Hunt, P., & Goetz, L. (2001). Critical issues in the inclusion of students who use average and alternative communication: An educational team perspective. *Augmentative and Alternative Communication, 17,* 62–72.

Taylor, S.J. (February, 2001). On choice. *TASH Newsletter,* 8–10.

Wacker, D.P., Berg, W.K., & Harding, J.W. (2002). Replacing socially unacceptable behavior with acceptable communication responses. In J. Reichle & D.R. Beukelman (Series Eds.) & J. Reichle, D.R. Beukelman, & J.C. Light (Vol. Eds.), *Augmentative and alternative communication series: Exemplary practices for beginning communicators: Implications for AAC* (pp. 97–121). Baltimore: Paul H. Brookes Publishing Co.

Warren, S.F. (2000). The future of early communication and language intervention. *Topics in Early Childhood Special Education, 20*(1), 33–37.

Wehmeyer, M.L. (1997). Self-determination as an educational outcome: A definitional framework and implications for intervention. *Journal of Developmental and Physical Disabilities, 9,* 175–209.

Yoder, P.J., & Warren, S.F. (1999). Maternal responsivity mediates the relationship between prelinguistic intentional communication and later language. *Journal of Early Intervention, 22,* 126–136.

Yoder, P.J., Warren, S.F., McCathren, R., & Leew, S.V. (1998). Does adult responsivity to child behavior facilitate communication development? In S.F. Warren & J. Reichle (Series Eds.) & A.M. Wetherby, S.F. Warren, & J. Reichle (Vol. Eds.), *Communication and language intervention series: Vol. 7. Transitions in prelinguistic communication* (pp. 39–58). Baltimore: Paul H. Brookes Publishing Co.

CHAPTER 12

Mealtime Skills

Dianne Koontz Lowman

A teacher of students with severe disabilities is concerned about a student in her class. Carol has a degenerative disorder; she chokes on small pieces of food and falls asleep with food in her mouth. The teacher is becoming afraid to feed Carol in school.

A paraeducator has just observed Joseph's mother feeding him. When placed in the Rifton seat, he attempts to straighten, which forces his head into extension. His mother feeds him by using his teeth to scrape the food off the spoon. Because his head is extended, the food naturally falls down his throat.

The staff of the vocational program have become concerned about Frank. Recently, he has started ruminating daily after lunch. The staff are worried that this behavior will threaten Frank's health as well as his ability to participate in the workplace.

Eating meals is an essential activity that occurs several times a day in all families, including those with and without a child with disabilities. Farlow and Snell (2000) emphasized that eating meals is the most functional and frequently used self-care skill. Meals provide children with the nutrition needed for growth and survival, the pleasure of enjoyable tastes and aromas, the opportunity for positive social interaction, and the chance to increase independence in eating skills. Feeding difficulties that affect the child's health can be extremely upsetting for caregivers. In addition to the nutritional aspects, mealtime is a social process that helps caregivers and children form relationships and impart culture, traditions, and values. Disruption in the mealtime process can interfere with caregiver–child interactions (Case-Smith & Humphry, 2001; Lowman & Murphy, 1999).

Many children with severe and multiple disabilities have difficulty eating their food. Although exact figures are not available, it has been reported that as many as 90% of children with disabilities have feeding difficulties and that children with the most significant disabilities are at the greatest risk for malnutrition (Dahl, Thommessen, Rasmussen, & Selberg, 1996; Reilly, Skuse, & Poblete, 1996; Schwarz, Corredor, Fisher-Medina, Cohen, & Rabinowitz, 2001). Eating problems, inadequate food intake, and decreased appetite are reported to be common in children with cerebral palsy (Gisel, 1996; Reilly & Skuse, 1996). Disorders of muscle tone may make lip closure difficult, interfering with the child's ability to take food from a spoon or hold liquids in the mouth. The presence of primitive reflexes (e.g., tonic bite reflex) may make chewing difficult or impossible. Structural abnormalities such as cleft lip can further complicate eating (Case-Smith & Humphry, 2001). Clearly, there are a significant number of students with severe and multiple disabilities who require some form of assistance in mealtime skills.

This chapter describes a holistic process for observing and assessing complex but common mealtime concerns and presents intervention methods to achieve specific mealtime objectives. This process will examine the numerous factors that influence mealtime performance. Both eating and feeding skills are included in this discussion. *Eating* (sometimes called *self-feeding*) refers to the child being able to actively bring food to his or her mouth. *Feeding* refers to the child being assisted in the activity of eating (Avery-Smith, 1996).

THE ASSESSMENT PROCESS

Because feeding and eating are complex skills, this chapter emphasizes the use of a comprehensive assessment process using observations and interviews to gather as much information as possible about all aspects of feeding, eating, and the mealtime process. Figure 12.1 includes a holistic feeding observation form that can be used to gather information on a student's eating routine.

The components of the assessment process described in this chapter include the family's feeding concerns, respiratory concerns, positioning needs, oral-motor skills, sensory aspects, communication and socialization skills, behavioral issues, and nutritional and dental concerns. Assessment of eating and feeding skills requires a determination of both what the child can and cannot do and which skills are critical to improving the child's functioning in current and potential future environments. Each child's assessment must be individualized,

Holistic Feeding Observation Form

Child's name: _____ Age: _____

Dates observed: _____ Time: _____

Environments observed: _____ Observer(s): _____

The questions provided under each heading are suggestions to help guide your observations.

I. **Collaboration with the Family**
   - Has a positive family dialogue been established?
   - Has information been gathered from the family about relevant past experiences concerning feeding and medical experiences (e.g., NICU, feeding tubes)?
   - What is the feeding routine: at home? in the school or center?
   - Issues identified by the caregiver:
       What is pleasurable specific to the feeding interaction?
       What is difficult specific to the feeding interaction?
   - What cultural implications are important to consider?

Observations:

II. **Respiratory Concerns**
   - Is the gag reflex present and effective (not over- or under-responsive)?
   - Is the swallow reflex present and effective (not inhibited or delayed, no paralysis)?
   - Is the feeding pace determined by the child (not the feeder)?
   - Is swallowing relaxed and without gagging, coughing, or aspiration?
   - If a respiratory infection is present, is enough extra time allowed for coordination of breathing and swallowing?
   - Is the coordination of breathing, swallowing, and talking difficult?

Observations:

III. **Positioning**
   - Is optimal postural alignment achievable?
   - Are feet and arms supported by a flat surface (not dangling)?

(continued)

Figure 12.1. Blank holistic feeding observation form. (From Lowman, D.K., & Murphy, S.M. [1999]. *The educator's guide to feeding children with disabilities* [pp. 231–233]. Baltimore: Paul H. Brookes Publishing Co; adapted by permission.)

Figure 12.1. *(continued)*

- Is there adequate flexion at the knees?
- Are hips resting symmetrically against a supportive surface?
- Is trunk upright and symmetrical?
- Is a neutral head position ensured for most-effective swallow and eye contact?

Observations:

IV. Oral-Motor Skills

- What reflexes are present?
- Are there any structural problems?
- Has overall muscle tone been determined (normal, high, low)?
- Have tone issues specific to the face and mouth been determined?
- Have needs for oral-motor treatment been identified? Some common examples include

  Jaw: thrust, clenching, retraction, instability

  Tongue: retraction, thrust, limited movement

  Lip and cheek: low tone, lip retraction

  Palate: nasal reflux, cleft
- Which of the following feeding techniques that enhance oral-motor skills are appropriate for this child? Lip closure, tongue lateralization, munching, chewing, cup drinking, swallowing

Observations:

V. Sensory Aspects

- Are any limitations of the sensory modalities present: visual, auditory, tactile, gustatory, olfactory, proprioceptive?
- What type(s) of touch are most easily tolerated (arousing versus calming)?
- What temperatures are most easily tolerated (note preferences)?
- Which tastes are most easily tolerated (likes versus dislikes)?
- Which textures are most easily tolerated: thick liquids, thin liquids, smooth solids, lumpy solids, chewy solids, crunchy, mixed textures?
- What are appropriate stimulation techniques and tools?

Observations:

VI. Communication, Behavioral, and Socialization Skills

- Does the child have the maximum control possible?
- How does the child indicate hunger: food present? not present?
- How does the child indicate need for a change of pace/pause?
- How does the child indicate a choice of food or liquid?
- How does the child indicate readiness for more?
- How does the child indicate that he or she is finished?
- How does the child indicate desire for social closeness/distance?

Observations:

VII. Nutritional and Dental Concerns

- Have the child's nutrition needs been identified?
- What has been tried in the past to increase calories, dietary diversity, and nutrients?
- Has the family implemented alternative diets?
- Have any dental concerns been identified?
- How is dental care currently being addressed in the classroom?

Observations:

VIII. Feeding Process and Implementation Plan

- Has the family, all feeders, and needed specialists participated in the development of this plan?
- Has needed medical information (including physician orders and nutrition requirements) been received and factored into this feeding plan?
- Has needed feeding equipment been identified and obtained?
- Has the most effective sequence been determined?

Observations:

occur over a period of time, and include a variety of team members (Lowman & Murphy, 1999). The team can pull together the results of this assessment to develop a comprehensive feeding plan. The first step in this process begins with the team.

Collaborating with the Team

Difficulties during mealtime may be complex and require planning by a team of individuals from a variety of disciplines (Hall, Yohn, & Reed, 1992). One person, commonly the classroom teacher, usually takes overall responsibility for organizing the assessment and planning process, integrating information from the entire team. The teacher also brings expertise in training methods to the team. Classroom assistants and any other caregivers involved in daily feeding activities also should be included in the planning process. The speech-language pathologist can contribute expertise that will help with potential speech as well as eating skills, because motor patterns developed in eating will influence those used in speech (Alexander, 2001). The physical therapist can contribute valuable information about motor skills, reflexes, positioning, and therapeutic interventions. The occupational therapist is often an excellent resource for information about sensory preferences, food presentation, and adaptive utensils. The school nurse may help train staff to prevent choking and recognize signs of aspiration. A nutritionist or dietitian has important expertise that should be included to positively affect the child's health, growth, and development. Similarly, the dentist should be part of mealtime planning. Many decisions made by these professionals and other members of the feeding team interact with the physician's treatment decisions. Therefore, the physician should also be included. Although it is not possible to have all of these professionals attend team meetings, input should be gathered from them prior to team planning, and the feeding plan should be circulated to them for input and approval prior to implementation (Lowman & Murphy, 1999).

Parents and other primary caregivers must be included as full members of the team for numerous reasons. Parents typically know their child, the history of previous interventions, and what has and has not been successful. In addition, parents generally are responsible for feeding the child most of his or her meals. It is important to gather information from the family concerning the feeding routine(s) at home, including identifying anyone who might feed the child, what is pleasurable about the feeding routine, what is difficult and needs to be changed, and any food allergies the child might have. Care should be given to consider cultural values and preferences for feeding and mealtimes (Lowman & Murphy, 1999).

Consider the following situation described by a teacher of students with severe and multiple disabilities:

———————————

I was concerned about Carol—a student in my class. Carol had a degenerative disorder that had really begun to take its course over the past 2 years. Carol had a munching pattern, required food to be cut into tiny pieces, and took more than an hour to be fed. She choked on small pieces of food. The therapist had had to do the Heimlich maneuver a few times. In addition, Carol fell asleep during meals, even with food in her mouth. Carol's mother was opposed to putting her on ground meals (Carol had always been able to eat food off the school lunch menu). Carol's mother wondered if the school was cutting the food into small-enough pieces. This became a huge issue for school staff.

The principal and I worked closely with the mother, realizing that she was having difficulty dealing with the changing needs of her daughter. After several meetings and long discussions, the principal was able to convince the mother that Carol needed ground meals. Carol is now doing well, eating in 30 minutes, and does not choke during meals.

In addition to emphasizing the importance of working closely with the family, this vignette illustrates the need to deal with safety issues during mealtimes. The first safety consideration must be issues related to breathing.

Dealing with Possible Respiratory Concerns

Once a positive dialogue has been established with the family, the team must next address safety during mealtimes. Safely taking food by mouth requires coordination between breathing and swallowing. The team must consider two health concerns related to respiration—total airway obstruction and aspiration—before beginning oral feeding with a child with severe or multiple disabilities.

Total Airway Obstruction

First, all caregivers involved in mealtime routines need to be trained to recognize, prevent, and treat airway obstruction. Total airway obstruction (discussed in Chapter 8) typically occurs without warning and requires prompt action. Warning signs and procedures for dealing immediately with airway obstruction should be determined by the team and specified in advance in writing as part of the individualized education program (IEP) or an emergency management plan, sometimes called a health services plan (HSP) (Lowman & Murphy, 1999). Warning signs might include significant difficulty with breathing or signs of oxygen deficit (e.g., blue tint of nail beds or lips). Procedures specified in the written emergency management plan might include notifying a health care professional immediately, suctioning, or administering oxygen. If the airway is completely obstructed, the Heimlich maneuver (described in Chapter 9) can open the airway and save the person's life. Procedures for dealing with airway obstruction *must* be outlined in advance (Ault, Rues, Graff, & Holvoet, 2000; Graff, Ault, Guess, Taylor, & Thompson, 1990). A sample HSP can be downloaded from www.brookespublishing.com/store/books/lowman-3750/excerpt2.htm.

Signs of Aspiration

Aspiration refers to the entry of fluids or particles of food into the lungs. At mealtimes, aspiration can occur when food or fluids are on their way down to the stomach or when the contents of the stomach back up the esophagus. Gastroesophageal reflux (GER) involves the backward flow of stomach contents into the esophagus. Stomach contents can be aspirated into the lungs during GER. If only a few drops are aspirated and the child has typical reflexes, the body's natural defenses (e.g., coughing) often will resolve the problem in a few minutes. However, children with severe or multiple disabilities are at increased risk for aspiration due to disorders affecting motor coordination or protective responses (Eicher, 2002). Recurrent aspiration can result in accumulation of food in the airway, causing irritation and inflammation, aspiration pneumonia, and scarring of the lungs. These effects can be life threatening; consequently, prevention is essential (Loughlin & Lefton-Greif, 1994; Rogers, Arvedson, Buck, et al., 1994; see also Chapter 8).

In other cases, sometimes referred to as "silent aspiration," the child may exhibit no immediate signs of difficulty or efforts to cough, particularly if he or she has hyposensitive reflexes. In these cases it is critical that caregivers and classroom staff closely observe the child's behavior during meals (Hall et al., 1992; Lowman & Murphy, 1999).

Figure 12.2 includes a form to record the signs of aspiration that are observed, how long they last, and the context surrounding the incident. Suspected aspiration should be documented and reported to the team and/or the child's doctor. Using this form, for example, Carol's teacher was able to document the episodes of choking and fatigue with meals; these observations helped the principal and mother understand the safety concerns during meals at school.

Prevention and Treatment of Aspiration

A referral to health care professionals should be made to evaluate and identify appropriate treatment for chronic aspiration problems. A videofluoroscopic swallow study (VFSS) is a procedure that is used to visualize the swallowing process in action to help determine if anatomical or functional problems exist. A VFSS can be used to determine if aspiration is occurring, with what size bolus, and on what consistency of food and liquid (Morris & Klein, 2000). A VFSS can help identify both the safest positions as well as the most risky positions for feeding (Arvedson & Lefton-Greif, 1998; Rasley et al., 1993).

Indicators	Date and time of each observed symptom and how long it lasted	Position of the child	Feeding procedure in use	Foods/liquids involved (note texture)	When during the meal (e.g., beginning, middle, end, after meal) signs occurred	Any treatment given
Pneumonia, bronchitis, asthma						
Coughing, gagging, choking						
Wheezing or "noisy" breathing						
Rapid breathing with meals						
Fatigue with meals						
Vomiting, reflux, or regurgitation						
Drooling or food falling out of the mouth						

(continued)

Figure 12.2. *(continued)*

Spurting or forceful ejection of food from mouth					
Delayed, uncoordinated swallow					
Poor oral awareness, packing food in mouth					
Mealtime behaviors (e.g., fear, reluctance, slow pace, unusual eating patterns)					
Other:					
Other observations, comments, notes:					

Figure 12.2. Blank observation form to record signs of aspiration. (*Sources:* Hall, Yohn, & Reed, 1992; Lowman & Murphy, 1999.)

Positioning is an essential strategy to prevent as well as treat aspiration. A child receiving meals by his or her mouth should be fed in an upright position with the head flexed slightly forward, which encourages active swallowing and prevents food from passively running down the throat. Because reflux may occur after the meal is finished, the individual should remain in an upright to semi-reclining position for at least 45 minutes after finishing a meal (Arvedson & Lefton-Greif, 1998; Snyder, Breath, & DeMauro, 1999).

Other factors may contribute to aspiration problems. Pureed foods and thin liquids increase the risk of aspiration because they can easily run down the throat without stimulating a true swallow response. The swallow response closes the airway and protects against aspiration. Using solids, soft solids, or coarsely ground foods and thickened liquids may provide better stimulation for swallowing and reduce the risk of aspiration (Alexander, 2001; Arvedson & Lefton-Greif, 1998). For some children, a limited diet of liquid or pureed foods causes constipation. Because of this constipation, the intestinal system may be blocked and as a result, the contents of the stomach are more likely to be pushed up into the airway. Taking precautions to prevent constipation, watching carefully for signs, and treating it quickly are measures that help ensure that food in the stomach is free to move into the intestines, which helps reduce the risk of aspiration (Eicher, 2002). The team should identify the best combination of prevention and treatment procedures for each child. Although no prevention program can totally eliminate risk, a well-designed feeding program can reduce the risks of aspiration.

In addition to making changes in positioning and food textures, a variety of medications are used to manage reflux. Medications such as antacids, antisecretory drugs (which reduce the amount of acid in stomach), proton pump inhibitors (which block the production of gastric acid), and prokinetic drugs (which increase upper gastrointestinal motility) are used to manage the symptoms of reflux (Jepson & Nickel, 2000). These medications are not always effective in the overall goal of reducing aspiration, however. For example, aspiration of stomach contents is dangerous, even if the stomach contents have reduced acid. Many children experience a variety of side effects from medications, as well. Surgery is considered when positioning, modification of food, and medication are not successful in managing reflux. Fundoplication is a surgical procedure that tightens the lower esophageal sphincter so that food and drink cannot move upward from the stomach to the esophagus, which reduces an individual's risk of aspirating these stomach contents (Eicher, 2002; Jepsen & Nickel, 2000; Morris & Klein, 2000).

After the team has determined that the child can safely take food by mouth (without compromising the child's respiratory system), the next step in the planning process is to determine the most appropriate position(s) for eating and feeding.

Determining the Optimal Position

In order to assume, maintain, or change positions, a child must have postural stability, which is defined as the ability to maintain stability of the body against gravity. During mealtime, children must assume a variety of positions and demonstrate stable postural control to eat or drink successfully. Children who are typically developing will eat and drink without any awareness of the underlying postural control mechanisms that help maintain stability. Children with physical disabilities may lack the motor control needed to perform these tasks independently, however (Snyder et al., 1999). For children unable to maintain stability independently, positioning by caregivers is necessary to provide a stable base of support and as much alignment as possible (Campbell, 2000). Two factors that affect motor control are the presence of abnormal muscle tone and atypical reflexes.

Abnormal Muscle Tone

As discussed in Chapter 6, inadequate muscle tone (hypotonia) or excessive muscle tone (hypertonia) are frequent problems among children with severe and multiple disabilities. These problems often affect the oral musculature as well as many other parts of the body and result in significant eating problems. Inadequate tone is called *hypotonia, low tone,* or *floppy.* Hypotonicity makes it difficult for the child to move against gravity and may result in drooping of the child's head, jaw, and lips, as well as weak chewing patterns. Inadequate tone may result in the inability to maintain stability of the trunk, neck, and head, which makes control of fine oral-motor movements difficult (Campbell, 2000; Morris & Klein, 2000).

Excessive muscle tone is called *hypertonia, high tone,* or *spasticity.* Hypertonicity may result in extreme rigidity that limits any movement of the oral structures and may deform some of these structures as a result of constant pressure. Because increased tone may be present in the muscles controlling movement in opposing directions, great effort may be required for any movement (Campbell, 2000).

Abnormalities of muscle tone do not typically affect all muscles in the same manner or to the same extent. Most children with disorders of muscle tone exhibit uneven tone across muscle groups. Typically, patterns of extension or of flexion predominate as a result of uneven tone. This may result in the chronic retraction of lips, protrusion of the tongue, limited voluntary control, or a number of other problems (Campbell, 2000). Some children have fluctuating muscle tone that may result in involuntary movements of oral structures or that make precise, coordinated movements of lips, tongue, and jaw impossible (Morris & Klein, 2000). All of these disorders of muscle tone have adverse effects on mealtime skills, and intervention to normalize tone is an important component of a mealtime intervention program. The suggestions for positioning and stimulation described later in this chapter are useful in normalizing muscle tone.

Atypical Reflexes

Several types of the involuntary motor patterns called reflexes can create feeding problems for children with severe or multiple disabilities. *Primitive reflexes* (described in Chapter 7) may persist in children with severe or multiple disabilities well beyond the time of typical integration or disappearance. For example, when the asymmetrical tonic neck reflex (ATNR) does not integrate or go away by 4 months of age, it creates specific problems for eating and feeding (Nichols, 2001). As the child's head rotates to one side, the arm on that side involuntarily extends, and the other arm flexes in a "fencing pose." Not only does the turning head make it difficult to put food into the mouth but also muscle contractions generalize to the tongue and jaw, interfering with normal oral-motor control. Figure 12.3a illustrates how presence of the ATNR might affect feeding and eating.

In addition to primitive reflexes that are integrated or go away within the first year of life, protective reflexes or responses exist that persist throughout life. For example, the cough reflex is present in all children and protects the child's airway from foreign objects. Some children with disabilities have *hyposensitive reflexes* (that may require much higher levels of stimulation) or *hypersensitive reflexes* (that are triggered by much lower levels of stimulation). These atypical responses to stimuli may affect feeding; for example, hypersensitivity of the startle reflex may create problems. Any loud noise, change in position, or sudden movement may result in total flexion or extension patterns. Patterns such as this may interfere with voluntary movements and may also contribute to excessive muscle tone (Case-Smith & Humphry, 2001; Nichols, 2001). The control of the reflexive patterns is important for improving feeding, eating, and drinking skills.

Importance of Positioning

Positioning refers to the use of adaptive equipment techniques or external supports to provide optimal alignment to enhance the child's functional performance. The importance of positioning for performance of eating and feeding skills cannot be overemphasized. Postural alignment during mealtimes is needed for

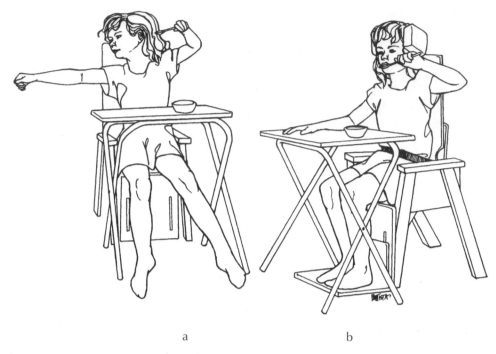

a   b

Figure 12.3.   How the use of adaptive positioning can lessen the influence of asymmetrical tonic neck reflex (ATNR) and promote independent eating: a) child attempts to feed self, but ATNR interferes with the child's ability to feed self; b) child positioned in adapted chair with external supports. The influence of the ATNR is lessened. (From Snyder, P.A., Breath, D., & DeMauro, G.J. [1999]. Positioning strategies for feeding and eating. In D.K. Lowman & S.M. Murphy, *The educator's guide to feeding children with disabilities* [p. 74]. Baltimore: Paul H. Brookes Publishing Co.; reprinted by permission.)

the preservation of an open airway to enhance breathing and decrease the risk of aspiration (Geyer & McGowan, 1995; Snyder et al., 1999). Because there is a close relationship between the child's body position and his or her oral-motor skills, optimal positioning enhances specific oral-motor skills, such as lip closure on a spoon. The final benefit of positioning is hastened digestion, which might decrease the severity of reflux. Upright sitting might enhance the management of constipation by promoting the outflow of stomach contents (Snyder et al., 1999; Wolf & Glass, 1992). Eating and drinking skills may be enhanced by optimal positioning. Although positioning varies from child to child, the considerations given in Table 12.1 are important for all children (Case-Smith & Humphry, 2001; Snyder et al., 1999).

   One of the goals of positioning is to provide only the amount of support needed to ensure stability, using the least amount of adaptation necessary. The finer muscle coordination required for eating and feeding is impossible unless larger muscle groups provide a stable base. Appropriate supports might be a firm

Table 12.1. General principles of positioning for feeding and eating

When positioning a child for feeding and eating:
- Provide support as required to ensure stability, using the least amount of adaptation
- Use positions that keep the child as upright as possible
- Positioning should encourage postural alignment and symmetry of the body
- Consider the practical and motor requirements of the task
- Use positions that promote function and as active participation as possible
- Choose positions that are useful for and acceptable to the child, parent, or caregiver
- Facilitate comfort and ensure the safety of the child and feeder

Sources: Case-Smith & Humphry, 2001; Snyder, Breath, & DeMauro, 1999.

table or tray surface on which to rest the elbows, and/or foot supports at the appropriate height for the child's height. Providing more support than is needed can be restrictive, discourage independence, and actually weaken muscles that the student would otherwise use for support. Dynamic or temporary support is often adequate and makes more restrictive, static support unnecessary.

Another goal of positioning is to keep the child as near to upright as possible. Most children are more successful if they are seated upright with their necks slightly flexed, but the degree of flexion required must be determined individually through careful observation. Positioning should encourage postural alignment and symmetry. The great majority of children will eat best if positioned in a manner as nearly symmetrical as possible. For some children with unilateral reflex patterns, slightly asymmetrical postures may work better. It is important to consult with the physical and occupational therapists to determine the most appropriate position for each child.

Positioning should be as normalized as possible. It is important to use positions that promote function and active participation, facilitate comfort, and ensure the safety of the child and the feeder. They should also be useful for and acceptable to the parent or caregiver. The optimal position for eating and feeding varies from child to child. The principles listed previously are general; the key to determining the best position for each student is careful collaborative assessment and planning (Case-Smith & Humphry, 2001; Snyder et al., 1999).

Joseph is a child with severe spasticity. When placed on the floor, his muscle tone is so strong that he straightens out and becomes "hard as a board." When he is seated in a Rifton corner seat that is reclined slightly, he attempts to straighten out. This forces his head into extension (sometimes called "bird feeding"). His mother feeds him by scraping the food off his teeth. Because his head is extended, the food naturally falls down into the back of his throat. When working with Joseph and his mother, the therapist demonstrated ways to reduce Joseph's tone and emphasized placing him in the seat a short time (often 10 or 15 minutes) before the meal begins in order to allow time for him to relax and adjust to the new position. The therapist also emphasized that the "bird feeding," although effective in getting food down Joseph's throat, put Joseph at risk for aspiration and interfered with the acquisition of appropriate eating and feeding skills. The therapist showed Joseph's mother how to flex his head forward and provide jaw support to facilitate normalized oral-motor patterns.

Examining Oral-Motor Skills

Although eating and drinking are generally considered to be under voluntary control, oral-motor behavior is a combination of reflexive and voluntary patterns. As described earlier, a newborn is born with primitive reflexes such as the rooting, gag, or suck-swallow reflex. As the infant's nervous system matures, these primitive reflexes disappear as they are integrated into learned motor patterns (Eicher, 2002; Nichols, 2001). Other reflexes, such as the gag reflex, persist throughout life. For this reason, it is important to study typical development to better understand the effects of atypical development.

Typical Development

A newborn who is typically developing nurses using a total sucking pattern that allows him or her to breathe and eat simultaneously. Dominated by physiological flexion (sometimes called the "fetal position"), the newborn's jaw, cheeks, lips, and tongue move together as one unit (Murphy & Caretto, 1999a). As physiological flexion decreases, a suckling pattern emerges. *Suckling* refers to obtaining liquid as a result of rhythmic licking of the nipple and does not require lip seal for suction. By the age of 6 months, true sucking can be observed. *Sucking* refers to obtaining liquid as a result of the suction created by raising and lowering the tongue after sealing the oral cavity by pressing the lips against the nipple. Swallowing is integrated with all of these patterns (Alexander, 2001; Alexander, Boehme, & Cupps, 1993; Eicher, 2002; Murphy & Caretto, 1999a).

For most children, the next stage of eating occurs when semisolid foods are introduced at 6–7 months of age. The exact age varies greatly depending on caregiver expectation and cultural values. If the infant is still using the suckling pattern, much of the food is pushed back out of the mouth by the tongue at this stage. Gradually, as the child's oral-motor skills mature, he or she learns to keep the tongue in the mouth and to use the lips to take food from the spoon (Alexander, 2001; Alexander et al., 1993).

As more solid foods are introduced, children learn to bite and chew. At about age 5 months, *munching* is exhibited by most infants. Munching combines vertical jaw movements with a flattening and spreading of the tongue. *Rotary chewing*, which combines lateral tongue and rotary jaw movements, replaces munching as increasingly more solid foods are presented over time. The emergence of teeth makes chewing more effective, but the chewing pattern is typically fully or nearly fully developed by the age of 6 to 9 months, well before the molars emerge. Drinking from a cup is also commonly introduced at this time. Again, the child typically responds with a suckling pattern, but, gradually, he or she learns to control excess tongue movements and to accept and hold liquids in the mouth before swallowing them (Alexander, 2001; Alexander et al., 1993).

Atypical Oral-Motor Development

As discussed previously, problems may be associated with typical reflexes or responses that are hypersensitive or hyposensitive. A gag reflex is present in all children and adults and protects against the inadvertent swallowing of things that might obstruct the windpipe. When hypersensitive, it may interfere with normal swallowing by producing unnecessary gagging and coughing. A hyposensitive gag reflex is also problematic because it will not protect against the swallowing of pieces of food or foreign objects and may even allow fluids to enter the airway (Morris & Klein, 2000). Generally, hypersensitivity of oral and facial areas may exaggerate these and other reflexes. Such hypersensitivity is frequent among children with severe and multiple disabilities; often, children are reluctant to accept new textures, tastes, or temperatures in food and resist any feeding intervention that requires facial contact.

Atypical muscle tone and responses to reflexes may result in atypical oral-motor development. The most common atypical feeding patterns observed as a result of atypical oral-motor development are listed (Alexander, 2001; Case-Smith & Humphry, 2001; Murphy & Caretto, 1999a):

- *Inadequate lip closure*: The ability to keep the lips closed makes it hard to keep food inside the mouth and might increase the tendency to drool.

- *Jaw/cheek/lip/tongue retraction*: Retraction of the jaws, cheek, lips, or tongue is a common compensatory pattern observed in the child who is hypotonic. The child tries to adjust for low tone in his or her trunk by increasing the tone in the facial and oral muscles. This pattern of retraction reduces oral mobility needed for eating.

- *Tonic bite:* The tonic bite reflex is exhibited when stimulation in the mouth produces a forceful, involuntary, and generally prolonged clamping of the jaws. This response pattern obviously interferes with spoon feeding and also often makes chewing extremely difficult.

- *Tongue protrusion and/or tongue thrust:* Tongue protrusion is when the tongue rests outside of the mouth. In tongue thrust, the child's tongue is bunched or forced out of the mouth. Both patterns push food or fluids back out of the mouth and over time, may also push the teeth out of position.

Structural Abnormalities

Structural abnormalities such as cleft lip, cleft palate, micrognathia, high-arched palates, and missing or displaced teeth may cause or complicate eating problems. Uncorrected cleft lip and cleft palate make sucking and swallowing difficult, requiring the infant to develop abnormal patterns (e.g., increased use of the tongue to obtain milk from the nipple). *Micrognathia* refers to the small jaw structure often seen in children with Pierre-Robin and Down syndromes. When the child's jaw is small, the tongue often protrudes rather than resting on the floor of the mouth. High-arched palates are also commonly observed in children with physical disabilities. Food may collect on the roof of the mouth and be impossible for the child to reach. Similarly, missing and/or displaced teeth can cause difficulties with spoon feeding, cup drinking, and biting and chewing (Murphy & Caretto, 1999a). These abnormal patterns may lead to secondary eating problems later in life (Wolf & Glass, 1992). Surgical correction, as early as possible, is frequently the best treatment for these conditions.

Strategies to Improve Oral-Motor Functioning

Many oral-motor patterns are not under voluntary control; therefore, successful interventions will either facilitate more typical patterns or inhibit atypical patterns. When addressing these atypical patterns, the team should look at the child as a whole and not just focus on the mouth. It is important for the team to examine the physical and emotional needs of the child, the environment, and the interaction between the child and feeder. Specific suggestions include the following (Morris & Klein, 2000; Murphy & Caretto, 1999a):

1. Rule out medical reasons for the oral-motor problems. Contact the child's doctor before any significant changes are made to the child's mealtime.

2. Be especially careful to identify food allergies. Food sensitivities may cause increased sensory or oral-motor problems such as drooling or respiratory congestion.

3.   Examine the environment in which mealtimes take place. Overstimulation from the environment may heighten the child's hypersensitive responses.

4.   Ensure proper positioning of the child. As described earlier, proper positioning can provide stability to the child's trunk, therefore facilitating mobility of the muscles of the face and mouth.

5.   Identify activities that can help normalize the child's muscle tone. Please refer to Chapter 7 for techniques to increase or reduce the child's tone so that the benefits of normalized tone can carry over into eating.

6.   Provide oral/facial stimulation to the child. Specific techniques to normalize a child's response to sensory stimulation in and around the mouth will be discussed in the next section of this chapter.

7.   Examine how the sensory properties of utensils and food can affect the child's oral-motor patterns. Specific techniques are discussed in the next section.

8.   Provide oral support when needed by determined by the team.

9.   Develop appropriate interactions between the child and the feeder. The feeder should read the child's cues/communication correctly to provide the appropriate rate or timing of feeding.

Providing Oral Support

If changes in positioning, utensils, and sensory properties of foods have not normalized the child's oral-motor skills, the team should discuss the use of oral support or physical assistance. Although research has supported the use of oral support with infants (Einarsson-Backes, Deitz, Price, Glass, & Hays, 1994), it should be used as sparingly as possible with older children (Alexander, 2001; Morris & Klein, 2000). Overusing physical assistance is unnecessarily intrusive and interferes with independent mastery of skills. It can also create dependency on external stimuli rather than on stimuli that are typically part of the behavior that is being learned. Some suggestions for providing oral support include the following:

•   The feeder may provide head control by placing his or her hand on top of the child's head or on the neck area. Because many children are especially hypersensitive to touch on the head and face, head control can also be achieved by static positioning of the head using positioning aids (e.g., cushions).

•   Direct control of the jaw and lips can be accomplished by applying jaw control from the front (e.g., the feeder places his or her hand under the child's chin to provide stability). This method is typically suitable only for minimal assistance.

- More intensive control of the jaw is usually better applied from the back or side of a child. Usually, the feeder uses the nondominant hand to control the jaw and the dominant hand to feed the child. Morris and Klein (2000) suggested that the feeder place the middle finger under the child's chin just behind the bony part, placing the index finger between the tip of the chin and the lips, and placing the thumb on the side of the face near the eye. This allows the feeder to assist and control the opening and closing of the jaw.

- Most authors agree that jaw control should not involve control of the upper lip because pulling down the upper lip will stimulate more lip retraction (Alexander, 2001; Morris & Klein, 2000; Murphy & Caretto, 1999a).

Overall, these procedures can be very helpful with some children, but extreme caution should be exercised in their use. Muscle strength and tone are developed by working against resistance; external control may produce the movements required but will not contribute to the child learning to produce those movements independently. When jaw control must be used, it is essential that the minimum effective force be used and that other procedures (e.g., exercises outside mealtime) be used to help the child to develop independent responses (Alexander, 2001; Morris & Klein, 2000; Murphy & Caretto, 1999a).

Considering the Sensory Aspects of Feeding

One of the most important aspects of feeding is the understanding of how a child processes sensory input and the effects of sensory processing on eating and drinking. A child receives sensory input from many sensory systems, including visual, auditory, olfactory, gustatory, and tactile systems. Information from the environment is collected through receptors throughout the child's body and sent, via electrical signals, to the brain and/or spinal cord. This sensory information is interpreted by the central nervous system and used to plan, organize, and execute movements. Stimuli that are pleasant can help calm the child or improve attention to a task. Stimuli that are unpleasant or threatening will result in a protective response (Arkwright, 1998; Kranowitz, 1998; Murphy & Caretto, 1999b). For example, a hot bite of food is placed in the child's mouth. Through a "feedback loop," the electrical signals travel to the brain, the decision is made that the food is too hot, and the child spits it out.

Some children have milder (or hyposensitive) reactions to input from these systems than expected. Elevation in the sensory threshold of these children means that the children register less sensory input. Reductions in the sense of taste and smell can cause indifference to eating. Other children have stronger (or hypersensitive) reactions than expected. The sensory thresholds of these children are lower, meaning that they react more intensely than normal to sensory input. These children might become overly excited by the senses surrounding eating (Kranowitz, 1998; Morris & Klein, 2000). Children who demonstrate abnormal sensory reactions during feeding might refuse to accept solid foods, demonstrate picky eating, gag or vomit while eating, stuff food into the mouth, or suck food. Specific techniques are available that address children's atypical response to touch, taste, temperature, or texture during mealtimes (Murphy & Caretto, 1999b).

Sensory Stimulation Programs

Therapists and teachers have used various stimulation procedures to help "normalize" the sensitivity in and around children's mouths before and during meals (Murphy & Caretto, 1999b). Empirical evidence supports the use of these programs for improving feeding and eating skills (Fucile, Gisel, & Lau, 2002; Gisel, 1994; Gisel, 1996; Gisel, Applegate-Ferrante, Benson, & Bosma, 1996). For children who have a high sensory threshold (or hyposensitve reactions to sensory input), sensory stimulation is designed to give the child increased sensory input. For children who have low thresholds (or hypersensitive reactions to sensory input), the goal of sensory stimulation programs is to desensitize the children's reaction to incoming sensory input (Case-Smith & Humphry, 2001; Morris & Klein, 2000). The team, including a therapist who is trained in sensory integration, must determine the specific procedures appropriate for a particular child. Ongoing assessment is required to determine whether the treatment is producing the desired results for the child, especially because results appear to be inconsistent among different children. Table 12.2 highlights the basic guiding principles to consider before providing sensory stimulation (Alexander, 2001; Case-Smith & Humphry, 2001; Morris & Klein, 2000; Murphy & Caretto, 1999b).

Facial stimulation can have significant effects on sensory awareness. When done before the meal, this stimulation helps prepare the muscles for eating.

Table 12.2.   Principles for providing sensory stimulation

Begin to work from distal to proximal.
Stimulation should begin away from the child's face and move gradually toward the face. The areas away from the face, such as the hands and arms, are more familiar to touch, and touching them is not considered to be as intimate as touching someone on the mouth.

Use deep, firm pressure.
Light touch is arousing to the central nervous system. Deep, firm pressure works best to activate the sensory system and allow input into the joint and muscle receptors.

Stimulation to the body should be done in a symmetrical manner.
What is done to one side of the body should be done to the other side as well.

Examples of specific techniques for providing facial stimulation include the following:

- Using the palm, stroke downward on the cheeks toward the corners of the lips.
- Stroke downward from the nose toward the upper lip with the side of one finger.
- Stroke upward from the chin to the bottom lip with the side of one finger.
- Stroke around the lips in a circular motion.

A child's therapist should always be consulted before providing stimulation inside the mouth. The most common techniques for oral stimulation within the mouth are brushing the child's teeth before a meal or providing items for the child to chew on. Items such as NUK toothbrushes and Chewy Tubes are available from the companies listed in the resource list at the end of this chapter.

Incorporating Touch, Taste, Temperature, and Texture into the Meal

Changes in food selection and preparation can provide a variety of tastes, temperatures, and textures into the child's meal and can heighten a child's awareness of the food in his or her mouth (Alexander, 2001). Often, children with severe and multiple disabilities are given diets that consist wholly or primarily of puréed foods. Alexander (2001) and Arvedson (1998) recommended avoiding thin purées whenever possible and using more coarsely ground table foods if the child cannot chew solids. Because many normal eating skills (e.g., chewing) require the stimulation of having solid food in the mouth, puréed foods do not allow the development of these skills. Puréed foods also contribute to constipation, dental caries, and vitamin deficiencies (Acs, Ng, Helpin, & Rosenberg, 2002; Morris & Klein, 2000). Unfortunately, many children who are not exposed to whole foods in infancy may resist them later in life.

Several techniques for increasing the texture of the child's food include adding a new texture to a food that the child prefers (e.g., breaking up graham crackers into pudding), combining two preferred foods (e.g., steamed carrots and mashed potatoes) into one new food, and gradually increasing the texture of a given food. For those children who do not tolerate mixed foods or textures, the use of a commercial food grinder is a measurable way to gradually increase texture of a single food. A commercial food grinder allows the feeder to more accurately control the texture of the food and to chart the number of times the food is ground, and is therefore preferred over the use of a blender, which produces evenly blended or puréed food (Murphy & Caretto, 1999b).

Similarly, consideration needs to be given to the choice of foods. Because not all solid foods have the same texture, tastes, or temperature, careful matching of the food to the current abilities and preferences of the child is essential. Some children find it easier to start with new foods that dissolve easier with saliva, such as graham crackers. Foods that combine liquid and solid textures, such as soup, are difficult for some children. Some children may exhibit better performance if hot foods are avoided; other children may have better results if cold foods are avoided. Other children prefer spicy foods to "wake up" their sensory systems. The team should make careful selections while considering nutritional concerns, the child's preferences, and the cultural and personal preferences of the family (Alexander, 2001; Arvedson, 1998).

A good rule to remember when presenting a new food or texture is to place the food on the side of the child's mouth directly over the chewing surface of the teeth (also called side placement). By placing this new food directly on the chewing surface, food can be kept off the child's sensitive tongue. Side placement gives the child more oral-motor control to manipulate the food in his or her mouth (Murphy & Caretto, 1999b).

The manner in which food is presented to the child is extremely important, especially when another individual is feeding the child. The person feeding the child should be seated on a low chair so that the food is well below the child's face and the person doing the feeding's face is at or below eye level when the child is properly positioned. This encourages the child to be positioned with a slightly flexed neck, which makes swallowing without aspiration easier for the child and minimizes abnormal reflexes. Exceptions may be when the child has excess flexion and needs extension or when the person doing the feeding must be positioned behind or beside the child to provide physical assistance (Case-Smith & Humphry, 2001; Snyder et al., 1999).

Similar attention must be given to the way in which the spoon or cup comes into contact with the child's mouth. When encouraging spoon feeding, food should be placed in the middle of the mouth on the tongue. To encourage chewing and tongue movement, it is often helpful to place food directly between the teeth. The rim of the glass or cup should be placed on the child's lower lip, encouraging good lip seal and avoiding stimulation of the bite reflex, which often occurs if the rim is placed between the teeth. Cups and glasses must be tipped up just far enough to allow a controlled flow from the vessel to the mouth. If the cup or glass is tipped up too far, it will encourage the child to use an extension pattern to compensate or to assume a sudden and extreme flexion posture. Either of these extremes will interfere with drinking (Case-Smith & Humphry, 2001; Snyder et al., 1999).

The timing of presentation also is extremely important. The pace and cues provided by the feeder can enhance relaxation or increase tension in the child. The pace of feeding should be slow enough to allow the child to coordinate eating and drinking behavior with his or her breathing patterns. Failure to do so will result, at a minimum, in increased difficulty eating or, at worst, in life-threatening aspiration or airway obstruction (Murphy & Lowman, 1999).

In addition to food selection and presentation, utensils can be modified to encourage appropriate oral-motor patterns (Alexander, 2001). Regular glasses and cups require hyperextension of the neck because when they are tipped up far enough for the contents to pour into the mouth, the rim hits the drinker's nose unless the head is tipped back. Unfortunately, many children with severe and multiple disabilities choke, gag, or have other difficulties when they tip their heads back to drink. A cup with part of the rim cut away (called a cutaway or flexicup) can be tipped up farther without hitting the child's nose or requiring the head to be tipped back (Morris & Klein, 2000). For children who are being fed, clear plastic cups are best. These allow the person doing the feeding to observe the fluid in the cup and the child's mouth without having to move to an inappropriate position for presentation.

Some children with hypersensitive bite or gag reflexes may demonstrate less intense responses when using modified spoons. Nylon, plastic, or rubber-coated spoons may work well for children with hypersensitivity, especially those who react strongly to hot or cold stimuli, because metal utensils conduct heat to or from the oral structures very rapidly. Nonmetal spoons are also useful for children who bite down on utensils because they are generally softer and are less likely to cause injury. Although small, disposable, plastic spoons are excellent for some children because they minimize stimulation, they are not suitable for a child who may bite down on them because they break, often leaving sharp splinters of plastic in the mouth (Alexander, 2001).

Modified utensils can be extremely useful for many children with disabilities when used in combination with other interventions. Other children, however, eat as well or better with regular utensils. It is important to remember the normalization principle and to use specialized eating utensils only when a clear benefit over regular utensils can be demonstrated. Careful, ongoing observation and assessment is the best method for determining whether modified utensils have value for a specific child, and it allows planning for their introduction and use as well as planning for a return to regular utensils as soon as possible.

———————————————

Frank is 15 years old and recently began a new vocational program connected with his school program. Frank has severe mental retardation as well as severe visual and auditory impairments. His mode of communication has always been a tactile sign language, such as stroking his throat in a downward fashion when thirsty. Recently, Frank started ruminating daily after lunch. The staff was puzzled by this new behavior. As part of a functional analysis, the vocational staff, the school staff, and the family observed Frank over a period of time. Based on these observations, the team brainstormed a number of hypotheses for the motivations behind Frank's behavior, which include the desire to gain attention, escape a task, or receive additional sensory input. They decided that if the ruminating was sensory motivated, say, a matter of taste, they could give Frank a wider choice of foods to select at lunch. Thus, prior to each lunch he was given a choice of at least three different foods. Because Frank's only method of selecting food was to smell and touch it, those foods not selected were wasted. Although wasteful, it was the only way to give Frank more choice about what he ate. The team made an interesting discovery here. Although Frank did refuse some of the choices presented to him, he ate two servings most days. With enough food to satiate his hunger, he stopped ruminating. The lunch provided by the vocational center was not typically his favorite foods and the quantity was not enough for Frank. Clearly, Frank was hungry and did not like some of his lunch choices so he was ruminating to "feel" more full. (Lowman, Kientz, & Weiseman, 1999, pp. 169–170)

Facilitating Communication and Socialization During Meals

In addition to considering positioning, oral-motor skills, and sensory aspects, communication and socialization are critical components of mealtimes. "At the heart of every successful feeding session lies a respectful interaction between the child and the feeder" (Murphy & Lowman, 1999, p. 127). It is critical for the feeder to read the child's cues, establish trust during the feeding session, and allow the child to be in control of the interaction as much as possible. Important guidelines to establish this respectful interaction include

1. The feeder should watch and listen carefully to the child and coordinate presentation of food with the child's natural breathing and movement patterns.

2. The feeder should ensure appropriate lighting and positioning so that the child has a clear view of food or drink.

3. The feeder should establish a smooth and predictable pace while feeding.

4. For many children, a verbal (or tactile) ready signal from the feeder is helpful. It should be pointed out that many children will not require this signal and some children with hypertonicity may respond with an increase in tone (Campbell, 2000).

5. Children should be given the opportunity to signal (e.g., look up, move, verbalize, point) when they want the next bite of food or drink. The feeder should encourage this by waiting, observing, and reinforcing any sign of readiness.

6. Distractions and interruptions (to feeder and child) need to be minimized.

As described in Chapter 11, children with severe and multiple disabilities should be given every opportunity to make choices and indicate preferences during mealtime. The turn-taking behaviors developed during the feeding interaction build an essential foundation for more advanced communication skills. Feeding is also one of the important interactive contexts for the development of attachment between children and their caregivers, and attachment is also a powerful force in the development of communication. The oral-motor skills that are refined in eating are fundamental to the development of speech (Alexander, 2001). These influences on the development of communication skills make mealtimes an important context for teaching early communication. Teaching more advanced communication and social skill objectives is also easily integrated into mealtime activities because these behaviors are natural elements of mealtime routines.

Dealing with Possible Behavior Problems

Up to this point, this chapter has focused on oral-motor feeding problems. It is beyond the scope of this chapter to present a comprehensive overview of behavioral feeding problems, such as food refusal, food selectivity, mealtime tantrums, excessive meal duration, rumination, and pica (ingestion of nonfood items). It has been estimated that as many of 50% of children with developmental disabilities also have behavioral feeding problems (Kedesdy & Budd, 1998). Behavioral feeding problems may have serious implications for nutrition and growth; for example, long-term rumination of stomach acids can burn and damage the esophagus and teeth. For this reason, procedures to address behavioral mealtime problems are mentioned briefly.

Mealtime behavioral programs are often viewed as fitting into two categories: 1) building desirable behaviors and 2) eliminating undesirable behaviors. In practice, the development of desirable behavior at mealtime is often adequate to eliminate inappropriate behavior. Therefore, there is no need to institute direct intervention to reduce the inappropriate behavior. This focus on building appropriate behavior is consistent with the increasing awareness that behavior that is inappropriate (in the eyes of caregivers) is typically extremely functional for the child, and that teaching a more appropriate functional alternative may be the best means of behavioral control (Horner, Albin, Sprague, & Todd, 2000).

For example, if a child finishes his or her food and then grabs food off of other children's plates, this behavior may function to satisfy the child's continuing hunger. The team might try to use punishment procedures to eliminate food stealing, but such procedures will have little chance for success if the child has no more acceptable way of asking for a second helping. If the child is taught to obtain food through an acceptable requesting behavior (e.g., hand raising, picture symbol, AAC device), the unacceptable behavior may be eliminated with no other intervention or with less intrusive intervention than otherwise might be required.

Of course, the success of this approach depends on correctly identifying the function (or communicative intent) of the undesired behavior. Certainly, attaining food is the most obvious function one might ascribe to food grabbing. If the child does not really want the food and instead grabs food to attract the caregiver's attention, teaching the child more appropriate requesting behavior may do little to control food grabbing. Therefore, it is important to consider all functions for this behavior; for example, if a child grabs food off of another child's plate, he might be trying to convey one of the following messages (Lowman, Kientz, & Weissman, 1999):

- "I don't want what is on my plate" (protest)
- "I want more of what is on that child's plate" (request)
- "Please talk to me" (socialization)
- "That just burned my tongue" (protest)
- "This feels awful in my mouth"(sensory)

Therefore, the success of this program depends on a careful analysis of the child's behaviors. Considerable attention has been given to the process of conducting a functional analysis as a way of understanding the behavior of children with severe or multiple disabilities (O'Neill et al., 1997). The functional analysis process (or ABC analysis) involves observing the antecedents, behavior, consequences, and circumstances within the environment that might influence a child's behavior. As emphasized earlier, an important component of the functional analysis is determining the function or communicative intent of the behavior. Once the purpose(s) of the child's behavior have been identified, the goal of intervention is to teach the child replacement skills or a more appropriate way to meet his or her needs (e.g., teaching the child to ask for more rather than grabbing food). Two important references on behavioral feeding problems are Kerwin's (1999) systematic literature review of 32 articles describing psychosocial or behavioral interventions and Kedesdy and Budd's (1998) book on the biobehavioral assessment and intervention of feeding disorders.

Addressing Nutritional Concerns

Any observation and assessment of the eating and drinking skills of children with severe or multiple disabilities should consider nutrition. After all, one of the major goals of intervention surrounding feeding and eating is to ensure that the child receives adequate nutrition for growth and development. Children with developmental disabilities appear to be at greater risk for nutritional deficits than their peers without disabilities (Beker, Farber, & Yanni, 2002; Jepsen & Nickel, 2000). A position paper from the American Dietetic Association (1995) estimates that as many as 40% of the children with disabilities are at risk for nutrition problems.

Risk Factors

Children with severe or multiple disabilities may have the following risk factors that contribute to problems with nutrition (Beker et al., 2002; Case-Smith & Humphry, 2001; Jepsen & Nickel, 2000):

- Difficulty with ingestion or digestion (e.g., food refusal, rumination, food selectivity)

- Limited oral-motor skills, which leads to decreased food intake (e.g., tongue thrust, bite reflex, hyperactive gag response)

- Limited movement and/or atypical tone, which leads to a diet of puréed foods

- Structural impairments (e.g., cleft lip and/or palate)

- Gastrointestinal dysmotility (e.g., reflux, delayed gastric emptying)

- A metabolic condition affecting nutritional requirements (e.g., phenylketonuria)

- Medications that change appetite, interfere with absorption, or increase excretion of nutrients

- Inability to communicate that leads to problems maintaining hydration

- Mealtime interactions/interventions that can be difficult and frustrating for the child and the feeder

Signs and Symptoms

Problems in nutrition might be both the cause and the result of the developmental problems (Beker et al., 2002). One of the major difficulties of providing better recognition of nutritional deficits in children with severe and multiple disabilities is that signs and symptoms of these deficits are often ascribed to other causes. Lethargy and poor resistance to infection, which may be signs of anemia, are often considered to be a result of the child's diagnosis or to the medication given to the child. Retarded growth and scoliosis, which may be signs of inadequate calcium or vitamin D, are often seen as resulting from a genetic syndrome or disorder of muscle tone and posture. Thus, nutritional problems may be masked by other risk factors. This means that screening, assessment, and monitoring of nutrition in children with severe and multiple disabilities must be particularly thorough.

Nutrition Screening

Because of the high risk for nutrition problems, members of the team should conduct regular nutrition screenings with guidance from the nutritionist (Case-Smith & Humphry, 2001; Story, Holt, & Sofka, 2000). Areas to note during a screening include the following:

- The child consumes less than 16–32 ounces of milk (adequate amounts depend on the child's age).

- The child has constant diarrhea, constipation, or other medical conditions such as reflux or vomiting, known to affect nutrition.

- The child has significant food aversions or allergies that limit diet.

- The parent expresses concern about the child's weight or growth.

- The child's nutritional intake is not consistent with his or her chronological age.

- General observation of color or texture of skin, hair, and gums raises concerns.

- The child's weight for height is below the 10th percentile, weight for height is above the 90th percentile, or height and weight are below the 5th percentile.

Answering yes to the above might indicate the need for referral for an in-depth nutritional evaluation and services (Case-Smith & Humphry, 2001).

Meeting the Child's Nutritional Needs

All of the risk factors listed previously contribute to nutritional problems for a large percentage of children with severe and multiple disabilities. Awareness of these concerns by all team members and careful periodic assessments by a professional in dietetics and nutrition are important components of service delivery to children with severe and multiple disabilities. Improved nutrition can make a major contribution to health, learning, and quality of life for children with severe and multiple disabilities. Improved nutrition should be a part of every feeding plan. On a daily basis, children with disabilities should be encouraged to learn to participate in choosing their own food. Pairing choices between reasonably nutritious foods allows children to make choices and to learn to enjoy nutritious foods. The reader is referred to Morris and Klein (2000) for a comprehensive description of a variety of techniques for increasing calories, increasing dietary diversity, and increasing nutrients. Additional information can be found in Story, Holt, and Sofka (2000), including the description of a way to calculate energy needs for children and adolescents with special health care needs.

Alternative Diets

Much has been written about specific dietary interventions that aim to produce substantive changes in behavior and learning potential. These include participating in megavitamin or orthomolecular therapy to reduce hyperactivity and improve learning; reducing sugar intake and eliminating common food allergens to prevent hyperactivity; and the Feingold diet of eliminating natural salicylates, artificial colors and flavors, and certain preservatives. The Feingold Association of the United States (2002) has an extensive list of published research that has supported these kinds of intervention. Other sources report that there is no conclusive evidence that a specific diet works for all children with a certain disability (Beker et al., 2002), however. Such conflicting results suggest that some small subgroup of children may be helped by these interventions. Therefore, it is suggested that the team carefully weighs the benefits of the diet with the costs to the child and family.

Considering Dental Needs

Children with developmental disabilities are at a higher risk for dental disease than their peers who are typically developing (Acs et al., 2002). Families of children with severe or multiple disabilities may face additional barriers to receiving adequate dental care, including transportation difficulties, physical barriers, unprepared dental providers, lack of awareness of services, and an inability to pay for dental care (Acs et al., 2002; Schultz, Shenkin, & Horowitz, 2001).

Special Dental Concerns

Some particular dental concerns exist for children with severe or multiple disabilities. Children with cerebral palsy often have more cavities, more periodontal disease, poor occlusion, and damaged teeth due to bruxism (grinding of the teeth). Children with Down syndrome appear to have fewer cavities than other children, but they often have increased periodontal disease and poor occlusion. Children with epilepsy are at risk for damaging teeth in a fall or may have an abnormal overgrowth of the gums caused by medication. Children with mobility problems have difficulty cleaning their own teeth and gums thoroughly; in addition, abnormal reflexes and limited ranges of motion may make dental treatment more difficult. Puréed, sticky diets provided to some children promote cavities and increase the need for brushing. All of these factors contribute to the need for ongoing, high-quality dental services. These services can best be provided through close cooperation between dental specialists and other team members (Acs et al., 2002; Agins, 1999; Pilcher, 1998).

An example of dental problems addressed by team members can be seen in the case of children with gum overgrowth. Approximately 50% of children who receive Dilantin (phenytoin) have significant gum overgrowth. A reduction in phenytoin can reduce this overgrowth if the child can tolerate this reduction. If phenytoin cannot be reduced, ascorbic acid may be prescribed to reduce some of the negative effects. Such intervention, however, must require careful consultation with the physician to determine the potential effects on seizure activity. If overgrowth of gums cannot be prevented, the dentist should be consulted to determine how careful cleaning of teeth and gums will reduce the infection and irritation that can lead to serious dental disease. The occupational therapist should be consulted regarding adaptations to the toothbrush. As always, the parents must be involved at all times (Acs et al., 2002).

Dental Care and Prevention

Good dental care requires the teamwork of dentists, dental hygienists, parents, teachers, and other caregivers. Introducing solid foods to the child as early as possible while avoiding puréed foods can reduce cavities and encourage normal development of oral structures (Morris & Klein, 2000). Avoiding the use of sweets as reinforcers and snacks will reduce cavities. Snack foods that promote dental health include raw vegetable sticks, unsweetened plain yogurt, and cheese. Perhaps most important, regular brushing and flossing are major preventers of cavities and periodontal disease. As discussed earlier, frequent brushing also helps to provide needed sensory stimulation. Whenever possible, children should be taught to brush their own teeth, but caregivers may need to supplement this by helping to clean the children's teeth. Electric toothbrushes and oral irrigators, disclosing solutions to show what is missed during brushing, may help to ensure the quality of cleaning for many children. The introduction of mouthwashes that contain ingredients (e.g., chlorhexidine) that inhibit formation of plaque has been a significant advantage in oral hygiene. Applying the mouthwashes directly to the teeth and gums with swabs has proven effective in decreasing plaque and gingivitis among people with disabilities who are unable to use an oral rinse properly (Acs et al., 2002). Additional suggestions for oral care can be viewed at http://www.brightfutures.org/oralhealth/index.html.

THE FEEDING PLAN: PUTTING IT ALL TOGETHER

A comprehensive feeding plan can be developed with all of the information gathered about the family's mealtime routines and concerns, respiratory concerns, positioning, oral-motor skills, sensory aspects, communication and socialization skills, behavioral concerns, and nutritional and dental concerns (Lowman & Murphy, 1999). In addition to information gathered in each of the preceding areas, the following questions should be answered during the development of the comprehensive feeding plan:

1. Did the family, the child, all potential feeders, and specialists as needed participate in the development of this plan?

2. Was the needed medical information, including physician's orders and nutritional requirements, received and considered?

3. What is the most effective sequence for the mealtime/feeding process?

4. What feeding equipment will be needed?

5. Where will meals and feedings be conducted?

Considerable controversy exists regarding the best times and places to teach eating and drinking skills (Farlow & Snell, 2000). Some teachers and therapists suggest that quiet times and places may produce better acquisition than busy lunchrooms in the school cafeteria. Others argue that skills taught in a natural environment, under typical conditions, are most likely to be generalized and maintained over time. One way to approach this discussion is to determine the goal of the feeding session. If the goal is for the child to eat meals with classmates or family members, then the normalization principle dictates that meals be provided at regular times in the typical environment. If the goal of the feeding session is for the child to acquire a new skill, then supplementing regular mealtimes with specialized training sessions might be appropriate. For example, requiring a child to use a new oral-motor pattern at his regular mealtimes may have two disadvantages. First, it will reduce fluid intake and may threaten his health. Second, the child will almost certainly resist because the new pattern at first will lessen fluid intake. By teaching initial acquisition outside regular meal and drink times, more fluids are provided instead of less, and the additional fluids provided at these special times reinforce the newly acquired pattern. Providing small meals for training purposes in addition to regular mealtimes may also be useful for training in eating skills because this provides distributed rather than massed practice (Farlow & Snell, 2000). Although providing small meals has advantages for all learners, it may be particularly useful for children who tire quickly or become distracted or disruptive during longer meals. Other children may benefit from additional or alternative eating and drinking times because they take advantage of their peak learning times. Peak learning times are easily identified for many students who may be active, alert, and attentive at some times during the day and may be lethargic, unresponsive, or irritable at other times. Finally, it should be noted that snacks are common in the United States, and few people restrict their eating to only three meals a day. Using snacks for either structured or incidental learning is consistent with typical patterns of everyday life.

NON-ORAL (OR TUBE) FEEDING METHODS

Children with disabilities are sometimes placed on feeding tubes to make it easier for them to grow and thrive. For some children, the feeding tube is the sole source of nutrition, and for others, the tube supplements what can be taken orally. Feeding tubes are used for a number of reasons, including prematurity, anatomical abnormalitites, neurological issues, aspiration, fatigue, pending surgeries, and failure to thrive. The various types of feeding tubes are described in Table 12.3.

Although oral feedings are preferred whenever possible, some children's nutritional status is greatly improved with tube feedings. In some cases, tube feedings reduce the stress levels of families and other caregivers as well as the children involved because unsuccessful attempts at oral feedings can produce great frustration. It is important that parents and others involved in decisions about feeding alternatives are fully informed about the potential benefits, costs, and risks of all possible alternatives (Morris & Klein, 2000; Wolf & Glass, 1992). Planning should begin at the time of tube insertion for the maintenance of the child's oral-motor skills, prevention of oral hypersensitivity, and the transition back to oral feedings (Jepsen & Nickel, 2000).

Tube feedings should occur during the natural times for meals and snacks for the children in the class. Tube feeding during mealtime gives the child the experience of feeling full as food is being served as well as participating in mealtime through as normal a process as possible. If specified in the HSP, the child should be offered food by mouth at the same time as the tube feeding. If oral feeding is not allowed, oral stimulation should be conducted to have the child make the connection between oral stimulation and feeling full (Ault et al., 2000).

Those administering tube feedings should be trained to follow procedures carefully. General procedures for administering tube feedings are available from a number of sources (e.g., Graff et al., 1990; Porter, Haynie, Bierle, Cald-

Table 12.3. Types of supplemental feeding tubes

Type of feeding tube	Insertion/ destination	Strengths	Limitations
Nasogastric tube (NG)	Nose/stomach	No surgical placement required Oral feeding possible with tube in place	Insertion and presence in nose/throat is uncomfortable and may be aversive May trigger bradycardia May be cosmetically unacceptable for long-term use
Orogastric tube (OG)	Mouth/stomach	No surgical placement	Same as NG, also, difficult to feed orally with tube in place
Duodenal tube	Nose/duodenum	No surgical placement Bypasses stomach so decreases risk of gastroesophageal reflux (GER)	Same as NG, though softer, so may have fewer hypersensitive responses Must use continuous-drip feeding Difficult to place and maintain in correct position
Gastrostomy (standard, percutaneous, button, peg)	Surgically placed in stomach	No aversive oral-facial stimuli Despite surgical placement, can be removed easily when no longer needed	Requires surgical placement Site needs daily care, and trip to doctor might be necessary if tube falls out Potential risk for increased GER after tube placed
Jejunostomy	Tube surgically placed in jejunum, possibly in association with gastrostomy	Same as gastrostomy Bypasses stomach, so reduces risk of GER	Requires surgical placement Site needs daily care, requires trip to hospital if tube falls out Requires continuous-drip feedings

From Wolf, L.S., & Glass, R.P. (1992). *Feeding and swallowing disorders in infancy: Assessment and management.* Tucson, AZ: Therapy Skill Builders; adapted by permission.

well, & Palfrey, 1997; Urbano, 1992), but it is important to individualize the procedures (e.g., positioning, rate of flow) for each child.

Transitioning to Oral Feedings

Not all children who receive tube feedings will transition back to oral feedings for a number of reasons, including

- Often, the problems that led to the initial decision to use tube feeding are still present.

- The initial problem is often aggravated by a weakening of the oral structures as a result of not being used.

- Because the oral structures lack stimulation typically provided by feeding, they may become hypersensitive.

- Although the oral reflexes of some children receiving tube feedings become hypersensitive, other children may develop hyposensitive oral reflexes. For example, children who frequently have an NG tube in place may have hyposensitive swallow reflexes because they are desensitized to feeling something in the back of their throats.

- Children who have become accustomed to tube feeding sometimes resist the reintroduction of oral feedings.

- The motivation of family and team members may be reduced because the availability of tube feeding makes oral feeding less vital (Morris & Klein, 2000)

Programs to reinstitute oral feedings must be individually developed. Usually, the best time to begin the program is as soon as the child starts tube feedings or even before tube feedings are started. Morris and Klein (2000) described many stimulation procedures designed to ease the transition to oral feedings. Often, the mouth, tongue, lips, and other oral structures are hypersensitive as a result of deprivation of the stimulation typically involved in eating. Morris and Klein suggested encouraging or assisting the child to explore the environment with the tongue and lips. Voice and sound play are also useful components of a transition program. Stimulating the child with smells and tastes throughout the tube-feeding phase may also be useful, even if the child cannot be allowed to actually swallow food during this time. If it is possible to allow some oral feedings concurrently with the tube-feeding phase, this should be done with an emphasis on making the experience as pleasant as possible for the child.

A critical component of the transition plan is to help the child make the connection between feeling hungry and being fed (Case-Smith & Humphry,

2001). Children who are on continuous tube feedings may never experience hunger. One of the first steps is to change the tube feedings from continuous feedings to feedings conducted over a short period of time (bolus feedings). Once the child's system has adjusted to the bolus feedings, the team should work with the doctor to determine if the total number of bolus feedings can be reduced. Shauster and Dwyer (1996) suggested reducing food at 25% to stimulate the feeling of hunger. Because children who have tube feedings are sometimes not medically stable, reduction in calorie intake and transition from tube to oral feedings can take a long time (Case-Smith & Humphry, 2001). Parents need constant support and encouragement during this long transition period.

EATING SKILLS

Basic eating (sometimes called *self-feeding*) skills include handling finger foods, drinking from a cup, and eating with a spoon. More advanced food skills include more complex sequence of skills involving serving, preparing, and purchasing foods.

Basic Eating Skills

For children with movement difficulties or skill deficits, modeling the desired behavior may be helpful. As discussed in Chapter 3, however, graduated guidance is the most common instructional method used to teach basic eating skills. Generally, the caregiver will find it easier to work from behind the child and to guide the child through the required movements with assistance as needed. Assistance is gradually withdrawn as the child becomes more independent. For example, the instructor might initially use hand-over-hand assistance to help the child scoop food and bring it to the mouth. As the child becomes more proficient, assistance might be faded from wrist guidance to elbow guidance (Farlow & Snell, 2000; Klein & Delaney, 1994).

Generally, teaching children to feed themselves with their fingers is best accomplished at the beginning of a meal when they are hungry. Some children, however, may become easily frustrated at this time and will tolerate instruction better after having something to eat. To be successful initially, it is important that the child knows and likes the foods. Larger foods such as a cookie, strips of food such as toast, or food with a "handle" such as broccoli are easy to hold and put into the mouth; smaller pieces of food can get lost in the grasp. As the child becomes more proficient, smaller pieces of food allow for isolation of the thumb and finger. It is, however, important to avoid finger foods that are round and similar in size to the airway: Foods such as grapes, hot dogs, nuts, and popcorn can cause choking. Many children begin finger feeding independently, in which case, instruction may focus on improving grasp and release or establishing a suitable pace (Morris & Klein, 2000).

Learning to drink from a cup is a messy but rewarding experience for almost any child. For many children, the only requirement is caregivers' willingness to provide ample learning opportunities. For other children, the coordination of arm, hand, head, and mouth movements is extremely challenging. Stable positioning is critical, especially in terms of the child having a solid place to rest his or her feet. It is also helpful to rest the child's elbows on the table while drinking. As was the case with finger feeding, graduated guidance is useful for teaching children to grasp the cup, raise it to the mouth, and return it to the table. For some children, thickened liquids may be easier to control at first. Consultation with a child's occupational therapist will help in the selection of the cup with the best shape and weight. Although spout cups reduce spilling, these types of cups are not generally recommended because the spout encourages an infantile sucking pattern (Morris & Klein, 2000). A variety of adapted cups are available from the companies listed at the end of this chapter.

Graduated guidance is also a common method of teaching children with disabilities to eat with a spoon. Because spoon-feeding involves a fairly long chain of discrete responses, task analysis is often useful in determining exactly which steps need direct instruction. As shown in Figure 12.4, a variety of adaptive spoons are available for children who have difficulty gripping, bringing the spoon into their mouths at the appropriate angle, or keeping food balanced on the spoon while bringing it to their mouths. Consultation by the team with the occupational therapist will help determine which type of spoon is most appropriate for the individual child.

Foods that stick to the spoon, such as pudding, yogurt, oatmeal, mashed potatoes, and macaroni and cheese, help the child get food into the mouth. Using a slightly deeper bowl on the spoon means that food does not fall out as easily as it does from a flat spoon. Children with difficulties with motor coordination or wrist control will find a shorter handle easier to control than a longer handle (Morris & Klein, 2000).

Advanced Mealtime Skills

For children who master basic eating skills, instruction in more advanced mealtime skills will increase their level of independence and allow them to function in a wide array of environments. The selection and order of skills taught will not be the same for all children. Specific skills should be selected on the basis of the needs and skills of the child and requirements of his or her current and potential future environments. For example, tray-carrying skills may not be relevant

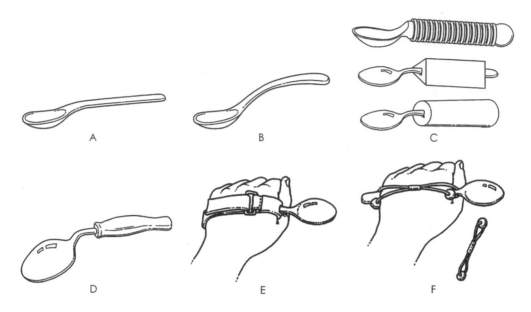

Figure 12.4. Different types of spoons and adaptations to aid in holding spoons: a) spoon with a flat bowl, b) spoon with a deep bowl, c) spoons with large handles, d) spoon with a bent handle, e) universal cuff, f) elastic handle made from a ponytail holder. (From Lowman, D.K. [1999]. Adapted equipment for feeding. In D.K. Lowman and S.M. Murphy. *The educator's guide to feeding children with disabilities* [p. 148]. Baltimore: Paul H. Brookes Publishing Co.; reprinted by permission.)

for children who eat only family-style meals at home and in their classrooms, but these same tray-carrying skills may be extremely important for children who eat in a school cafeteria. Some advanced skills include demonstrating table manners and mealtime social skills, serving food, setting the table, preparing food, selecting nutritious foods, requesting desired foods, ordering in restaurants, and shopping for food. As stated previously, task analysis is an important instructional method for teaching the various components of advanced mealtime skills. Using the principle of partial participation, instructors can teach children with severe and multiple disabilities to master as many of these basic skills as possible (Farlow & Snell, 2000).

SUMMARY

This chapter presents information and discusses issues concerning mealtime skills and related concerns for children with severe and multiple disabilities. Mealtime skills are essential for survival, health, and a good quality of life. Ongoing observation and assessment of respiration, physical development, oral-motor skills, sensory issues, communication skills, and nutrition are critical to the development of an appropriate plan of intervention. A carefully designed feeding plan can do much to promote development, health, and quality of life by providing instruction in eating and feeding skills, creating a typical and relaxed mealtime environment, protecting against the dangers of airway obstruction and aspiration, and ensuring good nutrition and dental care. Collaborative teamwork is required to assess the child's current abilities and the demands of the environment and to implement effective mealtime instruction.

REFERENCES

Acs, G., Ng, M.W., Helpin, M.L., & Rosenberg, H.M. (2002). Dental care: Promoting health and preventing disease. In M.L. Batshaw (Ed.), *Children with disabilities* (5th ed., pp. 567–578). Baltimore: Paul H. Brookes Publishing Co.

Agins, A.P. (1999). *Parent & educators' drug reference: A guide to common medical conditions and drugs used in school-aged children.* Baltimore: Paul H. Brookes Publishing Co.

Alexander, R. (2001). Feeding and swallowing. In J.L. Bigge, S.J. Best, & K.W. Heller, *Teaching individuals with physical, health, or multiple disabilities* (4th ed., pp. 504–535). Upper Saddle River, NJ: Merrill Prentice Hall.

Alexander, R., Boehme, R., & Cupps, B. (1993). *Normal development of functional motor skills: The first year of life.* Tuscon, AZ: Therapy Skill Builders.

American Dietetic Association. (1995). Nutrition services for children with special health needs—Position of ADA. *Journal of the American Dietetic Assocation, 95,* 809.

Arkwright, N. (1998). *An introduction to sensory integration.* San Antonio, TX: Therapy Skill Builders.

Arvedson, J.C. (1998). Management of pediatric dysphagia. *Dysphagia in children, adults, and geriatric, 31,* 453–476.

Arvedson, J.C., & Lefton-Greif, M.A. (1998). *Pediatric videofluoroscopic swallow studies: A professional manual with caregiver guidelines.* Tucson, AZ: Communication Skill Builders.

Ault, M.M., Rues, J.P., Graff, J.C., & Holvoet, J.F. (2000). Special health care procedures. In M.E. Snell & F. Brown (Eds.), *Instruction of students with severe handicaps* (5th ed., pp. 245–290). Upper Saddle River, NJ: Merrill Prentice Hall.

Avery-Smith, W. (1996). Eating dysfunction positions paper. *American Journal of Occupational Therapy, 10*(10), 846–847.

Beker, L.T., Farber, A.F., & Yanni, C.C. (2002). Nutrition and children with disabilities. In M.L. Batshaw (Ed.), *Children with disabilities* (5th ed., pp. 141–164). Baltimore: Paul H. Brookes Publishing Co.

Campbell, P.H. (2000). Promoting participation in natural environments by accommodating motor disabilities. In M.E. Snell & F. Brown (Eds.), *Instruction of students with severe handicaps* (5th ed., pp. 291–329). Upper Saddle River, NJ: Merrill Prentice Hall.

Case-Smith, J., & Humphry, R. (2001). Feeding intervention. In J. Case-Smith (Ed.), *Occupational therapy for children* (4th ed., pp. 452–488). Princeton, NJ: Mosby.

Dahl, M., Thommessen, M., Rasmussen, M., & Selberg, T. (1996). Feeding and nutritional characteristics in children with moderate or severe cerebral palsy. *Acta Paediatrica, 6,* 697–701.

Eicher, P.S. (2002). Feeding. In M.L. Batshaw (Ed.), *Children with disabilities* (5th ed., pp. 549–566). Baltimore: Paul H. Brookes Publishing Co.

Einarsson-Backes, L., Deitz, J., Price, R., Glass, R., & Hays, R. (1994). The effect of oral support on sucking efficiency in preterm infants. *The American Journal of Occupational Therapy, 48,* 490–498.

Farlow, L.J., & Snell, M.E. (2000). Teaching basic self-care skills. In M.E. Snell & F. Brown (Eds.), *Instruction of students with severe handicaps* (5th ed., pp. 331–380). Upper Saddle River, NJ: Merrill Prentice Hall.

Feingold Association of the United States. (2002). *Studies on diet, health & behavior.* Retrieved April 2002 from http://www.feingold.org/research1.html.

Fucile, S., Gisel, E., & Lau, C. (2002). Oral stimulation accelerates the transition from tube to oral feeding in preterm infants. *Journal of Pediatrics, 141*(2), 230–236.

Geyer, L.A., & McGowan, J.S. (1995). Positioning infants and children for videofluoroscopic swallowing function studies. *Infants and Young Children, 8*(2), 58–64.

Gisel, E.G. (1994). Oral-motor skills following sensorimotor intervention in the moderately eating-impaired child with cerebral palsy. *Dysphagia, 9,* 180–192.

Gisel, E.G. (1996). Effects of oral sensorimotor treatment on measures of growth and efficiency of eating in the moderately eating-impaired child with cerebral palsy. *Dysphagia, 11,* 48–58.

Gisel, E.G., Applegate-Ferrante, T., Benson, J., & Bosma, J.F. (1996). Oral-motor skills following sensorimotor therapy in two groups of moderately dysphagic children with cerebral palsy: Aspiration vs nonaspiration. *Dysphagia, 11,* 59–71.

Graff, J.C., Ault, M.M., Guess, D., Taylor, M., & Thompson, B. (1990). *Health care for students with disabilities: An illustrated medical guide for the classroom.* Baltimore: Paul H. Brookes Publishing Co.

Hall, S., Yohn, K., & Reed, P.R. (1992). *Feeding students in school: Providing guidelines and information on safe feeding practices for special students.* Salem: Oregon Department of Education.

Horner, R.H., Albin, R.W., Sprague, J.R., & Todd, A.W. (2000). Positive behavior support. In M.E. Snell & F. Brown (Eds.), *Instruction of students with severe handicaps* (5th ed., pp. 207–243). Upper Saddle River, NJ: Merrill Prentice Hall.

Jepsen, C., & Nickel, R.E. (2000). Nutrition and growth. In R.E. Nickel & L.W. Desch (Eds.), *The physician's guide to caring for children with disabilities and chronic conditions* (pp. 78–98). Baltimore: Paul H. Brookes Publishing Co.

Kedesdy, J.H., & Budd, K.S. (1998). *Childhood feeding disorders: Biobehavioral assessment and intervention.* Baltimore: Paul H. Brookes Publishing Co.

Kerwin, J.E. (1999). Empirically supported treatments in pediatric psychology: Severe feeding problems. *Journal of Pediatric Psychology, 24*(3), 193–214.

Klein, M.D., & Delaney, T.A. (1994). *Feeding and nutrition for the child with special needs.* Tucson, AZ: Therapy Skill Builders.

Kranowitz, C.S. (1998). *The out-of-sync child: Recognizing and coping with sensory integration dysfunction.* New York: The Berkley Publishing Group.

Loughlin, G.M., & Lefton-Greif, M.A. (1994). Dysfunctional swallowing and respiratory disease in children. *Advances in Pediatrics, 41,* 135–162.

Lowman, D.K., Kientz, M., & Weissman, R.A. (1999). Behavior strategies for feeding. In D.K. Lowman & S.M. Murphy, *The educator's guide to feeding children with disabilities* (pp. 155–172). Baltimore: Paul H. Brookes Publishing Co.

Lowman, D.K., & Murphy, S.M. (1999). *The educator's guide to feeding children with disabilities.* Baltimore: Paul H. Brookes Publishing Co.

Morris, S.E., & Klein, M.D. (2000). *Pre-feeding skills* (2nd ed.). Tucson, AZ: Therapy Skill Builders.

Murphy, S.M., & Caretto, V. (1999a). Oral-motor considerations for feeding. In D.K. Lowman & S.M. Murphy, *The educator's guide to feeding children with disabilities* (pp. 49–64). Baltimore: Paul H. Brookes Publishing Co.

Murphy, S.M., & Caretto, V. (1999b). Sensory aspects of feeding. In D.K. Lowman & S.M. Murphy, *The educator's guide to feeding children with disabilities* (pp. 111–125). Baltimore: Paul H. Brookes Publishing Co.

Murphy, S.M., & Lowman, D.K. (1999). Communication strategies for feeding. In D.K. Lowman & S.M. Murphy, *The educator's guide to feeding children with disabilities* (pp. 127–140). Baltimore: Paul H. Brookes Publishing Co.

Nichols, D.S. (2001). Development of postural control. In J. Case-Smith (Ed.). *Occupational therapy for children* (4th ed., pp. 266–288). Princeton, NJ: Mosby.

O'Neill, R.E., Horner, R.H., Albin, R.W., Sprague, J.R., Storey, K., & Newton, J.S. (1997). *Functional assessment and program development for problem behavior: A practical handbook.* Pacific Grove, CA: Brooks/Cole Publishing Company.

Pilcher, E.S. (1998). Dental care for the patient with Down syndrome. *Down Syndrome Research and Practice, 5*(3), 111–116.

Porter, S., Haynie, M., Bierle, T., Caldwell, T.H., & Palfrey, J.S. (1997). *Children and youth assisted by medical technology in educational settings: Guidelines for care* (2nd ed.). Baltimore: Paul H. Brookes Publishing Co.

Rasley, A., Logemann, J.A., Kahrilas, P.J., Rademaker, A.W., Pauloski, B.R., & Dodds, W.J. (1993). Prevention of barium aspiration during videofluoroscopic swallowing studies: Value of change in posture. *American Journal of Roentgenology, 160*(5), 1005–1009.

Reilly, S., & Skuse, D. (1996). Characteristics and management of feeding problems of young children with cerebral palsy. *Developmental Medicine and Child Neurology, 34,* 379–388.

Reilly, S., Skuse, D., & Poblete, X. (1996). Prevalence of feeding problems and oral-motor dysfunction in children with cerebral palsy: A community survey. *Journal of Pediatrics, 6,* 877–882.

Rogers, B., Arvedson, J., Buck, G. et al. (1994). Characteristics of dysphagia in children with cerebral palsy. *Dysphagia, 9,* 69–73.

Schultz, S.T., Shenkin, J.D., & Horowitz, A.M. (2001). Parental perceptions of unmet dental need and cost barriers to care for developmentally disabled children. *Pediatric Dentistry, 20,* 321–325.

Schwarz, S.M., Corredor, J., Fisher-Medina, J., Cohen, J., & Rabinowitz, S. (2001). Diagnosis and treatment of feeding disorders in children with developmental disabilities. *Pediatrics, 108,* 671–676.

Shauster, H., & Dwyer, J. (1996). Transition from tube feedings to feedings by mouth in children: Preventing eating dysfunction. *The Journal of the American Dietetic Assocation, 96*(3), 277–281.

Snyder, P.A., Breath, D., & DeMauro, G.J. (1999). Positioning strategies for feeding and eating. In D.K. Lowman & S.M. Murphy, *The educator's guide to feeding children with disabilities* (pp. 65–109). Baltimore: Paul H. Brookes Publishing Co.

Story, M., Holt, K., & Sofka, D. (Eds.). (2000). *Bright futures in practice: Nutrition.* Arlington, VA: National Center for Education in Maternal and Child Health.

Urbano, M.T. (1992). *Preschool children with special health care needs.* San Diego: Singular Publishing Group.

Wolf, L.S., & Glass, R.P. (1992). *Feeding and swallowing disorders in infancy: Assessment and management.* Tucson, AZ: Therapy Skill Builders.

For More Information

HEALTH SERVICES PLAN

The components of a Health Services Plan can be viewed at http://www.brookespublishing.com/store/books/lowman-3750/excerpt2.htm

ADAPTIVE EQUIPMENT

Achievement Products, Inc.
Post Office Box 9033
Canton, OH 44711
800-373-4699
(scoop bowl, plate, spoons, utensil cuffs, Dycem)

adaptAbility Products for Independent Living
Post Office Box 515
Colchester, CT 06415-0515
(Dycem nonslip products)

Abilitations
One Sportime Way
Atlanta, GA 30340
800-850-8603
(Whistle Sippers, no-spill bubble tumbler, whistle kit)

AliMed
http://www.alimed.com/product_list.cfm?VMID=11&CategoryID=324
(Rolyan Millicup, maroon spoons, Nosey cutout cup)

Beyond Play
http://www.beyondplay.com/CATALOG/ORA1.HTM#T309
(Infa-Trainer, NUK toothbrushes, Infa-Dent, Chewy Tubes)

Collis Curve Toothbrush Catalog
302 North Central Avenue
Brownsville, TX 78521
800-298-4818
(Collis-Curve toothbrush)

DeRoyal/LMB
200 DeBusk Lane
Powell, TN 37849
800-541-3992
(plate guards, cups, weighted and soft-grip utensils, universal cuff)

Equipment Shop
http://www.equipmentshop.com/Product2.asp?CategoryID=6
(NUK massager and toothbrushes, chewy tubes, maroon spoons)

Exceptional Parent
Post Office Box 3000
Department EP
Denville, NJ 07834
800-562-1973
(This magazine for parents reviews and advertises a variety of adaptive equipment)

Flaghouse, Inc.
601 Flaghouse Drive
Hasbrouck Heights, NJ 07604
800-793-7900
(utensils, cups, plates)

Mealtimes
http://www.new-vis.com
(A resource for oral-motor, feeding, and mealtime programs; a variety of massagers, chew toys, utensils, and books)

Medela, Inc.
Post Office Box 660
McHenry, IL 60051-0660
800-435-8316
(Haberman feeder)

Rifton
Box 901
Rifton, NY 12471
800-777-4244
(variety of adapted equipment)

Psychological Corporation
http://www.psychcorp.com/index.htm
(M.O.R.E: Integrating the Mouth with Sensory and Postural Functions)

Sammons Preston Rolyan
http://www.samsonspreston.com/
(scooper bowls, cups, sure-grip utensils, universal cuff, Dycem, electric self-feeder)

Sassy, Inc.
1534 College SE
Grand Rapids, MI 49507
(Sassy training cup)

Smith & Nephew, Inc.
One Quality Drive
Post Office Box 1005
Germantown, WI 53022
800-558-8633
(a variety of utensils, cups, plates
and plate guards, toothbrushes, oral swabs)

Southpaw Enterprises
Post Office Box 1047
Dayton, OH 45401
800-228-1698
(oral stimulation kit)

The Kennedy Cup
888-THE-KCUP
http://www.kcup.com
(spillproof cup with straw)

Therapy Skill Builders
555 Academic Court
San Antonio, TX 78204
800-211-8378
(Maroon spoons, dysphagia cup, flexi cups)

VIDEOTAPES

Blind Children's Center
4120 Marathon Street
Los Angeles, CA 90029
800-222-3566
(Let's Eat: Feeding a Child with a Visual Impairment)

Clinician's View
6007 Osuna Road, NE
Albuquerque, NM 87109
505-880-0058
(Therapeutic Management of Children with G-Tubes)

Ellyn Satter Associates
http://www.ellynsatter.com/
*(Feeding with Love and Good Sense: The Infant,
the Older Baby, the Toddler, and the Preschooler)*

Lerner Managed Designs, Inc.
Post Office Box 747
Lawrence, KS 66044
800-467-1644
(Home Gastrostomy Care for Infants and Young Children,
Feeding Infants and Young Children with Special Needs,
Nutrition for Infants and Toddlers with Special Needs
Universal Precautions in Schools: Protection from Blood-Borne Diseases)

University of Nebraska Medical Center
Meyer Rehabilitation Institute, Medical Resource Center
600 South 42nd Street
Omaha, Nebraska 68198-5450
402-559-7467
(videotape series on feeding and swallowing)

CHAPTER 13

Self-Care Skills

Dianne Koontz Lowman

Anquan, a 10-year-old student with significant motor disabilities and no traditional means of communication, just transferred into a teacher's room. After observing this boy for a month, the teacher is convinced that Anquan not only knows when he has urinated but also is uncomfortable with wet diapers.

———————————

Jamie's mother has asked that Jamie's individualized education program (IEP) be rewritten to address toilet training. Jamie is unable to attend the local after-school program with her brother because she is not toilet trained, and the staff in the program are not prepared to deal with changing diapers. Toileting has suddenly become a high priority for this family.

———————————

Suzanne screams and physically resists every time the teacher tries to take her into the bathroom and seat her on the toilet.

———————————

Because Nate is now 15 years old, Nate's mother would like him to dress by himself. Instead, Nate and his mother have huge battles every morning about getting up, dressed, and ready for school.

———————————

Self-care tasks such as toileting, dressing, grooming, and personal hygiene are some of the most important tasks children learn as they grow and mature (Shepherd, 2001). In addition to the mealtime skills discussed in the previous chapter, development of toileting, dressing, grooming, and personal hygiene are viewed as particularly important for a number of reasons. All of us will use toileting, dressing, and grooming skills every day throughout our lifetimes. Dressing and undressing a child or dealing with wet and soiled clothes numerous times throughout the day requires much parental and caregiver time, energy, and resources. Teaching students to perform even parts of these skill sequences will be helpful to caregivers. Wet or soiled clothes or poor hygiene can interfere with a student's social acceptance (Wheeler, 1998). Participation in self-care skills can improve a student's skills in the areas of sensorimotor (e.g., strength, range of motion, coordination) and cognition (e.g., sequencing, memory). In addition, the ability to dress, groom, and, especially, perform self-toileting will give a student a sense of accomplishment, independence, and pride in his or her abilities. Successful management of self-care skills will improve a student's health by preventing rashes, sores, and, in some cases, bladder and kidney infections (Shepherd, 2001; Wheeler, 1998).

Farlow and Snell (2000) proposed some general principles for developing and implementing self-care programs for students with significant disabilities. Initially, the team, including the student (if possible), should work together to select specific skills and goals for instruction. Any instructional methods used should be socially valid, age appropriate, and respectful of the family's culture. Involving the child's peers in planning will help the team determine what is socially and age appropriate. Meaningful assessment of the child's abilities is critical; in this chapter, the use of task analysis will be emphasized to determine what the child can and cannot do.

Although independence in self-care skills is the ultimate goal, encouraging partial participation is an important way to involve the child in learning part of a skill sequence that might not be mastered independently. Techniques for facilitating the child's partial participation in a self-care skill sequence might include adapting materials, changing the sequence of the activity, or having the caregiver provide physical assistance as needed. Caregivers are encouraged to select appropriate environments and schedules for instruction using uncomplicated and effective methods as much as possible. Caregivers should consider teaching related skills, such as social and communication skills, in addition to the primary goal (Farlow & Snell, 2000).

This chapter builds on these principles to explore approaches to teaching students with severe or multiple disabilities to become more independent in toileting, dressing, grooming, and personal hygiene. Suggestions are provided for assessing the child, the tasks, and the environment and for making adaptations (Case-Smith, 1994).

TOILETING SKILLS

Independent toileting at appropriate times and places is a critical developmental milestone with wide variation among children with and without disabilities. Children without disabilities follow a predictable developmental sequence with regulated daytime toileting occurring between 2 and 3 years of age. Total independence in the toileting routine is usually achieved between 4 and 5 years of age (Shepherd, 2001). Deciding when a child with disabilities is ready to start toilet training can be difficult, especially when the child is below 5 years of age and the social impact is minimal. Training should not begin before 18 months. Beyond 4 years old, toilet training usually becomes a priority (Wheeler, 1998).

Toileting skills are some of the most difficult skill sequences to teach because toileting requires an awareness of internal stimuli (e.g., bladder fullness) and a long sequence of related skills (Farlow & Snell, 2000). Several of the more advanced toileting skills, such as managing clothes and seating oneself on the toilet, may never be possible for some students with severe and multiple disabilities.

Assessing Toileting Skills

A number of factors need to be considered when determining readiness for toilet training. Assessment in toileting encompasses three areas: 1) the child's physiological readiness, 2) current elimination patterns, and 3) ability to perform a number of related skills.

Assessing Readiness

The following physiological prerequisites reflect the maturity of the child's central nervous system and the muscle sphincters involved in elimination. These prerequisites should be considered when determining if a child is ready for toilet training (Farlow & Snell, 2000; Wheeler, 1998); namely, the child should have

- Chronological age of at least 2 years
- Daily periods of dryness, usually lasting 1–2 hours
- A stable pattern of elimination, usually three to five urinations a day occurring at certain times of the day
- Regular bowel movements, usually one bowel movement a day
- Level of awareness regarding elimination, such as acting differently when diapers or clothing are wet or soiled

Students who are ready for toilet training usually demonstrate these prerequisites; however, some students with severe or multiple disabilities may not. In these cases, it is recommended that a student have a thorough medical examination to rule out any medical or organic problems. If the team determines that toilet training is an important goal, it is recommended that training be initiated regardless of level of disability, assuming that the child is medically sound and physiologically mature (Farlow & Snell, 2000). Once the determination has been made to start toilet training, the next step is to determine the child's patterns of elimination and dryness.

Assessing Elimination Patterns

Developing a chart of the student's toileting behavior proves helpful to detect when the child typically urinates or defecates and whether the child has voided in a toilet or had an accident. A sample daytime toileting chart is presented in Figure 13.1. As with traditional toilet training methods, this chart is important to establish a baseline and to determine the child's natural routine. In addition, this chart can be used during and after the training to monitor training and progress (Farlow & Snell, 2000; Wheeler, 1998).

The child should be checked at half-hour intervals and the appropriate notation marked (e.g., a check for urinating at 11:00 A.M.). This particular chart covers a 12-hour period and can be marked by both parents and school staff. An important reason for including the parents is to gather a complete picture of the child's pattern of elimination as well as to involve the parents in the planning process. Farlow and Snell (2000) suggested that, to determine the toileting patterns, baseline charting be conducted for at least 2 weeks; charting can be continued up to 30 days if needed to establish clear patterns of elimination. In addition, 15-minute intervals could be used instead of 30-minute intervals to get a more accurate picture. It is also important to change the child's clothing after detecting accidents to avoid confusing new accidents with earlier ones (Farlow & Snell, 2000).

Researchers have recommended that caregivers begin with developing a schedule for daytime only (Farlow & Snell, 2000; Wheeler, 1998). Nighttime training should be started only after the child has been successful during the day (Wheeler, 1998). In addition to determining the child's patterns of elimination, it is important to examine the child's ability to perform all skills in the toileting sequence.

Assessing Related Skills

Successful toileting involves a rather complex series of skills such as removing and putting on clothing, wiping, flushing, and washing hands. To work toward

	Sunday	Monday	Tuesday	Wednesday	Thursday	Friday	Saturday
7:00 A.M.							
7:30							
8:00							
8:30							
9:00							
9:30							
10:00							
10:30							
11:00							
11:30							
12:00 P.M.							
12:30							
1:00							
1:30							
2:00							
2:30							
3:00							
3:30							
4:00							
4:30							
5:00							
5:30							
6:00							
6:30							
7:00							
7:30							

Figure 13.1. Blank daytime toileting chart to keep track of successful eliminations in the toilet and accidents. Such a chart allows user to see a child's pattern of elimination to assist in toilet training. (Key: U=Urinated in toilet; B=Bowel movement in toilet; XU=Accident [urination]; XB=Accident [bowel movement].)

independent toileting with students with severe and multiple disabilities, the caregiver must regard each skill or step in the process as a separate goal. The caregiver should observe and assess each skill in order to choose the correct starting point for instruction. A task-analysis format is an excellent way to determine which skills in this sequence the child can perform and which skills need assistance (Farlow & Snell, 2000). As shown in Figure 13.2, the components in

Child who is ambulatory	Child who uses a wheelchair
1. Request to use restroom	1. Request to use restroom
2. Go into restroom and into stall	2. Go into restroom and into stall
	2.1 Position chair
	2.2 Lock brakes
	2.3 Undo seat belt
	2.4 Move to edge of seat
	2.5 Assist with assisted standing
	2.6 Hold on to handrail
3. Unfasten pants and pull down	3. Help unfasten pants and pull down
3.1 Unfasten belt	
3.2 Undo zipper	
3.3 Pull down pants	
3.4 Pull down underwear	
4. Sit on toilet	4. Sit on toilet
5. Urinate	5. Urinate
6. Wipe self	6. Call for assistance to wipe
6.1 Take toilet paper	
6.2 Pull paper off roll	
6.3 Wipe self from front to back	
7. Stand up	7. Request assistance to stand
	7.1 Hold handrail and assist with standing
8. Pull up clothing	8. Assist in pulling up pants and fastening
	8.1 Pull up underwear
	8.2 Pull up pants
	8.3 Zip up zipper
	8.4 Fasten belt
9. Reach for handle and flush	9. Move into chair and reach for handle
	9.1 Assist with turning and sitting
	9.2 Move back into seat on wheelchair seat
	9.3 Put on seat-belt
	9.4 Unlock brakes
	9.5 Move wheelchair near handle and push to flush
10. Go wash hands	10. Go wash hands

Figure 13.2. Components in the toileting process using task analyses, for toileting for children with and without physical limitations. (From Heller, K.W., Forney, P.E., Alberto, P.A., Schwartzman, M.N., & Goeckel, T.M. [2000]. *Meeting physical and health needs of children with disabilities: Teaching student participation and management* [p. 253]. Belmont, CA: Wadsworth; adapted by permission.)

the toileting process are broken down into steps and the child's performance on each can be recorded (Heller, Bigge, & Allgood, 2001). The child with limited use of motor or sensory systems can be taught to do parts of the related skills through individualized adaptations and the use of partial participation. Once the child's elimination patterns have been established and the child's performance on the various steps in the task analysis have been determined, it is time to begin toilet training.

Toilet Training Methods

Several broad approaches can be taken to teaching toileting. Traditional schedule methods—sometimes called trip training method, distributed practice training, or a child-oriented approach—focus on training students when they are most likely to use the toilet, when the bowel or bladder is naturally full. Massed trial or rapid training methods, such as the Azrin and Foxx procedures, require students to consume extra fluids, creating more opportunities for toileting (Bailey & Wolery, 1992; Farlow & Snell, 2000; Lowenthal, 1996).

Consider the story of Anquan, the 10-year-old student with significant motor disabilities described in the chapter opener. Anquan has recently transferred into a teacher's classroom. After observing him for a month, his teacher is convinced Anquan not only knows when he is wet but also is uncomfortable with wet diapers. In a conference with his mother, she indicates unsuccessful toilet training was attempted when he was 4 years old. Because of his significant motor limitations, his mother has not tried again because she doesn't think he will ever be toilet trained. Anquan's teacher and his mother decide to chart when Anquan is wet and dry for 2 weeks. After looking at the chart, it appears that Anquan has four periods during the day when he is wet. The teacher meets with Anquan's mother and his therapists to discuss strategies needed to start habit training.

Traditional Toilet Training Methods

As children with disabilities learn to use the toilet, they might move through various stages of toileting, including habit or trip trained, self-initiated, and independent toileting. Students with severe disabilities may attain complete independence or may only attain habit or self-initiated toileting. These practices are described in the following sections (Farlow & Snell, 2000).

Stage 1: Habit Training The goal of a habit training program, also known as *trip training,* is to foster regular bladder and bowel control by having the student go to the toilet on a regular schedule. Once the student's pattern of elimination is determined, the student is taken to the toilet 10 minutes before he or she typically urinates. The student sits on the toilet for 5 minutes and then is returned to the classroom. No reprimand is made for not using the toilet. After use of the toilet, the student is reinforced. Because some students with severe disabilities have a preference for routines, it is important to begin toilet training as an entire routine, rather than just as sitting on the toilet. As the child becomes more proficient in each step of the task analysis, caregiver intervention can be faded (Bailey & Wolery, 1992; Heller et al., 2001; Heller, Forney, Alberto, Schwartzman, & Goeckel, 2000; Wheeler, 1998). Boswell and Gray (2002) suggested using a visually supported routine, incorporating the symbols used by the student's communication system (e.g., Mayer-Johnson symbols, photographs). For more in-depth description of the habit training or trip training method, please see the chapter on toileting training in *Meeting Physical and Health Needs of Children with Disabilities: Teaching Student Participation and Management* by Heller, Forney, and colleagues (2000).

Fredericks, Baldwin, Grove, and Moore originally described distributed practice, a variation on the habit training method, in 1975. As in habit training, the child's pattern of elimination is recorded during half-hour blocks. In distributed practice, the child's elimination chart is then reviewed and the two times of the day when the child is most likely to urinate are identified. Training is initiated only during these two identified times. Axelrod (2000) also suggested starting training with the two most probable times when working with children with deafblindness. During these two half-hour blocks, the child is seated on the toilet and reinforced if successful. No comments are made if the child is not successful. When the child is able to use the toilet with at least a 75% success rate during these two blocks, training is extended to other periods of the day until the child is dry throughout the day (Axelrod, 2000; Bailey & Wolery, 1992; Fredericks et al., 1975).

An important consideration during this first stage of habit training is to establish a comfortable position for the student on the toilet. Ideally, the child's head and shoulders should be slightly forward and in midline, the arms relaxed and close to the body, the hips at an approximately 90° angle, the knees bent, and the feet supported (Finnie, 1997). A variety of regular and adapted toileting seats are available, ranging from stand-alone toilets to devices that fit over toilets (Heller et al., 2001). The child's physical therapist should be consulted to determine the most appropriate seating arrangement. Because voiding requires voluntary relaxation of muscles, it is important for the child to feel comfortable and secure.

Toileting adaptations for young children with cerebral palsy are illustrated in Finnie's (1997) book titled *Handling the Young Child with Cerebral Palsy at Home.* Several other possible adaptations for the training area include 1) using a stepping stool to help a small child get on the toilet, with rubber matting on the stool and underneath it to prevent slipping; 2) installing a nonslippery floor, with either well-fastened carpeting or a rubber mat around the toilet; and 3) removing the bathroom door to allow the child using a wheelchair, walker, or crutches to enter more easily (Shepherd, 2001). Occupational therapists or physical therapists can provide much help in determining and fashioning specific adaptations.

Habit training is a socially acceptable way to improve the hygiene of a child who is not ready for self-initiated or independent toileting. Habit training might be appropriate for those students who have no awareness of the need to urinate, have no awareness when diapers are wet, and/or who are older than 6 years of age and have not been successful with other toilet training techniques. Successful habit training may result in preparing the child for self-initiated toileting. Helping the child to stop eliminating in his or her clothing may develop the habit of regular elimination and may help the child realize when he or she is wet, thus paving the way to self-initiated toileting (Wheeler, 1998).

Stage 2: Self-Initiated Toileting   The second step toward complete independence in toileting is recognizing and indicating the need to go to the bathroom. During Stage 1 and Stage 2, the caregiver helps the student to make the connection between the internal feeling of bladder fullness and eliminating in the toilet by giving feedback such as praise as soon the child eliminates in the toilet (Farlow & Snell, 2000). The choice of underwear can also help the child make the connection between fullness and elimination. Pull-ups or diapers wick wetness away from the body, preventing the child from feeling wet. Even though accidents in underpants will require more time in clean up, underpants and training pants do not retain wastes, allowing the child to immediately feel when accidents occur (Wheeler, 1998). In addition, wearing regular underpants is more age-appropriate than pull-ups and might increase the child's social acceptance.

During Stage 2, it is critical for caregivers to determine the most appropriate way for the student to initiate the toileting sequence. A student may begin to spontaneously go to the familiar bathroom in the classroom. A student still needs a way to communicate this need when a toilet is not immediately available. Initially, the caregiver can look for any behaviors or signs that indicate the need to eliminate, such as crossing legs, grimacing, going to the corner, and so forth. When these behaviors are observed, the caregiver can help the child use a systematic communication system such as objects, pictures, or words to communicate the need to go (Boswell & Gray, 2002). An effective communication system should be used consistently throughout the toilet training process and be available at all times following completion of toilet training (Wheeler, 1998).

Stage 3: Toileting Independence   The final stage in toilet training is complete independence, which involves 1) realizing and indicating the need to go to the bathroom and 2) managing all steps in the task analysis of using the toilet. At this point in the training, the focus shifts to generalizing skills and making skill performance more proficient; the caregivers will thus fade themselves out of the bathroom. For some students, nighttime training may be initiated at home at this time (Farlow & Snell, 2000).

Jamie is a 6-year-old with cerebral palsy and cognitive delays. She is very small for her age and still wears diapers. Because Jamie is so small and needs to be carried, it has been easy for her parents to think of her as a younger child. Now that Jamie is in school full time, her mother has gone to work. She wants to place Jamie in the same after-school program with her brother, but enrollment was denied because Jamie was not toilet trained. Until this last IEP meeting, Jamie's parents had not been particularly concerned about her self-care skills. The parents now want to add toilet training to her IEP; in fact, they want to make it a high priority!

Massed Practice or Rapid Method

The techniques described by Azrin and Foxx in their book, *Toilet Training in Less Than a Day,* although published in 1974, are still used by parents of children with and without disabilities. Their method is called "rapid" because the training is delivered with high intensity, allowing multiple opportunities for practice. Some components of their package include increased fluid consumption, dry pants inspection, accident treatment, self-initiation training, and moisture-signaling devices.

Modifications of the Azrin and Foxx procedures have been used successfully with children with various disabilities. Didden, Sikkema, Bosman, Duker, and Curfs (2001) used Azrin and Foxx's procedures to successfully establish toileting skills in six children with Angelman syndrome (a genetic disorder that results in developmental, speech, and motor/balance delays). Taylor, Cipani, and Clardy (1994) modified Azrin and Foxx's procedures through a careful analysis of the antecedent stimulus for accidents and were able to successfully reduce the accidents of a 10-year-old boy with autism.

Main Components   The main components of the Azrin and Foxx (1974) program are as follows:

1. Increase the child's intake of fluid to induce more frequent urination. It should be noted that the Azrin and Foxx procedures were developed with adult residents in a state school for people with mental retardation (Azrin &

Foxx, 1971). Parents or school staff contemplating using a rapid technique for students with severe or multiple disabilities should consult the student's physician to determine an appropriate liquid to use. It is best to avoid giving children large amounts of caffeine and sugar or other fluids (e.g., apple juice) that might cause or aggravate constipation or other health problems. Perhaps more important, forcing liquids over an extended period may lead to a condition called hyponatremia. Marked by nausea, vomiting, seizures, and even coma, hyponatremia requires emergency medical care. No toilet-training program that uses hydration should begin without first having the student medically evaluated (Farlow & Snell, 2000).

2. Seat the child on the toilet for a set period of time (e.g., 10 minutes) and then take the child off the toilet for a set period of time. This phase of the toilet-training program, bladder training, is designed for the student to gain control over his or her bladder and bowel muscles so that elimination occurs only on the toilet. A prompting–fading procedure is used throughout bladder training. Prompts appropriate to the learner's skill level (e.g., verbal, gestural, physical) are provided to teach the acts of approaching the toilet, pulling down pants, and so forth and are faded as soon as possible.

3. Reinforce the child for using the toilet and for staying dry. If the child's pants are dry, the child is reinforced with praise. If the pants are wet, the trainer indicates their wetness with disappointment and withholds reinforcement.

4. When accidents occur, do several things. Verbally reprimand the child for wetting. Six positive practice trials should be provided for the child to walk to the toilet, lower pants, sit, arise, raise pants, and so forth. Opportunities should be provided for the child to feel his or her wet pants, and the child should be required to take off the wet pants, wash them, and put them away when dry.

5. Once the learner initiates toileting without prompting, self-initiation training begins. This step involves components such as lengthening the time between dry pants inspections, intermittently rewarding using the toilet, removing the urine alert from the toilet bowl (see the section on moisture-signaling devices), and having the child indicate that he or she can locate and get to the toilet from various areas.

Questions About Intensive Toilet Training Programs   Even though intensive, or rapid, toilet training programs are available and used, questions have been raised about how appropriate these methods are for students with disabilities (Axelrod, 2002; Farlow & Snell, 2000). Several drawbacks to intensive toilet training programs are listed next:

- The rapid training programs require an intensive time commitment for caregivers working with the child. In school, several adults might share these responsibilities in the classroom; however, at home, a family might be overwhelmed by the amount of time devoted to this effort.

- Learning a new skill involves experiencing at least a 70% success rate (7 correct responses for every 10 attempts). Toileting programs that use long periods of sitting on the toilet without voiding increase the percentage of errors and make learning more difficult (Axelrod, 2000).

- Students with severe or multiple disabilities might not make the connection between overcorrection or positive practice and a toileting accident. Activities such as raising and lowering pants a number of times do not teach the desired behavior of voiding in the toilet.

- Overcorrection and positive practice might feel like punishment to the child, who then might attempt to escape or avoid the activities viewed.

Improved Traditional Methods

Two components of the rapid toilet training methods, dry pants inspection and moisture-signaling devices, have been successfully incorporated into traditional training programs when traditional training methods alone have not been successful.

Dry Pants Inspection   The dry pants method is designed to teach children the difference between wet and dry sensations and to deliver reinforcement for having dry pants. This procedure includes 1) asking the student, "Are you dry?" (using gestures as appropriate), 2) prompting the person to feel his or her crotch area for wetness, and 3) reinforcing the person for having dry pants. If the pants are wet, a neutral expression is given and reinforcement withheld (Farlow & Snell, 2000)

Moisture-Signaling Devices   The function of these devices is to alert the caregiver at the moment the child has voided, allowing the caregiver to immediately reinforce the child for success. One such device is a pants alarm, which signals the presence of wetness. The other device is a urine alert, which fits into a toilet bowl and signals urination or defecation. Lancioni and Markus (1999) used urine-triggered alarm signals and prompts combined with positive reinforcement to successfully establish daytime urinary continence in a 9-year-old boy with severe disabilities. The use of electronic devices may facilitate toilet training but cannot be viewed as an essential part of a training procedure. They certainly should never be used to replace techniques of systematic prompting and reinforcement. Moreover, Farlow and Snell (2000) criticized moisture-signaling equipment as being potentially stigmatizing and simply not feasible in general education classes and in the community. These devices might, however, be appropriate for at-home use or in specialized summer training programs.

Suzanne screams and physically resists every time the teacher tries to take her into the bathroom and seat her on the toilet. The teacher has tried using a potty chair instead of sitting her on the toilet, with no success. After meeting with the collaborative team, a program was implemented to desensitize Suzanne to the bathroom/toilet by using a fuzzy rug and a nightlight instead of overhead lights and reinforcing positive behaviors by using her favorite music.

Specific Problems and Solutions

Children with severe and multiple disabilities might experience fear of going into the bathroom, sitting on the toilet, or flushing. In addition, children may urinate outside the toilet or smear feces. Some children also may have a strong reaction to wiping or using paper. Some excellent suggestions for coping with these problems have been suggested by Boswell and Gray (2002) and by Wheeler, in her comprehensive resource titled *Toilet Training for Individuals with Autism and Related Disorders* (1998).

Fear of Bathroom, Toilet, and Flushing

Children may resist bathrooms that are unfamiliar, especially in school or other public places. This fear might be related to size, noise, coldness, or the presence of unfamiliar people. Fear of sitting on the toilet might come from not liking the feel of the porcelain, feeling unsafe on the tall toilet, or being afraid of the water or noise of the flushing. Some suggestions for calming these fears and desensitizing the child to the bathroom include the following (Boswell & Gray, 2002; Wheeler, 1998):

- Have the child go in without sitting on the toilet at some time that he or she does not feel the urge to eliminate, or have a bathroom visit paired with something the child enjoys, such as washing hands.
- Have the child sit on the toilet without removing clothes.
- Use a potty seat rather than have the child sit up high on the toilet.
- Take turns sitting or using a doll for a model.
- Wait to flush until the child is away from the toilet.
- Give advance warning of the flush.
- Allow the child to flush.

Urinating Outside the Toilet

Some children urinate outside the bowl because of distractions, because they do not understand, or because they are not physically able to aim. Suggestions to ameliorate these difficulties include the following (Boswell & Gray, 2002; Wheeler, 1998):

- Minimize distractions.
- Place child in a stable position.
- Supply a target in the water, such as a Cheerio.
- Add food coloring in water to draw attention.
- Use picture cues to visually show the reward that will follow urinating in the toilet.

Smearing Feces

Smearing feces is not a common behavior, but when it occurs, it can be highly offensive and unsafe. The best way to deal with this problem is to prevent it from happening. The following are a few suggestions (Wheeler, 1998):

- Include picture, symbol, or command in toileting routine for wiping.
- Provide paper that is comfortable to the child.
- Provide assistance with wiping if needed.
- Check child frequently or provide a signal for child to indicate finished.

Strong Reaction to Wiping

Some children have very strong reactions (which may be caused by tactile defensiveness) to different textures or types of touches and resist using toilet paper. The following are some alternate strategies that might be used (Boswell & Gray, 2002; Wheeler, 1998):

- Try different materials such as different types of toilet paper, wet wipes, or a warm washcloth.
- Try to determine what temperature is preferred.
- Provide assistance with wiping.
- Include a picture or symbol in the sequence reminding the child to wipe.

The preceding lists of ideas are not inclusive but are offered as examples of how the team might problem solve solutions to specific problems encountered by children with severe or multiple disabilities (Boswell & Gray, 2002).

Nighttime Toilet Training

Teachers and parents often work together to address problems that occur at home as well as at school. A common problem among children with severe and multiple disabilities (and among children who do not have disabilities) is nocturnal enuresis (i.e., bed-wetting). This section briefly examines procedures that have proved successful in nighttime toilet training.

Traditional Procedures

Farlow and Snell (2000) summarized the following components of traditional nighttime procedures:

- Reducing fluids 1–2 hours before bedtime
- Toileting just before bedtime
- Giving simple instructions to the child about receiving a reward for a dry bed in the morning
- Performing regular awakenings during the night and recording the child's accidents and successes every 1–1½ hours
- Guiding the child to the toilet and having the child sit on the toilet for 5 minutes without allowing him or her to sleep
- Praising on-toilet eliminations and recording them
- Changing wet linens and awakening the child at an earlier time the next night

Rapid Nighttime Training Procedures

As with rapid training procedures for daytime toilet training, rapid nighttime-training procedures include increased fluid consumption. The rapid nighttime training program (Azrin & Foxx, 1974; Foxx & Azrin, 1973) includes positive practice in toileting before getting into bed, drinking fluids before bed, hourly awakenings, reinforcement for dry bed, and cleanliness training for wet bed.

Interventions for Nocturnal Enuresis

Pharmacological, behavioral, and alarm interventions are used for children with nocturnal enuresis. Behavioral interventions include star charts, reward systems, overlearning, dry bed training, and scheduled waking. In a systematic review of the literature, Glazener and Evans (2002a) examined 12 trials involving 748 children, of whom 365 received a simple behavioral intervention. In small trials, reward systems, lifting, and waking were each associated with significantly fewer wet nights than controls. They concluded that, although further trials are needed, these simple methods could be tried as first-line therapy before considering alarms or drugs, which may be more demanding and have adverse effects.

Alarms

Enuresis alarms might be an auditory alarm located in a mattress pad, a visual signal, or a vibration. With body-worn alarm systems, the sensor is placed in the child's pants. In a systematic review of the literature, Glazener and Evans (2002b) concluded that children who used alarms were significantly more likely than children who were not given alarms to control enuresis to become dry during treatment. Insufficient data existed to judge whether one type of alarm was better than another. When the decision is made to use a moisture-signaling device, the team must understand how the equipment works, make sure that the student understands why the equipment is being used and how it works, and ensure that the student will not be hurt by this equipment (Farlow & Snell, 2000).

Bowel Management

Many children with severe and multiple disabilities have bowel movements less frequently and less regularly than the typical individual. It is common for students with severe and multiple disabilities, in fact, not to have bowel movements during the school day. Bowel management programs in the school, therefore, should be coordinated carefully with home interventions. Children with severe and multiple disabilities may have constipation, diarrhea, encopresis (described later in this section), or impaction. Any bowel management program should be designed for regular emptying of the bowels with no leakage of stool in between (Graff, Ault, Guess, Taylor, & Thompson, 1990; Porter, Haynie, Bierle, Caldwell, & Palfrey, 1997).

Constipation is a common problem in children with multiple disabilities because of generalized hypotonia and limited muscle function of the bowel, lack of physical activity, inadequate fiber and liquid intake, and poor health (Beker, Farber, & Yanni, 2002; Nickel, 2000). Prolonged constipation can lead to urinary tract infections, especially in girls (Graff et al., 1990).

A treatment program for constipation may include a review of positioning and seating, behavioral management, dietary alterations, a cleanout program to treat the impaction, and a maintenance program (Nickel, 2000). Although laxatives and enemas are often used, adjusting the child's diet is the best approach to this problem. Additional fiber may be added by replacing low-fiber goods, such as white bread, with higher-fiber foods, such as whole-grain bread, or with fiber-rich beverages or fiber supplements. Increasing daily exercise also helps prevent constipation (Ault, Rues, Graff, & Holvoet, 2000; Beker et al., 2002).

Diarrhea is often a symptom of an illness or food intolerance (Beker et al., 2002). The most serious consequence of diarrhea is the loss of water, which usually is reabsorbed into the body during the passage of normal feces through the colon. Water loss can lead to dehydration, a serious condition needing prompt medical care (Graff et al., 1990). Signs of severe dehydration include lethargy, sunken eyes, dry mouth, and inability to drink. Some parents will use commercially available oral dehydration liquids, such as Pedialtye, Ricelyte, or Resol (Beker et al., 2002). The child's physician should be consulted before making any adjustments in the child's diet.

Encopresis refers to the involuntary passage of fecal material. If a child holds the bowel movement for long periods of time, a large stool mass stretches the walls of the colon and rectum. This causes the anal sphincter to relax and, while the hard stool stays put, soft stool or liquid leaks out involuntarily (Brazzelli & Griffiths, 2002; Hill, 1999). Dietary modifications, medical treatments such as enemas and laxatives, manual evacuation, and behavioral programs are all used to soften the stool and empty the intestine. In a systematic literature review, Brazzelli and Griffiths (2002) found that there was some evidence that behavioral intervention and laxative therapy together, rather than either therapy alone, improves continence in children with encopresis. Consultation with a dietitian can prove very helpful, but it is critical to consult with the child's physician before planning any program to treat constipation or diarrhea in children with severe and multiple disabilities.

DRESSING AND PERSONAL HYGIENE SKILLS

Now that Nate is 15 years old, his mother would like for him to dress by himself. Instead, Nate and his mother have been having huge battles every morning about getting up, dressed, and ready for school. After a functional analysis of the morning routine, the team suggests preparing a visual routine to guide Nate throughout the steps of dressing. The night before, Nate picks out his clothing from three different choices. The clothing is arranged in order on a small table in his room. When Nate comes downstairs dressed, he may choose a reinforcing activity while waiting for breakfast. Nate and his mother wake up 30 minutes earlier to complete this routine.

When a child with multiple disabilities has the ability to participate, at least partially, in dressing and personal hygiene activities, it lightens the load for caregivers and gives the child more opportunities for control and choice. For this reason, instructional goals in dressing and hygiene are often priorities for families (Farlow & Snell, 2000). Interviewing the family members can yield valuable information about the child's abilities, environmental characteristics, and the goals for intervention (Shepherd, 2001). Decisions on which dressing and grooming skills to teach and how to teach them should be based on the following general guidelines (Farlow & Snell, 2000; Heller et al., 2001):

1. Select skills that consider the wishes of the student and/or parents or care-giver.

2. Select skills to make the student as independent as possible.

3. Consider the frequency with which the student needs to use the skill during the day.

4. Select skills that reflect practices typical for the student's age.

5. Consider the importance of learning the skill for moving into a vocational setting.

6. Consider the degree to which learning the skill would facilitate acquisition of other important skills (e.g., toileting).

7. Choose settings for instruction that are the most natural for the activity.

8. Teach the simplest skills first, moving later to more complex skills.

9. Use peers as models and teachers for some skills (e.g., hair styling).

As was the case with the toileting sequence, specific dressing and hygiene skills are made up of a sequence of skills or steps that require relatively sophisticated and coordinated movements of almost every body part. In order to assess a child's performance on a specific dressing or hygiene sequence, Heller et al. (2001) suggested conducting a discrepancy analysis to determine the skills or steps required to master a sequence, whether the student can perform these skills, and if adaptations or modifications to the skill are required for mastery. An example of a discrepancy analysis for a student learning to wash his or her hands is shown in Figure 13.3 (Heller et al., 2000).

After talking to the family and completing the discrepancy analysis, the team can determine the most appropriate instructional strategies to use (Heller et al., 2001).

Strategies for Teaching Dressing and Hygiene Skills

Caregivers should follow several general guidelines when designing instruction to teach students with severe or multiple disabilities self-care skills. Caregivers should analyze current self-care skills using a discrepancy or task analysis, provide assistance only at the minimum level needed, generally teach undressing before dressing, teach special techniques and modify clothing if needed, and teach what to wear and when to wear it (Heller et al., 2001).

Student: Jamie

Task analysis	Score I = independent V = verbal prompt P = physical prompt	Student error	Adaptation or alternative performance options
1. Go to bathroom	I		
2. Position body for hand washing	V	Not getting close enough to sink	Provide verbal and pointing prompt
3. Turn on faucet	P	Difficulty manipulating	Use elongated handles
4. Adjust water temperature	P	Unsure which is hot	Mark hot and cold with red and blue marks
5. Thoroughly wet hands	I		
6. Put soap on hands	P	Difficulty manipulating	Change dispenser
7. Rub together, creating lather	P	Difficulty moving hands together	Provide elbow support
8. Continue rubbing, count to 15 slowly (15 seconds)	V	Kept stopping	Continue counting and use sticker chart
9. Rinse soap off hands thoroughly	P	Did not get all of soap off	Point out soapy areas
10. Dry hands	P	Did not thoroughly dry	Provide pointing prompt
11. Turn off water with paper towel	V	Wanted to turn off water without towel	Provide verbal prompt

Figure 13.3. Sample discrepancy analysis for the task of washing hands. (From Heller, K.W., Forney, P.E., Alberto, P.A., Schwartzman, M.N., & Goeckel, T.M. [2000]. *Meeting physical and health needs of children with disabilities: Teaching student participation and management.* Belmont, CA: Wadsworth; adapted by permission.)

627

General Instructional Techniques

Teaching dressing and hygiene skills at naturally occurring times during the day provides numerous opportunities to practice a skill as well as teaching the student to initiate a sequence in response to a naturally occurring cue (Farlow & Snell, 2000). Another benefit of providing instruction throughout the day is the opportunity for the student with disabilities to watch classmates in the general education classroom perform the same sequence. Recent studies have supported the benefits of learning by watching other children (Biederman, Fairhall, Raven, & Davey, 1998; Sewell, Collins, Hemmeter, & Schuster, 1998; Wolery, Ault, & Doyle, 1992). In addition to teaching dressing skills at naturally occurring times, it is important to teach dressing skills in context, using the child's own clothes. To avoid the need to teach generalization from an artificial setting to a naturally occurring environment, dressing dolls and fastener vests, frames, or balls should be avoided.

The needs and preferences of the child and the task will help the team decide on a prompting system to use. Reese and Snell (1991) successfully used graduated guidance to teach three children with multiple disabilities in an inclusive elementary school to put on and remove their jackets and coats. The teaching techniques also involved using clothing initially that was one or two sizes too big for the child and subsequently reducing the size to the one typically worn by the child. Sewell and colleagues (1998) showed that simultaneous prompting during the natural routine was an effective way to teach two preschoolers with developmental delays to take off and put on shoes, socks, pants, and skirts. The teacher first gave an attentional cue to look at the article of clothing and then provided full physical assistance and verbal explanations throughout the task.

The principle of partial participation should be considered for those students who experience significant physical restrictions in movements and who may be unable to complete most dressing tasks with total independence. The principle of partial participation capitalizes on the fact that most students can perform at least part of most tasks, making the student as independent as possible while relieving the stress of caregivers to complete the entire self-care sequence. An example of a partial participation sequence for tissue use is shown in Figure 13.4.

Positioning

As with all other activities, self-care is facilitated when the student has been properly positioned. The choice of position is largely determined by the child's postural tone, movement patterns, and the actions required in the specific sequence. Consultation with the physical and occupational therapists is critical.

Student	Caregiver
1. Indicate on communication board the need to wipe nose with tissue	Acknowledge request
2. Visually locate tissue	Move student to tissue box
3. Reach for tissue	Hold tissue box in place
4. Grasp tissue in hand	
5. Turn wrist so hand is facing toward body/face	Provide wrist guidance if needed
6. Bring hand up to nose	Provide elbow guidance to stabilize if needed
7. Place tissue over nose and mouth	
8. Blow through nose into tissue	Provide verbal prompt
9. Wipe nose with tissue	Complete wiping with hand over hand
10. Bring hand down from face	
11. Indicate need to throw tissue away on communication board	Acknowledge request
12. Visually locate trash can	Move student to trash can
13. Drop tissue in trash can	
14. Repeat if needed	

Figure 13.4. Task analysis for tissue use using partial participation.

Parents also can provide helpful information because they have more practice than other team members and often develop useful tricks.

Campbell (2000) and Finnie (1997) provided some useful guidelines for positioning children for dressing activities. Avoid dressing children in the supine (on their backs) position. Most children in this position have a tendency to push their head and shoulders back and to straighten and stiffen their legs. Children on their backs also are unable to see and are likely to become uninterested in the activity. If it is necessary to dress an older and heavier child in this position, a hard pillow should be placed under the child's head to raise the shoulders slightly. If at all possible, children should participate in dressing while seated. Individuals who are typically developing will put on pants, hosiery, socks, and shoes while seated. This position bends the child forward at the hips to enable the caregiver to bring the child's arms forward. When assisting children who are blind, the caregiver might work from behind the child. Children who cannot sit and maintain their balance unsupported are easier to dress if they sit with their backs to you and lean forward. Children who can maintain their balance unsupported can use hard surfaces, such as walls, for stability. If sitting is not possible, children can be dressed on their sides. Sidelying often relaxes children, makes bringing their shoulders and head forward easier, facilitates bending their legs and feet, and enables children to see (Campbell, 2000; Finnie, 1997).

Selecting and Adapting Clothing

The ease with which children learn to dress (or to be dressed) is linked to the type of clothing they wear. Although the goal of any dressing program is to teach the child to put on and remove his or her own clothing, it may prove helpful to use oversize shirts, sweaters, and so forth to allow easier movement and greater success in early phases of training. Similarly, the size, shape, and location of fasteners may facilitate speed of learning. Special, permanent modifications of clothing and fasteners may be required (e.g., Velcro fasteners for buttons). When use of permanent adaptations is not anticipated, however, materials that resemble the student's own clothing in size and orientation are best used whenever possible. The choice of clothing not only can facilitate dressing but also can make the student feel and look better. This section presents both general and specific guidelines for selecting clothing (Farlow & Snell, 2000; Finnie, 1997; Heller et al., 2001; Shepherd, 2001).

Fabric

The choice of fabric influences comfort, durability, and ease of care. Loosely woven natural fibers (e.g., cotton, wool) that breathe can help with regulation of body temperature. Although synthetic materials are not as breathable, some stretch and may increase comfort by not binding the student. Durability is greater in more tightly woven or knit fabrics. Many synthetic fibers are stronger than natural fibers. Ease of care is enhanced with synthetics that stand up well to repeated machine washing. Print, textured, and dark fabrics show stains less than light, solid-color fabrics. Slippery fabrics (e.g., nylon) may make it harder for students to maintain balance or for caregivers to pick up and carry students. Some children with tactile defensiveness reject fabrics that are slippery, shiny, or noisy (Case-Smith, 1994).

Design Features

A garment's construction helps to determine the student's comfort and the garment's durability. Regularly cut clothing will bunch in the back, ride up in the lap, or ride down in the back while a student is seated in a wheelchair. To accommodate the needs of people with disabilities, a company called Special Clothes, Inc., cuts their styles longer in the crotch, wider in the seat and legs, and with a special waistband elastic that allows for size adjustment (http://www.special-clothes.com). At the time of the publication of this chapter, middle school and high school students were wearing oversized clothing, which reinforced the social validity of students with disabilities using loose clothing.

Design features that increase the durability of clothing include the following: double-stitched seams; adequate seam allowance with small, even stitches; reinforcement of all openings (e.g., pockets, fly); and reinforcement with double fabric on areas of heavy wear. Other design features to consider are included in Table 13.1 (Shepherd, 2001).

Fastenings

Buttons are manipulated more easily if they are medium to large in size and have a shank. Zippers are easier than buttons for children with the strength and coordination to pull them up. Larger-toothed nylon zippers and zipper pulls facilitate zippering. Most hooks, clasps, and buckles are difficult for children with severe and multiple disabilities to close. Velcro is an ideal solution to most fastening problems (Shepherd, 2001). As was the case with loose fitting clothing, Velcro can be found on many garments and shoes worn by children with and without disabilities.

Specialized Clothing

Sometimes the student's use of mobility aids (e.g., crutches), orthoses (e.g., braces), or health-related technology (e.g., gastrostomy tube) also requires special clothing accommodations. A book written by an individual with multiple sclerosis, *Dressing Tips and Clothing Resources for Making Life Easier* (Schwarz, 2000) contains hundreds of practical tips as well as contact information for more than 100 companies that sell adaptive clothing for children with disabilities. One simple suggestion for a child using a tracheostomy tube is to have him or her wear a scooped neckline that does not interfere with the tube. Gastrostomy tube access can be created by sewing a pocket on a garment. The access opening is concealed in the pocket, where it can be reached easily. The pocket is lined with waterproof fabric to keep fluids from staining clothing. Patterns and ideas for adapting garments for children are also available from specialty stores. (See For More Information at the end of this chapter for more on specialized clothing).

Latex Allergy

Children who have had multiple hospitalizations and surgical procedures are at particularly high risk for developing an allergy to latex. Allergic responses can range from minor skin irritation to reactions requiring emergency treatment to prevent death. Some clothing items that might contain latex include rubber-soled shoes, athletic shoes, slippers, adhesive used in many shoes, and elastic in clothing. Teachers and caregivers should be especially vigilant about exposed elastic in underwear, pajamas, and swimsuits and rubberized clothing such as appliques on bathing caps. Even covered elastic can cause reactions (see Special Clothes for Children, http://www.special-clothes.com/).

Dressing Aids

Another form of assistance is the use of specialized adaptive devices or dressing aids. Many of these devices require sufficient upper extremity strength or dex-

Table 13.1.   Design features of clothing for easier dressing

Pull-up garments
- Large size
- Stretchy materials
- Loops sewn into waistband
- Elastic waistbands

Pullover garments
- Large opening for ease of pulling over head
- Flexible, rib-knit fabric
- Large armholes and sleeve openings
- Raglan sleeves
- Elastic cuffs and waistbands

Front-opening garments
- Loose style
- Fullness in back of garment
- Collars may be different color than rest of garment
- Short-sleeve garments first, proceeding to long-sleeve garments
- Raglan sleeves

Buttons
- Flat, large buttons
- Buttons contrast in color with garment
- Buttons sewn on loosely
- Buttons sewn on one side, Velcro tape on both sides to close shirt

Zippers
- Nylon zippers
- Zipper pulls
- Velcro instead of zipper
- Front zippers first, proceeding to side and back

Socks
- Soft, stretchy socks
- Large size
- Tube sock with no set place for heel
- Loops sewn into socks

Shoes
- Long-opening shoes (many eyes) with loose laces
- Slip on shoes
- Velcro closures
- Elastic laces already tied

From Shepherd, J. (2001). Self-care and adaptations for independent living. In J. Case-Smith (Ed.), *Occupational therapy for children* (4th ed., p. 514, copyright 2001). St. Louis, MO: C.V. Mosby; reprinted with permission of Elsevier.

terity to use, but can be modified by the occupational therapist to suit an individual child's needs. Some common dressing aids include reachers to grab the waistband so that pants can be lowered; dressing sticks to help pick up, pull up, and push off clothes; stocking aids to help pull up socks or stockings; adapted shoe horns; and buttonhooks (Heller et al., 2001; Kohlmeyer, 1993; Melvin, 1994; Shepherd, 2001). The occupational therapist can recommend companies who specialize in these types of dressing aids, such as Sammons Preston Rolyan (http://www.sammonspreston.com).

Personal Hygiene Skills

Teaching students personal hygiene skills such as washing hands, face, and body; brushing teeth; brushing hair; using a tissue; or managing hygiene is important for a number of reasons. First, being clean makes most people feel better about themselves. Second, a well-groomed appearance makes individuals more approachable, promoting socialization. Third, cleanliness and good personal hygiene help prevent illness and infection (Heller et al., 2001).

As stated previously in this chapter, the general instructional strategy most effective in assessing and teaching personal hygiene skills is a discrepancy analysis or task analysis. Because cultural expectations and social routines for some personal hygiene skills vary, the team should consider family preferences when developing an instructional plan (Shepherd, 2001). The discrepancy analysis presented in Figure 13.3 illustrates how the task of hand washing could be adapted to meet a student's individual needs. The sample task analysis of tissue use presented in Figure 13.4 illustrates the use of partial participation for those students unable to complete a sequence independently.

Whenever possible, equipment used by other members of the family should be used. Items such as liquid soap in a pump dispenser instead of bar soap or a self-soaping, long-handled bath sponge might be appropriate materials that can be used by everyone in the family. If needed, additional modifications can be made. For example, the soap dispenser may require an extension of the handle and more secure mounting to the sink or wall. Other assistive devices might require more individualization, such as creating special splints and cuffs to allow someone to use a hairbrush or razor. The occupational therapist will be an excellent resource for designing instruction for personal hygiene skills. In addition, a variety of companies manufacture and sell adaptive devices that facilitate personal hygiene skills. The team might wish to consult local specialty stores and pharmacies that sell items to older individuals or individuals recovering from illness.

Special devices and equipment for bathing and showering may be less familiar to school personnel and may be more applicable to the home. (Children who participate in physical education classes, especially at the secondary level, may be required to shower after gym class, however.) Some of the following items may be helpful to provide to the family for use at home (Shepherd, 2001):

- Safety stripping for the bottom of the tub or shower
- Permanent safety guard or grab rail
- Bath mat made from the foam pads that are used for backpacks
- Hammock chair with oversize suction feet
- Plastic laundry basket with front cut out
- Shower bench
- Inflatable bath collar
- Hand-held shower head
- Shower caddy to hold soap, shampoo, and other items

Feminine Hygiene

Although boys as well as girls need instruction on personal hygiene skills, an important area of personal hygiene for girls is menstrual care. Because this is a private matter, the involvement of the parent(s) is critical. The most effective way to teach menstrual care is through on-self instruction. Epps, Stern, and Horner (1990) found that teaching menstrual care to students with mental retardation using on-self instruction was more effective than using simulation training with dolls.

Figure 13.5 shows the task analysis for changing a menstrual pad. Many of the steps in this task analysis involve gross and fine motor skills akin to those involved in toileting and may be very difficult for the typical female with multiple disabilities. If the student is unable to perform all steps independently, she may indicate that the pads need to be changed, hold supplies, or direct the caregiver through a communication system (Heller et al., 2001).

SUMMARY

This chapter has presented strategies for assessing and teaching toileting, dressing, and personal hygiene skills to students with severe or multiple disabilities. Because of the personal nature of these skills, it is apparent that the family members and child, if possible, need to be involved in planning for instruction. Occupational therapists and physical therapists play major roles in ensuring proper positioning, adapting materials, and modifying the environment. Other

Steps	Completed
1. Identify need for menstrual bag.	
2. Take bag to bathroom.	
3. Remove necessary clothing.	
4. Pull down underwear.	
5. Sit on toilet.	
6. Remove small sandwich bag from menstrual bag.	
7. Removed soiled pad.	
8. Place in sandwich bag.	
9. Fold over bag two times.	
10. Determine if underwear is soiled.	
11. If soiled, take plastic bag from menstrual bag.	
12. Remove soiled underwear.	
13. Place soiled underwear in plastic bag.	
14. Take clean underwear from menstrual bag.	
15. Put on clean underwear.	
16. Take clean sanitary napkin from menstrual bag.	
17. Remove adhesive strips.	
18. Place sanitary napkin in crotch of underwear.	
19. Clean vaginal area.	
20. Pull up underwear.	
21. Examine external clothing for soiled areas.	
22. Replace clothes as necessary.	
23. Place soiled clothes in plastic bag with underwear.	
24. Flush toilet.	
25. Place soiled napkin (in bag) in trash.	
26. Place adhesive strips in trash.	
27. Place plastic bag with soiled clothes in menstrual bag.	
28. Wash hands.	
29. Return to locker/personal storage area.	
30. Put plastic bag with soiled clothes in locker.	
31. Replace used items in menstrual bag.	
32. Return to class/work.	

Figure 13.5. Task analysis for changing a menstrual pad. (From Bigge, J.L., Best, S.J., & Heller, K.W. [2001]. *Teaching individuals with physical, health, or multiple disabilities* [4th ed. p. 544]. New York: Merrill; reprinted with permission.)

specialists, including urologists, nurses, physicians, dietitians, and family and consumer studies (formerly home economics) teachers, among many others, can provide important consultation and direct services. Clearly, in self-care skills, as in all other parts of the curriculum, team efforts are essential.

REFERENCES

Axelrod, C. (2000). *Toilet training children with deafblindness: Issues and strategies.* Available on the web at http://www.tsbvi.edu/Outreach/seehear/summer00/toilet.htm

Ault, M.M., Rues, J.P., Graff, J.C., & Holvoet, J.F. (2000). Special health care procedures. In M.E. Snell & F. Brown (Eds.), *Instruction of students with severe disabilities* (5th ed., pp. 245–290). Columbus, OH: Charles E. Merrill.

Azrin, N.H., & Foxx, R.M. (1971). A rapid method of toilet training the institutionalized retarded. *Journal of Applied Behavior Analysis, 4,* 89–99.

Azrin, N.H., & Foxx, R.M. (1974). *Toilet training in less than a day.* New York: Pocket Books.

Azrin, N.H., Sneed, T.J., & Foxx, R.M. (1973). Dry-bed: A rapid method of eliminating bed-wetting (enuresis) of the retarded. *Behaviour Research and Therapy, 11,* 427–434.

Azrin, N.H., Sneed, T.J., & Foxx, R.M. (1974). Dry-bed training: Rapid elimination of childhood enuresis. *Behaviour Research and Therapy, 12,* 147–156.

Bailey, D.B., & Wolery, M. (1992). *Teaching infants and preschoolers with disabilities* (2nd ed.). New York: Macmillan.

Beker, L.R., Farber, A.F., & Yanni, C.C. (2002). Nutrition and children with disabilities. In M.L. Batshaw (Ed.), *Children with disabilities* (5th ed., pp. 141–164). Baltimore: Paul H. Brookes Publishing Co.

Biederman, G.B., Fairhall, J.L., Raven, K.A., & Davey, V.A. (1998). Verbal prompting, hand-over-hand instruction, and passive observation in teaching children with developmental disabilities. *Exceptional Children, 64,* 503–511.

Bigge, J.L., Best, & Heller, K.W. (2001). *Teaching individuals with physical, health, or multiple disabilities* (4th ed.). New York: Merrill.

Boswell, S., & Gray, D. (2002). *Applying structured teaching principles to toilet training.* Available on-line at http://www.teacch.com/toilet.htm

Brazzelli, M., & Griffiths, P. (2002). Behavioral and cognitive interventions with OT without other treatments for defaecation disorders in children (Cochrane Review). *The Cochrane Library, 4.*

Campbell, P.H. (2000). Promoting participation in natural environments by accommodating motor disabilities. In M.E. Snell & F. Brown (Eds.), *Instruction of students with severe disabilities* (5th ed., pp. 291–329). Columbus, OH: Charles E. Merrill.

Case-Smith, J. (1994). Self-care strategies for children with developmental deficits. In C. Christiansen (Ed.), *Ways of living: Self-care strategies for special needs* (pp. 101–156). Rockville, MD: American Occupational Therapy Association.

Didden, R., Sikkema, S.P.E., Bosman, I.T.M., Duker, P.C., & Curfs, L.M.G. (2001). Use of a modified Azrin-Foxx toilet training procedure for individuals with Angelman-Syndrome. *Journal of Applied Research in Intellectual Disabilities, 14*(1), 64–70.

Epps, S., Stern, R.J., & Horner, R.H. (1990). Comparison of simulation training on self and using a doll for teaching generalized menstrual care to women with severe mental retardation. *Research in Developmental Disabilities, 11,* 37–66.

Farlow, L.J., & Snell, M.E. (2000). Teaching basic self-care skills. In M.E. Snell & F. Brown (Eds.), *Instruction of students with severe disabilities* (5th ed., pp. 331–380). Columbus, OH: Charles E. Merrill.

Finnie, N.R. (1997). *Handling the young child with cerebral palsy at home* (3rd ed.). Woburn, MA: Butterworth Heinemann.

Foxx, R.M., & Azrin, N.H. (1973). Dry pants: A rapid method of toilet training children. *Behaviour Research and Therapy, 11,* 435–442.

Fredericks, H.D., Baldwin, V., Grove, D.N., & Moore, W.G. (1975). *Toilet training the handicapped child.* Monmouth, OR: Teaching Research.

Glazener, C.M., & Evans, J.H.C. (2002a). Simple behavioral and physical interventions for nocturnal enuresis in children (Cochrane Review). *The Cochrane Library, 4.*

Glazener, C.M.A., & Evans, J.H.C. (2002b). Alarm interventions for nocturnal enuresis in children (Cochrane Review). *The Cochrane Library, 4.*

Graff, J.C., Ault, M.M., Guess, D., Taylor, M., & Thompson, B. (1990). *Health care for students with disabilities: An illustrated medical guide for the classroom.* Baltimore: Paul H. Brookes Publishing Co.

Heller, K.W., Bigge, J., & Allgood, P. (2001). Adaptations for personal independence. In J.L. Bigge, S.J. Best, & K.W. Heller, *Teaching individuals with physical, health, or multiple disabilities* (4th ed., pp. 536–565). Columbus, OH: Charles E. Merrill.

Heller, K.W., Forney, P.E., Alberto, P.A., Schwartzman, M.N., & Goeckel, T.M. (2000). *Meeting physical and health needs of children with disabilities: Teaching student participation and management.* Belmont, CA: Wadsworth.

Hill, J.L. (1999). *Meeting the needs of students with special physical and health care needs.* Upper Saddle River, NJ: Merrill.

Klein, M.D. (1988). *Predressing skills.* Tucson, AZ: Therapy Skill Builders.

Kohlmeyer, K.M. (1993). Assistive and adaptive equipment. In H.L. Hopkins & H.D. Smith (Eds.), *Occupational therapy* (8th ed., pp. 316–320). Philadelphia: J.B. Lippincott.

Lancioni, G.E., & Markus, S. (1999). Urine-triggered alarm signals and prompts to promote daytime urinary continence in a boy with severe intellectual disability. *Behavioural and Cognitive Psychotherapy, 27*(3), 261–265.

Lowenthal, B. (1996). Teaching basic adaptive skills to young children with disabilities. *Early Child Development and Care, 115,* 77–84.

Melvin, J.L. (1994). Self-care strategies for persons with arthritis and connective tissue disease. In C. Christiansen (Ed.), *Ways of living: Self-care strategies for special needs* (pp. 157–187). Rockville, MD: American Occupational Therapy Association.

Nickel, R.E. (2000). Cerebral palsy. In R.E. Nickel & L.W. Desch (Eds.), *The physician's guide to caring for children with disabilities and chronic conditions* (pp. 141–184). Baltimore: Paul H. Brookes Publishing Co.

Porter, S., Haynie, M., Bierle, T., Caldwell, T.H., & Palfrey, J.S. (1997). *Children and youth assisted by medical technology in educational settings: Guidelines for care* (2nd ed.). Baltimore: Paul H. Brookes Publishing Co.

Reese, G.M., & Snell, M.E. (1991). Putting on and removing coats and jackets: The acquisition and maintenance of skills by children with severe multiple disabilities. *Education and Training in Mental Retardation, 26,* 398–410.

Richmond, G. (1983). Shaping bladder and bowel continence in developmentally retarded preschool children. *Journal of Autism and Developmental Disorders, 13,* 197–205.

Schwarz, S.P. (2000). *Dressing tips and clothing resources for making life easier.* Verona, WI: The Attainment Co., Inc.

Sewell, T.I., Collins, B.C., Hemmeter, M.L., & Schuster, J.W. (1998). Using simultaneous prompting within an activity-based format to teach dressing skills to preschoolers with developmental delays. *Journal of Early Intervention, 21,* 132–142.

Shepherd, J. (2001). Self care and adaptations for independent living. In J. Case-Smith (Ed.), *Occupational therapy for children* (4th ed., pp. 489–527). St. Louis, MO: Mosby.

Taylor, S., Cipani, E., & Clardy, A. (1994). A stimulus control technique for improving the efficacy of an established toilet training program. *Journal of Behavior Therapy & Experimental Psychiatry, 25*(2), 155–160.

Wheeler, M. (1998). *Toilet training for individuals with autism and related disorders: A comprehensive guide for parents and teachers.* Arlington, TX: Future Horizons, Inc.

Wolery, M., Ault, I., & Doyle, P.M. (1992). *Teaching students with moderate to severe disabilities.* White Plains, NY: Longman.

For More Information

BOOKS TO READ TO CHILDREN ABOUT TOILET TRAINING

Cole, J., & Chambliss, M. (2000). *My big boy potty/My big girl potty.* New York: HarperCollins.

Cole, J., & Miller, M. (1989). *Your new potty.* New York: William Morrow.

Dorman, T. (1993). *No more diapers: Personalized edition.* Gulf Breeze, FL: Hefty Publishing Co./Create-A-Book, Inc.

Frankel, A. (1999). *Once upon a potty: Boy/Once upon a potty: Girl.* New York: Harper Festival.

Gomi, T., & Stinchecum, A.M. (1993). *Everyone poops.* La Jolla, CA: Kane/Miller Book Pub.

Lindgren, B., & Eriksson (1986). *Sam's potty.* New York: William Morrow.

Miller, V. (2000). *On your potty.* Cambridge, MA: Candlewick Press.

Rogers, F., & Judkis, J. (1997). *Going to the potty.* New York: Puffin Books.

RESOURCES ABOUT DRESSING

The Attainment Co.
Post Office Box 930160
Verona, WI 53593-0160
http://www.attainmentcompany.com/

Special Clothes, Inc.
Post Office Box 333
Harwich, MA 02645
Phone, TDD, and Fax: 508-896-7939

Anitavee's Adaptive Apparel
3000B East Main Street, #277
Columbus, OH 43209
Toll-free: 1-888-246-8203
24-Hour Fax: 614-258-5380

Specially For You, Inc.
15621 309th Avenue
Gettysburg, SD 57442
605-765-9396

Index

Page numbers followed by *f* indicate figures; those followed by *t* indicate tables.